W9-BYP-736

Clinical Sexuality

*A Manual for the Physician
and the Professions*

Clinical
Sexuality

A Manual for the Physician
and the Professions

JOHN F. OLIVEN, M.D.

Attending Physician (Psychiatry), Columbia-Presbyterian Medical Center, New York; St. Vincent Hospital and Medical Center, New York and Harrison, N.Y.; United Hospital, Port Chester, N.Y.

Consulting Physician, Community Hospital, Peekskill, N.Y.; Putnam County Hospital, Brewster, N.Y.; Butterfield Memorial Hospital, Cold Spring, N.Y.

THIRD EDITION

J. B. Lippincott Company
Philadelphia and Toronto

THIRD EDITION

Copyright © 1974 by J. B. Lippincott Company

Copyright © 1965 by J. B. Lippincott Company
Copyright 1955 by J. B. Lippincott Company

This book is fully protected by copyright and, with the exception of brief excerpts for review, no part of it may be reproduced in any form, by print, photoprint, microfilm, or any other means, without the written permission of the publishers.

ISBN 0–397–50329–6

Library of Congress Catalog Card Number 74-1058

Printed in the United States of America

1   3   5   4   2

Library of Congress Cataloging in Publication Data

Oliven, John F
    Clinical sexuality for the physician and the professions.

    Published in 1955 and 1965 under title: Sexual hygiene and pathology.
    Includes bibliographies.
    1. Hygiene, Sexual.   2. Sexual disorders.
I. Title. [DNLM: 1. Sex behavior.   2. Sex deviation.   3. Sex disorders.   WM610   046s   1974]
RC556.044 1974   613.9'5   74-1058
ISBN 0–397–50329–6

Preface to the Third Edition

This work endeavors to describe and explain the range of human sexual life—developing, normal, aberrant and disordered—from its earliest manifestations in the child, through the puberal phases in the teens, and during the ever-lengthening existence of the adult. This third edition reflects current developments and research as far as they enhance clinical understanding and usefulness.

Many of the longitudinal study cases—tomboys, pedophiles, castrates, rapists, pseudofrigidae, child rape and incest victims, feminoid boys, to name a few—have now been observed for another 10-year period of their lives. Again, as in past editions, long-term study has helped in understanding and describing the various sexual states and conditions as they arise, manifest themselves, and, perhaps, as they change or resolve. Another source of clinical insight again have been the in-depth retrospective explorations of patients as the histories of their sex lives came under scrutiny at some point while they were being attended for related or unrelated difficulties.

The emerging generation of sexually liberated young people may well bring its own style of medical attendance and increase professionalism with it, notably women and their physicians: the latter knowledgeable, willing to tune in on their patients, and unabashed in discussing anything and everything that may be of interest to a sexually alive woman. Whether these doctors are willing to forego adapting at least some of their advice to their own moral convictions remains to be seen.

The author wishes to express his gratitude to friends, authorities and consultants in various specialties who were kind enough to read sections or chapters of the manuscript and offer suggestions, and to the colleagues who kindly permitted him the use of clinical material to supplement his own.

JOHN F. OLIVEN, M.D.

Preface to the First Edition

This book is designed to fill the needs of practicing physicians, medical students and certain groups of ancillary medical workers for information on sexual matters as they are of interest to the physician. The normal has been dealt with in some detail so that deviations from normality can be more easily recognized, understood and treated. The author assumes throughout the text that the reader has a medical background and that he is engaged with patients and their problems.

Awareness among physicians of the medical importance of sex matters appears to be increasing rapidly. In our day and age people are entitled to physicians who know the answers to certain personal health and hygiene questions and problems and will not shrug off, or skirt around, the subject of sex when the need for advice or treatment arises.

The plan for this book first came into being when medical students kept asking to be referred to a comprehensive, up-to-date text relating to sex matters, both for their general information and for future reference. The plan took more definite shape when much favorable interest followed in the wake of a Round Table on the Sex Instruction of the Medical Student (Drs. F. J. Gerty, L. G. Lowrey, J. F. Oliven [Chmn.], S. Rado, M. F. Reiser, E. Stainbrook; American Psychiatric Association, 1951). A number of physician friends in general practice, in several parts of the country and some abroad, have been kind enough to make a record of all sexual problems which happened to come to their professional attention, and of the information they would have liked to have. These data have been a great help in keeping close to the practicing physician's viewpoint. The author has tried to keep this book practical, but avoided the cut-and-dried, symptom-prescription type of approach, while at the same time enough theoretical data have been included to facilitate use of the volume as an adequate reference and text book.

The author desires to express his appreciation to those colleagues and students who have helped in collating and following up the clinical material, in making observations, in checking on the usefulness of certain approaches to treatment, and in searching the literature, both American and foreign. Grateful appreciation is expressed also to Drs. Earl T. Engle, Sol W. Ginsburg, Robert W. Laidlaw, Lawson G. Lowrey and Arthur M. Master, for their kindness in reading chapters or sections of the manuscript and offering appropriate comment.

JOHN F. OLIVEN, M.D.

Contents

Part 1

SEXUALITY IN CHILDHOOD

Part 3

SEXUALITY OF THE NORMAL ADULT

Part 4

SEXUAL PATHOLOGY

PART 1

Sexuality in Childhood

CHAPTER 1

Sexual Development of the Child

Origin of Male and Female — Child's Organs and Functions —
Psychosexual Phases of Childhood — Precocious Sexual
Development.

ORIGIN OF MALE AND FEMALE

The basic tendency of all human embryos is to develop as females; when
a male is programed to arise it must keep imposing masculine development
every step of the way. Thus many biologists now consider maleness technically an androgen-induced variant of the basic femaleness. The very first
choice, the original programing, appears to be random (see also p. 219):
the genetic sex is fixed at the moment of fertilization as either an X-bearing
or a Y-bearing spermatozoon unites with an ovum—all ova have one X sex
chromosome—to form an XX (female) or an XY (male) zygote. However,
it remains uncertain by what chemical device the genetic sex determinant
information is transmitted into the structural guidance system of sexual
development.

Bipotential Gonad. Evoking development of the appropriate gonad
is probably the earliest task. The fetal gonad is formed early. It organizes
at first as an indifferent structure which can differentiate into either ovary
or testis. As it arises, ridge-shaped, on each side from a patch of specialized
peritoneum, it is simultaneously invaded by numbers of large primitive germ
cells from the yolk sac which move like amebae and seek out the gonadal
tissue with great determination. It is assumed that male and female germ
cells exist, although they cannot be distinguished. The presumably female
cells, the future ova, settle, divide and multiply rapidly; the others form
linked cell cords, the future seminiferous tubules. Before the gonad differentiates, the primitive ridges begin to change into a pair of rounded
structures. Testicular structures develop earlier than ovaries: Leydig cells
are formed, and the invading germ cells have each brought its own nurtur-
ing—the future Sertoli—cell. Thus, before the end of the second month of
gestation* the basic testicular morphology is complete. After the second

---

* Refers to Gestational Age, calculated from day of expected ovulation following
last known menses, thus about 2 weeks younger than clinical reckoning by Nägele's
Rule (p. 224).

month the testicles become capable of secreting androgen. The ovaries develop considerably more slowly.

Genital Differentiation. Just before this, during the seventh week, the beginnings of the internal genitalia have emerged, in the form of a double set of primitive reproductive tracts: the wolffian ducts, to become vasa and seminal vesicles in a future male; and the müllerian ducts, to become fallopian tubes, uterus and uppermost vagina in a future female. For a while they exist side by side.

If a little boy is being produced, the newly completed testicles must now secrete substances to keep modifying intrauterine development along masculine lines. The ovaries in every fetus remain hormonally inactive; a female simply develops whenever no testicles are programed. At this stage—the third month—the testes are believed to produce 2 substances: an unknown inductor substance which suppresses the müllerian ducts, and an androgen which promotes development of the wolffian structures. Without androgen the wolffian ducts do not survive; for unknown reasons the left duct reacts more sensitively to the presence of androgen. Androgenic stimulation continues to be required for the development of the epididymides, the external genitalia, their midline fusion, and the suppression of vulvovaginal development. The time schedule for these various gender-differentiating steps appears to be rigidly set down; the process is completed by the fifth month.

Masculinizing the Brain. A period of relative inactivity of fetal testicular activity follows; the Leydig cells gradually regress, but little is known about this phase. There are indications that the central nervous system of the male fetus is dependent on a minimal androgenic level being maintained if subtle interference with masculinization of gender traits due to stressing of the mother is to be avoided. No equivalent need exists for the female fetus, and her neural centers seem to achieve maturation in a different hormonal environment. However, there is every indication that late during fetal life, or just possibly soon after birth, there is a postulated brief critical period during which the male fetus, stimulated by maternal chorionic gonadotropin, irreversibly differentiates his own brain toward maleness with a surge of testosterone. The basic pattern of all fetal brains is cycling, i.e., female: a cyclic release—by a built-in clock—of gonadotropin releasors; these, in turn, have the task of controlling the ovarian cycle including the all-important ovulatory LH surge (a remnant of the animal estrus). The intrinsic cycling mechanism is situated in steroid-sensitive centers of the hypothalamus; in the presence of testosterone the mechanism is washed out, bringing into operation the dormant male, constant ("tonic") releasing mechanism (Gorski, Barraclough, others). The parts played in subsequent cycling by the reticular activating system in the brain, by hypothalamic sensitivity to ovarian humoral signals, and by some other factors are being actively explored at present by workers in the important field of neuroendocrinology.

Inborn vs. Learned. Androgen is not everything in the process of becoming a human male, but it is much: the cruel incompleteness of androgenization, possible at several junctions, does not make the fetus revert to the basic femaleness, but it neuters the male in a number of ways. However, in normal humans, assumption of either the male or female gender role is not simply the result of testosterone exposure in utero or its absence. Rather, male and female neonates come into the world with a disposition to acquire certain ways of behaving, perhaps no more and certainly no less. Yet it is quite unrealistic to say that the child, apart from anatomic differences, is born psychosexually neutral, a tabula rasa, a unigender awaiting conditioning input to sway it one way or another. In certain respects masculine and feminine behavior are so inescapably entwined with sex-specific physiology that the innate disposition will not be denied. At the other end of the scale, traits heretofore unquestioningly regarded as being gender-specific are turning out to be cultural stereotypes. In prehistoric days the skills and behavior pattern of the slayer of beasts differed vastly from that of the nurser of children; in today's technologic society even certain biologically differentiated traits are becoming irrelevant, and may be gradually dropping away from the classical gender role profiles. But to speak of a "culturally prescribed gender role" is vastly irrational: cultural roles grew around differences in physiologic function; secondarily, a cultural overgrowth begins to exert a dynamic effect of its own on role attribution. The overgrowth may hide the neurohumoral wiring for gender, but the latter does not just disintegrate and disappear.

Mother-Infant Feedback. It is a matter of conjecture at this time how much the behavioral differences between male and female are determined by indoctrination, and how much by genetic mechanisms. Ascending the phylogenetic scale, learning probably becomes increasingly important for masculine-feminine differentiation. Under normal circumstances the infant seems to induce its own gender role learning. Its genitalia and what they imply, and perhaps certain other differences already observable in the hospital nursery, convey the original message to the mother; they create a specific gender response in the mother-infant unit in the form of a sensitive, dynamic feedback mechanism (theory). Mothers are profoundly sensitive to the reactions of their babies (Coleman-Kris-Provence); e.g., from the earliest they talk more to girls because infant girls seem to respond more to words, thus stimulating the mother to keep talking; later, the earlier greater verbal aptitude of girls—and of "Mamas' boys"—is observed. Generally, the female neonate seems to relate more actively to faces and people because of some unknown difference in neural organization; she thus molds the quality of the mother-infant relationship and probably the nature of the pleasing cycle. The young mother, from the earliest stage and even more so later, responds further to the gender cue by projecting different "hopes and hang-ups" into a male and a female infant, thus additionally modifying the response cycle. Unwittingly she thereby promotes, develops, or represses specific gender attitudes; she also overinterprets certain responses, and may over-respond to them in turn. Altogether, she clearly contributes defining influences to future sex-specific conduct.

Conditioning. With toddler age social conditioning and reinforcement of gender differences escalate. The mother gives the cues by the type of play encouraged, the degree of fussing with clothes, the amount of aggression tolerated, the toys supplied, or the child's just being labeled boy or girl. At the same time the effects of the combined dimorphism and earliest conditioning begin to show: girls hover closer to mother; males disperse their toys and toddle after them. Reactions to fences and other frustration differ; boys show a higher level of exertional activity and a tendency to competitive stances. The nature of play remains controversial, although, for instance, maternalism will emerge a few years later as a specific feminine trait, even after isolation from learning experience. This may not be true of girls' doll and house playing, which some unigender-rearing observations show to be conditioned; it may or may not be true of astronaut and Indian games deemed characteristic of boys. However, other play patterns in our culture remain differentiated even years later. In late childhood toy experiments boys construct fortifications with cannon and exterior action scenes; girls build low enclosures with elaborate doorways and organize and furnish the inside space. This may be paralleling the unconscious genital body image: out-directed organ versus internal reception space (Erikson).

Coding. Secondary learning of gender role and hardening of gender identity next is believed to proceed by yes-no coding in the brain. YES, in a boy, for instance, is the retrieval-comparison system (e.g., "that's the way *he* always does it"); the NO code is a cross-checking device (e.g., "this is a no-no, a girl thing"). It matters less what the culture allows each gender to be like and to do than does clarity and consistency of role distinction (Money). It may be mentioned that parental role blurring, now practiced in a small subculture, is believed to lead mainly to neuterizing and confusing the more vulnerable males; reproductive function may also be affected in that the mode and quality of sex expression have never been divorced from gender identity in our era. Around this time the child's father enters the picture as a direct communicator of gender attitudes; boy-girl names become meaningful; clothing and hair may assume some conscious differentiating importance, and genitalia are noticed, compared and reacted to. Code learning merges with role model imitation and identification. The differentiating task here is all the male's again, as it has been from earliest

MASCULINITY—FEMININITY AND GENDER IDENTITY
Some Psychologic Tests and Measures

Some of the alternative choice questionnaires in this group are useful mainly as group screening devices rather than as methods of individual personality diagnosis.

Draw-a-Person Test (J. Pers. Assess., *36*:307, 1972)

Toy Preference Observation

Games Observation (family set of dolls)

Minnesota Multiphasic Personality Inventory Mf scale (older adolescents and adults)

Thematic Apperception Test (TAT) BM-cards 3,6,7,8,17. 13MF

It Scale for Children (under 6) (J. Consult. Psychol., *21*:197, 1957)

Gough True-False Questionnaire (Educ. Psychol. Meas., *12*:427, 1952)

Franck Drawing Completion Test

Three Wishes Test

Guilford-Zimmerman Temperament Survey, masc-fem scale

Embedded Figure Test (Witkin, H.: Personality through Perception. New York, Harper & Row, 1954)

California Personality Inventory, masculine-feminine scale

Transsexual Attitude Scale (Barlow-Agras) For pathologic cases (Arch. Gen. Psychiatry 28:570, 1973)

House-Tree-Person (drawing) test (HTP)

Jenkins Personality Test (J. Psychol. Stud., *12*:237, 1961)

Bender Visual-Motor Gestalt test

Male-Female Vocabulary Test (Slater) (Brit. J. Med. Psychol., *21*:61, 1947)

Terman-Miles Test for masc. & fem. mental traits (Terman & Miles: Sex and Personality. New York, McGraw, 1936); 456 items but imperfectly discriminant. Little used now.

fetal life: the little boy must first "overcome" and disassociate from the mother and seek out the same-gender parent; the female has but to abide; she is thus less subject to mislearning and psychosexual derailment.

Imprinting. The child's self-concept as a boy or girl is probably completed at around 2½ years of age (Gershman); others have placed it as late as age 4. A short critical, high-susceptibility period may occur around that time during which the imprinting of the core gender identity, the unquestioned certainty of being male or female, takes place. Once imprinted, it appears to be permanent and unalterable. The stage of development at which gender imprinting occurs is not known. It is possible that it coincides with urination training—sitting or standing; that "the call of nature is the moment of truth" (Valentine).

Abnormalities. The human infant can be manipulated into a gender pattern counter to its chromosomes, its gonad and/or its genitals by means of a major brainwashing conspiracy followed later by surgical alteration if necessary. This is occasionally done for good and valid medical and humane reasons (see Intersexed States, p. 361), and the sex of assignment hopefully becomes the sex of rearing and leads to the desired gender identity. Apart from these anatomically severely stigmatized cases there are also assumed to be derailed little boys—certain future unmodifiable deviants— whose partly neuterized (androgen-starved?) brain is cued from the earliest to gender stimuli counter to the pattern: delight in esthetics, feminine ornaments, frocks, colors, cooking, etc. Their genitals are normal and they cannot be recognized as deviants at birth, but they mislearn and often misidentify genderwise in a manner as yet incompletely understood. Some of the observations and conclusions on sexual categorization now current may quite possibly have been marred by having been based too heavily on atypical—subtly neuterized and psychically derailed—infants.

CHILD'S ORGANS AND FUNCTIONS

The child's reproductive system is essentially formed, although unmatured. A functioning brain-pituitary-gonadal axis is in existence prior to puberty; i.e., gonadotropin is being secreted, although the set of the feedback signals is as yet low-keyed. Children produce small amounts of sex steroids: testosterone production in boys resembles the amount present in the adult woman (42 mg per 100 ml of blood plasma); estrogen is produced in very small amounts by both male and female children; in the latter it increases first at age 7 or 8.

In the Male

The Penis of the infant averages slightly less than 1 inch in length (20 to 25 mm) and slightly more than 1 inch (28 mm) in circumference. It grows somewhat until mid-childhood, reaching a length of from 1½ to 2 inches before age 7; then it remains stationary until the growth spurts of pubescence set in. The circumference increases a little until age 2, then remains more or less stationary at 1½ inches until pubescence. In uncircumcised boys, the prepuce adheres to the glans. If necessary, it can be detached with gentle force, but at birth only 4 per cent of boys have a fully retractable foreskin; 50 per cent have it at age 1 and 90 per cent within a few years. The need for routine circumcision of the infant continues to be disputed sporadically; "the prepuce of the newborn is normally so tight and adherent that no information can be obtained as to later need for circumcision." (McKay)

Micropenis (microphallus) is a rare congenital anomaly. The organ usually has no corpora cavernosa. Testicular deficiency may be associated. Must be differentiated from the hidden penis of the obese boy. Treatment: phalloplasty in mid- or late childhood, following trial with testosterone.

Epispadias. Fairly rare. Partial or complete defect of dorsal fusion of the urethra which may include bladder sphincter. Penis tends to be short, squashed-looking. Treatment: surgery before school age.

Hypospadias. Fairly frequent. Urethra ends and opens ventrally somewhere along the shaft. Often a symptom of intersexuality, requiring careful diagnosis (p. 361). Associated chordee makes the penis curve downward. Prepuce partially overgrows the glans. Treatment: early surgery.

The Scrotum of the newborn is dark red in color, flaccid, has a distinct raphe and is covered with a sparse growth of lanugo. At about the seventh to the tenth month it becomes smoother and less flaccid, and its (proximal) base increases in width. It undergoes no further changes until pubescence when it begins to darken and wrinkle, and its distal end becomes enlarged to accommodate the growing testicles.

The Testicles are not always in the scrotum at birth, but in most cases they have descended by the second to the eighth week. By 1 year of age 80 per cent of undescended testes have also descended (Scorer). At birth the normal testicle averages 12 to 15 mm in length, shape is ovoid as in the adult, but position in the scrotum is more nearly vertical. At birth, testicle and epididymis are of equal size and almost completely separated from each other, while the adult epididymis is about one ninth the size of the testis. Following postbirth involution of the Leydig cells, the testicles change only very slightly during the first half of childhood. Massive development sets in at pubescence. In about 50 per cent of boys the 2 testes are of unequal size; their consistency is normally harder than in the adult.

Undescended Testicles (cryptorchidism, cryptorchism). A frequent, often vexing pediatric anomaly in which one or both testicles remain in the abdomen or in the inguinal canal instead of being in the scrotum. It may be recalled that the fetal testicles migrate from the abdomen in the seventh month of pregnancy. A peritoneal pocket evaginates through the abdominal muscles along the inguinal canal, just ahead of testicle and epididymis as they are drawn by a fibrous band, the gubernaculum, toward the as yet rudimentary scrotum. After exiting from the inguinal canal the peritoneal pocket (processus vaginalis) closes behind each testicle, the gubernacula disappear, the vasa deferentes elongate and the testes enlarge; they reach—the left one first—the bottom of the scrotum in the ninth month or soon after birth. The descent is controlled by maternal chorionic gonadotropin.

Undescended differ from ectopic testicles; the latter have deviated from their normal course while descending. Also to be differentiated are retractile (migratory, hypermobile, pseudocryptorchic) testes, a benign variant of normal descent involving intermittent retraction or easy retractability out of the scrotum by cremasteric muscle action; the condition is self-correcting near pubescence and the testicles remain undamaged. Very rare is congenital uni- or bilateral anorchia which can be ruled out by evoking a testosterone reaction—congestion and pigmentation of scrotum, increased erections, inguinal discomfort—by injecting chorionic gonadotropin 1000 units 3 or 4 times, 4 days apart, in the small boy.

The undescended testicle remains relatively small, the ipsilateral side of the scrotum remains undeveloped, while the controlateral testicle undergoes some compensatory hypertrophy even before puberty. About 5 per cent of cases of bilateral cryptorchism are associated with major endocrine or developmental pathology. In most other cases the causes of failure to descend are incompletely understood. There is no unanimity on the onset and extent of damage to the undescended testicle, but the following appears ascertained.

Microscopic damage develops progressively from age 2 while from the fifth or the sixth year substantial degenerative changes in the interstitial tissues, deficient spermatogonia and reduced seminiferous tubules have been demonstrated by microphotography. The damage to the seminiferous structures is probably due to increased abdominal temperature. In bilateral cryptorchism, the testicles secrete about one half of the normal amount of androgens; sterility is the rule. The hormone-producing cells resist damage better than the sperm-producing structures. The age at which the spermatogenic damage first becomes irreversible continues in dispute; however, spermatogenesis is irrevocably lost in almost all cases past the age of 17. In unilateral cases, sterility is probably not to be feared, because even a portion of one healthy testicle supplies enough normal spermatozoa to ensure fertility. Even bilateral cryptorchism does not interfere with normal sexual development and maturation. In the rare case where it does, anorchia rather than cryptorchism may be suspected to exist, calling for rapid intervention (see p. 342).

Prostate and Seminal Vesicles and other accessory genital structures are very little developed in the child. The prostate is usually not palpable rectally, and no secretion can be massaged from it.

Erections can occur from birth—and prenatally—and are observed throughout infancy and childhood. In infants they occur either without apparent cause or in conjunction with bowel movements, after urination, during cleansing manipulations, from excitement of any kind, or during REM sleep; they may last from 30 seconds up to 1 hour. Prolonged erections are sometimes a cause of fretting, restlessness and inability to sleep. A search of the area may reveal local irritation; if not, the infant should be kept generally quiet except for gentle arm-rocking; sedative medication, cold-wet envelopes or sitz baths should not be used to detumesce the organ.

In young boys erections are occasioned, in about equal measure, by erotic and nonerotic stimuli. The former include pleasurable erotic or quasi-erotic fantasies and genital self-stimulation. Among the nonerotic sources are prolonged sitting, for instance in school, church, or a vehicle; accidental friction from tight underclothing; rhythmic motions such as bicycling, swimming or gently jolting rides; and various emotions, notably acute fear, fearsome dreams, pain, startle, joyous anticipation or "thrills," such as the sight of marching soldiers, fires or climactic rescue scenes in adventure books or movies. Most very small boys show only moderate interest in their erections, and there is little recollection later. It is not unusual for a boy who reaches late childhood to be startled when he notices his own erection "for the first time." Copulation is possible in boys as young as 5 or 6 years of age, although their erective endurance and copulatory skill are limited at this early age, and there is little satisfaction.

Orgasm has been observed to occur as early as the fourth or fifth month of age, but relative peak incidence of first orgasm in boys is probably between 6 and 8 years of age (e.g., through masturbation or companionate sex play). Prepuberal orgasm is characterized by the absence of an ejaculation (dry throb) and by quick-succession multi-orgasmic capacity.

Spermatogenesis does not occur in the normal child.

In the Female

The Vulva of the little girl, even with thighs in close apposition, is more conspicuous than in the adult woman; there is no pubic hair; a slight relative anterior tilt of the pelvis makes the external genitalia appear situated more anteriorly ("higher"); and the lack of labial development tends to expose the introitus more and makes the vulva appear more pouting and/or slit-like. The memory of the clearly visible hairless "slit" or "crack" vividly preoccupies some pubescent boys until the reality of the teenage or adult vulva supersedes it. Some males do not make this transition: the obsessive imagery of some heterosexual pedophiliacs (p. 472) seems to center mainly on this image rather than on the child's person. The relatively exposed introitus contributes to the ease with which infection ascends into the immature vagina. The vulva is also more easily traumatized than in adults (e.g., in edge and straddle falls). The clitoris in childhood is relatively large; it may attain a considerable proportion of its growth before pubescence. The clitoral prepuce may be asymptomatically adherent or redundant. The Bartholin glands are rudimentary and not believed capable of harboring infection.

Hymen. The child's hymen is located relatively high in the vulvovaginal passage; it may not be easy to visualize unless the child is made to strain or cry. Its early appearance differs from that in the adult woman: it lies somewhat bunched upon itself in an irregularly redundant fold. The average opening is usually less than pencil-size; this does not appear to change during childhood. The same atypical openings as in the adult (p. 183) may be found. The hymen is sensitive to touch in children from age 3.

The Vagina of the small child is relatively longer and directed more toward the vertical than in the older girl or woman; it measures from 3 to 4½ cm in length. Its length increases only slightly during childhood. Except during the first few weeks of life the child's vaginal walls are thin and fragile, until puberal changes take place. Rugae formation is marked, but the walls are closely approximated and not always easily separated. The child's vaginal secretion is neutral or slightly alkaline, which contributes to the low resistance to local infection.

Uterus, Ovaries and Fallopian Tubes. These organs occupy a relatively high intra-abdominal position in the small girl and do not descend into the true pelvis until pubescence. The uterus immediately after birth is disproportionately large due to the effect of maternal estrogen; postnatally it rapidly decreases to the size of a large hazelnut, and grows only slightly and gradually before pubescence. Unlike the adult's, the child's uterus has an almost straight axis; there is no anteflexion and little anteversion. In infancy the cervix constitutes about two thirds of the length of the uterus, but in the second half of childhood the corpus grows relatively faster than the cervix. The cervical canal is poorly developed and probably closed tightly due to circular elastic tension, so that usually no patent uterovaginal connection exists. The ovaries, at birth, are narrow and flat and usually the size of a lima bean, although considerable variations within the same age group occur. Ovarian cysts without clinical significance are frequent in children. The fallopian tubes in childhood are tiny, thin, tortuous structures.

Ovulation and **Menstruation** do not occur in normal children.

Orgasm may be experienced in childhood, or even in infancy. It is not known with certainty if masturbatory arousal produces vaginal transudation as in the adult, although a moist vulva is described by nurses and mothers of some girls.

PSYCHOSEXUAL PHASES OF CHILDHOOD

Throughout infancy and childhood, the development of instinctual patterns appears to follow an intrinsic timetable of its own. As programed maturational changes in peripheral receptors and central nervous system tracts take place, and in keeping with the postulate that psychologic development follows underlying biologic growth in the immature (Alexander), the young infant keeps up with how its own developing neural organization equips it to react. This instinctual progression parallels such sequential changes as progress from crawling to walking, or from vocalizing to talking.

Timetable. The development occurs in stages or zonal phases. The nature of these phases, together with their sequence, is reasonably well established, although there are differences in their onset, duration, intensity and in the manner of their overlap. The basic scheme in each child cannot be modified by any direct effort of the mother or anyone else. However, the circumstances of life can tamper with the orderly course of the phases; e.g., an unhealthy emotional milieu, extended illness, or disruptive interaction between mother and child can hinder transition from one stage to the next, thus unduly prolonging the previous one; traumatic events can severely frustrate the natural pleasure content of some phase; or undue affect—pain, anxiety, excessively pleasurable indulgence—can become fixedly associated with some zone or stage. There are substantial indications, but no certainty, that such disruptions during a specific critical period can have a lasting and defining influence on future psychologic, especially psychosexual propensities.

The forerunners of the various stages are found in the diffuse, practically undifferentiated sensuosity of the small infant, in the bodily pleasure and delight he derives from kinesthetic and vegetative stimuli and impulses, and especially from the total surface of his own body. At first the small infant obtains sensual delight through his entire skin and from proprioceptive sensations (e.g., stroking, cuddling, warmth, satiety); and somewhat later from rolling, squirming, kicking, rocking, etc., with the degree of responsiveness varying from baby to baby. Somewhat later, the sources of bodily pleasure become especially concentrated in a number of zones, notably around the mucocutaneous junctions. These primitive erogenous (erotogenic) zones displace one another in sequence.

Orality. The first such zone is the mouth. In most children this oral phase is believed to predominate between the fourth and the tenth months, although vestiges of this predominance sometimes remain for years. Drinking and eating are not the only pleasurable stimuli: the infant seems to enjoy all tactile and pressure sensations about the lips and the tongue and may produce them himself by fingersucking, etc.; even orgasmlike responses from excessive mouth stimulation have been observed here. A subdivision into a receptive-retentive and an aggressive-biting phase has been postulated also. The sense of smell may play some part at this stage.

Anality. Next, approximately during the second year of life (range: 10 months to 3 years of age) the mouth phase is displaced by the predominance of pleasurable interest in the perineal openings and their functions. Initially the source of the pleasure is kinesthetic and tactile, e.g., sensuous delight in the feeling of a distended bladder, of fecal masses in the rectum, or of the outflow of the voiding stream. Soon this is intermingled with a new kind of cerebrally higher pleasure found in the toying with, owning and controlling at will of these functions. This anal phase coincides with toilet training and with the first pronounced showing of self-assertion by the child. The pleasurable controlling sensations become tied to a primitive sense of power when the infant learns that by way of the bowels he can center on himself various kinds of pleading, commendatory or similar attention on the part of the parent-trainer. Current thinking on toilet training favors waiting until the child is less contrary (boys near age 3, girls at 2) and to interrupt training voluntarily rather than have a battle of wills. Among permissive mothers median training starting age was 16 months, completion age 1½ to 3 years. A few children with older siblings initiate their own training; 20 per cent started at younger than 12 months, and a few completed after age 4 (Thomas-Chess-Birch).

Genitality. At about 2½ years of age—sometimes much earlier, sometimes later—sensuous interest becomes gradually centered in the genitalia (i.e., the penis or the vulva). The child discovers these parts and explores them, and this is accompanied by vaguely pleasurable sensations. Characteristic of this phase are curiosity about the presence or the lack of a penis in oneself or in other children. Masturbatory maneuvers, of a rather casual nature, are not unusual here for a period of 1 to 3 years in both sexes.

Narcissism. While the early genital phase is still in progress, fairly close to kindergarten age now, there occurs an incompletely understood personality shift which marks the transition, usually fairly rapid, from primitive, zone-centered autoerotism to the more advanced object love (allo-erotism). The first love object to emerge is the self: self-love of the child for itself as a total object, known as narcissism (narcism). Symptoms of this new fascination include mirror-admiration, exhibition of pretty underthings, mannerisms of cuteness, and a suddenly developing bodily modesty. Narcissism is not extinguished by subsequent developmental progression, but continues to develop and coexist with object relationships and, to a widely varying degree, probably throughout life (theory).

Oedipal Phase. The next love object to emerge, with onset approximately between 4 and 6 years of age (range 3–7 years) is usually the parent of the opposite sex or, where circumstances dictate a fantasy image of him (her). This is the most turbulent psychosexual developmental period of childhood, although it often passes unnoticed. The genital phase is not extinguished at this point, and the principal source of sensuous pleasure often are still the genitalia. Erotic interest may range from a tenuous, barely noticeable infatuation—"I want to marry Mummy (Daddy)"—to the most intense erotic fantasies and impulses. The child fantasizes in accordance with the sex information he possesses, e.g., that intimately loving the parent means looking at each other's private parts, or some way of babymaking, or going to the toilet together. The child clings to the conviction that there is now no physical intimacy between the parents. In boys this phenomenon has been called Oedipus situation, after the well-known ancient Greek myth of filial incest and retribution. In girls, the phase frequently has been designated the Elektra complex.

In the wake of this attachment there is usually some subsurface jealousy and rivalry with the parent of the same sex, feelings of guilt, and fear of the rival's retaliation. A boy may hate his father intensely during this phase, or a girl her mother, yet, at the same time, dependence on and love need for the father does not cease in the normal child (ambivalence of feelings). Even though no actual hostility has been shown him, a boy may have fearful fantasies that retaliation will be aimed at the organ which is his main source of bodily pleasure perception at this stage, i.e., he may fear mutilation of the penis. Girls, in whom the conflict situation appears to be less intense, are believed, with less certainty, to imagine that the mother will vent her jealous anger against them, or already has, or they may fear that the father will retaliate against them because of their hostile, occasionally mutilating fantasies against him. In a negative resolution of the oedipal phase the boy, fearful of angering the powerful father, fantasizes and acts himself into an essentially undesirable masochistic, passive-submissive relationship with him. Excessive fear here is believed capable of damaging his masculinity (disputed). In a resolution by crisis, also undesirable, the rival parent may happen to leave home, or die, or otherwise change status; or in single-parent upbringing overexposure (p. 74) may occur as the mother is tempted to allow acting-out of a romantic attachment.

Under normal and generally favorable circumstances this irrational sexual competitive conflict is ended by moderately rapid lysis, as the father provides the continued warm, unstifling rapport which is necessary for a meaningful reality testing. The boy perceives, as it were, that Mother belongs rightfully to Father; that he must grow up to be like Father—whom he now begins to idealize—to attract such a mate to himself. At the same time most erotic interest recedes and stays relatively dormant for the remainder of childhood.

The Oedipus situation had been assumed to represent a normal and necessary stage in the child's development. It may be that, but, according to newer views, it does not appear to be a universal, quasi-biologic phenomenon, and its intensity and importance appear to be subject to, and to vary with, cultural and social circumstances.

Latency. Beginning at about school age and lasting into early pubescence, slightly longer and more marked in boys, the latency period ends the intense emotional, psychosexual upheavals of the genital and oedipal phases. It gives the child respite from the intense erotic fantasizing of the preceding years, as well as an opportunity to develop social traits, learn new interests, make companions and explore the wider world (Lief). The rudiments of ethical traits emerge which will later keep sexuality within civilized bounds. The average child becomes markedly less absorbed in his own person and more outwardly directed. Children now herd with same-sex peers, ignore or denigrate the opposite sex and tend to draw apart from them. Girls find boys uncouth and may fear them; boys think of girls as sissies who can't do any real, interesting things. Sexual behavior is not absent, especially in the second half of latency, but it is more a social manifestation. Kissing parties are a game, or a rehearsal for skills and feelings soon to come. Any companionate sex play is often motivated by social pressures, e.g., fear of being considered a sissy, or wanting to be a good sport, or a form of competition. Crushes are on safe adults: there is no rejection in yearning and dreaming. Coitus is in imitation of others (e.g., in crowded slum dwellings, or by adult seduction). Only where the environment is excessively restrictive or punitive of naturally widening sex curiosity and experimentation may sex feelings, often negative now, become florid again. Any massive irruption of sexual stimuli during the latency phase which is beyond the child's power to ward off is apt to have an unsettling effect (see also p. 74).

PRECOCIOUS SEXUAL DEVELOPMENT
(PRECOCIOUS PUBERTY, PUBERTAS PRAECOX)

Premature sexual development, more frequent in girls, produces an often vastly precocious emergence of sexual characteristics, together with early height growth. There are two principal types: true precocity, with steroid production by the gonads induced by premature activation of the hypothalamic releasing mechanism; and precocious pseudopuberty due to independent steroid secretion by adrenal or gonadal tissue (tumors, hyperplasia). In the former, the gonads mature and there is a regular puberty at an irregular age, including fertility. In the latter the gonads remain immature and there is neither ovulation nor spermatogenesis (diagnostic first step: a serum LH level by radioimmunoassay to determine if the pituitary is suppressed by excessive amounts of sex hormones; many other tests must follow). In true precocity the development is always in accord with patient's own gender (isosexual); in pseudoprecocity it can be either way. Onset varies: precocious puberty is deemed to exist if menarche occurs before age 8⅔ and sexual maturation begins before 6⅔ years of age, adding 2 years to the latter in boys (Tanner). Other observers postulate as precocity onset before age 9 in girls, age 10 in boys.

Growth. Some sexually precocious children, especially those with tumors, are chronically ill or have a short life span, but most enjoy fair to excellent health. They are very tall for their ages: height increase and skeletal maturation are very often (always, in boys) the earliest signs, and at present nothing can safely be done to arrest this growth. Unfortunately the epiphyses close early, and final adult stature is reached between 9 and

14 years of age; it is not much above dwarf size as a rule, although the range reaches a few inches above 5 feet. The earlier the onset, the sooner they stop growing (Thamdrup). Many such children look, move, and talk as if they were teen-agers, but their range of interests usually remains childlike. Few have unusually advanced social poise or emotional maturity, but most become unsuited for keeping company with their age mates (e.g., "a woman among kids") and by drift and/or arrangement—earlier-begun or accelerated schooling if of good intelligence—they seek friends somewhat nearer their somatic age.

Behavior. Behavior varies; most adjust quite well with proper handling and with professional guidance of the parents. While normal children often engage in sex play without ever coming to adult attention, chances are greater that the precocious child will be reported by a playmate who is frightened or startled, especially by the pigmentation and the hairiness of the patient's private parts. A sense of frustration, partly expressed as rage, enters the picture; these children are often deprived of the normal demonstrative affection of their parents and others: a father may be reticent to hug and caress a full-breasted girl seemingly in her early teens who comes to sit on his lap, or a mother may be startled when her 4-year-old son, cuddling in bed innocently, thrusts an erect phallus into her side. These children are children, with the emotional needs of children; it is very easy for an adult who faces a sexually precocious child to lose sight of the child's chronologic age and to expect too much (Hampson). Truly disturbed behavior appears to occur mostly in the posterior hypothalamic type of precocity; some of these children are so restless, unstable and difficult to control that they require behavior-modifying medication under psychiatric supervision.

Sexuality. In girls, if it is apparent from the diagnosis that menses will occur, the mother should prepare the child for this. Increased erections of their relatively large organs bewilder or even panic some very young boys. Boys' ejaculations are accompanied by some degree of orgasmic sensation, either while masturbating or in the form of involuntary nocturnal emissions; some kind of "exciting" dreams may accompany these emissions. Where erotic daydreaming is present—possibly to the same degree as in normal pubescents—it may be a mixture of childlike notions, romanticism, crude genital imagery and generally "exciting" situations.

Although their genitality may be use-ready, precocious boys infrequently appear to be sexually aggressive, nor are the girls especially seduction-prone, unless their upbringing has been grossly mismanaged, or in some cases of endogenous, e.g., cerebral behavior disorder. Their childlike range of interest tends to act as a check on the unfolding instinctual drive, although patterning in this respect tends to be labile more often than not, and much attention needs to be given by parents to the continuous re-channeling of energy and curiosity (Money). On the other hand, precocious children require unobtrusive protection from sexual victimization, especially little girls who are able to conceive. Both sexes should receive adequate sexual instruction at an accelerated rate, and an effort should be made to condition them to earlier concealment of their private organs than one would expect from normal children.

Treatment deals firstly with the underlying condition where possible. Hydrocortisone is specific in adrenal hyperplasia. Thyroid suppresses the manifestations of precocity in cases associated with hypothyroidism. Tumors are treated surgically. In cryptogenic precocity Depo-Provera (medroxyprogesterone acetate) 100 to 250 mg i.m. at 2-week intervals, suppresses precocious girls' menses, breast growth and other biologic estrogen manifestations, but it does not slow height growth or bone maturation. Some antiandrogenic compounds seemed to do this, but they were discontinued because unsuitably dangerous. The search for an effective, safe gonadotropin suppressant has continued.

The following principal varieties of precocious puberty may be mentioned.

Cryptogenic (Idiopathic, Constitutional) Precocity. The most common variety. Sexual maturation is complete, and only in this type are girls known to become pregnant (youngest mother on record: full term delivery by Caesarean of a son at 5 years and 8 months of age; Peru 1939. Other, well-documented cases at 6 and older). Development of feminine contour, breasts, pubic hair, vagina and internal genitalia usually begins before age 5; these children skip all or part of their physiologic childhood. Boys have concentrations of plasma testosterone and androstenedione very similar to those of normal adult men; their ejaculations contain live spermatozoa; youngest father on record reportedly 7 years old. These children are in good health. Diagnosis can only be made by excluding all other types of precocity, especially the cerebral. However, most cryptogenic EEGs are abnormal, and symptoms of undetected brain symptomatology may appear only later: prolonged vigilance is necessary to avoid missing tumor signs. Otherwise, as the name implies, the cause is unknown. A genetic theory— there are a good many heredofamilial cases—exists. There are also indications that a part is played by undetected hamartomas, a malformation of up to egg size, consisting of nervous tissue, at the base of the hypothalamus, with connecting fibers between the two only in cases where the mass and precocity coexist. There is no treatment for cryptogenic precocity, but the prognosis, except for final stature, is excellent.

Cerebral (Neurogenic) Precocity. This is a true precocity, with early fertility, although the children may be too ill or do not live long enough to have conceived or begotten offspring; there are no known cases of this. The condition is recognized most often in boys, although McCune-Albright's

PRECOCIOUS PUBERTY

Frequency of Principal Types among 770 Cases (Wilkins)

	Girls	Boys	Total
A. True Precocity			
Cryptogenic	52.1%	14.4%	66.5%
Cerebral	2.3%	6.6%	8.9%
McCune-Albright			
Syndrome	4.3%	0.2%	4.5%
B. Pseudoprecocity			
Testicular Tumor		2.3%	2.3%
Ovarian Tumor	10.1%		10.1%
Congenital Andreno-genital Syndrome in Boys. (Girls, technically, develop pseudo-hermaphrodism, q.v.)		7.6%	7.6%

With refinements of neurodiagnostic techniques and longer observation the ratio of cyptogenic:cerebral cases of true precocity has shrunk, mostly in boys.

polyostotic fibrous dysplasia, where the bony skull lesions seem to be the prime culprit, is a disease largely of girls. A vast variety of intracranial disorders and abnormalities have been identified as causes, some diffuse (postmeningitic or postencephalitic states, convulsive disease, etc.), some localized; the latter always in or near the posterior hypothalamus. This includes hamartomas, pineal gland tumors, various tumors of the floor of the third ventricle, tuberous sclerosis, etc. Onset of precocity is after age 6, except in hamartomas where it is very early.

Precocious Pseudopuberty due to Congenital Adrenal Hyperplasia (formerly adrenogenital syndrome). Sexual development here may, but need not, start as early as the first year of life. Onset after age 2 requires differentiation from an adrenal tumor. There is rapid height growth and early bone and dental maturation as well as masculinization of habitus, skin, hair, and voice, but the internal genitalia including gonads remain immature. The progressive virilization of girls is checked by the early-begun cortisone treatment which most of them receive today, and nothing much out of the ordinary happens; but unless treatment is started very early, their build, voice, hair distribution and personality, and perhaps the clitoris, remain somewhat characteristic. Treatment tends to be late-begun or even omitted where congenital changes of the external genitals are slight or where virilization sets in post-birth. There is no female puberal development in untreated girls. In late-treated prepuberal girls it sets in rapidly, and earlier than normally as treatment is started. Untreated boys show hypermasculinity; the big penis contrasts with the small testicles, although scrotum and prostate are also large (macrogenitosomia praecox; infant Hercules). They are stocky, muscular, deep-voiced, hirsute and bearded. With early diagnosis and appropriate steroid treatment these children will grow and develop normally. The cause of the disease is inherited defects in the enzymatic synthesis of corticosteroids; syndromes of hypertension or chronic sodium loss are associated in some.

Pseudoprecocity as a result of maternal progestational medication (some types of birth control pills) during the critical fetal period is observed at times. The syndrome in females is a form of intersexuality; see p. 107 and p. 363. In boys the precocious, muscular infant Hercules results, with large penis and scrotum and accelerated motor development (e.g., walking at 7 months). Associated disturbance of the sleep mechanism, unremitting hyperactivity and reckless day-and-night adventurousness have been seen to strain the parents' stamina during the first year of life (Russell).

The untreated hyperadrenal boy—some are still encountered—may develop difficulties in pubescence due to the suddenly imposed change in body image and social regard: linear growth stops and they suddenly fall way behind their peers ("from Lord Strongman to the pip dwarf"). Untreated boys also fail to develop puberally. Timely-treated girls become physically normal girls with minor stigmata at most (see above), but there is a high incidence of tomboys (q.v.) among them, mostly of moderate degree and largely reversible following menarche. The girls accept marriage; there are no lesbian inclinations. In childhood many are bright, quick-witted, imaginative and intellectually ahead of their age mates. In pubescence they seem to become plodding, dull, depressive; some timid, inhibited, lacking initiative, passive and withdrawn; others irritable, even irascible, with permanent chips on their shoulders. In adulthood, after finally receiving treatment, equilibrium is largely regained. If intelligence was high to begin with, it probably remains high—on paper: high intelligence buried in torpor or aloofness, or wrapped in irritation barbed to the point of inaccessibility, is functionally no better than dullwittedness. Besides, the effect of sex steroids on intellectual functioning remains largely unexplored.

Gonadal Tumors. These are fairly rare types of pseudoprecocity and, very occasionally, of true pubertas praecox. Most often one testicle is involved, the other being immature and atrophic. Orchiectomy is followed by regression of the precocity, but not in all cases. Adrenal rest tumors in a testis may reproduce the adrenal variety of precocity. Girls with an ovarian tumor may menstruate, even from infancy, but do not ovulate. One ovary is most often affected. Treatment is chiefly surgical.

Precocity from Various Causes. Cases of sexual precocity have been reported in small numbers following prepuberal excision of the spleen with hepatoblastoma; in some types of chronic nephritis; and in gonadotropin-producing tumors in various locations. Precocity has occurred in hypothyroid children. Transient, mild physiologic precocity occurs in the first weeks of life due to the high hormone level retained from the maternal circulation. Virilizing adrenal hyperplasia may be produced in utero through hormones administered to the mother. An infant or a child may develop degrees of transient or even permanent hypergenitalism, bone growth changes, breast and nipple growth, hirsutism, or bloody vaginal discharge through excessive response to hormone medication for cryptorchism (chorionic gonadotropin) or for vulvovaginitis (estrogen); from contact with the hands of a mother who uses hormone cream; from accidental ingestion of birth control pills; or possibly due to contamination of children's medications during manufacture.

Incomplete Precocity. Premature pubarche, i.e., pubic and some axillary hair growth in childhood or even infancy (mostly girls) without other major precocity is now increasingly considered as an incomplete form of adrenal pseudoprecocity (adrenarche). Because of the relatively high concurrent incidence of mental defect, epilepsy or cerebral palsy in these cases, a hypothalamic origin has also been suggested. In premature thelarche, isolated precocity of breast development in females in late infancy, without other evidence of heightened hormonal activity, is assumed to be due to isolated end organ overresponsiveness. Differentiation from drug (estrogen) induced mammary growth can be made by the absence of areolar and nipple pigmentation in the former.

Spurious Precocity. Some early maturers merely represent the extreme end of the normal curve of distribution of puberal onset, often a familial or ethnic trait, which may be rendered more conspicuous in a certain environment or when associated with delinquency. A child who is conspicuously curious sexually, unduly provocative or aggressive in his (her) sex interest and possessing some early sophistication in the use of the spoken word, but with normal childlike build and sex characteristics, may be called "precocious" in everyday language, but this does not represent precocious puberty. Some parents mistakenly expect early pubescence in such cases and have been known to become anguished when it was not forthcoming. Some little girls with a sonorous voice, an early tendency to facial down rendered conspicuous by its color and consistency, with seemingly intense interest in sex, a slightly large clitoris and known to masturbate but with normal laboratory tests, fall under the benign heading of a constitutional viriloid variant, and can probably be left alone with impunity. Episodes of true priapism sometimes occurring in small boys with sickle cell disease are not evidence of precocity.

FOR ADDITIONAL READING

Beach, F. A. (ed.): Sex and Behavior. New York, John Wiley & Sons, 1965
Erikson, E.: Childhood and Society. New York, W. W. Norton Co., 1963

Freud, A.: Normality and Pathology in Childhood: Assessment of Development. New York, Internatl. Universities Press, 1965

Gardner, L. I. (ed.): Endocrine and Genetic Diseases of Childhood. Philadelphia, Saunders, 1969

Maccoby, E. E. (ed.): The Development of Sex Differences. Stanford Univ. Press, 1966

Patten, B. M.: Human Embryology, ed. 3, New York, Blakiston-McGraw Hill, 1968

Sharman, A.: Reproductive Physiology of the Precocious Puberty. Livingston, 1966

Somjen, G.: Sensory Coding in the Mammalian Nervous System. New York, Appleton-Century-Crofts, 1972

Spitz, R. A.: The First Year of Life. New York, Internatl. Universities Press, 1965

Stoller, R. J.: Sex and Gender. On the Development of Masculinity and Femininity. New York, Science House, 1968

Thomas, A., Chess, S., Birch, H. *et al.*: Behavioral Individuality in Early Childhood, New York, N.Y. University Press, 1963

CHAPTER 2

Sex Education of the Child

Principles of Sex Education — Typical Questions and Answers — Unsound Attitudes and Reactions — Sex Education in Lower Grade School.

PRINCIPLES OF SEX EDUCATION

Sex education in childhood is essentially an attitude, rather than a rational course of instruction designed to acquaint the child with the physiologic facts of reproduction. Under ideal circumstances, gradual knowledge of the facts of life does not result from a separate effort by the parents but is a by-product of affectionate upbringing.

Perhaps the most important fact of life that the child must learn is the meaning of love. Unfortunately, comprehension cannot be transmitted by purposeful instruction. It is learned in the course of the years, mainly as the child watches the parents treat each other with affection. With this knowledge firm, much of the subsequent advice becomes relatively easy to give and easy to accept. Where, for instance, an older child need be told that genital activity is characteristic of, or reserved for, people when they have grown up and love each other ("as Father and Mother do"), this evokes a clear picture in the child's mind. Obversely, references to love are likely to be meaningless if they come from parents living in a chronically discordant marriage.

Seeding Furtiveness. Proper sex education is a continuous process which begins soon after infancy and does not end before the later stages of adolescence. Sooner or later the child who can talk begins to express interest in why the sky is blue, why Daddy leaves the house in the morning, where babies come from, or why boys' things and girls' things are different. If certain subjects are persistently singled out for evasion or disapproval, the normal child quickly understands that there is something wrong with the object of his curiosity, since at that early age concepts of modesty, privacy and discretion are beyond his comprehension.

The child then knows that some things he is concerned with are disapproved, bad, or—pursuant to the pars pro toto principle governing much of child mentality—perhaps that he himself is bad. It is only somewhat later that it becomes apparent that a substantial element of distrust and furtiveness already has been introduced into the child-parent relationship. Many of the problems that arise subsequently are probably only a pyramiding of guilty (i.e., unapproved) knowledge (street type) on top of furtiveness. Although any number of things are declared off limits to the small child from time to time—matches, glass, poking in baby's eyes—this type of thwarting is based on reasons, the reasons are often given, and they do not relate to some of the child's tensely exploratory own-body concerns. One can also predict that parents unable to be relaxed about the earliest curiosities of a child will be at least as tense about the even more "embarrassing" or "improper" questions bound to arise by midchildhood.

Results of Evasion. Where no one takes responsibility for answering the child's early questions, these children often seem to become overpreoccupied with elimination, genitalia and babies. Falling back on a mixture of their own imaginings and fragments of hearsay, they are apt to build up rather worrisome explanations for themselves. Parents who fail the child in his early curiosity are usually also the ones who harshly discourage early genital self-exploration, thus producing additional sources of bewilderment or anxiety. It may be several years before the child connects the genital prohibitions with the subject matter of some of its unanswered questions. Some of these children can be expected to display more than casual interest in companionate sex exploration and sex play, which, in turn, is likely to generate additional feelings of guilt in them.

A little later the normal thrill that such unguided children experience when doing something secret invests sex vulgarity with an excessive aura of "fun" which is quite unrelated to any biologic or psychological needs. Still later, when the need for counsel and guidance is especially acute, the child cannot turn to the parents because it has been conditioned not to expect answers from them, or because of a wholly conditioned sense of embarrassment when "certain subjects" come up. The totally unguided child, as it grows up, must rely on miscellaneous information, often from irresponsible sources. Facts and distortions intermingle to build up separate images of love and of sex. Excessively cavalier, or unduly romanticized attitudes, or an otherwise distorted code of sex behavior may result and carry over into adulthood. To their child's lifelong detriment, the parents thus have failed to bestow what is the ultimate goal of all sex education: the eventual ability to merge biologic impulses with a fully satisfying family life.

Question Asking. Sex instruction proper begins when the child begins to ask questions. Most often one may expect a normal child to translate his interest into his first sex questions at about 2½ years of age. As a general average, questions are asked for the first time about the mother's breasts at 2½, about urination differences between 2½ and 3¼, about sex differences between girls and boys generally between 2½ and 3½, where babies come from between 3¼ and 3½, about how the baby gets out of a mother between 4 and 4½, about how it gets in (i.e., father's role in a general way) probably some time before 5, and about the father's role in somewhat greater detail between 6½ and 8, or slightly later. Girls ask corresponding questions earlier than boys. Such individual variables as temperament, alertness, articulateness or parents' permissiveness also play a part. Very bright children may ask questions before 2 years of age.

SEX VOCABULARY

Suitable for Young Children

At the earliest age, often the *genitalia* are called by the term for urination: wee-wee, pee-wee, pee-pee, trickle, etc. Somewhat later the *penis* is identified as penis—("peanuts" to some boys), or commonly as peenie, peter, pecker, tailie, dingus, hinie (or hiney), dick (or dickie), private, boy's thing(s) (to girls), and others. Best avoided are perhaps piece, worm, dickie bird, thing down there, or anything shaming or implying dirty or bad. The *foreskin* is the skin or simply foreskin or sometimes ding-ding. The *testicles* and the *scrotum* rarely interest a boy before school age; they are most often called balls or ballies, in their little sack or bag. When *erections* are mentioned at a later age, it is the tailie that hardens up or gets large.

The *vulva* of little girls, past the stage of the wee-wee hole, is the sissie, susie, tushie or private parts. Best avoided are crack and hole, and probably baby hole. A separate term for the *vagina* is neither of interest nor appropriate below the age of 9 to girls, and probably not until well into the second decade to boys. At that time, the most suitable terms are vagina or passage. The girl's pectoral wall, before the *breasts* bud, is the chest. Nipples are nipples or buttons to children of either sex; the umbilicus is the navel or belly button.

The child whose vocabulary differs too conspicuously from that of his playmates tends to discard what is greatly different and adopt the words the other children use. Parents are well advised to go along with a child's outside vocabulary, so long as it is not frankly vulgar.

Some parents who have all the factual knowledge they are going to need evade answering their children's questions simply because they do not know the proper words to use or are uncertain about the propriety of words they do know. Where adults since their early youth have not spoken a reproductive word aloud, merely the unembarrassed frankness of the physician counselor in reciting suitable terms can help.

Answer Giving. Generally, it is best to answer the child's questions as they are asked. Small children require very little information at any one time. They may ask when something in connection with their play comes up, or when they have observed something. If the answer is simple, brief and relaxed they will pass on to something else. Occasional evasion of a question (e.g., by distracting a young child's attention elsewhere) does no harm, so long as it is not done too obviously or tensely, or habitually. With advancing age, different details need to be supplied. To the question, "How did the baby get inside you?" the 3½-year-old will be satisfied that it grew from a tiny thing. The 5-year-old may insist until he is told that Daddy put the seed in; while a 7- or 8-year-old may want knowledge or confirmation on how Father did it (see below). A 4- or 5-year-old who asks how babies are made would be badly confused by a description of the mechanics of sexual union.

Shockers and Loading. Children may ask the same question over and over. This is not a sign of unduly intense curiosity. Children forget; or they confuse facts and their own fantasies and primitive theories; or at different ages the same question may express different levels of puzzlement. Probably it is best to repeat the same answer until the child shows, through its follow-up questions, that it is ready to have additional details supplied.

Sometimes a question strikes the parent as being a real shocker. A 4- or 5-year-old, for instance, may ask, "What does Daddy do to the baby with his stick inside?" The shock should pass off quickly as the mother realizes that somewhere the child has picked up a fragment beyond its level of comprehension and almost certainly beyond its level of interest. Here the answer can deliberately be partially unresponsive, as the mother makes a single, calm restatement of the last "official" information the child has been given on this subject, disregarding the fancy addition. If the question is repeated, the same answer is pleasantly but firmly repeated or paraphrased. After a few times around, the normal child is likely to have lost interest, his faith in the parents' information is preserved, and in fact he may put the playmate-informant sternly in his place for lying or being dopey.

Sometimes a child loads a question. A 5-year-old may say, "So-and-so told me babies are made when people go to bed together and have lots of fun." Probably, no adult source has said anything remotely similar; the information stems from some random source. Without entering into denials, disputing or checking with the other source, the immediate situation again calls for partial unresponsiveness (e.g., "children come when grown-ups love each other very much and get married") reiterated as necessary. Repeated loading may be interpreted as a sign of impending difficulties (e.g., that the child has been losing trust in the parents for some time), and a general review of their own attitude for possible flaws is called for.

TYPICAL QUESTIONS AND ANSWERS

Home sex education cannot be planned. Parents must be prepared to meet the child's questions. Where they feel apprehensive or unsure of themselves, they may be aided by discussing sample answers and questions such as can be anticipated with each phase of the child's development. It is less important for them to have their facts absolutely straight than to avoid unwholesome attitudes toward the questions. Sex instruction of little girls and boys need not differ substantially before 8 or 9 years of age. Questions before that age are more usually asked of and answered by the mother; thereafter by the parent of the same sex. The following represents a cross section of questions and answers frequently encountered in childhood:

"Why have I no little dingus like brother has?" (or, "Where is sister's?"; see also p. 37). All baby boys and baby girls are made different. Little girls do not have any so they can grow up to be mommies. Only mommies can have babies. All little boys have one, but they can't be mommies; they can't have babies.

"Why doesn't Daddy have any breasts?" Only mommies have breasts so they can feed their new baby milk if they want to.

"How does one know a father cat from a mother cat?" Same as one knows a little boy from a little girl.

"Where do babies come from?" (or, "What have you—or Mrs. So-and-so, or the cat—in your tummy?" or, "Where did I come from?") Babies come from inside Mother. They grow under Mother's heart. Mommies have a special place inside for babies to grow in where it is safe and warm, a baby nest. (References to the "stomach" are best avoided, as they may reinforce the oft-encountered oral impregnation fantasies and theories of small children—more often girls—a suspected source of subsequent troublesome reactions in at least some children and adults.) Girls make babies when they are old (big) enough to be mommies. That is what is called pregnant. The place inside is called the womb.

"How does the baby get out?" (or, *"What does 'born' mean?"*) It came out by itself (yourself). When the baby is new, it is tiny and can come out easily. You were so tiny. The baby grows inside until it is old (big) enough to be born. Or, you have seen the opening when we take a bath; it looks the same as yours.

"Where does the baby come out?" It comes out through a special opening. Every girl has one. It is not the opening where she goes to the toilet. It is very small. When she is ready to have the baby the opening gets bigger for the baby to come out. *"Where is your opening? Can I see it? Can I touch it?"* It looks the same as yours (or sister's). Or, yes, you can see it for a moment; when mommies grow up they have a little hair there. Yes, you can touch it for a moment (hairy mons pubis only). Or, no, you

cannot touch it; we (people, children) don't do that; I will tell you what you want to know. Exceptionally, very tense parents may indicate the navel as birth outlet, rather than shy away from the whole subject altogether; the correction can be made before age 5, when topical interest in the genitalia has become less intense and the child is less likely to want a detailed description.

"Does it hurt to have a baby?"   Yes, a little, but the doctor knows how to help the pain and make it easier. He helps the baby come out. It's worth having some pain to have a baby (you).

"How does the baby eat?"   Through a tiny tube. It is called the cord.

"How does the baby get in?" (or, *"Where was I before I was inside you?"*)   The baby starts as a tiny seed inside. When mommy is ready to make a baby it begins to grow. When people want a baby that makes the seed start to grow. Or, God sent the baby when he was very tiny and he grew in mother's body until he was born. For boys in the latency phase the race of millions of sperms for the egg holds special fascination. Later: The baby comes from two seeds, one from the mother, one from the father.

"How does the seed get in?"   Daddy plants the seed. Daddy puts the seed in with love. "Can I see the seed?" It is very tiny. It cannot be seen.

"How does Daddy put the seed in?"   The seed flows in from Daddy. Father puts some fluid inside mother. They make the baby together, so it belongs to both of them. Later:

"How does Daddy put the fluid inside?"   He has a special organ, like the penis of the little boy. It fits in mother's opening. He puts it inside there, then the sperm flows in. The sperm fluid passes from his penis into the little opening inside mother. That is called intercourse. People do that when they love each other very much and are married and want to make a baby. They only do it when they are married, so the little baby will have a home, and a father and a mother. More graphic or crude descriptions, such as "they put piss to piss," or, "the woman lies on her back and the man gets on top of her and puts it in"; or emphasizing that the act requires at least a degree of undress, etc., although they have found their advocates, do not appear to be suitable representations in the instruction of a child.

The child may ask about the meaning of certain words and phrases picked up from various sources. In younger children these words often surpass their capacity to comprehend as well as their level of interest. In such instances it is quite acceptable to promise an explanation "later, when you are older." Examples:

"What does sex mean?"   It means several things. It can mean male and female. Or the things that have to do with love. Or when grown-ups are married they love each other in every way, with the heart, the mind and their bodies. Sex has to do with people's private organs, and whether they make proper or improper use of them.

"What does being intimate (or being lovers) mean?" When grown-ups love each other very much and are together all the time. Later: when two people like each other very much and do the things married people do.

"What is a bad woman (prostitute)?" Girls who ran away from home, or have no home, and don't behave nicely. Later: Girls (women) who get paid for being nice to (entertaining) strange men. This is obviously for the relatively sheltered middle-class child. The most highly exposed children from the most dissocial urban environment, if they happen to ask mother, a relative, teacher, clinic nurse or worker, may best comprehend such statements as: She can't wait to give it with love to a man of her own. Later: She has a sort of sickness in the head to let every bum do it to her for a few dollars, and then the miserable pimp takes it all.

"What is a brothel (whorehouse, etc.)?" An apartment or house where people can amuse themselves with other people for money; play grown-up games for shame; rent sex partners, loose women; for older men who have not married anybody.

"What is a pervert?" They are sick people (men); they do fresh, stupid, nasty things because there is something wrong with them. They want to touch people (children) sometimes and do things normal people don't do. They never learned how to love. *"What is a homosexual (gay, fag)?"* Some boys have something wrong with them. They don't like girls; when they grow up they cannot love them. They grow up and they never get married. Sometimes it gets them into trouble. People don't like them always. It is all right to like another boy (girl) very much if he (she) is your best friend; people love their very best friends, but it isn't the same as boy and girl love (making out).

UNSOUND ATTITUDES AND REACTIONS

Suppression and Evasion

Some parents either recognize no obligation to satisfy the child's natural or anxious curiosities or they are too inhibited or apprehensive to enter upon these matters. Approximately one half of all children are believed to grow up without ever receiving a single word of sex explanation, reassurance or advice from their own parents.

Such parents may shush the child ("don't bother me"); or reproach it directly or indirectly ("Let's talk about something nice,"); or otherwise discourage it ("Wait till your father—or teacher, clergyman, etc.—hears what kind of things you have on your mind," or, "Have you been playing with yourself to get ideas like that?"); or defer the subject indefinitely and habitually ("You are too little for that"); or forever defer to another, perhaps equally unwilling person ("Ask So-and-so, she (he) knows more about it than I"); or plead ignorance ("I don't know"); or simply get mutely angered or flustered.

Discoveries. Children may accidentally discover traces of *menstrual blood* on an undergarment, bed sheet, or a carelessly discarded sanitary device, belonging to a member of the household. This will lead to questions. Unless the child is small, or the spot inconspicuous, one cannot very well deny that it is blood if it obviously is, or blame a scratch or insect bite for it, or patently refuse to reveal its source. In the child of early school age the explanation need not differ substantially from that given the pubescent girl (p. 130), except for necessary simplifications, and sufficient reassurance to counteract the natural association of blood with hurt. Boys may be given substantially similar explanations as girls, although they are usually less observant in this respect. Questions about advertisements for *sanitary devices* in magazines, or discovery of such devices at home, are either answered in the same manner or, to smaller children, explained as a device for general cleanliness and hygiene.

Untimely discovery of *contraceptive devices* may occur. Children can find discarded condoms outside (park, beach), or a carelessly discarded one in a toilet bowl at home, or a diaphragm or box of condoms in a drawer. They may ask, "What is this for?" or, "Can I play with it?" or, "Can I show it to my friend?" Hands-off directives must forestall children's picking up discarded condoms as playthings, or showing domestic devices to their little friends. One may motivate the prohibition as, "this is for grown-ups who have had babies, to keep them healthy; the doctor prescribed it." This rarely leads to further questions. Factual contraceptive explanations are unintelligible, perhaps improper, for most children below age 9 or so, as are antivenereal aspects of such devices.

Causes of Suppression. There are many causes. They range from apathy, mental retardation or sociopathy of the mother, or neglect, to the most complex sex fears or revulsions. Timidity and apparent prudishness may be due to a lack of a vocabulary, or to ignorance of simple biologic facts in spite of having given birth. Some unsophisticated parents have a vague belief that a child, once encouraged, will not stop asking until the most delicate subjects are reached. They worry about "What will he ask next?" or about how the child may use the knowledge to embarrass the parents in public by untimely remarks or questions, or that he will corrupt his playmates, thus giving the neighbors "the wrong impression of our home."

Some are afraid of the disapproval of an "old-fashioned" mother or other relative. Others have erroneous ideas about the attitude of their church, although all denominations favor adequate and properly graded sex education of children, certainly by their parents; emphasis on a spiritual and moral, rather than a predominantly materialistic approach may be an added requirement.

In some mothers anxiety is the main inhibitant, more often so when dealing with a little boy. Sometimes it is difficult to visualize how intense this inner fear or repugnance to masculinity and its appurtenances actually is. The young mother appears to be a cheerful and calm person on the surface. At times one may begin to anticipate a negative attitude when, half in jest, she is a little unsure of how to handle the infant boy's "little gadgets" or "those boy things." There may be a history of continued marital tension or discord, perhaps chronic orgasm failure or other sexual maladjustment; occasionally, there is overattachment to her own mother. Some admit that they have a feeling that they must keep sex out of their own child's mind as long as possible and not "spoil its innocence."

Gross misapprehensions may be advanced as the reason for avoiding sex topics, frequently by the father. These are often subconscious masking devices for underlying timidity or anxiety. Examples include, "It will upset the child," "It will arouse sex interest prematurely," "It will make him (her) a sex delinquent," "Adolescence (or before getting married) is soon enough," "Allow nature to take its course," "We want to keep our home clean." Actually the children with the most patent sexual misconduct are often the ones who received the least sex education from their parents. On the other hand, of course, sex education is no guarantee against behavior or impulse disorders. An occasional child can become upset by reproductive explanation; however, these are usually "slow" children who have been overexposed to explanations before they showed interest.

One can attempt to reassure such parents that the child's simple questions are the result of natural curiosity; that birth and conception are decent and approved processes; that unsatisfied curiosity leads to furtive exploring and eventually to trouble; that sex cannot be kept forever out of the child's life (newspapers, magazines, companions, etc.); and that it is better if the parents tell the child what is right and proper than that its untutored mind should be exposed to sundry fragments of sex information. Although parents may have defaulted on their obligations during the child's early stages, it is undoubtedly better to make belated amends than to continue in an attitude of reticence, disapproval or neglect.

Instant Sex Education (Dosing)

Parents who believe that they can get rid of their obligations by one-shot dosing of the child with sex facts on special occasions, perhaps "once and for all," are the butt of popular jokes, but they are still with us. We-must-have-a-good-talk-about-all-this-soon, tonight-let's-discuss-something-important, he (she)-is getting-into-trouble (or has-been-playing-with-self) so-we-must-tell-the-child-the-facts-of-life—all these bespeak past omissions which this delayed expounding of a set of sex facts cannot be expected to remedy.

Comparative excursions into botany and animal biology are a sound accompaniment of the midchildhood phase of sex education and a major contribution of early grade school, but they are of no interest and not in the least illuminating to the child during those years when interest and anxious curiosity center around its own and other children's bodies and the mysterious tangibles of human origin. Thus it can be asserted with confidence that, where such approaches represent the parents' first effort to inform, already they have failed the child at an earlier stage.

Encyclopedism

Some parents, seemingly anxious to conform with what they understand to be progressive child rearing, may overstuff the child with knowledge that he cannot absorb. They tend to respond to the child's simplest questions with too much detail, at too early an age. Later they may probe anxiously to determine whether the child got its facts straight, and they may be greatly perturbed if it seems to have forgotten or garbled them. Some have an almost obsessional fear of giving the wrong answers; others have so little confidence in themselves that they feel impelled to document their presentations with printed illustrations or diagrams, or even request the physician or other professional to lecture the child. Still others may argue that their child is unusually advanced for his age which, even where true, would rarely justify an overly intellectualized approach to reproductive matters, certainly not during the first half of childhood.

Younger children cannot be expected to build up an orderly concept of human sex facts. In the young child's mind any combination of fact and fantasy is possible. Male, female, animals, children, adults, storybook characters, babies mingle freely. Whatever they hear, they comprehend in terms of familiar functions and sights. Also, it is apparently impossible to prevent the formation of gastrointestinal theories of reproduction in the young child, regardless of the information presented. Parents should try not to reinforce these theories and thus confuse the child beyond this passing phase; but probably it is even more confusing to the child when parents dispute such theories after exposing them through undue probing. Many of these parents are rather compulsive or obsessional personalities, and the physician may find it difficult to make them desist completely without causing them to become tense or dejected and grossly unsure of themselves. It is preferable to curb only the most flagrant excesses of their teaching zeal, and to disabuse them of the belief that thorough sex instruction is a panacea which can prevent a child's jealousy about a newborn sibling, listening to other children's sex talk, participating in sex play, masturbating and the like. In severe cases, psychiatric consultation for the parent may be considered.

False Images (Storkism)

Some parents explain in reply to a child's question about the origin of babies that "the stork brought you"; or you were bought in a store, at the hospital, dropped down the chimney; or brought in the doctor's little black bag; or came out of a rosebud, cabbage leaves or bulrushes; or sent by an angel. Such fiction represents undue evasiveness and is undesirable. However, it is one of the relatively less noxious of parents' unsound attitudes toward sex education.

It is fairly certain that these tales are more often frightening and confusing to a child than having its questions answered in a natural fashion, in keeping with its level of understanding. Observations and random remarks from various sources will soon cast doubt on the story in the child's mind, thus converting even inherently innocuous facts into guilty (i.e., unapproved) knowledge. It will also make the child feel that the parents lied. The argument that if Santa Claus and nursery fables are acceptable, the stork story should also be acceptable is a spurious one. Sooner or later the normal child will be exposed to starkly factual data about reproduction, while Santa Claus may remain a sweet holiday tradition for which reality testing never will become a confrontation problem. The stork-type mystification cannot even be maintained for long by the parents themselves without resort to increasing evasiveness and suppression of curiosity.

Peculiarly, an occasional child will not believe that it has grown inside the mother but will insist on the stork or a similar story. Here one may suspect either that someone else, unbeknown to the parents, has fixated the child on the fictitious version of its origin; or that some strongly disagreeable association with "inside mummy's tummy" exists in the child's mind (e.g., a thought chain "in tummy—too full—throw up—messy—reproach"; or some elaboration of overheard remarks about some pet animal with a "big belly" which is "going to make a mess again"). When such a child insists, the stork theory is best not disputed, nor attempts made to disprove it. Of course, such theories are relinquished eventually.

The Non-Asking Child

The parents may report, or even boast, that their 8- or 9-year-old child—boy or girl—never has shown any curiosity about the functions of elimination, sex anatomy and sex differences, the origin of babies and similar subjects. The child either appears pleasant and happy or, less often, somewhat timid. In some cases the parents may report an exaggerated modesty, such as a little boy trying not to touch his penis when urinating, or a little girl locking herself in or hiding behind a closet door when undressing.

Having excluded mental retardation, speech impairment, serious emotional disorder, extreme stolidity and simple concealment of interest because of an intimidating parental attitude, there emerge a few children who are such timid personalities, or their parents so obtuse or detached that they do not understand when the child hints at some sexual subject of interest to him. An occasional child may have been subjected to early genital manipulations or frightening sex tales by an adult and warned, for instance, "not to tell your parents that you know about (or do) such things or they would die with unhappiness." The most frequent cause is probably that at an early age the child has been conditioned to be deeply afraid of its own curiosity: earliest questions or explorations may have been brushed aside or inhibited crudely. This disapproval may have been perceived by an especially sensitive small child as a threat to its basic security.

Some parents require an explanation of the difference between innocence and inhibition. In most cases the mother may be advised to broach sexual topics casually and briefly on suitable occasions (e.g., by calling attention to a pregnant woman or animal, or asking the child where he thinks he comes from before he was born). Children who are concealing guilty knowledge from the parents need to be approached gradually, by taking more interest in their general activities. Such efforts must be consistent and may have to precede broaching of sexual topics by a period of 6 months, until a relationship of trust can be assumed to prevail. In every case of overinhibition there probably should be a positive corrective effort on the parents' part, in order to avoid excessively erratic attitudes during the second decade.

Embarrassing Frankness of the Child

An occasional child below school age may greatly embarrass an adult by asking sex questions, or making unsuitable remarks, in public. Fear of recurrence may cause the parents to withhold all further mention of reproductive topics.

One must distinguish between naïvely innocent questions or impulsive verbalizing by a child who has not been trained to limit mention of certain subjects to the home and his parents, or similar conventions of privacy, and public sex questions which serve a child as an attention-getting device. Some children are well aware of the shocked embarrassment caused by their remarks. These occurrences cannot be blamed on the fact that sex education has been given, but the child makes use of the subject which he has observed the parent to be most squeamish about. The cause of the attention-getting or tension-creating impulse must be sought in a personality disturbance of the child or in a major flaw of the parent-child relationship. An occasional, seriously disturbed or psychotic child may bring up sexual subjects in public in a compulsive and irrepressible manner.

SEX EDUCATION IN LOWER GRADE SCHOOL

Since sex education of the young child is essentially a product of a continuing attitude of the parents, a part of general upbringing, it is characteristically the business of the home. But the lower school, beginning with kindergarten, is bound to contribute importantly to the understanding of simple reproductive biology and family life during general classroom study.

Separate and specific instruction in these fields is not—and should not—customarily be given below the fifth or sixth grade. The controversy which has embroiled sex education in the schools (p. 118) does not involve children below the middle (seventh and eighth) grades.

By prevailing custom the area is divided into 4 broadly relevant educational levels: early grades, kindergarten to third or fourth grade; the preteen fifth and sixth grades; the middle grades (seventh, eighth, sometimes the ninth); and the high school years.

The curriculum, ideally, provides that in the first years the child begins to understand that life comes from life. Plants come from seeds, as observed by planting flowers or vegetables, and watching them sprout and grow. Animal families consist of father and mother animals rallying around and nursing animal babies, just as a new baby (e.g., in a classmate's family) is cared for by its mother and father.

In the second and third grades pregnant hamsters or guinea pigs bring babies into the world: the wonder of life. Animals come from eggs, or animal babies grow in the mother's body; so do human babies. Tiny eggs in the mother animal, and seeds in the male, must meet (fourth and fifth grade). When a litter or baby is ready, there must be a family, father and mother, waiting for it, each with a function. There are siblings. Also, people not related can form friendships. Mother and father were children; they grew up. They became friends. People fall in love when grown up. The focus remains on animal life, switches mostly to humans in the fifth and sixth grades: internal body organs, endocrine glands, heredity. Human marriage and family, the family unit, the trek of ovum and sperms, human gestation and birth, perhaps some anatomic models, but nothing technical on genito-genital contact is necessary as a rule.

The fifth grader is factually interested, and still not self-conscious and emotionally involved with his (her) own puberal changes. "In the fifth grade it is good to tackle more detail. The fifth grader is a factualist, a realist. They filter out what they're not ready for. Every one of these kids has a different receiving set." (a school principal).

All first decade instruction is by classroom teachers, except possibly by the school nurse when a fifth (occasionally sixth) grade Personal Hygiene (menstruation) movie is shown and commented upon to the girls; today this or a similar movie is sometimes also shown to the boys (e.g., a year later). Some informal questions and answers in classes are at the teacher's discretion, with wide individual or district-wide variations of what is encouraged or discouraged, and how it is handled. Ideally, the lower grade school supplements and slightly trails behind family-supplied information. In practice, grade school may sometimes be the only supplier of information, counteracting as best it can confusing tidbits of street information: very occasionally the opinion is heard that such planned familiarizing of young children with certain facts of reproduction merely exposes some parents' ignorance without there being proof that anything of value is being contributed to the child's education.

SOME HELPFUL BOOKS

Arnstein, H. A. and Staff, Child Study Assoc. of America: Your Growing Child and Sex. Indianapolis, Bobbs-Merrill, 1967 (parents)

Berenstein, S. and J.: How to Teach your Child about Sex. New York, Ballantine Books, 1971 (parents)

Calderwood, D.: What Shall I Tell my Child? New York, Crown Publ., 1966 (parents)

Child Study Assoc. of America (Staff).: What to tell your Children about Sex. New York, Meredith, Revis. 1968; also Pocket Books (parents)

Cosgrove, M.: Eggs and What Happens Inside Them. New York, Dodd, Mead, 1966 (ages 8 to 10)

Goldstein, M. (transl. fr. German: Haeberle, E. I.): The Sex Book. A Modern Pictorial Encyclopedia. New York, Herder & Herder, 1971 (Protestant orientation; very candid. Photogr. Illustr.)

Gruenberg, B. C. and S. M.: The Wonderful Story of You. Garden City, N.Y., Garden City Books, 1960 (ages 9 to 12)

Gruenberg, S. M.: The Wonderful Story of How You Were Born. New York, Doubleday, Revis. 1959 (ages 5 to 9)

Kind, R. W. and Leedham, J. You Grow Up. London, Longmans, Green, 1968 (ages 9 to 12)

Lerrigo, M. O. and Cassidy, M. A.: A Doctor Talks to 9 to 12 Year Olds. Chicago, Budlong Press, 1964 (ages 9 to 12)

Levine, M. I. and Seligman, J.: A Baby is Born. The Story of How Life Begins. New York, Golden Press, Revis. 1966 (ages 5 to 9)

Power, J.: How Life Begins. New York, Simon & Schuster, 1965 (fourth grade)

Rubin, I. and Kirkendall, L. A.: Sex in the Childhood Years. New York, Association Press, 1971 (parents)

Showers, P. and K. S.: Before You Were A Baby. New York, Crowell, 1968 (ages 5 to 9)

Wyden, P. and B.: Growing up Straight. What Every Thoughtful Parent Should Know About Homosexuality. New York, Stein & Day, 1968 (parents)

Zeichner, I.: How Life Goes On. Englewood Cliffs, N.J. Prentice Hall, 1961 (fourth grade)

CHAPTER 3

Common Sex Problems
of Childhood

Discovering Genital Differences — Observing
Parents' Sex Act — Domestic Nudity — Sex
Play — Masturbation and Pseudomasturbation.

DISCOVERING GENITAL DIFFERENCES

At 2½ or 3 years of age practically all children understand that they are
either boy or girl, and that other children and adults are classified as either
he or she. The child must be ready for this recognition, each at his individual time; it does not seem to occur earlier even when all along there
had been opportunity to view a child of the opposite sex. Readiness seems
to coincide approximately with the phallic phase of instinctual development
(p. 14), which in turn may well depend on maturation of neural apper-
ceptive mechanisms. The first indication often is that a boy who has learned
to urinate standing up will try to, or insist on, doing it sitting down, and
vice-versa. At the same time there is curiosity about these differences,
resulting in questions, inspection and/or fingering.

The Parents. It is not certain what if any difference it makes whether
the child makes the discovery in a sibling or in a little playmate, although
many parents are more perturbed by the latter. When misguided parents
believe that they have concealed all comparative genital knowledge, they
are frequently deluding themselves, certainly by kindergarten or early
school age. Instead, an only child for instance usually acquires some kind
of "guilty knowledge" from various sources. Excessive delay of actual discovery after discovery-readiness has been established seems to lead to increasingly unfavorable reactions to the actual confrontation. The sensible
mother does not interfere with a young child's first curious or fascinated
inspection of divergent genitalia (e.g., those of an infant sibling) but allows
the child reasonable opportunity to absorb the new sight, including some
fingering. Of course discouragement of fingering must be undertaken in due

time. The period of discovery may be attended by casual explanations that all children are made different from the beginning, and that without exception all little girls grow up to be mommies and all little boys daddies. According to circumstances a certain amount of eulogizing of the female role is desirable ("little girls can be mommies who have babies").

Pride, Envy and Anxious Worry are the affective reactions believed most often associated with the discovery of genital differences. In a little boy penis pride would result if a little girl expresses envy; qualitatively it may not differ much from toy pride: a smug sense of possession (e.g., of a rare trading stamp or autographed baseball). However, children at that age tend to compare in terms of lack rather than of addition: that something has been taken away which is identified with disapproval by the parent. Thus, depending on what pertinent observations the child has made in the household, one may reasonably assume that a child's awareness of genital differences is accompanied by the impression that, for instance, little sister's dingus has been cut off, broken off or such by whichever parent does the taking away and the cutting in the home, and that she is now left with a hole or crack to pee through.

The boy's anxiety revolves around a threat to a possession, his dismay that what he had taken for granted could really be absent, and that this could happen to him if he is bad or displeases. He may hold or handle his organs excessively—to make sure of their continued presence as it were; or the parents may report that the child is easily and greatly worried about anything that is broken, hurt or out of place, such as toys, utensils, cracks in the plaster, invalid people, or minor blemishes and injuries on his own body. Sometimes a little boy just seems easily worried about all manner of things without apparent reason. Some go through a reactive phase of breaking and injuring things. The cruelty to animals in early midchildhood may be a related phenomenon; the well-known phobias of childhood may have their origin in excessive genital recognition anxiety. In adult psychopathology certain personality and sexual disorders seem to have part of their origin in anxious misrecognitions at this stage of childhood.

A little girl's recognition anxiety is assumed to arise in connection with feelings of being injured, deprived or punished, with perhaps an admixture of envy of the boy, or all boys. The result in the normal boy a few years later is probably a vague sense of pride in his special possession. It is less certain how the untutored little girl eventually copes with her withoutness; possibly through a denial-of-loss reaction ("the one I have will come out soon, it's still inside"), and through other fantasies and games simulating possession. But major ill effects are unlikely to result, in accord with the tenet that girls are less swayed by what happens, in matters of sexuality. An older, now discarded theory held that the phase of genital recognition had importance in shaping the attitudes of the two sexes; that females, unconsciously burdened by a lifelong sense of inferiority or injury, develop into the characteristically yielding, passive personalities; while males, un-consciously elated throughout life by a sense of pride, possession and superiority, develop the psychic traits stereotypically identified with mas-culinity.

In a general way the child who is happy and secure probably shows the least amount of anxiety in connection with the discovery, while unhappy, tense, neglected or insecure children, or those threateningly castigated for self-manipulation can be expected to react most unfavorably, with anxious fantasies and worry-theories about loss of the organ recurring again and again.

OBSERVING PARENTS' SEX ACT

The child who chances upon the parents in the act of sexual intercourse ("primal scene"), especially if uninhibited, is frequently affected in a greatly and sometimes lastingly (disputed) unfavorable manner. The child awakened or attracted by the parents' commotion, or accidentally awake and about, usually remains to observe in fascinated horror. Mere over-hearing is much less disturbing to most children, but it is likely to attract the child to leave his bed and investigate more closely. Descriptions—by observed parents, by third persons, by direct recall—speak with great frequency of the little boy or girl standing with fist stuffed in mouth to prevent an outcry, weak and shaky with a mixture of fear, sometimes rage, and a strange sense of excitement. Some children cry out, either in fear or to make themselves noticed and halt the perpetration. Those viewing from their own bed stare tensely with bated breath.

An impression of violence and aggression often prevails, regardless of what information the child may have of the father's role in producing babies. As the two parents moan, groan, posture and struggle about, either the father or the mother is often perceived in the role of a brutal aggressor. There are vivid images of choking, sticking, biting or eating the other, beating, even killing. In the naïve child the sight seems to produce mostly confusion, fear and an acute sense of helplessness and impending abandon-ment. Children possessed of secret sex knowledge and those with mastur-batory guilt or apprehension experience a peculiarly intense sense of guilt as well as fear. In some cases, especially where much has been made of the mother's "purity" or "sanctity" by a father trying to keep a boy from masturbating or from talking sex in the home, a sense of violation or degradation of the mother may be mingled with a feeling of helpless rage and anxiety. Only an occasional older child is believed to feel simply revulsed or ashamed. It is uncertain at what age or stage exactly a child can intuit the erotic or sexual character of the happening. It may be a factor that from age 2½ children apparently can perceive sexual odors and are known to react negatively to them. Where the father's erection and the details of connection happen to be discernible, fright mingled with a sensation of guilty excitement is frequent.

Nonparental Acts. For reasons which are not altogether understood, the impact on the child's psyche in these cases seems to be conspicuously greater than when persons other than the parents are observed under similar circumstances. Even for children from extreme poverty areas, with several families and boarders crowded into a small apartment and the sights and sounds of cohabitating adults almost commonplace, the effect of observing parental coupling is known to have differing, more noxious significance, although observing sex in other adults and adolescents under the same circumstances undoubtedly attenuates the impact. The sight of copulating large animals may be temporarily disturbing to children who are not accustomed to it, perhaps especially if they happen to be weighed down by a sense of guilt regarding masturbation, companionate sex play or "dirty knowledge." Ranch and farm children who are familiar with the sight of large animals in the act of copulation have been known to be adversely affected by observing the primal (i.e., parental) scene. The sight of children and younger juveniles, and of small animals, engaged in some type of coital activity leaves a distinctly lesser impression, and often none. Cultural factors undoubtedly play a part, witness the many anthropologic reports of past customs among Eskimos, Indian and African tribes, Archipelagian islanders, etc., permitting children freely to watch adult intercourse. But did this include the parents?

Sequels. If exposure remains undiscovered, the parents may notice that the child's behavior has changed inexplicably. Some children become generally unruly and defiant—"fresh" or furtive or "less honest"; others become markedly subdued or "suddenly shy." A fully trained child may resume wetting the bed at night, possibly because of fear of going to the bathroom so as to avoid repetition of the sight; another theory considers enuresis in these excited-frightened children a symptom of sensuous regression, as genital interest is sharply repressed and ontogenetically earlier urinary pleasure impulses are substituted during halfsleep or sleep. In others again there is a sudden intensification of companionate sex play as the child acts out the observed scene with playmates or younger siblings. It has little practical significance whether the child's mate here is of the same or opposite sex. In these games the traumatized girl peculiarly tends to take the masculine role. There may be mere posture imitation, with or without some degree of undress, or genital maneuvers may be approximated or, occasionally, reenacted. One may be fairly philosophic about these occurrences, because they seem to act as a safety valve and may forestall more serious sequelae.

More to be feared for instance—although it is not certain if a single incident can precipitate them in the absence of major predisposition—is the development of school or animal phobias, tics, habit spasms, stuttering or the elements of an obsessive-compulsive syndrome with its eminent chronicity. Symptoms here begin insidiously, and often the early stages are overlooked. At times the parents notice only that the child's behavior is "a little bizarre," and that he—less often she—is developing little peculiarities of breathing, coughing, gesticulating, or that he "keeps himself awake in bed without doing anything." Actually, the child may be evolving elaborate, "magical" rituals of protection. They often involve his breathing (e.g., "every night if I don't breathe or make a single noise until I count 23, and do this 3 times and press my back hard against the bed, mother won't die tonight."). Phobias in such children practically never have sexual content, but displacement of the fear (e.g., on dogs) may occur. The memory of the traumatic event itself tends to fade in these children before the onset of pubescence, although frequently it can be reevoked even many years later, during psychotherapy. Long-term sequelae may involve sexuality more directly. It is suspected that a sadistic concept of sexuality can develop in a few of these children, although predisposing factors probably must be present here. Some boys already predisposed to expect aggression from the mother may come to identify the sexual act with violence on the part of the female. There are indications that some girls, after viewing the enormous size of the father's phallus in conjunction with an image of assault, may become predisposed to various sex fears later in life.

Prevention. Ideally a child should not be exposed (i.e., sleep within sight or hearing) to parental intercourse after the age of 15 to 18 months. Most parents will deem such a toddler too small to understand, and frequently this is true. However, there are a fair number of reasonably plausible observations where later psychiatric symptoms seem to have been precipitated by observation at this early age. It may be best to avoid this risk if at all feasible. Under no circumstances should there be exposure after age 2½ or 3. The incidence and the seriousness of psychic ill effects due to exposure seem to mount rapidly from this age to reach a peak at the approximate age of the first-grader, after which the risk decreases again, although it may not disappear completely until well into the second decade. Where small children share the parents' bedroom, it need be remembered that rooms at night are rarely completely dark, the sexual act rarely completely noiseless, and that the depth of a child's sleep is not always the same. Some couples tend to become careless after a child has slept through the act on a number of occasions.

Corrective Action. Where observation is known to have taken place, the child should be reassured and comforted by the parents at once in as unobtrusive a manner as possible, even when he shows no outward signs of being upset. One of the parents may sit at his bedside until the child falls asleep (but no taking an older child into bed with the parents!). There should be no insistent questioning on how much has actually been observed.

Small children may be told casually about "fun battles" or "playing grown-up games," but it would be unwise to call the activity a "quarrel." It is best to give older children no immediate explanations, but in the course of the next few weeks the parents may give appropriate attention to the child's sex knowledge in keeping with his age and capacity to understand. At the same time the legitimacy of adult married love may be pointed out to the older child, giving him to understand that love in parents is a private affair not to be peeked in on, the same as one does not peek in on bathroom privacy. Where observation of the primal scene is merely suspected, the general procedure may be similar, but it is usually best not to make an effort to find out if observation has actually taken place. Even truthful children may be pressured into lying here, thus arousing additional guilt feelings.

DOMESTIC NUDITY

The reaction of children to nudity is largely conditioned by the attitude of the total environment. In our civilization, with its long tradition of genital concealment, deliberate individualistic overfrankness by the parents in this respect is almost bound to have unfavorable effects of some kind on the child; nor is contrived exposure a suitable way for the child to learn the details of genital differences between the sexes, nor can it be expected to teach the child greater acceptance of his own body.

A child could be exposed unreservedly to almost total nudity at home if one could guarantee that all his childhood playmates will have had a similarly nudist upbringing; that all the adults in the environment will not conceal their bodies on the occasions when the child's own parents would not conceal them; that no one will put the child to shame for his upbringing; and that the parts "down there" will not be mentioned in a derogatory or scandalized fashion by anyone, adult or child, at any time. Since this cannot be expected in our culture, one must advise parents to practice at least a reasonable degree of conformity. An exception in this country would be children reared in families that are long-term devotees of the nudist culture (see p. 461).

There are a substantial number of observations in which undue exposure to parental nudity—whether self-consciously deliberate display, misguided overpermissiveness, or merely dissolute laxity—has been a source of major emotional and social difficulties in subsequent years, even if no seductive attitude was involved. It is difficult to predict which children will adjust easily to the patent differentness of their childhood mores from what they will encounter outside, and which children will become disturbed by the contrast. The earliest, minimal complication one may predict is a sense of being different in the child, or actual isolation at times (e.g., after the 5- or 6-year-old naïvely tells the peers that "at home we show us everything" or boasts that "I can touch my dad's tail all the time."). Admiration may quickly change to ostracism after these stories, with added embellishments, have reached the ears of the playmates' scandalized parents. Even where this early reaction of the environment is less severe and immediate, the normal child himself usually becomes increasingly embarrassed and resentful at the parents' continued display or their disregard of privacy.

On the other hand a reasonably relaxed attitude of the parents is quite compatible with normal, gradual training toward conforming manners. For instance it is probably better if a little girl who accidentally happens on the scene while the father is in undress has a fleeting glimpse of the pubic region—but never of an erection!—than for the father to make near-panicky concealing maneuvers, or even react with violent remonstrations or a slap. Such overreactions can be expected to make the child furtively determined to find out more about what makes the man parts so forbidden. It has also been suggested that children up to age 10 or 11 be permitted occasionally to view parents in the nude in casual situations (Gardner); it would seem, however, that only in rare families would such procedure fit into the overall life style.

Same Sex Parent exposure to a child in the home under appropriate circumstances is usually no great problem until the "modest phase" of pubescence arrives, although many parents of either sex abandon the practice of joint bathing, showering, toileting, etc., at a considerably earlier age. Observing use of the toilet, including father's urination by small boys, is a legitimate learning experience for children up to about age 3. Certain unusually shy, "soft" boys probably should not be exposed to the father's nudity after age 5 or 6, and almost certainly should not be compelled to undress in locker rooms with adult or adolescent men as this has been noted to be a greatly distressing experience to them at times.

Opposite-Sex Parent. Bathing with the mother is a normal pleasure for children of both sexes. In the case of little boys it probably should cease near age 4. The presence of little girls at father's intimate bathroom activities is not advisable at any age above toddling. Exposure of the mother's breast, if nursing, is a normal occurrence of family life and need not be concealed from children. Where babies are bottle-fed, the breasts may constitute an object of occasional curiosity for children of either sex up to age 3 or 4, after which interest seems to cease. Brief exploration of the hairy mons pubis is permitted by many mothers to small children (up to age 2½) of either sex when the occasion happens to arise, but anything beyond that is not advisable. The first necessary lessons in the customs of privacy are often learned by the child in connection with such touching. Similar exploratory handling of the father's genitalia by children of either sex—although advocated by extremists from time to time—must be deemed unnecessary, and by age 9 most children do not wish the opposite sex to see them nude. Beginning midway during pubescence, but certainly by the time puberty is reached, children should no longer be required to be viewed nude by the parent of the opposite sex under ordinary circumstances. For instance it is undesirable for a father to intrude on a bathing or dressing daughter after that age, or for a mother on her son.

The casual viewing of nude sibling by sibling is a normally accepted occurrence; it is, in fact, desirable as it is the main source of learning about sex differences for many children. Joint bathing of brothers and sisters need not cease before the oldest has reached age 8 or 9, although many families discourage it after age 5 or 6. Below age 4 few children seem to have any qualms about disporting total nudity on occasions. In the home, children up to the age of 5 cannot be held strictly accountable for concealing their lower bodies on all occasions.

SEX PLAY

It is extremely likely that a normal child at one time or other will engage in at least occasional companionate sex exploration or sex play. This can be expected at any time after age 3 and short of being oppressive it is not possible for parents or guardians to "protect" a normal child from at least some participation in such activity. Nor is this ordinarily desirable. It is not known if the lessons taught by the Harlows' famed motherless monkeys—frequent failure to develop reproductive behavior later, reduced only by an opportunity for sex play with other infant monkeys—are in some way applicable to humans, but there are indications that they are.

Before School Age much of the sex play is of an exploratory nature, motivated by curiosity or perhaps by a degree of anxiety about genital intactness. For some subdued or tense children on whom harsh genital prohibitions had been imposed from an early age, an experience of this type has a reassuring effect. They see another child interested in the same area, the incident passes without consequences, and this may relieve them of an inner fear that something terrible will happen if the lower parts are exposed or touched. As a rule only the mildest of pleasure sensations are elicited during these early activities, and orgasm is an exceptional occurrence in either sex. Little boys frequently do not even have an erection during such games, although they are well capable of this. The thrill of doing something secret or forbidden often helps in making these activities interesting. There is much interest in other children's urinary functions near age 4, although competitive urinary games between boys occur more characteristically only some years later. At this age there is relatively little significance in whether sex play takes place with a companion of the same or the opposite sex, whether the vulva or the anus is the center of interest, or whether a finger, a stick or the penis is used for poking maneuvers.

The types of companionate sex activities in childhood are practically limitless, but with a few exceptions no type has inherently more abnormal significance than any other. Whether there occurs a simple game of "show," or playing "doctor," "nurse" or "house" with embracing, smooching or poking is most likely due to such circumstances as example, opportunity or individual inventiveness. It is not known if these early sexual role playing games are invented over again by each generation or whether they are passed on from older to younger children (Beigel). Abnormality chiefly enters the picture in the form of unusual frequency, persistence, aggressiveness or seductiveness. For instance, a little boy whom nothing can deter from lifting the skirts of little girls is likely to be more disordered emotionally than a little slum boy who participates in a gang-up on another boy resulting in anal immission.

In Older Children both the nature of sex play and the participating pattern differ. Past age 9 the overall incidence is less, while the ratio of boys now distinctly surpasses that of girls. Girls at this age, in our culture, become more reticent or disdain to participate. Pleasure sensations from all manner of direct genital stimulation are frequent, and orgasm is now often the goal of these activities; on the other hand older children are often less intensely interested in what they are doing sexually; the activity frequently is more in the nature of a companionable event, a sporting activity, including occasional all-boy group sex play and group masturbation. The abnormally seductive or aggressive child now stands out more from the rest and is more disturbing to, and more disliked by, the group. At this age boy-girl activity is perhaps more characteristic of children on the lowest sociocultural levels, while boy-boy sex play prevails as one ascends. Among prepuberal boys nearly 3 times as many boys from a blue-collar background have had or tried intercourse than those from white-collar surroundings (Gebhard-Elias).

Parents may require detailed reassurance that occasional sex play is harmless; that it is not an indication of precocious erotism; and that it usually represents no hazard as to future sex attitudes. Two children who secrete themselves and giggle may not be concerned with genital, urinary or similar explorations at all. On the other hand most mothers know that where two children have secreted themselves and are suddenly altogether silent, a quick investigation is in order. It is always advisable to intrude on such situations, as children need directive reminders that certain activities are unacceptable. Where an adult chances on such secret activities, however harmless they may be, it is normal and proper to register disapproval. Anything else would only bewilder normal children and hinder them in their development toward normal standards of conduct and attitude. There is no need to frighten such children ("will make you sick," "unheard of"); a combination of calm reproach ("these things aren't done") and cheerful distraction toward other games is sufficient. For repeaters who are essentially normal and happy children, ordinary disciplinary measures are in order. The sex play of a child should not be discussed with other adults, perhaps especially not a physician, within the child's hearing.

Swift, harsh punishment is rarely a suitable way to deal with sex play, especially not in the anxiety-ridden or otherwise disturbed, recidivist child whose interest in such play seems to be excessive. The best preventive is a normal amount of natural, properly guarded frankness toward the child's early questions and curiosities (see p. 24); of course, this offers no guarantee that occasional participation will not occur. Children who are bored, have no opportunities for interesting activities, or are unacquainted with games and possibilities for fun, are probably more susceptible to participation in joint genital or urinary ventures. The same may be said of those who are unusually suggestible, chronically overstimulated by a sensual attitude in the home, of highly sensuous endowment, or lacking all adult supervision, interest and direction. An overpermissive attitude in the home is disturbing to children in our culture.

Brother-sister sex play requires special mention. Its beginning—most often between ages 4 and 7—is innocuous enough as the children explore their parts together; at this stage it is not an alarming manifestation regardless of the frequency and length of time spent on mutual exploration, and it should not then be designated as incest. However, it is, in our culture, an undesirable and potentially harmful situation. The activity is more frequent than is commonly assumed, especially where there are no other siblings in the family, and where the two children share a bedroom.

Because of the unique opportunity, and perhaps for other reasons, siblings are apt to indulge in more complete types of sex activity, and to make it a more regular practice than playmates. The activity tends to progress from genital exploration and manipulation to apposition and interfemoral immission, and thence to vulvar, rarely vaginal, but not infrequently rectal immission. Orgasm may be sought in this fashion almost every night for many months, often years, on end. There can be no question that such habitual heterogenital activity in children is noxious. The danger of overt incest fixation in adulthood is slight, although such cases have occurred. Much greater is the risk of psychic fixation on the other sibling throughout life, which can make both of them thoroughly unsuitable to conduct good marriages, especially where the affair carries over well into the second decade or is resumed near puberty. There are indications that girls with protracted domestic sex entanglements often tend to promiscuous sex behavior beginning in the second decade.

Where such activity is discovered by the parents, the children should be assigned separate sleeping quarters without much fuss except for normal remonstrations. No other measures are usually indicated. This applies equally to fraternal twins. From the beginning of the second decade, latest from menarche, mixed-gender siblings should not share a bedroom whenever possible. Some existing and unusually intense attachments, of course, will always find the means for expression; such major problems require individual consideration. Brother-brother sex play occurs at times in late childhood or pubescence (e.g., when an older brother shows the younger one how to masturbate, or involves him in mutual masturbation). These are almost always transitory activities. Sister-sister sex play seems to be rare.

The Child Instigator. One of the problems of childhood sex play involves the so-called instigator (i.e., the boy or girl who is a chronic seducer or aggressor). The compulsive chronic instigator belongs in the field of child psychopathology. But even the merely impulse-disordered little wrongdoer may greatly perturb a whole group of children and mobilize undue guilty erotism in the more labile members of the group. Sometimes these children can be identified when a stable child who has a trusting relationship to his parents admits sex play with the disturber but indicates that he "hates" him (her). This alone would be hazardous grounds on which to single out a chronic instigator, but frequently a number of children will make similar statements to their parents about one particular child. It is often with a heavy heart that unhysterical parents band together to label another family's child a chronic undesirable. At other times social considerations make parents look the other way. But where a group of calm parents are reasonably sure of their beliefs, it would seem to be proper and necessary for them to seek a suitable, direct and honest solution for the sake of their children.

A different situation exists where blindly enraged parents—usually the father—elicit from their child caught in major sex play the statement that the other child was the instigator. Actually one cannot often speak with certainty of an instigator in the sex play of two essentially normal children, especially if below school age. This attitude of parents is almost bound to mobilize a particularly noxious type of guilt feeling in the child. As there is also likely to be agitated talk of "ruination" and such, the child may become quite perturbed. A parent requesting a physician to make an obviously needless genital examination of the child, motivated by indiscriminate vindictiveness, perhaps by a plan to sue for damages, should be refused for the child's sake, together with appropriate explanations and reassurances. It may be noted that where a boy and a girl of school age are involved in major sex play, it is perhaps at least as often the little girl who entices the boy and, if necessary, instructs him, as vice versa.

MASTURBATION AND PSEUDOMASTURBATION

Following generations of alarmist views concerning childhood masturbation there has been put forward in recent decades a rather sweeping assertion that masturbation in the first decade is a normal phenomenon. This may be a helpfully soothing formulation for the benefit of disturbed parents, but the physician cannot overlook the fact that genital self-stimulation in infancy and in childhood can represent a reaction to adverse psychological conditions in the environment which may need to be identified. Because of its habit-forming propensities, such a reaction may become an end in itself, even long after the original adverse circumstances have ceased.

Normal Infant: Self-exploration. Early Sensuosity. Not all genital activity in childhood constitutes masturbation. Beginning at 5 or 6 months of age, the infant quite normally discovers and fingers the parts of his body everywhere, including the various projections and openings. Sometimes parents are overimpressed by how often the genital region is fingered as compared with the nose and such, forgetting that the diapers come off only in an adult's presence. Before the tenth month no sensuosity probably is connected with these explorations even though baby boys may produce erections in this fashion; but then almost any type of stimulus can make the penis of the male infant erect itself.

Late during the first year the infant first derives some enjoyment from handling the genitals. This is the stage in which the sensuous perception which temporarily invests the mucocutaneous junctions and the functions of the perineal openings are discovered. Some children pass through the perineal phase with little manifest interest in this region, while others— perhaps constitutionally more highly sensuous—are obviously and at length responsive to it and may show a great deal of delight in eliciting sensations. More little girls than boys continue the sensuous exploration and exploitation of their genitals during the remainder of early childhood, not rarely to the point of producing orgasm ("shivers"). Such manipulations include prolonged fingering, poking, rubbing or squeezing of the vulva, rubbing against the edge of the crib or a chair, rolling over a pillow or toy, or rubbing against the mother's or another unwary adult's body. Some lie prone and beat their heels against the buttocks. All these maneuvers remain characteristically unconcealed.

Distressed Infant: Genital Self-excitation, etc. Distress-induced self-gratification occurs even in very early infancy, but this group of manifestations is poorly understood; what has been observed is variably interpreted by different observers. The manifestations include dreamy-withdrawn diddling, rhythmic rocking, thrusting self-excitation and possibly accessory movements of ludeln.

Causes. Among the causes is low tolerance for or overexposure to excitement, tension or various other stressful insults to the infant's level of neural organization: noises, overexcitement, overebullient caressing, premature tossing and swinging games, etc. A part may be played by continuous frustration of an infant's or small child's dependent needs by a depriving mother (mother's disinterest, overburdening, tiredness, advent of a new baby), or else by her inconsistent, erratic or contradictory behavior—sometimes overindulgent, sometimes depriving, or rejecting detachment immediately followed by effusiveness. Some infants exposed to insufficient pleasurable stimulation act as if they had to recompense themselves from whatever endogenous pleasure source is currently (i.e., developmentally) available to them. Some observers have been impressed by the relative frequency and the tense-anxious characteristics of masturbation in small children who have been prematurely or force-trained in toilet habits. Why different children react differently to similar insults is not definitely known; constitutional factors may play a part, also the total affective climate, including the quality of the "pleasing cycle" (the pleased mother pleases her infant, and vice versa). Where a previously good visual-tactile-auditory image of the mother has been lost by the infant, hallucinatory (some say fantasized, improbable at this age) substitution of her pleasurable stimulations, accompanied by such substitute activities as sucking or rubbing of various parts, including the genitals, may occur. Genital play appears to be relatively infrequent in institution-reared infants.

Manifestations. The most primitive pleasure source is believed to be rhythmic rocking, either supine, prone, standing, or on knees and elbows or hands, sometimes with head bumping. Pleasure sensations here may be centered around the genital area, but in boys, for instance, there is no penile erection. Not all stereotyped rhythmic activities in infants represent masturbatory equivalents. Rhythmic motor discharges in the small child can be a generalized response to frustration; they tend to be massed between maturation stages, when satisfaction from one source is declining while the new source is not yet functional or satisfying. In some children near toddler age who have been left much alone, given few toys or similarly deprived, genital self-manipulation may be accompanied by a peculiarly flaccid, immobile posture and a "far-off" absent facial expression, while the eyes have a humid shine. This is apparently quite similar to the "dreamy withdrawal" of some of the infants who engage in persistent fecal play. The meaning of the latter has been variably interpreted, but it is probably a substitution symptom, and clinically it cannot always be taken lightly. Certain accessory movements of "ludeln" (suctus voluptabilis) are a separate manifestation. Ludeln is the well-known rhythmic finger-sucking in infants with its attendant "voluptuous" facial expression which may be accompanied by rhythmic rubbing of the body and, at times, of the genital region, with the free hand. The activity is traceable to the characteristic finger-hand movements of the infant during the feeding act.

Least frequent, but most dramatic is the thrusting self-excitation of infants. The infant is seen lying supine, making rhythmic body movements including pelvic thrusts of gradually increasing rapidity until, after a final tensing, an acme occurs after which there is relaxation. During the act the eyes are shiny, the face flushed, and in male infants the erect penis may throb. The average act lasts a few minutes (reported range: 10 seconds to 10 minutes); at times it is repeated 2 or 3 times in succession. Contact of the genitals with surfaces or objects is absent here, and the act is non-manipulatory. Occasionally in older infants there is up-and-down motion of the pelvis in the prone position. The parents may be advised to crib- or arm-rock and cuddle the infant when an episode appears imminent. A sharp command with raised voice or a slap on the buttocks at the onset has been found helpful by experienced infant nurses. It is best to avoid excessive swinging, bouncing or tickling of such infants. Cleansing of the perineal region need not be feared by the mother. Local irritations almost certainly play no part in the causation. The condition is self-limiting.

Childhood Masturbation. Sensuous automanipulation of infancy extinguishes itself before age 3 except for a minority—probably less than one fifth of the total, mostly little girls—who continue to exploit the newly discovered fricating sensations of the vulva until, within a year or two, they have learned to produce orgasm in this fashion. But near age 5 or 6 two broad new groups of children are found resorting to masturbation, now a large majority of them boys: the chronically unhappy or otherwise distressed self-comforters, and those who have socially discovered how to "play with themselves."

Play-experimenters. This group gets to know masturbation as something which "feels good," a sport or game among their peers, something serving to express momentary defiance or rebellion, a plaything entailing the thrill of the forbidden, or practiced because of boredom and social understimulation. Some are essentially self-indulgent, and constitutionally highly sensuous children who readily recompense themselves for hurts and slights by extracting pleasure from their bodies without much conflict. It may become an almost automatic self-comforting response at the slightest distress (e.g., for being sent to bed, loneliness, boredom, apprehensions or upsets). In some children the picture is complicated by the existence of a secondary gain pattern; here the symptom is retained, as it were, because it has proved to be effective in worrying, scandalizing, dominating or simply gaining attention from the adults concerned. Fantasies—probably infrequent before age 8—are mildly erotic and rarely fully sexualized as they will be during the hothouse years around puberty, now still several years away. Complete spontaneous relinquishment of masturbation in this group during the latency phase (p. 15) seems to be somewhat easier for girls, except perhaps for tomboys who also seem to be more subject to conflict about masturbation than their more feminine peers.

Chronically Unhappy Children resort to masturbation for its comfort value when something depresses or upsets them but lose interest when the underlying distress improves. In children's institutions a disciplinarian teacher or a harsh housemother may send the masturbation rate—solitary or mutual—soaring; but when a warm and sympathetic person enters the scene the rate often declines again very sharply unless one or a few "instigators" keep reinfesting the group. A more serious problem are the chronically tense, anxious or otherwise emotionally distressed children with a low capacity for tolerating even moderate disapproval; they tend to exploit genital sensations in a compulsive fashion and eventually stimulate themselves regardless of comfort need. An increasing loathing for themselves and a continuous fear of the consequences of masturbation is characteristic for this group of often very intelligent children. Many become progressively more troubled, but more than other masturbating children, they deny the practice and evade counsel and clinical help. Some of the males one encounters again in adulthood, among the so-called neurasthenoid type of habitual masturbators (p. 432); most of them probably never stopped.

Physical Causes. In an undetermined, but probably small number of cases, local irritations are a contributing or indirect cause of early masturbation, more often so in little girls. The local itching or discomfort directs the young child's attention to the area, leads to manipulations, and pleasurable sensations may first be aroused in this way. However, it has not been shown that in the absence of predisposing factors such children persist in manipulating themselves once the cause has been removed. Itching vulvo-vaginitis, various rashes, herpes, balanitis and occasionally penile or clitoral phimosis may be at fault. The pellets of smegma imprisoned under a tight clitoral prepuce with its midline raphe intact may cause irritation and congestion (Clark). Some small children may reproduce or prolong the pleasurable sensations they associate with passive distention of the rectum and derive masturbatory impetus from it; such induced constipation may be considered a co-symptom of a self-comforting syndrome. Because of their relative frequency one need be attentive to the possible presence of pinworms (Oxyuris or Enterobius vermicularis) in self-manipulating little girls. The female worm migrates out of the anus and deposits its eggs in the perianal area, sometimes even the vulva, giving rise to pruritus. Inclusion of oxyuriasis among the etiologic factors in childhood masturbation is traditional, although it has never been proved.

Modalities. There is little significance in how a child masturbates. Small children often stimulate themselves in a distinctly monotonous, stereotyped fashion, but a few more enterprising ones soon discover additional ways of eliciting pleasurable sensation. In midchildhood one observes a great variety of masturbatory technics, some of which may appear disconcertingly bizarre at first glance. These methods depend partly on the way in which masturbation was first discovered and partly on a tendency of normal children to experiment with their sensations. For example, self-stimulation may be limited to bicycling, tree- or rope-climbing, or banister sliding. Boys above age 6, besides the usual manual frication, may finger the organ through a pants pocket with or without a hole (in school), rub against mattress or ground while prone, or against the wall while standing, introduce the organ into cracks or holes in furniture, plaster or earth, between closet door and jamb, toilet seat and rim, rub it between the thighs in any position, or simply beat, squeeze or punish it with the hands or between two hard objects. The pummeling modality, most often encountered in late childhood or pubescence, may originate when a boy, seemingly for the first time, becomes aware of a vigorous erection and is frightened that it will never go down again and the parents will find out. Then in near-panic he may try to beat the member into subsiding, thereby accidentally producing his first orgasm. If repetition is sought later, it is done in the only manner known to the boy. Little girls, in addition to the previously mentioned modalities, may also squeeze the vulva between the thighs, or introduce the rubber tip of a pencil, a bobby pin or a twig into the urethra.

The fantasies and imageries which accompany masturbation in childhood involve a variety of subjects, only a minority of them of an erotic nature. One encounters, from the age that they are accessible to later recall, fantasies of comforting nearness of an adult, thrills of rescue and gratitude, grandiose achievement, revenge, fire, torture, killing and even terror. However, one cannot with any degree of certainty predict abnormal tendencies from any of these at this stage of development.

Parents. For some parents it is virtually impossible to watch the infant or toddler explore, diddle and toy in the genital region. They almost compulsively remove or impulsively slap the infant's hand while by mien or word they give unmistakable expression to their disapproval. Such parents require explanation and reassurance; at times a word about unreasonable interference may be necessary. An occasional casual removal of the infant's hand, for parents who simply cannot tolerate the sight, has no consequences, but continuous brusque interference with self-exploration may greatly bewilder the baby.

Later, many parents feel that in spite of all that is being said and written today they must stop the child from masturbating at all cost. Some become blindly infuriated for reasons darkly recessed in their own minds. Some are genuinely misinformed about possible damage to the child's body or mind. Others have a vague feeling that if their child masturbates, they have been remiss in some way in his upbringing; they either want to remove the evidence of their remissness or make amends by restoring the child's "innocence." Still others are afraid that a teacher, a nurse, a physician or a clergyman may notice it, and that it will reflect on the moral climate or the competence of the home; or that other people's children may pick up the habit from the child, and that they will be blamed ("the Joneses would never forgive us"). The consternation is often greater when a little girl is discovered masturbating. One may observe that it is the father who is more greatly disturbed at a daughter's masturbation. Mothers seem often most disturbed about little boys when their own vita sexualis is unsatisfactory; and about little girls when they are building daydreams of vicarious achievement around their little daughter's future.

Advising normally affectionate parents to disregard masturbation—not to look for it or not to let on that they suspect or know of it—is excellent advice. In our culture few parents can reasonably be expected to stand by with approval in such situations. By ingrained and age-old instinctive tradition nothing much is said or done in the case of girls. In the case of a boy, ideally the father unobtrusively takes greater interest in his activities, friends and thoughts, reinforces or establishes mutual trust, and eventually discusses masturbation in an informal, nonthreatening manner. He may point to the desirability of a wholesome way of living with "each thing at its proper time," and casually correct guilty knowledge or distorted fragments of sex information. He should avoid unduly detailed sex-physiologic data reminiscent of medicine and sickness.

As a rule the symptom of masturbation cannot be suppressed with impunity. Unfortunately it is fairly easy for parents and others to do so, either by frightening the child or by playing on his sense of guilt which is at least minimally present in masturbating children even when parents have been permissive. Negative conditioning is induced, for instance, by giving the child to understand that "mother has worried herself sick over you," that "people will see it in your face and think you are dirty," or a chagrined suggestion "not to go near nice children." One can similarly frighten a child out of masturbating by threatening remarks that "you will not grow up," "can't marry and have children," or "will become stupid like so-and-so." Of inordinately great effect in little boys are threats to "cut it off"; this means much more than threatening to cut off his nose for eavesdropping, or chopping off his fingers for stealing because he knows of no noseless or fingerless people, but most probably he has learned that little girls haven't got it any more, but just have a hole instead; he may understand that they have been bad and "that's why they had it cut off." Sealed night clothes, arm splints, tape cuffs, mittens and similar restraining devices as well as nocturnal bedside vigils are considered an anachronism today. Reward incentive systems with cumulative symbols such as star charts, and especially tangible or edible rewards, are now generally considered to achieve nothing of value.

An inadvertently noxious situation has been observed in certain chronically ill children, notably with rheumatic heart disease, in whom cautioning about overexertion has been combined with ill-advised remarks about avoiding masturbation. Some of these children seem to combine severe guilt feelings (e.g., that they made themselves sick and caused all the trouble by "doing it") with a nagging fear that each repetition will "ruin me for keeps."

CHAPTER 4

The Child as Victim of Sexual Aggression

Forcible Assault — Seduction and Molestation — Father-Daughter Incest — Unintentional Sex Aggression — Sequelae of Sexual Abuse — Preventive Measures — Imaginary Assault.

FORCIBLE ASSAULT

Related:
Teen-age Child Molesting p. 152
Sexual Aggression p. 436
Pedophilia p. 472

The prepuberal victims of forcible sexual attempts most often are girls 6 to 11 (peak 8–10) years of age. The perpetrator usually is a male adult or, less often, an adolescent. There is a seasonal peak from June to September. The act usually results in intercrural or incomplete vulvo-vaginal immission. Complete vaginal immission of an adult-sized phallus is rarely accomplished unless sufficient violence is used to cause major genital lacerations. Impotent, senile or intoxicated men may go through the motions of forcible assault without accomplishing genital contact, although in cases of ejaculatio praecox ante-portas traces of semen may be found later on the child.

Some deviates find gratification in forcibly uncovering a child without desiring genital contact, but the incidence of mutilating and violent acts seems to be especially high in those cases. Beating, choking or various mutilations in connection with forcible assault can have been inflicted either before, during, after, or instead of the sexual act. A relatively large proportion of mutilated or otherwise injured child victims die before they can be found and succored.

When first seen, a forcibly assaulted little girl may present a picture of acute fright, expressed by sobbing, crying and trembling; others are in a protracted daze, although their eyes may be open and roving; still others are stolid and show little concern. The acute fright seems to be caused largely by the general violence of the attacker's behavior rather than by the sexual maneuvers themselves. Small children may be totally unaware of the sexual nature of the assault (e.g., "a dirty man peed all over me" or "he tried to hurt me all over."). Hysteroid manifestations in an assaulted child may set in hours later: an apparently calm little girl may suddenly scream, seek to hide, or thrash about when the physician approaches to examine, or at the sight of a hypodermic syringe or instrument.

On Questioning, the child's story may be vague and contradictory, even if the assault took place very recently, and this must not be regarded as evidence of hysterical or deceitful fabrication. With each successive questioning the child's actual memory of the event tends to become more blurred and is increasingly filled in with hearsay, fantasy and secondary memories. A child whose initial story was vague, though real, who displays sudden lucidity about the event on requestioning a few days later, probably has been prompted by ill-advised parents. Psychiatric consultation to help question, evaluate or handle difficult child rape cases is often desirable.

Examination. The child in status post raptum should be kept in quiet surroundings, and as a rule should not be separated from her mother unless the latter is obviously agitating the child with her behavior. The presence of one cooperative parent implies consent to examine, but needs to be recorded. The examination has 2 separate purposes: to assist the victim medically and to conduct a medicolegal procedure. With the latter the physician serves the processes of justice and protects the rights both of the community and of the accused; he is the guardian of perishable evidence to which no one else has access. All findings, including negative ones, should be recorded immediately. Garments or undergarments with blood, grass or semen stains are evidence. All assaults require a search for traces of semen about the body, especially the vulva, thighs and lower abdomen; for details of specimen collection see p. 265, except that vaginal specimens are rarely indicated in younger children. All evidence and specimens need to be labeled and kept admissible-in-court by passing directly from examiner's hand to those of the next responsible person. Color photography of lesions, etc. is frequently recommended.

Complete physical examination of the child is advisable, as injuries may be present elsewhere. Total absence of bruises, abrasions or other trauma anywhere raises the possibility of fabrication or acquiescence. On the other hand, head injuries and trauma to ribs, larynx, spine, pelvis and peritoneal cavity all have been present in such children but were overlooked initially. Necessary gynecologic examination requires the usual cautions applicable to children: non-elaborate draping, placement of mother at the child's head, nondisplay and prewarming of metal instruments, use of lubricants where indicated, etc. When the genitalia are traumatized, rapid general anesthesia is preferred by many surgeons. Pre-cocainizing the parts by sponge prior to examination has been advocated in certain cases. Malsedation or excessive tranquillization may lead to fitful somnolence or partial clouding of consciousness, giving undesirable results. Exceptionally, a seemingly unhurt but very panicky child in need of immediate gynecologic examination requires a general anesthetic.

Genitalia. The vulva of an assaulted child may merely show minor bruising and oozing abrasions, or perhaps major degrees of swelling and a large hematoma. The latter are evidence of blunt trauma, although not in themselves evidence of genito-genital contact (i.e., rape): they may have been produced by rough handling preparatory to attempted rape. Redness and congestion of the part may also be due to the mother's emergency use of concentrated disinfectant wash, or to prior manipulation in companionate sex play. The child's sensitive hymen, when exposed to view, may show the characteristic fresh circumferential tears due to recent defloration; however, the possible variation of hymenal appearance in the child needs to be kept in mind. In brutal rapes there may be vulvar midline tears extending from urethra to perineum. Lacerations may include the vagina in depth, even extending into the peritoneal cavity; they have involved anus and rectum at times. In the most brutal attacks severe, deep injuries are more usually caused by forcible intromission of a heavy stick or umbrella rather than the phallus; few children have survived such sadistic attacks. Generally the thin covering of the child's vulva and vagina bleeds easily and profusely or forms a hematoma upon moderately severe traumatization; but it also stops bleeding rapidly with pressure and cold packs, and heals well, according to experienced observers.

VD-prophylaxis. If the assailant is unidentified or cannot be examined at once, it is not unreasonable to assume in principle that simultaneous infection of the child with both syphilis and gonorrhea has taken place, regardless of the age of the attacker or victim. In one series of rape cases a 4-year old girl became infected with primary syphilis (Hayman). In another series of 180 venereally infected children there were 42 children under age 9 with gonorrhea acquired by nonvoluntary sexual contact (Branch-Paxton). Fortunately, adequate gonorrhea prophylaxis with dosage-adjusted penicillin (e.g., procaine penicillin G in aqueous suspension 1.2 million units i.m. on two successive days) will also abort co-acquired syphilis during its incubation phase; however, this is not safely applicable to any older girl who may conceivably have been infected within a few weeks before the assault (see p. 266). A follow-up serologic test for syphilis 4 weeks later is desirable; the purpose of the specimen should be veiled from the child at that time. In an occasional older girl with a history or suspicion of prior exposure both a syphilis test and a cervical culture for gonorrhea at the time of first examination are valuable as a medicolegal baseline.

Management of the Child Victim. Hospitalization of an abused child should be avoided whenever possible and is practically never indicated on psychiatric grounds. The objective in almost every case is to return the child to her accustomed activities and environment with the least possible delay; for this reason, prolonged bed rest or seclusion at home and other oversolicitudes should be discouraged. The mother may accompany a frightened child in the street the first few days, but this should be discontinued as soon as the child will tolerate it.

It is often advisable for the parents to prepare the girl for the curious questions of neighbors and playmates (e.g., by telling her, "These people want to be nice, but you can just tell them politely that you are trying to forget this," or "Tell them the man tried to hurt you but you screamed and ran away," or "Tell them your parents said not to talk about it.").

The Parents' Own Attitude is important, and counseling them appropriately should routinely be part of the care rendered in child rape cases. They will need an opportunity to ventilate feelings, particularly if there is guilt about negligence or their failure as parents. They should also be cautioned against expressing undue suspiciousness ("maybe she looked for trouble"); against future overstrictness in supervision, as well as against prolonged overprotective attitudes. They must avoid referring to the incident in such terms as violated, ruined, dirty or "lost her innocence," as this may produce baseless anxiety and feelings of guilt in the child.

It is highly unwise for parents to instill in the child any excessively vindictive feelings against the assailant which they themselves may have. Some children may have experienced a vaguely pleasurable sensation at some point during the attack, or else they may even have allowed liberties initially, but later panicked and balked, provoking a forcible attempt. This can have happened even if the girl shows great and genuine distress when first examined. It can be a source of guilty conflict and anxiety in such a child, especially later, if she is compelled to aid in the attacker's conviction and possibly is expected to gloat about it. Actually she is expected to condemn certain impulses in herself which perhaps she did not, and does not, understand to be wrong.

The parents may be puzzled about giving additional sex information to the child who has been exposed sexually. They may think it best to let the child forget by keeping all mention of sexual topics from her and evading any questions relating to the reproductive functions. Experience has shown that this "conspiracy of silence" is not advisable except in the case of very young and patently naïve children to whom the whole incident can be explained as a simple assault. Prepuberal girls harbor a certain amount of fanciful sex notions, and having been assaulted may come to mean to them that they have somehow been "torn open" or permanently hurt; or will become forever marked or different or even diseased; that they cannot have children any more; or that now no boy will ever like them or no man will marry them later. These notions, if uncorrected, may persist below the level of consciousness and can give rise to disturbances throughout life. An assaulted child should be encouraged to come to her mother with any questions and anxious doubts concerning her body, or the mother may even want to take the initiative in presenting a reassuring view of the incident. The counseling professional needs to satisfy himself that the mother has a basic vocabulary of sexual terms which can be used in discussing these matters with the child (see p. 25).

Moving to a new neighborhood or community may occasionally be planned by the parents, especially if the incident has received much public notice, or if the child remains very fearful and upset. Generally, this should not be encouraged as it tends to increase the shamefulness and stigma of the mishap in the girl's mind, and she may come to live in continuous fear that her new companions will find out about her dark secret. If the attacker happens to be a member of the child's own household (e.g., a relative or a boarder) he should be removed from the child's environment. Some families try to shield such a man for various reasons and do nothing in the hope that it will not happen again. But because of the danger of recidivism and the exceptionally pronounced psychological ill effects on the child in these cases, this should be discouraged.

The parents may beg the physician not to report a criminal assault, although the law in this respect varies. Because of the high incidence of repeaters among sex offenders against children, whenever feasible the parents should be encouraged to cooperate fully with the authorities, in the interest of possible future victims. Most children with good general emotional equilibrium, and if properly handled, will not be unduly upset by making a statement to the police or the prosecuting authority, nor even by the task of identifying the assailant. If the child must testify in court she can be told about this one or two days in advance. An assigned social worker should prepare both the child and her parents for the court experience through such methods as role playing, behavior rehearsals and mock trials (Schultz). Efforts should be made to speed the legal proceedings, prevent delays, and insure privacy in court. The social worker should accompany the child and family at every court appearance, and generally everything should be done to spare the victim embarrassment and upset.

SEDUCTION AND MOLESTATION

Seduction of a child, most often a girl, by an adult or an adolescent lacks the element of force and requires at least the toleration of the victim. It is resorted to ultimately in search of sexual contact, either genito-genital, or a manipulatory or other intimacy is performed on the child's genitalia, or the child is enticed to manipulate the adult's organs. Seduction can be accomplished through small sums of money, candy, a treat, or the promise of some favor or job for pay. Flattery ("beautiful . . . practically a young woman") can be effective in hypersuggestible and certain unstable children. A child brought up without much warmth eventually may permit intimacies even to a total stranger who has been friendly and pleasant over a period of weeks or months. Curiosity and the example of companions sometimes are sufficient, especially if a treat is involved ("he'll give you candy just for lifting your skirt a little"). Deception combined with a self-assured approach ("I am a doctor and must examine you," "All children do this here," "I'll show you what to guard against with bad people") is effectively used even by complete strangers on small children who have a serenely trusting attitude toward the adults in their own environment, and on slightly older children by persons the child knows well and respects.

On the other hand it is almost never possible to induce a child to co-operate with a seducer by arousing her sexually in the adult sense. Bodily fondling, the sight of exposed genitals, sex stories or pornographic material do not arouse the normal child's libido, although these maneuvers may render her sufficiently curious, flattered, bewildered, fascinated, intimidated or vaguely excited to tolerate additional advances. Some disturbed and character-neurotic children tend to provoke seduction (e.g., because they derive a certain morbid delight from watching the discomfiture of a susceptible man whom they keep tempting erotically in various ways, or from observing his alarm and remorse after they have permitted intimacies). Others will engage in sex play with an older male as a neurotic defiance reaction against their parents or other environment. Some character-neurotic girls have an outspokenly charming and seductive manner, but by every legal and moral standard the adult is responsible for avoiding and resisting the advances of a child.

Molestation of a child most often takes the form of furtive fondling, hugging or uncovering; kissing and "jocular" spanking on the buttocks by an unauthorized adult; exposing the genitalia; peeping on a child who is urinating or in undress; accosting with obscene propositions; and the showing of pornographic material. Although these maneuvers may simply be the forerunners of a seductive (less often a forcible) attempt, most habitual child molesters shun major intimacies with children but resort to subsequent solitary masturbation. Some emotionally unstable and character-neurotic children appear to invite molestation, although they will not permit genital contact.

The molested child's emotional reaction to the incident depends largely on her general emotional stability and on what attitude the parents and other adults take; if undisguised neighborhood agitation happens to be high because of a recent series of similar incidents, some children panic belatedly. Otherwise the immediate effects are usually minor or absent.

FATHER-DAUGHTER INCEST

Occurrence. Sexual relations between a father and a female child or children is practically always a continuing affair, often of 5 to 10 years' duration, and not necessarily carried on furtively. Such incestuous concubinage in our culture occurs more often than had originally been believed. Only a minority are found out; retrospective exploration of former victimized females in psychotherapy has been an added major source of information. It is not typically a lower-class phenomenon, nor associated with substandard housing or low moral standards, nor yet with subnormality, shiftlessness or general criminality of the father. Most of these men are of average intelligence and education, and working steadily. In a midwestern series of 203 detected cases the men's age averaged 39 (range 20 to 56); the daughters ranged from 3 to 18 years of age (Cavallin). Onset of the relationships most frequently occurs at the girl's age 9 or slightly below.

Cultural Incest. Only in a small number of cases, hardly ever reported except in case of pregnancy, is the family essentially free from psychopathology. Such cultural (functional) incest occurs in some overcrowded, disorganized patriarchal subcultures. Here the incest barrier may have lost much of its significance. A father may exact his "rights" from a daughter, or a mother may persuade her to gratify the father temporarily during her incapacitation by childbirth, etc. The environment would view this with tolerance or even accept it as a matter of course. The girls here appear to be somewhat older. Nothing is known about ill effects if any.

Family Pathology. The more typical incestuous situation tends to evolve in an outwardly unbroken, but otherwise grossly dysfunctional home. Only in a minority of cases has the man been widowed or deserted; almost always the wife has in one way or another abdicated her role as sex partner. However, both parents wish to maintain the public façade, while a gradual, tensely conflict-laden, often destructive mother-daughter role reversal takes place. These families tend to be large and the father may begin with the oldest girl and subsequently engage one or more of the others as they grow up.

The Mother is the fulcrum and catalyst of this family pathology. Few father-daughter affairs could continue for long without her subtly manipulatory or even overt collusion. Such mothers foist adult responsibilities on their daughters and rush them toward maturity so as to free themselves from the burden of sexual relations. Mother and daughter may quarrel over attention from the father (e.g., involving small money presents). In other cases the mother resents being deprived by the affair, yet does not seem to have the personality resources to stop it. When questioned these dependent, immature women will stress their helplessness, their ignorance, etc. In extreme cases a mother will tolerate incestuous cohabitation right in the marital bed. She may pretend to sleep while the girl, feeling "lone-

INCEST

Occurrence. Medically, incest is sexual intercourse between two members of the immediate family. Legal blood kin prohibitions have been codified almost everywhere and an act of close degree constitutes a crime even without the added offense of abuse of a minor. Incest occurs most frequently between brother and sister, but the most often reported and clinically and sociologically best explored type is father-daughter incest (Irving, others). Counting reported cases only, incest occurs at the rate of 1 to 3 cases per million population per year, with the rate probably rising.

Offspring. Incest babies, usually born to healthy teen-age mothers from a normal brother or father show a striking inbreeding effect: death in infancy, hereditary illness, or congenital anomalies occurred in 54 out of 124 such babies in one series, as compared to 3 out of 136 controls (Seemannová); in another series 8 out of 13 died or were defective (Carter); and 11 times the control rate in still another group (Adams-Neel). Normal incest progeny is believed to be of generally duller than average intelligence. The risk of first-degree consanguineous parents sharing a deleterious recessive mutation is 4 times that encountered in the notoriously high-risk first-cousin marriages.

Theories. Avoidance of incest, according to most 20th century theories, is not instinctive (Briffault, Dunlap, Freud, Seligman, Westermarck, others), but its widespread horrified rejection shows the deep-rootedness of the cultural prohibitions or "incest taboo." A possible instinctive-bioprotective component in incest fear has not been disproven, however. In view of today's increasing separation of pleasure-seeking sex activity from reproductive function, the basis for controlling incest behavior may have to be rationalized anew.

some" or such, is allowed to lie between the couple. The father then reassures himself that in the dark he always mistakes one for the other and, this type of man being an inveterate rationalizer, may even almost believe this himself; at least he may try to make the girl believe that he believes it.

The Father tends to be a passive, immature individual, sometimes highly susceptible to seduction, and often with a childhood background of a broken home and severely affectionless upbringing. In one series 75 per cent of the men were involved with alcohol, but other observations disagree with this frequency. Only a proportion are classifiable as pedophiliacs (Weinberg). All observers agree that practically none of the men are grossly disordered psychiatrically at the time of the affair.

The Girl. The very young girl is initiated with caresses and mutual erotic play "as a treat" or "to help you sleep" or in the course of "sex lectures" or fiend warnings. Complaints about mother's coldness, loneliness, etc. often go with this. Crude early intromission occurs mostly in alcoholized states, but even in these cases the girls, no matter what age, do not often seem to complain. As the affair progresses, lubricants may be brought into play, and a condom after menarche. The girls' acceptance and conspiratorial cooperation increases over the years, although there may be grumbling. The father, perhaps made angry by his own remorse, may treat the very young girl alternatingly with harshness and with tender promises and stimulation. While most girls bear the father no ill will, even years later, almost all come to hate and resent the mother, although this hostility is ambivalent and interspersed with anxiety over usurping her place, and dread of being abandoned by her. Death wishes against her are an inherent part of father-daughter incest. In the teens some girls keep away from all boys, encouraged in this by the father ("Robert—he is rarely called Dad—didn't want me to date anyone"). They become fiercely defensive of the home, the family group and especially the father. A minority of the girls are seductive instigators, even at a very young age, highly sensual and charming; their acting-out behavior, together with a poorly integrated, highly seducible father does, in fact, initiate some chronic incest situations.

Sequelae. For the duration of the incestuous relationship the girls display only minor psychologic morbidity. The spectacular breakdowns—adolescent psychoses such as catatonic states or suicidal depressions, and runaway social disintegration via prostitution—are mostly precipitated by termination conflicts (see below). There are indications that relatively late-commencing affairs tend toward the more spectacular ill effects, while those protracted from early childhood have a subtler but more chronic effect. The very young girl who is engaged in erotic dalliance with her father becomes enormously confused as her dependent need is made to intermingle with his orgastic impulses and the implied conflict with the mother. As childhood fantasies and, later, normal instinctual urges are being acted out and fulfilled directly, there is little incentive to progress beyond that developmental stage and toward more mature love objects. Instinctual retardation, even arrest occurs and the girl becomes increasingly incapable of future normal love relationships. Later, some suffer dissociative episodes bordering on schizoid states; in times of crisis they tend to denigrate their husbands (Lustig). Even in the early and midteens the incestuous conflict is acted out sometimes by drifting into a compulsively promiscuous pattern (e.g., by organizing sex groups among younger children or contemporaries, or by self-debasing modes of adolescent multi-partnerism). With their peers they become either withdrawn or furtive, or else boastful and immodest. Often they come to prefer the company of older age groups ("I felt I was different from the girls my age") and they tend to display pseudomaturity. Chronic low-grade mental depression, destructive behavior, learning difficulties, psychosomatic (e.g., abdominal) symptoms and compulsive-masochistic reactions (Bigras) are noted at times.

There are two critical occasions during the affair at which a rapid, sometimes fulminating—less than 24 hours—break into the pathologic tends to occur; dethronement and termination. Symbolic dethronement from the fantasied position as surrogate wife can occur if the mother happens to become pregnant, or if in a major decision the father sides with his wife, or when a widower announces that he will remarry. The impact on the girl's psyche of being rudely awakened to her actual status in the family exceeds even that of accidental incestuous pregnancy. However, there is good toleration when a younger sister takes the girl's place, usually a gradual affair. Hurtful termination of the affair occurs either with the father's arrest or when he, in panic or in fear of arrest, deserts the home. The resentment of the mother usually forces the girl to leave the home soon or later, or else she becomes a runaway with probability of winding up as a prostitute.

Neoplasia of Cervix. From present knowledge, incestuous fathers are exposing their young daughters to a substantially heightened risk of developing premalignant lesions of the cervix later in life. (See p. 258.)

Break-up. The law protects all minor children against sexual abuse by the father or others. The offense is punishable by imprisonment everywhere. Adoptive daughters, stepdaughters and foster daughters are protected similarly. Where the physician is the primary recipient of a girl's claim that she has been victimized, a degree of skepticism toward such charges is in order, as some girls vindictively implicate the father or stepfather in various incestuous relationships. Having excluded this, the first impulse may be to confer with the mother, but chances are that if her hand is forced, the mother will manipulate or testify the daughter into delinquent status and save the family breadwinner; practically all fathers can be assumed to go along with these maneuvers. When a mother presents the complaint to the physician, it must be assumed from present experience that she is not motivated primarily by concern about the child's welfare. The physician who attempts to confront a father with what he has learned most often faces an incensed or even belligerent and threatening man, without in the end having accomplished much, as the affair is likely to be resumed after a period of time.

Management. However, something effective must be done. These girls cannot be left at home once the case has been opened up, nor would any family court tolerate such a solution. Some observers, placing their trust in family therapy, dispute this, but there is little evidence of success so far. The individual practitioner is well advised to request the assistance of a youth-protective or children's aid organization even if he has "known" the family for many years. From social agency and individual psychiatric experience with incest victims, the prognosis is generally guarded (i.e., only a minority among reported cases make a satisfactory adjustment and maintain it). Experience also seems to show that these girls do better when placed in a good protective institution for rehabilitation, and that frequently they do poorly when placed in a foster home (disputed). The girl in process of avulsion from the home situation needs close observation and support, psychiatric if possible, during the separation period. Temporary but adequate preventive psychotropic medication (e.g., perphenazine 2–4 mg t.i.d. with imipramine 10–25 mg hs) can be valuable in taking some of the jolt out of the changes about to take place in the hapless girl's existence.

UNINTENTIONAL SEX AGGRESSION

The possible noxious effect, on some children, of enemas and spanking is in part based on retrospective evidence (i.e., the frequency and the manner in which these measures turn up in the recollections of character disordered, sex-deviant and other patients during psychotherapeutic exploration in depth).

Spanking.   Views differ on the desirability of corporal punishment, but in itself occasional spanking on the buttocks by hand or flat paddling device does not seem to be damaging to the psyche of a normal child; however, it can produce definitely erotic sensations, including orgasm, in some children. Some such children have been known to cause themselves to be spanked, usually by the same particular person. The discipliner may be unaware of this; in other cases there has been culpable awareness and toleration of the child's sexual reaction. Pseudo-disciplinary spanking for the adult's own perverted gratification has rarely been encountered in the recent past. Nonerotic erections can occur in small boys being spanked; if noticed, further and future spanking may lead to a morbid conditioning process connecting pain and pleasure, or sex and chastisement. However, post-spanking solitary masturbation is almost always a self-comforting device.

The following modalities of spanking seem the most noxious as regards future psychosexual development of susceptible children: spanking exclusively by opposite-sex parent or other adult past age 3 or 4; use of narrow or flexible whipping device (cane, rod, possibly belt), especially if the child is made to kneel or lie supine with legs held up-raised; spanking on bare buttocks in front of expressly invited witnesses (siblings, companions, mother, etc.); tantalizing (i.e., lengthy pauses between strokes); lingering of hand or device, or their post-stroke straying to perineum; consoling (e.g., effusive hugging during or immediately after spanking).

Enemas.   There are indications that repeated, more rarely single enemas given a child of either sex between ages 3 and 7 can under certain conditions lead to future psychosexual or related difficulties. This is especially true if there is no preceding explanation or reassurance and the enema is administered rather harshly. In little girls still somewhat confused about the nature of the various perineal openings, with garbled notions about sexual penetration and childbirth and oral impregnation fantasies (kissing on mouth bad, baby comes from mother's tummy), forcible evacuation of the digestive tract can become associated with having done something bad; that the product of badness is now being removed by the incensed adult, or even that some sort of birth process—messy, painful, dangerous by hearsay—is now in progress. In other children reactions of a sensual nature and physical discomfort augmented by fright may come to coexist with a sense of shame and guilt: intensely pleasurable erotic sensations from an enema, occasionally to the point of orgasm, seem to be anything but rare, no matter who administers the clyster. Repetition of the experience through chronic voluntary constipation may be sought; this can be combined with an anxious, fearful or hostile reaction toward the administering mother. Children unacquainted with enemas have experienced a harshly administered clyster as if it were an act of genital aggression, sometimes frightening and pleasurable at the same time. Especially susceptible here seem to be children who have previously witnessed parental intercourse (p. 39) with its vague sense of excitement associated with the general impression of hurt and violence. Especially to be discouraged on general principles are enemas administered to a boy whose upbringing is solely in the hands of females; to any girl by a male adult; to any child continuing to resist even after explanation; and to any girl recently sexually exposed or molested.

SEQUELAE OF SEXUAL ABUSE

In a general way the most serious and lasting ill effects on the child's psyche seem to occur when a child has been seduced repeatedly by the same adult (i.e., child concubinage), whether incestuous or not. The incidence of personality disturbances and maladjustment resulting from this type of exposure, from the vantage point of retrospective observation, clearly surpasses that resulting from a single incident of forcible assault. Additionally, any type of sexual trauma is worsened when the child has no reasonable opportunity to complain about or ventilate the happening or for some reason (e.g., in a small village or because of family relationships or parents' economic dependence) cannot break away from the perpetrator. In one series of 75 child victims only 33 told their parents (Henningsen). Other observations place the figure of children reporting sexual victimization at an average of about 50 per cent. Girls are somewhat more secretive —or fearful or self-assured—than boys.

Benign Course. In most cases of forcible assault, if the child has no pronounced guilt conflicts and has been dealt with calmly and reasonably, the memory of the event tends to dim progressively; in very young children it may disappear permanently from consciousness in less than 18 months and leave no detectable trace. However, in the immediate period following the assault, even stable and properly managed children tend to show an increased interest in companionate sex games; this can be regarded as the child's way of relieving inner tension, and unless the activity is pursued overaggressively or overrepetitiously it can be viewed without concern. Some children who acquiesced in at least part of the act may feel impelled to commit a minor, often rather transparent offense of a general nature; the punishment for this may supply some vicarious relief from their guilt feelings about the sexual venture. Others similarly display general naughtiness and wildness in sharp contrast with their usual behavior.

Terror and Amnesia. For a period of time many forcibly assaulted children, as well as a small proportion of victims of exhibitionistic molestation, have fears of being alone, staying in the dark or going in the street, recurrent nightmares, pavor nocturnus, eating difficulties, or vomiting before going to school. Where pavor nocturnus is frequent and pronounced, the traumatic experience has intruded into sleep. The dream life and sleep itself—separating the child from the mother, immobilizing her as the dream exposes her to threat and attack—becomes a thing to be feared. However, the very act of waking from the dream supplies the extricating and mastering mechanism as it brings back to life the protective existence of the mother. This experience of relief seems to promote self-healing if the child is basically healthy and not overdependent. Night terrors thus are a post-traumatic transition symptom; only if they persist for more than 2 or 3 months they presage little good. All immediate post-traumatic symptoms tend to disappear within 1 or 2 months with unexcited, sympathetic handling by the parents. Somewhat more stubborn symptoms are the reappearance of enuresis or of uncertainty of daytime urinary control, facial tics and habit spasms, and various minor obsessions. Among other measures, these call for a diligent search for unwholesome parental attitudes toward the incident or toward sex matters in general. After the initial period of ventilation and reassurance well-guided parents will drop the subject of the incident. The child's natural amnesia, if preceded by ventilation and defusing, is promoted by normal activities, school interests and, of course, by separation from the perpetrator. Judiciously small amounts of psychotropic medication can be helpful at times.

Bad Results. In poorly managed child victims, and in some of those with marked prior instability, chronic sequelae are likely to develop, often in a progressive fashion. Early manifestations may be subclinical or are easily overlooked (e.g., an endless, obsessional hunting for sex words and sex meanings in books or conversations; protracted, aggressive curiosity about the genitalia of other children or even of unsuspecting adults, or excessive masturbation). Any conspicuous change of personality following a major sexual incident should be investigated carefully. Later (e.g., beginning in the teens), there may be a tendency to sexual promiscuity or other delinquent behavior, or various emotional disturbances. Some prepuberal character-neurotic girls tend to boast about their "conquest" or about the hold they have over the seducer.

PREVENTIVE MEASURES

The majority of sex offenses against children, female or male, are committed in fairly private surroundings by persons the child knows well. But in many other cases the perpetrator is a stranger, and the locale is a public premise. Many men with erotic interest in children do not loiter persistently where children congregate, but act on chance opportunities. However, a substantial number compulsively stalk an individual child for days

PRECAUTIONS AGAINST CHILD MOLESTING

DON'T RULES

Don't play alone in deserted places, empty buildings or in alleys.

Don't let anyone you don't know touch you or fuss with your clothing.

Don't play or loiter near a roadhouse or tavern; don't wait around public toilets.

Don't accept candy, money or treats from persons you don't know.

Don't go anywhere with a stranger no matter what he offers, or when he asks directions.

Don't accept rides from people you don't know or get into their car.

Don't go on hikes alone.

If a stranger is insistent, it is all right just to run away.

PUBLIC MEASURES

Closing of unused school areas, including basement; closing or patroling of toilets in isolated locations.

Children leave their classroom only under the buddy system.

All visitors in school buildings wear large visible passes.

Separate children's sections in movie theaters.

Blockmother or volunteer blockwatcher system.

Proper probationary and psychiatric supervision of known pedophiliacs.

or weeks before they come forward. Or a prospective molester becomes friendly and tries to join the games of a small group, or else he may invite 2 or 3 children together to his abode the first time or two and merely entertain and treat them; later the chosen victim may not consider him a stranger any more and visit him willingly alone. Few preventive measures or advice can effectively protect a child from someone thought of as a friend.

Most children seem to learn appropriate conduct toward strangers automatically (e.g., from the remarks of other children or older siblings, or as they observe the parents' disapproving or worried mien when un-authorized adults try to caress them). However, beginning at about age 5 little girls are ready to be instructed more specifically by the parents. Although the child may ask, "What would a stranger do to me?" usually he or she is satisfied with explanations such as "Nice people don't touch children they don't know," or that some men are just "nosey," "fresh," "nasty," or "not right in the head." A few years later it can be indicated that there are people abnormally interested in children, boys or girls; people who do not understand that some things in other people are private; people who have no modesty themselves. With advancing years, but well before puberty, an even more realistic warning regarding sexual offenders is well tolerated by the normal child. In places and during periods where need for special precaution exists, in-class warnings in the appropriate settings in school may be added. Care must be taken by all to avoid excessive zeal in prevention so as not to construe a sex fiend out of every lingering stranger in the minds of overly danger-conscious children, or to lead to indiscriminate defamation and harassment of all kinds of innocuous offenders.

A child tends to be least suspicious of strangers who are dressed and behave approximately like his own father or other men in his environment. Thus warnings of strangers should not be made to mean strangely behaving, which few pedophilic deviates do, nor being either shabbily or overelegantly attired. Children should be in the habit of telling their parents about every new friend, especially adult, they make; and parents always should lend an interested ear to their children's exploits and not just perk up when they "smell" something improper or dangerous. This latter attitude also contributes to the invention of erotic incidents by the child (e.g., as a means of self-dramatization).

IMAGINARY ASSAULT

Children of either sex sometimes fabricate, or grossly exaggerate, an incident of sexual abuse at the hands of an adult or adolescent. This is not limited to anxiety-ridden, high-strung or character-neurotic children, but it will be found that in most such girls and boys their early natural curiosity about sex matters was handled poorly in their homes, and that the parents maintained a tensely forbidding attitude toward sex questions.

Motivation. Often, but not always, the child's choice falls on the alleged molester quite by accident and at random. An incident may be invented simply to avoid being punished for staying out late, to explain clothing torn in rough play, or even when the mother discovers vulvar scratches from a stick or twig produced during companionate games of "doctor" or such. A child overwrought by agitated neighborhood talk regarding recent sex crimes may misinterpret an adult's simple affability as an erotic liberty; having been severely warned against having strangers touch her, she may interpret this quite literally and report the gesture as "he did something bad." Some parents, uneasy about asking for details, then may become agitated over nothing. A child who has tolerated an adult's minor sexual advances may afterward become panicky with fear and guilt feelings and seek to absolve her(him)self by exaggerating the happening into an assault. Sometimes a molestation, actual or imaginary, is embellished and added to after the child observes the dramatic interest which the story has produced in the adults. Some children who happen to have observed intercourse between their parents or some other disturbing sex-related incident become intensely preoccupied, worried, even guilty about this and eventually translate the brooding about sexual aggression into a first-person story. Actually this represents a protective mechanism by which the child subconsciously forces the subject into the open and which affords considerable emotional relief, especially if dealt with reasonably—reassuringly and without major recriminations or accusations—by the parents.

Role-playing in certain suggestible and/or imaginative children can be a factor. In the pseudologia fantastica syndrome seemingly unmotivated invention of a dramatic erotic incident, usually first-person, can occur. Two prepubescent girls trying to trump each other with how much attention is being paid them by a shared adolescent male idol eventually may come up with a wholly invented physical intimacy; later this may reach adult ears and be taken seriously. Maladjusted borderline retardates or children with major emotional disturbances have been known to identify themselves with a child in an actual case they have heard about and may attempt to play out the role of victim.

Criteria for Judging. Universally applicable criteria for judging the veracity of a child's version of a sexual incident do not seem to exist. The degree of realism in the account can be severely misleading: a wholly invented story may be so realistic in its detail that the parents and the authorities feel that it could not possibly have been invented by a child, while actually such knowledge was acquired through hearsay, various observations and sex play with companions. On the other hand, an actually assaulted but naïve child may give an unlikely-sounding account of the event. Clarity and coherence of the story are equally unreliable yardsticks; an abused child may sound vague and evasive, while sometimes a fabricated incident is told in a lucid and convincing manner. In doubtful cases, a psychiatric examination of a child-accuser may be helpful in this regard, but a single interview is not usually conclusive. Evaluating the child's personality by means of psychological tests is a valuable addition to such an examination, but by itself can be misleading (e.g., even the most mendacious little psychopath may actually have been victimized). Exploration of a child-accuser under hypnosis or under intravenous drugs is neither advisable nor usually even permissible.

Parents. It is not unheard of that parents, although themselves disbelieving the reality of a sexual incident, have forced the child to adhere to her story rather than embarrass them as being the parents of an unstable, hysterical or lying child. Other parents who suspect that an incident of forcible assault was in reality at least partly tolerated or provoked may prompt the child to adhere to her forcible version lest doubts as to her innocence and niceness arise in neighbors' and relatives' minds. Although it may be assumed that such attitudes have an unwholesome effect on the formation of the child's value system and may help produce future personality difficulties, it has not usually been possible for professionals to dissuade parents once they have adopted such a stance. Parents may ask whether future contact between pseudomolester and child-accuser should be prevented; the common-sense answer is "yes," especially if the incident was publicly known.

CHAPTER 5

Abnormal Sex Behavior
in Children

Spurious Abnormality — The Overexposed Child — Disordered
Sexual Conduct — The Pre-Deviate Child.

SPURIOUS ABNORMALITY

All sex behavior in children, including the merest physiologic self-exploration, is subject to a great deal of overrecognition. Even today, parents,
having totally forgotten pertinent experiences in their own childhood, may
be puzzled, alarmed or shocked when they first notice some type—any
type—of sex activity in a child. They sometimes appear less than reasonable when they complain that their boy or girl is displaying "abnormal"
sex behavior.

Sex Games. For example, parents have called it abnormal that a little
boy had erections, or that a small child persisted in exploring his genitalia
after disapproval had been expressed. Young children have been called
"sex delinquents" because of mutual urinary or genital showing games or
other curiosity-impelled sex play. An 8-year-old boy was called a "mental
case" because, in experimenting, he had placed his organ in the neck of a
beer bottle where it became stuck. Two boys of 8 were called "budding
perverts" because they nightly hid in the shrubbery for a week, watching
a woman undressing with the blinds drawn up and the room illuminated.

Where two children are engaged in mutual sex play, it is always possible
that one will know more than the other (e.g., one boy may teach the other
how to masturbate). By itself this neither makes him necessarily the
instigator nor—unless it is a pattern with him—a pathologic aggressor.
Children who come from homes with nonconforming views and habits concerning sexual frankness, or those transplanted from social or geographic
backgrounds with divers customs, may display sexual interest in a way
which seems abnormal in a more conventional setting. Occasionally dis-

turbed, paranoid or otherwise abnormal adults read into a child's action, or his mere glances, an abnormal sexual intent.

Blind Child. Caution should be used also in evaluating the sex behavior of handicapped children. The child blind since birth or early infancy may serve as an example. When he masturbates, for instance, it is found out more easily, which can lead parents to alarming conclusions; or he may manipulate himself innocently undisguised because parents often have an overprotective, overtimid attitude about explaining genital matters to blind children. Somewhat later, when the characteristic tense self-consciousness of congenitally blind youngsters about being observed sets in, he may go to unusual lengths to hide self-manipulatory sex activity, giving the erroneous impression of engaging in ritualistic practices like those of prepsychotic children. The characteristic shaking or body-rolling movements of some blind children when they are excited ("blindisms") also may occur in conjunction with masturbatory excitement and give the appearance of pathologic sensuosity. Some sightless children possibly masturbate a great deal because they are confined to relative inactivity and are understimulated or isolated by the tense attitude of the environment and thus more likely to extract additional satisfaction from their bodies. Like sighted children, the sightless do not need instruction or imitation to discover early masturbation; unless mental retardation is associated, they probably experience the same early biologic sensations and tensions at about the same age as other children.

THE OVEREXPOSED CHILD

Normal Exposure. Sexual exposure of a child is ubiquitous, an unavoidable part of growing up. The normal child is exposed to sex talk and sex play with contemporaries, to experimentation, comparing and showing games. Farms and streets are replete with copulating animals; graphic newspaper stories on sex subjects abound for those who can read, and unsubtle illustrations are on view for those of all ages. Snatches of adolescent conversation, smutty jokes, obscenity, graffiti, petting couples on beaches and in parks, venereal disease posters, feminine hygiene ads, encounters with exhibitionists, or the sight of non-disguising effeminate homosexuals and soliciting prostitutes and, in the most crowded slums, the daily sights and sounds of reproductive processes all are part of today's total experience which the child shares with most other children in the same culture. Not all of it, although perceived, penetrates into meaningful consciousness, and if it does it may be categorized offhandedly as "grown-up stuff," especially during the latency years (p. 15). If an experience penetrates and threatens, and it cannot be ventilated freely at home, it can always be ventilated and compared within the peer group, in exchange for bits of ever-so-reassuring misinformation. The overall exposure to these matters, unless unremittingly force-fed and inescapable, cannot be considered harmful to the normal child.

Sexual Overexposure, on the other hand, is neither commonplace nor is it an innocuous part of growing up. Although it is more subtle than victimization in its various forms, it is nevertheless at least as noxious— probably more so in the long run—to the child's psychic welfare. Overexposure may range from leeringly lax condoning of early sex delinquency to outright incestuous concubinage; from veiled erotism directed at the child to sensual tempting or lascivious provocation at the hands of an adult or adolescent in his (her) own home. The culprit may be a parent, parent substitute, houseworker, relative, hetero- or homosexual boarder, a bored and horny adolescent; it is worse when it is a person on whom the child is largely dependent, and has no way to avoid or resist or even complain about. Unlike normal exposure, adult seductive maneuvers are flatteringly, excitingly aimed directly at the youngster and only at him (her), both satisfying and disquieting him. However, the tensions and experiences forced on him are beyond his capacity to tolerate or ward off; the stimulation can generate a continuous state of erotic tension which he can neither abreact nor disperse as the stimulating parent deprives him simultaneously of the safety valve of peer ventilation by prohibiting or even preventing contact with them. The sensual stimuli do not gratify a present need of the child; they artificially create a pseudoneed, a tension state which gradually worsens as the parent or other agent inconsistently— irresolutely or perhaps teasingly—grants or withholds gratification of some kind, not excluding induced orgasm.

Overexposure is most often encountered in girls, from mid- or late childhood, in relation to their fathers (see Father-Daughter Incest, p. 61), and in boys in relation to their mothers.

Sexualized Mothering. This is not the demasculinizing mother who suppresses her son's virile role as she binds him to her. The boy is not the mama's boy, nor the effeminate future deviate, nor the puer mollis. The woman, if she fits any pattern at all, is the "seducing mother," the incestoid mother (von Henting), the hostile seductress-coercer (A. Johnson). Most often she has been encountered as a single parent who lives alone with a male child, perhaps entertains men as a means of livelihood or merely has a succession of boyfriends, but where all goings-on almost inescapably involve the child. The frequency of drug abuse and borderline psychosis among these women has been mentioned (Finch).

She sensually stimulates and teases as she—in a composite of manifestations—hugs and mouth-kisses the boy, bathes him, inspects and cleans his genitals with lingering care, questions him at length on masturbation and sex play or warns him off with a wealth of detail or takes him into her bed on the slightest excuse or per custom, even though fully aware of his erections which she may "prohibit with a wink." She may dress and undress in front of him without modesty or, when drunk, with startling abandon pose seductively in his presence, examine her breasts, bathe with him and not avert her gaze from his erections, or encourage him to fondle her breasts for comforting when he complains that he is not happy or not feeling well. Altogether she stimulates his prepuberal or pubescent maleness, yet she prohibits genito-genital contact at all times, producing, even in the child, a state of chronic frustration.

Such boys manifest blocked, sullen behavior subsequently; or outbursts of sexual aggression and menacing violence (Bender). While the over-exposed boy—no matter how guilt-ridden or frustrated and enraged—tends to preserve a tensely, almost fiercely loyal silence, the incestoid mother more easily betrays the child (e.g., under the influence of alcohol she may boast of her "little lover boy"); or she may panic, become tearfully distraught and righteous and complain that the boy is oversexed, totally shifting the blame. It should be noted that such incestoid relationships occur on practically all socioeconomic levels.

The Seductive Child. Some youngsters play an active part in their own overexposure, mainly the budding asocial and unsocialized-aggressive personalities. At the time of first overexposure these children essentially are already as pathologic as they ever will be. Adult sex contact may help to pattern their future difficulties or even render them more antisocial, but their personality, or their disorder, is not produced by such experiences. Overexposure here is often almost exclusively of the child's own making, in that he (she) may play an actively enticing role not excluding vis-à-vis a suggestible, seducible, perhaps mentally retarded parent.

On the other hand, not every child who entices or provokes an adult into sex contact is eo ipso a psychopath incapable of being harmed greatly by the experience. The child who compulsively re-enacts some erotic domestic exposure may seem to solicit adult advances, but almost certainly does not desire them, cannot absorb them and probably is psychically further injured by them. Brain-impaired and schizophrenic children also may accost grown-ups, but it takes an adult of rare obtusity to dally with so visibly abnormal a child.

DISORDERED SEXUAL CONDUCT

In the second half of childhood certain brain, personality and mental disorders can produce disordered conduct pertaining to the sexual sphere. Symptoms vary from the relatively benign to some of the most spectacularly abnormal.

Symptoms. Boys may incessantly instigate other children to group sex play, irrepressibly talk sex and use obscene language even when it is wholly inappropriate to do so, tell interminable, witlessly smutty tales,

decorate walls with pornographic symbols, indulge in undisguised masturbation, exhibit themselves before children or adults, attempt to seduce or
rape smaller children of either sex, molest or try to attack adult women,
including strangers or even the mother, or commit cruel acts against
animals in connection with sexual acting-out. Girls may bodily and
aggressively accost boys or men, familiar or strangers, invite coition or
other familiarities, and generally behave in a fashion similar to that of the
boys.

Organic Brain Syndromes. Characteristic is the impulsiveness and the
uncontrollability of these acts which can give the impression of organically
driven behavior. In the acts of aggression these children seem to experience no fear, nor do they manifest any particular sense of remorse; the
child often is generally impulsive as well as hyperkinetic. Rapid mood
swings, excitability and personality changes ("more selfish," "less reliable," intolerance of frustration) are frequent. They tend to deny or isolate
bad attitudes ("I didn't do it . . . my mouth—hands, pecker—did it").

These are the brain-disordered children. Most frequent among these
syndromes—and often unrecognized—are what have been designated as
the postencephalitic syndromes of childhood; they differ greatly from the
adult (and adolescent) type because of the preponderance of behavioral
symptoms. The history may include a bout of encephalitis, perhaps most
often viral, in early childhood (e.g., in connection with one of the childhood diseases); or there may have been one or more unrecognized episodes of high fever or even repeated, insidious minor febrile illnesses
without clear symptoms. It has been suggested that the younger the child
is at the time of illness, the greater is the likelihood of psychiatric sequelae.
The behavior disorder and change in personality may follow the illness
immediately, or unexplained changes in the child may develop gradually
over a period of 1 or 2 years. Major sexual manifestations rarely occur
before school age. Anomalous sexual behavior may follow head injuries,
including concussions, as well as toxic (e.g., lead) encephalopathies. Similar disturbances occur in early hepatolenticular degeneration (Wilson's
disease), and they have been reported following tuberculous meningitis.

Epileptoid Patterns. In another group the acts of sexual aggression,
promiscuous seductiveness, exhibitionism or poorly disguised masturbation
are seen to have a distinctly episodic character; such episodic conduct may
represent seizure equivalents or other pathologic discharges. In a few
severe cases children have shown continuous sexual overaggressiveness or
a prevalently cruel, sadistic attitude. Both the hyperkinetic and the unsocialized-aggressive reaction patterns include children in whom behavior
is marked by a fusion of sexuality and aggressiveness. More than in other
organic brain syndromes, disordered behavior here is incorrigible without
appropriate medication, but often highly responsive to it (e.g., dextro-

amphetamine, and primidone or methsuximide), adding an antihistamine (e.g., promethazine) and/or an ataractic (e.g., perphenazine) p.r.n.

Antisocial and Asocial Personality Defects. The socially most disruptive children with abnormal sex behavior are those designated as impulsive psychopathic personalities. This is an eminently chronic and at present intractable disorder in which the individual acts either with unpredictable, even explosive impulsivity; or with a joyless, guiltless trouble-making malice; or as if he (she) were motivated solely by the pain-pleasure principle in its crudest application.

In boys, the reckless sexual aggressiveness or brutality may surpass anything seen even in the postencephalitic syndrome, although they usually follow a "smoother" and more consistent pattern than that of the brain-impaired child. A proportion of these children seem to have no impulse control to speak of. A fair number, perhaps more noticeably girls, appear to be charming, even sweet and disarmingly innocent, and display attractive, affectionate personalities at first glance. But many cannot seem to understand or learn the line of demarcation between affectionate-demonstrative and erotic-seductive behavior toward and from adults; they may be almost totally indiscriminate in making provocative advances to men, on impulse or from boredom or curiosity (". . . to see if he'd pee in his pants after I said I'd tell on him"); all aided by the absence of a sense of shame ("What's to be ashamed? It's his look-out; I'm the kid."). The varieties of unchildlike, abnormal sexual conduct encountered in these children are practically endless, and the indiscriminate seeking of erotic gratification—in any form and from anybody—is an early pattern in them. Most are unabashed liars. They lie with ease and conviction, and effortlessly shift the blame for misdeeds on another child or person. Total absence of a sustained sense of guilt and absent capacity to experience more than superficial anxiety are pathognomonic.

Childhood Schizophrenia is accompanied at times by disordered sexual behavior. The behavior may resemble that of the postencephalitic child. A characteristic finding in some boys with schizophrenia is excessive masturbation, sometimes undisguised. In both sexes one may find intense, pervasive sexual fantasies and preoccupations, often of a sadistic or masochistic nature. There may be phobias revolving around sexual subjects, which is unusual in the phobias of nonschizophrenic children. Bizarreness of the sex manifestations occurs occasionally (e.g., masturbation with a dead animal or self-fellatio).

Obscenity. Unmotivated, seemingly irrepressible outbursts of obscene language may occur. Occasionally this may constitute an aura preceding an epileptic discharge or its equivalent in the youngster. In some other cases the early signs of the Gilles de la Tourette syndrome (p. 461) can be identified. However, in most cases the excessive use of obscenity represents but one of the symptoms in the major psychopathologic syndromes of childhood.

Compulsive Acting-out. Sexual overexposure in children (p. 73) leads a number of them, in turn, to become themselves active molesters and seducers of other children, whom they bribe, incite or browbeat into participating. In addition, all manner of repetitious sex manifestations occur, including peeping or exhibiting of the genitalia. There is often a compulsive quality about these activities, and reasonableness, threats, punishment or the rejecting attitude of other children cannot halt them for long. The little boy whom nothing can deter from lifting little girls' skirts, or who cannot pass a wall without scrawling a genital symbol on it, frequently belongs in this group of tensely compulsive overexposed children. Many are erratic distress masturbators (p. 51). Such compulsive sex behavior, even where it is unaggressive, is often greatly disturbing to other children. It cannot be considered unreasonable of the other parents if they try to keep their own children from associating with such a child, or if the school feels impelled, following psychiatric consultation, to exclude him. Obstacles to both treatment and self-healing are substantial here: these children must not only cope with the adversity of the environment and their own compulsive pattern, but also with the guilt and anxiety engendered by the massive sexual irruption into their own latency phase (p. 15), which gave rise to their acting-out in the first place.

THE PRE-DEVIATE CHILD

Certain major forms of sexual deviance encountered in the male adult are recognizable already in childhood. They include transsexualism, transvestism, effeminate homosexuality, often the self-assured, highly masculinized type of homosexual deviance and a proportion of cases classified as fetishism. Female deviance recognizable in childhood is more uncertain; it includes the general group of the future non-reversing tomboys (p. 109) who mostly develop into masculine-mannered lesbians and the closely related small number of female transsexuals.

The Feminized Boy. Most profoundly deviant are the future transsexual males (p. 486). Incidence of the condition is no longer considered rare, and may be rising although as a rule only the most pervasively disordered cases come to medical attention (Green, Lebovitz, Robins, Stoller, Zuger, others). These boys have persistent unboylike attitudes from a very early age; many can be clearly recognized at age 2 or even younger. They are genetic males and there is no ambiguity of the genitalia. Very early they have a distaste for boys' games and will not play with boys. They prefer the company of little girls and women generally, often giving the impression of hanging on their mothers' skirts where they cling and cry when they feel threatened. They have a phobia of being physically hurt.

Many secretly or openly wish they were girls and they may be clearly envious of the mother and sisters. Some have a precociously well-developed appreciation of decor, ornaments and esthetic beauty generally; also of acting and the dance. A talent and predilection of some for arranging female hair, choosing colors, combining ensembles of women's wear and other style skills may be evident already in childhood. The degree of interest in cooking, sewing and domestic arts generally probably depends on the specific encouragement given by the environment, notably by the mother: a few of these women are domestically oriented; others, notably the residual tomboy mother, are not. A few of these boys are fascinated by dolls and infant care, but others manifest no maternalism.

In the school years the feminized boy is rarely part of the group, but often the butt of scorn and cruel jokes, the victim of the way young boys in groups are wont to act vis-à-vis contemporaries who are different as well as sensitive. He is fastidious in manner and dress and has an aversion to sports, outdoor activities, fights, and rough games. Some are giggly, others whiny, still others placid. His posture, walk and gestures, which often are not typically boylike, help set him apart. The feminine type of suspension of his elbows known as "carrying angle," for instance, prevents him from male-type ball throwing (he throws sideways or underhanded) and may be responsible for the fan-like motions of his hands and other gestures, although the role of cultural imitation is not clear here. The female-type configuration of both the humeral head and glenoid fossa and the head of the femur and acetabulum have been noted; the latter together with changes in knee joint suspension are believed to affect his running stride. With teachers and most other adults he tends to relate passively (i.e., through ingratiation, clinging and charming). He is eager to please, worried about the impression he makes, and often disarming. Because for the feminized boy the going in school is rough and the separation from the mother frightens him anew every day ("maybe she won't be there when I get back"), school phobias develop with some frequency.

Milder cases begin even now to develop compensatory and camouflage mechanisms whose extremes, over the years, may include general delinquency, motorcycle gang capers or the choice of highly-visible-risk vocations and avocations. In fact, by a process of subconsciously self-administered operant conditioning, these milder cases seem to modify their own behavior to sufficient gender-appropriateness so as to submerge comfortably among other males; they thus come to constitute merely the feminoid end of a theoretical spectrum of masculinity rather than deviance.

Causes. From substantial indications the feminized boy is the combined product of a functional aberration during fetal development—possibly hormonal damage to a steroid-sensitive area in the brain—and the effect of parental attitudes in the early years. The observation that in some animal species the stressed pregnant mother demasculinizes her male offspring through changes in the fetus' neurohormonal milieu may have relevance here. At any rate, the cerebrally neuterized male infant cannot dissociate himself from the mother at the proper time, after he has charmed, bound and seduced her into total pleased devotion. She, in turn, being the woman she is, keeps demasculinizing him, as it were, by un-remitting, overwhelming closeness to this usually beauteous boy whom she may also intuit as in special need of close protection. She makes no effort to introduce masculinity into his life, may even discourage it. A useful father model is often not available to this young in-between: father was turned off early, puzzled, disappointed, perhaps bitter, more so when the small boy rejected what he had to offer. Other observers have argued that the father is a detached, passive man to begin with, one whom this male-envying kind of woman is apt to have attracted to herself as a husband. However, a father who is absent in person or in spirit is, as such, most probably not a cause of severely faulted gender role development. Societies in which fathers are frequently absent—seafaring people, for instance—do not produce effeminate men. The way an absent or deceased father is carried in memory or esteem and presented (idealized) by the mother, and how identifiably he comes across to the child, may be enough of a masculine cue to serve as role model. A number of cases are known in which Klinefelter's syndrome and transsexualism coexist.

Cross-dressing. All feminized boys have an interest in female (mother's, etc.) clothing, but most especially the future transvestite and the female-clothing-responsive fetishist. While the future transsexual considers them his kind of clothes, the cross-dresser does not, but is erotically aroused by them. Transvestism first becomes overt somewhat later in childhood, often between 4 and 5 years of age, after some masculine identification and role development have taken place.

Most normal boys don some of the mother's apparel sporadically, often as a form of masquerading play, or because of transient exploratory fascination or, just possibly, as part of occasional intensely erotic fantasies about the mother during the oedipal phase (q.v.). Normally, this ceases at about the age of 6 or 7, although there may be another flurry of interest in early adolescence in the form of cross-dress clowning. On the other hand, the feminine boy with cross-dressing interest continues throughout childhood until somewhat after puberty, when the tendency may become temporarily attenuated or cease. In a few the interest never ceases.

In childhood pre-transvestite boys, whenever they have the secret opportunity, feel compelled to put on mother's apron and heels, perhaps lipstick and mascara, to obtain a "warm," "hot," "loving-like" sensation. At the same time mother and sisters may take delight in dressing them as girls and calling outsiders' attention to "this cuteness," which does not seem to faze these children at the time. As teen-agers, they may have hiding places for their female clothing, including mother's, which is now donned to masturbate, and very occasionally to dare the world to recognize them in cross-dress; however, the latter is mostly an adult manifestation.

Non-Deviate Clothing Erotism. There is another type of clothing urge in some male youngsters which is mostly sensuous and bound to the erotic image of the wearer. Boys as young as 10, but mostly teen-agers, have been known to burglarize empty neighbors' and other homes to obtain pieces of female clothing, often nylon or fur, of a particular, to them provocatively exciting woman, with masturbation into the material often taking place right on the spot. The psychodynamics of this manifestation are in dispute.

Effeminate Homosexual Boys. Partway between the feminine boy who identifies as a female and the budding transvestite whose urge is an erotic compulsion rather than a personality-warping aberration, one encounters the effeminate homosexual in the making. While the majority of homosexuals come to self-recognition of their deviance in the mid- to late teens, the effeminate deviate has passive romantic feelings for other males well before he even knows what a homosexual is. His fascination dates back "as long as I can remember," actually probably most often to age 5 or 6. Most know themselves to be boys, although later they sometimes wish fatuously that they had female genitals and breasts so as to attract and please their favorite type of masculine male. However, there are a few feminized and female-identified individuals among them; in these the homosexual behavior probably constitutes an avoidable complication of the teens. For reasons poorly understood it is also among effeminate homosexuals that one encounters a great deal of the aberrant construction of the arm and leg joints mentioned above. The mincing and tripping quality of the gait, the hip-swishing and shoulder swaying, and some of the characteristically swishy hand motions are acquired characteristics which appear near adulthood; however, a few children do manifest the beginnings of these mannerisms. These boys differ from certain vulnerable youngsters, some with slender gracile physiques, some soft, rounded, almost gynecoid in appearance who are basically normal, but inadequate, suggestible and flattery-prone and who may be late-conditioned into homosexual orientation in their teens (p. 144 and p. 502).

Seduction and Homosexuality. Often characteristic in the effeminate homosexual's childhood history are repeated incidents of seduction and molestation by adolescents and adult men. These boys are not merely prone to enticement into sex contact; usually they are actively interested in such contacts. It is well established that not all children are asexual and unwilling victims in their sex contact with adults, as sentiment and the codified law will have it. On the other hand, while homosexual contact with adults can probably advance, perhaps initiate these boys in their pathologic aim direction, these relationships cannot produce homosexuality. Some predeviate children can be so aggressively seductive toward a man who had no prior designs on them that the latter, if in any way sexually unstable, may succumb to the temptation.

Masculine Homosexual Boys. On the other extreme of a theoretical scale of personality characteristics encountered in homosexual males is the self-assured, strongly masculine individual. He, too, tends to emerge into self-recognition earlier than the average, often in the first decade. Relatively little of a systematic nature is known about him because he rarely will discuss his deviance with any physician or counselor, and rarely if ever cooperate with professional attempts to modify his aberration. In this he resembles his effeminate counterpart. But when he emerges to awareness in childhood, he does not become involved in sexual activity.

To his peers and teachers he is known as a perceptive, self-assured young person, always seeming in control of himself—when he disputes, when he smiles, even when he denounces in anger. He has leadership qualities, but he often discourages the formation of any group around him, nor does he join groups or make friends except later in the teens when he may fall deeply in love with another, sometimes younger, softer but never an effeminate boy. His sexual behavior encompasses the most rigid continence, pierced, in some cases and occasionally, by episodes of wild sexual debauchery under secret circumstances. He is careful, polite, and often repels others by his seemingly unmodifiable arrogance. He takes great care of his appearance, his person, his health, and he can be an outstanding all-around athlete as well as a student of excellence. He is often cultured to the maximal extent his background permits, but dilettantism rather than scholarship seems the rule. Others develop into well-versed professional or technical students. In most people he inspires a mixture of fascination and awe, while he himself is not awed by any adult.

Treatment. Psychotherapy of pre-deviate children has not been very successful, and the emergence of deviance in adulthood essentially cannot be prevented at present, even if the condition is recognized early. Some groups of pre-deviates, even in childhood, are not interested in cooperating with professional efforts to modify the progression of their aberration. No effective biologic methods of treatment are known. However, the prevention and treatment of secondary maladjustment and of avoidable psychologic complications by means of guidance of both patient and parents remains a worthwhile task.

Guidance. Guidance of the parents is a prime need to avoid homosexual drift or "sidestepping" into homosexuality by basically nonhomosexual youngsters, or the precipitation of a psychosis in late adolescence. Some fathers badger or taunt such a boy into sex role conformity, or even to toughen and masculinize him, in a highly undesirable fashion. An alarmed mother may either increase her hovering, protective stance or else stand off in panic and withdraw her support, which can be a highly unsettling experience to such a boy. All vigorously corrective attempts by the parents should be discouraged. Especially inadvisable appears to be the boarding of this type of youngster in a military-type school. The mother must be cautioned against a sudden attitude of horrified repudiation of any prior bosom-friend-and-confidant relationship with the boy; but tutoring of the boy in the domestic arts and any major overindulgence by the mother should cease.

The father needs to be encouraged to take the most active possible interest in the boy, if he will undertake to do so consistently rather than further alienate the patient with sporadic withdrawal of interest. Where no father is present and the boy is past mid- to late childhood, precipitous remarriage by the mother with the sole object of giving the boy a father is likely to lead to more complications than benefits. Generally, it seems desirable in such a family to superstress that the father is "a man in the world of men," and a person whose voluntary activities make it clear that he thinks "kids are worth working for"; a living image of the precept that it is right and proper for a man to be venturesome and even impatient at times with the female's domestic detail and fussing.

The boy may be encouraged subtly to seek the company of his male contemporaries. If even a spark of erotic interest in girls is present, it may be encouraged. Where such interest is totally absent, suggesting it is probably useless at best. Any pronounced esthetic, decorative or similar interests and talents are best encouraged while trying to channel them into a constructive and satisfying vocation. Where marked cross-dressing tendencies exist, an attempt to discourage them would always seem to be worthwhile.

FOR JOURNAL LITERATURE AND ADDITIONAL READING

Bakwin, H. and R. M.: Clinical Management of Behavior Disorders in Children, Philadelphia, Saunders, 1966

Birch, H. G.: Brain Damage in Children: Biological and Social Aspects. Baltimore, Williams & Wilkins, 1964

Buxbaum, E. Troubled Children in a Troubled World. New York, International Universities Press, 1970

Shaw, C. R. and Lucas, A. R.: The Psychiatric Disorders of Childhood. ed. 2. New York, Appleton-Century-Crofts, 1970

PART 2

Sexuality in the Second Decade

CHAPTER 6

Puberal Development, Normal and Abnormal

The Phases of Development — Physiology of Sexual Development — Sexual Development in Detail — Puberal Delay and Puberal Failure — Masculinization and Pseudomasculinization in Girls — Deficient and Pseudodeficient Masculine Traits in Boys.

THE PHASES OF DEVELOPMENT

The second decade in humans is a period of somatic growth, physical development and sexual maturation. Gender differentiation, started in the embryo, now becomes completed and the mental processes of thinking, feeling, experiencing and reacting undergo transformation.

The stages of puberal development have been classified in a variety of ways, none of them perfect; the one followed here appears to be rational. The latency phase of childhood is followed by a period of intense growth spurts and development of the sexual apparatus of 2 or more years' duration, known as *pubescence or prepuberty*. This is followed by *adolescence,* comprising approximately the mid- and late teens; here much of the final maturation of genital and other sex characters takes place. The two stages —child in transition and adult in the making—are divided by *puberty*. This is the somewhat theoretical moment when ovulation or spermatogenesis have been established. Some authorities employ the term puberty to signify the phase of genital growth; others consider it synonymous with pubescence; still others include in it all phases until full sexual maturity is attained. It is also believed to be the critical maturation point of the hypothalamus at which a shift in the control of gonadotropin release is induced (see below).

The sequence of changes in the teens largely evolves in fixed order, but both onset-age of each stage and tempo vary widely. Girls are about 2 years ahead of boys of the same chronologic age during most developmental phases.

Girls as a rule go through the most active puberal changes between ages 9 and 13. They begin visible pubescence with a gradual widening of the pelvis, first noticed at 9 or 10, followed shortly, usually after age 10, by some nipple elevation. First observation of nipple growth usually permits the prediction that menarche is at least 2 years (extreme range 6 months to 5½ years) away. Nipple growth is followed by thelarche (i.e., the conical-type budding of the breasts), closely followed, but occasionally preceded, by the appearance of a soft pubic down, some nipple pigmentation, intense skeletal growth spurts, and major growing of the genital organs themselves. Within 1 year, provided the peak of the height growth is over, menarche follows at the statistical mean age of 12 years 8 months (U.S.), with up to 1 to 1½ years variation either way not uncommon, coinciding with a bone age of somewhat over 13 years, and at an invariable mean weight of ca. 96 lbs. (a theory; Frisch-Revelle). Body shape and contour now soften further, and motility becomes more graceful. Adult-type pubic and then axillary hair appears. Many girls reach final height 1 to 2 years after menarche (i.e., at 15 years of age or less), others only by age 18. At 16 the adolescent girl has emerged fully, but complete reproductive maturity, including monthly ovulation, may not be reached before the late teens, or even beyond.

Boys as a rule undergo most of the active developmental changes sometime between 11 and 15 years of age. Earliest clinical changes are signaled by some modest increase of testicle size, often near age 11 (normal onset range 10 to 13½). Bone age at the beginning of boys' sexual development averages 11 years, regardless of chronologic age. Near age 12 the scrotum first becomes wrinkled and then reddens or darkens somewhat. This coincides with growth of the penis and acceleration of linear growth, but unlike in some girls, the height spurt is not the first sign of male pubescence. Downy hair then appears at the base of the penis. If breast hyperplasia is to appear, it does so most often now (see also p. 111). The first seminal emission most often occurs around this time, although cultural and psychologic factors co-determine this event. Penis and testicles grow rapidly now. In normal boys full pubic hair rarely occurs in the absence of substantial genital development. At 17 at least half of non-beard-oriented boys shave at least once or twice a week. Some of them are still gaining in height and stature at that age; male height growth continued into the twenties is believed much rarer today than it was at the turn of the century.

PHYSIOLOGY OF SEXUAL DEVELOPMENT

Brain. The impetus to develop in orderly sequence, beginning at a certain time, is an endowed characteristic of living organisms. Its primum movens defies human rationalization, while its mechanism in the human mammal is being increasingly understood. Primary control of puberal development and of the signal to start is vested in parts of the brain, but is mediated by a complex relay chain of hormones. The major controlling structure of this neuro-endocrine axis is the phylogenetically stable limbic system, including hippocampus, septum, pyriform cortex and amygdalae, but most especially the corticomedial nuclei of the latter.

Hypothalamus. Fibres from these structures converge upon the hypothalamus; they are joined by neural input tracts from other cortical, autonomic and sensory areas of the brain. These convey perceived environmental and body-endogenous information important to the puberal process, such as climate, emotional deprivation, nutrition, intercurrent somatic damage, etc. The hypothalamus acts as a switchboard-like final common pathway for the input from the various controlling parts of the central nervous system. Next in the chain the neural signals are transformed into neurohormonal information by cells in the ventral hypothalamus which secrete, at a controlled rate, specific releasing hormones. These hypophysiotropic releasors are then transported, via a system of local portal vessels, to the nearby adenohypophysis (i.e., the anterior lobe of the pituitary gland).

Pituitary and Hormones. The anterior pituitary, as one may recall, furnishes the specific tropic (or trophic) stimulating hormones for each of the endocrine glands (e.g., ACTH, thyrotropin, gonadotropin). In pubescence, as the specific releasors reach the pituitary, they permit the gland to increase its synthesis and output of gonadotropin. This is the first clinically measurable event in the internal puberal process. One of the gonadotropins—FSH—helps develop the germinal epithelium eventually leading to spermatogenesis, as well as the ovarian follicles; the other—LH (or ICSH)—induces the gonads to secrete their sex hormones. Sex hormones, in turn, acting in the manner of embryonic inductors on local receptor cells via synthesis of messenger (RNA, DNA) hormones, stimulate the unfolding of the preformed end- or target-organs (i.e., they promote accelerated growth of such steroid-sensitive structures as the penis, nipples, larynx, vagina, etc.).

Cyclic vs. Tonic. As her breasts begin to bud the female develops a cyclic pattern of gonadotropin secretion, while the glands of males have acquired a steady or "tonic" type of secretion. This sexual differentiation is not inherent in the pituitary, but in the brain, which was bathed by differing hormonal compositions in males and females as it developed. The controlling factor is the presence or absence of testicular androgen: at a postulated critical point in fetal or neonatal life males masculinize their own brain irreversibly, as the fetus' own androgen alters the steroid receptor mechanism. This probably occurs in the stria terminalis fibres which link the amygdala with the preoptic area of the hypothalamus (a theory).

Feedback. A built-in system of checks and balances surrounds the brain-gonadal mechanism. A series of inhibiting (negative) and stimulatory feedback effects is continuously operating. While for example the discharge of gonadotropin into the circulation controls the rate of sex hormone production, high levels of circulating sex hormone (notably estrogen) in turn inhibit gonadotropin secretion, either at the pituitary level itself, but mostly by blocking the hypothalamic relay, probably at some point between the limbic system and the releasor terminus in the median eminence of the hypothalamus. In fact, the current concept is that, apart from the necessary maturation of the amygdalae, it is maturational changes in the feedback system which help activate the mechanism of pubescence. In the child of either sex the small amount of circulating estrogen helps to inhibit the hypothalamic releasing hormones and thereby the gonadotropins. This is a reciprocal mechanism; the immature gonad restrains pituitary gonadotropin whose absence, in turn, leaves the gonad immature.

For unknown reasons, at a certain point in development, the hypothalamic receptor cells become less sensitive to sex hormones and can no longer be made to block tropin releasor production. As more gonadotropin is released, inducing more circulating estrogen, the whole negative feedback operation is reestablished but with the gonadostat, as it were, set at a higher level of circulating hormones, enough to sustain sexual development. There also appears to exist a stimulatory short-loop feedback mechanism, by which pituitary hormones can affect their own rate of secretion. In men the androgens, particularly testosterone, influence secretion of LH but not of FSH. In fact, testosterone is believed to be a potent inhibitor of the LH releasor. However, spermatogenesis influences the secretion of FSH by an unknown mechanism.

The Pineal Gland, in animals, is a major contributing factor to the timing of puberal development and in the modulation of gonadal activity. Knowledge in humans is much less substantial. The pineal is a neuroendocrine traducer, like the adrenal medulla, as it receives instructions by neural pathways only. Actually it consists of two diverse parts: one secreting hormone, and a photoreceptor structure.

The now well established effect of light on the gonads in animals is mediated by the principal pineal hormone, melatonin. Environmental light, including day and night rhythm, acts—via retina, an accessory optic pathway, upper cervical sympathetic and adrenergic links—to reduce melatonin, thus probably disinhibiting gonadotropin releasors in the brain and ultimately increasing size and activity of both male and female gonads. Melatonin formation is inhibited in light, stimulated in the dark. The pineal is also known to block pubescence until it undergoes partial or temporary regression at the end of the first decade. Generally it inhibits reproductive function and thus is a pituitary antagonist as regards gonadal control.

SEXUAL DEVELOPMENT IN DETAIL

Sexual Dimorphism. During pubescence and throughout the first half of the teens the body changes rapidly in shape as well as in size and composition. Boys, as part of the masculine habitus, acquire somewhat greater stature than girls, their shoulders expand while the hips stay relatively narrow, the chest deepens and widens, and limb fat tends to disappear. In Tanner's original Discriminant Androgyny Score, for instance, which applies to final stature, the formula 3x bi-acromial diameter minus 1x bi-iliac diameter, in centimeters, furnishes an average male score of 90.1 ± 4.7, and an average female score of 78.9 ± 4.6. Males have androgen-sensitive cartilages in the rib areas near the scapulae and clavicles.

Male arms and legs are longer relative to the trunk. Especially marked is the relative length and size of the male forearm compared with whole arm length. Muscles of the male acquire greater size and power with concomitant biochemical differences in muscle cells and a higher creatinine excretion rate. Under the indirect influence of testosterone higher hemoglobin and hematocrit values are found in males. Other differences involve body temperature, respiration and gastric acidity.

These puberal changes, says Tanner, which specifically adapt the male to his primitive role of dominating, fighting and foraging, occur generally in primates, but more in some species than in others. Man lies at about the middle of the primate range as regards degree of sexual differentiation. As maximum strength achievement in the male lags about 1 year behind the maximum height spurt, for a while boys have the stature of young adults but not the strength of a same-size adult. As dimorphism is maintained by sexual selection, and as rawer features of maleness become less important for the sustaining of existence, it is possible to assume that these gender earmarks will become less pronounced traits and will gradually be bred out.

In girls, the pelvic inlet begins to widen as early as age 8, but often this process is too gradual to have clinical significance; the pelvic outlet of girls is already wider at birth. As estrogen concentrations rise, skin water content and thickness increase as does subcutaneous fat, and body fat distribution generally is altered. The rounding of hips continues through much of adolescence, but other feminine contour changes are nearly completed at menarche. The width of the pelvis increases shortly before puberty by appearance of a new ossification center between ilium and pubis whose cartilage is estrogen-sensitive. The bony pelvis of the female may be adequate for passage of the full-term newborn in less than one year after puberty.

Of interest to the behavioral scientist are certain peculiarities of the female elbow and knee joints. The average girl, beginning in midpubescence, develops a "carrying angle" at the elbows which differs considerably from boys': there is more flexion, and few girls can pitch a ball overhand without a stiffly awkward downward motion. The angle is believed to be a phylogenetic residue connected with infant holding. Most females are also knock-kneed and when running their lower legs for the most part are "thrown around" in a characteristic arc-like motion, while most boys—and tomboys—run straight-legged and more gracefully. These differences are perpetuated into adulthood.

Penis. The male organ begins to grow shortly after the onset of testicular growth; the increase in size becomes noticeable during the early teens. Circumference at puberty averages 3 inches. Growth in length of the penile shaft and growth in skeletal height spurt together. However, penile growth is completed earlier than linear height, often near age 15. Individual variations in onset and tempo of penis growth are very large: in a random group of contemporaries some boys may have completed penile growth, while at the other end of the scale a few have not yet begun visible enlargement.

Testicles and Scrotum. Growth of the testicles becomes noticeable early in the developing boy (e.g., at 10½ or 11). Development is intense for several years. Adult microscopic structure probably is reached before the end of the midteens, but final adult size not before the late teens. Increase in size is mostly due to growth of the seminiferous tubules. The endocrine Leydig cells reappear during pubescence, scattered interstitially between the tubules throughout the substance of the testicles. As these cells and their enzyme systems mature, they acquire the ability to convert androstenedione, a weakly androgenic precursor, into testosterone. Because of the internal changes, the testicles become temporarily softer in mid-development. Unusual positions of the testes in the scrotum during this period are common; also, one testicle may now be larger and/or suspended higher than the other. To evaluate testicle size in a developing boy, the Prader orchidometer, a string of graded plastic models, is helpful.

The scrotal sac distends, beginning at about age 11, and the proportionate dimensions of its base and bottom become inverted. Increased scrotal wrinkling, vascularization and pigmentation, in that order, also take place.

Prostate, Seminal Vesicles and other accessory structures must have developed and become functional before ejaculation can take place. First activity in the prostate can be discovered early (e.g., between 10 and 11). The lobes, except possibly the anterior, grow rapidly during pubescence, and secretion can be massaged out of that organ toward the end of this stage.

Mons, Vulva, Vagina. During pubescence, soon after the breasts bud, the labia majora develop and come together until they hide the other structures of the vulva from view. The labia minora also develop, especially at their upper pole. The mons pubis becomes more prominent. The bartholinian glands begin to secrete. The clitoris completes its vascular organization and may first become fully erectile at this time (disputed). Generally, the tissues around the vaginal introitus appear more vascular and fleshy and undergo some color changes. Vaginal secretion becomes acid, the pH decreasing to 4 or slightly less, from approximately 7½ in the child. The dominant vaginal organism is now the bacillus vaginalis Doederlein instead of the child's cocci. The vaginal mucosa thickens and the surface layers of epithelium become cornified and contain glycogen, while overall dimensions increase.

The Uterus, same as the vagina, develops simultaneously with the breasts, accelerated growth beginning near age 12. As estrogen concentration rises, its most dramatic impact anywhere is probably on the uterus. Intensified activity of estrogen-sensitive enzymes and newly activated protein and lipid (DNA, RNA) synthesis lead to hypertrophic cell changes in the myometrium. Cylindrically lined simple tubular glands in the endometrium give way to more intricate secretory structures. The most rapid changes occur in the cervix as the characteristic biophysical and chemical properties of the cervical factor and the steroid-sensitive glandular structure of its mucosa develop. Anatomically the corpus uteri grows most rapidly, the proportionate lengths of the infantile organ being reversed to a 2/3:1/3 corpus:cervix ratio early in adolescence. The corpus now assumes the normal adult anteflexed position and changes its shape. Descent of the internal genitalia into the true pelvis takes place at or near puberty.

The Ovaries. Small amounts of circulating estrogen are demonstrable throughout childhood, but only between 8 and 10 years of age do the ovaries become active glands of internal secretion. At this time larger follicles on their surface contribute enough estrogen to start and sustain development of the reproductive apparatus and of secondary sex characteristics. Estrogen cycles are established by the brain about one year before menarche, approximately at the time the breasts bud and the height spurt begins. However, transformation of the follicular cells into the corpus luteum is absent or erratically insufficient during the maturation process; thus there is no progesterone to participate in the cycling until well past menarche.

The organs themselves tend to grow slowly: at menarche the weight of the average ovary is probably only 30 per cent of ultimate adult weight. Growth is not completed before the late teens. The Fallopian tubes increase in length and diameter, especially in the months before menarche. Peristaltic action and cilia in their lumen make their appearance during early adolescence.

Breasts. The mammary glands are target organs for almost every hormone in the body. Of the pituitary hormones prolactin and growth hormone (GH or HGH) are the most important for breast growth, although for optimal effectiveness they require the presence of the ovarian steroids. On the other hand, the ovaries are not essential when the endocrine mechanism governing breast development and lactation is activated by suckling. Virgin girls, women and, in a few cases, men have responded to vigorous suckling by infants with mammary growth and lactation (Meites).

The first sign of puberal breast maturation is an increase in nipple height, most often between ages 10 and 11, followed by a slightly increased pigmentation and enlargement of the areolae. Shortly before age 12 (at 143. ± 14.5 months) the breasts bud into conical shape (thelarche). Towards menarche the final, rounded shaping begins and continues for several years. Early discomfort, even from garment contact, can occur during the budding phase. A girl's height or weight rarely influences her breast size, as long as she is within the 5′ to 5′10″ height and the 105 to 148 lbs. weight range.

Breast development in girls can be atypical. In premature thelarche the breasts attain final rounded shape as early as at menarche. In the rare isolated breast retardation they may still be in the areolar budding stage at the first menstrual period. One breast may develop several months before the other, although usually the two become equal again, except in congenital unilateral aplasia which can only be treated surgically. Following contact X-radiation with doses of 300R or more in childhood (e.g., for angioma), breast maturation on that side will be incomplete, giving rise to hypoplasia. However, slight degrees of breast asymmetry are no rarity in women; if pronounced it may eventually require one-sided augmentation surgery. Coarse long hairs around the areola can appear in normal adolescents; they have no significance but require electrolysis for permanent removal.

At times breasts just keep growing after menarche, and the sometimes huge pendulous breasts may hang below the navel; reductive surgery then becomes necessary for this disfiguring gigantomastia ("virginal hypertrophy"). Newer mammoplastic technics do not interfere with subsequent lactation. Normal but large breasts in young girls are uncomfortable in the gym, and misdirect the attention of boys. They should be supported by a brassiere early as Cooper's suspensory ligaments and the supporting skin tend to stretch irreversibly, causing excessive pendulosity (ptosis, sag). The anti-bra splinter group of the Women's Liberation Movement believes that suspension is a purely male-pleasing option and that ptosis is in no way harmful.

The male breast undergoes some permanent changes in the teens (e.g., the diameter of the areolae increases by over 70 per cent); but in adult men it is still smaller by ⅓ than in adult women (21.5 vs 35.5 mm).

Gynecomastia, a temporary enlargement, occurs in about one out of three actively developing boys. It is discussed on p. 111.

Pubic Hair. From antiquity this had been considered one of the most sensitive indicators of the state of puberal development in both sexes, but especially in the female the triad of pubarche (incipient pubic hair), thelarche (budding of breasts) and menarche does not always occur in a fixed sequence. Pubarche, in girls, is presumably brought on by a spurt of androgens produced by the adrenal cortex, or else by testosterone produced in the peripheral tissues such as in the skin, or from androstenedione. In boys, testicular testosterone is believed to be the controlling factor.

During childhood a colorless, downy vellus covers the abdomen and pubes. First hair growth starts, in boys, shortly after scrotum and testicles begin to grow at about age 12 ± 2.5 years and in girls at 11¾ years ± 14 months of age. Premature pubarche—before age 10 in boys, age 8 in girls—is a benign variant. First pubic hair is longish, slightly pigmented, straight or slightly curled, centered around the base of the penis or along the labia majora. Later, darker, more curly, kinked hair appears; it becomes progressively coarser and denser, and extends laterally and up to the mons. When hair has become adult in type, it still covers less area than in the adult. Final spread to the thighs and up the abdomen may come in the late teens or early twenties. The function of pubic hair is undetermined; one theory believes it to be, together with axillary hair, a rudiment of the abdominal hair cover by which primate mothers can be seen to transport their clinging young. A function of control of genital skin temperature is debatable.

Axillary Hair usually lags behind the appearance of pubic hair by anywhere from 2 to 24 months, although it does in an occasional youngster precede the pubic growth. Age in American girls was recently reported to be 12 years ± 15 months (i.e., less than 3 months after the median age at pubarche in the same group). Underarm hair begins to grow as a down and undergoes texture and pigment changes comparable to those of pubic hair. Together with the hair, there develop in the axillae the apocrine sweat glands; they play a part in the decomposition of resident gram-positive skin bacteria, keratin and other debris, and emit the characteristic axillary odor which is absent in childhood and wanes again in involution. Unlike the eccrine, sudoriferous glands of the skin, the apocrines are histologically related to the scent glands of mammals and had been considered afunctional rudiments in humans. According to newer findings and theories these glands, especially the axillary ones, not only emit sex-specific, cyclic steroid odors, but are the principal dermal organs for the emission of External Chemical Messengers (ECM).

Skin. Increased pigmentation of the axillary fossae, the perineum and the external genitalia parallels the development to final structure of the apocrine-type sweat glands. Increased activity of sebaceous glands during the teens contributes to acne vulgaris. Peak acne incidence in boys is at 16. The texture of the general skin usually assumes adult characteristics after puberty.

Voice. The larynx of boys begins to grow from about age 12. Under the influence of testosterone the cricoid and thyroid cartilages gradually increase in size. The latter, which forms the laryngeal prominence or Adam's apple, becomes especially pronounced during this period. A sudden acceleration of growth of the larynx and the vocal cords between 12 and 15 causes difficulties in controlling pitch and "the voice breaks" (mutation). Between 14 and 18 years of age the male voice drops as much as 1 or even 1½ octaves. Changes may be abrupt in some boys and the whole breaking and dropping period can occur within a month or so. No choral singing should be permitted during mutation (Brodnitz). Girls' voices also deepen normally as much as 2 or 3 semitones, but only slowly and without breaking. See also p. 106.

Beard and Male Body Hair. The beard begins, most often between 14 and 15, as a down (pappus) on the upper lip, first at the corners, then spreading to the midline as it coarsens. Later it grows under the chin and in its cleft, and on the sides of the face. Full beard often is not attained before the late teens. Chest, scrotal and perianal hair develop slowly from about the time of onset of axillary hair. Hair on the distal ends of the extremities begins as a downy growth during pubescence; no data for its completion are available. In exceptional cases of isolated end organ receptor unresponsiveness appearance of beard growth may lag to the early twenties and that of the general body to the mid-twenties.

Erections of the penis can occur from earliest infancy, and probably prenatally. In girls the clitoris probably gains full tumescent capacity only in midpuberal development. The propensity of adolescent boys to have frequent strong erections, even in public, is well known to observers as a source of embarrassment and confusion to many of these youngsters during this androgenically active stage of their development.

Orgasm can occur in young children, at times even in infants, but is not accompanied by transudation or secretion in girls before puberty and is "dry" in boys during the early part of puberal development.

Ejaculation and Spermatogenesis. Ejaculation is not possible before the prostate and seminal vesicles have become functional, although development of the sperm-producing testicular structures need not be completed. Timing of the first emission is not strictly a biologic event, but is influenced by cultural and psychologic factors. Median age in American boys is between 12½ and 14 years of age; it is also reported to take place about 1 year after the acceleration of penis growth.

Mature spermatozoa are most usually formed towards the end of the midteens; this is preceded by the ability to ejaculate by variable periods. However, paternity by normal boys in the early teens, perhaps even earlier, has been observed from time to time. For Precocious Puberty see p. 16.

Menstruation and Ovulation. First menstruation (menarche) occurs at the age of 12¾ years in most American girls. The mean age in 1970 was estimated to be 151.8 ± 14.1 months; it is one of the world's lowest. Zacharias' empiric equation for age at menarche is

$$Y = 57.8 + 0.373X_1 + 0.286X_2 \pm 22.2$$

where Y = age at menarche; X_1 = age at breast budding; X_2 = age at pubic hair appearance; all expressed in months.

Menarche is a landmark in a girl's developmental staging, but it does not signify that reproductive function is now mature. First vaginal bleeding may in some cases represent a true menstrual period (i.e., one preceded by the first ovulation); however, most often it is pseudo-menstruation: circulating estrogen simply has reached the production point at which uterine bleeding is stimulated. Thus only infrequently can conception occur right after menarche. It must be noted that neither ovulation nor even every conception means that full reproductive competence has been established. Regular—thus presumably ovulatory—menstruations in American girls today are established at 13¾ ± 2 years; permanently adult-type ovulatory cycles are believed to begin at 14.6 ± 2½ years of age.

For 100 years or more menarche in the U.S. and at least some European countries has occurred progressively earlier at a rate of 4 months every 10 years of time in the overall Western World, but only about 2 months per decade on upper socio-economic levels. Just lately there are some indications that this trend to accelerated biologic maturity has slowed, as disadvantaged girls everywhere are catching up to the statistical mean age of their front-running sisters. The latter may have arrived at or near a point where further biologic shortening of childhood may not be possible. In fact, some observers have postulated the existence of a historical cyclical trend of the maturation age pattern.

In a satisfactory environment, age at menarche appears to be largely under genetic control. A familiar pattern is often recognizable (e.g., among sisters); but the mother-daughter rule must be adjusted for the secular acceleration trend: age of American mothers at menarche was 4.5 months older recently than that of their teen-age daughters. A recent theory proposes that at a critical range of body weight (ca. 96 lbs.) changes in the metabolic rate occur which reduce the sensitivity of the hypothalamus to estrogen, altering the ovarian-hypothalamic feedback and triggering menarche (Frisch-Revelle). Race plays much less of a part than used to be thought. Short, stocky, dark-eyed, strongly pigmented Western world girls tend to menstruate genetically earlier than tall, thin, blue-eyed ones.

Environment overrides genetic influences when extraordinary factors, good or bad, are present. Conditions of hygiene and nutrition probably are the chief variables. Present-day earlier menarche may be largely due to better protein utilization from infancy on. Overweight girls, if no more than 30 per cent above ideal weight, menstruate earlier. Urban girls have always menstruated earlier than rural ones; contemporary U.S. regional studies show the youngest menarchial ages to occur in the East, the latest in the central and western states; or in a recent survey reported from Poland farm girls there menstruated at 14.30, nonrural girls at 13.77 years of age. It is no longer believed that menarche appears earlier in hot, humid climates. However, relative lateness in high altitudes is an established fact, possibly via chronic hypoxia. For example, in Denver, Colo., almost a mile above sea level, menarche occurred at 13.1 ± .12; in Berkeley, Cal. (sea level) at 12.8 ± .14 years of age (Frisch-Revelle). Exposure to atmospheric light, possibly photoperiodicity, is a disputed factor. Ethnic factors are considered important, but are incompletely understood.

PUBERAL DELAY AND PUBERAL FAILURE

Sexual development in the teens can be delayed, or arrested, or fail to occur altogether, in boys as well as in girls; a lag in bodily growth, or atypical growth, is often associated. The average American boy is considered late by his parents if secondary sex characteristics have not started to appear at 14½ or 15 years of age; a girl, if she shows no breast development at 13. At 14 most girls without genital development or menarche begin to worry about not being normal and at the end of the 16th year the outer reaches of benign delay are at hand. Past 17 years of age—some say 18—menstrual delay becomes primary amenorrhea, and developmental lag becomes puberal failure, making full investigation mandatory.

Late Maturing. Many of the youngsters who visibly lag behind their contemporaries are simply constitutional late-maturers. Such late blooming, more frequent in boys, occurs familially in about 50 per cent of cases. Biosocial, ethnic and racial factors also play a part. Such temporary nondevelopment is a normal variant. Provided bone age is in line with height age, hormone levels are normal, buccal smears for sex chromatin gender-appropriate, and there is no subacute or chronic systemic disease, prognosis as to spontaneous development is excellent and no medical treatment is needed. Once such children start developing they do so rapidly and completely.

However, the youngsters feel conspicuous and fretful if most or all their peers are average-maturing. Only where, for instance, a substantial ethnic enclave of slow-ripening people exists, both the youngsters and their parents derive reassurance from this and local physicians report less pressure on themselves to attempt hastening of puberty.

On the slow-late extreme of the normal distribution curve are the "runty" or "shrimpy" late-maturers in whom height growth has lagged behind all through childhood. They are most often normal on examination, free from disease, although differentiation from isolated growth hormone deficiency and from an undiagnosed maternal deprivation syndrome is difficult. However, their bone age is retarded by as many as 5 years. Developmental prognosis in this variant is also good, except for genetic limits on final height (e.g., if both parents are short-statured).

Delayed Development. Failure to normally pubesce, menstruate, spurt in height, etc. can result from many systemic disorders, if they are sufficiently severe, prolonged or stressful. A frequent and complex cause is malnutrition. A direct blocking effect of even severe semi-starvation on sexual development remains in dispute, but so-called internal starvation (i.e., impaired utilization of nutrients due to a variety of metabolic and intestinal diseases) seems well established as a cause of puberal delay or arrest. Also capable of inhibiting development are stressful sieges of such diseases as poliomyelitis, sickle cell disease, osteomyelitis, chorea, rheumatic fever, unresponsive bronchial asthma, juvenile diabetes, and others. Zinc deficiency is an established cause of maldevelopment in the Middle East. Inadequate oxygen saturation of the peripheral tissues (e.g., in some chronic pulmonary disorders and in congenital heart disease with a large shunt), can fault puberal development by several years.

Puberal Failure is the most severe form of nondevelopment; it follows in the wake of endocrine and brain disorders which affect the controlling brain-pituitary-gonadal axis. Two principal causes exist: direct failure of the gonads, and pituitary failure with secondary silence of the gonads.

Primary Testicular Failure has been observed in congenital anorchia and in the related syndrome of rudimentary testes, both fairly rare; in the early type of myotonic dystrophy; in variants of the Klinefelter syndrome; occasionally following infarction complicating testicular torsion; following orchiopexy when the blood supply has been severely interfered with; in atrophy following scrotal hematoma as a birth injury; and in traumatic or prepuberal surgical castration. These boys remain immature; pituitary gonadotropin excreted in the urine usually is high, and their eunuchoidal body proportions often are marked. Because of inadequate testosterone their long bones do not stop growing: their epiphyses may still be open in the early 20s. The eunuchoid is tall, at times near-gigantic. His arm span, from fingertip to fingertip, exceeds his total height; his soles-to-symphysis exceeds his symphysis-to-crown measurement. But his contour tends to be neuterized or "gynecoid": shoulders slope, muscles often are weak or underdeveloped, his hip girdle broad and pelvic circumference may exceed that of his inspiratory chest. His sexual infantilism, as it is commonly called, may be quite marked, although the clinical picture rarely reaches the spectacular symptomatology seen in the worst cases of pituitary-induced failure (see below). If the eunuchoidal youngster is left with palpable testes they most often remain small; there is generalized hypogenitalism and no seminal emissions take place. The voice remains high and piping, the skin soft, and the face smooth, beardless and free from acne, although pubic and axillary hair may be present. Interference with emotional maturation can be marked.

Female: Primary Ovarian Failure. Girls with primary ovarian failure for the most part also develop eunuchoidal body proportions. The causes, none of them frequent, include ovarian agenesis, surgical castration due to malignant tumors, destructive tubercular lesions and other ovarian insults. Such a girl keeps growing taller, with relatively long legs and arms. The pelvis stays small, muscle development usually is poor and the skin is inelastic and later will wrinkle early. There are no breasts, or some breasts and underdeveloped nipples. The degree of hypogenitalism varies: in the most severe cases the genitals remain infantile; one finds, even in the later teens, a low retracted perineum, absent labia minora, a short and narrow vagina with vulnerable mucosa, shallow fornices, a small pointed cervix and a sharply anteflexed uterine corpus. Urinary gonadotropin is elevated and there is child-type vaginal pH and cytology. There is no menarche, or else menses are scant, persistently irregular and anovulatory. Pubic and axillary hair may be present but sparse. Special body build and signs are present in girls with gonadal dysgenesis (q.v.), in some cases of the polycystic ovary syndrome (q.v.), and in the testicular feminization syndrome (q.v.).

Secondary (Central) Failure. Centrally induced or secondary non-sexing occurs in youngsters in whom a defect of, or damage to, the pituitary-hypothalamic end of the axis has occurred. Such lesions directly or indirectly impair the secretion of the pituitary gonadotropins. Lacking gonadotropin stimulation the gonads remain unawakened and immature: they secrete no sex hormones, and without these target organs such as the genitalia and breasts cannot develop. As other pituitary hormones (e.g., thyrotropin, growth hormone) can also be involved, as well as adjacent brain areas, a variety of clinical syndromes with metabolic, sensory and neurologic manifestations can coexist. Also, only some of these youngsters develop eunuchoidal proportions. Some remain very short-statured, even dwarfed; others are dysplastic or obese; still others have normal body configuration.

The most severe syndrome is panhypopituitarism; it results in the sexually infantile pituitary dwarf, male and female, although today much can be accomplished for them with timely treatment. Hypopituitarism in the teens may be idiopathic, or else caused by tumors encroaching upon the area, notably the craniopharyngioma group, as well as carcinoma, optic glioma, pinealoma and, less often, meningioma. Histiocytic infiltration, including the Hand-Schuller-Christian syndrome, can be a cause. Infection and head injury affecting the anterior pituitary are rare causes in non-adults. Certain juvenile pituitary brain syndromes are accompanied by severe hypogonadism: the Prader-Willi syndrome (males only have hypo-genitalism) with dwarfing, obesity, mental retardation, diabetes mellitus, muscle weakness; Froehlich's adiposogenitalism, usually a suprasellar tumor, with obesity and diabetes insipidus; Kallman's syndrome with hyp-or anosmia; cases of Simmonds' disease with teen-age onset; and half the cases of the Lawrence-Moon-Biedl syndrome with obesity, dwarfing, mental retardation, retinal degeneration and supernumerary toes and fingers. Of unknown etiology is Werner's syndrome, related to progeria, with dwarfing and premature aging.

Obesity can be associated with delay or disruption of sexual development. While moderately overweight youngsters with evenly distributed subcu-taneous fat often are early-maturing, girls who weigh more than 30 per cent above the standard and boys with large fat deposits simulating a gynecoid habitus tend to be sexually delayed. As pseudosmallness of the genitalia is associated in these boys, as well as certain physical and mental softness traits (see p. 112), there used to be over-recognition of what was considered a benign variant of adiposogenitalism. Today the pendulum has reversed towards under-recognition, the syndrome being classed as exogenous obesity, the mild hypogonadism being considered merely ap-parent. However, the syndrome exists as a clinical entity, presumably based on a transient functional insufficiency of diencephalic mechanisms of adaptation. Almost all of these boys later grow into essentially normal, fertile men, although it is possible to be retrospectively aware of some residual traits.

Psychic Stress, if prolonged, is strongly suspected of having an anti-puberty effect in vulnerable youngsters. There is no longer any reasonable doubt that psychologic stimuli can influence hypothalamic-pituitary ac-tivity. The developmental ill effects of the maternal deprivation syndrome, if unrecognized and uncorrected, may make themselves felt beyond child-hood (a theory). Clinical follow-up, alas unsystematic, of some schizo-phrenic and some severely phobic children points to a delay of sexual development beyond the mean standard deviation. Children interned during the Second World War experienced sexual delay of up to 3 years beyond expectancy. Although degrees of malnutrition played a part, there is evidence that it was the coexistence of emotional deprivation which led to the delay. Isolated psychogenic menarcheal suppression—the view that the dread of menarche can delay menarche in the absence of somatic pathology—has not been proven. Its equivalent in boys is even more diffi-cult to prove. Anorexia nervosa occurring in the early teens has a distinct development-inhibiting effect.

Psychic Complications of Nondevelopment arise as a result of parent and peer attitudes and of self-comparison. As peers grow in height, develop the characteristic contour, acquire pubic hair, larger genitalia, budding breasts or deeper voices, gossip about menstruations and ejaculations and develop a new type of interest in the opposite sex, the late-maturer's ego essence—self-esteem, body image and emotional stability—are at risk of becoming severely disturbed.

The psychic hazards of delayed maturation are more pronounced in boys. The sexually delayed boy easily becomes the center of hostile attention on the part of his peers and even of his family, especially if he is also markedly runty, gynecoid or obese. Relentlessly dissatisfied parents—overanxious, derogatory, or merely perceived as rejecting—can help ingrain a sense of shame. In others a syndrome of withdrawal, brooding and deep feelings of worthlessness arises; still others reflexly adopt an inordinately passive-dependent attitude with display of exaggerated ineptness and helplessness. Some others again resort to aggressively antisocial conduct, especially to stealing, to prove masculinity.

Delayed girls have a somewhat easier adaptive task, partly because they are less conspicuous among their contemporaries. However, many of these girls worry greatly about their marital and reproductive future, especially if the mother's attitude is disquieting.

School performance of delayed youngsters tends to lag, because often they are tense, anxious and excessively preoccupied with themselves, although intelligence is not affected. Increased fatiguability, mental and physical, contribute to this, as their more childlike somatopsychic economy is not geared to the tasks and pursuits of their more developed contemporaries.

Late maturers may carry into adulthood residual symptoms of their disturbed adaptation, and it is suspected that in the worst cases chronic proneness to hysteroid behavior, panic states, obsessive tendencies and even major personality disorders can ensue. On the other hand, where the family's attitude has been supportive, the very fact that the latency stage of childhood (p. 15) was so prolonged and the early teens relatively free from puberal turbulence, can enhance ego functions such as determination and venturesomeness, and can broaden the outlook.

Treatment. Ideally, all minor variants of delayed development are treated by reassurance and watchful waiting, while all major development-inhibiting disorders require prompt, energetic treatment. This is based on the assumption that sexual development and somatic growth must be maintained as close to the normal pattern as possible: at a certain point of development at least some of the sexual target organs seem to reach their optimal response readiness; after that critical point they may develop only partially in response to sex steroid stimulation. Where a disorder causes midpuberal disruption, practically each few months during which development is suppressed can mean up to several years or partial hypogenitalism later, as the organism tries to catch up with its own gradually diminishing puberal impetus.

Concern mounts as the youngster advances through the teens and the gonads remain silent. There arise insistent demands from the understandably worried parents for some kind of action, while the youngster's increasing psychologic stress and social difficulties threaten to approach the point where they cannot be easily reversed, especially in those who have come into the teens with a history of emotional instability in childhood. Clinical decision-making if and when to treat must take into account that parents pressing for early action do not always do so out of deep concern over the boy's ultimate manhood and size: their own personality make-up may make the presence of a lagging, peer-rejected child intolerable to them. Conversely, in cases where the height problem is not primary, the youngsters themselves today may disdain any hormone treatment as being an artificial thing. Where the physician decides he must proceed with treatment the boy should be reassured that this is merely for the purpose of hastening his development and that normal maturation would have occurred spontaneously, although somewhat later.

In Boys the therapeutic trend is to hasten lagging development more readily and earlier, but not generally before age 14. The principal hazard is advancing the bone age and premature closure of the epiphyses of the long bones, thus exchanging accelerated "now" development and height spurt for a possible permanent loss in final height. The responsible factor is estrogen secreted by the stimulated testicles.

The preferred method of stimulating the testicles, once primary testicular failure has been ruled out, is by means of human chorionic gonadotropin (HCG) given intramuscularly in slightly uncomfortable courses somewhat larger and longer than previously used (e.g., up to 15,000 I.U. per week in 2 to 5 divided doses) for several—up to 5—months, the course to be repeated, if necessary, after an interval. The Leydig cells mature and the plasma testosterone rises before there is visible evidence of puberal development. However, the enzyme system fabricating testosterone must have sufficiently matured; if not, no sex development occurs. The advantage of HCG over testosterone here is that induction of sexual development is more gradual, probably less likely to close the epiphyses, and that it eliminates the negative feedback effect of circulating androgen. However, antibodies may develop, and some observers have found permanent testicular damage from lengthy courses. HCG should probably not be administered while natural pituitary evocation of the testicles is in progress: if on testicular biopsy the tunica propria of the tubules is being formed, sexual development may be predicted to follow within a year. Anabolic analogs of testosterone have beneficially been added to gonadotropin treatment.

The use of testosterone is necessary as replacement therapy in primary cases (i.e. in hypergonadotropic hypogonadism). Useful has been oral methyltestosterone 10 to 30 mg a day, or one half this dose as sublingual tablets, or the equivalent in depo-testosterone injections in 3 to 4 month courses. Major penile stimulation—overfrequent erections or temporary priapism—may be watched as an indicator of disproportionate virilization; many of these boys are quite sensitive to the sudden influx of unaccustomed testosterone. Bone age must be assessed radiologically every few months and treatment stopped if undue acceleration occurs.

In practically all cases the relative abruptness of induced maturation may find the youngster unprepared, and undue emotional reactions, some perhaps due to the sex steroids themselves, are observed in a number of these young people. This is aggravated by their contemporaries having long since passed this stage and having lost interest in talking about the wondrous changes of budding manhood, reassuring each other just by comparing notes. This leaves the late-developing boy isolated at first and without the supporting mechanism of peer gossip. To dissipate some of the impact, the same-gender parent or a counselor may make an acceptable substitute here.

In Girls chorionic gonadotropin is ineffective in hastening sexual development and is not in use. In severe hypogonadism, especially in the Turner syndromes, continuous estrinization (e.g., Premarin 1.25 mg daily) for up to 6 months, followed by cyclic administration with an added progestin, will produce breast and uterine development as well as psychologically helpful withdrawal bleeding. In physiologically normal but late-maturing girls continuous estrogen administration may produce negative feedback and ovulatory suppression, uterine pathology, irregular bleeding, and cystic breast changes. Between menarche and past the 16th birthday ovulation-depressing hormones are avoided, to allow the cycle to establish itself firmly. More so than in boys, all effective hastening therapy in late-maturing girls would also endanger the final height. On the other hand, safe results are obtained in 8 to 11 year old premenarcheal girls for whom excessive final height has been predicted, with parenteral cyclical estrogen being administered until their epiphyses fuse with the metaphyses of the long bones, taking away up to 4 or 5 inches from the projected giantess' stature.

MASCULINIZATION AND PSEUDOMASCULINIZATION IN GIRLS

Pseudomasculine Habitus. A girl's build may deviate from the stereotypic feminine norm. She may be of unusually lanky or stocky build, or the shoulders may be broad and/or the pelvis narrow. In the absence of eunuchoidal body proportions (p. 100), and of residues of adrenal virilization with short legs and small breasts, these constitutional variants have no or little clinical significance. A prominent variant is the girl of Amazon build as she emerges in the middle teens—long-limbed, well muscled, slightly husky-voiced, her stride loose and easy, the feet pointing straight ahead, often even when running, and using the whole sole of the foot from heel to toe in propelling herself. The masculine quality of her gait is largely due to a differing maculine-type suspension mode in the knee joint, corresponding to the less pronounced carrying angle in the masculine-type elbow; the latter, in turn, permits less awkward ball throwing and catching. However, the Amazon possesses all the appurtenances of femininity—physical, physiologic, psychologic and sexual.

Athletic Interest and competitive spirit in sports participation for girls is now almost universally considered appropriate and desirable. The menstrual handicap is considered minor (see p. 132). Successful performance by teen-age sportswomen is now commonplace in swimming, gymnastics, skating and many other endeavors, some requiring litheness and agility, others muscle power, still others stamina, with none of them, in essence, being considered unfeminine. A difficulty brought to light in recent years concerns certain individual competitors in international competitions, including the Olympic games: the intrusion of males masquerading as females (rare), and the unwitting participation of intersexed or certain sex-inappropriately reared individuals who would be competing unfairly. The test now favored for Olympic competition is fluorescent microscope examination for Barr and Y bodies of the cells of quinacrine-stained sheaths of scalp hair roots of every female competitor. Controversy has arisen regarding the classification of some of the chromosome mosaicisms which carry no clinical masculinizing changes.

Hirsutism.   Variations of body hair most often include unusual or excessive growth on thighs, abdominal mid-line, face, nipples or between the breasts. They appear in pubescence, but often disappear in late adolescence. Where they remain, racial or ethnic-geographic factors may play a part; for instance, 1 of each 5 Mediterranean females is believed to have a somewhat masculine-type pubic escutcheon, while few are found in females of Scandinavian extraction. Most frequently irreversible is hirsuteness of the extremities, especially the legs, in an otherwise normal girl, most of it probably due to hypersensitivity of the hair follicles, rather than adrenocortical pathology. Onset is a few years after menarche. Acne may precede and/or coexist with hirsutism. Adrenal pathology may be suspected if clitoral, voice and Adam's apple changes are also present and the breasts remain small (hydrocortisone treatment). The presence of polycystic ovaries would have to be ruled out. Some drugs (e.g., Dilantin) can induce transitory hypertrichosis. Girls with an innate tendency to release ACTH and produce androgen in the adrenals when under physical or mental stress also can develop excessive hair transitorily on those occasions. It may be noted that the growth rate of hair in humans is markedly more rapid in summer than in winter. Treatment of hirsutism in major cases, after age 16 or 17, may be with estrogen in fairly large doses, administered cyclically and offset by an end-of-cycle progestational hormone. The antiandrogen cyproterone acetate, not generally available now, has reportedly given creditable results.

Voice. A sonorous or chronically raucous voice, in the absence of other atypies of clinical import, is encountered in some girls; it has no significance and there is no known treatment. A startlingly deep voice, although rare in the second decade, on the other hand, would be evidence of evolving endocrine pathology or possibly sex-inappropriate rearing. During puberal development, moderate deepening of the voice in girls occurs slowly and without breaking.

Flat-chestedness. Persistent bilateral flat-chestedness can occur in an otherwise normally developing, well-nourished girl without endocrine or chromosomal pathology. Actually it is not so much a masculinizing as it is a nonfeminizing trait. It is assumed to be due to end-organ failure (i.e., permanent un- or subresponsiveness of the breasts' receptor cells to hormonal stimulation).

Such micromastia constitutes a potentially major psychologic hazard. It can be associated with (precipitate?) ambivalence toward growing up. Depressions with suicidal ruminations have occurred in girls obsessively preoccupied with their hypoplastic breasts. Such girls may first come to nurse's, counselor's or medical attention when repeatedly seeking to be excused from school swimming programs for trivial reasons. Counseling here emphasizes their being normal and feminine in every other respect.

POSITION OF IDEAL BREAST

Ideal breast-nipple positioning was postulated by a South African plastic surgeon in 1955 (Penn, Brit. J. Plast. Surg. 7:357) thus: Standing upright, arms at sides, with all points projected on one plane as in a photograph, a female's internipple, nipple-sternal notch, and nipple-midclavicular point measurements are equidistant (8 to 8½ inches). Nipple-inframammary grove distance 2½ to 3 inches. Nipple lies 1½ inches below mid-humerus. The latter is a point halfway between acromion level and lateral epicondyle.

Others, favoring less pendency, have postulated the nipple lying at mid-humerus, an internipple distance of 9 + inches and a nipple-sternal notch distance of 6 to 7½ inches. This appears to correspond to Tanner's developmental stage 3.

Ratio of internipple:thorax width, the latter at nipple level and measured by P-A chest x-ray, is 0.640 ± 0.040 (Fleisher). Abnormal width occurs in Turner's syndrome and hypoplasia of kidneys.

Where breasts are merely small lactation may be possible later. Padded bras and "falsies" today no longer satisfy most teenagers in view of prevailing styles of dress and conduct. Estrogen in the early and midteens is inadvisable as it may depress pituitary function, cause uterine pathology and close the epiphyses too soon, thus impairing final height.

Beginning in later adolescence a trial of hormone treatment for small breasts is feasible. Breasts respond unpredictably to different estrogenic compounds (Kupperman). Estrogen also tends to enlarge best those breasts already generously endowed. However, a few hypoplastic breasts respond to very large dosages (e.g., natural conjugated estrogens 2.5 mg. t.i.d. by mouth continuously), adding medroxyprogesterone acetate 10 mg. b.i.d. in the last 7 days of each calendar month (Young). If no results after 6 months, success is unlikely. The effect may be temporary when stopping treatment. Exercises for enlarging the breasts do not exist, but the underlying pectoral muscles can be strengthened and thickened, thus improving the contour. Implantation of a silicone prosthesis (augmentation mammaplasty) is considered a safe and worthwhile method, but is best withheld until young adulthood, partly because adolescent breast surgery tends to produce unsightly scars. Implantation of the prosthesis most often is made over the pectoral muscles except where there is little covering breast tissue, in which case the added thickness of the pectorals make palpability of the gel-filled rubber container less likely. Injections of silicone, etc. into the breasts have fallen into disuse. Implanting of fluid-inflatable bags has gained some acceptance. Local inunctions with concentrated steroid lotions have been recommended, if systemic effect is avoided by proper dosing; others have held them ineffective.

Virilism. The degree of virilization in the female corresponds roughly to the production rate of testosterone in the body. In virilizing adrenal hyperplasia (e.g., the delayed prepubescent type), androgen is secreted as androstenedione by the adrenal cortex and then bioconverted to testosterone. Certain ovarian and adrenal tumors—usually in adult women—secrete testosterone directly. In prepuberal children and normal post-puberal females about one half of the circulating testosterone is secreted by the ovaries, and one half converted from other plasma steroids of adrenal origin.

Carry-over virilization from childhood (e.g., late or incompletely treated adrenal hyperplasia with or without intersexing) continues to be picked up in practice, although adequate maintenance treatment is universally available. There appear to be differences in personality make-up between the residual classical and the delayed forms of adrenal virilization. While the former does well in childhood where she is superior to most of her peers in strength and drive, she often does poorly during much of the teens when suddenly the attainment of femininity is her female peers' main striving and measure. She tends to moroseness, feelings of inadequacy, depressive reactions and defeatist withdrawal; her intellectual functioning is now average at best; she is lesbiophobic, sexually much preoccupied and probably masturbating a great deal. In late adolescence and early adulthood these girls recover a more adequate personality and functional drive, but treatment efforts during the teens may have played a part in the known cases. On the other hand, the girl who begins to newly virilize somewhat just before pubescence, seems to literally burst upon the scene of teen existence—bright, ebullient, often forward and noisy, with aggressive personality traits resembling those of some of the most pronounced idiopathic tomboys. Although these girls make very good athletes during the second decade, they seem to slacken off during late adolescence and soon merge inconspicuously with their peers (see also p. 20, p. 354 and p. 363).

Tomboyishness in Girls. The average idiopathic tomboy is a girl of prepubescent or pubescent age, sometimes younger, sometimes older, free from detectable endocrinopathy and virilizing signs and, by random sample, genetically female. The condition is carried into the second decade from childhood. Because of present-day patterns of rearing, play and attire recognition is infrequently possible before age 7. In childhood she is inclined to roam, climb trees or explore empty buildings, shout, and prefer the company and the gross-motor games of boys rather than stay close to home and associate with girls in girl-type play. She does not show early mothering behavior and later has little patience with smaller children. She disdains primping and may masculinize her name. She may fervently wish that she were a boy because "boys have all the fun"; she resents or even despises her growing breasts and the prospect of menarche. Unlike the adrenocortically virilized but treated type of tomboy the idiopathic tomboy not infrequently manifests increased erotic activity (e.g., continuing masturbation or even ostentatious pre-adolescent promiscuity), the latter perhaps as a form of bravado or challenge vis-à-vis the peer group. However, others are reticent with boys and extremely prudish.

Characteristic is the close attachment to the father and the negative relationship with the mother, including reciprocal jealous hatred of an intensity rarely encountered in any other parent-child relationship. She is the apple of her father's eye from an early age. She may not be the only child, may even have one or more brothers, but in that case she is usually the first born. The father takes her fishing or camping, teaches her woodcraft or shopwork or stamp collecting and proudly explains his business or trade to her in every detail; if he cares about schooling he supervises her schoolwork. He imparts most of the sex information and counsels on boys and dates, sometimes in a subtly discouraging fashion. She may say, proudly, "Dad always wanted a boy." She seeks his ear with her problems and is accustomed to having him complain to her about her mother. If he drinks to excess she may help him to conceal this from her mother. He teaches her "not to need anyone" and diffidence about being pitied. There appears to be nothing overtly erotic about this relationship; these girls are not represented among father-daughter incest victims (p. 61).

In the early midteens, sometimes as early as menarche, the vast majority experience a softening of their nonacceptance of the feminine role. They continue to disdain frills and cosmetics for a long while, but later accept dating and marriage without great struggle. In adulthood, their life styles become indistinguishable from those of most other women, although the practiced clinician can often pick them out. They seem to make good wives and mothers who dote on a son but seem slightly bewildered by the psychology of a daughter. In the opinion of some observers it is the ex-tomboy turned mother who tends to feminize a son by means of a compelling, intimate symbiosis in infancy (see p. 488) and by discouraging masculine behavior (Stoller, others). One may suggest that quite possibly the infant carries the cue, having been prenatally subtly demasculinized in an altered humoral environment; its femininized make-up and reactivity then precipitate this type of maternal response. Unlike the adrenocortically virilized and some intersexed (p. 361) girls, idiopathic tomboys as a rule are not outstanding or even good athletes in the teens nor later. A small minority do not make the pubertal transition into the appropriate gender role, but continue into severe deviance, i.e., the rare female transvestism (p. 484), transsexualism (p. 489) or lesbianism (p. 525).

The cause of idiopathic tomboyism is not known, although the theoretical possibilities are limited. In all probability the over-affectionate intrusion of the father into the girl's rearing is not a primary cause, but part of the often complex cause-and-effect interplay of personalities in these nuclear family triangles. The presence of some kind of partial prenatal masculinization of female brain structures is purely speculative at present. Lack of sisters or of female playmates during the early years are not causes.

There is no effective treatment for this condition, which is far more acceptable in our society than its opposite, effeminacy in boys. Sympathetic but unobtrusive guidance towards acceptance of bodily changes during the critical preadolescent period can prevent an unwholesome distortion of body image and perhaps some future psychosexual difficulties. Advising a mother to force feminine attitudes leads only to increased rebelliousness and alienation. Group therapy in carefully selected teen-age groups can be of value.

DEFICIENT AND PSEUDODEFICIENT MASCULINE TRAITS IN BOYS

Few bodily or psychic traits in boys cause more anxious over-recognition in parents than deficient masculinity. Lack of drive, emotional lability, feminine appearance or motility are perceived as sex-divergent traits which arouse a more striking negative reaction than a girl's divergence of corresponding degree. Such a boy often is aware of, and may distort and adopt, the doubts of his parents and other adults as to whether he is a "real man."

Variants of Individuality. Although a cultural reaction has begun to set in, sissyphobia still dominates present societal thinking which regards with diffidence most sensitivity, creativity, tender demeanor and confidingly close same-sex friendships in males. Variations may take the form of artistic-esthetic or one-sided intellectual inclinations, or lack of interest or talent in competitive athletics, spectator sports, business or politics in an otherwise normal boy. This also includes dreamers, idealists and gentle souls. These patterns are discernible from midchildhood and can rarely be altered, nor should this be tried. The picture is most often misrepresented to the physician by a greatly disappointed father who naïvely measures masculinity by the a-real-boy-has-skinned-knees criterion. These boys have, as a rule, normal masculine habitus, although one may suspect a prevalence of asthenic physiques. Their sexuality, including development, libido and drive, is normal. This does not include the genuinely girlhood-oriented boy (see p. 144 and p. 146) who is passing through the teens bound for adult transgender deviance.

High-pitched Voice. The voices of some boys fail to deepen or to remain deep before late adolescence, the twenties or even permanently, although all other development may be normal. The cause is probably an isolated end-organ defect (i.e., the vocal apparatus is constitutionally unresponsive to normal androgenic stimulation). Absent or incomplete mutation differs from the falsetto voice which, in turn, differs from the clear, high, piping quality of the completely unmatured child's voice. Falsetto, considered a conversion hysteric manifestation (Franklin), is infrequently seen today; its quality is that of a shrill, unnatural, tense-sounding treble with limited range; during phonation the larynx is held high in the neck, the cords are overstretched by the cricothyroid muscles, and respiration is tense. A cough or throat clearing will show the normal nature of the voice. To differentiate psychogenic falsetto voice from delayed or incomplete mutation, the Gutzman Pressure Test (Ann. Otol. 67:235, 1958) has been recommended. The treatment of failed mutation is essentially expectant and reassuring; it rarely responds to testosterone (caution during active development). Specialized voice training may be attempted. Also, these boys must be cautioned against developing chronic vocal spasms and intermittent aphonia due to forced attempts to "talk deep."

Beardlessness is observed sometimes. Facial hair growth may lag or be permanently scant in the absence of other developmental deficits. Occasionally this is a racial or ethnic trait (e.g., American Indians), but again the most frequent cause is probably a constitutional end-organ defect of the hair follicles. A trial with androgenic medication during post-adolescence is sometimes worthwhile. No other treatment is known.

Gynecomastia. Transitory ("physiologic") growth of the male breasts occurs in over one third of all boys between 12 and 14½ years of age, with peak incidence near 14. Enlargement ranges from small painless, subareolar nodules palpable directly underneath the nipple to pendulousness. The latter is more apt to occur if adipomasty coexists with the mammary tissue hyperplasia. Pain, tenderness and, at times, colostrum secretion may occur. In 1 out of 5 boys the condition is unilateral, more often on the left. Gynecomastia tends to disappear, usually before 2 years have passed. In 3 or 4 per cent of cases the breasts stay permanently enlarged, without other abnormalities being manifest, including some of the unilaterally enlarged breasts. Occasionally the condition may last only very briefly (evanescent gynecomastia). Where small testicles are associated with gynecomastia in the midteens, closer examination is necessary to rule out Klinefelter's syndrome. Spurious gynecomastia (adipomasty) (e.g., in marked obesity) must be differentiated.

With conspicuous breast enlargement, especially if pendulous, the boy may become greatly embarrassed and inhibited, while minor degrees rarely seem to cause perturbance. Those with large breasts are apt to avoid shower rooms, athletics and school vaccinations, giving various excuses; these excuses in themselves sometimes are encountered again years later, embedded in all manner of neurotic avoidance reactions. Boys with major degrees of gynecomastia avoid dates; some get into disciplinary difficulties at school because they equate defiance with masculinity and are anxious to prove the latter. Others worry a great deal that they are changing into a woman or into a homosexual; some are subject to pseudohomosexual panic states. Those with the most intense pre-existing conflicts about growing up or fears of not growing up seem to have the most intense anxiety reactions.

Treatment of minor hyperplasia is expectant for a period of at least 2 years, but pendulous breasts do not regress spontaneously no matter what their composition (Schonfeld) and mammaplasty without delay is indicated, by intraareolar semicircular incision which leaves a minimally visible scar. Testosterone is not indicated; in fact, pubertal breast hyperplasia often seems to occur in boys who are virilizing rapidly. Some preparations, notably methyltestosterone, can worsen gynecomastia. Reassurance and, in major cases, psychotherapy are necessary.

Puer Mollis. A syndrome of obesity of gynecoid distribution, puberal delay, softness of psychic traits, emotional immaturity and minimal or pseudohypogenitalism occurs in boys. Formerly designated as pseudo-Fröhlich or pseudo-adiposogenitalism—terms no longer in general use—it may be due to decreased release of pituitary gonadotropin, either of unknown etiology or an effect of the obesity itself (Lloyd). The condition probably differs somewhat from other types of obesity in boys. The course is benign and essentially transient and patients grow into normal, fertile men, although minor residual traits remain recognizable at times.

These boys are sissified but not girlish, shy but not coy, socializing poorly. Their sense of maleness, of being boys, is never seriously in question. As to overweight, girdle obesity—of upper thighs, hips, buttocks, mons pubis and lower abdomen—prevails, and the chest shows adipomasty (pseudogynecomastia). Stature and growth are unremarkable, the skeleton is slender, even gracile, especially wrists and ankles. A tendency to knock knees and flat feet exists. Muscle development is weak, posture often slouchy; joints, especially elbows, may be overrelaxed. The face is immature, often cherubic, conveying an impression of fatuousness or of petulance. The skin is soft. Testicles may or may not be smaller than normal. The penis may be somewhat small, but often it appears even smaller than it is because it is partly buried in pubic fat; in pronounced cases urination standing up can become difficult and embarrassing because the mons almost covers the penis. No major pituitary pathology and low urinary 17-ketosteroid and gonadotropin excretion values have been noted.

Most of these boys are passive, emotionally immature and lack enterprise. They are affectionate and good-natured, easily led and easily frightened, self-pitying, and cry easily. A few are mostly irritable; some others are torpid, slow, clumsy and forgetful, although there is no unusual impairment of intelligence. Most experience themselves as vulnerable to control by others and they may despair of developing adequate defensive equipment against taunts and what they perceive as contempt, and to each occasion they overreact with further withdrawal. Their sense of ineffectualness and disturbed awareness of their own body image conveys to them that they look unmasculine and brings flashes of confusion and doubt as to whether they were not meant to be females after all; however, this differs sharply from chronic boyhood effeminacy (see p. 81). School phobias also occur, resulting from a combination of fear of taunts, a state of depression and consuming fear of not finding the mother again when they return home. In his emotional make-up the puer mollis during his critical puberal years somewhat resembles the case of Klinefelter's syndrome (q.v.) passing through the teens, except that he generally lacks the latter's not infrequent tendency to suspiciousness, bitterness, temper tantrums or aggressive grandiosity growing out of the basic sense of gender inadequacy.

Treatment, basically, is expectant. Reassurance and emotional support are as important as regulation of caloric intake and energy output. However, a routine prescription of reducing and dieting with the promise that it will solve all their problems may precipitate mental illness when the symptoms are part of a long-standing maldevelopment (Bruch). Disturbances in the emotional make-up and parental rapport is not an invariable or even a prominent part of the background history; the overprotective, over-indulgent mother is more typically present in the simple exogenous obesity of boys. The father's intensified interest in the boy should be encouraged, however. These boys should not be pushed into situations in which they are likely to fail out of a mistaken purpose "to make a man out of him"; they must have a fair chance to succeed.

FOR JOURNAL LITERATURE AND ADDITIONAL READING

Donovan, B. T. and Van der Werf ten Bosch, J. J.: Physiology of Puberty, Baltimore, Williams & Wilkins, 1966

Federman, D. D.: Abnormal Sexual Development: A Genetic and Endocrine Approach to Differential Diagnosis. Philadelphia, Saunders, 1967

Heald, F. P. and Hung, W.: Adolescent Endocrinology. New York, Appleton-Century-Crofts, 1970

Huffman, J. W.: The Gynecology of Childhood and Adolescence. Philadelphia, Saunders, 1968

Hurlock, E.: Adolescent Development. Ed. 3. New York, McGraw-Hill, 1967

Jones Jr., H. W. and Heller, R. H.: Pediatric and Adolescent Gynecology. Baltimore, Williams & Wilkins, 1966

Martini, L., Motta M., and Fraschini, F. (eds.): The Hypothalamus. New York, Academic Press, 1971

Steiner, M. M.: Clinical Approach to Endocrine Problems in Children. St. Louis, Mosby, 1970

Wolstenholme, G. E. W., and Knight, J. (eds.): The Pineal Gland; A Ciba Foundation Symposium. London, Churchill Livingston, 1971

Wurtman, R. J., Axelrod, J., and Kelly, D. E.: The Pineal. New York, Academic Press, 1968

CHAPTER 7

Adolescent Sex Education

Sex Education in the Home — Guidance — Sex Education in
School — Premarital Sex Standards — Adolescence and
Contraception.

SEX EDUCATION IN THE HOME

No responsible adult today doubts that the normal teen-ager should have substantial information on sexual matters. Under ideal circumstances the child has brought with him into the teens a warm rapport with the same-sex parent, and an ingrained feeling that he (she) can turn to the parent for most explanations and be assured of a basically trusting, benign and helpful response. The amount of sex information an adolescent should have need be no problem to the parents if a simple trio of requirements is kept in mind: it should be sufficient to enable him (her) to evaluate his own sexual drive and any transient peculiarities without worry; nearing the late teens he ought to know enough to enable him—as he well may—to enter marriage adequately prepared for it except perhaps for its most intimately technical aspects; and by that time he should also be able to react without panic to unfamiliar aspects of sexuality he may encounter, including pathologic ones. As regards the conveying of physiologic detail, there is wide agreement today that it should be essentially complete by the end of mid-adolescence.

The Central Affirmation. The greatest single hurdle to domestic frankness in matters of sex education is a reluctance on the part of a great many parents to admit to the youngster, boy or girl, the existence of sexual intercourse, namely the fact that the hardened penis enters the vagina when adults make love. This is a pivotal acknowledgment, and when it has been made, it tends to make all other sex information easier to ask and to give. There exists hardly a subject relating to sex which cannot be discussed more easily once the primal fact has been acknowledged. It does not seem to matter that usually the parent is not telling the youngster anything he (she) did not know already; nor does it seem to make much difference, at

114

what stage of upbringing—early, timely, or belatedly—and in what context this bare fact was acknowledged.

Parental Failure. Where a parent feels impelled to ask, "how do we tell our child?" or whenever a mother complains, "I cannot get my husband to talk to the boy about these things," or when a physician or counselor gets the request to "give the boy (girl) a good talking to" or "explain a few things to her," it is virtually prima facie evidence that the parents have failed to fulfill many of their natural obligations to the child that was, as well as to the youngster that is. When a father complains that he cannot "get through" to his son, most likely it had first been the boy who could not get through to his father.

Where timidity has kept a father from attempting to gain the son's trust on sex matters and worries, but where the basic relationship is good, some fathers have done well by simply admitting that they are timid "because of how I was brought up by my own father." Once the midteens are reached it is, in our time, too late to establish a meaningful trust relationship between parent and child ex novo. The role of the mother vis-à-vis a son's sex education in the second decade is close to nil under normal circumstances. In fact, where the father is accessible, but the mother-son relationship at this stage is such that the mother appears best suited to assume the boy's sex education, one is most likely in the presence of psychosexual pathology, in statu nascendi, in the boy.

Checking with Peers. On the other hand, any amount of sexual information by parents or other adults remains relatively meaningless unless the youngster can put it into proper perspective by exchange of information with contemporaries. Such exchange also reassures the midteen-ager, with his physiologic worrisomeness, that his impulses and conflicts are not unique. The normal youngster with the most secure background of sex education is, of course, also the one least likely to buy the distortions and half-truths which are apt to infiltrate this juvenile trading of sex information, while the one who throughout his teens is isolated—or through psychic peculiarities isolates himself—from the normal sexual probing and groping for concepts among his peers is experiencing a deficit in his psychosexual maturation which probably cannot be altogether recouped.

GUIDANCE

Limit Setting. The youngster of early and midteen age who is trying to develop a standard of sex attitudes, is also testing out his (her) limits; he requires, and subconsciously desires, a set of controls to butt his (her) head against, not silence or total permissiveness or, worse, adulation. With the parents who set no limits the child develops the uneasy feeling that they are not really interested in him. Clamor for too-early grown-up status must be denied; there must be refusal to be intimidated. Antagonism between adolescent and parent is necessary and normal; without conflict there is no growth (Blos). The most wholesome image parents may hope to convey at this stage is "a reliable father you can trust and possibly admire, and a mother who has understanding."

Normal Turbulence. This is an age of transition. Conflicts and apprehensions are the norm here. Even in the most normal youngster the inexorability of his biologic progression to adulthood produces flare-ups of panicky conflict between his urge to experience a separate identity and a wish to remain a child, dependent, looked after. The desire to prove bodily competence—prowess in boys, beauty in girls—and the struggle to establish success with the opposite sex engender spasms of insecurity. Erratic shifts in the midteen years affect even the hitherto stable youngster. The peak physical modesty stage—between 10 and 13 in many girls, almost 2 years later in boys—may be interrupted by the most immodest exhibitionistic impulses. Episodes of regression to primitive instinct indulgence alternate with phases of ascetic idealism, and there are unpredictable shifts from sloppiness to overfastidiousness, from hero worship to cynicism, or from quixotic enthusiasms to taedium vitae.

Controls. Values. The important task for parents here is to share their values with the adolescent, even if he seems to disparage or disregard them continuously. This is also the rebellious age (Flegeljahre, Ger.; l'âge ingrat, Fr.). The protective rulings of adults often appear to be frustrating and arbitrary to the midteen-ager; yet, be it ever so dimly, they very often constitute a source of prideful identification; a rock bottom support for his temporarily disarrayed impulse-conscience balance; a check on his more chaotic experimentations; or perhaps a counterbalance to the example of perturbingly freewheeling eroticism among some peers or older idols. As one parent said, "We owe it to our children to be unpopular with them sometimes."

Many parents deny their children such a frame of reference. A variety of profoundly personal parental hang-ups first seem to come to light when parents reach the stage where they must deal with ethical and moral values vis-à-vis an adolescent son or daughter. The fact that a youngster seems to be wise and knowing—or socially adroit, or a great sex theoretician, or intellectually brilliant, or a student of biology—may frighten some parents into subsiding; yet almost certainly none of this is a guarantee that the youngster is free from conflict and tension, or genuinely emancipated. To permit "choice" of sexual attitude in the midteens is to expose the young person to the hazard of covert panic reactions.

Some Parental Misfits. Here one encounters the excessively permissive father who tells his son, "We don't care what you do as long as no one gets in trouble," perhaps adding hypocrisy ("just don't disgrace us"); the father steeped in erroneous beliefs ("it's a biologic need at this age"); and the one who regales his growing son with tales of his own erotic exploits, sometimes including extramarital ventures—subconsciously urging the boy to follow in his steps. To encourage such license is counter to all principles of juvenile psychology. The midteen-ager almost certainly experiences relatively more anxiety than fun in connection with his more unbridled erotic exploits. To his elders he looks for restraining gestures as well as an attitude of reassurance with respect to sexual manifestations. When he is egged on instead and feels that he cannot show that he is less of a man than seems to be expected of him, noxious conflicts tend to ensue.

Also maladapted is the mother whose sex explanations to a daughter may consist of a "you will get your surprise" coupled perhaps with oft-repeated laments that "men are beasts," with hints at her own frigidity or father's brutality and demandingness. Ideally, sex education does not stress the dangerous or the wicked in sex, nor does it resort to excessively unrealistic appeals ("think that every girl is someone's sister"; "help the frail girls preserve themselves").

Earlier Social Experimentation. At the young end of the teens, mothers of girls increasingly countenance, possibly even press for, earlier and earlier social experimentation and demonstrations of feminine appeal, forcing those unready for it into endeavors for which their rate of maturation has not as yet fitted them. Instinctively, slower-maturing youngsters protect themselves; the snack bar at dances may be a sanctuary to retire to; exaggerated tales of erotism may bring the parents' stern veto; or unready girls may eat themselves into overweight or a recrudescence of acne, or otherwise manage to make themselves temporarily ungainly so that they can rationalize their unfashionable fear of boys more acceptably to themselves.

Another manifestation is increasingly early steady dating. The practice sometimes leads to fairly early sexual intimacy. Occasionally one finds such couples quite evidently merely playing the role of people in love, but the intimacies are quite real. However, a desire for date security and romantic twinship often is also involved, and there is some evidence that such youngsters do steadier work in school.

SEX EDUCATION IN SCHOOL

The value of sex education in high school has by no means been established. Knowledge is not wisdom, and the programs do not seem to influence sex behavior. Home, ideally, is the place for sex education but many parents are poorly equipped; besides, during the teens even greatly worrisome concerns cannot always be comfortably discussed with parents, even though this is a traditional obligation of a father toward a son, and of a mother toward her daughter. At any rate, in view of the prevailing reality—probably no more than one fourth of parents today assume this responsibility—reliance on other sources (e.g., church, school or clinic rap sessions) is a practical need. The churches, through their Sunday schools,

---

FAMILY LIFE EDUCATION

Position statement on Family Life Education in the Schools (condensed).
American Psychiatric Association

"Responsibility . . . must be divided between the home and the school. Parents do not always have the competence to assume sole responsibility; they need the assistance of the school resources. It is recommended that:

    a. Parents, clergy, and school-related health professionals . . . be involved with educators in developing the curriculum.

    b. The rationale (and justification) of the curriculum (content and objectives) be clarified by open discussion until rational doubts in the minds of the participating adults are allayed.

    c. Student representation in planning, in the junior and senior high school grades, helps achieve effectiveness.

    d. Sex education be part of a more extensive curriculum dealing with other health, family life, and community life matters.

    e. Teachers be selected on the basis of ability to deal with the subjects . . . with poise, honesty, scientific accuracy, and matter-of-factness and after having been prepared to lead small group discussions.

    f. Individualization be permitted through voluntary participation in this curriculum and through provision of individual counseling if and when the need arises.

    g. Evaluations and feedback be built into the plans and teaching methods."

Approved by the Board of Trustees,
December 1969
(Full text: Amer. J. Psychiat.
126:1551, 1970)

---

do not at present seem to reach the most exposed youngsters at the most vulnerable ages, although some are engaged in a major effort in this direction, and Catholic parochial high schools have always included programed sexual education in their curricula. Some religious counselors to older adolescents are abandoning a spiritual appeal in favor of a more down-to-earth one—"this hybrid approach has attracted very few" (Blaine Jr.). Teen clinics, many sponsored by Planned Parenthood/World Population and contraception-oriented, are spreading quite rapidly. In a typical program, boys and girls may drop in after school, participate in group discussion on sex matters, then see a counselor, if desired, be examined including routine VD testing, and provided with contraception (Goldsmith).

Opposition. Actual opposition to school sex education chiefly revolves around the philosophy of approach: there are objections to the belief of some that the approach to sexual matters should be dispassionate; that teachers should not impose their own morality views but let youngsters reach their own conclusions; and that, in fact, there is no universally established norm of sexual behavior. Those in opposition believe that adults unwilling to face the moral issue and take a moral position should not be allowed to instruct on such matters; and that youngsters will take their cue from a respected instructor who treats the subject of sex as beyond moralistic considerations and without reference to a spiritual dimension, thus contributing to the undermining of family values based on Judeo-Christian ethics. Less reasonably parents have feared that school sex education courses will lead to increased sexual experimentation by being received as a kind of how-to-do-it course—too specific, too early and too stimulating; that classroom programs are contrary to the normal intimate nature of sexuality; and that schools are illicitly pushing to take over an educative function belonging in the home.

However, most observers with substantial interest in the area believe that the needs of youth in our time are best served if the school curriculum of the teen-ager does not turn its back on the realities of sexual growing and functioning (Cavanagh, Gadpaille, Mathis, B. Mead, Sands, others).

Teaching VD in High School. Gonorrhea, now officially classed as an epidemic-out-of-control, is today a disease largely spread by teen-agers of both sexes. Although knowledge of VD does not seem to reduce its inci-

---

THE SEX EDUCATION TEACHER

The course really depends on the teacher. If he gets embarrassed, forget it; you may as well study plants or something. BONNIE H., *High School Student*

Until competent teachers with high moral integrity can be properly trained and until guidelines for proper supervision can be established, I am opposed to such a program in the school curriculum. F. F. ROYAL, M.D.

In the public schools, who are the teachers? Physicians as a whole have not distinguished themselves in their understanding of sexual matters. R. R. PARLOUR, M.D.

Most teachers don't give any arguments for continence. Nobody believes in it. The teachers are cowards. BENGT N., *High School Student* (Sweden)

Many teachers are well equipped, even have special competence, others unfortunately are poorly informed or emotionally unprepared. Each has to develop his own approach to the subject out of his own inner feelings and convictions. All teachers should know basic facts, but they may find it useful to refer to an expert. HELEN SOUTHARD, *Consultant on Sex Education*, Natl. Board of YWCA

Why bring in a doctor to discuss the reproductive system, as if other people didn't understand it—we make it look like a big deal. *A Teacher*

dence, ignorance of VD has been shown to contribute further to its spread, and mightily so. In some urban schools, with practically half the school population infected at any one time, teaching about the venereal diseases becomes a purely defensive undertaking. And once VD is taught, there is no point in playing down the fact that it is spread by sexual intercourse which, in turn, opens the gates wide for other sexual topics. However, even with skilled teaching there remains, among many of the socially most overexposed youngsters, a puzzling lack of motivation to protect themselves, an indifference to the possible consequences of infection. If remnants of the old penicillin faith are a major cause of this, as some observers think they are, somebody obviously must come forward and teach these

---

A HEALTH AND FAMILY LIFE COURSE IN SCHOOL

Format. Most often recommended 6 to 8 weekly sessions of a separate course. Sometimes preferred: at night. 20–30 students. No assignments, texts, examination. Trained teacher. Relaxed, informal atmosphere. Realism, but no vulgarity.

When Taught. Seventh to twelfth grades. In high risk areas emphasis on earlier years for benefit of prospective dropouts.

Course Name. Life Science, Family Living, Marriage and Family, Health and Family Life Education, Personal Health, Community Health, etc.

Sexes. Segregate boys and girls first 3 to 5 sessions. Girls more comfortable in same-sex group on intimate hygiene subjects. In mixed groups both masturbation and homosexuality have been found deadening, embarrassing subjects.

Parents' Consent. Attendance voluntary. Parents to preview programs by invitation. Best to modify or omit what is objected to even by a few rather than risk polarization and endanger project. Community leaders, political or others, probably need to be heeded; cooperation with media important. Some districts and schools require parents' written consent; others merely solicit cooperation.

Visitors. Almost always discouraged, to prevent self-consciousness. But exceptions such as father-son, mother-daughter nights in seventh, eighth or ninth grades (e.g., a film, then question period; parents in rear). Can open new channels of communication.

Subject Matter. Audiovisual presentation or short formal talk, followed by question period (live or written). Some prefer neutral base subject (heredity, infant care, age at marriage) and let it expand. Talks by guest lecturers need to be followed by question period to dispel misunderstandings. Biologic matter is organized either "upward" (ovulation-sperm entry including organs and coitus—conception—pregnancy—childbirth—infancy—puberty—social factors—marriage); or centrifugally (female organs including menses, puberty, childbirth, their difference from boys', functions of each, etc.)

young people about penicillin-resistant gonococci, asymptomatic carriers, symptoms and so forth. This is not the old fashioned scare-tactics approach designed to ensure continence, but tendered in a spirit of prevention, helpfulness, and immediate concern.

Contraceptive Teaching in High School. Ideally, the premarital pregnancy rate is controlled by attitude. But where attitude is out of control, there opens up the need to bring something—anything—to bear to ward

---

CLASSROOM SEX QUESTIONS

A sampling of sex questions asked of teachers in school, viva voce or via anonymous question box, by boys and girls aged 11 to 16, collected from across the U.S. Illustrates prevailing range of pre- and early adolescent preoccupation with sex.

Does too much sex make your glands old?

Are homos really women inside?

How does the pill against babies work?

How can one make breasts grow?

When a girl gets raped can she have babies later?

What happens when a man and woman can't get apart?

When kids fool around in a car is that against the law?

Is sex good or bad for pimples?

How much can a girl let a boy do?

Why do some women try to get rid of their babies?

What is a douche for?

Why are some girls boy-crazy?

What is syphilis?

How do you know that you have a disease?

Can a man like 60 or so still do it?

Why do women die sometimes when they have children?

What is it if a man is a man and a woman?

Why do some men try to hurt little girls?

Does the baby stand inside the mother?

Do people get a baby every time they do it?

Is intercourse the same as sex?

What is eloping?

Why does a woman use cotton?

Is it OK to have intercourse while the girl is having her period?

What is a condom?

Can you get syphilis from a toilet seat?

Can you get pregnant in your sleep?

Do boys have periods like girls?

How can a girl be popular with boys?

What is a prostitute?

What should a girl do on her first date?

How can you tell if you're pregnant?

How does the baby go to the bathroom in the mother?

Do girls have wet dreams?

What is the test the doctor makes?

Can a woman have a child when she is not married?

Is love possible without sex?

Can a person get pregnant the first time you have intercourse?

How can you tell when a person is homosexual?

Is VD more common among poor people?

off these often tragic situations. Logic points to the contraceptive devices. Although it is apparent by now that devices cannot completely control the unwed teen pregnancy rate either, in some urban schools with huge pregnancy rates among 14- to 16-year-old girls, device teaching, at least the fundamentals and where to turn for additional help, would seem to be a realistic need. Disadvantaged girls were found to be less likely to drop out of school and become public welfare dependents if they had contraceptive protection. Emphasis on moralizing would make much of sex education irrelevant to the thinking of these overexposed young people. Nor does age probably matter much here ("if they're big enough to do it, they're old enough to get shown how to stay out of trouble.").

On the other hand, and in less vulnerable areas, contraceptive information tendered to teen-agers of high school age has its undesirable aspects. It offends those whose basic decision (for abstinence) is anchored in their parents' trust ("It's like Dad saying, 'I know you wouldn't do anything, but here is a prophylactic just in case' "). It perturbs those already struggling with problems of instinctual control ("she loves me and I love her, and we are really trying not to do anything, and here comes this nurse and tells us . . ."). To the labile and suggestible young person information may equal license ("they practically told us it's O.K., as long as I didn't get knocked up"). Also, the teacher of an official course—by role a parent figure—may appear confusingly permissive, even conniving about something which by deeply embedded covenant a parent figure must be opposed to: unpostponed libidinal acting out. It tends to pervert the parent image which is basically asexual at this age.

PREMARITAL SEX STANDARDS (DUVALL'S GROUPING)

1) Chastity before Marriage an Absolute Requisite. Their number today probably about equals that of youngsters pressing for unlimited sexual freedom; they are the two minorities at the extremes of the spectrum. In many the negative motivations of fear and deterrence continue to prevail, of pregnancy, VD, hellfire, or because when found out there descends on them the overwhelming censure of parents, school, clergy, relatives, even police (Pomeroy). The more insecure may seek professional counsel, even under a cover problem, when a psychosocially tantalizing, conflict-laden situation arises: should they, should they not? By rule of thumb: if they have to ask, the answer is no. Highly permissive colleges, declining to act in loco parentis, help pressurize unready youngsters (e.g., via all-night dormitory visiting privileges). It deprives them of important protection in curbing their own impulses or in marching to their own, slower drummer.

2) Chastity of Women but not of Men (Double Standard). The classical tenet here imposes that every girl is to keep herself pure (i.e., virginal) for her future husband. It implies social penalties for girls who engage freely (e.g., "As a man I set my own standards, but when I marry it will be to a virgin"). In our time this extreme position is an anachronism. Besides, meaningful interest in the physical intactness of the hymen is eroding rapidly in much of the Western world, and there is growing impatience with hypocritical compromise solutions such as the old demi-viergism (Fr.) (i.e., "everything except all the way"). Nevertheless there continues to be greater tolerance for premarital sexual experimentation on the part of the male than of the female, and only one or two love affairs by the girl are generally tolerated, says Reiss. The rebellion against traditional masculine sexual prerogatives (male chauvinism, machismo) keeps mounting, but of late the possibility of a biologic basis for the latter has again arisen. Based on the study of primates, newer embryologic knowledge and a variety of clinical observations, it is being increasingly held that male sexuality, being but a chromosome-imposed variant wrested from the unwavering basic femaleness of the embryonic organism (see p. 4), is brittle and easily disrupted. There are indications that it is important for males to "learn" as well as reinforce the use of adult sexuality between puberty and young adulthood. In human males, abstinence past the early twenties is associated with an increased rate of subsequent sexual difficulties.

HIGHLIGHTING ADOLESCENT NOW MORES

I blow him. I quiet the beast the least messy way I know of so I can be with him and talk friend to friend. I long for later (marriage), sometimes. *A college coed*

It's quite fantastic how some kids are not motivated to prevent pregnancy and VD. DR. M. TOTTIE, *Swedish and W.H.O. VD expert*

The best guarantor of a young girl's virtue is a strong, watchful father and strong brothers whose mother has instilled a strong sense of family in them. *Author of Italian descent*

That sex evolution thing—flesh trips, stud tripping, making it in the sack. Mess around and be a big man. You're not supposed to be hung up on morality. Nobody wants to be a kid anymore. Lots of kids are plenty frightened. Sex is to show you really like somebody, so if you have a lot of sex it means you care for a lot of people. Lots of kids get hurt and do some hurting. *Teen-age musings audited by* PROF. THOMAS J. COTTLE, 1972

I wouldn't ball a fellow if I didn't really love him enough to marry him; it wouldn't be right. *High school girl with several past affairs*

Suppressing sexual expression leads to ogling topless night club waitresses or buying pornography. *College*

Only a nitpicker would make an issue over a little bit of membrane. *High school*

3) Sexual Freedom for Lovers. "We love each other, we know and understand each other, sex is simply an expression of our love for each other." Premarital intercourse is approved by many if it occurs in a stable and affectionate relationship. Others restrict it to an exclusive, committed relationship. "In some very complete relationships it seems wrong to hold back something you want the other to have, that you really want to give him." Or, "Why should we wait for marriage, frustrate each other? Why deny ourselves the pleasure? Society will not suffer from it." There are no reliable data to show that premarital sex either improves or lessens the chances of a good marriage.

4) Sexual Permissiveness. Premarital sex is not a loaded issue today. Sex serves young people as a defense against alienation; to express and confirm identity; to escape depersonalization; to gain comfort, security, reassurance, relaxation; to obtain companionship and sharing; or simply for pleasure or fun. "It is the best way to get to know somebody." Sought more often today is a twin, not a sweetheart or lover; security is found with someone who resembles oneself closely (Greenson). Hopefully, self-assertion grows through sexuality. "The necessity to cling rigidly to a set of fixed attitudes is a sign of anxiety. Better to grow in the judgments that are made, to make choices." Slum Negro boys and girls often engage in sexual relations as a test and symbol of their maturity, and their ability to be in the swing of things. Over time some develop appreciation of sex, but competitive and exploitative attitudes on both sides often make sex relations a tense and uncertain matter (Rainwater).

5) Sexual Irresponsibility. It is less sexual love than it is genital sex in the service of the contemporary triad of fun morality, libidinization of the life style and the quest for instant gratification. A composite of pronouncements by free love advocates: "The only tests of sexual conduct should be, do I want to do it? Does it hurt anyone else? It's a human right to go to bed with someone you like without being insulted by society. . . . Chastity is just a sacred cow without relevance for the swinging youth of the 70's. . . . If you're big enough, you're old enough. . . . Abstinence is a sign of neurotic inhibition in our day and age." One hazard is that those testing out the limits of experience tend to escalate into stimulant and other drugs, and into deviate patterns on which some of them may become hung up or impaled.

ADOLESCENCE AND CONTRACEPTION

Physician Prescribing. Many states have lowered the age of consent which governs marriage and statutory rape (p. 261) but this age does not necessarily constitute the age of majority which governs medical consent. No medico-legal problems regarding contraceptive prescribing exist where the physician deals with a person of major age; or with a minor who has written parental or guardian's consent (signing the routine college medical consent form is considered insufficient); with a married (emancipated) minor; and wherever state law specifically permits care of minors on their own consent. Many physicians also modify their attitude in women with a history of previous pregnancy and in parous women; in those engaged but deferring marriage; and in those living in an established pattern of common-law marriage.

Physician Opposed. Prescribing and supervising contraception for single minors is not a generally accepted part of medical practice. The statutes and the courts have clearly defined the conditions for assuming majority; they also restrain a minor from assuming responsibility for her own decisions. A physician cannot be expected to make such an invalid decision by a minor the basis of his offer of treatment without parental consent. Nor is it the physician's place to condone or facilitate an immoral act by prescribing for an unmarried minor, nor would he wish to potentially damage a patient by abetting promiscuity in those lacking control of their impulses. Acceding to these youngsters demeans the professional relationship and makes the physician a partner in their transgressions. Besides, testing the limits of the permissible is not part of the educational experience (e.g., in college). What some girls making such a request are

---

**CONTRACEPTIVE SERVICES FOR UNMARRIED MINORS
POSITION OF THE AMERICAN MEDICAL ASSOCIATION**

In June 1971 the House of Delegates adopted the following Report which reads, in part and in essence, as follows: Physicians may proceed in prescribing contraceptive materials and devices to unmarried minors in accordance with their best medical judgement and discretion. They are advised to observe closely the following safeguards: 1) Make efforts to obtain consent from parents wherever possible. 2) Consider the patient's total situation; obtain and record a full case history. 3) The medical record should reflect the basis for the physician's judgment that pregnancy would constitute a more serious health hazard than birth control measures. 4) The minor to sign consent indicating awareness of the nature, problems and consequences of the contraceptive recommendations. 5) Insist on follow-up whenever indicated.

The above was, in part, based on a review by the A.M.A. General Counsel which concluded that "liability for providing contraception . . . appears to be unlikely" (JAMA *216*:2059, 1971).

---

really asking is that the physician approve their having sexual intercourse and to make a judgment for them. Even if his attempts to dissuade the girl are unsuccessful, at least he has not encouraged her in a direction which she may later regret.

In Favor. A single woman, even if of minor age, seeking contraceptive protection from the physician, is not seeking advice about morality, but medical help. In college, for instance, each female student is free to decide for herself whether or not she should have contraception; sex is a private concern of the individual student. The physician, recognizing the serious hazard of abortion or illegitimate birth, has the responsibility to respond with the best medical help the state of the art permits. He must protect the girl from herself while she is immature or experimenting; somewhat later he must protect her from having a quasi-permanent relationship upended because of unwanted birth. He may counsel her towards a more chaste pattern of behavior, if in his judgment this is indicated, but he must not enforce a code of morality by threat of pregnancy. By turning her down, he also helps create a medical problem; some even say that the physician who fails to give protection to a single woman whom he knows to have intercourse regularly is negligent, shirking his responsibility and malpracticing. His only concern should be how to motivate those not using contraception. Also, no one has yet devised a way to eliminate sex from the campus, and the realistic thing to do is to eliminate some of the consequences. Besides, the patient can, and does, go elsewhere. It does not behoove a physician to get hung up on contraception for minors on the basis of fear of being prosecuted, or sued, or exposed to parental anger. In the 1970s the momentum of the law has gone beyond the old concept that parental consent is necessary to guard a minor child's rights and shield her from injury. (Ayd, Blaine Jr., Calderone, Farnsworth, Reiss, others).

Failure to Use. The newer medical technology has shifted most contraceptive responsibility to the female. Among single persons most men today believe that they can assume that a female consenting to sexual relations has "taken care." However, among relatively untutored teen-agers (e.g., the younger female undergraduates on college campuses) the newer birth control methods have been found to be unpopular. One reason, apart from the usual concern about complications, may be that the most reliable methods are physician-controlled which may conjure up images of pelvic examinations, history-taking, records, appointments, perhaps searching questions, all of which may deter some girls. Besides, being on pills or carrying a diaphragm implies overeagerness, ever-readiness, perhaps promiscuity. It would also deprive the consenting girl of such possible rationalizations as being unexpectedly swept off her feet, or of having been forced into the experience. Some girls even omit—hide—available precautions so that they can pretend spontaneity in certain situations. They thus subject themselves to the hazard of relying on an inexperienced boy who may not know how comfortably to buy or borrow condoms when the occasion is at hand, or who may be too high on beer or marijuana to remember to withdraw before ejaculating, or who has not yet developed this kind of control. These girls often reassure themselves blithely with the existence of the morning-after pill, or the new ambulatory mini-abortion. In others, failure to use contraception may be caused by ignorance, non-availability, opposition in principle, personal carelessness, apathy, or a belief that pregnancy is something unreal and remote which happens only to others (Sorensen).

Medically, oral contraceptives are rarely prescribed before age 16 (i.e., before the cycle is firmly established) and progestin administration presupposes that bone growth is completed. In the midteens one pill-free cycle is often interposed every 6 months.

SOME BOOKS FOR THOSE DEALING WITH TEEN-AGERS

Breasted, M.: Oh! Sex Education! New York, Praeger, 1970

Brown, T. E.: A Guide for Christian Sex Education of Youth. New York, Association Press, 1968

Burt, J. J., and Brower, L. A.: Education for Sexuality. Concepts and Programs for Teaching. Philadelphia, Saunders, 1970

Fletcher, J.: Situation Ethics: The New Morality. Philadelphia, Westminster Press, 1966

Kirkendall, L. A., and Whitehurst, R. N. (eds.): The New Sexual Revolution. New York, D. W. Brown, 1971

Offer, D.: The Psychological World of the Teen-ager. A Study of Normal Adolescent Boys. New York, Basic Books, 1969

Rubin, I., and Kirkendall, L. A. (eds.): Sex in the Adolescent Years: New Directions in Guiding and Teaching Youth. New York, Association Press, 1968

Schulz, E. D., and Williams, S. R.: Family Life and Sex Education. Curriculum and Instruction. New York, Harcourt, Brace and World, 1968

Singer, L. J., and Buskin, J.: Sex Education on Film. A Guide to Visual Aid Programs. New York, Teachers College Press, 1971

Sorensen, R. C.: Adolescent Sexuality in Contemporary America. New York, World Publishing Co., 1973

Usdin, G. (ed.): Adolescence: Care and Counseling. Philadelphia, Lippincott, 1967

SOME BOOKS FOR THE TEENS

Bauer, W. W.: Moving into Manhood. New York, Doubleday, 1963 (early and midteens)

Borowitz, E. B.: Choosing a Sex Ethic. The Evolution of Jewish Morality. Schocken, 1970 (mid-late and late teens)

Butcher, R. L., et al.: Teen Love, Teen Marriage. New York, Grosset & Dunlap, 1966 (early and midteens)

Cain, A. H.: Young People and Sex. New York, John Day, 1967 (mid-late and late teens)

Demarest, R. J., and Sciarra, J. J.: Conception, Birth and Contraception. New York, McGraw Hill, 1970 (late teens)

Duvall, E. M.: Why Wait Till Marriage? New York, Association Press, 1965 (middle and late teens)

Hettlinger, R. F.: Living with Sex. The Student's Dilemma. New York, Seabury Press, 1966 (late teens)

Johnson, E. W.: Sex—Telling It Straight. Philadelphia, Lippincott, 1970 (mid-teens)

Landers, A.: Ann Landers Talks to Teen-agers about Sex. New York, Fawcett, 1968 (middle and late teens)

Levinsohn, F.: What Teenagers Want to Know. Chicago, Budlong Press, 1967 (middle teens)

Lorand, R. L.: Love, Sex and the Teenager. New York, Macmillan, 1965 (middle and mid-late teens)

Pierson, E. C.: Sex is Never an Emergency. A Candid Guide for College Students. Philadelphia, Lippincott, 1970 (late teens)

Roy, R., and D.: Honest Sex. A Revolutionary Sex Ethic by and for Concerned Christians. New York, World Publ. Co., 1968 (late teens)

Sarrel, P., and Student Committee on Human Sexuality (Yale Univ.): The Student Guide to Sex on Campus. New York, New American Library, 1970 (late teens)

Southard, H. F.: Sex Before Twenty. New Answers for Youth. New York, E. P. Dutton, 1967 (middle and late teens)

FOR INFORMATION ON AUDIO-VISUAL MATERIAL

Association Films Inc., New York
British Film Institute, London W.1
Canadian Film Institute, Ottawa, Ont.
Encyclopedia Britannica Corp., Chicago
McGraw Hill Films, New York
H. Newenhouse Distrib., North Brook, Ill.
Siecus (Sex Inform. and Educ.), New York
and the Audio-Visual Centers of many Universities

CHAPTER 8

Sexual Concerns of the Second Decade

Nocturnal Seminal Emission — First Menstruation — Erotic Daydreaming — Petting — Exposure to Pornography — Juvenile Masturbation — Juvenile Homoerotism.

NOCTURNAL SEMINAL EMISSION

(Involuntary Emission. Vernacular: wet dream. Antiquated: pollution)

The first nocturnal emission occurs most frequently when the boy is between 12½ and 14 years old. Although the physiologic ability to ejaculate precedes puberty (i.e., the theoretical moment when mature spermatozoa are first produced) by at least several months, a continent boy probably has his first nocturnal emission only about 1 year after the ejaculating mechanism is ready. In practice, a majority of boys experience their first ejaculation through masturbating or companionate sex play rather than in the involuntary manner. Yet, the boy who masturbates moderately still seems to experience nocturnal emissions; in fact, it is believed that his first one occurs slightly earlier than it would have had he been continent.

Once begun, nocturnal discharges recur periodically throughout the sexual life span, at an average frequency of once every 10 to 35 nights, provided that the individual's voluntary sex activity is scant or nil. During the teens emissions on 2, perhaps more successive nights are entirely possible, at times even in non-continent boys. Acute illness or malaise may delay the rhythm, while intense erotic excitation sometimes hastens it. The effects of strenuous physical exercise or overfeeding on the frequency of involuntary emissions are uncertain.

Nocturnal emissions most usually occur during a period of REM sleep without any manipulation of the penis. The member erects during an erotic dream, and orgasm is reached while the individual is still asleep. Occasionally the sleeper will awaken just before orgasm sets in and feels impelled, often in a half-sleep, to produce the climax by a few masturbatory motions. Most individuals awaken after the orgasm has occurred, at least for a brief period, but sleep may be resumed promptly. In the morning there may be amnesia for the event and the stained nightclothes or damp bedsheet may come as a surprise.

Every boy should be prepared for the impending onset of nocturnal emissions by the father sometime during active pubescence. He should stress that all boys have these emissions at this age; that they are entirely natural and harmless; and that they are not under the control of the will and thus in no way constitute an unchaste act. The father should be cautioned against making remarks such as, "It is normal unless it happens too often."

An unprepared boy may fear, upon his first nocturnal emission, that he has injured himself internally in some way through his masturbating or such. He may have heard that loss of semen weakens the mind or hinders development. Some boys simply believe that they have been enuretic when they have had an emission. Others are greatly afraid that the parents will discover the evidence in the morning and that they will not understand or will even criticize the mess he made. Some boys dread that the mother will discover the evidence of their sexual activity; in this case the father, on first preparing the boy, should mention that mother is familiar with this occurrence and does not mind it. However, direct preparation or reassurance concerning seminal emissions by the mother seems inadvisable at this age, under most circumstances.

FIRST MENSTRUATION

(Menarche, Menstrual Onset. Generally: Menses. Catamenia. Vernacular: period, monthlies, sickness, my friend, curse, have rag on, being unwell, etc.)

The first menstrual period occurs most often at 12½ years of age, in mid-development. Variations in onset of a year or more either way are common. Throughout the civilized world the age at menarche has been steadily reduced for more than 100 years, although the trend may be slowing now (see also p. 97). In many girls a regular cycle is not established for up to 1 or 2 years after onset. The resulting skipping of menses can be a source of needless anxiety for the girl or her family. Usually, girls are not able to conceive during the months following menarche because all or many of the early periods are anovulatory.

Advance Notice. Every girl should be told well in advance by the mother what to expect, even if only to make certain that garbled childhood notions are corrected. Age 9 or 10 is not too early for this. Emphasis should be placed on the fact that this is not a real bleeding such as occurs in injuries, but that once every month, for many years, the female womb gets ready to receive a tiny egg. If this egg is not fertilized it passes out, together with the shedding of some superficial inner lining of the womb and a little blood, rarely more than 1 or 1½ ounces. A new nest is started by the body right away. Boys may be given the same information, but perhaps one or two years later in age. Menarche, even untutored, seems to usher in concern with privacy of the body and a period of several years of modesty with overtones of secretiveness in the young female. An unprepared girl may fear that she has injured herself internally (e.g., through masturbation), or that she has a disease; some have assumed that they are giving birth, having an abortion or bleeding rectally, and even enlightened girls have been known to look for glass or a nail in the toilet seat the first time.

Mother-daughter. Psychologically the mother is a major factor in shaping the girl's attitude toward her first and all future periods. A re-kindling of mother-daughter conflict occurs at this stage, and its labile physiologic equilibrium seems to be mirrored in emotional instability. Hostility, moody withdrawal or quarrelsomeness, despondency, a flurry of phobias or psychosomatic (often gastrointestinal) manifestations beset some girls here. Undue influence is exerted by the mother who talks much of sickness in connection with her menses, emphasizes how delicate a girl becomes at that time, or customarily takes to her bed or acts like an invalid; however, this is no longer believed to be the principal cause of perimenstrual discomfort; cultural factors appear to play a part also. Occasionally encountered are hostile and even cruel, vicious reactions to a daughter's menarche by a mother who is an emotionally arrested individual or else a conspicuously paranoid personality, perhaps an untreated psychotic. The impact of this on the girl is severe at this vulnerable junction, more so if there was no preparation for the event, as is apt to happen here. Such girls respond to menarche with unrelieved feelings of helplessness or a sense of abandonment, possibly with panic; others are hastened on the road to social rebelliousness, including delinquency.

Juvenile Dysmenorrhea. Primary pain at menstruation is a spasmodic cramping of the uterus which starts with the first day of the flow. It appears only in ovulatory periods, thus is largely absent until about age 15. It worsens to peak occurrence at about 18, then diminishes gradually until in many cases it ceases in the early or midtwenties. It is rare after the first pregnancy. Five per cent of young females are disabled by pain during the first day or two. The cause remains obscure, although several theories exist. To be differentiated is secondary (organic) dysmenorrhea in which pain is produced by organic pelvic conditions such as endometriosis, pelvic stenosis or—rare in the midteens—fibroids, pelvic inflammatory disease, etc. The congestive type of dysmenorrhea, the precursor of the adult premenstrual tension and bloating syndrome, occurs much less often in the teens. Here the discomfort precedes the flow by several days; pain is less severe, diffuse rather than localized, and irritable or moody tearfulness may co-exist. The syndrome is related to progesterone sensitization, and response to treatment is better than in the cramping type. The role of emotional factors and faulty attitudes in dysmenorrhea is not well defined, but the girl who seems to follow in her mother's footsteps and the girl with much ignorance of the reproductive apparatus—a frequent cause of symptom aggravation—can often be spotted by the examining physician. The approach to treatment includes that he elucidate, reduce fears of abnormality and advise the mother. Experienced observers have advised that the youngster be examined without the mother present the first time, and that in major pain cases no mental probing be attempted, but that 1 or 2 anovulatory cycles, with bleeding but without pain, be induced to prepare a more receptive setting for subsequent counseling.

Athletics and Menstruation. In an international survey of top female Olympic athletes (track and field, gymnastics, swimming, volley ball) reported in 1967 about one third continued training during menses, more than half trained sometimes and sometimes not, while 12 per cent always interrupted training, notably the swimmers; however, all took part in all actual meets when menstruating. In the same group menstrual disturbances when training or competing—stronger bleeding, longer duration, abdominal pain—were absent in 50 per cent, present in 41 per cent, while 7.7 per cent had an improved menstrual course (Zaharieva). However, as regards average teen-agers it is widely agreed that no major curtailment of ordinary gym activities is necessary when menstruating. As regards heavy athletic training and competition it has been discouraged, especially on the first day or two, for such categories as swimming, diving, rowing, tennis, skiing and gymnastics, while in lighter sports only those may compete who are in perfect gynecologic health and whose athletic performance does not tend to suffer during the period (Erdelyi). Long hikes, heavy lifting, basketball and similar exertions are also best avoided on the first or second day. Especially in girls aged 15 to 17, athletic overtraining during menses is believed capable of inducing some irregularities in the cycle. On the other hand, a tendency to dysmenorrhea has been relieved by regular, moderate exercising. Athletic performance efficiency seems to be best just after, and lowest just before, the period; in adolescents it is diminished in sports requiring prolonged effort (tennis, rowing, etc.).

Girls need reassurance that in swimming and bathing no blood oozes through an internal tampon. There is continued uncertainty as to whether athletic participation benefits painful menstruation in juveniles; it can, however, be said that fewer athletes seem to have primary dysmenorrhea than is found in a randomized population, but that athletics do not seem to cure an established pain pattern.

SANITARY PROTECTION

Two principal types in use today: disposable perineal pads or napkins pinned front and back to a small belt; and disposable tampons for intravaginal absorption of menstrual fluid. The internally worn tampons, dating to the 1930's and praised as an advance in hygiene (Israel) have encountered some emotional resistance and suspicion of their possible ill-effects—none established, almost all disproved—which are disappearing only now. Some women with copious early bleeding use a pad the first two days, then switch to tampons. Malodor of the discharge develops only on contact with air, thus is absent in tampons; deodorant powder should be applied to pads.

Objections raised to use of tampons by young girls:

Blocks menstrual flow from cervix (no merit; tampon's tip rests loosely in fornix, not against os)

Attention prematurely directed to vagina (True but neither premature nor undesirable)

Dilatation of juvenile vagina (not possible)

Causes erotic excitation (No merit. Tampon cannot be felt; also no known case)

Incomplete protection against external contamination (Bathwater does not enter tamponaded vagina; also, "contamination" not harmful as vagina is intact during menses)

Contributes to cervical erosion, dysplasia, cervicitis; worsens leukorrhea; interferes with puerperal healing of cervix (all disproved by well-controlled studies except some slight question regarding erosion)

Reflux of blood into peritoneal cavity; contributes to endometriosis (Reflux believed possible, may even be physiological at times, but tampon neither promotes nor impedes it. No known connection with higher incidence of endometriosis)

Destroys hymenal evidence of virginity (Some hymenal stretching occurs; hymenal tears highly unlikely with small-size tampon and lubrication of tip in beginning; 10% of adolescents believed unsuitable for tampons because of unusual consistency or patency of hymen)

EROTIC DAYDREAMING

(Erotic or Sexual Reveries)

The content of teenage reveries is often frankly sexual, but it is by no means exclusively so in the normal youngster. Many parents, teachers, and youth leaders regard daydreaming as undesirable, fearing it indicates undue preoccupation with sex or that it may lead to social isolation.

Theories. There are indications that daydreams are a possible manifestation of REM (p. 174) in the waking state, perhaps part of a 24-hour cycle of the circadian rise and fall of the level of certain hormones and neurotransmitter substances in the organism. One may further speculate that the daydream fulfills a protective purpose, as it absorbs and buffers some of the normal threshold anxiety of the pubescent as he (she) feels himself pushed toward new and unknown experiences, some inviting, some frightening. In daydreaming, the reality ahead, as yet vaguely perceived, is being pre-tested as it were; responses are rehearsed and rehashed, roles are tried on, and in the process the youngster experiments with and reconstructs his (her) image of himself.

Content. Girls' erotic fantasies often begin with role trying: a femme fatale, a devoted helpmeet, a noble prostitute; they then acquire intensely romantic overtones, the girl picturing herself in connection with wooing, being adored, eloping, being engaged, seduction or disdainful discarding until with the advent of puberty the daydreams tend to become increasingly more reality-centered and to relate to one or a succession of specific boys. Frankly voluptuous imageries participate in the pattern to varying degrees. In boys nonerotic daydreams greatly outnumber erotic ones during the earlier teens, but the latter tend to be more crudely sensuous. At the youngest, preteen level it may be a fantasy of having the reputation that every girl in the 6th grade would allow him to touch her breasts. Later it may be being feared as a sex fiend; or the awe his huge, tireless phallus inspires at an all-night orgy as his girls, rarely more than 3, try to pull him away from the food and his friends. Also normal in boys in our culture are voyeuristic and slightly sadistic fantasies, although they tend to wane as daydreams merge with normal masturbation fantasies. In most boys, daydreams abate at a somewhat later age than in girls.

Interference. Some youngsters quite obviously daydream more often and longer than their peers, and frequently at inappropriate times. They may or may not be socially withdrawn and awkward at the same time. Such inward-centered girls and boys are not necessarily beset by pressures too great for them nor emotionally disturbed, although this may of course be the case. Interference with such, or with any, daydreaming by exhortation, scolding or warning of its supposed dangers is inadvisable, nor should dream content be pried into by overanxious parents. Where daydreaming is obviously excessive or greatly protracted beyond its usual age limits, it occasionally presages a developing schizophrenic process. It is also important to differentiate anxious brooding about sexual matters from true erotic reveries: the feeling tone of the latter is either pleasurable or bittersweet, while that of worried brooding is persistently distressing.

PETTING

Necking. Preteeners as they grow out of the stage of party kissing games experiment with necking (theoretically "from the neck up") which is platonic in intent, an exploratory over-the-clothes groping with lip-kissing and hugging embraces. The maneuvers are often self-conscious, and rarely effect true sexual arousal, although the idea of doing this can be arousing in itself. The proceedings may follow an unwritten limit-setting code prevailing in a peer group, although a 12-year-old may boast of his lip-brushing and breast-fondling encounter as a "heavy session."

Petting. Soon after age 14 or 15 the socially accelerated, coitus-bound minority of girls and boys branches off in the surveys. But the majority experience of all (middle class?) high school couples, the 16- and 17-year-olds, is petting. It is generally under-the-clothes, and when "making out" becomes heavy it includes direct stimulation-to-climax of at least one partner's genitals by body appression (rarer today), by hand or, increasingly often today, by mouth.

At first there is little drive to work up to climactic intimacy. The boy is still largely experimenting with his masculine assertiveness; also, the knowledge that he is getting as far as other boys in his crowd is usually sufficient satisfaction. The mid-adolescent girl is still greatly preoccupied with her ability to attract and fascinate the male, and her ego tends to be satisfied with the boy's gesture of sexual demand. Consequently, their petting is usually self-conscious. Besides, her love interest, which may appear to be sensual, is often mainly romantic or impelled by curiosity, even if she may seem to want to touch and cling to the point of being provocative. This is how young people learn about their sex and the other side's sex. In the midteens a frank sexual response by the boy often comes as a shock and is rebuffed indignantly: the girl sets the limits, and she would not forego the privilege of setting these limits herself. However, what constitutes an acceptable degree of intimacy at various levels of interpersonal commitment seems to be a matter of mores and varies with the time and place (Broderick).

Group-psychological Factors also tend to keep midteen petting within bounds: an unwritten group code often prescribes what is allowable at dates. In girls, early blatant transgression of the code can bring social ostracism, because all the girls in the crowd feel cheapened if one of them misconducts herself grossly. Boys also tend to enforce group conformity at this age. They may tolerate boasts of rapid or complete intimacy if the girl is outside their own circle, but even then they tend to condone it only in boys whose physical development is noticeably advanced. However, among certain crowds maximal petting or even coitus may be the thing to do, and a youngster who is reluctant or unready for this may still feel compelled to participate because he is afraid of being considered different and because he wants to belong.

Petting and Marriage. In late adolescence petting, especially extended same-partner petting, is clearly a substitute for sexual intercourse which the couple eschew for their own reasons. Surveys have been inconclusive in predicting marriage success or failure for couples with extensive heavy-petting experience (Reevy; others). In the marriages of virgins any statistically predicted high rate of success probably occurs because they often also have other marriage-preserving virtues (Shope). To the extent that non-virgins, male or female, have these same attributes, their marital expectations would be equally as good. Besides, the promiscuously petting technical virgin (demivierge, Fr.) to whom petting is "anything-except-all-the-way", is notoriously difficult to categorize in any kind of survey.

Effects of Petting. Casual petting is not known to produce ill effects in males or females. But habitual extended petting of a couple (e.g., for a year or more) seems capable of interfering with their subsequent sexual responses in a proportion of cases. Petting goes straight to the target—to climax; it eliminates the "waste motion" of intercourse, but also its sharing. Physiologically the orgasm experience may be, but has not been proven to be, similar, but the total experience in affectionate intercourse probably differs. To the female partner especially, subsequent sex in the marriage bed has been disappointing at times: missing were the speed and one-track intensity of purposeful manipulation, the high excitement of exposing or groping for an erogenous zone with the clothes on. Such conditioning has not always been irreversible, but then again, in a proportion of cases it has been. Also, there is not usually more than one climax for the petting female, or there may be none. She may be intensely aroused and then left high and dry; symptoms of the chronic pelvic congestion syndrome (p. 412), the "engagement pelvis" of past generations, are reportedly still encountered in such girls. In boys, petting that frequently stops short of immediate orgasm produces testicular and perineal discomfort, symptoms of a minor subacute congestive vesiculoprostatitis. Delayed masturbatory climaxing 1 or 2 hours later, when the date is over, does not appear to afford the male the same degree of detumescent relief as it does in the female.

EXPOSURE TO PORNOGRAPHY

See also Pornography p. 461

Hazard and Non-hazard. An emotionally stable adolescent with a reasonably well balanced personality, a variety of interests, and freely communicating with his contemporaries is not likely to display more than a moderate, passing interest in pornography, although, of course, he would not be expected to turn away from it when an opportunity arises. There is no substantial evidence to prove or to disprove that his emotional and moral development would be impaired by normal obscene material, although there is every indication that it will not. However, this does not equally apply to the boy in midpuberal development who is of borderline stability (see below), nor to material which is massively morbid or "freakish" (deviant). The proportion of these youngsters cannot be estimated, nor is there a feasible way of limiting distribution of pornographic material to some youngsters while excluding others. There are, in fact, no dependable criteria for singling out the vulnerable individuals, just as no practicable censoring line can be drawn between normal pornography and escalated or specialized deviant material. It is this knowledge, or lack of knowledge, which furnishes the foundation for the doctrine that pornographic material is collectively hazardous to the juvenile mind.

Legislatures and courts almost everywhere have taken the view that it is especially the vulnerable among us who need protection even if they cannot be singled out. Also, not all parents possess the wisdom or ability to guard their vulnerable young. Thus the state, the law, must act in loco

---

PORNOGRAPHIC PACKET 1973

A packet of photographs approximately 3 × 4 inches recently purchased by a 15-year old boy in a town on the East coast. Price $6.00. A mixture of the normal and the pathologic, probably for "sampling."
Naked woman reclining, legs up and spread apart.
Same, with dressed man's exposed phallus being handled.
Same, with 2 naked men being tended.
Two naked girls side-by-side fondling each other.
A girl entwined with 2 men.
Naked teenage boy kneeling in front of dressed man mouthing latter's exposed phallus.
High-booted, spike-heeled woman stomping on man with erection.
Fettered nude woman, her breasts being cigarette-burned by male.
Woman masturbating with dildo being implored by fettered nude male.
Several others depicting groups, costumed tortures, etc.
P.S.   Almost all commercial pornography is aimed at men, except for a small specialized sadolesbian, etc. output.

---

parentis. The power of the state, said the U.S. Supreme Court in 1944, to regulate and protect the conduct of children surpasses the scope of its authority over adults. In practice, the law must protect the young from having obscenity thrust upon them through the mails or through open public display.

Some Vulnerables. In a developing boy who already is struggling severely to achieve impulse control, pornography can implant distortions as to what constitutes a normal vita sexualis. In the hypersuggestible pubescent with low-reality testing endowment the repeated experience encourages worrisome preoccupation with unreal genital shape and size, or with what performance will be expected from him. The introverted or otherwise isolated adolescent with little opportunity for obtaining balancing information from his peers may develop morbid degrees of autoerotic conditioning while his level of erotic expectation rises. For those raised in affect-cold homes frequent pornographic perusal can make sex become even more depersonalized, more centered on genital pleasure, more separate from loving affection. The picturing of sexual excitement in conjunction with cruelty or debasement may expand and intensify sadomasochistic potential (e.g., in pet torturers). Similarly a case can be made for the borderline feminoid-homosexual boy overexposed to deviant pornography. The cases exist although the cause-effect relationship remains uncertain. Of some interest here are the Bandura and the Walters experiments on the acting-out of aggression after viewing aggression; also the theoretical possibility of deviate imprinting at some critical developmental point in the teens (e.g., through concentrated exposure to portrayal of the abnormal) (Egan). Pornography is least meaningful to predatory antisocial teenagers who may roam freely across the spectrum of deviant sexual opportunities, who do not read well, and to whom dirty pictures and comics merely mirror what they can grab from the environment almost any day or what has already been forced on them by older peers and others.

Free Access. The ideal of youth's free or self-selective access to reading material, including erotica and moderate pornography, promoted by some

---

TWO QUOTES

By exposing children to pornography we are exposing them to the expression of precisely those covert and lewd attitudes that sex education is designed to prevent. MARGARET MEAD in *Redbook Magazine*, March 1972

A society mustn't organize its moral system on the basis of what applies only to children. We must be permitted our adulthood, with all its risks. RICHARD GILMAN in *N.Y. Times* 1968

---

inspired educators and tested in a few residential schools, mainly in Europe, to date has remained just that: an ideal. These schools had and have offered an abundant variety of activities and alternative interests and a unique esprit of purpose not available elsewhere; also, co-ed raising in the second decade always has been a major anti-pornography factor. Free access is also practiced in a relatively small number of wholesomely, maturely nonrestrictive homes where eventually nothing these youngsters may reasonably desire to read or see is denied them. Where the results of such an upbringing are optimal, the youngster's interest in pornography tends to be perfunctory. Upbringing of this type is perhaps a fairly rare gift some parents have; and attempts to learn such attitudes may end in failure: a cramped overpermissiveness intermingled with covert but tense vigilance. "I simply can't stand it to know he's looking at all these nude women," such a misguided mother reports, "but he wouldn't respect me if I were old-fashioned." Such attempts at misunderstood modernism at all costs are best discouraged.

JUVENILE MASTURBATION

(Sexual self-stimulation, -excitation, -gratification. Autoerotism, autoerotic manipulation, automanipulation, autosexual practices. Ipsation. Unsuitable: self-pollution or -abuse, onanism, silent or solitary vice. Vernacular: play with self, solo-sex.)

Incidence. More than 90 per cent of normally developing boys masturbate at some time during the teens, according to best available indications. Peak onset of male juvenile ipsation is near 13; peak incidence is between the ages of 14 and 16; gradually thereafter they lose interest in self-gratification, some sooner, others not before they reach the midtwenties. There is less agreement on the incidence of masturbation in teen-age girls. The consensus seems to be that not less than one half of all girls masturbate at some stage in the second decade, while the incidence for females of all ages seems to be between 70 and 80 per cent. Peak incidence in girls is during the one or two years after menarche, but onset frequently occurs 1 or 2 years before menarche. Unlike in boys there seems to be no distinct pattern of cessation, but the practice is pursued irregularly until the time of marriage or other regular coital activity and not infrequently throughout sexual maturity and beyond.

Cause. One cannot properly speak of an external cause of masturbation as the practice develops largely in response to internal stimuli. With the puberal outpouring of sex steroids, intensified sensations and new powers, and with them new awareness, are experienced with which the young person feels impelled to experiment in some fashion. Learning can be by accidental self-discovery (e.g., in bed, or during a boring solitary task, or on waking near the climax of a wet dream); or else through a companion, an adult seducer or perusal of pornographic material. The significance of the mode of discovery for the future shaping of sexual expression is not known, but it is believed insignificant; contrary views have referred to special circumstances of initiation in the etiology of fetishism. A proportion of youngsters carry childhood masturbation directly into the second decade without major interruption. For others it actually is a relearning; they seem to discover it completely anew because of the teen-ager's normal amnesia for childhood situations.

Frequency of masturbation in normal boys varies, the average range probably being 2 to 20 times a month. Boys masturbate at fairly evenly spaced intervals; the spacing becomes more even as they grow older. At times several acts may be "bunched" within a short period, for instance during a temporary low in physical or mental well-being or, less often, due to outside erotic stimuli. In girls, bunching of masturbatory acts seems to be the rule rather than the exception, but unlike in the adult female, no relationship to menstrual periods seems to exist.

Where heavy bunching recurs with some frequency (e.g., 6 or more times per 24 hours in boys, 10 or more times per 24 hours in girls, including multiorgasmic acts) it may be evidence of major chronic anxiety; it can also accompany an intense homoerotic phase in either sex. Pathologically excessive masturbation is infrequent in the second decade, unless accompanied by psychotic symptoms such as excitement states, bizarre thoughts, major compulsive-ritualistic behavior, mutism, grimacing or undisguised masturbation. The use of marijuana in connection with or sometimes for the specific purpose of enhancing masturbatory sensation pertains more to the second half of the teens in both sexes (see also p. 443); it has little or no pathognomonic significance.

Method. Normal boys past puberty soon acquire a preferred technic which tends to remain fixed as long as masturbation is practiced. Most boys masturbate manually by enclosing the penile shaft and proceeding with a rubbing-pumping motion until orgasm occurs. The body position is incidental; he may lie on his back or side, stand, sit, kneel or squat. Nonmanual methods in boys are much less frequent but not rare: some boys, especially those who discovered masturbation by themselves, lie on their stomachs and rub the organ against mattress, floor or ground. Intercrural masturbation in supine or squatting positions may occur, or pseudocoitus into pillows, fabric, hay, etc. The more bizarre methods so often encountered in masturbating little boys (p. 52) are rare in the second decade. For masturbation utilizing animals see p. 493. Masturbatio reservata, abandoning the act just before climax because of fearful beliefs, has been known to be a habitual practice in boys with a recognizable obsessive-compulsive personality. Certain persistently bizarre methods forebode the development of psychosexual or mental pathology (e.g., compulsive use of female garments in the act, preparatory setting-up of elaborate mechanical contraptions, re-enacting hanging by the neck, simultaneous introduction of a finger in the rectum, or sticking or squeezing the organ during the act). Some boys with a long childhood illness or arrested puberal development may carry bizarre childhood methods of masturbation (p. 52) over into the second decade.

Girls in the second decade probably masturbate nonmanually as often or oftener than by handling the vulvoclitoral area. They may press or rub the vulva against the heel of the drawn-up foot (e.g., in a swing or rocking chair); or rub the vulva between the appressed thighs while sitting cross-legged; or hunch forward to bring the vulva against the seat edge (e.g., in a gently jarring vehicle). Psychic masturbation—climax reached without physical stimulation, by mere imagery or viewing—may be possible, or else it may unwittingly be accompanied by slight contractions of the adductor longus so that its tendon presses the labia majora against the clitoral shaft (Sherfey). Electrovibratory stimulation of the clitoris does not seem to be a characteristic teen-age practice. Self-stimulation of breasts and nipples (e.g., before a mirror) can excite some girls, occasionally to orgasm. Introduction of small objects into the urethral meatus is resorted to by some girls. Introducing a stimulatory object into the vagina is not characteristic of the second decade. Distinctly pathologic technics of self-gratification in adolescent girls have not been identified.

Fantasies. In most boys, and many girls, masturbation is normally accompanied either by picture viewing or by fantasies or imageries. The latter seem to be more intense and vivid the oftener masturbation is being practiced. In boys, the fantasies are of an erotic nature; with growing age they normally assume an increasingly heterogenital or coital character. In girls the fantasies more often resemble erotized daydreams: only during later adolescence are they frequently of a frankly sexual nature. They may, however, even then remain purely romantic (being admired, courted, petted, kissing, elopement, etc.). It is not certain what part, if any, cultural inhibitions play in keeping them so relatively asexual. Exploration of masturbatory fantasy content is a specialty tool in the diagnosis of sexual deviance; its significant portion occurs just preceding the climax. Most youngsters are defensive about discussing this, and it should not be attempted indiscriminately. It may be noted that in boys fantasies of beating, control and rape are not rare and do not necessarily signify an abnormal trend.

Ill Effects. We may disregard the more fantastic claims of past generations as to juvenile masturbatory ill effects which ranged from chorea to epilepsy, from stunted growth to the Insanity-ex-Onania of 19th century physicians; we may even disregard surviving beliefs by responsible adults considering autoerotic practices in young people abnormal, sinful, degrading, or evidence of moral weakness, disease or depravity. However, a body of hearsay beliefs concerning teen-age boys remains, and seems to defy all reassurance proffered in print or by counsel: that masturbation, the discharge of semen, will weaken the body and the stamina, cause impotence early in life, is evidence of intrinsic lack of will power and that the habit, once acquired, never stops. When a boy feels impelled to continue to practice what he perceives to be so dangerous, so shameful or so conspicuously stigmatizing, masturbation becomes the center of a guilty or self-contemptuous conflict with a sweltering overtone of fear which makes the teen years a hated experience.

The predisposed youngster becomes distraught, intensely worried and self-absorbed, or morose, furtive and irritable. His social behavior becomes increasingly timid and withdrawn, and his self-consciousness makes him afraid of girls. The more he withdraws the more lonesome he feels, and the more he will masturbate; and the more he masturbates, the more isolated he is likely to feel. As he struggles with his conflict each lapse into masturbation signifies defeat to him, and depressions are frequent. These, in turn, help further to impair his school work and add to his social difficulties. Depressions are also likely to increase his masturbating even further because of a transitory feeling of hopelessness ("it doesn't matter any more"), self-debasement and, perhaps, as an unconscious wish of self-injury ("raging against his own body"). One thus encounters the classic, severe case of the conflict-ridden juvenile masturbator. The ensuing difficulties may be somatized—headaches, various gastric symptoms, dizziness, photophobia, insomnia, perhaps precordial discomfort—or else they manifest themselves as symptoms of a slowly worsening juvenile anxiety-tension syndrome with its disquieting depressive interludes. Extreme manifestations of masturbatory contributions to psychiatric syndromes are infrequent today, but the phenomenon is by no means extinct.

Management. The troubled juvenile masturbator requires, as a minimum, sympathetic handling and reassurance. It is often surprising what immense relief some youngsters experience even today when given an opportunity to ventilate their masturbation problem with a sympathetic adult, even if they seem to be fully acquainted with society's views on the harmlessness of masturbation. Merely the frank, repeated use of the word masturbation or a similar term seems to rob the phenomenon of its aura of guilt and furtiveness for some boys. Attention may be directed to the temporary nature of the masturbatory phase. Urging troubled youngsters indiscriminately to practice self-denial is neither realistic nor perhaps even without some hazard in the presence of major anxiety. Those who are greatly reluctant to go into these matters should not be pressed; they may return spontaneously for counsel at a later time. Encouragement of socializing, more constructive use of free time, and appropriate physical activity are desirable as general measures, as is advice regarding unsuitable dietary habits including excessive use of coffee or other xanthine beverages or of spices. Examination of the genitalia rarely shows anything noteworthy as regards masturbation. Parents are best advised to disregard masturbation, not to look for it nor try to prevent it, but to be prepared to talk about it or other sex matters when information, advice or mere ventilation appear to be desired by the youngster.

JUVENILE HOMOEROTISM

Emotional attachments to members of the same sex are common in the first half of the second decade or somewhat later; sexual experimentation may or may not accompany this juvenile homoerotism. This is a normal phase of psychosexual development. In many cases—perhaps 50 per cent or more—the overt erotic aspects of this phase may be so little troublesome as compared with other nonsexual but more conspicuous transitions of this age that it passes unnoticed by the environment. The phase is self-limiting in normal individuals; where juveniles are segregated by sexes during most of the second decade, without opportunity to form hetero-erotic attachments and interests, the tendency may persist somewhat longer, and sometimes into the late teens (e.g., when highly frustrated and/or intoxicated, a homosexual act may be sought on impulse). This is most likely a residual manifestation and resembles the substitute indulgence of the isolated adult. The normalcy of juvenile homoerotism has been disputed by a few recent observers. It has been called phase-appropriate only in cultures with sexually repressive child rearing. It has also been called nonnormal, conflict-producing and hindering maturation (Ollendorff).

One needs to take issue with the overly narrow view—conducive to an ostrich-like attitude if applied to the second decade—that a diagnosis of clinical homosexuality cannot be made if no overt sex activity takes place. Some very demonstrably gay teen-agers, especially boys, elect to keep themselves chaste; or they abstain for a variety of other reasons; and the great inner turmoil of a homosexual youngster just "coming out" into overtness can be unmistakable even without overt acts.

Homoerotism in Boys. In boys the tendency is at its peak between 13 and 14 years of age, but variations occur. Most common are early close friendships between two contemporaries. At some point these are practically always at least slightly tinged with erotic overtones; this may or may not lead to mutual sexual acts. Where such practices occur, they are most often groping or casual, but even repeated, fairly intense mutual sex activity for a period of time can be considered within normal limits at this age.

Also encountered are emotional attachments to an older adolescent or young adult male. Most often this takes a form which is, or resembles, hero worship. The idol's admired qualities may be of an athletic, social, intellectual, financial, erotic, venturesome, artistic, criminal or any other desirable or undesirable nature. This depends largely on the boy's social milieu, the personality of his father and, of course, the youngster's own aspirations, needs and shortcomings. At least some homoerotic reveries are practically always spun around the person of the idol regardless of whether attachment is par distance or personal contact exists. These reveries may be fleeting and unintense, or they may be pursued intently and be accompanied by masturbation; again this is not evidence of abnormality by itself.

Teen Body-building and Homosexuality. A teen-age boy not yet involved intimately with a girl may suddenly go on a body-conditioning spree (weight-lifting, judo, etc.), supposedly, as he confides, to improve his attractiveness to girls. From clinical experience, however, this can be a danger signal (i.e., that he is acting out a fantasized fear of being attacked homosexually). Such undertakings have been observed to be: 1) motivated as stated by the boy; 2) the forerunner of emerging homosexuality; 3) followed by overt paranoid ideas and/or a schizophrenic break. The significance of these observations has been disputed, however.

Muscle Magazines, Pornography and Juvenile Homosexuality. The continued secret perusal of muscle and body-building magazines with pictures of male torsos with prominent genital bulges should be regarded as a fairly substantial basis for the assumption that deviant homosexual overtness is at hand. This practice is unrelated to psychotic symptoms. It needs to be noted with care that muscle magazines are not known to produce homosexual tendencies. This is probably not true, however, of the continued perusal, by vulnerable youngsters, of frankly suggestive, pornographic homosexual material; it probably includes the regular reading of non-pornographic news and club material issued by the homophile movement with its unwittingly proselytizing appeal for the fascinated and vulnerable boy.

The Vulnerable Youngster. Certain hypersuggestible or passive-inadequate boys—often markedly handsome in a soft, prettyish way, with slender gracile physiques or of rounded, near-gynecoid habitus—seem unwittingly to attract older homosexual men and may become enticed into a mutual attachment, with or without intimacies. They make up the bulk of the endangered or homosexually vulnerable boys, the borderline cases whose future sex direction depends on fortuitous circumstances as often as it does on an endogenous trend. In the course of the first homosexual attachment they may lack the psychic strength to forsake the flattering, satisfying feeling of being desired and esteemed instead of being derided by contemporaries or regarded with a measure of distaste by their own families. They become unwilling, as it were, to exchange this contented state for the uncertainties of the competitive quest for the female. The result, at best, is an unduly prolonged juvenile homoerotic phase; at worst, they become conditioned to a type of chronic facultative homosexuality which, although reversible in theory, often goes unreversed in practice for lack of will, means or opportunity. See also p. 502.

Parents' Anxiety. A great deal of unnecessary apprehension and self-consciousness have been stirred up among parents of young boys by the popularization of some well-executed but faultily interpreted research work on the vitiating role of parents in causing homosexuality (e.g., the binding mother, and the hostile or detached father). This work lumped together different types of homosexuality, although actually this is not a uniform disorder but the common ultimate path for several aberrant sex patterns; it also disregarded the nature of the earliest mother-infant pleasing cycle. Certain male infants, possibly unusually beauteous and attentive—responsive like girl babies—induce certain mothers to adore, protect, and intimately bind them to themselves. From the toddler stage they have no interest in the father's activities, and as their feminoid pattern and identification become more marked they severely disappoint, bewilder or frighten and turn off even some highly motivated fathers. But, always it seems to be the child who carries the cue. But be that as it may, in the teens the effeminate prehomosexual is no great diagnostic problem, as his pattern was established and patent years ago, and his future course is fixed. Differential diagnostic uncertainty exists chiefly regarding late-transitional (vulnerable) homoerotic boys and the "regular," non-effeminate gay adolescent who emerges into self-recognition at this time. The normal boy passing through a homoerotic phase has usually subsided into heterosexuality by the time the true gays come out into overtness.

Parents are chiefly concerned that a pubescent homoerotic attachment can lead to adult homosexuality (i.e., that the tendency will not be outgrown). The physician cannot give a generalized answer here, but there is rarely justification for anxiety where all signs point to a transitional type of behavior. There is justification for a fair amount of anxiety, and a genuine need for careful guidance, when the boy's personality and recent history place him in the vulnerable borderline group. There must be a great deal of pessimism when the evidence points to the emergence of true deviance (see following table).

Management.   The transitional homoerotism of normal boys requires no specific treatment. Parents should be encouraged to avoid undue alarm or interference. A bewildered boy's questions as to masturbation, homosexuality, etc., should be answered with all possible frankness and without implied health threats. Some modern mothers are quite alarmed by the problem of homosexuality and out of fear of its widening scope support aggressively their son's precocious heterosexuality. However, no boy should be pushed in an area of such delicacy, especially if it is possible that he does not feel ready for it or if he has a phobia of rejection or failure, and especially not by his mother. Some kind of informal guidance is often desirable if the boy accepts it. Heteroerotic interests (dates, dances) can be encouraged, but insistent emphasis in this regard is pointless.

In susceptible (endangered) boys, more active preventive measures are in order. Attachments to considerably older males should be interfered with efficiently but tactfully and quietly. Boarding in all-male institutions should be avoided. Involvement with hippie-type groups who are into group sex and not being hung up by gender differences in picking a love partner are especially traumatic for these boys. Athletic, competitive and similar pursuits should not be interfered with. Minor psychotherapy (guidance, support, suggestion) is desirable, especially in conjunction with a suitable but not over-emphatic program of social and occupational activities.

DIFFERENTIATING TEEN-AGE HOMOEROTIC BEHAVIOR

The difference between columns 2 and 3 below is somewhat schematic and subject to shading and exceptions. Not only the effeminate, but also the future highly masculine homosexual (i.e., the two untreatable extremes) tend to emerge into overtness in childhood. The late-induced, vulnerable youngster is not included in this table. The boy in column 2 is sometimes misdefined as the boy who didn't outgrow the normal homoerotic phase; he was never in it (theory).

	Transitional Homoerotism	*Homosexual Emerging into Overtness*	*Established Effeminate Deviate Passing Through Teens (See also p. 81)*
Onset and Course	Homoerotic Phase peaks between 11 and 14 (average 13½); somewhat longer in all-male environment. Residuals into late teens.	Emerges between 13 and 17, occasionally later. Tendency increases instead of diminishing and persists beyond teens.	First manifest at age 2, even earlier. Pattern progresses evenly. Mild cases learn to disguise somewhat.
Interests and Pursuits	The whole range of boys' interests. Usual degrees of group participation.	Turmoil of self-discovery may bring detachment from group, at least temporarily. Later preference for "select circle" activities. May excel at arts, sports, speech or other skills. Dilettantism first noticeable in teens.	Avoids competitive pursuits and groups generally. Loner, sissy. May befriend another outcast. Interests along non-masculine lines; domestic, dramatic and decorative arts, least often fine arts. Misfit if forced into unsuitable activity, depending on degree of effeminacy.
Girls and Dates	Normal interest in girls begins in midteens, or even concurrent with homoerotic phase. Where interest is delayed this is often due to immaturity and shyness.	Several possibilities: 1) No interest at all at any time; polite, but aloof; not markedly hostile. 2) Interest dwindles rapidly after first homoerotic infatuation, or latest within 2 or 3 years after puberty. 3) Gynecophobia 4) Bisexual, without clear pattern in teens.	Associates with girls as companions or equals, very comfortable in their company; or even competes with them for attention of male athletes, etc.
Homoerotic Attachments	1 or 2 attachments which may be moderately intense. Possibly 1 or 2 fleetingly erotized hero worships, personal or par distance. Casual sex experimentation in groups carried over from latency. Homoerotic attachments last 2 to 12 months, rarely longer. Terminations uneventful, friendship may outlast erotic phase. Only interested in individuals he knows fairly well.	Infatuations can be devastatingly intense or prolonged. Break-ups are major crises. Some boys very shy in approach; cruder ones go in search of sex partners in parks, rest rooms. Decisions for chastity not rare at this stage.	History of repeated "seductions" by men or adolescents in childhood; or infatuations with older men or masculine heros. Greatly neuterized boys have scant libido. Others notice and may be attracted to various males, and may actively try to be picked up.
Homosexual Practices, if any	Wrestling, hugging, groping leading to mutual masturbation or such. No great interest in other's genitals as such. No or little interest in mutual denuding. Oral or rectal experimentation, but rarely repeated. Forcible rectal gang rape of smaller boys in institutions, even repeated, is nonmorbid delinquency.	Same as in normal group, but often deep fascination with other's genitals. Actively promotes undressing. May seek oral or rectal sex repeatedly. In boy's rape by gang may be instigator (often while still latent), or decline to participate.	Sometimes the habitual victim of gang-shags. Passive in sexual play which he may have instigated. If passive-aggressive personality, may provoke favored activity by pouting, etc.

Homoerotism in Girls. In girls, transitional homoerotic tendencies take various forms, including a crush on a girl the same age or on a young adult female. Such attachments are infrequent after 17 or 18 years of age, except possibly when there is prolonged segregation (e.g., in an all-female institution or school); or in some cases in which maturation is delayed.

The Crush. In the normal girl, emotional attachments to a contemporary seem to last somewhat longer than they do in boys, and a duration of up to 1 or 2 years is not unusual. The beginning of a crush is often sudden, and a great emotional pitch may be reached quickly. However, all degrees of intensity can be observed: some bosom friendships are devoted and serene; others are turbulent and unsettling. Periods of romantic elation, despondent brooding and erotic preoccupation alternate. Erotic reveries, either fleeting or intense, are almost always present at some point. Erotic manifestations such as hugging, cuddling, kissing, unsystematic fondling or other intimacies are not rare during the relationship, but activities involving the genitalia, especially mutual masturbation, probably are relatively less frequent than in boys passing through the same phase.

Secret Sisters. During pubescence these attachments are basically egocentric and possessive in nature; the quality of tenderness is usually scant or absent until about the time of puberty. These less mature girls tend to demand absolute faithfulness, exclusion of other friends, and baring of all thoughts, feelings or information to each other. Frequently, messages in a personal code, secret words and double meanings are exchanged, some relating to the puzzling facts of sex and puberal development, others seemingly to nothing particular at all. So-called sisterly tendencies (e.g., dressing alike) are frequent before puberty. Lately the spreading trend to minimally erotized boy-girl "twin" relationships in the teens may be taking the place of some of these minor homoerotic attachments.

Break-up. Even in normal girls these attachments rarely seem to end as serenely or casually as they do in most normal boys. Frequently a separation crisis is precipitated in some way (e.g., by one girl's "disillusionment" about the other who is accused of wearying and breaking away). Gradual transition into a more mature type of friendship, as may occur in boys, is apparently rare; but the friendship may be resumed after an interval of some years. Passage through the homoerotic phase does not preclude interest in boys and dates, except possibly in younger girls during the period of an intense crush. Sudden spurts of interest in boys may be motivated by spite against the bosom friend.

The Ideal. Older females may be worshiped as "my ideal" (idol) either from afar, or close contact may be sought ceaselessly. Characteristics frequently sought in the ideal—who may be a teacher, a celebrity, an older sister or friend—are elegance, worldliness, beauty, kindness. A degree of subsurface protest and antagonism against the girl's own mother usually coexists. Two closely attached girls may share their worship for the same ideal without jealousy.

Differential Diagnosis. At this age the differential diagnosis between transitional homoerotism on the one hand and incipient lesbianism on the other is frequently difficult, perhaps even more so than in boys. The occurrence of numerous, excessively protracted attachments and crushes, especially if characterized by either a markedly passive longing or an aggressively seductive attitude should arouse suspicion; most so if the tempo of puberal development is normal but is combined with a persistent absence of genuine interest in boys after puberty. However, even a markedly passive-longing attitude in a girl appears to be quite compatible with an expectation of normal heterosexual interest in adulthood, or at least with a socially inconspicuous type of bisexuality.

Treatment. Transitional homoerotism in girls requires no treatment. The mother should maintain a sympathetic attitude and be ready with counsel, comfort or reassurance when and as the girl appears to be receptive for this. An obvious or suspected crush on an older female may at times arouse a degree of jealousy and hostile unrest in the mother. Interference with crushes (e.g., forcible separation of the girls) serves no constructive purpose under ordinary circumstances. An endangered (susceptible) category corresponding to that in boys includes, among others, certain inadequate or hypersuggestible but beauteous girls; they require greater protection especially in connection with attachments to older females who may seduce and condition them toward a facultative type of lesbianism.

CHAPTER 9

Disordered Sex Behavior
in Adolescence

Aberrant Sex Behavior in Teen-Age Boys — The Teen-Age Male
Prostitute — Promiscuity in Teen-Age Girls — Sex Problems in
Mental Retardation.

ABERRANT SEX BEHAVIOR IN TEEN-AGE BOYS

In no other phase of life is mere escalation of normal sexuality rubbing
shoulders as closely, and is as difficult to distinguish from, genuine pathology as in the adolescent period of the developing male. Adolescents are
in the process of learning to keep their primary drives satisfied within
accepted limits and to gain satisfaction from both social and self-approval
that comes with such control. The new biologic drives, as yet undisciplined,
involve the sporadic emergence of erratic appetites which, when blocked,
cause frustration which the young person has not yet learned to deal with
and may release as aggression. According to another theoretic formulation,
residual infantile libidinal drives as well as primitive aggressive behavior
resurge strongly during adolescence and may momentarily break through
the controls. The results are antisocial acts involving sex—some, no doubt,
unspeakably crude as well as punishable under the law—but they do not
necessarily carry a profoundly pathologic label, nor do they necessarily
portend an unfavorable prognosis.

Predatory Opportunism. Many of the predatory antisocial teen-agers
who roam the streets victimizing and exploiting also roam freely across
the spectrum of sexual deviance. As part of their non-caring, often establishment-hostile life style they become involved in a variety of crudely
hedonistic acts of opportunity—whatever their older peers have forced on
them, or whatever they can grab from the environment to try and soon
discard: rape—which here is merely "ripping off some loving from the
bourgeoisie"—homosexual hustling (p. 153), zoostuprum, voyeurism, child
molesting, frottage, sadism or exhibitionism. None of these are sought very

149

actively, but few challenges are passed by. This is the non-pathologic sexual delinquent: a smash-bust aggressor when in the mood, socially dangerous, even destructive frequently, but in most cases his tumultuous sexuality is only transiently so. Adolescent perversity, orneriness, a compulsive need to do the unexpected, to shock; and an overriding fear of the peer group's contempt and disapproval makes him persist, until he, with the majority of his peers, outgrows this pattern together.

Instigator's Role. Some boys are more susceptible to the adoption of sex delinquent patterns than others. Some are suggestible, easily led and strongly craving approval by their more aggressive peers, trying to be no better than they so as not to incur rejection. In such a setting it is most often the emotionally disturbed, the truly sick youngster who comes along and "talks up"—and acts out—the free-floating libidinal aggression, escalating it into organized sexual delinquency. Often he succeeds—by dint of the wondrous psychology of the juvenile mind—in pulling a whole peer group with him. Gang abuse of a consenting girl becomes gang rape. Baiting of homosexuals becomes queer-hunting (i.e., decoying, beating and robbing of hapless deviates). Aimless sexual experimenting may become systematic and vicious for a time; but when the others grow out of all this, the susceptible youngster remains behind, morbidly fixated (e.g., a recidivist rapist, a late-conditioned homosexual, a sadist or a voyeur).

Parents' Contribution. Other factors may coexist. Some parents not only condone but actually foster delinquent sex behavior. A mother may encourage her adolescent son's escapades as a sign of virility, because she feels that her own husband is a milquetoast. Occasionally, the parents subtly seem to suggest a choice of sexual misbehavior to the youngster; here their fantasizing provides a compelling guide, for instance as the father quizzes the boy suspiciously on what he possibly might have done or barely avoided doing, or warns him explicitly on what he might be tempted to do, or what he, the father, himself was or was not able to avoid doing in his own youth; or as the parents, sometimes with ill-concealed and unaccustomed rapturous interest listen to this child's exploits, the father vicariously living out his own impulses or vicariously taking pride in his own virility, as he—with prideful disapproval, as it were—makes much of the chip-off-the-old-block sentiment and in the process also finds unconscious satisfaction in mortifying his wife as she is being apprised of the acts of predatory sexuality of which the men in her family are capable.

Juvenile Phase of Chronic Sexopathies. There are some types of adolescent sexual acting-out which are neither caused, worsened, improved or prevented by anything that happens in the second decade. Two principal groups exist: those carried over from childhood, and those emerging into overtness in the teens. Carried-over aberrant sexual behavior is a direct continuation of childhood pathology, but now more

patently sexualized; it includes certain antisocial (psychopathic) personalities; certain brain-disordered (postencephalitic, epileptoid, etc.) youngsters; and the feminoid trio of male transvestism, male transsexualism, and
the effeminate type of homosexuality—each clinically different from the
other, but just possibly etiologically related. Some of the chromosomal
XYY and related genotypes would belong here, but the existence of a
genetic factor in their personality problems remains uncertain. Those
belonging to the ill-starred trio of functional and psychologic gender aberrations are socially innocuous in the teens, mostly bewildered or in emotional turmoil, perhaps experimenting with cross-dress. Among them the
maturing homosexual is most disturbing to his normal peers as he may
represent a threat to their final shedding of the normal homoerotic phase
of the second decade (p. 142). This whole group does not often come to
relevant medical attention at this stage, although some of these youngsters
can be treated. See also Chapters 5, 20 and 21.

Pathologic and Borderline Delinquents. The antisocial sexopaths and
the brain-disordered are a small but socially highly disruptive group, especially the former. These child sex delinquents of yesterday often cause
consternation and mayhem even as they pass through the teens, on their
way to developing almost predictably into some of the worst adult trans-
gressors and corrupters.

The Antisocial Psychopath. The youthful sadistic psychopath, for
instance, with a history of 2 or more forcible rapes by the time he is 17,
with a discernibly cruel bend, is an exceedingly poor social risk. He is
incapable of responding to either kindness or a disciplinary approach. He
experiences no guilt; apprehension yes, but neither concern nor sorrow
and only shallow joy. He meets denial with violence, is often cruel to
animals, tantrum-prone, perhaps impulse-ridden, incapable of forming
meaningful relationships other than exploitatory ones, unable to learn from
experience; he is an instigator, but the first to be turned off, or to turn
away or run; surfeit-prone, not averse to relieving his libidinal urges of
the moment on male, female, child or animal, and in almost any deviant
fashion that tantalizes him at the moment (composite description). Next to
nothing reliable is known about the cause of this syndrome, nor can he,
nor his female counterpart, be effectively reclaimed at present. However,
some of these patients seem to lapse into asymptomatic quiescence during
the middle and late teens, only to emerge again as sexual offenders during
young adulthood, or even later.

The Organic Delinquent emerges into the teens as an excitable, impulsive
and sometimes very cruel aggressor, although in some temporal lobe disorders, by retrospective history, sexual apathy seems to prevail. A more
explosive aggressiveness and greater susceptibility to alcohol, a greater
capacity for remorse, and a quality of "drivenness" adhering to his im-

pulses distinguish him from the young male with an antisocial personality. Here one also encounters the compulsively smutty-tongued boy, the "dirty weak coward" despised by his contemporaries, teachers, even his own family, until occasionally he becomes warped and brutalized by rejection to the point that one has on one's hands a potentially very cruel sneak despoiler of children. A possible similarity in some such cases to the Gilles de la Tourette syndrome (p. 461) has been raised. Newer findings, mostly outside the U.S., relating demonstrable small brain injuries due to falls or other trauma in infancy to abnormal sexual tendencies opens interesting avenues. The prognosis as to subsequent sexual transgressions is somewhat better than in the sociopath. Explosiveness may give way gradually to irritability and instability, and medicinal control is substantially more feasible here. Spontaneous improvement of sexual conduct in mid- to late adolescence is no rarity.

Emerging Sexual Anomalies. Among chronic sexual abnormalities emerging into overtness in the teens are the majority of cases of homosexuality and bisexuality, and many of the compulsive sexual deviations which will afflict the individual later (e.g., exhibitionism, sadomasochism, voyeurism, possibly fetishism). These are discussed in Chapter 20. A schizophrenic syndrome may be precipitated into overtness in the teens; while other symptoms may go unrecognized, the young patient's symptomatic impulsive-aggressive sex behavior may attract attention because it is so grossly out of character with his previous personality. This condition is not a continuation of childhood schizophrenia (p. 77); the latter usually subsides into a residual state by the time of puberty.

Teen-age Child Molesting. Sexual delinquency in the form of aggressive molesting or raping (rarely vaginal) of small girls occurs as an acting-out of impulses by either predatory or sociopathic youngsters; as a delayed reaction of rectally abused boys without an opportunity to abreact their deep confusion about maleness and the passive sex role; and in fatherless boys sexually overexposed by an erotically tantalizing mother (p. 74), as rage and confusion follow the abrupt ending of the affair near puberty. The child victim of abuse later becomes a victimizer himself. Often sexual aggression against little girls is so obvious, repetitive or cruel that it seems to be a signal of appeal to the authorities to rescue and remove him from his own abuser. Another type of molester is the budding homophilic pedophile, usually a timid, socially isolated teen-ager who tries to touch and seduce only smaller boys. In one series of 80 male teen-age child molesters the mean age was 14.4 years. Mean IQ was 108, but most were underachievers, as well as loners with a prevalence of passive-aggressive personality traits. The victims' mean age was 5.1 years (Shoor).

Sex Hanging. An estimated minimum of 50 deaths annually occurs in adolescents who strangulate themselves, probably accidentally, while masturbating (Resnick). Such erotized hangings are usually repetitive and progressively more dangerous, and may serve as an experimental search for escalated sexual sensation; possibly they are a form of autosadism (q.v.) or other deviation. However, no live self-strangulators have been examined psychiatrically in depth. Self-trussing or binding ("bondage") including of the genitalia, nudity or, sometimes, female attire, pornographic material, padded rope, chain or leather strips, and often a mirror for self-viewing have usually been part of the scene. There is evidence that no desire to die is involved. The deed sometimes has, wrongly, raised suspicion of a sex killing.

THE TEEN-AGE MALE PROSTITUTE

They are known as hustlers, collectively as trade. Boys aged about 13 to 16 (chickens) cater to ephebophilic men (chicken hawks, p. 474), a borderland between pedophilia and homosexuality. The majority, aged 15 to early adulthood, serve homosexual men who seek them out (cruise them) in certain streets and localities, or in specialized houses of prostitution for homosexuals, or from their ever-changing list of call boys. A small number of effeminate boys hustle, but mainly for anal immissions. Male hustling flourishes flagrantly in the big cities and can be assumed to exist underground in most medium-sized towns. Adolescent trade seems invulnerable to arrest, but the younger boys' pimps are more vulnerable.

Teen-age hustlers as a group are members of a subculture of delinquents and petty hoods, mostly of limited intelligence, with little schooling and no skills. They come from broken or unstable homes, are shiftless, confused about themselves, not very enterprising and tend to drift (Cory-LeRoy, Ginsburg, Hoffman, Humphreys, MacNamara, Pittman, Reiss Jr., Sonenschein, others). They are introduced into prostitution either by pimps who often beat or drug them to start them off, or else by the peer group which also remains the arbiter of whether the boy is a true hustler (i.e., strictly out for an easy money job) or whether he shows signs of liking it and thus turns out to be (? become ? become overtly) a homosexual and lose his peers' respect. This is an overriding obsessive fear with them; they are extremely sensitive to any threat to their prized masculinity or its façade. To a customer's tenderness, kiss or wrong-way proposition they may react with panic, followed by explosive, knocking-down violence, with secondary cruelty and robbing. Peers may join in this. Especially older ones who sport masculine style (butch) leather-and-boots attire or working man's get-up (rough trade) can be highly dangerous to an occasional hapless deviate.

In most instances the sexual ritual is rigidly maintained to avoid homosexual labeling by self or the peers. The score fellates (goes down on) the hustler. Neither one undresses and no other body contact is permitted. The boy avoids expressing pleasurable satisfaction and the client may not attempt to treat him as a lover. However, one may suggest that those staying in the life for any length of time are latent homosexuals to begin with. Of those still soliciting in their 20's the saying may often be correct: today's trade is tomorrow's queen. Even if the teen hustler should be aware of homoerotic stirrings—and some customers are attractive youngish men —he will hide it, as scores prefer straight partners, although usually they do want to arouse and pleasure them, and presumably proselytize them.

The outcome, from what is known, is often not good. Suicide, alcoholism, crime, drug addiction are not infrequent in follow-up reports. Highly motivated professional attempts have been made to seek the boys out and provide them with vocational training and social rehabilitation (Deisher).

PROMISCUITY IN TEEN-AGE GIRLS

Related:
Promiscuity in Women p. 425
Prostitution p. 447

All sexual multipartnerism before the mid- to late teens must be considered a pathologic manifestation, either an individual behavior disturbance, or a sociopathic phenomenon; among the latter belong teenyboppers, some groupies, gang-bang volunteers, shared juvenile gang auxiliaries, floating pad girls, midteen urban prostitutes, high school sex club queens, and other juvenile delinquents. It is only in late adolescence that the concepts of variant personal or group life styles begin to have applicability. Except for some schizophrenic, brain-disordered or neglected retarded girls maximal promiscuity—the indiscriminate granting of sexual liberties to all comers— does not seem to occur before the late teens or young adulthood. Younger teen-agers do discriminate—by age, race, physique, moneyedness, group membership or even some form of limiting geography.

The term promiscuous, as used in the general language, is subject to much over-recognition; this is especially true when it is applied to female adolescents. Girls are called promiscuous because occasionally they display a lack of reticence on dates; or it is considered evidence of promiscuous tendencies if a girl acquires a vaginal fungus or a venereal disease or becomes pregnant out of wedlock. To the clinician, on the other hand, the term has largely retained its original meaning of "not restricted to any particular person" (Webster).

Promiscuous acting-out in a teen-age girl is almost always a symptom rather than an independent clinical entity; hoping to bring about improvement, one must go below the surface and try to pinpoint the aberrant impellent or compellant motive, or diagnose the emotional illness. As most juvenile female delinquents live in a world of semi-fantasy, with their behavior often compulsive and unconsciously motivated, neither disciplinary measures nor threats, shaming or cajoling, nor even social ostracism by their own peer group, can reclaim these girls for long, as a rule.

Environment. However, what constitutes promiscuous behavior in one social setting may be considered unremarkable in another. Where a girl's indiscriminate sex behavior does not differ substantially from that of all her daily companions, and where such behavior does not seem to cause concern to the adults responsible for her, the physician most often is dealing with group delinquent reaction rather than with an individual aberration, although, of course, pathologic promiscuity is also found among the socially diverse. Girls coming from a morally relaxed home background (e.g., where the mother entertains men for sexual purposes, either in the absence of a husband or with his tacit acquiescence, or where she is sexually involved with a boyfriend and repeatedly accused of being so by her husband) sexual promiscuous acting-out by a young adolescent daughter is no rarity. It is reactive behavior rather than due to any like-mother-like-daughter or imitative or inheritable mechanism. In such cases the mother—although the father is always involved in some way—has been noted unconsciously to encourage the amoral or delinquent behavior of the girl. This differs from the vicarious pleasure which some mothers with a background of counter-erotic upbringing seem to derive from the sexual acting-out of a young daughter.

An insecure but otherwise normal girl who is transplanted suddenly into a neighborhood dominated by an aggressively promiscuous crowd of juveniles may feel that she must imitate their behavior to be accepted by them; this is especially frequent if the parents suddenly relax their supervision and day-to-day interest in her. Community-wide social upheavals are another possible factor: if a community suddenly becomes host to numerous free-spending transients (military installation, mining camp, vacation resort) with characteristic cash affluence, relaxation of anti-vice enforcement and distraction of parental interest, this may result in the rapid deterioration of sex mores among certain groups of exposed teen-agers. If alcohol and narcotics become more widely available, usually this trend is accelerated.

The Highly Sexed. Contrary to what is sometimes believed, excessive sexual desire seems rarely to be the cause of promiscuity in teen-age girls. Some girls, of course, are highly sexed (i.e., they have a high degree of erotic responsiveness as well as a relatively low sexual arousal threshold); but this by itself does not lead to promiscuous behavior. In fact, where a highly sexed girl happens to become promiscuous—probably less than one third of promiscuous girls are highly sexed—treatment can be directed only at the emotional pathology, as drive intensity (sexual temperament) is most probably an endowed trait which defies attempts at correction short of the crudest kind of suppression.

The Hapless Ones. In the cases of girls being systematically used and abused by groups of male juveniles or by grown men, without affection and with only chattel sentiments entering the picture, the males' usual justification is, "they asked for it." This is more often true than not, if one disregards such social pressures as group identity, fear of isolation, and competitive popularity measured by number of questing boys, or the wide range of internal emotional impellents (see below)—all tugging at the vulnerable, fun-hungry girl with an undistinguished ego, a superego like a Swiss cheese, and only adult situation-ethicists watching over her. Some girls maneuver actively to participate, others wander in harm's way blithely or dumbly or uncaringly, or just gullibly anxious to show some boy that they like him and then not knowing enough to get out when he begins passing her around among his friends. Girls volunteering for line-up abuse (gang shack-up) were found to be seriously disturbed individuals, with almost no ability to relate on a one-to-one basis with a boy, and remaining ungratified by the sex acts (Kimsey).

Internal Impellents. Among the promiscuous girls who are neither intellectually understimulated and perpetually bored nor thrill-hungry, one encounters a variety of mental mechanisms leading to compulsively repetitive sexual misconduct. Certain ingrained morbid convictions can arise either early in life (e.g., the ruination beliefs of some poorly managed child victims of sex aggression) or more recently (e.g., the obscured rage following break-up of a long-term father-daughter affair) (p. 64); or as the result of chronic endogenous depressive morbidity. These root impellents are hidden from the casual observer, and almost always from the girl herself.

All she or anybody usually knows is that she simply "can't help herself and just does it." But if one takes the time to examine the conduct of such a girl more closely, often it is not difficult to recognize underlying patterns. In one type the girl acts as if she possessed no sense of personal worth; her conduct is patently self-disgracing or even potentially self-injurious, as if she were saying, "Nothing matters in my case." Other girls, deeply convinced that they are bodily or sexually "different" or in some way unlovable, seem to be engaged in a frantic pursuit of every male within reach, as if they had to prove unceasingly that boys still want them after all. Still others seem to be engaged in endless defiance of the sex mores of their environment, as if "everything is their (parents', society's) fault—now I'll really be bad and hurt them back."

Less often promiscuity is observed in girls who have conscious feelings of inadequacy so pronounced that they amount to a chronic obsession. They, too, seek acceptance, a sense of identity as a person. Pelvic contact gives them a momentary sense of acceptance, but their feelings of personal worthlessness continue (Auerback). They may indiscriminately tolerate sexual advances because they are convinced that for them this is "the only way to hold a boy" or to be popular. It is rarely possible to persuade them otherwise, and in some respects the condition resembles the depressive variety described above, except that treatment here is more difficult.

Another type of girl, although of normal intelligence, possesses vastly passive-inadequate and hypersuggestible traits, sometimes coupled with strong libidinal responsiveness. Some of these girls seem to be totally unable to resist the sexual demands of any male whose manner is self-assured or whose flattery is persuasive. Some others, even in early adolescence, are habitually complaisant but also secretive and difficult to establish rapport with. These girls act as if longing to satisfy sexually all the males of their small world, although they themselves seem to gain little if any orgasmic gratification from this. This is the beginning of what has been termed "the passive succorer" (p. 426) among promiscuous women, characterized by an unusually high rate of unfavorable outcomes (psychosis, addiction, suicide).

Asocial and Antisocial Personality. This is a group of girls who, once started on a promiscuous pattern, follow no predictable direction. Some continue and rather quickly make the transition into prostitution, perhaps addiction; others drift restlessly between jobs, crime, marriages and prostitution without persevering in any of these; still others, more fortunate, attach themselves permanently to a stable male or female and build a domestic menage resembling a family. Intelligence here is mostly normal or even superior, but they are impulse-ridden and may lack any sort of judgment. They tend to be amoral rather than immoral, have limited or no capacity for feeling guilt, shame, sorrow, friendship or deep anxiety, and cannot learn from experience. Some are incorrigibly cruel and callous. All lie with ease. They can experience sexual pleasure and impart it to a partner, but sex is simply one more tool in their manipulative armamentarium. A few are chronically irritable, but many have a charming and ingratiating manner or display an appearance of extreme naïveté and wide-eyed innocence. Cause and nature of the condition are unknown and no effective remedy seems to exist, although a few claims to the contrary have been made.

The Predatory, Aggressive Psychopath is a variant of the above, and explosive personality traits may be associated. She is exemplified by the brutalized, establishment-hostile teen-age street prostitute who gladly cuts the customer with a knife rather than be denied an extra few dollars when she feels she deserves it or when her pimp or lesbian lover or she herself is hungry for a drug fix. Some travel on the streets of large cities in small packs late at night, using prostitution as a pretext for armed robberies.

General Corrective Measures. Short of systematic psychotherapy, some results can be obtained by simply allowing the patient to unburden her mind. A search for sex fears and misapprehensions always is indicated, although it may take time to make the girl overcome her apathy, suspicion or defiance. The physician's attitude must be completely uncritical toward her past conduct from the very beginning. It is often worthwhile to correct some bad condition in the girl's home or some faulty attitude of her parents. The patently self-injurious type sometimes responds very well if treated as if suffering from a subacute depression, while omitting all emphasis on her sexual conduct. An attempt to separate the girl from obviously undesirable companions is always worthwhile, but there should exist at least the prospect of other, better companionship. Leisure-time activities and dates should receive parental scrutiny, but this must not become oppressive (e.g., to the point of prohibiting all dates).

The girl may bring suitable dates home, after the parents make certain corrections, such as ceasing to be embarrassingly quarrelsome or unmannerly at home, or refurbishing a neglected living room. Sometimes the conspicuous presence of a disgracing relative (senile grandparent, retarded sibling) discourages a teen-ager from seeking contact with desirable companions. Occasionally a girl's lagging sense of personal worth can be enhanced simply by encouraging her to decorate her own room and to feel at home there. Major unhappiness and worries regarding her school or job adjustment should be explored, hobbies and hobby group activities encouraged. Usually the physician can secure the help of a social case worker or family agency in order to arrange for an endangered girl's temporary sheltering or placement.

Parents should not forbid a promiscuous girl the use of all cosmetics or attractive clothes, nor impose indiscriminate punishment (e.g., an excessive schedule of domestic responsibilities "to take her mind off boys"). In the vast majority of cases there should be no hasty marrying off. Summary expulsion by the parents from the home is an egotistical and pointless measure, to be especially condemned because it tends to lead to runaway status and eventual prostitution rather than to halting the promiscuity.

SEX PROBLEMS IN MENTAL RETARDATION

Defining the Terms.   3 per cent of the population have an IQ of 70 or less, but only 1 per cent are genuinely mentally retarded, defined as having significantly impaired intelligence with concurrent, similar general maladaptation, both overt before age 17 (Heber, Tarjan). About one fourth of the latter are "clinical," usually organic retardates, having concomitant somatic defects, both dating from infancy, with many secondary handicaps, and not confined to any social class; they constitute the bulk of today's institution cases. The other three fourths are "socioculturally" or "functionally" retarded, a condition found almost exclusively among the underprivileged, mostly diagnosed on entering school, not usually requiring institutional care, and its clinical overtness tending to disappear in late adolescence or early adulthood (disputed). Sexual problems arise most frequently with borderline, mild (IQ from 53 to 68) and some of the moderately (IQ from 36 to 52) retarded youngsters. Proper care of the mentally retarded transcends general medicine and psychiatry.

Mental retardation as such rarely produces abnormal sex expression. However, in childhood many retardates—least often the mongoloids—do get into sexual difficulties, and conspicuous degrees of sexual delinquency are sometimes encountered when they reach adolescence. The principal causes are their failure in social adaptation and coping, their vulnerability to exploitation, and their suggestibility. On the other hand, the more severe retardates not rarely are hypogonads, and general as well as libidinal apathy may be associated; also, coping with the demands of an institutional environment is an easier task.

Parental Handling. In childhood, most mildly retarded boys and girls can be expected to have the same tensions, stirrings and curiosities as other children, although dimmed, perhaps delayed, and certainly less well verbalized. However, they will act out their curiosity, impulses and tensions with cruder directness, less well concealed, and less adroitly denied when caught. Parents of such children, many themselves intellectually limited, often lack access to guidance on how to deal with the special problems of a retarded child, although they are well-meaning. Others are too impatient, or frightened, or ashamed. Such a limited or frightened mother may shy away from all sex questions including the origin of babies, boy-girl differences, etc., out of a vague apprehension that this "will get him into trouble." In an effort to protect the child, she may reduce all sex teaching to the stereotyped formula that everything "down there is bad . . . phooey . . . don't ask, don't look . . . don't touch, don't allow touching." The resentful and rejecting mother is likely to treat all self-manipulation in childhood with excessive harshness. Since the retarded child is obviously less adroit at concealment, he is more often exposed. This may stir the parents to even greater suppressive efforts because they fear that they are dealing with an abnormally sexed child, or that other parents will blame them for any mutual sex play that may be discovered. Occasionally one encounters the opposite, a rejecting or guilt-ridden mother who is excessively permissive, possibly even subtly exhortatory, regarding sexual exploration.

At Risk. Because of their vulnerability to victimization, some retarded children are overexposed (e.g., where a retarded young mother without a husband brings up one or more children while resorting to semi-prostitution). A father, an alcoholic, or sufficiently retarded himself to be the consort of a retarded woman, may abuse his retarded young daughter sexually, often on repeated occasions and beginning in early pubescence; or the mother may permit men she is entertaining to take such liberties with the youngster. There may be no concealment of nudity, or of marital or nonmarital intercourse, the adults reassuring themselves that the child is "too stupid to understand." Actually, these children appear to perceive and absorb sufficiently to become perturbed in a manner rather similar to that of the normal child.

A characteristic result is a child who is tense and anxious, or insecure and unhappy. Both overexposed and harshly suppressed children may have a compulsive urge to explore the genitalia of other children or to repeat with other children parental intimacies which have vaguely excited and perturbed them. Since contemporaries often will not consort with a retarded child, there may be tampering with smaller children.

Childhood Misconduct. The retarded child, especially the nonaggressive boy, who is rejected by and isolated from the activities of his normal contemporaries in the neighborhood, is likely to experience substantial anxiety at each rebuff; increasingly so if rebuffs occur in series because transfer of experience from occasion to occasion is not easily accomplished. If he has learned to extract compensatory pleasure from his own body by masturbating he may, when acutely rebuffed, immediately crave solace from his genitals, and with characteristic lack of judgment proceed to do so nearby, only lightly concealed; later this is often reported simply as undisguised masturbation. The very dull child may also learn that the only way to get the attention of other children, at least momentarily, is to do something unusual. In the sexual sphere this may consist of exhibitionism, undisguised self-manipulation, cruel manipulation of animals, or such. Retarded children may misconduct themselves sexually vis-à-vis adults. A neighbor woman may stir a vague longing for demonstrative, maternal affection and interest in the child; but from daily experience with his own harsh mother the child knows that he cannot count on such interest. To obtain some affect reaction, even of dismay, the child may impulsively approach and, for instance, lift the woman's skirt or exhibit himself. Boys consistently frustrated or exploited and left to their own devices in a rough environment become somewhat brutalized, and even in childhood major degrees of aggressive sex-related behavior may develop. Passive homosexual seduction of such boys by pedophilic men and others is no rarity and may lead to a lifelong deviant pattern.

Teen-age Boys' Sex Delinquency. The retarded boy who has been persistently rejected, neglected or overexposed becomes even more maladjusted during the teens. The contribution of certain chromosomal aberrations to sexual delinquency is not well understood at present. There also emerges now the brutalized retardate who is potentially dangerous, especially if he has substantial physical strength. He tends to utilize this strength to express whatever emotions are taking hold of him at the moment, including sexual ones. Brutalization may result from thwarting:

a girl who has aroused his interest may reject him while other boys egg him on to "fight for his girl," then he may vent his rage by attempting rape. If the arousal-thwarting-rape pattern becomes a fixed reaction, eventually sexual brutality may be his stereotyped response to all sexual arousal. Left uncared for, the retarded adolescent may submerge among the subculture of vagabonding drifters, especially in the large cities. The least desirable among them are crafty in a primitive fashion, brutalized and unpredictably predatory; others are harmless derelicts who seem to age rapidly. The incidence of true, compulsory homosexuality appears to correspond to the general population's, but the late-conditioned, potentially reversible type, and bisexuality, may be somewhat more frequent. Drifting in and out of male prostitution (p. 153) is no rarity in mildly retarded urban adolescents.

Female Adolescent Retardates are somewhat subject to promiscuous sex behavior and usually are exploited in the process. This is often more marked if the girl has recently been discharged from an institution. The adolescent girl whose level of retardation is mild may be able to hold a job in her community, yet be incapable of protecting herself. Those who are more markedly subnormal may not even understand at first what is happening to them in a sexual encounter; others were never conditioned to espouse a fairly rigid moral and social code so necessary to effective self-care of the retarded female at liberty (Ollendorff). Often they are credulous and easily led. If they have been given poor training and insufficient sex education they may not be capable of handling boy-girl situations and often do not know how to turn down persuasive requests for sexual favors. In their often overriding desire to be "just like all the other girls" they crave to have a boy friend or a good time as the others do; yet they are much more quickly deserted by boys.

Lack of good judgment may cause them to dress and make up in an excessively provocative manner, although they merely may intend to look as pretty as some idol. Some act impulsively on minor emotions, without being capable of considering or comprehending the consequences of their acts. A few are subject to manic-type episodes of overstimulation and impulsivity. Those on the lower levels of intelligence who come from a harshly loveless or insecure home situation may become totally indiscriminate in tolerating sexual liberties because they crave the few affectionate or flattering words with which a male regales them prior to quick seduction. These girls are often rather pathetic victims of exploitation by gangs of adolescent boys or vagabonding men. As they have less resourcefulness than most normal girls, the rate of infection and pregnancy probably is high among them. Those drifting into prostitution are believed to profit little because of exploitation by hangers-on living off the proceeds, on whose guidance they have to depend for almost everything.

Sex Education. This is imperative for the mildly or moderately retarded boy or girl who is expected to live a reasonably normal existence. Ideally it starts in the home although untutored parents tend to be uncomfortable in this, especially with problems of the male. The child should be told everything that the normal child is told, although at a later time (up to 5 years later), in a slower and more repetitious manner and without abstractions. Questions of "why" or such can be answered simply (e.g., "that's the way girls are made, different from boys" or "God makes boys different from girls" or "all girls have this"; this usually satisfies) (Bass, Morlock-Tovar, others). It is often desirable actively to call the child's

---

RETARDATES' SEX EDUCATION IN SCHOOL

Because of the limitations in many retardates' homes, courses in Family Life, in connection with their special classes, assume great importance. Some choice procedures:

Classroom teacher, if properly prepared, should participate.

No crash courses.

Separate sexes from pubescence.

Simple answers to questions, according to age and mental level.

Applicable examples always; repetition according to demand.

Simple language consistent with decorum.

No medical, few biologic terms if possible.

No choices of behavior presented. In teens reassurance added to all answers.

Parental permission rarely a problem, but moral tone should be responsive to preponderant domestic (community?) standard.

Gradual, early start with birds-and-bees biology (disputed).

For pubescent boys: erection, nocturnal emission, masturbation, outline of female and male anatomy; menses, pregnancy, and childbirth lightly; attitude toward girls.

For girls: dating manners, what and where to stay away from, outline of female and male anatomy and function. Lightly on pregnancy and childbirth, as many will not procreate (see p. 199).

Little VD talk beyond "see the nurse or doctor right away if sore, etc." except in high-risk areas.

---

attention to boy-girl differences, if the presence of other young children makes this feasible. Later, a girl needs to be told about menstruation, together with exact and detailed training on how to use sanitary devices. Of course, there should be a somewhat greater than ordinary emphasis, especially in girls, on avoidance of genital display or genital contact with others, in order to minimize the hazard of victimization. These children can be trained to report to the parents whatever has happened to them each day.

Protection against Impregnation out-of-wedlock is necessary for a proportion of young female retardates. Stern suppression of erotic interest by the family has been shown to be of little value. Religious beliefs and conditioning to a rigidly moral pattern of conduct are good barriers, but under special circumstances they have been seen to vanish suddenly and completely in these girls. An oral contraceptive schedule is excessively subject to errors; barrier and chemical methods often are too complicated. Among IUDs only the newer shield and copper devices are believed to be suitable for insertion in the retarded nullipara, but these girls cannot be relied upon to check on the device's presence on each occasion. Thus for the retarded girl at risk, elective permanent sterilization, on parent's or guardian's application, may be preferable. Since 1973, in federally funded cases (Medicaid, etc.), sterilization of retarded minors judged incapable of giving informed consent also requires approval by a special review committee. It has been held that a Catholic girl with a mental age of 7 as a minimum guideline lacks proper understanding of the meaning of marriage, so that she is merely "an unwitting party to biological intercourse, a form of rape," and that there is nothing in the teachings of the Church which precludes the physician's use of contraceptive agents to protect his patient from the consequences of rape (Hellegers, paraphrased).

Problems in Institutions. The hospital or school being responsible, morally and legally, for the welfare and safety of all who shelter, work or visit there, sexual or any other aggression cannot be tolerated and must be humanely controlled. The use of discipline and controls also being an important conditioning and therapeutic agent, institutions often use various systems of reinforcing—usually tangible rewards—to promote avoidance of a set of well-defined infractions. Pharmacal sexual suppression and inhibition of drive (e.g., in males) is necessary at times for the safety and well-being of all. Combined-type oral contraceptives or, in young boys, pure progestational compounds have been employed. The menstruation of severely retarded girls can produce difficult hygienic problems due to bloody soiling. Systematic menstrual suppression by continuous administration of combined-type contraceptive pills has been found helpful and without deleterious effect in suitable cases. Sex education of severely retarded inmates of either sex is arranged according to the need to know, and thus differs according to what is planned for each patient. In the sexual guidance of the multiple handicapped—retarded but also burdened with deafness, blindness, phobias, psychosis, epilepsy, chromosomal anomalies, endocrine pathology, dwarfism or neuromuscular disease—the counsel of a psychiatrist and/or pediatrician is usually sought in each individual case.

FOR JOURNAL LITERATURE AND ADDITIONAL READING

De la Cruz, F., and La Veck, D. (eds.): Human Sexuality and the Mentally Retarded. New York, Brunner/Mazel, 1973

Easson, I. M.: The Severely Disturbed Adolescent. New York, International Universities Press, 1969

Osofsky, H. J.: The Pregnant Teen-ager: A Medical, Educational and Social Analysis. Springfield, Illinois, Thomas, 1968

Semmens, J. P., and Lamers Jr., W. M.: Teen-age Pregnancy. Including Management of Emotional and Constitutional Problems. Springfield, Ill., Thomas, 1968

Vedder, C. B. B., and Somerville, D. B.: The Delinquent Girl. Springfield, Ill., Thomas, 1970

PART 3

Sexuality of the Normal Adult

CHAPTER 10

The Sexual Apparatus

Male Organs and Functions: Penis — Scrotum — Testicles and
Epididymides — Excretory Ducts and Accessory Glands — Erection
— Ejaculation and Orgasm — The Semen.
Female Organs and Functions: Mons Pubis — Vulva — Labia
Majora — Labia Minora — Clitoris — Hymen — Vagina. Vaginal
Cervix — Sexual Arousal. Orgasm.

Male Organs and Functions

PENIS

*(Member, Membrum Virile, Male Copulatory Organ, Phallus—
When Erect.)*

The male organ is structured so as to subserve its twofold function: it is
basically pendulous for the controlled run-off of liquid waste; and rendered
rigid and properly angulated for the deposit of male genetic material inside
the female reproductive tract. The organ contains a corpus cavernosum
with 2 crura, one on each side (formerly believed to be 2 corpora), and the
smaller corpus spongiosum underneath. The latter surrounds the urethra;
its distal end is enlarged and helps to form the glans. These cavernous
bodies, whose engorgement with blood causes the organ to erect, are
actually vastly enlarged capillaries interposed between the penile arteries
and veins. They are covered by the strong, fibrous tunica albuginea which
also sends out the septa dividing the bodies into separate cavities and forms
their supporting structure. Engorgement of the corpora cavernosa affects
penis thickness chiefly, while the spongiosum may affect length. A penis
bone (os priapi), encountered in many animals, does not exist in man.

Size. Size of the organ is a fairly unimportant factor for the fulfillment
of either function, but in humans it has assumed psychologic significance,
and numerous men, especially adolescents, are preoccupied with genital
size. Despite reassuring medical data their number may be increasing.
Possible causes are sought in the male phobia of microphallus; the survival
of early juvenile fantasies of gigantic impact; informational spread regarding genetic maldevelopment; and in a spreading, almost obsessive appre-

hension of militant female demandingness, selectiveness, and the implied privilege of rejection.

SIZE OF ERECTION

According to best available data length of the adult erect penis, measured dorsally in a straight line from skin surface of penopubic junction to tip of glans, is approximately 15 cm (6 inches), with an average range from 11 to 25 cm. Flaccid length in normal men averages 9.5 cm; average range 8.5 to 10.5 ± 1 cm. Median breadth (i.e., diameter) at midshaft is 3.75 cm. Median girth (i.e., circumference) at midshaft is between 8.75 and 10.5 cm. Circumference may exceed length in short, thick erect organs. Recently proposed erective size categories: Small: 8.75 cm average. Medium: 15 cm average. Large: longer than 20 cm. Greatest recorded length 35 cm (14 inches), presumably acromegaly.

MEASURING ERECTION: THREE METHODS

1. Direct Measurement. Preferably with ruler, always along dorsal surface. Circumference is measured by string or tape, breadth by gauge or outline.

2. Self-Measurement. By tracing penile outline or marking tip of glans on underside of piece of cardboard held closely on phallic dorsum, edged against penopubic skin: distance between cardboard edge and tip of outline represents length.

3. Flaccid Measurement. Although flaccid size can vary with prevailing conditions, fully stretched flaccid length permits a fair estimate, especially in young people. Measurement is dorsal by tape. Applicable is the Schoenfeld-Beebe equation

$$Y = -.0095 + .985X$$

where Y is erect length and X stretched flaccid length.

Except for extremes of clinical pathology there exists no definable relationship between body structure and penile size. Nor is a penis which is small in the resting stage also necessarily small when erect, nor a large pendulous organ necessarily transformed into a large-sized erection. Racial differences in erective size do not exist to any significant degree in the U.S. population. The penis of many black men appears relatively large in the flaccid state, even without the often characteristic long prepuce, but there seems to be a proportionately lesser increase in erective length. No observations on relative erective girth and breadth are available. In some groups of Asians a tendency to relatively small copulatory organs is believed to prevail.

The potential or maximum size of the organ at full maturity appears to be genetically precoded for each individual; it is not increased by vigorous or early-begun sex activity, nor is it lessened by prolonged continence.

Hormone treatment or local application will cause size increase in an adult only if there was a subclinical endocrine deficiency which escaped notice. True shrinkage of the penis is observed in demasculinizing syndromes (see p. 345). In older men the organ may appear elongated, probably because of shrinkage of pubic fat pads.

Shape of Erection. Slight upward arching of the phallus is normal. Pronounced arching—prow type—is usually combined with a characteristically shaped glans; it is a congenital trait in some men and, dubiously, is said to interfere with proper insemination. A slight lateral curvature of the organ, more often to the right, is frequent and has no known clinical significance; it may be due to the shape of the crotch of men's trousers. The angle of erection in most adult men is 20° to 40° to the horizon when standing up and at the height of arousal. With advancing age it tends to decrease. Angles of up to 50° are no rarity, however, nor are near-horizontal and near-vertical positions. Maximal erections pointing below the horizontal in a vigorous young man occur occasionally.

Sensitivity. Maximal erotic tactile sensitivity usually is encountered at the lower surface of the glans, especially at the preputial frenulum, in the coronal sulcus, and at the dorsal rim of the corona glandis. The uncircumcised foreskin is highly sensitive, especially its inner surface. Most of the remaining epidermis of the glans, especially in circumcised men, is fairly insensitive to voluptuous touch, but it is uncertain if copulatory endurance (i.e., time elapsed between coital immission and ejaculation) of the average circumcised man exceeds that of the average uncircumcised man. The lower and lateral aspects of the penile shaft are fairly sensitive both to touch and pressure; however, there are many individual variations. Where an apprehensive man complains of diminished sensitivity of the penile skin, objective validation needs to include impaired sensation to pinprick and light touch of the saddle area skin; the scrotum is included, but its often rugose skin makes clinical sensory responses difficult to evaluate.

SCROTUM (SCROTAL SAC)

The principal function of the scrotal sac is thermoregulatory with respect to the testes, whose sperm-producing function is thermosensitive (see also p. 350). Its exposed position, large surface area, thin walls, absence of subcutaneous fat and plentiful sweat glands make it a cool repository. The testicles are kept at a temperature 10° or 15° F. below that of the body and at a fairly uniform level. Equally important among the several protective thermoregulatory mechanisms protecting the male genetic repository is the complex testicular circulation which cools by arterio-venous heat exchange.

Developmentally the scrotum corresponds to the female labia majora. Its layers represent the layers of the abdominal wall which the descending testis pushed ahead of itself during its descent through the inguinal canal. The sac can distend and contract quite rapidly in response to various external and internal circumstances: it is more pendulous with warmth, fatigue or a relaxed psychic state, while it contracts with fear, cold, physical exertion and sexual arousal. The touch and temperature receptors in the scrotal skin are so sensitive that mere touch can change the shape and temperature of the sac. However, the erotic sensitivity of the scrotum resides in subsurface proprioceptors which respond to light pressure, especially posteriorly and laterally near the base. During the sexual act the sac contracts and thickens as it follows the rising testicles and the shortening ducts to the point of lying close to the perineum just before ejaculation.

The scrotum thins with age, and chronic relaxation with a limited or absent coital reaction is frequent in older men. However, erotic sensitivity of the sac to light pressure may be one of the last scrotal functions to be lost. Scrotal size is not a reliable indicator of testicle size.

TESTICLES (TESTES) AND EPIDIDYMIDES

The adult testis is of ovoid shape and averages 2 to 3 cm in width and 3½ to 5 cm in length (4.3 ± 0.6 cm in Caucasoids, 4.6 ± 0.6 cm in blacks; Tishler). A length of 3.4 cm or less signifies hypoplasia. Measurement of size may be made with the Prader orchidometer, a string of graded testicle-shaped models. Normal consistency of the organs is medium-hard and somewhat elastic. In the adult their upper poles point somewhat obliquely outward. In almost one half of adult men one testicle is suspended lower than the other. The two testes are separated by a septum. During sexual activity, near ejaculation, one or both testes rise until they lie close to the perineal end of the inguinal canals. This appears to happen in conjunction with the rapid shortening—and widening—of the vasa, part of the process of seminal emission (see below).

Function of the testicles is twofold: production of spermatozoa and secretion of sex hormones. These functions are controlled by the central nervous system via pituitary gonadotropin and its fractions. With loss of one testis the other hypertrophies and overproduces, with no loss of function. Even fairly small remnants of one testicle probably suffice to maintain hormonal adequacy. For hormonal function see p. 171.

Spermatogenesis. The main substance of the testicles consists of a system of coiled seminiferous tubules, arranged like a three-dimensional spider web, and subdivided into a few hundred lobular compartments. Each tubule, uncoiled, averages 1 to 2½ feet in length; altogether they furnish a sperm-producing channel estimated to be 250 to 300 meters long. Here spermatozoa are produced in continuous cycles, some groups resting, others active, so that a supply always comes to maturity. Spermatogenesis is not believed to be affected by sex activity, although some unknown feedback action of germinal epithelium on the production of pituitary FSH appears to exist.

The time it takes most germ cells to mature through the various stages and be discharged into the lumen of their tubule as spermatozoa averages close to 2½ months (72.1 days; other observers: 74 ± 5 days). The newly formed spermatozoa are moved out of the testicles by the high secretory pressure (vis-a-tergo) constantly prevailing in healthy, active gonads; by a perpetual, slow (10 to 13 minutes) rhythmic contracting-relaxing cycle of the tough tunica albuginea which envelops each testis; by tiny contractile smooth muscle fragments surrounding the seminiferous tubules; or by a combination of these. The tubules discharge their product into a spongelike network of canals, the rete, situated posteriorly near the upper pole of each testicle; the rete, in turn, via the efferent ductules, drains into the epididymis on its side.

The Epididymis is attached to the upper pole of each testis; each is about 1/9 the size of the latter. Here the efferent ductules form a vast coiled conduction system until they combine into the long tightly convoluted epididymal duct with a total length, if uncoiled, of 4 to 6 meters. The final tail portion (cauda) of each epididymal duct, just before it emerges to form the vas (ductus) deferens, is the principal storage reservoir for spermatozoa.

In the epididymis the spermatozoa undergo final maturation of their ultrastructure, and acquire some motility. Transport through the epididymis—from the lumen of the seminiferous tubule into the cauda or ampulla, ready to be ejaculated—requires 1 to 2½ weeks (median 12 days; known maximum 21 days; fastest about 20 hours). Forward motion is via whipping by cilia lining the duct and by peristalsis of the walls; possibly also by vis-a-tergo, and by remote vacuum suction during ejaculation. Although 300 million sperm mature each day, the maximum output per 24 hours is believed to be one half of this (i.e., one half of all sperm produced are broken down and phaged in the epididymis).

One device in exploring the speed of sperm travel through the male ducts is by marker representing quality change (e.g., certain major systemic disturbances—allergic syndromes, disorders of liver function, virus infections and others—cause changes in the structure of the spermatozoal head). These are first detectable in the ejaculate within 2 to 3 weeks after onset of the disorder, and may persist for weeks, even months, after apparent recovery.

The Leydig (Interstitial) Cells of the testes are the producers of both androgen and estrogen. They lie scattered singly or in groups in the loose connective tissue in the interspaces of the seminiferous tubules; by bulk they constitute only one eighth of the seminiferous apparatus. They are vastly more resistant to stress and insult—radiation, toxicity, systemic infection, starvation, etc.—than the easily disrupted germinal epithelium. The main product of the Leydig cells is testosterone converted by enzyme action from acetate and cholesterol, the latter being the principal stored precursor. Ninety per cent of the testosterone present in the circulation of the human male originates in the testicles. Its synthesis is controlled by pituitary LH, the luteotropic fraction of gonadotropin. It remains uncertain whether any of the human male's circulating estradiol, the most powerful estrogen, is directly secreted by the Leydig cells, or whether all of it is derived from bioconversion of testosterone and immediate precursors. The role of the Sertoli cells in the testicles remains incompletely understood. They are director cells, each responsible for transporting nutrients to a group of maturing germ cells in their immediate area, but via an unknown hormone of their own may also mediate some form of interdependence between spermatogenesis and testosterone production.

EXCRETORY DUCTS AND ACCESSORY GLANDS

The Vasa (vas or ductus deferens) are the continuation of the epididymal ducts. Each is 40 to 45 cm. long; its lumen is about 0.5 mm. From the scrotum each traverses the inguinal canal as part of the spermatic cord, courses upward along the side of the pelvis, crosses the dome of the bladder and reaches the proximity of the prostate where it enlarges to form the *ampulla*. Each vas is joined there by the tapering outlet of the *seminal vesicle* on its side to form the narrow, 20 mm. long *ejaculatory ducts*. These, in turn, pass through the *prostate* and open into the *posterior urethra* as 2 tiny slits close to each other. The prostate gland opens into the urethra nearby with up to 3 dozen small ducts. The *bulbourethral (Cowper's) glands* open into the urethra just below the prostate. The small *urethral (Littré's) glands* are widely present throughout the urethra.

All accessory structures—glands and ducts—secrete chemically differing, specialized fluids which combine into the seminal plasma in which the spermatozoa become suspended. The seminal plasma is the necessary diluent for the thick mass of spermatozoa as found in the epididymides. Both too little fluid and excessive dilution (e.g., after several short order ejaculations) impair sperm motility and cause degradation of the spermatozoa. Cowper's and Littré's glands secrete first, usually during arousal, alkalinizing and lubricating the urethra in anticipation of the passing ejaculate, possibly also supplying some spermatozoal coating. The prostate probably supplies the bulk of most ejaculates, its contribution being a thin fluid with pH 6.5, rich in acid phosphatase, fibrinolytic, proteolytic and other enzymes, calcium, citric acid, and a characteristic high zinc content. The ampullae, in addition to producing secretion, serve as secondary storage for sperm and for other accumulated epididymal products. The role of the seminal vesicles in humans remains incompletely understood. They do not serve as sperm storage, although some spermatozoa are always present, possibly due to reflux. Their pigmented gelatinous product includes the bulk of the fructose and other sugars needed to energize sperm locomotion. In addition to many other organic and inorganic substances they are the source of the more than a dozen E- and F-type prostaglandins active in semen. They seem to replenish ejaculated fluid faster than other accessories, and the fluid pressure prevailing in them at the time is believed to be a factor in the degree of orgasmic intensity experienced.

ERECTION (TUMESCENCE, TURGESCENCE)

Observable during erection are enlargement, elastic hardening and up-righting of the organ. The glans does not harden, although it becomes enlarged. Uprighting can be fairly rapid (e.g., a matter of seconds in young boys and adolescents, but may take a minute or more in many normal men as they leave the age of youth). Arousal and erection are accompanied by a drop or two of clear mucoid precoital secretion from the bulbo-urethral (Cowper's) and urethral (Littré's) glands in about two thirds of adult men (urethrorrhea libidinosa; antiqu. distillatio). To some adolescents this is a source of baseless worry. The secretion may contain viable spermatozoa, without ejaculation having taken place. During sexual arousal there also occurs an increase of secretion from some of the preputial (coronal) glands. During erection the nutritional circulation of the penis is fully maintained and the urethra is in no way compressed.

Stimuli. Erections can be induced by erotic as well as nonerotic stimuli. Nonerotic excitation can occur autonomically, or else reflexly by a variety of touch and pressure sensations. Examples are the prolonged pressure of tight undergarments, a constipated lower bowel, rhythmically jarring gentle motion, or a nonspecific state of physical satisfaction from postprandial satiety. Neither these nor erectant stimuli arising anywhere in or near the genito-urinary tract need penetrate to cortical levels of awareness. Erotic excitation in the adult most commonly is obtained from erotic sights, sounds, smells, imageries, reminiscences, anticipation, thought association or dreams (psychocortical and subcortical induction of erection). However, to sustain the erection for sexual purposes, tactile stimulation of the external genitalia usually must be added; in fact, some stimulation of the penile glans probably must occur in order to initiate the ejaculatory process.

Morning Erections. Of interest is newer knowledge about what is known as morning or "full bladder erection." It is now assumed that urinary accumulation most often does not cause the phenomenon. Waking erection probably is the last of a series of spontaneous erective cycles occurring during sleep, averaging 4 or 5 per night, and becoming longer and stronger as the circadian rhythm of plasma testosterone accumulation is rising towards its early morning peak; a direct cause-effect relationship here remains unconfirmed, however. These erections and semi-erections coincide closely with cyclic dream periods known as REM sleep, which include rapid eye movements, an unusual EEG pattern and various fleeting autonomic changes (Karacan, Fisher, others). These periods occupy about one fourth or one fifth of the total sleep. Daytime sleep may produce a similar pattern. Nocturnal tumescence occurs even following evening coitus, but beginning in the late 30's it then appears to be limited to the latter part of the night.

Mechanism of Erection. A vagal mechanism is chiefly operative in erection, the ultimate impulses being derived from postulated spinal erection centers situated in S-2 to S-4 or S-5 and reaching the penis via the pelvic plexus and the nervi erigentes. Vasodilatation of the arterioles and cavernous sinuses is stimulated, resulting in hugely increased arterial blood inflow. Simultaneously there is inhibition of sympathetic vasoconstrictor impulses. Inflow appears to be aided by a valve mechanism, consisting of longitudinal muscular pillars on the intimae of the small penile vessels and shunts, under neural control. In erection these bolsters open the lumen of the arterioles and partially close the venules. The deep veins of the penis have side-branches—sluice channels—into which blood appears to be reflexly diverted and trapped. It may also be recalled that in vascular stasis the CO_2 content of blood rises, increasing its viscosity, while the fall in oxygen tension alters the red corpuscles and, in turn, increases stasis.

Through the overloading of the blood volume and the resulting mechanical compression the venous outflow is retarded further and engorgement thus maintained. The bulbocavernous muscle and spiral fibers of the ischiocavernous—in the past misnamed erector penis—are subject to tonic reflex contractions and, in theory, additionally compress the corpus cavernosum and the underlying veins, but it is now thought that these muscles contribute negligibly to erection. They can be contracted voluntarily, and briefly increase hardening, but their functional absence does not impair erection. While reflex erection is mediated in the sacral spine, with secondary circuits reaching the thalamus, psychocortically induced erections —visual, olfactory, fantasy, etc.—are represented elsewhere in the brain and appear to be conducted through lumbar segments L-1 to L-3, possibly with some emphasis on adrenergic pathways and mechanisms. It is not known if and what subtle differences exist in the quality of such differing erective mechanisms.

Most types of erections in humans are somewhat under the control of the will in that they can be terminated, initiated or prolonged by directing thought, imagery and participation of the senses in an appropriate manner.

EJACULATION AND ORGASM

Orgasm is somewhat similar in men and women, but ejaculation is a uniquely masculine function. In the adult male orgasm is rarely possible without preceding stimulation of the external genitalia (one major exception: involuntary nocturnal emission), while in women climax following extragenital or even psychic stimulation is not uncommon. In the man, the pleasurable orgasmic sensation centers predominantly in the phallus or the immediate genital area, while in women a pelvic spread of sensation is more usual. Male orgasmic sensation terminates abruptly and is followed by a refractory period—even though brief in very young men—during which the glans penis may be acutely sensitive to touch; in the female sensation tends to cling off more gradually, and multiple, rapid-succession orgasms are feasible for many women.

In principle, ejaculation and orgasm are a functional unit in the normal male adult. Ejaculation without pleasurable climax occurs in certain spinal disorders, some cases of petit mal, heroin and morphine withdrawal syndromes, in severe neurasthenoid potency disorders (p. 385), in electro-ejaculation, etc. Orgasm without ejaculation (dry orgasm, coup sec) occurs physiologically only in prepuberal boys; in adults it is either due to retrograde ejaculation into the bladder (p. 374), or else it follows several preceding close-order sex acts with the stimulus remaining high, but the amount of available fluid, perhaps a drop or two, not enough to reach the meatus.

Ejaculatory Vigor varies from man to man, often from occasion to occasion, depending chiefly on the state of general well-being, the tonus of the man's muscles, his age, his basic sexual drive, degree of arousal, length of prior continence and perhaps fullness of the accessory glands. Ejective vigor can range from forceful to feeble and slow, or even seeping. However, ejaculatory vigor is not a fully reliable indicator of the intensity of the accompanying orgasmic sensation.

The Ejaculatory Process consists of two phases: emission, under sympathetic control, includes the rapid assembly of seminal components, from as far away as the epididymis, and their propulsion into the posterior urethra; and ejaculation proper of the semen, under parasympathetic control, through the anterior urethra and out in the open.

The process begins when repetitive genital stimulation results in a summation of impulses in an ejaculatory center postulated to exist in the superior intermediolateral nuclei of the lateral horns of spinal levels D-12 to L-2 or L-3 to a point where a threshold level is reached. A broad charge of sympathetic impulses is fired via the rami communicantes and the pelvic plexus, together with a probable release of oxytocin from the posterior pituitary. This results chiefly in contraction of smooth muscles surrounding the excurrent ducts and the accessory glands. As the powerfully spiral-muscled walls of the vasa contract rapidly, straightening, widening and shortening their length to less than one-half, the resulting vacuum probably helps suck semen from the epididymal duct. Simultaneously autonomically aroused epididymal cilia and contractions of the epididymal cauda help deliver the semen. This is assisted by the cremasteric lift of one or both testicles against the external inguinal ring. The bladder is now inhibited, and sympathetic stimulation of the internal (urethral) sphincter keeps the bladder neck in involuntary contraction, thus keeping urine out of the urethra as well as preventing backward flux of the semen. The engorged colliculum seminale (verumontanum, urethral crest) may constitute an additional barrier. The anterior urethra has become distended at this point.

Emission. First to expel its secretion into the posterior urethra is the prostate; during earlier stages of sexual stimulation its cortical or "masculine" portion—in response to vagal impulses via the hypogastric nerves—had rapidly and markedly increased its fluid production. Probably next to discharge are the seminal vesicles, by means of 7 to 10 contractions, followed by emission of the spermatozoa and secretions of the ampulla, followed, in turn, by the ductal and epididymal load.

Ejaculation. As the various components of the seminal fluid are emitted into the posterior urethra, where their rapid intermingling takes place, a secondary reflex, this one vagally controlled, sets the perineal (ischiocavernous, bulbocavernous, constrictor urethrae) muscles in spasmodic motion, causing expulsion of the ejaculate in several (5 to 7 usually) jets within less than 10 seconds. While the onset of the climax can frequently be delayed or even somewhat accelerated by an act of will, once the seminal fluid has reached the posterior urethra, ejaculation becomes inevitable and cannot be halted except by brute mechanical obstruction.

Neural Manifestations. During orgasm both autonomic and other neural excitation spreads broadly. The rise in pulse rate, blood pressure and cardiac output which had begun during the arousal stages now reach a rapid peak; intestinal peristalsis is temporarily arrested, breathing becomes disorganized, perspiration may be profuse; the pupils are dilated, and the visual fields shrink to virtual tunnel vision. These changes vastly exceed what one would expect during other kinds of physical exertion of similar intensity. The muscles of the neck, the back and the legs are in extensor spasm, and there may be spasmodic contractions of the face and elsewhere. Semiautomatic vocalizing, compulsive verbalizing, autonomic-type pseudo-weeping and involuntary aggressive impulses (e.g., biting, slapping, beating) may occur. Depending partly on the intensity of the orgasmic experience, degrees of suspended sensory perception and apperception occur; the individual in orgasm may become incapable of responding even to major threatening occurrences or painful stimuli. At times there may be a temporary loss of consciousness.

OBTAINING SEMEN SPECIMEN FOR EXAMINATION

Best Method: After 5 days (others say 4 or 3) of continence, masturbation or coitus interruptus directly into clean or sterilized, dry, dark, widemouthed 2-ounce glass container, tightly capped. Keep or transport at room temperature or slightly below (i.e., jar not to be pocketed in transit). After 20 minutes at room temperature, stir well with blunt glass rod. Examine after 30 to 60 minutes (others say immediately), but not more than 2 to 3 hours. Loss of first drop(s) in coitus interruptus invalidates the sperm count. When an average-type specimen is desired, no set period of prior continence is prescribed. Also, it remains incompletely certain that masturbated ejaculates are identical with coital ones. Obtaining 3 specimens and averaging the results is preferred for accuracy.

Condom Method: Less desirable. Total specimen difficult to measure and/or assemble. Unless withdrawal is practiced some semen is distributed up the condom along penile shaft; if first drops are lost, miscount is likely. Rubber condoms, even prewashed, dry and unpowdered can impair sperm motility; skin-type (sheep's gut), plastic and nylon condoms are safe. Coitus with pin-punctured condom has satisfied religious objections. In transit condom should not be stored in vagina, as temperature is too high.

Other Methods: Vesiculoprostatic expression, needle aspiration, vaginal collection pouch, electroejaculation, etc.; these can be applicable under special circumstances. Modes of specimen collection for artificial insemination differ somewhat.

THE SEMEN

(Seminal Fluid, Liquor Spermaticus. Colloqu. The Sperm.)

Physical Properties. Semen is a white or grayish-white, alkaline substance, opaquely glassy, and sticky to the touch; after prolonged abstinence it has a faintly yellowish tinge. Its consistency when fresh can vary from watery to thickly gelatinous; occasionally it is stringy. The slight but characteristic odor resembles that of chestnut blossom and is derived from amines in the seminal plasma. On contact with the air ejaculated semen curdles and forms a tenacious gel, but by action of its own fibrinolytic enzymes it undergoes spontaneous reliquefaction in less than 30 minutes, becoming more opaque. Semen drying on fabric leaves a pale, sharply demarcated stain with a sinuous, more deeply stained border, stiff-starchy and later brittle to the touch, and somewhat difficult to wash out. Semen fluoresces clearly in ultraviolet light, but this test is not specific; other albuminous material also gives bluish fluorescence.

Volume. Sperm Content. The amount of semen ejaculated after 3 days of continence averages less than a teaspoonful: median amount 3.5 ml, average range 2½ to 6 ml, known record 15 ml. Normally volume varies considerably with age, prior emissions and probably the intensity of sexual arousal. In successive ejaculations, if in close order, the amount diminishes progressively to the point of a practically dry orgasm. The spermatozoa in late close-order ejaculates have scant fertilizing power. This appears equally true for spermatozoa in the first specimen after long —more than a week—continence. High frequency of ejaculatory sex activity has been associated with an increased availability of semen, possibly also of mature spermatozoa, but it is uncertain which of three possible cause-effect relationships applies: use stimulating production, production inducing use, or both being stimulated endocrinally.

The number of spermatozoa in normal human semen, after several days of continence, averages 80 to 100 million per milliliter, and not rarely up to double this amount. The first portion—in fact, the first drop(s)—of the ejaculate contains the greatest concentration of normal, motile spermatozoa in the vast majority of men; based on this are modern split-ejaculate techniques leading to more concentrated inseminating fluid. Couples highly anxious to conceive may cohabitate too frequently, and thus excessively lower the count of mature spermatozoa in the ejaculate. A conservative estimate of the total ejaculate during a normal man's lifetime is 18 quarts, but up to ten times this amount has been calculated for some sexually extremely active (homosexual) males. Lifetime production—but not emission, which is less by about half—of spermatozoa in humans is believed to average 4 trillion.

Quality of Semen (i.e., ultimately its fertilizing capacity) is determined microscopically. Macroscopic features—amount, appearance, viscosity, turbidity—are not considered reliable indicators of seminal quality. A man's semen—morphology and motility percentages, but not the count— appears to remain constant throughout his reproductive life while he is in good health; the characteristic patterning has been likened to that of a fingerprint.

The most important yardsticks of the quality of spermatozoa are their number and concentration on microscopic analysis (spermiogram, spermogram), their morphology, the percentage of those in motion, and the speed energy, direction and formation of their locomotion. The minimum number of spermatozoa compatible with fertility is assumed to be 20 million/ml (oligospermia), although exceptionally impregnation has occurred with counts as low as 500,000/ml sperms if highly active. As regards morphology, at least 80 per cent of spermatozoa must be of normal shape and size; or else not more than 15 per cent to 30 per cent deformed, and not more than 2 per cent immature (spermatids). As regards sperm motility, good quality is evidenced according to some authorities by 70 per cent to 80 per cent of spermatozoa showing strong forward progression, especially

THE HUMAN SPERMATOZOON

Anatomy: Average length 55 microns (0.05 to 0.06 mm), mostly tail. Components are the head, neck, midpiece and subdivided tail (flagellum). Head, except for a thin layer (headcap) is mostly nucleus; carries genetic material, nutrient lipids, metabolites, barrier penetrant and other enzymes as well as defensive and aggressive (cumulus and corona-dispersing hyaluronidase; lysin for zona surrounding ovum?) coatings in the acrosome. Outer enveloping and inner membranes exist. Round-headed, small, speedy Male-(Y chromosome)-carrying and larger, slower, oval-headed Female-(X)-bearing sperms exist in equal numbers (see box p. 219). Morphologic variants include taperforms, double heads, pin heads, double tails, megaloforms, etc.

Locomotion and Viability. Forward movement produced by whipping motion of tail via a system of contractile fibres, fibrils and riblike structures; with necessary energy being created chemically, then transferred, from tightly coiled mitochondrial helices in the midpiece. Velocity varies with the medium, fastest probably in uterine and tubal secretions. In vitro sperm swims average of 3½ to 5 mm per minute (6 to 8 mm for the strongest, swiftest one third). Sperm rotates as it moves. Nonmotility is not proof of death. No fertility without motility, but motility is not proof of fertilizing capacity.

Payload. Nucleus of head is tightly packed with nucleoproteins, the seat of all hereditary traits. Average deoxyribonucleic acid content:
$$2.2 \text{ to } 2.6 \times 10^{-9} \text{ mg. DNA per sperm.}$$

in phalanx-like formation, with not more than 10 per cent or 20 per cent wandering about feebly, aimlessly or in stationary motion (asthenospermia). Not less than 60 per cent must be motile after two hours.

However, serially repeated motility determinations appear meaningless, as seminal plasma is not the physiologic medium of spermatozoa beginning a few minutes after ejaculation. Clinically preferable in a specific-partner fertility work-up would be a postcoital test, either by capillary tube or in vivo, to measure interaction of sperm motility and the cervical factor: coitus is performed during the predicted fertile (ovulatory) period; within 4 to 6 hours cervical mucus is examined in a hanging drop under a cover slip. Normalcy is presumed with at least 4 actively motile spermatozoa per high power field.

Female Organs and Functions

MONS PUBIS (MONS VENERIS)

This adipose prominence overlies the pubic symphysis and is not part of the genitalia proper. It is covered with thick, rather coarse and curly hair, but this is scantier and softer in most blonde women. This hair forms the characteristic female escutcheon. The mons, as a rule, is not sensitive to erotic tactile stimulation, but rhythmic pressure stimulation of the general area is excitatory in many cases because of the direct and probably indirect (traction) effect on the underlying crura of the clitoris, the ischiocavernous muscles inserting into them, and on the suspensory ligament of the clitoris.

VULVA

(Vulval Cleft, External Genitalia, Pudendum, Pudenda.)

The vulva includes the labia majora and approximately all structures which can be detected when the labia majora are drawn apart: chiefly labia minora and Bartholin's glands, clitoris and preputium, urethral meatus, vestibule and its erectile bulbs, and hymen. The vulva is richly vascular and during sexual excitement some of its components become bluishly engorged or swell. The pattern of these swellings varies with the individual (i.e., it may take circular, bipartite or similar form). The position of the vulva with respect to the body varies slightly from woman to woman (i.e., it may be located more rearward or more forward) but in the normal, nongravid adult these variations are more apparent than real and probably due to varying pelvic tilts in conformity with each woman's habitual posture.

LABIA MAJORA

These are 2 thick (1 to 1½ cm.) adipose cushions, covered with fine hair, particularly on their upper-outer surfaces, and containing numerous sebaceous and other surface glands. The inner surfaces are pink or bluish, smooth and moist, although in the multipara their appearance may be more skinlike. In the well-nourished virgin with small labia minora they are in apposition; in other women they may gape somewhat. Embryologically, they correspond to the male scrotum. During sexual excitement the labia majora of multiparous women become engorged to double or more their size, thus adding to the entry funnel of the vulvovaginal passage. In the nullipara this is preceded by outward flattening of the structures during the early stage of arousal.

LABIA MINORA

(Lesser Labia, Inner Lips, Nymphae.)

These 2 folds of tissue are thin but quite firm, smooth, moist, devoid of hair, often redundant, and of pink—bluish in brunettes—hue. Their across width ("length") varies greatly; average is 1 to 2 in. Very long nymphae may occur familially in conjunction with copious sex activity; racial differences may also exist. Moderately hypertrophic ("marital") nymphae sometimes protrude through the labia majora in repose, either at their upper end or in toto. Such protruding nymphae may appear more skinlike, and very long ones may distinctly hang. With old age the nymphae tend to disappear due to atrophy. Sometimes additional or accessory labia occur.

Anteriorly (i.e., at their upper pole) the labia minora become two folds which form the preputium and the frenulum of the clitoris, respectively. The labia during coitus usually are subjected to both friction and a rhythmic lifting-descending motion by the thrusting phallus which indirectly involves the clitoris (see below). The nymphae are well innervated and richly vascular. At the height of sexual excitement there is considerable swelling and expansion in length, which adds to the overall length of the coital canal. During sexual activity they also undergo a distinct color change, turning bright pink or red in the nullipara, a deeper wine red in the multiparous woman, about a minute prior to orgasm, and disappearing shortly thereafter. In fact, Masters and Johnson during their direct visual observation of many female laboratory subjects engaged in sexual activity saw none reaching orgasm without first having these labial color changes; they consider the change proof of impending climax, providing the stimulation is maintained.

The labia minora have sebaceous glands, but few if any sweat glands. The two bean-shaped *bartholinian glands,* one in each labium minor, 5 mm long, have their opening on the inside surface of the labia near the introitus. They secrete a small amount of mucous—least in the nullipara—upon coital friction, but the amount is greater when the act has been prolonged. Bartholin's glands may also be scent glands.

CLITORIS

This small vascular structure is the embryologic counterpart of the man's penis; major differences include small size, absence of canalization and lack of a third cavernous body. The body (shaft) of the clitoris is suspended by a ligament from the front of the bony symphysis; it divides into 2 crura which are attached to and follow the pubic arches downward and outward. Length of the clitoris is measured from the dividing point of the crura; although difficult to measure and unreliable in vivo, combined length of shaft and glans seems to average close to 3 cm with many variations both in length and thickness. The clitoris is freely—up to 1 inch—mobile up and down the midline. It can rarely be visualized on inspection even when fully tumescent. In aging women the organ may appear to be more prominent, partly because of shrinkage of surrounding fat pads. Under the clitoral prepuce (hood) smegma may accumulate; sometimes it is malodorous, and often in the form of small hard pellets.

The glans of the clitoris can be felt in the approximate size and shape of a pea or a pencil eraser. It is richly vascular and often, but not always, well innervated with genital sensory corpuscles; the latter are also found inside the corpora cavernosa. The clitoris, notably its shaft, is highly responsive to erotic stimulation, while the glans is often too sensitive to permit prolonged direct tactile stimulation. However, erection proper with elastic uprighting and hardening as is observed in the penis, probably does not occur in the clitoris. Instead the stimulated female's shaft thickens—elongation is unusual during coitus—while the glans, especially if it is fairly large to begin with, swells palpably in a proportion of women. The congestive changes in the female are slower to appear than corresponding erections in males; they also take longer to disappear.

The organ probably responds with some minimum tumescence to any erotic arousal, but for maximal local response rhythmic stimulation is ordinarily necessary; this may be either direct (tactile), or indirect by traction and motion via labia minora and prepuce or from above through the mons pubis. At the height of arousal the clitoris retracts against the anterior symphysis so that the preputial hood seems to be empty; upon lessening of arousal it descends again, moving to and fro at times during the sexual act. At the height of arousal the clitoris has been said to throb rhythmically at the rate of 1 or 2 times per second (disputed).

Frequent and prolonged clitoral self-manipulation seems to produce some thickening and perhaps lengthening of the clitoral body. How lasting this is once the stimulatory pattern ceases, and what the biomechanism is, largely escapes us today. Neither a frequent clitoral petting pattern nor a moderate amount of masturbation, even if lifelong, seem by themselves capable of producing similar hypertrophy. While the potential maximum size of the adult penis seems to be genetically precoded for each man, this is probably not the case for the clitoris, which tends to increase in size with an increase of the plasma concentration of androgenic compounds, especially of testosterone. In virilization (p. 358), as the increased circulating androgens enlarge and vascularize the clitoris, they also sensitize the organ erotically in a proportion of women. Masturbatory release may be the result, especially if normal contacts are unavailable or insufficient, and it is this simultaneous appearance of an urge to masturbate and clitoral hypertrophy in virilizing women which seems to have been the source of misconceptions about manipulatory clitoromegaly. However, the longer the androgenic changes persist, the less likely they are, as a rule, to completely regress after the cause of virilization has been removed.

HYMEN

(Virginal Membrane, Maidenhead.)

The hymen is a thin fold of tissue, a perforated membrane, which partially closes the vaginal introitus of the virgo intacta. It is completely concealed from unaided external view by the labia minora which are in apposition over it. It is formed of connective tissue and covered by mucosa, all of it well vascularized. Consistency varies from parchment-like thinness to, occasionally, that of a thick, ligament-like membrane, average thickness being 2 to 3 mm, less at the free lip. Ordinarily the hymen has little elasticity, but in a small number of women it can be sufficiently elastic not to be torn by months or even years of marital intercourse and, in a few known cases, not even by 1 or 2 childbirths.

The hymenal opening in the adult woman is round or semilunar in shape, less often septate, slit-shaped or eccentrically situated. Even rarer are sieve-like, denticulate or fimbriate apertures, the latter sometimes giving the appearance of pseudodefloration. An imperforate hymen leads to vaginal distention and hematocolpos after menarche, and incision is necessary. A completely absent hymen is a rarity. The average diameter of the unentered opening is between ¾ and 1 inch upon gentle stretching; openings originally admitting less than a fingertip probably are infrequent. The virginal opening may become somewhat enlarged as a result of vaginal examinations, douches and the use of indwelling sanitary tampons. The "marital" but nulliparous opening averages 1½ to 1¾ inches, while the parous one averages 2 inches, thus admitting 3 fingers. Following a period of cohabitation the hymen usually becomes a ring of nodular fragments, the carunculae hymenales (or myrtiformes). After childbirth or copious sex relations the hymenal rests may become ironed out close to the point of disappearance.

Spontaneous hymenal tears have been seen following perineal and crotch injuries, including kicks, and possibly some falls; also from ballet split positions, from hurdle jumps on horseback and from hurtling rides astride a motorcycle back seat. However, most non-impaling crotch falls and injuries, as well as ordinary athletic overexertion, cause defloration rarely, if ever.

Function of the hymen is not known; it is most probably an afunctional rudiment. The importance ascribed to it in various cultures has ranged between the extremes of elaborate, ritualistic concern with its physical presence and routine incision during childhood. In our present culture preoccupation with anatomic intactness is giving way to a more matter-of-fact attitude, or even to a studied disregard of its existence. Nevertheless, for those so motivated, the hymen frequently remains a symbolic rallying point for chaste resolves and moral scruples.

VAGINA. VAGINAL CERVIX

In repose the vagina is an irregularly shaped passage whose walls are partly collapsed and adherent. Its general direction is cephalad, parallel with the rectum. In the flatly reclining woman it is directed only slightly below the horizontal; with legs hyperflexed it angles toward the tip of the sacrum; standing or sitting it points toward the midsacrum. Vaginal length—fourchette to posterior fornix wall—of the nullipara in repose is 7 to 8 cm and about an inch longer at the height of sexual excitement. Length of the complete coital canal or vulvovaginal passage, from subpubic ligament to sacral hollow, recumbent, subtracting the thickness of the posterior vaginal and 2 empty rectal walls, averages 5½ to 6 inches (14 cm or slightly more); vulval excitatory congestion can add further to this length. In obese women thick external genitalia may give the man the illusion of an additionally lengthened coital canal. Basic vaginal length is not notably affected by either parity or age. The proportional relationship between body size and vaginal size in the normally developed woman has not been established. Foreshortening of the vagina occurs in pregnancy, some uterine malpositions, sexual infantilism and some other conditions.

Innervation. Sensory nerve endings in the vaginal mucosa are scant or absent, except probably for fine fibres in a touch-sensitive mucosal area in the anterior wall near the introitus, extending upward for less than 2 cm and about 2½ cm from side to side (Krantz, others). However, sexual sensation is perceived in the perivaginal tissues which are endowed with proprioceptive nerve endings sensitive to movement, pressure and stretching (e.g., when the copulatory organ distends the vagina). Vater-Pacini and Herbst corpuscles—the presumed receptors—and associated ganglion cells have been identified in the perivaginal fat, in the bulbocavernous muscles, near the numerous blood vessels forming the submucous erectile tissue, especially of the lateral vaginal walls, and in the epineurium of large nerves.

Size and Tonus. The vagina is distensible in all its dimensions. Its across-distensibility and tonus, thus ultimately its "size" (width) during the sex act depend partly on congenital characteristics, on the woman's general and pelvic muscle tonus, and occasionally on sequelae of childbirth. Relaxed vaginal walls offer little contact and resistance to the intromitted phallus (see p. 406). Also "size" is confused by some couples with relative introital tightness or gaping, although the size factors determining introital size seem to stand in no definable or constant relationship to either width or tonus of the vagina. The amount of endogenous lubrication may also alter a mate's subjective impression of size. In past eras astringent applications and packing (alum, rock salt, etc.) were used to produce the illusion of tightness of the coital canal; this also served to suggest hymenal intactness to an unsophisticated bridegroom.

Perivaginally, in its lower one third, and especially at the sides and posteriorly, muscle fibers from the levator ani group and their fasciae are inserted, notably the pubococcygeals. Somewhat lower, at the level of the introitus, the bulbocavernous muscles help form a vaginal sphincter group of variable strength (the old constrictor cunni). Size and strength of these voluntary muscles vary from woman to woman; they are subject to atrophy and atonia from disuse and from other causes, but often can be rehabilitated (see p. 418). As a rule these muscles contract reflexly (e.g., when stimulated kinesthetically by vaginal distention); but an occasional woman either has or develops a capacity for their voluntary activation and control, notably of the introital ring of constrictor fibers (e.g., a prostitute picking coins off a table in this fashion). Rotary (screwlike), thrusting and similar female coital motions depend on the muscles of the pelvic floor in toto as well as on gluteal, abdominal and other muscle groups.

At the height of sexual arousal the upper (inner) two thirds of the vagina widen considerably, doubling or tripling the canal's width near the cervix, at least under laboratory conditions. At the same time the lower third may begin to tumesce, narrowing the entry-area's lumen. The vaginal walls ordinarily are transversely rugose, as well as ridged. The rugae tend to flatten and stretch during sexual arousal. With copious sexual use the walls may become either more corrugated and even grossly folded, or else smooth and flabby depending largely on the musculofascial tonus of the walls. In women of asthenic build the vaginal walls tend to be thin. The numerous veins anastomosing beneath the mucosal layer of the vagina produce the vasocongestion which lubricates the canal by transudation early during sexual excitement. Local varicosities, possibly resulting from incomplete or delayed detumescence, may contribute to an irregular configuration of the wall.

The Cervix of the uterus protrudes partly into the vagina, helping form the well-known fornices and vaults. Its erotic sensitivity to direct stimulation by the glans penis varies; it is considerable in some women, but apparently is easily inhibited (e.g., by deep-thrust dyspareunia) (p.271) or, irrationally, by fear of pregnancy. It is not certain if some congestion of the cervix occurs during sexual excitation. At the height of sexual arousal the cervix, unless retropositioned, tends to follow the corpus uteri as it ascends into the false pelvis; it thus helps balloon out the upper vagina via a "tenting" effect. Following orgasm the os of the cervix has been seen to gape somewhat for 20 to 30 minutes, at least in nulligravidae. The mucus secreted by the endocervical glands is usually rather thick, viscous and tenacious. About 2 days prior to ovulation it undergoes a change, in response to the increase in the circulating estrogen: its volume increases, it becomes thinner and more translucent until it grossly resembles egg-white; it has increased flow elasticity, and greater threadiness in pulling apart (see also p. 221). The well-known arborization pattern of cervical mucus during the proliferative phase is also seen, somewhat less clearly, in the nasal mucus. With the progestational phase of the cycle the mucus becomes scantier, more viscous and relatively sperm-hostile again.

SEXUAL AROUSAL. ORGASM

(Climax, Acme.)

Sexual Storm. Sexual arousal in the female produces widespread transient changes in physiologic functioning. This "sexual storm" permeates the entire body, notably the autonomic nervous system. Cardiac output increases the rise in pulse and blood pressure may be steep and rapid, breathing deepens, the skin is warm and flushed, and many skin areas have heightened erotic sensitivity to touch. There are often tonus changes in the pelvic muscles and in those of the lower face, and some reflex abduction of the thighs. The pupils dilate, the visual fields narrow. As the sexual act proceeds the face increasingly expresses absorbed concentration. The mind becomes oblivious of the surroundings, and there is some inhibition of the faculties of the cerebral cortex, while a pleasurably tense "full-yet-unfilled" feeling seems to pervade the pelvic area. Still later, at the peak, there may be spastic contractions of the muscles of the neck and the extremities, with clutching, clawing or scratching motions of the hands. The flushed face reflects concentration, perhaps even more intense now, but less straining. Involuntary sounds may be emitted, or there may be repetitive verbalizing. Just before a climax sensory perception may be abolished in part; the eyes become "unseeing," sound is not heard, and pain not felt; there may be momentary clouding, possibly even loss, of consciousness.

Genital Signs. The overall picture is one of engorgement of the pelvic organs—internal, external and supporting structures, as well as the anorectal complex. Loading of the peripheral circulation also occurs, and these shifts produce a corresponding drainage of blood from the abdominal viscera. The first objective genital sign is the rapid secretion of mucoid moisture as a transudation (sweating) through the vaginal walls. It appears rapidly, increases as excitement mounts, but lessens during the orgasmic phase. A clear, tenacious, nonsticky mucus from the vestibular glands may also be secreted, but Bartholin's glands secrete their introital lubricant in more than minimal amounts only after stimulation has become intense or prolonged. Secretion may be scanty in some women even when maximally aroused, but this does not imply psychologic unreadiness for intercourse nor orgasmic incapacity. Conversely, even copious secretion does not necessarily mean psychologic readiness for intromission. As the vagina lengthens and widens, a series of swelling, flushing, gripping and throbbing manifestations of the vulvovaginal structures accompany the progression of sexual excitement to and through the climactic stage. The muscles and sphincters of the pelvic floor also contract. Oxytocin, released reflexly, helps set the smooth muscles of the uterus and tubes into peristaltic motion, as the organ together with its cervix is partially elevated into the false pelvis. Catecholamines are released into the circulation, and the relative balance of the steroid hormones may undergo some rapid changes (theory).

Extragenitally the veins in the mucosa of the nasal walls become engorged. The breasts become firmer and eventually larger. The nipples erect and may become turgid, even without tactile stimulation, very small and very large ones least, and sometimes one before the other. The Montgomery follicles may also erect, and eventually the whole areolar area of the breasts can appear somewhat puffy, even dwarfing the nipples. As sexual excitation heightens a transient measles-like rash or "sexual flush," more visible in blonde and redhaired women, has been seen to spread from the abdomen across the chest wall and the underside of the breasts.

THE GREAT CLITORAL CONTROVERSY

It is alive again, in new dress, after having been buried. Freud held that habitual clitoral orgasm preference in the grown woman was the product of an infantile feeling fixation, a failure to transfer to the maturity of vaginal enjoyment. The theory fell into disuse when a more holistic view —the genital apparatus as a whole, with fused or alternative site choices— was becoming accepted. Lately radical feminists, misinterpreting the Masters' laboratory observations, have held that the clitoris is the "key" to female orgasm. Think Clitoris! the most far-out among them exhort their fellow women, and escape reproductive enslavement and dependence on the phallus.

Climaxes may be alike in many observable ways no matter how they are produced—and they can, indeed, be produced in many wondrous ways in the female. But numerous women have indicated that the quality of what direct vulvo-clitoral manipulation can give them differs sharply from climaxing via a fused sex act (i.e., coital thrusting by an organ with a human male attached).

In female orgasmology intensity is not the same as quality, nor is relief the same as rapture.

Clitorally produced sensation is acute, more explosive (Moulton); the woman concentrates intensely on her own demands; she extracts pleasure. "It gets rid of the tension, but it's not really as good." Clitoral climaxing is instant-repeat-inviting (e.g., up to dozens of consecutive times with those super-pleasurizers, the electric stimulating devices which eliminate the tired-arm-barrier and which at least one observer has called addictive).

In Coital Stimulation the woman surrenders some of her transported feeling tone to her mate's desires and needs. It is a giving, in part. Climax here is more diffuse, harder to describe or localize, "more like voluptuous." Rarely more than a few orgasms per climactic plateau are needed for full gratification, although this is presumably as much a conditioned response as high multiple climaxing; besides, few male partners can hold on for more than this.

It has been suggested that a multipara with heavily arousal-congested genitalia may need about 3 orgasms in series for satisfying detumescence, and that a minimum of 4½ minutes of active, uninterrupted coital thrusting by the male is needed for this by the average woman. As any interruption of thrusting almost instantly lowers the level of the female excitement state, the male needs to be able to count on maintaining his erection for at least 10 to 15 minutes to complete the cycle of these females' coital arousal and detumescence.

Orgasm follows arousal after varying intervals whose extremes may range from seconds to an hour. Two to 5 orgasms may occur in fairly rapid succession during one sexual act, or there may be a prolonged suborgasmic plateau of voluptuous sensation spiked by individual climaxes each lasting several (2 to 10) seconds. Many of the observable physiologic effects of sexual arousal and orgasm are reportedly identical regardless of whether they result from intercourse, solitary masturbation, electric vibrator or motorized dildo, and regardless of whether the coital canal, the shaft of the clitoris or other erogenous zones are stimulated. Some of this can be accepted only with reservations. Visible genital phenomena may not differ, but there are weighty indications that psychomotor manifestations, quality of feeling tone and afterglow, local adrenergic and hormonal reactions, to name some, differ with the type of sex activity and the attendant emotive-affectional pattern mobilized in connection with it.

Mechanisms. In the majority of women the attainment of orgasm during sexual intercourse does not depend on any single structure or surface of the genital tract. All of the genital apparatus participates to some degree in triggering off a climax and, besides, general somatic and psychologic mechanisms of often equal power are also operative. As the thrusting phallus distends the vulvovaginal passage, sensations may arise from friction against various engorged portions of the vulva, from proprioceptive nerve endings outside the vaginal mucosa, from the clitoris as it is being subjected to rhythmic heave and pull via its envelopes and the nymphae or, more directly, as for some high-riding moments the clitoral shaft and crura are subjected to pressure against the dorsum penis or even between the bony symphyses. The cervix is not infrequently highly sensitive to direct stimulation by the glans penis.

At least some part is played by tactile-kinesthetic sensations relating to bodily nearness, weight and motion; by psychic stimuli due to the affectionate knowledge of being united and pleasing the other; by a sense of reception and possession; by feelings of anticipation and fulfillment; or by such varied but sometimes highly exciting feeling as a sense of being wanted, annihilated, subdued, penetrated, adored, taken, hurt, needed, impregnated or whatever, according to individual emotional needs, whether conscious or unconscious, healthy or neurotic. Observations of the mate's arousal is in itself a powerful stimulant; some wives are conditioned to climax at or near the husband's ejaculation and from almost nothing else. A part is played by the senses of hearing and smell; by simultaneous extragenital stimulation (e.g., breasts); or even by self-stimulation by way of fantasy and imagery. It may be reasonable to assume that orgasm-ex-coito, to be fully satisfying, usually must be produced by a composition of stimuli.

Variables. Not every woman exhibits every sign. Both subjective and physiologic responses of orgasm vary from woman to woman, and even from occasion to occasion in the same woman. Subjectively orgasm may range from tenuous (i.e., a mildly satisfying sense of fulfillment with some local congestion, and marked by no more than a slight sigh and a shiver) to the most intensely ecstatic and transported sensations together with spasms, throbbing, writhing and feelings described as "melting," "volcanic," "vanishing"; both extremes may be entirely satisfying to their respective possessors. Both constitutional factors and certain well-known variables account for the differences: the state of health and vigor, the feeling of well-being, length of previous abstinerce, intensity of sexual arousal, temperamental differences, the all-important constitutional androgenic endowment (degree of "sexedness"), possibly the phase of the menstrual cycle, parity perhaps, and freedom from interfering problems, preoccupations, fears, phobias, or unconscious feelings of guilt, to name the most prominent factors. Also the capacity of optimal apperception via the vaginal and perivaginal structures apparently must wait for full physiologic sexual maturation—not usually before the end of the teens or even later—but also for the establishment of a reasonably regular pattern of coition (theory).

In women orgasm may well be a conditioned response; not all women achieve it. But in the well-conditioned woman sex feeling and orgasm are hardy manifestations: they have survived hysterectomy, colpectomy, clitoridectomy, vulvectomy, bilateral ovariectomy and even complete exenteration of pelvic organs; they have been achieved by coition in the artificial (surgically constructed) vagina, although they have not survived adrenalectomy or hypophysectomy (e.g., in tumor cases).

FOR JOURNAL LITERATURE AND ADDITIONAL READING

Masters, W. H., and Johnson, V. E.: Human Sexual Response. Boston, Little Brown, 1966

MacDonald, R. R.: Scientific Basis of Obstetrics and Gynecology. Baltimore, Williams & Wilkins, 1971

McKerns, K. W. (ed.): The Gonads. New York, Appleton-Century-Crofts, 1969

Sigusch, V.: Excitation und Orgasmus bei der Frau. Stuttgart (W. Germ.), Enke Verlag, 1970

CHAPTER 11

Premarital Consultation

General Examination — Sex Information and Guidance — Some
Special Premarital Situations: Middle and Advanced Age —
Mental Retardation.

Premarital examinations are part of the expanding field of preventive
medicine. Most states make at least partial examination of each applicant
for a marriage license compulsory, but mere compliance with the minimum
letter of the law (e.g., a serologic test for syphilis and a cursory physical
examination) can no longer be regarded as optimal practice in our time.
Health is one of the fundamentals of happiness in marriage, and the health
of each consort is a major, legitimate concern of the other. Chronic sickness deprives and damages the other, detracts from the zest for living and
tends to reduce the couple's socioeconomic standard. Young people of all
social levels today—apart from those engaged in social experiments (see
p. 456)—show a growing desire to enter marriage prepared: courses for
engaged couples are· spreading; counseling on economic and emotional
aspects of couple existence is fairly widely sought; there is premarital
concern with the hereditary risk of certain afflictions by those planning
offspring; and there is frank interest in the reproductive aspects, mostly
contraception and sexual functioning.

The Need. Although young people appear sexually more sophisticated
and experienced today earlier in life than ever before, and ventilation of
reproductive topics and worries is less hampered today by shyness, a substantial number of marriage candidates possess much less essential sex
information than is commonly assumed. Often those seemingly most emancipated or engaging in intimacies for the longest time need to be told some
of the most elementary things. The former reigning belle and instigatress
of a high school sex club was sure pregnancy could not occur if the boy did
not go in "all the way, into the womb" but limited intromitting thrusts to
half the length of his penile shaft; a juvenile salpingitis had all along protected her against conception. A promiscuous 22-year-old bride with a
background of 5 years of continuous father-daughter incest until age 14

worried that her climaxing never brought a gush of liquid as in a man and requested treatment for retrograde ejaculation she had seen mentioned.

Reticent Physicians. Physicians should be at least as qualified as anyone else to respond to reproductive problems and sexual worries. Yet there has long been an almost traditional disinclination to discuss sexual questions with patients, including premarital applicants. Many persons continue to be a little afraid that they may be importuning their physician if they ask for sex information. Some physicians feel they have insufficient familiarity with the subject to venture into an advisory role. Others fear that they may offend one or the other's religious doctrine; which is groundless, as all of them permit or even encourage sex counseling. Also, there

---

RE: PREMARITAL CONSULTATION

"It is wise for the doctor's composure . . . if he refrains from detailed advice about . . . the wedding night until he finds out if the young lady is pregnant." DR. PAUL SCHOLTEN

A premarital examination is strictly the business of the young woman and her future husband. "This is not like former visits under your mother's apron strings to your pediatrician. From now on, you are establishing your own individuality as a mature woman . . ." DR. GOODRICH C. SCHAUFFLER

"We do not expect men to be endlessly fascinated by the ins and outs of feminine plumbing." BARBARA SEAMAN, Letter to the *N.Y. Times,* December 1972

---

survives a belief that "love always finds a way" or that "nature will take its course," or that advice on sex hygiene destroys the romance of an impending marriage, all of which have proven untrue. Contemporary pioneers such as Calderone, Lief, McHugh, Trainer, Vincent are contributing to a noticeable improvement trend as regards the preparation for sex counseling in medical and various graduate schools.

GENERAL EXAMINATION

Full Service. A complete premarital examination of a couple consists of a general health examination, compliance with the laws regarding venereal detection and an offer of sex counseling conferences with bride and groom. If a minor disorder is found, some flexibility in using the term "perfect (excellent) health" may spare a medically unsophisticated young couple needless worry. However, any major disorder in an incipient or latent stage should not only be brought fully to the patient's attention, but he (she) should be encouraged to be frank about this to the other party, especially if the disorder may conceivably affect life expectancy or earning capacity, or if it is a condition (in the bride) which may be aggravated by pregnancy. The physician, of course, cannot take it upon himself to apprise the other party of a positive finding without the patient's consent. For full service many experienced practitioners favor 2 or even 3 premarital visits and a follow-up appointment 6 to 8 weeks after the wedding. The first examination should take place 2 to 4 weeks before the projected day to allow time for any necessary further investigation and attention. Examinations are best conducted in a manner which encourages further questions.

Bride's Pelvic. The bride's examination is more complex than the groom's, as she is the fulcrum of the reproductive unit. Menstrual history, pelvic examination, contraceptive advice if desired, and search for potential childbearing obstacles are part of being of service to her. Gynecologically, in addition to the usual expeditious survey, there would be search for external malformations, hypoplasia of the internal structures, fungal and other infections, as well as appraisal of the status of the hymen with any necessary remedial action (see p. 229). Occasionally orthopedic problems or unusual obesity suggest special coital advice (p. 232). Some young women erroneously feel that no further genital examination is necessary as they have had premarital intercourse.

Advice on Child-spacing is legal in the vast majority of states if the physician believes that it is indicated for reasons of health or personal welfare. The prevailing practice is for the physician to do the necessary prescribing, instructing or fitting either at the time of the bride's pelvic examination or during a subsequent conference. It is done at the request either of the couple, or of the bride even without the expressed consent of the groom; or the physician may inquire of the couple if they desire such advice; or even, in some cases, advise, unasked, that it may be beneficial to postpone offspring and then inquire if they know how to prevent pregnancy. The best method for newlyweds is oral contraception as it permits full sexual spontaneity during the honeymoon. The pills should be commenced 2 months prior to marital onset to permit adjusting choice of product and getting used to minor initial discomfort. Brides who desire to eliminate the cyclic bleeding may continue on a combined pill for 6 weeks. Rhythm method by calendar must be commenced 6 months, or preferably 12, before the wedding to obtain a meaningful calculation (p. 301), but this is probably unnecessary if temperature rhythm is used.

Venereal Search. Legislation stressing compulsory premarital tests for syphilis had ceased being considered a rational measure by many physicians in the 1950's and 60's, but with the present epidemic proportions of VD, most opposition has abated now. One of the remaining valid arguments is that, apart from a false sense of venereal security, such laws popularize the erroneous belief that "a blood test is all that's needed," and that without this belief more patients would accept or request—and more physicians would make—more complete physical examinations which, in turn, would lead to other desirable premarital attention. At least one state permits physicians to disclose a diagnosis of VD to the patient's future spouse, and to parent or guardian, without subjecting the doctor to liability. The same law allows physicians to treat minors for VD without informing parents or guardian.

Genetic Advice. Basic genetic counseling, where indicated, is becoming increasingly expected as part of the premarital consultation, although in more difficult cases the physician may prefer to refer the couple for genetic analysis and counseling to one of the specialized practitioners or institutes to be found in many parts of the country. In cousin marriages an exceptionally careful search for inheritable disorders or defects including blood relatives' by history is indicated. In such unions there is an increased possibility that latent deleterious traits will be brought out in the open in the couple's future offspring. More than half the states prohibit marriage between first cousins. Cousin marriages may be fewer in our increasingly mobile and migratory civilization, but an increase in environmental mutagens—radioactive fall-out, clinical radiographic exposure—may make up for this by increasing the hazard for the children of blood relatives.

SEX INFORMATION AND GUIDANCE

Offering Information. The physician cannot assume that because a couple seem to be intelligent—or educated, perhaps sophisticated, or highly emancipated and asking no questions—that they are not in need of some frank information on one or more to them problematic aspects of sex. Possibly they cannot bring themselves to ask: timidity in this area has not ceased to exist. The subject of sex can be tentatively introduced while taking the menstrual history or examining the pelvis or while advising on how to recognize early signs of pregnancy. It may be asked, is she worried about the sex side of marriage? Is he? To whom have they talked—or, what have they read—about how to accomplish healthy marital relations? Men tend to be more reticent than their brides. The groom may not want the doctor to think that he is completely inexperienced; or he may be afraid that in talking he may have to acknowledge masturbation or some homosexual episode, past or recent. Embarrassment is most easily overcome where the physician uses words such as sex, intercourse, penis, vagina, erection—"private" or "a hard" is acceptable to most females—from the beginning, setting the tone of the talk at a level of clinical frankness. Couples requesting that all conferring be done jointly usually have dealt with the subject of sex between themselves in some manner and there is rarely need for being less expressive and frank than in individual conference.

Technics. Premarital group instruction and discussion, both joint and separated by sexes, is a desirable new trend; such groups have been sponsored by high schools, colleges, churches and temples, unions, service clubs, clinics, large medical groups, social agencies and counseling centers. A one-session course is best centered on explaining to each group the outlines of genital anatomy and function of the other sex. However, groups should be supplemented by an opportunity to ask questions in private conference with the physician.

Special charts or illustrations (e.g., those designed for high school biology classes) available in a physician's office or clinic help reassure the young couple that their desire for sexual information is neither unique nor beyond the doctor's experience and inclinations. Plastic anatomic models and moulages have been used successfully for the same purpose. Some physicians make it a practice to recommend a booklet on advice for the newlyweds, or a marriage manual. Others prefer to help an apprehensive virginal bride unused to menstrual tampons insert a lubricated Pyrex centrifuge tube or a tampon on the examining table to demonstrate to her the patency and the direction of her vagina.

Notions. Many young couples who have had a moderate amount of perhaps furtive premarital sex relations have no fewer, possibly more sex worries than continent couples, and instruction need not differ greatly between them. The bride may need reassurance that there are no rules about maximum frequency of sexual contacts; that coital positions, or the time, the place or any other modality of sex may vary with the couple's moods, and that erotic venturesomeness on the part of either mate is far removed from perversion (see also p. 210). The couple may need to be told that a woman cannot be considered immodest if she cooperates in the sex act by pelvic thrusting and other body motions, or if she guides phallic immission by hand; indeed, if she does almost anything which they both feel like doing. Instruction may need to include that women have no ejaculations as men have; surprisingly many women (and their husbands) believe that they are unresponsive unless they "discharge" copiously. It should be mentioned that it may take a few months before orgasm is attained by some women; that she may be naturally "slower in coming" than her husband; and that it is perfectly normal if she encourages her husband either to exercise patience by holding back, or to indulge in precoital foreplay, or both. Many men are unprepared psychologically for wives who are fairly uninhibited sexually and this possibility may be mentioned to the young woman. Young women have worried that drops of urine can contaminate their vagina, or that an excited husband will urinate into her by mistake. They should also know that the masculine sex appetite is not a hunger-like instinct which cannot be denied at times without causing physical or mental havoc. If the groom has a condition such as varicocele, an inguinal hernia or an undescended testicle, the bride may be reassured, with the patient's permission, that the condition is most likely without effect on sexual function or fertility, unless otherwise determined by the physician.

Early Anhedonia. It is also at the premarital examination that some young women first manifest what later in marriage will become a multi-disguised but chronic pattern of "reluctant invalid" pleading: protestatiÔns that she is not strong enough, too anemic, too old, too young, too tired out from the job, or from exams for frequent sexual relations (e.g., on the honeymoon); would the physician please caution the groom against making more than minimal demands upon her or against expecting too much? Or could he be made to give her time to accustom herself to such a large organ, especially since she is built so small? In the experience of some general practitioners the incidence of such female anhedonic states (p. 402) does not seem to have greatly decreased despite the prevailing attitudes toward sexual expression, although new sets of screen complaints are emerging. Few of these "cop-out" pleas are based on mere sexual ignorance, and instruction by itself will cure little or nothing; but attempts to uncover major underlying motives—sex fears, faulty conditioning at critical stages, latent homosexuality, etc.—are obviously beyond the scope of a premarital consultation. The physician rarely is doing such a bride a good turn if he simply transmits and endorses her request for near-abstentiousness to the groom. Reassurance in depth or consultative referral are in order here.

Honeymoon Advice will aim, in the bride, at dispelling undue apprehensions so far as they are accessible to explanation and reassurance; and, in the groom, at achieving the best possible balance between excessive trepidation and undue roughness. An unusually rough or crude attitude ("rape of the bride") may be caused by emotional obtuseness, by inexperience and physical awkwardness, or by an alcoholized state. In others, performance may be unduly hasty or give an appearance of brutality, because they are childishly anxious to demonstrate virile prowess, or trying to disguise their own apprehensions regarding erective endurance. A sub-sadistic, neurotic impulse to shock or to overpower is encountered in some men.

In women, ingrained negative feelings toward men, or sex, or marriage generally, remain fairly frequent, although a shift in relative incidence from subconscious fear to subconscious resentment is taking place. A fear of dependence and weakness, or a subconscious protest against being overcome by the man, may be a source of first-night difficulties in some females ("Brunhild motif"). In an occasional bride there also exists an exaggeration of the quite normal trepidations as to whether her body will be pleasing to the man, her organs normal and compatible with his, and her intimate responses the equal of his supposedly sophisticated and experienced expectations.

The groom faces trepidations of his own, many of them revolving around his performance and potency. His normal impetus and vigor may be partly "paralyzed" because of misapprehensions or overwarnings about the pain and the hemorrhage of defloration. Any fear of injuring a bride of small stature, or worries about having too small a penis for a woman of large stature, can be disposed of at this point. Also, there should be a discussion of defloration, although some caution is indicated here, as a husband may become morose or agitated if defloration should occur later with greater ease than the physician's talk made him anticipate; or if the bride is actually no longer a virgo intacta but the husband was unaware of this.

Frequently, it may be advisable to suggest that the first evening's intimacies be limited to petting. Even where eventually disregarded, such advice tends to ease the anticipatory apprehensions. Where the physician anticipates fatigue, strained or uncomfortable overnight accommodations, extreme apprehension in either spouse, emotional resistance in the bride or labile potency in the groom, the advice to delay intromission may be particularly helpful. The suggestion should be communicated to both parties, as for instance, nonperformance at the traditional moment may cause the bride anxiety as to her own qualities of attraction, or as to the husband's virile capacity. For some couples initial abstinence is required by religious orthodoxy.

Some Special Premarital Situations

MIDDLE AND ADVANCED AGE

An offer to counsel on sexual matters should not be routinely omitted simply because the parties seem to be experienced or are no longer very young. It is perhaps not easy for some younger physicians to do this, partly because of a deep-rooted attitude in our society resisting an association between sexual expression and nonyouth, in spite of well-documented observations on the latter's needs and capabilities (see chapter 15). The older persons themselves, in turn, may be equally reluctant to ask for sexual information. However, in many cases a pelvic examination is a good starting point for advice-centered dialogue.

Female Genitalia. With the advent of middle age, anatomy and function begin to change, especially in the woman. This may constitute an unpleasant surprise for the bride who has not been sexually active since some time in her youth. In postmature women who are not on estrogen medication intercourse may be painful, because during and after menopause the vagina begins to lose elasticity, shrinks in its dimensions, becomes slow to lubricate and is more easily irritated (see also p. 325). Dyspareunia is greater here the longer the act lasts, and prolonged intercourse is no rarity with an elderly mate who can maintain an erection, but not necessarily ejaculate readily.

Remedies. Regularity of use, gently pursued at first, tends to cure the condition; it also helps prevent recurrence, as well as help maintain better libido and potency in the male. The use of artificial lubrication (p. 207), perhaps with an anesthetic ointment added in the beginning, may be discussed. Topical application of estrogen cream or suppositories can be a necessity. The use of combined-type birth control pills—20 days on, 10 days off—is helpful; in the elderly bride with atrophic vaginitis natural or synthetic estrogen (e.g., stilbestrol 0.5 mg) p.o., alone or with added methyl testosterone 5 mg—to counteract any libido reduction from indirect estrogenic effect on the ovaries—is preferred by many. Instrumental dilatation is rarely necessary in physiologic shrinkage. Because of loss of tonus of the perivaginal muscles Kegel-type pelvic exercises (p. 418) may be helpful for sexual purposes. The inevitable general pelvic relaxation may have led to uterine descent; there may be some degree of cystocele, perhaps rectocele. If vaginoplasty is called for, the surgeon will remember that combined cystocele and rectocele repair is followed by a high incidence of severe dyspareunia, so that posterior repair is often omitted unless defecation is grossly impaired; also, that a tightly reconstructed introitus, regardless of the lady's wish to become her old nulliparous self again, can become the executioner for the no longer iron-clad phallus which will seek entry here. Vaginoplasty calls for early use of estrogen and dilators, and plans should be arranged so that regular intercourse can follow soon. Any middle-aged virgin, her hymen often slightly leathery by now, is a candidate for premarital hymenotomy (p. 229) to spare her new mate humiliation and both of them frustration. An occasional bride asking the physician's help in white-lie simulation of premenopausal status may be beneficially aided by inducing cyclic withdrawal bleeding (e.g., with conjugated estrogens 1.25 mg with progesterone 5 mg added on the last few days of the 20-day cycle).

The Groom—perhaps both consorts—may wonder about the male's remaining span of sexual vigor. A past history of reasonably regular and vigorous sexual activity in a healthy man permits a favorable prediction here for an indefinite period of time. The passage of the years does not leave the male's sexual performance unaffected, but changes are more benign—yet also less treatable—than in the female. Most noticeable, apart from slower erection and less vigorous ejaculation, is a progressively lessened sense of urgency to attain climax, including the intensity of sensation as he is performing the act. Both such spouses need to understand that not all acts of postmature men have to result in ejaculation; every second or third may satisfy the male need well, although many a woman believes that she has not accomplished woman's purpose unless her mate ejaculates (Masters).

Contraception. A middle-aged bride may inquire about the need for contraception. Menopause in the U.S. now occurs at close to 50 years of age on the average and not rarely a few years later. Pregnancy expectation

PREGNANCY IN MIDDLE AGE

Probable fertility of a middle-aged bride cannot be reliably predicted even if corpus luteum formation is demonstrated. Presence or absence of menstruation is not reliable, certainly not in amenorrhea of less than 12 months. Pregnancy expectation between ages 50 and 54 (diagnosis easily overlooked) has been estimated to be 1.9 pregnancies per 100,000 women in this age group (Douglas). Pregnancy in a primigravida of 47 or older is believed to terminate in abortion or miscarriage with 80 per cent probability.

Many claims for women past age 52 have been made but cannot be authenticated. Successful pregnancy after age 49 is rare in the U.S. but it has occurred. The oldest mothers giving birth to living babies, in presumably authenticated cases on record*, were 63 (U.S. 1910) and 59 (France 1891), both after approximately 10 years of amenorrhea. In modern times advanced mothers' ages were recorded at 53 years, 7 months (England 1959), 52 years, 4 months (New York 1963) and in the 53rd year (Maryland, 1959).

In men no general upper limit for capacity to procreate seems to exist.

grows progressively less from age 45, and live birth expectation diminishes even quicker. For live births past age 52 see box. Absence of menstruation is not a reliable guide for suggesting that contraception is unnecessary, certainly not below age 48. For more definite fertility data hormone assays and vaginal maturation index would be required. However, ovulation can occur well into the 50's (e.g., in 200 women past age 50 undergoing hystero-oophorectomy there was evidence of recent corpus luteum in 23 per cent) (Novak). A man who can ejaculate must be presumed fertile at any age unless proven otherwise by semen examination (p. 177). Among rules of thumb employed by practicing gynecologists and others, "12 months of amenorrhea at 48, or 6 months at 50 and beyond" seems to offer reasonable security. Preferred contraceptive methods after age 40 appear to be the combined oral gestagens, or an IUD, except in nulligravid brides (Tovell).

Birth Defects. With increasing age of the woman, the incidence of congenital anomalies in her offspring rises. A defective fetus is most commonly aborted, but among those carried to term mongolism (Down's syndrome) ranks high, followed by hydrocephalus, Klinefelter's syndrome (father's age?), malformed heart, and metabolic errors. In the age-related nondisjunction type of mongolism the risk is 100 times greater at a

---

* Am. J. Obstet. Gynec. *90*:673, 1964

woman's age 45 (1 in 40 or 50) than in her early twenties. In this sporadic type of Down's, unlike in the much rarer translocation-type of younger mothers, the risk of a second newborn being a mongoloid is relatively slight. The older father, regardless of the wife's age, is more likely to beget a stillborn baby than a younger man. The evidence as to his role in producing mongoloids remains inconclusive, although the weight of evidence now indicates that fathers play the same role as mothers. A major theory as to why aging endangers fetal normalcy is based on the experience that older parents have accumulated more—statistically confirmed—radiation (medico-diagnostic, radar, etc.) exposure. Another theory is based on the fact that older couples tend to have less frequent intercourse so that the germ cells' chromosome complement begins to deteriorate while the stale gametes still retain their fertilizing capacity; there is indirect confirmatory evidence for this from a higher incidence of mongolism among Roman Catholics who presumably use the rhythm method of birth control which in case of method failure has stretched the time elapsed between input and fusion.

MENTAL RETARDATION

Those mentally retarded young people who are able to maintain themselves outside of institutions have a basic human right to the succor of a close, reasonably permanent dyadic relationship and the physical intimacy derived from it. Where State law—much of it antiquated—permits, they should also be able to marry. On the other hand parenthood, even where legally permissible, can in good conscience only very exceptionally be advised, or should perhaps be actively discouraged, depending on whether one or both spouses are retarded and on the degree of their infirmity. In addition to the I.Q. a Vineland Social Maturity Quotient is helpful in predicting the prospects of such a couple. States prohibiting retardates' marrying often do little or nothing to enforce these laws, although the marriage can be invalidated and/or annulment sought (Robitscher). Institutionalized defectives, even when out on pass, can only marry with the consent of the superintendent of the institution which shelters them.

Mildly retarded girls (I.Q. from 53 to 68) often marry normal men, but retarded boys tend to marry girls more retarded than themselves (Bass, Thorne). Experience with retarded young parents has been poor on the whole; they become overwhelmed and someone else—often an agency —has to step in. Borderline retardates (I.Q. around 70 or 75) are reasonably satisfactory parents, if their environment remains familiar, and the number of children is limited and their advent well spaced. Retardates are unable to make consistent use of temporary contraception, and only long-term or irreversible—I.U.D. or surgery mostly—measures have been successful. Some states have laws requiring semicompulsory sterilization of retardates. Generally, the more retarded among them should be urged to undergo voluntary tubal ligation or vasectomy before marrying, with guardian's permission where necessary. If the bride is pregnant, the groom is still a candidate for sterilization before marriage. Sex information cannot be successfully conveyed by the physician at the time of retardates' premarital examination; this is best done in specially designed courses of instruction, a desirable part of educational programs for young retardates (p. 162). However, specific questions brought up by the applicants should be answered simply, clearly and, if possible, without emphasizing choices of behavior.

EUGENIC STERILIZATION OF MENTAL RETARDATES

At least 29 states have statutory directions as guidelines for the performance of eugenic sterilization of retardates of either sex for whom the hereditary background makes procreation inadvisable, as they are the probable potential parents of socially inadequate offspring. Most statutes include some mandatory provisions for certain cases (Sagall, 1972). The rationale of eugenic sterilization is fourfold:

To protect handicapped parents from responsibilities they are ill-fitted to carry.

To spare the prospective child: if retarded it will be handicapped in life; if normal it is exposed to hygienic neglect, lack of guidance and absence of early intellectual stimulation, with impairing results.

To relieve the community of potential burden.

To protect the human race: as each new defective, in turn, reproduces him(her)self he also will help depress the long-range quality of the population and the human race. Said Justice Holmes in the 1927 landmark decision of the U.S. Supreme Court upholding a sterilization law, "It is better for all the world if society can prevent those who are manifestly unfit from continuing their kind . . . Three generations of imbeciles are enough."

Opposing secular arguments: futility of the procedure, partly based on the phenomenon of continuous influx; incomplete knowledge of the degrees of heredopathic risk and the mechanisms of heredity; our inability to differentiate with precision between inherited and acquired retardation.

ADDITIONAL READING

Ingle, D. J.: Who Should Have Children? An Environmental and Genetic Approach. Indianapolis, Bobbs-Merrill Co., 1973
Robitscher, J. (ed.): Eugenic Sterilization. Springfield, Ill., Thomas, 1973

CHAPTER 12

The Sexual Act

Coitus or coition, copulation, consummatio, congressus sexualis, pareunia, immissio penis, intromission; sexual intercourse, union, communion, connection, consummation, embrace; intimate (sexual, marital) relations. Legal terms: cohabitation, fornication, conjugal (connubial) relations, carnal knowledge, sexual penetration and the Cannon law's copula (carnalis)

Nature of the Act — Coital Practices — Coital Positions — Conception — Intercourse in Special Situations — Complications of Intercourse — Forcible Intercourse (Rape) — Painful Intercourse (Dyspareunia).

NATURE OF THE ACT

In its barest essentials the sexual act consists of the insertion of the erect penis into the vulvovaginal passage followed by a series of continuous or intermittent rhythmic thrusting motions. With each stroke, the phallus advances through the vagina without leaving it, the glans brushing against the tip of the cervix and being carried briefly into one of the vaginal fornices. Penetrations may be shallow or deep, the thrusts slow or rapid, straight or with a circular screwing motion. For the male, rhythmicality and surface friction are key factors, while in the woman tissue traction and displacement and depth perception play a major part (see also p. 188). Most men tolerate interruptions better and can resume fairly readily; women's level of arousal is more easily put back by interruptions and distractions. Usually, the act is terminated after the man ejaculates. The woman's normal role is not passive, but she delivers pelvic counter-thrusts of varying vigor. In fact, the anatomic receptor role of the female does not preclude her playing a dominant, even aggressive part, just as a man, though anatomically the penetrator, can play a passive part in sex behavior which is satisfactory to both. Ideally, coital initiative is shared in long-term relationships.

Humans have no instinctive knowledge of how to copulate; they must learn this from hearsay, observation, instruction or other sources. Naïve couples have been known to resort to grinding pelvic appression, intralabial, intrafemoral, urethromeatal or similar pseudoimmissions. Although coitus may not require actual training to perform, a certain technical proficiency is learned only gradually after often awkward beginnings.

Sensation and Response. The potential capacity for sexual performance of women, by and large, greatly exceeds that of men; this is largely due to the absence of a lengthy refractory period in a fairly large proportion of women. Many females apparently can be conditioned, or condition themselves, to produce large numbers of orgasms in a row, especially by mechanical stimulation; men cannot. The curve of coital sensation usually differs in the two sexes. In most men it resembles a steep pyramid with unequal sides: a moderately steep ascent, the ejaculatory peak, followed by an immediate steep decline and a refractory period. In the woman the picture is more variable, but most often there is a gradual ascent, an orgasmic plateau of some length often spiked by one or more climaxes, followed by a slower downward slope.

In superimposing the two curves, optimally the male peak should coincide with some late part of the wife's plateau. Actual simultaneousness of orgasms is unusual and not an essential part of satisfactory intercourse. Many women tend to experience a climax most easily if and when they perceive that the husband is about to, or has begun to, ejaculate. Some women, many with a strong clitoral component in the coital responding mechanism, tend to have a fairly rapid climax, followed by a scaled-down male-type refractory period with hypersensitivity of the clitoral glans. Where a wife's orgasm tends to be delayed or the husband's performance rapid or cursory, this may place his orgasmic peak where the woman's arousal is still ascending, leaving her "high and dry" (see Pseudofrigidity, p. 410).

Duration of the Act. Measured from immissio penis to ejaculation, the vast majority of sexual acts is terminated in less than ten minutes, according to available American data; in fact, one may assume that a majority of husbands ejaculate in 3 to 5 minutes. However, most healthy adult men, if sufficiently motivated, are able to prolong at least one out of every few sex acts for 10 to 20 minutes without experiencing discomfort or loss of satisfaction. Unusually long coital endurance or "staying power" in some men is due to ejaculatio tardata (p. 391), a type of impotence, but can also be produced by certain drugs (p. 392) or with coitus reservatus (p. 319).

Coital Frequency in marriage varies from couple to couple, even where similar circumstances of age, health, life style and type of work prevail. Teen-aged mates may report 10 to 20 acts a week early in marriage and couples married in their twenties 9 to 12 acts a week during the same period. Later in marriage couples 25 to 35 years of age probably cohabit an average of 2 or 3 times a week, although not all surveys are in agreement with this. The frequency plateau which most couples seem to reach after 3 to 5 years of married life is apt to change only slowly with the passing years, if regularity can be maintained. Near age 45 1 or 2 acts of marital intercourse a week appears to be close to the average in our culture. The relatively steepest decline in coital frequency in healthy, affectionate couples most often occurs when the husband reaches the early or middle sixties.

There exists no known healthful or desirable optimum of coital frequency. Requests for specific advice in this regard are adequately answered with "as often as is mutually agreeable." There is also no need for concern about injuriously excessive frequency in healthy individuals acting by mutual consent. In obsessively worrisome individuals preoccupied with sexual frequency it is psychologically justified to name a limit of monthly acts, aiming perhaps slightly below what one would expect the patient to be capable of based on his age, marital harmony and past sexual performance.

COITAL PRACTICES

Light vs. Darkness

Initial insistence on intercourse in the dark by either spouse tends to disappear in most marriages once daily domestic intimacy has been established. In some couples darkness remains a custom, but there is enough flexibility so as not to interfere unduly with the vita sexualis. Some indications exist that dark-light preferences are not solely residues of early-conditioned shame, but are even in humans in some way associated with the well established optic-hypothalamic light effect on sexual questing, with participation of the pineal gland linked via an adrenergic mechanism. Insistence on darkness may be masking major sexual difficulties (e.g., in a woman a chronic sense of guilt, sex fears or subliminal revulsion; in men hard-to-eradicate subconscious horror feminae images, or obsessive fears of humiliation in the act). Where coitus is possible only with the help of substitution fantasies (see below), visibility of the real partner may inhibit them and disorganize the performance. Obversely, some highly narcissistic women insist on light as they require an opportunity to observe the sex partner's delight in order to feel gratified (see p. 409).

The Time of Day is a related problem. In our civilization bedtime has long been the traditional occasion for marital relations. The circumstances of daily living tend to make this one of the few practicable times; but also some women subconsciously may identify daytime lovemaking with non-marital dalliance: they feel as if engaging in a forbidden indulgence, although they may rationalize their avoidance. Bedtime may actually not be the most suitable and healthful occasion in many cases. In this connection one may recall that in men the level of circulating testosterone reaches its circadian peak early in the morning.

Coital Fantasies

Coital fantasies are common in men and women. They range from fleeting imageries which arise spontaneously on some occasions to indispensable enabling devices. Most commonly, on some uninspired occasions of marital intimacy, a wife may slip into reveries of the husband as he was or as he might be, or on how it might be as someone's lover; or a husband may fantasize an erotic encounter with an existing or non-existing female figure. Indulgence in coital imagining has, in fact, been described as one of the secrets of physical fidelity. The use of fantasies can help support the sexual aspect of marriage as it passes through a difficult period. Or a loving wife may use stimulus fantasy to intensify her response and to hasten her orgasm if she is notably slower in responding than the man, thus allowing him to feel free to release rather than overtire or frustrate himself.

Men's sexual fantasies, in the absence of major deviate or psychotic morbidity, concern themselves with various titillating stimuli and body contacts. In women fantasies of being overpowered and of exhibiting their charms or their acts to a group of onlookers appear to be quite common. Extramarital lovers may request and/or promise to substitute the other in effigy during domestic intercourse. Generally, the deliberate use of imagery during coitus, where the fantasied object takes the place of the real one, converts intercourse into a form of masturbation. This is probably much more common in men. Fantasy here serves as an enabling mechanism for individuals profoundly alienated from their spouses; for a variety of sexual deviates; and probably for many of the surfeit-prone habitual masturbators (p. 431). Such sexual acts may be characterized by insistence that the room be dark, the partner silent and undemanding, the frictional rhythm uninterrupted, and the position unchanged from act to act. However, over-recognition of such behavior must be guarded against.

Reverse imagery, either during intercourse or during sexual foreplay, is a device employed by men when they are highly aroused but wish to postpone ejaculation, usually for the partner's sake. For this purpose they must direct their thoughts to nonerotic matters and concentrate on them until the height of arousal has ebbed. This type of self-inhibition is not known to be inimical to sexual functioning.

Foreplay (Precoital Stimulation)

Some caresses and erotic banter are an integral part of intercourse in the average-affectionate couple; on some occasions it may be brief and cursory, on others more extended, but few marriages can flourish where the customary approach is demand for an "instant party" on the part of either spouse. The vast majority of women need a certain minimum of their specific kind of coital foreplay—genital, extragenital, audiovisual, romantic cuddling, or all of these—for an amount of time which is different for each woman and can vary from mood to mood, from (menstrual) cycle stage to cycle stage; also from partner to partner. But sheer length of coital foreplay is no guarantee of subsequent orgasm. Coital forepleasure should be a mutual experience, but its principal psychophysiologic aim in our civilization remains pre-pleasuring of the woman and increasing her state of coital readiness. For pre-pleasuring techniques applied to the male see p. 401.

Many women, even when acutely desirous, are not necessarily ready for immediate entry, especially where a husband's limited coital endurance requires that she attain orgasm fairly soon after intromission. The presence of vulvar moisture is not a reliable indicator of overall coital readiness.

The type of foreplay needed to bring about proper relaxation and gratification of the wife is best determined by trial and error. To some women it suffices to be closely, quietly held or cudded for a while; in fact, such sensuous body contact, implying affection and security, would be highly satisfying by itself to these women, at least some of the time, but the male sex urge being what it is, "they barter coitus for a cuddle." Other women respond to stimuli directed at sensitive (erogenous) zones. Apart from kissing and sucking of apertures and mucocutaneous junctions, this includes tactile skin arousal—touching, stroking or tickling—of ears, supraclavicular hollows, breasts, nipples, inner thighs, perineum, sacrum, etc. Other areas respond to kinesthetic stimuli (e.g., kneading the nape, lower buttocks, feet or breasts in some women, lower limb entwining, etc.).

Other women again respond most strongly to direct genital stimulation, which can range from performing gentle intimacies to purposeful masturbatory stimulation by the spouse, or even the use of an electrovibratory device. For most, the locus of non-self-manipulatory predilection are the inside of the labia minora and the clitoral shaft and attachments. Slow upward stroking of the shaft between 2 fingers, with lubrication dipped up from the introitus, is a mode of heterostimulation preferred by many women; it differs from the commonly used automanipulative techniques which often also aim more directly at a rapid climax. In a minority of women substantial clitoral prestimulation seems to interfere somewhat with subsequent coital pleasure, especially if the latter was carried to or close to climax. In these individuals orgasm depends heavily on the vulvoclitoral component, and their refractory period after climax tends to be prolonged. What excites a woman also varies with the moment (e.g., nipple touch may lead to near-orgasm one day and to nothing the next). Sites and responses in sensuous women, perhaps unlike in men, are not necessarily stereotyped unless both mates have conditioned and persuaded themselves to a one-avenue build-up of libido.

Oral stimulation is increasingly acceptable to males and females in many, but not all segments of the population; reticence has been identified with the most upward-striving groups, both caucasoid and negroid (see also Variant Practices, below).

A moderate amount of active precoital stimulation or love play tends to enhance the husband's subsequent erective endurance rather than shorten it. Obversely, where a woman at all times just passively suffers the husband to "work on her," foreplay can become a chore, deprive him of erection at times and, in the long run, can lead to loss of sexual interest. Hasty, abrupt or excessively mechanical fingering of the wife's parts tends to have little stimulus value for her. The use of electrovibrators by some husbands as a form of labor-saving foreplay device is reported with some frequency, but there are insufficient observations to evaluate its long-term effect on the vita sexualis. Where the woman frequently experiences orgasm during foreplay, this does not necessarily obviate the need for the latter, if the overall aim of achieving satisfying sexual union is kept in mind. Where the wife has impaired orgasm capacity, or the man's coital endurance is limited, her precoital climax is sometimes routinely sought by tacit agreement between the spouses.

Verbalizing

Verbal communications during intercourse most often include endearments and expressions of pleasure as well as signals and requests concerning the proceedings. The use of crude sexual folk words, if they are not in habitual use at home, or the exhorting the mate to use or repeat such words, mostly represents an excitatory device. Such verbalizing of "dirty indulgence" fantasies is more characteristic for men, while in women genuine peaking of coital arousal can occur more readily in response to a verbal assurance of love or a romantic endearment. The subclinical sadist may employ debasing, abusive obscenities compulsively, especially if this evidently repels the mate. The reverse (e.g., in mildly masochistic men) is less apparent or not well documented. A proportion of women tend to recoil from coital verbal crudity, partly because subconsciously they identify this with illicit sex or, if the situation happens to be illicit, because they feel thereby treated with disrespect or even exploited and humiliated.

Genital Lubrication

Lubrication of the vulvovaginal passage, natural or artificial, is a virtual necessity for intercourse, even where the canal is wide and the introitus gaping. The vulva tends to become moist, even wet with many kinds of sexual excitement (e.g., precoital anticipation, petting or simply erotic imagery). The vagina produces a lubricating transudate admixed with desquamated epithelial debris, but some women secrete substantial vaginal moisture only after coital entry no matter what prestimulation took place. In the estrogen phase of the ovulatory cycle the endocervix usually secretes a relatively large amount of light mucus, but this seems to enter the picture only during or shortly after the first orgasm.

In some women preliminary vulvar moisture is always scant regardless of the apparent degree of sexual arousal. Insufficient sexual arousal may but need not mean insufficient moisture. Even a proportion of raped women appear to self-lubricate automatically following penetration, although this does not signify mental acceptance. Women on oral contraceptives produce amounts of clear mucoid liquid during most of the cycle. Even with good initial lubrication vulva and vagina tend to dry out in many women during greatly prolonged, vigorous intercourse, especially in women not conditioned to this; more so in the presence of overrelaxed vaginal walls and with a gaping introitus as this is conducive to more rapid evaporation of moisture; and most markedly with interruptions of the act (e.g., where the phallus slips from the vagina). Insufficient genital moisture is frequently produced in sexual anhedonia; in postmenopausal women, especially as they approach the presenium; in many forms of developmental hypogenitalism; in genital yeast infections, and during medication with some anticholinergic and other drugs. In vaginitis, even copious discharge, the latter does not protect the already vulnerable female parts from coital traumatization; additional lubrication for the act is frequently advised.

Artificial Lubrication is employed where natural secretions are insufficient or slow to appear or have evaporated; when the genitals of either partner are abraded or otherwise traumatized; or where a man experiences artificial lubrication as stimulating, as many men do, especially in connection with a snug female tract. Some women resist the use of such applications, as it conveys to them a suggestion of sexual inadequacy, or else the feeling of being forced while unready. Most often the husband limits application of the lubricant to his own organ; where the wife employs a contraceptive cream or gel this may be used to moisten the vulva also, or preferably she may inunct the male organ with it.

Plain petrolatum (e.g., Vaseline) is often the handiest and least expensive, but it is not greatly desirable because of its greasy feel and its postcoital stickiness; also it tends to corrode rubber-type contraceptive devices (e.g., it may lead to a lacerated condom). Surgical lubricating jelly (KY, Lubafax, Koromex, Surgilube) is acceptable to most couples, although relatively expensive; it has been found to be significantly spermicidal in vitro. During protracted intercourse application may have to be repeated. Edible oils and fats are undesirable because they may become rancid in situ. Glycerine, soaps, and most perfumed cosmetic preparations irritate the mucosa including the male urethra; many are believed to have an unpredictable spermicidal effect. All fatty substances employed in quantity may interfere mechanically with insemination. Water is not a suitable coital lubricant, although any inert liquid, including saliva, can facilitate entry.

Coital Hygiene

In stably associated, average clean and healthy couples neither the man nor the woman needs special genital cleansing procedures before or after intercourse. However, a woman may elect to cleanse her external genitalia precoitally with water and soap, for esthetic reassurance or to remove vulvar malodor caused by menstrual debris, urinary residue, sebum or perspiration. Lately scented genital deodorant sprays have become available to mask real or illusory offensive body odors; some are also flavored to promote orogenital caresses. These sprays are not for intravaginal use. Women's liberationists have condemned these applications together with body hair shaving, referring to "the glabrous, odorless body of the feminine toy." The sprays have caused painful vulvar reactions and dermatitis of the thighs in some women. Prepacked moist deodorant towelettes are believed safer than sprays. A musklike odor emanates from the genitalia, possibly also from the total skin surface of some women, especially when erotically aroused; it cannot to any great extent be removed by washing. Its erotic effect on men is uncertain.

A related female hygiene problem concerns the cleansing of the vagina by douching either routinely or pre- or postcoitally. Generally it is believed that the healthy vagina needs no artificial cleaning out: it is self-cleansing in that the normal secretions carry organic debris to the outside as they gradually drain by gravity in the sitting or standing positions. Emotional stresses, erotic arousal and the midphase of the ovulatory cycle tend to increase the flow in many women. A continually profuse flow of clear mucus, once uterine lesions have been ruled out, may be due to simple leukorrhea, especially in the teens and early twenties; the condition can cause needless fretting about hygiene and esthetics; it has been well described as "not really a disease but a state of mind." To help reduce heavy leukorrheal flow, increased aeration of the perineum—skirts rather than jeans, soft knit cotton underpants rather than nylon, no panty hose or girdles, pads or pajama bottoms—should not be overlooked. Douches are not recommended for the treatment of simple leukorrhea by most authorities.

A major cause today of heavy flow is the use of birth control pills, especially those high in estrogen. The widely encountered Hemophilus vaginitis can cause a heavy flow with a characteristic odor; this and all other conditions presenting with malodorous, irritating, grey, yellow, white or blood-tinged discharge primarily require medical attention rather than routine cleansing which can only delay the seeking of treatment. Foul vaginal odor due to an old tampon pushed high into a fornix by another tampon and forgotten has been described. Routine cleansing douches in the absence of infection are best limited to 2 a week; overfrequent douching may remove the protective bacteria and the acid milieu. Postcoital cleansing douches are not necessary as a rule except possibly before removing a diaphragm, nor are they believed capable of preventing venereal infection, and there is no biologic necessity for flushing out the semen. For contraceptive douching see p. 319.

THE CLEANSING DOUCHE (VAGINAL LAVAGE)

Position
Preferred: reclining in bathtub, thighs moderately flexed, pillow under head. Others: supine in bed, with thick towel elevating buttocks; less satisfactory, sitting astride toilet bowl, bidet or douche pan.

Appliance
Douche bag, not used for enemas, 2-quart capacity, hung 2 to 3 feet above pelvis. Nozzle with large bulbous tip with openings only at sides. Others: bulb syringe; electric douche appliance.

Liquid
Warm tap water, circa 110° F. Total 2 quarts.

Additives
Plain water or various proprietary powders and liquids as per labels. Household additives: Salt: 1 teaspoon; lactic acid USP. ½ to 1 teaspoon or white or cider vinegar: 2 tablespoonfuls, all per quart of water. Use of vinegar is disputed.

Procedure
Nozzle is inserted 1½ to 3 inches depending on length of vagina. During procedure outflow is blocked a few times by pinching labia shut to permit better distention of vaginal folds, guarding against over-ballooning. The average distended vagina holds circa 8 to 10 ounces of fluid. Flow is shut off when pressure is felt behind symphysis. Vaginal filling and run-off are repeated until reservoir is empty. Procedure should take about 5 minutes. Not to be used during pregnancy.

Postcoital Phase

Upon ejaculation of semen the sexual act is essentially terminated. The male organ rapidly loses its erect consistency and some of its tumescence and, more slowly, returns to fully flaccid size. A refractory period has now set in for the man during which stimulation, perhaps the slightest touch of the penis, especially of the glans, is unwelcome if not acutely uncomfortable. However, aversion to caressing touch of other body parts at this time is not part of the male's physiologic refractory phase. The longer the preceding coital act, the slower, as a rule, the male's pelvic detumescence, including that of penis, rectum, prostate, etc. In the woman pelvic detumescence is more gradual as well as more complex. It is promptly reversible in a majority of women upon renewal of stimulation; a minority have a refractory period similar to but shorter than in men. Separation of the couple's genitalia within less than a minute after ejaculation is the rule, but sometimes couples find it more gratifying to remain united past cessation of the erection, and perhaps go to sleep that way. This is most practicable in one of the lateral coital positions.

Where marital intercourse takes place in bed and at night, sleep is the usual sequel. In the woman it may be preceded by a period of euphoric languor with a need to receive or express tenderness. It has often been suggested that for full marital contentment the husband should be discouraged from turning around and going to sleep, but that he should hold his spouse embraced to allow her a gradual clinging off. However, some men seem to require at least a brief sleep period following intercourse, or else they tend to be irritable. Some observers contend that this is not based on a physiologic need but on a psychologic aversion reaction, in view of instances of elated wakefulness in these same men on at least some nocturnal as well as on extramarital occasions; there is little proof for either contention. Postcoital tristesse—mild, transient melancholy or blues—in men, including a feeling of letdown, a sense of the temporal, is almost physiological; it is not a reflection on the underlying quality of his feeling for the mate. On the other hand, satisfying intercourse may stimulate some couples to animated or tender conversation or even to exhilaration. Most well-mated couples adapt to each other's postcoital moods and habits, wives more often to those of the man.

Variant Practices

In premarital experimentation and early in marriage situations young people often feel impelled to act out certain childhood fantasies and their residual adolescent curiosity regarding sex. This includes impulses to view close-up, touch all over, explore apertures, exhibit, impose contorting postures, assume novel positions, mock-overpower or submit and all manner of similar cavorting. This early acting-out is transitory in the marriage. The tendency is more pronounced in males, and is desired somewhat sooner by them than by females, although the distinction may be largely culture-conditioned. These are normal manifestations of the vita sexualis, as are varieties of frolic such as coitus under a soapy shower, in a tub, while swimming, and the like.

In certain cases, the need for one or the other variant practice, usually on the part of the man, persists or becomes more pronounced, sometimes relatively late in the marriage. There may be no problem because of mutual adaptability, but in other cases the compulsive practice of "kinky" variants constitutes a real problem and can endanger the union; this is especially true where certain acts are insistently forced on a reluctant spouse, disregarding mutuality, and where it has become an exclusive sex aim, regularly carried to orgasm.

Clinical discernment is needed in guiding such couples. Even where a wife expresses serious concern or a sense of outrage at her husband's "perverted" practices this does not represent a reliable history of sexual deviance, and diagnostic restraint is necessary. Borderline deviate men, and to a lesser extent women, can find in marriage an important outlet permitting them to partially act out and defuse minor fetishistic, homosexual, sadistic, masochistic, etc. compulsions and impulses, thus saving an otherwise good or promising marriage, and themselves from conditioning into overt deviance. However, where the marriage becomes disaffected for other reasons a wife's initial resolve that "I'll be anything he wants, anything he needs" tends to disappear.

Oral Practices (genital kiss, lambitus. Vernac. going down). From all available evidence, these have gained somewhat wider acceptance in recent years, apparently shifting from use in foreplay to the status of coital substitutes. The acceptance of heterosexual anal intercourse is believed to be rising also. Anal and oral immission continue to be subsumed under the outdated legal term of sodomy, still a statutory criminal offense in many states, although a substantial right to marital privacy may give de facto protection to married couples. The simultaneous practice of oral sex by 2 individuals is known in the vernacular as soixante-neuf (Fr., 69).

Fellatio consists of the purposeful apposition of the mouth to the male organ and its orolingual stimulation. It does not include brief nuzzling and mouthing during erotic foreplay. Intense initial sensation is produced not only by suction but also by slow lingual friction of the penile shaft and its wet manipulation. Where orgasm occurs, swallowing of the semen is common but not universal practice. Folk beliefs still hold that this benefits a woman's vigor, which is a fable; nor is ingestion known to be harmful. For possible venereal complications, see p. 243. The practice of fellatio has long been accepted in casual sex encounters; a proportion of married women continue to regard it as debasing.

Cunnilingus (cunnilinctio) signifies orolingual contact with the vulva, especially the clitoral area. Some woman cannot achieve orgasm easily in any other way; the reason is incompletely understood, although lesbian tendencies or conditioning were present in some. A large proportion of women appear to welcome the practice greatly, as part of erotic foreplay and increasingly men, especially husbands, feel pleased by so pleasing. Many men used to have an almost phobic horror of being known as cunnilinctors, and the practice tended to be a prized masochistic penalty service (see p. 475). An actual physical disgust may have been appropriate in the past because of inadequate female hygienic customs; today kitchen-flavored deodorant applications to the female parts are advertised and fairly widely sold.

Anal Practices in married couples continue to be an exception, but probably are growing in frequency. Rectal coitus is most often undertaken later in marriage, either because the tonus of the anal sphincter represents an enabling device for the man who cannot complete the act in the over-relaxed, atonic vagina of his multiparous wife, or as an answer to a difficult contraceptive problem. In the absence of large hemorrhoids or painful fissures the anus can, with some patience, be made to accommodate most lubricated male organs, as the woman spreads her own buttocks. The rectal mucosa, after some conditioning, is said to produce a transudate like the vagina's. Wives familiar with the practice have indicated that they can attain climax rectally. The anus being an erogenous zone, insertion of the man's wetted or lubricated finger during vaginal intercourse, possibly with counterfriction against the intravaginal penis, reportedly aids sensation and orgasm achievement of some women.

Minor Masochistic Wishes on the part of a husband may include that the wife use degrading or obscene words before and during coitus, or that she wear such paraphernalia as boots or high-heeled shoes, stockings, gloves, a small cocktail apron, a fur piece or a wide leather belt. If potency is adequate, the marriage may be endangered only in proportion to the degree in which the wife feels incapable of going along with such variants.

Minor Sadistic Acts can be more disturbing. A husband may "amuse" himself by introducing foreign bodies in the female tract or by acting out violent situations during coitus (e.g., laying a knife on the night table, holding a toy gun, asking the wife to beg as if for her life or using debasing language before the act). With counseling in milder cases, the wife may be guided towards an initial attitude of toleration which should gradually give way to amiable resistance. Where the wife's revulsion is marked and unabating, the marital outlook is not good. To be differentiated is the infliction of "passion pain" in the final stages of the sex act, such as buttock-clutching or -slapping, or digging into thighs. However, scrotum pinching and similar preclimactic, escalation-aimed acts are conscious erotic refinements. Love bites, nail scratching and neck hickeys—visible suction marks —may be more related to possessive feelings than to uncontrollable impulses.

COITAL POSITIONS

In our civilization the man-above recumbent position during intercourse, with its minor variants, remains undoubtedly the accepted norm. A great

.many theories have attempted to explain why this should be so; whether this is a biologic or a cultural phenomenon, or both. In some parts of the world other coital positions constitute the prototypes.

A couple may and probably should decide on their own to experiment with other positions for reasons of comfort, variety or enhanced gratification. In other cases it would seem that they are, on request, entitled to medical technical advice in this respect. The literature of the ars amandi enumerates a multitude of postures for the sex act: many vary from each other only in some minute details, some are bizarrely acrobatic, others tend to rob the act of some essential element, while a few are potentially injurious. Out of the many suggested only a few seem to merit professional interest.

Man-above Recumbent Position (Face-to-face recumbent, dorsal recumbent, ventro-ventral, vir incubus or incumbent, woman supine or underneath, habitual converse, front, basic, anterior, customary, normal, traditional, Western, missionary, standard, etc.). The standard coital position is satisfactory under most circumstances and probably affords more spiritual intimacy than any other. Technically, the wife reclines on her back, her legs slightly abducted and flexed and, if desired, a small pillow under her lower back—not buttocks—to raise the hips slightly. The man lies above her, his legs between hers, usually supporting his weight on his lower legs and forearms. The bodies may or may not be in contact. Where the woman is debilitated or fatigued she may support her feet against a wall or other fixed object.

Clitoral stimulation is average at best here. It is produced chiefly by the rhythmic to-and-fro traction on the clitoral hood and the shaft; this mechanism being less effective where the introitus tends to gape. By moving his body headward ("riding high") and possibly bracing his feet the husband can add direct friction of the clitoral body between the mates' pubic symphyses, at least for short periods of time. The maneuver is less suitable in the nullipara and with a generally tight introitus.

Flexion. A variant of the man-above position is flexion, as the wife draws her abducted and sharply flexed legs back towards her own abdomen. The loss of friction here can be compensated for by the woman pumping her knees up and down slightly. This position foreshortens the vagina and affords deep penetration. It is indicated where the penis is relatively small, the vagina relatively long, the introitus tight, or the organs insufficiently moist. In uncorrected sexual anesthesia due to vaginal overrelaxation (see p. 405) flexion affords compensatory friction to the phallus between the woman's symphysis and the edge of the perineum which is pulled taut and brought forward in this position. It is contraindicated in hypogenitalism of the wife, during pregnancy, whenever the cervix is

ADVISING ON COITAL POSITIONS

Some Indications and Contraindications

Many data empirical, some presumptive; individual variations in requirements exist. For descriptions, see text.

Cardiopathy, Convalescence, General Debility; *Male or Female:* Advise modified side-rear entry. No chair-seated.

Male: Advise woman above-sidesaddle facing, or woman low seated-man kneeling. Preferably no standard, especially not with woman hyperextended. No woman-above astride. No standing positions.

Female: Standard with moderate arching. No woman-seated. No woman above-astride.

Ejaculation, Premature: Advise modified side-to-side facing (man supine), or woman above-astride facing positions. Preferably no man-above positions (disputed).

Erections, lability of: Advise standard with woman's legs closed, or woman above-astride.

Frigidity (fem. orgasm failure): Advise arched variant of standard position with man shifting headward as tolerated. Also man chair-seated with woman astride-facing, or woman above-astride.

Genital Disproportions, marked: Advise woman above-astride generally. Male Larger: Advise standard with hyperextension. Male Smaller: Advise standard with hyperflexion.

Hemiparesis: *Male:* Advise side-to-side positions, keeping weak side lowermost. *Female:* Advise standard position.

Hypogenitalism, Contracted Pelvis: Advise standard position with arching. No standard with hyperflexion.

Infertility: Advise standard with hyperflexion or knee-chest rear entry.

Obesity: *Male:* Best is woman seated-man kneeling or standing. Possibly modified side-rear entry. No standard with arching unless man uses straight-arm crouch.

Female: Advise woman low-seated or across bed edge with feet supported, man kneeling. Possibly side-rear entry recumbent or woman above-astride; possibly rear entry positions. No standard positions suitable.

Both Obese: Advise as in male obesity. No standard positions.

Paraplegia (male): Woman above facing, astride or sidesaddle.

Pregnancy (last 3 months): Advise standard with moderate extension, or modified side-rear entry, or woman seated-man facing, standing or kneeling; possibly rear entry (knee-elbows). No standard hyperflexed nor extreme hyperextension. No woman above-astride.

Urethral Meatus Tenderness: Advise modified side-rear entry, or standard with hyperflexion; possibly rear entry positions.

Uterine Malpositions, Cervix Pathology: Same as in hypogenitalism.

Vaginal Overrelaxation and/or Hypesthesia: Standard position, but either hyperflexed or hyperextended.

sensitive or vulnerable, in adnexal inflammations, and in major uterine malpositions. Benefits and dangers of this variant are increased in hyper-flexing maneuvers, as the woman's legs encircle the man's chest or even his neck, or where one or both of her legs are bent up sharply at the hip and hand-held, by herself or the male, close to the body or sideways. Hyper-flexion has been recommended to improve the chances of insemination (see also p. 237).

Arching. The opposite variant of the man-above is arching (i.e., hyperextension of the female body). The woman places a thick firm pillow or folded towel or merely her own fists under her buttocks while elimi-nating pillows under her head and shoulders and resting her legs flat on the mattress. The position affords increased clitoral stimulation and is among those recommended in some cases of frigidity, as it adds stimulation for the female through the stretching of abdominal and thigh muscles. It is useful when deep penetration must be avoided, as with a relatively short vagina or a long penis, in pregnancy, and when the cervix is sensitive. It may be attempted where the vagina is overrelaxed. The position is rather tiring for the man and difficult with markedly overweight men. In a related variant the extension is more moderate, but the woman brings her legs together after insertion of the penis is accomplished; the husband positions his legs outside hers. It is indicated where erection is labile or incomplete. The effect is enhanced if one of the husband's legs rests inside, the other outside the woman's together with a minimal body shift so that the long axes of the partners' bodies are slightly diagonal to each other. The wife's thighs should envelop the man's inside thigh fairly tightly or even apply rubbing motions to it during the act.

Lateral Positions (side, side-to-side). Among the principal advantages of the various side positions apart from taking the man's weight off the wife's body is that they require relatively little physical exertion and permit comfortable resting positions including head and neck pillowing for both mates. This makes them especially suitable for prolonged coition, more so when pauses are desired, and in cases of fatigue, debility and invalidism of either spouse, as well as in pregnancy. Two principal types may be mentioned.

The Side-Rear Entry (posterolateral recumbent, lateral averted, cross position) is actually a modification of the regular, face-to-occiput recum-bent (spoon laying) posture, but the latter has little to recommend it for professional purposes. In the cross position the woman is on her back, with the pelvis somewhat twisted away to the side by raising the near buttock and leg. The man lies on his side facing her, their bodies forming a 60°, or even a 90° angle. The position, unless employed on the floor, requires a fairly wide bed. The man's comfort can be improved by sup-porting his back with pillows. This is one of the least tiring of all coital positions, and little body motion is necessary. It is also potentially a highly impersonal and noncomittal procedure, even more so than the notorious rear entry-standing. The reverse of the side-rear entry positions the male supine, with the woman on her side facing him; this has been recommended in the treatment of premature ejaculation.

The respective axes of vagina and phallus do not coincide in these lateral variants; sensation for the man is rarely intense, nor is there much automatic clitoral stimulation during the act; the latter can be supplemented by direct manipulation, or by the wife helping press the man's upper thigh against herself. The degree of penile penetration is controlled by the man as he angles his body closer or away. The cross position is also useful where statures of the mates are greatly disproportionate, and in dyspareunia due to tenderness of the woman's urinary meatus.

In the **Side Position-facing** (anterolateral) the wife lies on her side with knees drawn up and thighs spread apart. The man also lies on his side facing and embracing her; his hips may rest on her bottom leg, thus making it unsuitable for women with varicosities (e.g., during pregnancy). The husband's position is often slightly towards the supine as the act progresses. If the spouses reverse the relative positions of their legs it will be the wife whose body angles towards the supine and for comfort her back may be supported with pillows. The position is usually entered into by gently rolling on the side following immission in the standard position. It is most suitable for inexperienced couples in the process of acquainting themselves with the exercise of orgasm control. It is of some value in premature ejaculation.

Woman-above Positions (vir succubus, male succumbent, female dominant, equestrian, coitus inversus). Among the several variations in this group the most important and widely practiced is the woman astride-facing position. The husband lies on his back, his legs together; the woman straddles his hips kneeling, less often crouching or, for brief periods, squatting, and facing him; usually she assumes an active role regarding the tempo and vigor of the genital thrusts, their direction and depth of penetration. Insertion of the phallus is best manually assisted by the woman. Adequate foreplay is desirable in this position to promote sufficient lubrication of the vulvovaginal passage. The man may or may not employ pelvic upthrusts, or raise his knees, or move the woman's hips with his hands.

Since coitus inversus allows the woman to be almost uninhibitedly active during intercourse and to regulate her own stimulation, it is worth trying in cases of impaired female orgasm capacity. It is especially useful where orgasm cannot be attained without unfettered bodily motor expression, but where this is hindered when the woman is supine because of her husband's heavy build and weight or her own relative petiteness. Some wives with moderately aggressive personality traits go through periods during which they are acutely intolerant of the psychologically passive role which the standard position symbolizes to them. A role reversal by tacit agreement of the spouses here has a favorable psychic effect. In some men, however, a woman's insistence on coitus inversus can aggravate certain personality difficulties (e.g., where a basically passive-feminoid man unconsciously overcompensates for these tendencies by strict adherence to the trappings of masculinity including the incumbent role in coitus).

The woman-above position is not believed suitable for routine or exclusive use. Nor is it probably always relaxing and effortless for the man, as claimed by some observers, because uninhibited but inexpert female motion can cause the phallus to slip out and produce painful contusion of the male organ at the next unchecked downthrust; men reporting apprehensively straining protective maneuvers as the female approaches a climax are no rarity. On the other hand, with an experienced woman and/ or a couple well attuned to each other the inverse position has been found capable of affording exquisite refinements of genital sensation, especially to the man through the woman's rocking or rotary hip motions. It also permits the wife to demonstrate by her own motions to the husband what she would like him to do during traditional intercourse.

The position is helpful where either or both partners, but especially the husband, are markedly obese; and where the vagina is relatively long and the penis relatively short. It has been employed as part of a treatment technique for milder cases of premature ejaculation. Since deep penetration can take place in the male succumbent, it is probably inadvisable during the last trimester of pregnancy and whenever the cervix is vulnerable. It is contraindicated where the vagina is very short or foreshortened (e.g., in female hypogenitalism, and in some uterine malpositions).

Variant. An attenuated version of the woman-astride is the sidesaddle-facing position in this group. The man lies on his back, fairly close to the edge of the bed. The woman settles herself sidesaddle fashion on his erect organ facing headwards. Depth of insertion is controlled by the woman as she sits erect or bends forward. The position has less to offer to the woman, but it is more relaxing, and possibly reassuring to the man. As penetration tends to be more shallow the contraindications to the woman-astride position probably do not apply here. The sidesaddle position may be more suitable for multiparas and requires substantial lubrication.

Sitting Positions. In the chair-seated, woman astride-facing (frontal sedentary astride) position the husband sits on a fairly low, armless chair or a stool, his legs apart; the woman straddles his thighs close to him, facing him, while with his hands he lefts her pelvis and settles the genitalia in place. Activity during the act is about equally divided between both mates. The position is said to be capable of providing intense clitoral stimulation, and this would be its principal indication. Otherwise its indica-

tions are similar to that for the woman above-astride, as are the contraindications. It is often considerably fatiguing for the man. In the **Woman-
seated, Man-facing** positions the man either kneels or stands in front of the
wife, depending on whether she sits on the edge of a low bed or on a table
or such, supporting her feet on chairs. The position's main indication is
a large abdomen of either spouse (e.g., in obesity or advanced pregnancy).
The kneeling variant is considered comfortable and capable of providing
adequate gratification for both. The woman may semirecline on pillows
during prolonged coition without necessarily losing genital contact. As to
the standing variant, because of its potential for discomfort, lower back
strain and mild local injury the physician probably should not assume the
responsibility of advising it except for carefully selected indications.

Rear Entry Positions (Positio a posteriori or a tergo. Entry more
bestiarum, not to be confused with rectal intromission). Typical rear entry
takes place when the wife assumes the knee-elbow or the knee-chest position or stands bending forward supporting her weight on a bed or table.
The position has some medical indications (e.g., in some orthopedic im-
pairments of the wife, or when eversion or other tender afflictions of the
female meatus make frontal entry painful). The knee-chest position is
employed at times where malposition of the cervix is believed to impede
insemination and thus fertility.

CONCEPTION

Ovum. At ovulation time each month a single ovum is released from
its follicle on the surface of one of the ovaries. In preparation for this, at
the beginning of the menstrual cycle, 8 to 15 dormant follicles had begun to
develop rapidly from the diplotene stage of meiotic prophase in which they
had been arrested since before the woman was born. All but one, rarely
two, of this dozen then undergo atresia and degeneration. How a particular
one is selected for ovulation is not known, nor even has the alternate-ovary
release theory so far been confirmed.

Tubo-ovarian Mechanism. At this time the fallopian tubes, through
muscular contractions in their tubo-ovarian ligaments, bend and curve
sufficiently to let their fimbriae form a cone over much of the ovary on
their side. As the matured follicle swells and ruptures, the ovum with its
cumulus cells, all bathed in follicular fluid, slowly exudes from it onto its
waiting transport (i.e., the fimbriae of the fallopian tube on its side). The
delicate fimbriae are heavily ciliated; the beat is in the direction of the
ostium, guiding the ovum, as well as setting up an inbound current of fluid.
The ovarian surface epithelium is also ciliated and participates in the
process. No tubal sucking action has been demonstrated, although some
observers have noted a prostaglandin-mediated segmental contraction of
the tubes suggesting this. The tubal capture of the egg is a rapid process;

passage from the ovarian surface through the ostium of the tube is complete in a few minutes.

At times the tubal fimbriae may misattach themselves (e.g., to the wrong ovarian site or to the rectum); the ovum is then released into the peritoneal cavity (i.e., the cul-de-sac). It is possible that some such ova find their way into the tube by riding the ciliary fluid currents. However, the human ovum begins to degenerate if it has not been fertilized within perhaps 24 hours. Since mobile spermatozoa have also been observed in the abdominal cavity, failed tubal capture may result in primary ectopic (abdominal or ovarian) pregnancy if fertilization occurs in the abdomen. Ectopic pregnancy also can be secondary in case of accidental outmigration from the tube of an already fertilized ovum.

The Spermatozoa, following coital ejaculation, are inexorably impelled to make their way up the female reproductive tract. Each sperm represents a mobile package of genetic material, jetted on its way in huge cohorts, each package alike and all surrounded by supporting plasma. Each is equally provisioned with nutrients and energizers, endowed with enzymatic barrier solvents and digestants, pH stabilizers and buffers, coated with antigenic material, the all-important DNA within the nucleus armored by being

SEX DETERMINATION

Two types of spermatozoa, produced in equal numbers, exist: *round-headed*, smaller, lighter, probably speedier in vivo, Y-chromosome bearing androsperms; and *oval-headed*, larger, heavier, slower X-bearing gynosperms. Androsperm, in an electrical field, move to the negative pole; their life span and fertilizing capacity are shorter; the acid vaginal milieu hurts them, an alkalinity-raising female orgasm helps them. They prevail in ejaculates emitted after long continence. Gynosperms' life span is 2 to 3 days, but cervical mucus affects them adversely. In an electrical field they move to the positive pole; their motion is speeded by acetylcholine, this is blocked by atropine (Sanyal). The parent under greater psychosomatic stress seems to inhibit the viability of the same-sex spermatozoa (Schuster, others).

Accordingly, to predetermine sex, it has been prescribed *for male offspring:* lengthy precoital continence, intercourse at or very near ovulation, precoital vaginal douche with sodium bicarbonate (p. 209), to ejaculate deeply near cervical os; female orgasm desirable. *For female offspring:* frequent coitus up to 2 to 3 days pre-ovulation; precoital vinegar douches; to ejaculate shallowly (e.g., from rear-entry position); to avoid female orgasm (Shettles).

If people could choose their offspring's sex: At a 1973 international conference on chromosome research the participants estimated that the triple combination of access-to-amniocentesis (gender diagnosis), fetal-sex-revealing-to-parents, and abortion-on-demand would lead to an outnumbering of male births over females by a ratio of 3:1.

enmeshed in keratinic substance—and each highly expendable. Of, say, a quarter of a billion spermatozoa deposited in the vagina, only a few thousand seem to reach the correct tube and the vicinity of the ovum, and fewer than 100 are at the site when the front-runner fertilizes the ovum. The female tract can be either relatively sperm-hostile or else biologically helpful, depending largely on the prevailing phase of the menstrual cycle, this being a vestige of animal estrus with its rigidly limited occasions for copulation.

Sperm Migration.   Under favorable conditions spermatozoa ascend the female tract with great speed. Sperm has consistently been found in the endocervical mucus in 90 to 180 seconds (Sobrero-McLeod), and occasionally in less than 60 seconds, well embedded and no longer accessible to soluble spermicidal substances or to flushing. Under exceptional circumstances sperm was found in the fallopian tubes 30 minutes after deposit in the vagina, although more usually 12 hours are necessary for this. Fertilization in humans is believed to occur most often within 24 hours after insemination, and some observers believe that fertilizing capacity is lost by sperm after 48 hours at most, but live spermatozoa have been recovered from the female reproductive tract, during autopsy, up to 3½ weeks after sexual intercourse. There has to date not been found a way to determine maximum duration of fertilizing capacity—as distinct from viability—of human sperm in the female tract, although by rule of thumb, sperm maintain motility almost twice as long as fertilizing capacity. In cows and sheep the latter is 1 to 2 days, in horses close to a week, in hibernating mammals all winter, and reptiles can lay fertile eggs 4 to 5 years after contact with a male. Prolonged residence of sperm in the female tract increases the probability of its producing nonviable or abnormal embryos. Generally, the greater the time lag between germ cell maturation and fertilization, the greater the number of mutations that will develop.

Active swimming motion is the sperm's principal means of progression at the beginning of the journey in the cervical canal and at the very end when the winner traverses the ovum's zona pellucida. During the remainder of sperm migration transport is largely passive, by involuntary female muscle contraction and, to a lesser extent, by ciliary beat. The rate of transport is vastly influenced by the interaction of hormones prevailing during the phase of the cycle, and by alterations in alpha and beta adrenergic receptors mediated through changes in catecholamine storage and release.

Deposit.   In the vagina semen tends to be deposited as a pool in the posterior fornix, but in the normally strongly acid vaginal milieu the sperm cannot endure long; only 10 per cent are believed to survive after 2 hours, practically none after half a day, although prolonged sexual excitation of the female, as well as subsequently the seminal fluid itself, tend to neutralize vaginal acidity somewhat. Nonmotile spermatozoa can sometimes be recovered from the vagina after up to 24 hours.

Ascent into Cervix. Relatively rapid ascent into the more hospitable, alkaline endocervix, especially by the first, sperm-rich portion of the ejaculate insures survival for as long as 5 days or a week. In fact, the cervix may act as a reservoir, releasing additional spermatozoa gradually, possibly so as to ensure a supply at hand when the short-lived ovum finds its way into one of the tubes (theory).

The mode of semen transport into the cervical canal has been in dispute for a long time. Direct ejaculation into the endocervix, as in some animals, does not exist in humans, although sperm from the first seminal portion is found in the cervix sooner than their best estimated swimming speed can account for. The theory of an insuck effect on very small amounts of semen via uterine and abdominal orgasmic contractions has not been entirely disproved. An open-and-shut, snapping effect of the cervical os does not seem to occur. There does exist a rising of the cervix, in fact of the whole uterus, beginning when sexual excitement begins, although it is absent in retroflexed and retroverted organs. Also observed has been a dipping, wandering, "searching" movement of the cervix during midcycle coitus (unconfirmed). Immediately after female orgasm, and only after orgasm, a slight gaping of the external os has been observed in nulligravidae which persists for 20 to 30 minutes and may passively aid sperm ascent. However, even today the question of whether the quality of a woman's orgasm affects sperm ascent into and through the uterus and thus fertility, can only be partly answered. Obviously, orgasm is not needed, as evidenced by pregnancies of raped, frigid and artificially inseminated women. Nor has it been shown that markedly orgasm-prone women as a group are also the most fertile. While the surviving belief of some females that they can prevent conception by consciously suppressing the climax during the sexual act has little merit, the postcoital tension state of some pseudofrigidae is believed capable of interference with impregnation via cervical and tubal spasms.

Cervical Mucus. Optimal conditions for sperm ascent in the cervix exist during the ovulatory phase when the amount of circulating estrogen is approaching its peak. The mucus is now abundant and thin, secretion having risen from the usual 20 to 60 mg/day to 10 times this amount. Its pH is at its most favorable for sperm survival: 8.25 to 8.40. Its spinnability now increases to 10 to 20 cm. in length, thus lowering viscosity and with it surface tension. Sodium chloride content of mucus increases fivefold at this time; the resulting crystallization, well known from the fern-leaf test in dried specimens, favors sperm survival. The filament meshwork of sialomucin-type glycoproteins, the mucus' principal ingredient, has now widersized meshes, permitting better sperm passage. The external cervical os is more widely open at this time, with corresponding changes in the width and length of the cervical canal. A chemotactic attraction of midcycle cervical mucus on seminal fluid also appears to exist. Away from the midphase of the cycle sperm encounters substantially thicker and scantier cervical mucus, viscid, almost gelatinous in quality; the external os is also narrower at that time.

The cervix also acts as a major selective barrier in sperm migration, filtering out morphologically abnormal, and sub- or non-viable spermatozoa. Between the vagina's lethal chemical factors and the voracious phagocytes stationary in the center of the cervical canal, the number of spermatozoa emerging into the uterine cavity is vastly reduced.

Uterine Ascent. Ascent through the uterine cavity to the uterotubal junctions, a distance of approximately 2 inches, is a fairly rapid process effected largely by rhythmic contractions of the uterine muscles. These contractions are set in motion by an as yet incompletely understood interplay between oxytocin, various prostaglandins and the network of adrenergic nerve receptors in the female tract: sexual excitation as well as mechanical stimulation of the cervix by the thrusting phallus release the posterior pituitary hormones into the bloodstream, although emotional stress can interfere with this release; oxytocin, in turn, is believed to sensitize the nonpregnant myometrium to the effect of various prostaglandins; the latter, in their turn, mobilized from both the female tissues and from the semen pool deposited in the vagina, assist in sperm transport by stimulating uterine contractions, and possibly in other ways. The prostaglandin effect, in turn, is variable depending on their own quantity, the prevailing hormone milieu in the female tract, relative calcium and potassium levels, and possibly other factors.

Tubal Mechanism. Each uterotubal junction represents another barrier, and a further marked reduction in the number of sperms occurs at this point. Nonmotile, dysmorphic, perhaps species-foreign spermatozoa are barred by a number of mechanisms, such as swelling barriers, interdigitating constrictors, immunologic reactions and phagocytosis, although their relative effectiveness in humans remains uncertain.

In the tubes the surviving spermatozoa probably remain fertile for up to 48 hours, depending partly on their size and the shape of the head (i.e., the nature of the sex chromosome they carry). (See box, p. 219). Transportation is chiefly by contractions of the tubal muscle layers, but progress is counter to the ciliary beat. The oviductal fluid which fills the broom-straw-sized lumen of the tubes is subject to hormone-induced changes in volume and chemistry. It is in the tubes that spermatozoa are believed to complete the process of "capacitation," the final stage of their long maturation, without which they would be incapable of penetrating the investments of the ovum; freshly ejaculated sperm is functionally not mature; it lacks the capacity to fertilize until it has divested itself of one of its component factors, possibly a mucolytic enzyme group. The process takes several hours and as it gets under way the spermatozoon begins to age; its viability now runs down like a wound clock. The principal capacitating agent may be the follicular fluid brought into the tube by the ovum, or else a synergism between uterine, tubal and follicular fluids. The process is well established in animals; occurrence in humans is strongly probable but not proven.

The tubal dispersal and propulsion mechanism ensures that spermatozoa are transported into the upper portion of the ampulla (i.e., in the vicinity of the ovum's resting and reception site). It is not known with certainty how spermatozoa locate the ovum during the final distance of circa 1 mm. Both random encounter and chemotaxis (tropism) theories have been proposed, but more likely is a trapping mechanism similar to the fertilizin-antifertilizin interplay seen in lower organisms. The ovum's diameter averages less than 150 microns, the size of the smallest dot visible to the unaided eye, but being surrounded by several thousand cumulus cells makes it a larger target. Once a spermatozoon touches the mass, it stays attached. Less than 100 sperms seem to reach this stage; their combined enzyme systems are believed needed to digest the cementing matrix and to penetrate the cumulus layer. Their synchronized flagellar motion has been seen to rotate the ovum clockwise as rapidly as one full turn every 15 seconds for up to 20 or 30 hours.

Conjugation (syngamy). Although more than one spermatozoon is now believed to partly enter the ovum, following penetration of the zona pellucida a rapid chemical alteration propagates through the zona, and this together with changes in the egg's granular cortex make the ooplasm impenetrable to other spermatozoa. The tail of the elected fertilizing sperm detaches in the ooplasm; the head's shape becomes rounded and it forms the male pronucleus which slowly migrates to the center of the ovum. Within 12 hours the male and female pronuclei meet and fuse. The newly fertilized ovum (spermovium, zygote, conceptus) has been furnished with 23 chromosomes each from father and mother. Further cell division takes place by mitosis.

The first cleavage of the human ovum seems to occur about a day after fertilization. Further cleavage in humans occurs at about 22-hour intervals. The fertilized egg probably remains in the ampulla for 1 to 3 days, after which it is transported passively through the tube. It reaches the uterus at about the 16-cell stage.

Implantation (nidation, innidation) takes place approximately 6 days after fertilization, the conceptus being in the blastocyst stage and consisting now of up to 200 cells. In preparation the endometrium had undergone its cyclic post-ovulatory changes; thickening, softening, high vascularization, glandular proliferation, leukocyte infiltration. Delicate synchronization apparently is important, involving 2 days of progesterone activity followed by an estrogen surge, histamine release, catecholamine activity and an immunologic reaction. Although even ectopic implantation, presumably without some of these finesses, can succeed, in humans only about half of the fertilized ova are believed to survive the endometrial lodging process. When it does not, the woman rarely is even aware of having been pregnant; there is merely delayed menstruation.

DURATION OF PREGNANCY

Gestation, in the U.S., is medically usually calculated by Nägele's rule: 9 months, 7 days after the first day of the last normal menstruation. For quick calculation:

$$D_1 \text{ of LMP} + 7d - 3 \text{ cal. mos.} + 1 \text{ yr.} = EDD \pm 10d.$$

Average duration in this manner is 280 days (others: 282.2 ± 7.6 days median deviation). Embryologists measure length of gestation from day of conception (2 weeks later), or by crown-rump (CR) length.

Pregnancy is shorter in younger women, and possibly in multiparas; this is also believed related to race. Upper and lower duration limits are legally important, although, as a principle of law, in every state a child born to a married woman is presumed to be legitimate. A New York court recognized a pregnancy as lasting 355 days, while the husband had claimed his absence. A foreshortened gestation claim versus allegedly concealed pregnancy at time of marriage was adjudged for a wife at 222 days (Pennsylvania). Medically acknowledged range of birth variations for normally mature infants appears to be 220 and 315 days respectively, although much younger immature and later postmature birth ages are known.

At nidation the blastocyst burrows actively down into the loose, edematous endometrium, at the upper portion of the posterior wall in two thirds of the cases. Within a week epithelium has closed over it, sealing it from contact with the opposite uterine wall. Around that time, between the twelfth and fourteenth day after ovulation, placental villi and yolk sac begin to develop, and the conceptus becomes an embryo. This, according to present thinking, is the point at which life begins.

Impregnation without Penetration

A pregnant girl may state emphatically that she did not have intercourse near the time in question or even at any time in her life. In the latter case an intact hymen may be found exceptionally. As fresh semen must have reached the endocervix in some fashion, the following possibilities present themselves:

The chief possibility in every case is that the girl is not telling the truth, regardless of the impression she conveys. Also, intact appearance of the hymen does not necessarily disprove coital entry in some cases. A very naïve or retarded girl may believe the definition of coitus to include that the sex partners must be lying down or even "go to bed"; in all honesty she may believe that she merely petted when her boy friend effected vaginal entry while both were, for instance, in a standing or sitting position. Amnesia for an act of intercourse can occur (e.g., at alcoholic parties), both in inexperienced and experienced women. Cohabitation with an experienced, nondrugged woman who remains fully asleep has been claimed and perhaps is possible under exceptional circumstances.

Impregnation from semen deposited about the vulva is possible, although not frequent, exceptionally even with the hymen intact. Semen deposited on the lower abdomen or the thighs almost certainly cannot lead to impregnation. Accidental introduction of fresh semen adhering to a finger must be assumed possible but has not been proved. Accidental insemination through contact of the vulva with bathtub rim, toilet seat, washcloth, bed linen or handkerchief with fresh semen adhering have been claimed but are highly unlikely. Spermatozoal penetration through thin, average-meshed fabric (panties, handkerchief) is possible in vitro but not likely in vivo. Impregnation through sperm in the drop of pre-coital moisture must be assumed possible (e.g., in genital apposition).

Of related interest is a recent survey of 156 healthy student nurses as to their vaginal colonization with T-strain mycoplasma. Colonized were 5.6 per cent of women with no history of genital contact; 26.7 per cent of those with genital apposition without penetration; 37.5 per cent with 1-partner coitus; 54.5 per cent with 2-partner coitus; 75 per cent with coitus with 3 or more partners (McCormack-Lee).

Artificial Insemination

Instrumental depositing of seminal fluid in the female tract—mostly endo-cervical, occasionally vaginal, exocervical or intrauterine—is an alternative to adoption chiefly when the husband is either sterile or prevented from depositing semen by coitus. Indications have included erective impotence, some intractable ejaculatory disturbances, hypospadias, extreme obesity, paraplegia; also intractable trichomonal vaginitis, anomalies of the cervix, prior offspring with Tay-Sachs disease and other genetic impairment. Semen may be the husband's own (homologous insemination, A.I.H.), or from a selected donor (heterologous, A.I.D.). These are not "test tube babies." Because of the necessary secrecy surrounding the procedure, no reliable figures are available, but it is now well established and its acceptance spreading. A magazine, in 1971, quoted an estimate of 10,000 A.I. babies per year born in the U.S. (Time).

Obtaining Semen. Donor semen is obtained by masturbation under reasonably controlled conditions. Husband's semen is obtained, most often, by masturbation, coitus interruptus or condom. The Catholic Church disapproves of these methods, but is believed to countenance assisted homologous insemination by means of postcoital recovery of semen from the vagina; electroejaculation; vesiculoprostatic massage; needle aspiration from the excurrent structures; and semen involuntarily, nocturnally emitted into a pre-installed condom. A husband's oligospermic semen can be concentrated by separately catching the first sperm-rich portions of several ejaculates, freeze-storing, then thawing, pooling and centrifuging them and adding a freshly obtained split just before use. However, severely oligospermic specimens do not survive frozen storage well. On the whole, donor insemination tends to be more successful than A.I.H.

Donor Selection. The physician selects, and deals with, the donor. It is incumbent upon him to pass judgment on the donor's character, and his biologic and genetic fitness. Preferred are married young men with at least 1 child of known quality. The physician must match race, skin shade, height, habitus, eye color, hair color and curl, and possibly facial features as closely as possible to those of either spouse. He must ascertain quality of the donor's semen and freedom from genito-infectious diseases. Blood type should be related, and an Rh negative woman requires an Rh negative donor. By accepted practice the physician must absolutely shield and preserve the donor's anonymity from the couple forever, and the couple's anonymity likewise from the donor. Recipient couple and donor should not be in the physician's office at the same time.

Preparation and Procedure. The physician planning an A.I.D. must be satisfied as to the stability of the marriage because, from experience, marital strife and dissolution after a child was produced can lead to complications for everyone involved in the insemination, most sadly for the child. In all cases the motives of the couple desiring A.I.D. should be explored to some extent. Where the husband appears in the least suspicious, sullen, litiginous, disinclined but afraid to deny his wife, or still shocked by the discovery of his own sterility, experienced physicians have declined to inseminate, for the good of all (Kleegman). At times, irrelevant or trivial motives come to light (e.g., coital malimmission, sterility of the wife, a lesbian seeking asexual reproduction, or to cover up for extramarital pregnancy already in progress). A woman found to be suitable is scheduled for the endocervical procedure on 1 or more days, once or more times a day, near her ovulation time, with high spinnbarkeit of the cervical mucus. Insemination is done in the lithotomy position with hips elevated, a bivalve speculum in place. A sterile syringe with a special cannula attached is used with minimal pressure. The overflow is allowed to accumulate on the speculum blade, this pool to bathe the cervical os for 15 or 30 minutes while the woman maintains her position. Prior sedation and/or an antispasmodic to relax the fallopian tubes is sometimes administered. If necessary the procedures are repeated, month after month, but rarely for more than one year. Auto-insemination with husband's semen at home (e.g., by vaginal insert, by pipette, or a cervical suction cup with attached plastic tube to accommodate a syringe) has been employed with some success in certain cases.

Complications. Homologous insemination presents few legal or ethical difficulties, but many legal loose ends remain as regards A.I.D., although several states have sought to protect these children by legitimizing them by statute (Pilpel, St. John-Chivas, others). The concepts of adultery and illegitimacy continue to be brought into the discussion, although only wives of freely consenting husbands can obtain heterologous insemination today. Also, public policy in all U.S. jurisdictions is that all children born in wedlock are presumed the legitimate issue of the spouses. But can the husband disclaim the child later, or refuse to be liable for its support in case of separation, or can he obtain visitation rights if divorced? Can the state, or a court, force the donor's identity into the open and compel him to contribute to the child's support? Can the child claim himself heir to donor's property, if known? For inheritance purposes, is he to be considered the grandchild of his paternal grandparents? How can subsequent incest be avoided (e.g., in case of donor's multi-use donation)? Is the physician guilty of fraud or perjury if he—as is firm practice—gives the husband's name as the father on the birth certificate? And does A.I.H. make any future annulment of the marriage for nonconsummation impossible? There have been judicial proceedings for most of such questions without, as yet, clear answers.

Protection. Unlike in adoption, it is firm practice everywhere to conceal from the child his heterologous descent. It is desirable that the fact of insemination be kept from all relatives and friends. A blood relative or a close friend as a donor is not acceptable to physicians with A.I.D. experience. Written consent by both spouses is a firm rule; special release forms in case of stillbirth, prematurity, birth defects, etc. are the rule. It is held good practice where possible to mix some of husband's semen with the donor's in A.I.D. to ensure that at least a theoretical possibility exists that the husband was the father. The husband may be asked to be present during the insemination procedure. Some physicians request that the couple have intercourse on the day of insemination. If A.I.D. is successful, the inseminating physician frequently will not act as the obstetrician; the latter, unaware of the circumstances, can with equanimity list the husband as the father on the birth certificate.

INTERCOURSE IN SPECIAL SITUATIONS

Defloration — Coitus during Menstruation — Coitus during
Pregnancy — Coitus in Obesity — Coitus and Heart Disease —
Coital Techniques in Infertility.

Defloration

Defloration, enlargement of the hymenal opening, most usually occurs
when the vagina of the virgo intacta is penetrated for the first time. It
involves some stretching, as well as one or two small (approximately 0.5
cm) nick-like lacerations in the free edge of the hymenal membrane.

The Pain of defloration is brief and moderate in about one half of all
women, supposedly absent in 20 per cent and severe in the remaining one
third. An occasional bride may confuse vulvar chafing with hymenal pain.
An awkward, or too rough, or too hesitant approach of the male organ
can increase pain, especially if the bride's thighs are hyperflexed and the
phallus enters in an excessively upward (forward) direction, with its
underside too close to the virgin's high perineum. Fear or subconscious
resentment of genital penetration is believed to increase defloratory pain
sensations. Major pain may be due to atypical shape, thickness, rigidity or
hypersensitivity of the hymen. Artificial lubrication, if more widely used
by newlyweds, would in all probability reduce the number of sexually un-
satisfying honeymoons.

The Bleeding is usually slight and the lacerations heal over in a few
days, a week at most, with slight bleeding recurring from sex acts during
this time. If the bleeding causes concern the bride may rest flat on her
back with thighs in apposition. Intercourse in a moderately extended
position with a firm pillow under her hips may relieve discomfort, or she
can close her legs after entry has been effected so that the man's legs are
outside hers. An anesthetic cream may be useful. Bleeding is relatively
most copious in the very young, less so with advancing years, and it may
be altogether absent in older virgins. Racial and/or ethnic differences may
exist.

Nondefloration can occur (e.g., with an exceptionally elastic hymen and
a relatively small penis): there are no lacerations and little pain, as the
membrane is simply stretched and invaginated on intromission. Such
technical intactness can persist without impeding intercourse until childbirth irons out the membrane. In naïve couples brides have remained
unentered for years with the phallus always being sidetracked into a—sometimes deep—pocket between hymen and fourchette. In other cases (e.g.,
with an annular fibrotic hymen) inadvertent coitus per urethram for years
has been described.

Position. The basic coital position is almost always adequate for defloration, but hyperflexion of the woman should be avoided. It is preferable that the man place his body rather headward with respect to hers so that his organ enters well anteriorly, with the dorsum penis close to the pubic arch, even to the point of slight downward deflection of the phallus. This can minimize defloration pain and a shove-like thrust of average vigor will then suffice for penetration. A cooperating rather than shrinking or retiring motion by the bride facilitates the procedure. However, too anterior entry may bruise the woman's urethra, causing prolonged tenderness and possibly setting in motion a "honeymoon cystitis" (see also p. 242).

Defloration Problems are distinctly fewer today. The use of menstrual tampons from teen age tends to pre-stretch and desensitize the hymenal opening somewhat. Fewer young people today are crassly naïve or filled with frightening hearsay about "tearing and bleeding." There are fewer cases of unrecognized malformations and of hypogenitalism. Most young couples today have enough affectionate regard for each other to make undue brutality—"rape of the bride"—a relatively infrequent occurrence. For psychology of the bridal night see also p. 195.

Assisted Defloration, preferably applied before the wedding, is believed to be necessary in about 10 per cent of virginal brides. The principal indications are an unusually sensitive, rigid or thick membrane, a grossly atypical opening, the bride's overwhelming fear of defloration, and spontaneous request by the couple. Most often used is digital or instrumental dilatation, an office procedure done under local or topical anesthesia. The finger or else a series of prewarmed, well-lubricated dilators or a pyrex centrifuge tube is introduced into the opening by the physician while the patient is in the seated lithotomy position and instructed to bear down. After one to three sessions the introitus should admit at least two fingers.

In **Self-stretching** the bride, following speculum examination, is instructed to introduce first one lubricated fingertip as far as she can—pare long fingernails!—first under the physician's or nurse's observation, then once or twice daily for a few days, and then to progress to the introduction of 2 and finally of 3 fingers in toto pressing towards the lower back. This may be done in a warm bath or following warm douche irrigation of the introitus. The procedure takes 2 weeks altogether; it is most helpful where the virginal bride has expressed marked apprehension regarding her build or proportions.

Incision. Least often used, and probably best reserved for major local indications, is surgical defloration. Hymenotomy under local anesthesia consists of a few lengthwise snip incisions in the free hymenal margin. Fine catgut sutures are rarely needed, and the surfaces heal in less than a week, two weeks at most, but healing may restore the hymen's original status with added fibrous contracture. Hymenectomy if necessary, under general anesthesia, consists of removal of a wedge from the posterior quadrant, followed by dilatation. The use of rapid short-wave cutting current has been recommended.

Coitus during Menstruation (Coitus Intramenstruus)

Some women experience a heightening of sexual desire during the days they menstruate, and sexual intercourse at the time of the period is practiced regularly by some couples; many others shun it either because of custom, esthetic distaste, prohibitive hearsay regarding toxicity or health hazard, or some, because of religious orthodoxy (e.g., orthodox Jews, by Mosaic law—Leviticus 15:19), are forbidden coitus intramenstruus.

However, the frequency of the practice is increasing. Older taboos and warnings are being scrutinized more critically. The relative freedom from fear of conceiving makes it an attractive opportunity to some couples. And as women are becoming more assertive some tend to abandon the widely practiced perimenstrual masturbation—for many adult women the only occasion when they ever masturbate—to suggesting or requesting coitus intramenstruus; this is to many women a more satisfactory way of detumescing any uncomfortable pelvic engorgement occurring at that time and of relieving the urges manifesting themselves cyclically with the ebb and flow of gonadotropin plasma levels and sex steroid production. The above mechanism probably does not apply to the pseudomenses of the woman on oral progestins.

Some of the resistance to coitus intramenstruus comes from men. Not unusual is a shocklike reaction in some males at the sight of blood on their organ after intercourse, and they tend to avoid repetition of the experience. Some comfort-loving husbands may object to a choice between going to sleep in a "messy" state, or else arising postcoitally to clean themselves up, although a temporary diaphragm could contain the flow in such cases. Unless bleeding is copious (e.g., early during the period) spontaneous vulvovaginal lubrication may be scant and coitus can produce chafing in the absence of an artificial lubricant. Frequently the erotic arousal and sexual response level of the menstruating woman is heightened, but others dislike energetic copulation while they menstruate, or they feel too unwell generally, or they do not tolerate it well. A low-grade or negative reaction is more likely in women afflicted with major degrees of premenstrual tension-malaise. Where a husband persistently demands sexual relations during menses over his wife's objections, he may either be reacting with neurotically compulsive testing behavior to presumed sexual rejection, or else the presence of sadistic tendencies may be suspected.

Medically no generic contraindications to coitus intramenstruus seem to exist, although there are few systematic observations. Not all women tolerate it equally well; some seem to respond with a transient metritis during the late days, with crampy lower abdominal pain and reactivation of the flow. This is not to be confused with the well-known increase in rate of flow from the female tract which almost always follows toward the end of vigorous coitus and/or climax, especially in the first days of the period. An increased risk of upward spread of female tract infection and of endometriosis during menstrual intercourse has not been proven, but continues to be in dispute. It is equally uncertain if latent female gonorrhea regains virulence and increased infectivity for the sex partner during the period.

Coitus during Pregnancy

The physician's concern here is mostly with intercourse causing abortion in early pregnancy or premature labor during the late phases. Penile intromission as a primary (i.e., largely mechanical) cause of abortion has not been proven. Secondary mobilization of the uterine expulsion mechanism (i.e., neurochemically) is a substantial possibility. While habitual abortion is a well-established indication for abstinence, many practitioners continue to impose major restrictions for sometimes irrational indications during the early months. It is true that the highly permissive physician might expose himself to blame and litigation in case of fetal wastage, yet any family-protective prescribing of abstinence needs to be balanced against the heightened emotional and sexual needs of many gravidae, especially during the often highly sexed second trimester, and against the marriage-disruptive potential of imposed lengthy abstinence in borderline couples.

Prematurity. Toward the end of pregnancy intercourse may cause uterine irritability, thus a threat of prematurity, most so in primigravidae. In the last 2 to 3 weeks orgasm of the woman seems capable of precipitating labor, as does at times mere sex stimulation including of the nipples and areolas. Thus where a history of prematurity of birth and complications of labor exist, imposing abstinence in the final 2 months is not unreasonable; allowing intercourse but not orgasm leads to difficulties in some women, although in the last few months many are generally rather unresponsive. The factor of predisposition here is incompletely understood, as some couples have intercourse comfortably to the beginning of labor.

Absolute Coital Prohibition is universally advised after the membranes have ruptured and/or the cervix dilated, same as earlier in pregnancy any threat of miscarriage, any suspicion of placenta praevia, or even any uterine bleeding or staining contraindicate coitus. Introduction of contaminating material via the penis or semen is not a problem with the membranes intact and the cervix competent and shut. This does not include the major venereal diseases, of course, nor does it, perhaps, apply to primigravidae (see below). The risk of introducing abortion-inducing prostaglandins, unproven so far, into the female tract with the seminal fluid has led some physicians to advise against unsheathed intercourse during pregnancy, especially in predisposed women.

During the first pregnancy there should perhaps be no unsheathed intercourse at all. This is now emerging as one of the probable factors responsible for subsequent pre-cancerous changes of the cervix. During primigravidity women may be highly vulnerable to contamination with the mutagen-carcinogen whose source seems to be either type-2 herpesvirus hominis, or else DNA of sperm origin remaining in the genitalia after intercourse (see also p. 258).

Coital Positions during pregnancy may have to be adjusted to take the pressure off the woman's abdomen—for psychologic reasons, to obviate discomfort, later to avoid pressure on the cord and transmitted pressure on the deep abdominal vessels. Varicose legs need to be protected perhaps, clitoral orgasm minimized, and the vulnerable cervix spared. Recommended are the modified side-rear entry, woman above-sidesaddle-facing, the bed edge-seated man-kneeling, possibly the knee-chest rear entry positions and, if man-above posture is desired, a moderate amount of extension (see p. 215). Inadvisable are the hyperflexed and severely arched man-above and coitus inversus-astride positions.

Cunnilingus. Cases of sudden death due to air embolism have been observed, following the blowing of a substantial amount of air into the vagina of pregnant women during orogenital activity. Deliberate air blowing is described as conveying exciting stereotactic sensations; it also occurs inadvertently (dyspneically) during prolonged cunnilingus.

Resumption of sexual relations postpartum is generally allowed after 6 weeks (range 4 to 8 weeks); but many women are known to resume after 3 weeks or even less, not so much because they feel sexual needs—these tend to be still fairly low at that time—but out of concern over the husband, his contentment and his fidelity. Many men, especially those who are emotionally immature and/or with strong dependent needs, require this as a form of reassurance, as they feel neglected in favor of the infant. Some wives of highly needful or else labile men allow postpartum resumption as soon as the episiotomy is substantially healed, although the organs are as yet barely estrinized, erotic lubrication is all but absent and the cervix may not be firmly closed.

Coitus in Obesity

According to the available evidence sexual functioning is not essentially different from the average in obese individuals of either sex, except that in this group libido is more often either very high or very low. However, the condition imposes the need for certain technical adjustments in practicing the sex act.

Marked obesity of the wife, especially of thighs, pelvic girdle and abdomen, can make intercourse in the standard position well-nigh impossible. Even moderate stoutness, if it involves thick labia majora and a

COITUS DURING PREGNANCY

Absolute Prohibitions:
No coitus in threatened miscarriage, suspected placenta praevia or any uterine staining or bleeding. No coitus with ruptured membranes or opened cervix. No cunnilingus, to avoid even inadvertent air embolism.

Caution:
No female orgasm during last 3 weeks to avoid prematurity (unconfirmed). No sex stimulation, including of nipples, nor coitus, in habitual abortion. No coitus during entire first pregnancy to avoid subsequent carcinoma of cervix (unconfirmed). See p. 258. No haphazard sex prohibition and starving of heightened needs of emotionally labile couples. No seminal emission into the female tract of vulnerable women to avoid prostaglandin-induced uterine expulsion (unconfirmed).

Coital Positions:
Weight off woman's abdomen. Spare the cervix.
   Recommended: Modified side-rear entry. Bed edge-seated. Knee-chest rear entry. Moderately extended man-above. Woman-above, side-saddle facing.
   Inadvisable: Hyperflexed or severely arched man-above. Coitus inversus-astride.

Postpartum:
Usual resumption 6 weeks (4–8 weeks) postpartum. Coitus after 3 weeks not rare, although possibly uncomfortable.

prominent mons, can keep the male organ from penetrating to a satisfactory depth. In these cases an alternative position such as the woman semi-reclining across the edge of a low bed or a padded table, 2 chairs supporting the feet, and the man kneeling or standing in front of her, recommends itself. In lesser cases the modified lateral-averted coitus inversus, or even one of the rear entries may be suitable (see also p. 218).

In marked obesity of the husband (e.g., a protruding abdomen) the woman-sitting, man-kneeling position (p. 218) or the lateral-averted are feasible positions. Intercourse in the man-above posture, with the woman moderately arching up and his weight partly supported on his hands in a straight-arm crouch is feasible but may be too strenuous for most heavily overweight men.

Coitus and Heart Disease

The stress and strain on the heart of sexual intercourse cannot be truly measured at present. Such findings as those of the Case Western Reserve study of long-married, middle-aged patients with emphasis on energy cost (Hellerstein-Friedman) appear only partially applicable. Coitus does not merely represent muscular exertion with its measurable circulatory, oxygenation, etc. changes affecting the myocardium, but a plethora of incompletely understood neural, autonomic, hormonal and biochemical effects, triggered by often subtle emotional shifts; these in turn place an extra burden on the cardiac reserve.

The Physiology of a fully experienced orgasm represents a veritable autonomic storm which is not accurately mirrored by available functional measurements (see also p. 176). Also, sex-related affective stresses—most notably perhaps frustrational anger—induce an overproduction and/or rapid release from storage of potentially cardiotoxic catecholamines as well as of adrenocortical steroids, the latter perhaps acting via myocardial potassium depletion. It is believed to be the presence of these steroids which distinguishes the cardiac effects of high coital stress from the more benign stimulation of comparable physical exercise.

Resumption. When to resume coitus safely after a coronary infarction is an oft-asked question. There are no specific rules. Very few physicians seem to advise resumption in less than 6 weeks after onset. The most often used rule of thumb is "90 days," although for psychologic reasons this may be excessive where foreseeable circumstances are favorable. There may be a month's further delay in cases with complications such as arrhythmia or congestive failure. There is a tendency to allow return to work and resumption of sex together, and clinical judgment based on the tolerance of the general activities of daily life, such as walking, remains the principal yardstick at present. More rational criteria are based on successful exercise tests at levels of 5 to 8 calories per minute (e.g., when the patient can accomplish 1- or 2-flight stair-climbing or a Master 2-step without major EKG, BP, or pulse rate changes). Direct tolerance testing of coitus by bedside EKG, taped or radio-teletransmitted, has also been introduced. It has been asserted that occasional ectopic and ventricular premature beats during coitus, as well as ischemic ST-T complex depressions, are not cause for alarm. Patients with permanently implanted pacemakers, after wound healing, are subject to no special sexual restrictions beyond those imposed by the underlying condition (Rios).

Quality of Act. The quality of the sexual act is a major factor in cardiac care, sedate and moderate intercourse being the most desirable. One may describe as sedate or relaxed coitus relations between two mates stably and affectionately accustomed to each other, with the healthy spouse willing to cooperate in all necessary measures such as sexual frequency, intensity and positions. As moderate coitus one may describe activity indulged in with the minimal frequency necessary to fulfill the physical and emotional needs of both spouses. Although one may rather arbitrarily name an average frequency of 3 to 10 times a month, much higher rates probably do not per se constitute harmful excess in couples accustomed to and desirous of them.

Marital relations are more apt to be sedate than nonmarital ventures, especially if the latter involve prolonged effort to overcome resistance to seduction, significant age disparity, a hastily improvised locale, or fear of discovery or consequences.

Stressful Acts.   Marital sex can be equally tense and strenuous for the post-infarct patient. Coronary patients as a group have been found to have a distinctly high incidence of pre-illness sexual problems, including diminishing potency. Continuation of the pressures and anxieties arising out of such sexual maladjustment constitutes a risk requiring attention. Also, the coronary-prone type of individual, with his impatience with slowness and fumbling, his intense achievement drive and his general stress-blindness would be automatically at risk in pursuing his vita sexualis, regardless of the setting.

Some obsessively worrisome men are tensely apprehensive for months of how coitus will affect them each time, or how they will acquit themselves. Mild exertional pain panics some beyond all reason, causing additional psychogenic symptoms and stress and disorganizes performance. Feelings of bitterness keep nagging at some health-proud younger post-coronary men and can transform the sexual appetite into a would-be outlet for their rage, with ejaculatio tardata a possible result. A wife reacting with despondency or with angry hostility to the mate's illness and the changed sexual pattern can have a performance-disorganizing effect on the patient; so can the oversolicitous wife-turned-nurse even when in bed. These and similar interpersonal constellations help explain the postcoronary impotence rate of 15 to 25 per cent found commonly among middle-aged men during the first 6 months from coital resumption.

Female Cardiopathy.   Too few relevant observations on female cardiacs have been made or are available to permit meaningful summarizing. Some men, including husbands, require cautioning, however, about having relations with an acutely ill or decompensated woman; these men assume, probably falsely, that the woman's relatively passive coital role does not constitute undue exertion.

Counsel.   The physician can help greatly by anticipating his patient's concern about his future sexual life, including his often irrational fear of lifelong marital invalidism. Advice should not stop short of details such as coital frequency or preferred positions. It is often, but not always, best to include the wife in the counseling. Group counseling with couples is a worthwhile technique here. Group counseling for wives only has been attempted. Where pre-illness difficulties appear important in evaluating postcoronary progress and in programing assistance, psychiatric consultation may be desirable. Postcoronary patients seem to fare better sexually if they are participating in an overall supervised program of conditioning exercises: the duration, in months, of mild exertional angina may be shortened and vigor and enjoyment of sexual acts enhanced.

Sexual Technique and modalities are of some importance here. Foreplay is desirable and can be compared to the pitcher's wind-up: as a form of warm-up it facilitates neural pathways and reflexly helps reduce or close down the visceral vascular bed. Rest preceding coitus appears to be more important than a resting period following the act, although in many cases both may be desirable; thus marital relations in the morning may be preferable. A need to hurry is noxious, as is tense anticipation of possible intrusion such as by children. Intercourse should not take place with a full stomach, while wearing constricting garments or under unusual conditions of atmospheric heat, cold, humidity or unaccustomed altitude. Coitus interruptus is contraindicated, as is purposeful and frustrating pausing solely at the behest of an oversolicitous wife. Coital positions are chosen for comfort and relaxation including respiratory ease; the patient should be recumbent (i.e., all sitting and standing positions are best avoided). Most undemanding is the modified side-rear entry (p. 215), the man-kneeling, woman low-seated, and possibly the woman-above sidesaddle-facing. To be avoided are the woman above-astride and the arching variant of the man-above positions. Indiscriminate advising of the wife to take the more active role in coitus is unhelpful and at times irrational.

Restrictions. Patients who experience pain following effort, but no other signs—in mild postcoronary angina, in coronary insufficiency—need not abstain from sexual activity if the pain can be prevented or controlled by nitroglycerine. In fact, it has been suggested that in all cardiopathies— except acute myocardial infarction and its prodromal stage, in dissecting aortic aneurysm, during congestive failure or major arrhythmia, and perhaps with significant degrees of mitral or aortic stenosis—subjective discomfort should be the deciding factor as to whether coitus is permissible (Master). Exertional pain, if allowed to persist, may at times usher in subendocardial infarction.

Medication. Commonly employed for self-medication just before starting intercourse is nitroglycerin U.S.P. (glyceryl trinitrate) 0.3 mg 1 or 2 tablets sublingually, repeat $1\times$ stat if necessary; next repeat only after 20 to 30 minutes. The drug is very light- and heat-sensitive, and must be fresh. It acts rapidly as a coronary artery dilator, lowering myocardial oxygen consumption and reducing work of the left ventricle, thus increasing its work capacity. A long-acting preparation is preferred by some. No tolerance for nitroglycerin develops as a rule. A few individuals have paradoxical, adverse reactions to it. The ingestion of 1 or 2 ounces of whiskey has been suggested as a substitute vasodilator of opportunity. The preventive use of a beta-adrenergic receptor-blocking agent (propranolol) is a helpful adjunct. The use of monoamine oxidase inhibitors as adjuvants in some cardiopathies has been finding increasing acceptance, but its potency-depressant potential may annul its benefits in performance-conscious individuals. The same applies to many major ataractics, especially the phenothiazine derivatives; thus to neutralize general as well as precoital tension in the postcoronary patient the use of minor tranquilizers or of mild sedatives is preferable. Especially where a drug causes a major degree of ejaculatio tardata the patient should be advised to desist rather than to strain for release just to prove virile competence as some such men are apt to do.

Coital Techniques in Infertility

It is believed that the undisturbed presence, for anywhere from a few minutes to several hours after ejaculation, of a pool of seminal fluid in the posterior vaginal fornix bathing the tip of the cervix is essential for fertilization. Accordingly anything the couple with an incompletely diagnosed fertility problem undertakes to prevent premature outflow would promote conception. Postcoitally the wife assumes, or remains in, the knee-chest, or else a hyperflexed supine position with a buttock-raising pillow (p. 215) for at least 10 minutes, and does not get up from bed until morning. She avoids coughing, laughing, or anything raising the intraabdominal pressure. The husband stops thrusting immediately after his climax; he leaves the phallus in place until it is soft, to minimize dispersal of semen on withdrawal. The rationale is that dispersed spermatozoa, unlike those aggregated in a pool, seem to succumb quickly to the sperm-hostile vaginal milieu and do not get to take part in the reproductive process.

For this reason it may matter little if there is an anti-spillage barrier at the lower outlet (e.g., the natural one of the primipara's taut, high perineum, or the multipara's relying on prolonged vasocongestive outlet swelling by avoiding orgasmic release). Much seminal fluid is unavoidably spread, no matter what, by the final spasmodic thrusts of the ejaculating phallus. Whether much or any inunction of the tip of the cervix with semen occurs at this point is doubtful, nor is direct insemination into the external os known to occur in humans. Concern with malpositions of the cervix as a coital factor in sterility appears to have lessened among gynecologists today. In major uterine retrodisplacements (e.g., 3rd-degree retroversion) the knee-chest position has been recommended to help form a seminal pool anteriorly for the cervix to make contact with.

COITAL FACTORS IN INFERTILITY

Factor	Possible Measures
Adequate intercourse, proper penetration.	Gynecologic or urologic attention. Sex instruction. Psychotherapy. No lubricants, no douches.
Coital frequency and timing.	No overfrequency during fertile period, nor excessive prior abstinence. 48-hour interval believed best (range 1 to 4 days). Advice on fertile period.
Avoiding semen spillage.	Woman to remain in supine-hyperflexed or knee-chest position. No intraabdominal straining. Husband leave penis in place quietly until soft. No orgasmic release for parous women (disputed).
Female genital responsiveness.	Promoting female orgasm to activate cervical receptivity and neural factors aiding spermigration (disputed). No tense-anxious states in frustration-prone (?) women—marital or iatrogenic—to avoid tubal spasm.

COMPLICATIONS OF INTERCOURSE

Vaginal Lacerations — Fracture of Penis — Hemospermia — Penis Captivus — Sudden Death — Coital Headaches — Convulsive Seizures — Psychiatric Complications — Urinary Complications — Venereal Diseases — Other Genito-Infectious Diseases — Cancer of Cervix.

Vaginal Lacerations

The most serious coital injuries of women are tears in the upper vagina. Most are linear lacerations of the wall, running lengthwise, which may extend into the posterior vaginal vault or a lateral fornix, most often the right. Tears infrequently go beyond the mucosa, but perforations (e.g., into the rectum) are encountered. Associated lacerations of the uterine ligaments, unrecognized at the time, have been described in grossly abused women. Bleeding varies from scant to life-threatening.

As the soft glans penis acts as a buffer between phallic impact and female tissues, it requires major predisposing tissue changes and/or an unusual sex act to produce trauma of such severity. In fact, a majority of seriously injured women have had vulnerable genitalia because they were either postpartum, post-hysterectomy, postmenopausal, pregnant, grand multiparas, or suffering from hypogenitalism, an atypical vagina or vaginal carcinoma, in addition to rape victims who were little girls, old ladies or gang rapees. Brutal phallic immission (e.g., in an alcoholized state) is a major factor. Coital positions found conducive to major injuries in predisposed women have included rear entry, the standard with hyperflexion (woman's knees up on her abdomen) and the chair seated-facing. Emergency treatment includes vaginal packing, flat supine rest with legs in apposition, and attending to shock if present.

Milder—introital and anterior vaginal—injuries are often sustained at first intercourse; here conservative management suffices unless the laceration extends well up the vaginal wall. However, major hymenal and introital tears extending into the perineum are encountered (e.g., with a grossly atypical hymen or a neglected perineal laceration due to childbirth).

Fracture (Rupture) of the Penis

A fairly rare complication of coitus. Most such mishaps have occurred during unusually rough but missed re-entry thrusts—or counter-thrusts—in an unaccustomed coital position; also on forcing coital entry in the presence of advanced Peyronie's disease (q.v.). Sudden sharp bending leads to tearing of the tunica albuginea of one, rarely of both crura of the corpus cavernosum with variable injury to the cavernous tissues, and sometimes involving the urethra. Dorsal dislocation of the distal end of the phallus has occurred. Pain is severe and sudden and there is much swelling and discoloration. Active bleeding may continue for a period. Emergency treatment includes catheterization, cooling dressings, snugly encircling bandaging and splinting of the organ against the abdominal wall. Healing in followed cases was considered generally good but incomplete erections caused by lack of tumescence at and near the site of the cavernous scar can occur, as can permanent angulation of the organ.

Hemospermia (Hematospermia)

The appearance of bloody or blood-tinged seminal fluid upon ejaculation is not a rare condition, but its presence is easily overlooked. It has not been known to be the result of trauma connected with the sexual act immediately preceding its appearance. It is most frequent in middle-aged men with vesiculitis or chronic passive congestion of the accessory glands (see also p. 379). In these cases the semen is uniformly pink and there is no discomfort. The condition runs a limited course, but recurrences are frequent. Chronic and acute sexual overexertion in younger men has been suggested as a cause, but this appears unlikely. Occasionally the blood originates in the posterior urethra or is due to subacute prostatitis, but here the semen is streaked with blood and other local symptoms are usually associated. Cancer in the area of the seminal vesicles or papillomatous tumors of the bladder neck and the verumontanum should be ruled out. Most hemospermia may be considered harmless. Treatment is expectant including reassurance; others prefer more active therapy with antibiotics, estrogen and instillations into the ejaculatory ducts. In the treatment of congestive prostatic conditions frequent intercourse and ejaculation rather than abstinence may be encouraged.

Penis Captivus (Genital Interlocking)

The inability to withdraw the penis from the vulvovaginal passage during intercourse, an embarrassing and painful complication, has been becoming steadily rarer, as fewer women feel obligated to permit coitus in spite of acutely painful local conditions (e.g., severe introital moniliasis) and as sex fears relating to first intercourse are receding everywhere. However, the condition does exist despite recent skepticism.

The author has seen one case (fortyish newlyweds; treatment: intravenous amobarbital and caffeine sodium benzoate for wife); has treated one case over the telephone (advice: man's lubricated thumb up woman's rectum with woman bearing against it as if defecating); and was given a next-day verbal account by the husband in a case spontaneously resolved after 10 minutes.

Penis captivus in humans is unrelated to the oft-cited mechanism of copulation in dogs or any other animal copulatory pattern. The cause is reflex-type vaginismus (p. 271 and p. 420) occurring after intromission has taken place. The severe involuntary spasm encircles the male organ tightly: erection may not subside promptly, and the pain, for both, can be considerable.

Sudden Death

Coitus can be the proximate cause of fatal complications, either instantaneous or shortly after the act. The incidence is difficult to establish, especially in domestic incidents, because of concealment efforts by the surviving mate. However, there appears to be a growing belief among knowledgeable medical examiners and pathologists that intracoital fatalities are not rare. One large study (Japan, 1963) placed copulatory deaths at 0.6 per cent of all sudden endogenous deaths, but the figure may be higher. Confirmed cases have occurred mostly in middle-aged men engaged in extramarital ventures in an unfamiliar environment, probably under generally stressful circumstances (see also p. 235). About one half of these deaths are believed due to cardiac mishaps, mostly acute coronary insufficiency with or without acute infarction, or ventricular fibrillation in arteriosclerotic heart disease. Other causes include intracranial hemorrhage and rupture of a berry aneurysm. Massive pulmonary embolism due to unrecognized thrombotic changes in the deep leg veins, with coitus following prolonged inactivity in the sitting position (travel), has been put forward as a cause. A few cases of fatal intracoital hemorrhage due to unrecognized tubal pregnancy have been observed.

Coital Headaches

These remain an incompletely understood aggregate of vascular, psychogenic, histaminic and migrainoid manifestations. They arise regularly during or right after the sexual act, but otherwise they tend to be puzzlingly unpatterned or intermittent, many with unexplained onset after years of satisfactory marital intercourse. Most clearly identified is the pounding or throbbing vortex pain of probably hypertensive individuals, and the chronic major coital headaches of some hypothyroid patients. Migraine-type coital pain, with onset always late during or shortly after a sexual act, tends to be resistant to the usual measures; premedication with sublingual ergotamine preparations has proven irregularly helpful. Analgesic premedication, often resorted to by patients on their own, is unpredictable in effect and can be more hindrance than help in some cases. In men, a masturbatory act which produces the same type of headache can serve as a test to rule out specific psychogenicity; employing the test can save futile psychotherapeutic efforts.

Convulsive Seizures

These have been observed following intercourse in epileptic patients whose disorder was otherwise well controlled by medication. This is thought to constitute reflex epilepsy triggered by the autonomic storm of ejaculation, a sympathetic function. Alcohol consumption as a precipitating factor on each occasion needs to be considered. Treatment includes revision of medication schedules and exploration of covertly stressful psychosexual factors. A few unrelieved cases in men have sooner or later led to impotence.

Psychiatric Complications

Reactive emotional upsets can follow intercourse engaged in under traumatic or disquieting circumstances. Best known—apart from the sequels of rape (q.v.)—is acute hysterical retrograde amnesia following within hours or less upon a sex act involving, for instance, runaway girls, or else older women combining alcohol ingestion with a new sexual venture away from home. Treatment: best immediate results are obtained with brief psychiatric in-patient care, although longer-term therapy may be indicated later.

Severe depressions which seem to become overt after a sexual act are not specifically coital complications. The act here is a mere trigger event, part of the self-debasing delusional system of these patients (e.g., a husband's postcoital suicidal attempt because "I importuned this wonderful girl again with my filth . . .") or a depressive wife's postcoital suicide, as she was unable to respond and accused herself of ". . . my lack of love . . . he should be rid of me and free" (from a suicide note).

A paranoid schizophrenic woman may be convinced after a sexual act that another man impersonated the husband and cohabited with her. Another sexual delusion is the false belief of having been sexually possessed by an unknown or even a named, perhaps famous intruder during the night, as vague genital discomfort and soreness are perceived in the morning.

Syphilophobia (veneriphobia), in men, tends to be an obsession rather than a phobia; the act which is supposed to have caused the infection is a mere trigger event. In women, fear of venereal transinfection following a husband's disclosure of philandering, is more phobic rather than obsessional in nature, and more tractable.

Urinary Complications

The most common syndrome is immediate postcoital burning on urination, frequency, less often urgency, and occasionally slight hematuria, all lasting no more than a few hours, but often chronically recurrent. The symptoms occur in some postmature women because of altered structural relationships, but otherwise the cause of this urethral and bladder irritation, in the absence of evidence of major bacterial infection, is in dispute. A urethral diverticulum must be ruled out. Often tempting is a diagnosis of psychogenic urethra-bladder syndrome, but positive evidence for its presence in most cases is scant. More plausible appear theories of mechanical upward-stripping of indigenous flora from the distal urethra, including pseudomonas, E. coli, etc., combined with immunofailure. The urethra, which is less than 2 inches long, and the bladder lie close to the anterior vaginal wall; active coition, especially a phallus operating tightly anteriorly, tends to traumatize the urethral mucosa as well as massage urethral and periurethral material into the bladder. Additionally in some young women, coital thrusts pull the urinary meatus practically into the vagina, facilitating a transfer of organisms. Infection is abetted by the incompletely understood failure of intrinsic host resistance of the lower urinary tract which also explains the notorious frequency of "honeymoon cystitis," the female coital novice not having as yet developed a local immune mechanism in the bladder wall (theory). Treatment of the syndrome includes, most importantly, complete voiding right after intercourse, also urinary antiseptics p.o. for prophylaxis, copious fluids by mouth, and reassurance especially of the occasional veneriphobic bride. See also Dyspareunia p. 269.

Urinary incontinence can occur in females during intercourse. The least frequent cause appears to be stress (exertional) incontinence, due to sudden increase in intraabdominal pressure (e.g., while straining for a climax). Sudden urgency can produce incontinence during a lengthy act, as the woman is unable to tear herself away in time. In addition to urinary disorders and multiple sclerosis, some psychotropic and other drugs can produce this fairly infrequent complication. A vesicovaginal fistula can cause continuous wetting with urine. An occasional woman—usually a multipara—while cohabiting in the female-above position gushes her urine upon the man simultaneously with her orgasm. Some type of detrusor dysfunction is often involved—the so-called uninhibited neurogenic bladder—but in other cases only psychologic factors—deep hostility to men, slave-and-master fantasies—were identified. In some cases urinary wetting by the woman is deliberately sought by one or both partners and represents sado-masochistic acting-out.

Venereal Diseases

Syphilis — Gonorrhea — Chancroid — Lymphogranuloma
Venereum — Granuloma Inguinale — VD Prevention —
Medical Prophylaxis.

Infection is the most frequent complication of sexual intercourse. The term venereal disease, implying "contracted in venery," persists, although it refers to only some of the contagious diseases spread chiefly by sexual contact. Traditionally two major (syphilis, gonorrhea) and three minor (Donovanosis, chancroid, LGV) venereal diseases proper are recognized. Other genito-infectious disorders, epidemiologically separate, are to be found in the next following section.

Syphilis (Lues.)

Syphilis remains the potentially gravest of the venereal diseases. It has been called a disorder of signs rather than of symptoms. However, the face of syphilis has changed: the clinical manifestations today seem fewer, less florid and more atypical, both in early and late stages; diagnosis must increasingly rely on laboratory reports. Yet when the primary lesion appears, the standard blood tests are still negative and they usually remain negative until 1 or 2 weeks later, thus actually for 4 to 5 weeks after the patient became infected.

Pre-Onset. Incubation averages 3 weeks (range 15 to 35 days, extreme range 7 to 100 days). Subcurative amounts of penicillin or tetracycline received while syphilis is incubating—for an unrelated illness such as tonsillitis or acne vulgaris, or with inept self-treatment—will prolong incubation even further: the disease becomes camouflaged and all signs turn up weeks later including primary sore, lymphadenitis and positive serology; also, darkfield examinations become difficult. All this interferes with quick, early treatment and adds to the epidemiologic spread.

Signs. The classic primary lesion, the painless buttonlike single chancre, today is frequently replaced by smaller, often multiple sores. The classic primary site in the male is on or near the glans penis, especially at the frenulum, but often no such prominent primary lesion can be noticed. The sore may be macroscopically absent, or consist of a small linear fissure: or it is intraurethral or, even more frequently today, at the anus or in the rectum, or in or about the mouth.

In women the primary sore is even more difficult to detect, the clinical chancre detection rate probably being 4 males to 1 female. The classic genital sites are the labia, fourchette and clitoris, but in about 25 per cent of cases the primary chancre is in the vagina or at the cervix. Oral, anal, breast and other primary lesions are seen in women with increasing frequency. Late-discovered luetic females often cannot recall having had primary, or even secondary lesions; the number of untreated males with such non-awareness is also said to be rising.

Ano-rectal.   Moderate regional lymph gland swelling occurs bilaterally with most primary sores, but none is usually found with anorectal locations. Primary rectal lesions are often occult, or masked by coexisting gonorrheal proctitis. Not all anorectal lesions in a syphilitic patient, male or female, bespeak direct transmission a posteriori: similar lesions, also highly infectious, can occur spontaneously during the secondary stage.

Course.   The untreated primary sore disappears in a few weeks, but the patient's infectiousness increases. The secondary, highly contagious stage sets in anywhere within 2½ to 6 months following infection. Apart from its flu-like symptoms it is characterized by a variety of dry and wet skin and mucosal lesions, in many parts of the body. In this stage of an untreated syphilis all blood tests are reactive. If the patient is now treated adequately, reagin blood tests as a rule will become negative within a year or slightly longer. If treatment was given earlier, during the primary stage, the tests become negative within 6 to 9 months. Where these results do not occur, the patient is considered either a treatment failure or as having suffered a new infection.

Late Course.   If untreated, the secondary stage gradually subsides and the patient enters the early latent stage: he has no clinical symptoms or signs, but remains seropositive as well as potentially infective. This usually ends with the second year, although some health departments draw the line between early and late silent stages at the end of the first year. The early latent phase is followed by the late-silent phase and this, in turn, about 15 years (range 1 to 50 years) later, by tertiary or late syphilis with its chronic external and internal pathology in about one third of uncured luetics. Late lues is not infectious, except to the fetus. If treatment was given only late in the course of a neglected disease, some of these patients remain serofast (i.e., positive on the treponemal tests) for the rest of their lives no matter how much treatment they receive.

Contagion Hazard.   Syphilis is infectious during the primary, secondary, and early-latent stages. A recently infected person may transmit the disease before the blood has become serologically positive. In an undiscovered or untreated case the degree of infectious risk tends to rise during the first year following infection, then gradually lessens during the next year. However, because of unpredictably relapsing secondary symptoms in one fourth of untreated patients, a potential contagion hazard, cautiously calculated, persists for 4 years following infection. Untreated, the secretions of the cervix and vulva, and seminal fluid, are believed to remain potentially infectious for up to 4 or 5 years. Spontaneous immunity from luetic infection is incomplete and does not seem to prevent later re-infection. However, a new chancre does not occur while the old one persists and for some time thereafter. A syphilis vaccine is as yet not available.

Contact. Almost all syphilis is transmitted through some type of sexual body-to-body contact, onto any moist, warm mucous surface or any scraped, raw or abrased skin breaks even if they are tiny, anywhere on the body. The most usual sites are the genitalia, anus, and at or in the mouth, but also the nipples, fingers, nose, etc. Treponema pallidum, a fragile spirochete, lives only seconds on exposure to room air; this largely disposes of the drinking glass and barber's razor theories. Freshly introduced into the vagina, T. pallidum remains infectious for several hours. Mouth lesions, especially those of secondary syphilis, are highly contagious via oro-oral (wet kisses) or oro-genital contact. Blood itself is considered of low contagiousness unless massive doses are injected, and needle infection is believed rare. Transfusion syphilis is very rare today; under modern conditions of blood bank storage the T. pallidum dies in 24 hours.

Exposed Person. If the patient is known to have been exposed to syphilis, say the current U.S. Public Health Service guidelines, it is a fallacy to wait for the disease to develop to the clinical or the seropositive stages before treating, although every effort should be made to arrive at a diagnosis. These people should be given 2.4 million units of benzathine penicillin G; this constitutes effective preventive or so-called epidemiologic treatment.

Although not all named contacts of a confirmed new case will develop syphilis, there exists no way of predicting who will and who will not. The watchful waiting approach is unrealistic; such contacts cannot generally be expected to refrain from sexual relations for 2 or 3 months after exposure and to report regularly for examination during this time, especially in high-hazard populations. It may be noted that today, unlike in gonorrhea, a key factor here is the spread through homosexual contact, perhaps most so via bisexuals, especially highly promiscuous young men among those who swing both ways.

Treatment of Syphilis. Penicillin is the drug of choice, except where not tolerated. Unlike Neisseria gonorrhoeae the spirochete is destroyed by low but long-maintained (7 to 14 days) levels of penicillin. Fortunately, T. pallidum has not developed resistance to penicillin.

TESTS FOR SYPHILIS

Most important: Serologic Tests for Syphilis (STS) and microscopic (darkfield) examination. Test becomes positive ("reactive") as antibodies appear in blood serum 4 to 6 weeks after infection. Biologic false positive reactions (BFP) rarer today because of purified antigens; may occur in infectious mononucleosis, malaria, leprosy, collagen disease, some viral infections. Quantitative test results are obtained by diluting (titrating) the serum: a high titer (1:16 dils. or over) usually means active lues; a titer steadily falling with each testing signifies successful treatment. Specificity of a test refers to its ability to be negative if syphilis is absent; sensitivity is its ability to be positive if syphilis is present.

Non-Treponemal (Cardiolipin) Antigen or Standard Tests. Most commonly used: Venereal Disease Research Laboratory Flocculation Test, VDRL for short; qualitative and quantitative readings available. Next frequent; Kolmer Complement Fixation test, successor to the Wassermann. Kahn test still in occasional use, also Kline, Mazzini, a few others. Automated flocculation tests are replacing the VDRL for screening purposes.

Rapid Plasma Reagin Tests. These are simple, quick, economic screening and survey tests, some in ready-made disposable kits; may require finger prick only. All positives are retested with other methods. Examples: RPR Card test, PCT.

Treponemal Tests. Not for routine use; for diagnostic problem cases. Highly specific, but little usefulness in checking success of treatment, nor can need for treatment be based on them. They cannot differentiate between present and past syphilis. Some are technically difficult and expensive (use of animals). Considered most useful today: the FTA-ABS (Fluorescent Treponemal Antibody Absorption); especially permits earlier diagnosis of first stage. The TPI (Treponema Pallidum Immobilization) is used to standardize other tests. Others: KRP, RPCF. Automation of treponemal tests is in the process of advanced exploration and gaining agreement.

Darkfield Examination. Identifies T. pallidum by employing a darkfield condenser in the microscope. Uses needle aspirate from a lymph node, or serum oozing from a purposely gauze-irritated primary chancre. Persevering search and know-how required to pick out T. pallidum from other organisms and particles in motion. Especially useful in very early stages before serum is positive. Not suitable for oral lesions because of other treponemes found there; a Fluorescent Antibody Darkfield Test (FADF) can replace it here.

Subcurative doses of any antibiotic administered in primary syphilis will clean only the local chancre, but not the treponemia nor the total picture. If adequate syphilis treatment is given before the primary chancre appears or while the VDRL and other cardiolipin tests are still nonreactive, these tests will remain negative. In mixed infection adequate gonorrhea treatment given while the syphilis is still incubating will abort the syphilis, provided penicillin is used and provided there was definitely only a single sexual misadventure. As antigonorrheal penicillin dosage worsens the prospect of successful syphilis treatment once the chancre stage has been reached, it would be hazardous to use in any promiscuous patient with possible pre-existing infections.

Preferred Treatment. The following treatment schedules for the early stages of lues are currently suggested by the U.S. Public Health Service, with some modifications recommended by other authorities: benzathine penicillin G (Bicillin, Permapen, etc.) 2.4 million units deep i.m. at a single session, one half in each buttock. Some health services recommend this dose be repeated 1 week later. Alternative preparations are more costly, inconvenient and conducive to incomplete cures: PAM (procaine penicillin in oil with 2% aluminum monostearate) 4.8 to 6 million units given over a period of from 6 to 20 days. Also used: aqueous procaine penicillin G 600,000 units daily for 8 days.

A proportion of patients have a Herxheimer reaction after the first penicillin injection; it is regarded as innocuous. In truly penicillin-sensitive patients or merely those with a history of atopy (urticaria, hay fever, asthma, atopic eczema) there is danger of anaphylactic reactions. Penicillin reactions in the U.S. have occurred at the average rate of 7.5 reactions per 1000 penicillin treatments. Anaphylactic reactions have been seen at the average rate of 0.28 per 1000 patients (U.S. PHS). Treatment in vulnerable patients relies on tetracycline and oxytetracycline, or on erythromycin, 30 to 40 grams by mouth in equally divided doses over 10 to 20 days. These oral remedies require follow-up procedures which include spinal fluid examinations. Tetracycline treatment for syphilis in pregnant women will affect the baby's bones and teeth. Usually, local treatment of the lesions is not employed in syphilis. Bismuth and arsenicals are no longer in use.

Gonorrhea

Course. Gonorrheal infections are local first, then spread by extension and, in some cases, systemically. In males onset is most commonly seen as acute anterior urethritis, with yellowish seropurulent discharge, urgency and dysuria, 2 to 5 days (range 1½ to 14 days) following infection. In women asymptomatic infection is most frequent, or else after 3 to 10 days' incubation a moderate vaginal discharge and some discomfort ensue which may go unheeded. In the most acute cases the urethral meatus is fiery red and gaping, vulva and cervix look inflamed, Skene's glands are swollen, and a thick yellow discharge covers much of the area. In occult cases gonorrhea can be suspected clinically if moving the cervix is painful, Bartholin's glands are infected, and pus can be milked from the urethra. Presence of an I.U.D. is believed to increase the severity of female gonorrhea.

Rectal. Oral. More and more rectal gonorrhea is being seen, but it is often asymptomatic in both sexes. Half of all female gonorrhea patients reportedly also harbor the gonococcus in the anal canal, via drainage of vagino-urethral discharges, spread by wiping or other autoinoculation. Homosexual men with gonorrheal proctitis may first become aware of this when they infect a sex partner. For instance, in a series of 70 rectally largely asymptomatic homosexuals, one third harbored gonococci in the rectum upon culturing (Owen-Hill). Gonorrheal pharyngitis and tonsillitis, and very occasionally stomatitis, are encountered with increasing frequency in men and women; they are transmitted through either fellatio or cunnilingus. Only a few seem to have symptoms. Repeated cultures including sugar fermentation tests appear to be necessary for a diagnosis of some of these oral infections.

Complications. Frequent local complications in uncured cases include prostatitis, seminal vesiculitis, epididymitis; and in women vulvovaginal abscesses, salpingitis and pelvic inflammatory disease. Escherichia coli is believed to be the secondary invader causing salpingitis. Local late sequels include recurrent or chronic pelvic disease in women, urethral strictures and sterility in men. Among systemic complications are arthritis, endocarditis, perihepatitis, meningitis and ophthalmia neonatorum. Postgonococcal urethritis (PGU), actually a form of nonspecific urethritis (NSU), is the most frequent complication in men (see below). It requires careful exclusion diagnosis (trichomoniasis, gonorrheal relapse or re-infection, mechanical irritation due to inept-anxious self-examination). Treatment with tetracycline or expectant therapy (7 to 10 days) are the preferred choices; it does not respond to penicillin.

Transmission. Gonorrheal disease, in teen-agers and adults but not necessarily in children, is almost wholly transmitted through sexual contact. Neisseria gonorrhoeae, the gonococcus, is sensitive to air, and survival on a dry surface is very limited. However, infection via moist hands, moist towels and washcloths, and probably toilet seats, washbasins and other rest room surfaces is possible for several hours, but not for all strains of the gonococcus. Among persons exposed to a gonorrhea contact, less than half can be expected to develop the disease, possibly because a mucosal abrasion is not always present at the contact site. Women are more susceptible to being infected than men. Previous infection confers no known immunity, and many repeat infections, possibly with other Neisseria strains, can and do occur. Once infected, the patient remains potentially contagious until fully cured; once cured he (she) is almost immediately susceptible to reinfection with the same organism.

The Female Gonorrhea Carrier. A vast reservoir of infected but asymptomatic females exist; these are communicable carriers. It is not rare that a girl is unaware of being infected until someone names her as a contact. She may have been infected, remained uncaring or unaware, then received low-dosage penicillin for other illness resulting in a dangerous subcure. Or she may have stopped treatment prematurely after initial treatment failure (a rising occurrence today); or discarded, saved or shared part of her prescribed supply of tetracycline capsules. Asymptomatic presence of gonococci in the female rectum is believed a source of self-reinfection. In each case presumably she joined the pool of carriers. In an East Coast series of 231 asymptomatic middle-class private female patients reported in 1971, 2.6 per cent were found infected (Jones Jr.). In a West Coast series of 23,320 asymptomatic women aged 10 to 50, reported in 1971, 10.2 per cent were found to be carriers: 2.6 per cent of private patients and 25 per cent of poor clinic patients (Pedersen-Bonin). There are vastly fewer male carriers, probably for anatomic reasons, but more sensitive diagnostic applications have raised the number somewhat.

Uncontrollable Spread. Epidemiologic efforts against the disease have largely failed, worldwide. Some authorities maintain privately that public health efforts against gonorrhea are futile until serologic tests and a curative vaccine have been developed. The incubation period is so short that even identified contacts cannot always be reached and treated in time before passing on the disease. The spread of drug-resistant strains of N. gonorrhoeae results in many inadvertent subcures, converting acute cases into silent carriers; subcures are most frequent among passive, uncaring, restless and/or establishment-hostile individuals. A re-emerging public cavalier attitude toward gonorrhea ("just a little dose") leads to inept self- or drugstore-dosing, especially among teen-agers. In some uncured cases the gonococcus can remain latent but can be unpredictably rendered virulent and re-activated by strenuous intercourse, prolonged sexual excitation, an alcoholic binge, childbirth, or even menstruation (disputed).

Tests for Gonorrhea. In acute gonorrhea of the male Gram-stained smears of the exudate will demonstrate the intracellular diplococci; the test is specific and considered reliable. Specimens are obtained from the urethra by milking or by gently scraping just inside with a sterile wire loop. However, smears are deemed unreliable in subacute and chronic male cases, for all anorectal gonorrhea, and in most female patients. In all these, culturing of secretions on Thayer Martin VCN or similar medium is preferred. A woman with silent or suspected gonorrhea needs to have secretions obtained from the vaginal vault (disregard menses) and/or Bartholin's and Skene's glands; from the endocervix (remove mucous plug first); from the anus (insert swab 1 inch); and from the urethra (massage first). A Gram-stained slide of the urinary sediment can be helpful. For forwarding a culture to the laboratory, Transgrow tubes are now being widely used as a transport medium; they will keep gonococci growing for 4 days. For testing at the place of examination ready-made Clinicult tubes are useful. Fluorescent Antibody (FA) testing of secretions is considered a rapid, last-resort but expensive method.

Treatment of Gonorrhea is in a state of flux, largely because of the spread of high-virulence or antibiotic-resistant strains of the gonococcus, many introduced from Asia and prevailing mostly near the U.S. West coast and in some Midwestern cities, as well as in Europe. However, the upward trend in penicillin resistance is believed to be leveling off, while tetracycline resistance is said to be climbing rapidly. The gonococcus has been called almost as adaptable as the cockroach, but so far synthesis of new antigonococcal drugs and updosing of older ones has managed to keep the cure ahead of the disease.

Cure. The U.S. Public Health Service* currently (1972 revision) recommends as the treatment of first choice in acute, uncomplicated gonorrhea of men and women 4.8 million units of aqueous procaine penicillin G i.m. at a single visit, injected one half in each buttock, preceded by probenecid 1 Gm by mouth 30 to 60 minutes before the injections. As an alternative first-line treatment patients of either sex take 3.5 Gm ampicillin together with probenecid 1 Gm, both by mouth, as a single dose. Probenecid retards renal excretion of penicillin and steeply raises its blood level. For penicillin-sensitive patients with acute gonorrhea the choice is either spectinomycin, a single dose of 2 Gm i.m. for men or 4 Gm i.m. for women, or else tetracycline hchl. 9.5 Gm by mouth in divided doses over 4 days, at least ⅓ of it the first day, for either sex. The latter is not indicated during the second half of pregnancy because it tends to impair bones and teeth of the fetus. Of these four, only penicillin G is known with certainty to abort co-acquired incubating syphilis. Erythromycin is recommended for gonorrhea treatment by some authorities.

In treatment failures, determined by a test of cure 5–7 days later, the procedure or one of the alternatives is repeated. Except when the patient is well known to the physician, single-dose therapy for acute gonorrhea is preferable to multiple-dose treatment because of the notoriously high dropout rate with an incomplete cure, often leading to the socially dangerous carrier status. Patients who have made a diagnosis of treatment failure possible by returning are ipso facto more reliable as a group. Whenever an antibiotic other than penicillin G is used to treat gonorrhea, follow-up tests for syphilis during the next few months are advisable. Repeated gonorrhea treatment with penicillin, on the other hand, is believed to make subsequent treatment for syphilis more difficult.

No specific local treatment for gonorrhea is in use today. Hot or cold applications for pain, sexual abstinence, bland diet, no alcohol, bed rest in hyperacute cases and, in women, during menses even in less acute cases,

---

* Center for Disease Control (CDC), Venereal Disease Branch, Atlanta, Georgia 30333.

are frequently recommended. Patient should wash hands after any touching of own genitals, guard exposed wet towels, and not take small girls into bed.

Chancroid (Ulcus Molle, Soft Sore or Chancre)

The best known among the minor venereal diseases, Hemophilus ducreyi incubates 1 to 5 days. Onset is acute, with a ragged, necrotizing and painful ulceration on the genitals or anally, occasionally elsewhere. After 10 to 20 days half the patients develop a purulent inguinal bubo on one side. Some forms of chancroid are more destructive than others. Spread is through genital contact by the unwashed and the promiscuous, including homosexuals. Some prostitutes remain contagious but occult chancroid carriers for long periods, especially when the disease locates on the cervix, but mostly the pain, pus and swelling bring medical attention. Spread to fingers of those attending patients can occur. Syphilitic chancre, which may coexist, must be ruled out before treatment (sulfonamides, tetracycline). Incision of buboes is contraindicated.

Lymphogranuloma Venereum
(Nicolas-Favre Disease, LGV, Other Synonyms)

The potentially gravest venereal disease next to syphilis; now encountered more widely in the U.S. All races are susceptible, but Negro-Caucasian ratio is 5:1. Transmission of the highly contagious organism is usually by genital contact, with relatively high homosexual spread. This is primarily a disease of the local lymphatic system. Incubation is 7 to 12 days (range 5 to 21 days). The painless primary sore may be occult or so transient that the first symptoms consist of fever and severe malaise followed by lymphadenitis and eventually a painful femoral or inguinal bubo, especially in men. In others the primary ulcer extends and deepens to destroy the surrounding genitalia. Anorectal lesions, unless directly acquired, occur either by extension or by lymph drainage. Diagnostic is a high positive (1:40) LG complement fixation or the less reliable intradermal Frey test. The latter remains positive throughout life. Treatment (sulfonamides or tetracycline) results appear to be spotty; recurrences are frequent. Later elephantoid lesions of the genitalia occur, notably grossly enlarged labia and clitoris (esthiomene), and anorectal complications requiring surgery. The disease can lead to permanent invalidism, and probably predisposes to genital cancer.

Granuloma Inguinale
(Donovanosis, Many Synonyms)

This is a chronic subtropical and tropical as well as a dirt disease. The consensus is that it is acquired by coitus and homosexual relations, but some doubt remains as to its exclusive venereal nature. It is moderately contagious. Unlike in other venereal diseases there is selective racial immunity in various parts of the world. In the U.S. it is a disease of blacks, rarely acquired by Caucasians even after repeated exposure.

The etiologic agent is the Donovan body (Calymmatobacterium or Klebsiella granulomatis enclosed in large monocyte). Incubation is indefinite, may last up to 3 months; some observers say years. Onset is insidious: painlessly progressive skin ulcerations on the genitalia or near the anus which do not heal easily. Late lesions include chronic ulcerative forms, characteristic reddish exuberant granulomatous masses, or else incomplete keloid scarring. A pseudobubo in the groin, actually a skin tumor, is characteristic. Systemic dissemination occurs at times. Treatment: tetracycline or streptomycin. LGV may coexist as may syphilis; the latter must be ruled out before treatment. The disease predisposes to genital cancer.

V.D. Prevention

Venereal diseases have resurrected in a spectacular fashion, worldwide, and new control programs are being debated and attempted everywhere. Some are generally approved, others remain controversial.

The Contact.   The chief measure employed today is contact investigation, also known as field or "shoe leather" epidemiology. It relies, in part, on the universal reportability of V.D. and ideally is combined with outreach for latent or fearful cases. In principle, trained investigators try to find the person who infected the patient as well as the contacts to whom the patient may have passed the disease and bring them to treatment. Unfortunately, the method is not working too well at present, for various reasons.

Minors.   Laws permitting physicians to treat minors for V.D. without parents' or guardian's consent or knowledge are being sought in more and more states. This goes beyond the common-law doctrine of the "emancipated" minor (i.e., one who is married or permanently living away from the parents). Although such a law places the physician in loco parentis and may force him to make nonmedical decisions with legal and social implications, it is considered important in rolling back the spread of gonorrhea among teen-agers.

Reporting.   More stringent V.D. reporting laws by physicians and hospitals are probably not the answer, although physicians in private practice are estimated now to report no more than 15 to 20 per cent of the cases they see. Such laws are probably unenforceable. Moreover, they tend to be discriminatory, favoring those able to seek private care. Reporting laws aimed at laboratories appear undesirable chiefly because reports could not eliminate false-positive serologic tests. Expanded serologic mass screening, compulsory for some groups even today, has found objectors on constitutional grounds.

> **RE: EPIDEMIOLOGIC CONTROL OF V.D.**
>
> A kindly word by the admitting clerk, a friendly greeting by the clinic nurse, a professional attitude by the physician make it easier when the patient finally reaches the epidemiologist who will question him about intimate details of his sex life. C. WENDELL FREEMAN, M.D. in *Journal of the National Medical Association,* 1967

V.D.-teaching. Of much interest are a variety of educational efforts. Although V.D. scare-descriptions never have been an effective method of promoting chastity among youth, they need not be scorned as an aid in combating promiscuity. Public health authorities probably need to increase the intensity of their anti-V.D. fact-spreading campaigns to the fright level of 30 or 40 years ago to counteract persistent public attitudes of false security and complacency. Physicians are enhancing their spirit of community-mindedness regarding contact finding and the counseling of patients it entails.* There is need to raise physicians' index of clinical suspicion, regardless of a woman's age, a man's status, a teenager's wholesomeness or a family's cohesiveness. More controversial are efforts to intensify V.D. teaching in high schools, although in some high-risk schools with 25 to 50 per cent of their student body infected at all times, unpublicized anti-V.D. efforts are increasingly being made.

Medical Prophylaxis

The protection of the individual following hazardous sexual exposure includes mechanical, chemical and antibiotic measures.

Condom. The cornerstone of mechanical disease avoidance remains the condom, which affords some protection to both partners (disputed). However, its acceptance as a V.D. prophylactic by men has never been high in the U.S. It should cover the organ as fully as possible. Lubrication with petrolatum or mineral oil may damage some condom material. After the act the sheath should be removed without touching its outside with bare fingers. When cohabiting with a casual or pick-up partner, preliminary kissing as well as finger-fondling and mouth-genital contact constitute additional risks.

Local Measures. As soon as possible after exposed intercourse the man should scrub the penis and surrounding areas with water and soap, using a washcloth or gauze wipe; hexachlorophene (prescription item) or liquid

---

* Amer. Social Health Assoc. pamphlets VD-1, VD-5 and -6 (Spanish) are free or nearly so (1740 Broadway, New York City).

green soap are preferable. He should dry himself well but without abrading the skin. Urination under moderate pressure, by holding the meatus briefly shut against the stream, is traditionally recommended. There are no equivalent self-help measures for women because of their anatomy; the effectiveness of douches here has been questioned. However, washing of all parts that can be reached with soap and water, while squatting, has some value.

Chemical Prophylaxis has been discredited lately in many parts of the world, but past low failure rates under certain conditions and the increasingly necessary restrictions and cautions with the antibiotics make total discard seem unwise. The U.S. Armed Forces discontinued Pro-kits with calomel-sulfonamide ointment around 1960. 10 per cent and 20 per cent Argyrol solutions, if not too old and if properly instilled and held in the urethra, can give superior protection against gonorrhea, although urethral burns and sterility have been described. For chancroid exposure 2 per cent aqueous Zephiran rubbed in within 3 hours has been recommended. Mercurial inunctions into the genitalia and surrounding areas, although messy and having possible drawbacks, may give some protection against lues.

Antibiotic Prophylaxis, also known as preventive or epidemiologic treatment, is administered following known or suspected infected contact, similarly to treatment administered for the early stage of the disease: 2.4 million units benzathine penicillin for syphilis, and aqueous procaine penicillin G 2.4 million units for men—4.8 million for women—against gonorrhea, with the same substitutions for penicillin-sensitive patients. In suspected mixed infection adequate anti-gonorrheal dosage of penicillin, but not of tetracycline, will abort pre-primary syphilis.

Preventive Shots. Indiscriminate, preventive injection therapy, in anticipation of sexual exposure, for individuals or for groups, is discouraged by most authorities in the field. This is also true of the suggestion that individuals about to be exposed be enabled to obtain oral penicillin or tetracycline medication for self-dosing. Both this and routine pre-contact medication are considered risky, as they may lead to disease-masking and to subcures. In using benzathine penicillin, required against syphilis, the low plasma penicillin concentration would encourage gonococci to survive and help form treatment-resistant strains. Reportedly this also applies to tetracycline.

Other Genito-Infectious Diseases

Trichomoniasis — Moniliasis — Hemophilus Vaginalis — Herpes Genitalis — Nongonococcal Urethritis — Reiter's Syndrome — Molluscum Contagiosum — Venereal Warts — Crab Lice — Scabies

Trichomoniasis
(Trichomonal Vaginitis, etc.)

Trichomonas vaginalis is a flagellate parasite whose primary habitat is the vaginal epithelium in women of reproductive age. Here it can, but need not, produce vaginitis with an often copious, thin, frothy yellow discharge, and strawberry stippling about the cervix and posterior fornix. It can be confused with vaginal irritation due to soaps, bath oil, etc.

Transmission. Sexual intercourse is the usual route of transmission, with onset of symptoms several days after infection. T. vaginalis can remain dormant in the genitalia for a long time and flare up unpredictably following vigorous or prolonged coitus, first coitus after lengthy abstinence, lesions of the cervix, chemical vaginal irritants, a run-down physical or emotional state, even menstruation. The vaginitis may then subside spontaneously or following specific treatment (metronidazole, etc.). Also, the organism can survive on toilet seats for 45 minutes, on some enameled surfaces up to 6 hours, and on moist towels, etc. for 1 to 3 hours, occasionally up to 24 hours. The presence of T. vaginalis in men has been found, by different investigators, to be anywhere between 4 per cent and 100 per cent, the higher percentages perhaps with better search technics. Infested males are essentially asymptomatic, or else have a low-grade chronic, non-specific urethritis, with occasional prostatitis or epididymitis. Asymptomatic male carriers are an important reservoir of trichomonal infestation, and cycles of infection and retour-infection in spouses, known as trichomonal ping-pong, have led to unjustified marital, etc. suspicions of third-party sexual intrusion. Many physicians routinely co-treat the husband in cases of trichomoniasis in married women and impose coitus condomatus. Trichomoniasis is probably not spread by homosexual contact. T. hominis, another species, inhabits the lower bowel, and T. tenax the mouth, but neither invade the human genitalia.

Moniliasis
(Candidiasis, Candidosis, Vaginal Thrush, Mycotic Vulvovaginitis)

The yeast-like fungus Candida (Monilia) albicans is ubiquitous, and its latent presence in female genitalia, urine, stool, skin, sputum, etc. is not necessarily significant. However, it can produce an acute or subacute beefy vulvovaginitis with the characteristic, irritating "cottage cheese" exudate (not always present), severe itching and often secondary swelling and abrasions which can make coitus painful or impossible. Eruptions in the adjacent skin and anal thrush often co-exist. Unlike in trichomoniasis, there is relief from symptoms during menstruation.

Frequency of the disease is growing. Many women on contraceptive pills—least on the sequential type—develop moniliasis (disputed). Also predisposing are long tetracycline, etc. courses, a humid and very warm climate, unventilated underclothes, diabetes, and pregnancy. Treatment under any of these conditions is difficult. During childbirth C. albicans can invade the infant's mouth and nose and spread from there. Sexual transmission of the fungus is frequent but not essential. Men, especially if uncircumcised, are a potential reservoir of infestation via mycotic balanitis and groin or scrotal skin eruptions, although Candida apparently does not invade the male urethra. Homosexual spread is said to be possible. Transmission to the mouth (thrush) is possible, but rare in generally healthy individuals.

Hemophilus Vaginalis

This organism is believed present in the genitalia of one fifth of all women; it is transmitted sexually. Male partners harbor the organism in their genitourinary tracts, but without symptoms. In infected women it causes a mild vaginitis whose main symptom is a grayish, slightly pasty, characteristically odorous discharge. This benign genitoinfectious disease is often disregarded, especially by women indifferent to their own vaginal odor.

Herpes Genitalis

Herpes simplex genitalis (formerly H. progenitalis), occurs in both sexes and is produced by the venereally transmitted type 2 herpesvirus hominis (HVH 2). Onset is as a group of vesicles on a reddened area; they erode painfully after a few days and ulcerate. The lesion may resemble chancroid. Malaise and fever are not rare. The site in men is the penis; in women the vulva, vagina or cervix, sometimes diffusely. Cytologic (Pap) smears are diagnostically valuable in women. There is a tendency to periodic and often painful recurrences (e.g., after each menstruation). The disease appears to be associated with a high incidence of cervical carcinoma (see below). Because of serious danger to the newborn the link is close enough to call for subsequent regular examinations in women found infected. In pregnancy, caesarean section before the membranes rupture is the rule. Type 2 herpes vaccine is not available in the U.S., and treatment is generally symptomatic.

Nongonococcal Urethritis (NGU)

This is generally understood to be the sexually transmitted variety of nonspecific urethritis (NSU) of the male, although the entire group remains poorly delineated. Included are such entities as postgonorrheal urethritis (PGU), trachoma-inclusion disease, consort-specific and other allergies, urethritides produced by T-strain mycoplasma, Chlamydia oculogenitalis and pleuropneumonia-like organisms (PPLO), as well as others. Incubation is variable. Local symptoms tend to be fairly mild (e.g., single mucoid "morning drop" or chronic cloudy discharge, some itching, dysuria) but these often healthy young men can be greatly distressed, even disabled by the chronicity of some NGU and the anxiety it produces. Epididymitis, seminal vesiculitis and prostatitis occasionally complicate the picture; the latter must be differentiated from the intermittent painless mucoid prostatorrhea following urination or a hard bowel movement (see p. 380). Diagnosis of NGU is often by exclusion (e.g., of gonorrhea or of local allergy to urinary components and to trivial irritative urethrorrhea accompanying veneriphobia and overfrequent, anxious self-stripping of the urethra in search for secretion).

Reiter's Syndrome

This triad of urethritis, conjunctivitis and migratory polyarthritis is today no longer generally included among the venereally transmitted disorders, although such an etiology does seem to exist in some cases. More frequently the disease is associated with dysentery outbreaks. The infectious agent is believed to be a mycoplasma.

Molluscum Contagiosum

When venereally transmitted this infrequently encountered disorder occurs as multiple small growths on the genitalia and the general abdominopelvic area; they are waxy elevations with a central sore from which a cheese-like material can be squeezed. Perioral lesions have been observed. It is produced by a pox virus; incubation is up to 2 months. Spontaneous remission is observed, but the growths can recur, and either curettage or painting with cantharidin is the preferred treatment.

Venereal Warts
(Condyloma Acuminatum, Moist or Genital Warts)

Sexual relations are a frequent source of infection for these benign, soft, moist structures which tend to cluster into sizable pinkish cauliflowers in the anogenital zone, and occasionally at nipples or lips. The agent is a wart virus. The lesions often coexist with gonorrhea in females, and more generally with stubborn vaginal discharges or possibly with poor hygiene (disputed). As in other viral genito-infectious diseases, a connection with subsequent gynecologic neoplasia has been observed, but is incompletely understood (see also cervical cancer, below). An increased occurrence of genital warts has been ascribed to use of oral contraceptives; the disease may now be the most common venereal disease after gonorrhea (Roizman). Treatment includes podophyllin applications, various types of surgery and vaccinotherapy. Spontaneous regression can occur, but also stubborn recurrences.

Pubic Crab Lice
(Epidemic Pediculosis)

Infestation with the crab louse (phthirus pubis) is today increasing worldwide, especially among students and other young people moving about or living in primitive circumstances. It is transmitted through close personal contact, including sexual relations, but also via shared sleeping bags, bed blankets or clothing and possibly toilet seats, although, away from a host, this louse dies within 24 hours. Principal symptom is itching. Diagnosis is by visual search with magnifier and smooth forceps. The animals are seen as whitish bodies 1 mm (nits ½ mm) long cemented to pubic and perianal hair roots, occasionally to body hair elsewhere. Treatment for individual patients: application of 1 per cent gamma-benzene hexachloride USP (Kwell) as a shampoo, cream or lotion. Shaving is desirable but not necessary. Laundering and dry cleaning, or merely storing away, liberates clothing and sleeping bags.

Scabies

This skin infection is increasing worldwide, although still only sporadic in the continental U.S. and Canada, except the West Coasts. It is believed to regain virulence and flare up in 20-year cycles. It is a disease of poor hygiene and promiscuity, but if brought into a family, it spreads rapidly among all members, especially the children (e.g., via bed-cuddling). Generally, contagion is via intimate contact as well as shared clothing or bedding.

Sarcoptes scabiei, the itch mite, infects adults below the neck, mainly lower abdomen and breasts, male genitals, and inner surfaces of upper extremities. Onset of major symptoms is 5 weeks after contagion, as skin eruptions, superficial skin burrows ("runs") most visible in blondes, and intense itching, especially at night. It soon leads to scratching complications and secondary eruptions and, later, often to a stubborn parasitophobia in the predisposed. Systemic pyogenic complications can occur. Treatment is by means of various scabieticides. All family members need to be examined for mites. Best not to overstress the living mite to the anxiety-prone. The percentage of patients with coexisting syphilis reportedly is high.

Cancer of the Cervix

Squamous cell carcinoma of the cervix, unlike other female genital cancers, is now generally accepted to be a sexually transmitted disease, a coital complication. There is a long latency period—up to several decades —between entry of the carcinogen and detectable premalignant cervical neoplasia.

According to a plausible current theory the infectious substance transmitted at coitus is the genetic nucleoprotein DNA, which enters the nucleus of epithelial cervical cells during one of the female's 3 phases of highly active but normal squamous differentiation, and there produces genetic changes after fusing with the nucleoprotein of the host cell. The two critical active-metaplastic periods which are relevant here occur (1) at menarche plus at least one year immediately following it, and (2) during the first pregnancy. At those times the teen-ager or woman appears to be highly vulnerable to contamination with the mutagen (Coppleson, others).

This would agree with that part of the epidemiology of cervical cancer which seems to show the crucial importance of the age at first coitus: the younger the girl, the more she is at risk of future cancer, although multi-partnerism may be an additional aggravating factor. The epidemiologic importance of intercourse during the first pregnancy has not as yet been explored.

The suspected sources of the mutagen-carcinogen appear to have been narrowed down to two possibilities: genitotropic (type 2) Herpesvirus hominis (p. 256), or else DNA of sperm-head origin present in the genitals after coitus. However, the viral organisms of Donovanosis, LGV and venereal warts all have been associated with gynecologic neoplasia.

Generally, the epidemiology of cervical cancer closely resembles that of venereal diseases proper. A group of 900 women known to have had genital herpes had an 8 times higher incidence of cervical cancer than an uninfected control group (Nahmias). Gonorrhea has been suspected of being an inciting factor, the gonococcus being the piggy-back vector for the virus. Smegma from uncircumcised men is no longer considered a carcinogenic factor. The racial factor, in the light of newer findings, is now being discounted somewhat, but a low socio-economic level continues to be positively correlated, as does an ascending scale of risk from virginity, which gives absolute protection, to confirmed promiscuity, whose practitioners are at high risk. These and some similar factors may, however, merely circumscribe the background of females most apt to cohabit early in life.

Recent studies suggest that cancer of the prostate is influenced by factors closely similar to those encountered in the epidemiology of cervical cancer.

FORCIBLE INTERCOURSE (RAPE)
(Forced Sexual Relations, Stuprum, Stupration, Raptus.
Euphem.: Criminal Assault)

Related:
The Child as Victim of Sexual Aggression p. 55
Pedophilia p. 472
Sexual Aggression p. 436

Rape is sexual penetration, usually of a woman, against her will. Rape has taken place if the male organ touches inside the labia minora; full intromission is not necessary, nor need ejaculation have occurred. Thus, an intact hymen, for instance, does not disprove an allegation of rape. Where contact did not include actual genital penetration, the crime constitutes attempted rape, or felonious assault, even if ejaculation on or about the victim's body did occur. The essential element is penetration. It is not rape if a woman has given her consent and then withdrawn it at the last moment. She must struggle throughout the contact, exhaust all possible means in the struggle and have been made powerless to resist; she must not yield at the last moment, under the law. Unless prevented she must scream, in many jurisdictions. A woman can probably faint into unconsciousness at the height of the struggle, just before the act of rape is consummated, but such claims of blackout in the absence of significant physical injury have often been found associated with false accusations.

Coercion. In addition to physical force rape can also be accomplished by intimidation and verbal coercion (e.g., by threat to use a weapon or harm a child). Where a victim's general fear of violence and injury, but without direct threat, reduces her to a state of terror, inducing her to fail to resist and to submit, this does not constitute first degree rape in most U.S. jurisdictions. Submission via economic coercion (e.g., loss of job) is not rape in the U.S., but in some countries sexual exploitation of dependent or employed status constitutes an attenuated form of rape. Under the law, even a prostitute can be raped; however, being taken without getting paid is not rape. A wife cannot be raped by her husband.

Impaired Victim. Abuse of a disabled, helpless female constitutes rape under most circumstances. Relations with an unconscious woman constitute rape, even if the perpetrator was not responsible for her unconscious state. Intercourse with a mentally retarded or (hospitalized) psychotic female is rape, but probably only if the man knew that she was incapable of giving legal, rational consent and was taking advantage of her impaired state. Coitus with a woman who is drugged or intoxicated to such a degree as to be incapable of consenting is rape; it is considered one of the iniquitous provisions of the law that a woman who was a sexually consenting drinking companion before the act but quite toxic at the time of coiting may charge rape when sobered again. Intercourse through fraudulently obtained consent (e.g., by impersonating husband while woman was "half asleep," or by a bogus physician pretending treatment) is rape. Sexual submission under hypnosis or as part of posthypnotic suggestion has been described, but these cases probably constitute seduction, as hypnotized persons are not believed to cooperate in actions which they strongly reject.

Corroboration. In addition to a rape victim's testimony, the law in some states requires corroboration by other evidence (see below) or by a third party, when fully consummated rape is charged. The purpose is to prevent lodging of spurious charges by jilted, jealous, malicious, mistaken, paranoid or blackmailing women. Women's rights groups are protesting the often resulting impossibility to convict some obviously guilty attackers. It would, indeed, seem more equitable if corroboration were required only when the parties were pre-acquainted.

Statutory Rape. Sexual intercourse with a girl below the age of consent constitutes statutory or second-degree rape, even if she was willing. Prior unchastity of the underage female is no defense, nor even that she is married, divorced, or a prostitute. According to the law she is unable to consent and always is presumed to be resisting; "the law resists for her." However, some jurisdictions now are beginning to make cautious allowances for age mistake, consider the age spread between perpetrator and victim (less serious if small), and take previous reputation into account. The legal age of consent for intercourse in most states now lies at 16 or 18 years, although in a few states it is either higher or lower. Coitus with a girl under 12 usually constitutes "aggravated rape" and is punishable by life imprisonment (Slovenko). In a few states a woman can be prosecuted as a statutory rapist for coitus with an underage male.

Victimology of Rape. A lumbering term describing the subsurface interaction between victim and perpetrator, but a promising approach in modern medical criminology.

Not all rapes are grimly silent, on-the-spot assaults; there may be much preliminary discussing and negotiating even between strangers, attempts to divert or dissuade, repeated near-changing of mind, long car rides. Not all indoor rapists flee the scene leaving behind a shocked, agonized victim. After the act future dates may be asked for, occasionally even made; refreshments demanded or served; remorse expressed or sympathy offered; life histories elicited; affection demanded or pledged. Much of this occurs by way of the woman's fear of further violence, and probably more often with maturer, more educated victims, but sometimes empathy is genuine and mutual.

Some victims end up passively cooperating in a genuine rape situation (e.g., the woman may guide the phallus, or even help an erection along) the latter because some attackers are potent only when the woman struggles actively. Cooperation is almost certainly not given because true rape can be enjoyed by some women, but from desire to get out safely and from fear of further violence, as stories of murdered and injured women rise in the victim's mind. A vigorous woman may be able to successfully resist undesired immission by a basically friendly male, but brutal intimidation is not easily resistible. Other defeating factors here may be the shock of surprise, the unaccustomed crudeness and, perhaps, an initial choking or blow to the face.

Rapists have been known to return to the same victim, to telephone, or to secretly follow about and observe the former victim. They may add robbery while leaving the scene, or complete the burglary which the hapless victim had interrupted. Rapists have become severely infatuated with their victims; but the reverse has not been reliably observed. The rapist who expresses remorse, asks for signs of affection or declares himself in love post-rape appears to be the one most likely to return for another assault. Although a majority of all rapists are potential recidivists, the loquacious, pseudosentimental repeater fixated on a specific victim may be deemed somewhat more dangerous to life and limb than most, especially if enraged with jealousy, frustration or a sense of having been "betrayed."

Mental Sequels of Rape.   Some women endure the aftermath of forcible rape less well than others, depending on personality make-up. Social factors also play a part; for instance, an extreme attitude found among certain U.S. ethnics that a raped girl has been dishonored, and that the dishonor has nothing to do with her innocence in the matter, can crush the spirit of a passive, dependent victim, while a more self-assured woman may break away from the role being imposed upon her by the environment. Apt to malreact is also the compulsively scrupulous or perfectionistic woman who may endlessly torment herself—or become deluded—regarding her own weakness or complicity in the happening. Introverts and socially isolated girls seem to fare worse than extroverted ones. Apart from depressive episodes, rapes have in some instances been known to precipitate schizophrenic breakdowns, or occasionally have initiated a social downward slide via a pattern of promiscuity (Halleck).

Victim-precipitated Rape (Amir).   Sexual assault is followed by especially severe emotional sequelae where the victim has, or even merely believes she has, played a part in precipitating the attack. It may have been a single injudicious lapse, or else customarily negligent, reckless or indiscriminately seductive behavior: what has been called the unconscious need to be a victim. Some women derive excitement from fantasies of being watched, desired, perhaps attacked, vaguely wishing for a "forceful" man so that consciously at least they will not have to take responsibility for their own erotic impulses. These may be the women who frequently neglect to pull the shades when undressing; who seem to be fascinated by isolated locales or night-time strolls alone; whose garments tend to be just a shade too provocative on inappropriate occasions; or who urinate carelessly concealed in woods or field. Some teen-agers carelessly or defiantly hitchhike or pick up riders, or wear naïvely inciting buttons or sweatshirt inscriptions around non-peers obviously not accustomed to this. Some women implant themselves recklessly in culture-alien neighborhoods as a social gesture, or fraternize in the wrong drinking places, unaware of the nuances of erotic give-and-take among men of sharply different background, thus being presumed to be "asking for it." At any rate, after having unwittingly established an invitational pattern, they are shocked, enraged or self-pitying when the reality of sexual assault is as crude, ugly, dirty or painful as it usually is apt to be. Angry disbelief is mingled with guilt over their own suspected role. The acute phase subsides in less than a week and the usual life pattern—home, work, or school—is resumed while the woman tries to rationalize and forget, but these feelings keep smoldering and probably deepening below the surface. Weeks, even months later a related event—a wedding, identifying a suspect, a proposal, a rape story—can precipitate an overt depression with self-accusations and feelings of worthlessness (Sutherland-Scherl).

Examination of Victim. Privacy, some expertness, and compassion greatly enhance the results of both examination and care of the rape victim. For instance, silence during the physical examination is sometimes interpreted as a sign of the physician's disapproval or disgust by an overwrought woman. The emergency departments of some large metropolitan hospitals have developed excellent procedures for rape cases.

Except in medical emergencies, expressed or implied consent to being examined, preferably on paper and witnessed, is a medicolegal necessity. Findings, including negative ones, should be recorded in full and immediately, adding a sketch or color photograph when applicable. The rape history (see box) precedes or accompanies the physical examination; it is often most reliably obtained by a female nurse or caseworker. Specimens on slides, swabs and tubes for laboratory examination should be handed to the pathologist by the examining physician in person; a receipt may even be signed and stuck on the record.

Overriding concern, of course, is with major injuries, shock, etc. if present. Otherwise, primary observation takes notice of the behavior and the state of mind of the woman, her appearance, and the appearance of her clothing and underclothes (disarray, dirt, stains, tears). It is well to remember that a woman just raped may walk into a doctor's office, an emergency department or a police station appearing outwardly calm and unruffled. Advanced age, ungainly appearance, evident illness or obvious pregnancy do not preclude the possibility of rape having taken place. On the other hand, paranoid schizophrenic women sometimes hallucinate a sex act in part or in toto, blaming a mysterious intruder or, often absurdly, some prominent man, and request police action and/or gynecologic examination. Delay in reporting a rape, more often than not, should lead to suspicion of a false claim (Macdonald).

Search for Evidence. Post-rape examination combines medical attendance with search for medicolegal evidence. The purpose of the latter is to determine if rape truly occurred, and to help identify and prosecute the attacker. A photographic record of minor injuries about the face, neck, arms, breasts, thighs or vulva can indicate the rapist's use of force and/or the woman's struggle while resisting. X-ray examination of facial and chest

EXAMINATION FOR RAPE

(Medical Questioning)

Represents important medical and medicolegal answers needed. Preferably obtained by nurse or special case aide.

What time did it happen? What day? Exactly where?

Did you get hurt anywhere?

What did you do between the attack and now?

Have you washed or douched since the attack?

Describe the clothes and underclothes you had on. Where are they now?

How did the attacker threaten you?

Do you know the man or see him before?

Did you fight him? Scream? Scratch him? Faint? Did he bleed anywhere?

Was he on top of you, or what position were you in?

If outdoors, what were you lying on?

Did he get inside you with his organ? All the way?

Did he come off inside you? Elsewhere on you?

How many times did he enter you? Come off inside you?

Did he make you help him get an erection?

Did he make you look, use your hands, your mouth? Did he use his mouth?

Did he use a condom?

Did he say anything about being sterile, having vasectomy, not having V.D.?

Had you been drinking? What? How much?

Did you ever have intercourse before?

Have you had intercourse with anyone else in the last 24 hours? Since your last period?

Did you have a vaginal discharge, a sore? Were you getting treatment?

Are you menstruating now? When was your last period?

Have you taken any antibiotics lately, for any reason?

Are you allergic to penicillin?

Are you pregnant?

Have (will) you told (tell) the police?

Will you let the doctor examine you now? Can we take a picture of these bruises, of your torn clothes, etc.? Will you sign permission?

injuries is important. Also blood typing, a pregnancy test, a VDRL test and cultures for Neisseria from cervix and urethra, to rule out pre-existing venereal disease, etc., partly for the purpose of furnishing background evidence later. Gynecologic examination searches for introital and, in virgins, hymenal lesions. The fornices, usually the posterior, may show abrasions after vigorous coitus. All loose fibres, foreign hair and other material, as well as stained garments, should be collected, labeled and preserved; they can constitute crucial evidence. Encrusted blood on the woman's body, blood stains for grouping, and fingernail scrapings can be valuable. However, the most important part of the search is directed at the rapist's semen.

Semen Search. The presence or absence in the genitalia of seminal fluid and especially of spermatozoa is of legal import, as a criminal charge of rape is sometimes reduced to assault if no semen has entered the vagina. In some countries spermatozoa must be demonstrated to sustain a charge of rape. However, inability to demonstrate spermatozoa does not preclude that ejaculation took place (e.g., by an oligospermic or vasectomized attacker) or due to the rapid disintegration of spermatozoa in the vagina, especially in hot weather.

Seminal fluid can be encountered in the form of sticky material adhering to the abdomen, thighs or perineum; from these it is scraped or swabbed (sterile saline sol.). It may be found matting pubic hair from which it is snipped or rinsed off. From the vulva material is aspirated in several spots with a pipette after rinsing with a few drops of sterile saline solution. Vaginal material, notably from the posterior fornix, is obtained through a speculum by glass suction tube or by scraping with spatula or glass rod; swabs here are used only for storing material for subsequent chemical testing. Semen recovery from suspected fabric stains is best entrusted to a laboratory; the material should first be dried in the open air. On clothing semen stains can be seen and felt as sharply demarcated, starchy-stiff spots (see p. 177), but egg white, for instance, has similar feel and has been used for crude imitations in false claims. On clean fabric semen produces bluish fluorescence under ultraviolet light, but the reaction is not specific, as other albuminous material fluoresces also.

Scrapings can be examined for spermatozoa at once, by suspending material in a little saline solution, centrifuging, and examining the sediment microscopically on a slide; or else a drop of fresh material can be wet-mounted under a coverslip. For permanence a smear of the suspected material is made immediately, flame-dried, fixed in alcohol, stained with Gram or methylene blue, washed and dried. Both spermatozoa and gonococci are often searched for in suspected material. Finding spermatozoa is evidence of intercourse but not necessarily of rape. Finding gonococci is of uncertain value as evidence. One may recall further that negative smears in females do not exclude gonorrheal infection (see p. 248).

In the living vagina viable spermatozoa can be found for 1 to 6 hours, but only 10 per cent are believed to survive after 2 hours, slightly more and longer during menstruation. Nonmotile spermatozoa can be recovered up to 24 hours; however, numerous variations undoubtedly occur. Post mortem the vagina yields nonmotile sperms for many weeks. The endocervix can yield motile spermatozoa up to 5 days after insemination, and nonmotile ones for about 2½ weeks. From clean, properly stored fabric nonmotile spermatozoa can be recovered for up to a year, occasionally much longer; on soiled fabric, exposed to heat, cold and light they disintegrate quickly (Sharpe).

Chemically, the best known specific test for semen is that for acid phosphatase; it gives valid results in vaginal secretions for at least one day and in stains for several months. The high concentration of acid phosphatase in the prostatic fluid allows its differentiation from that found in blood and other body fluids; Phosphatabs-Acid (Warner Chilcott Diagn. Div.), including the quantitative determination, is a useful kit. Other approaches involve creatinine phosphokinase (CPK) level determinations, and the crystal-formation tests of Florence (iodine, potassium iodide) or Barberio (trichloracetic and picric acids). The specific blood group antibody substances A and B appear in the seminal fluid of most men, which may permit exclusion (i.e., exoneration of a suspect); the test has limited application as it does not distinguish group O secretors, some non-secretors, and negative preparations.

Cautious interpretation and reporting of the results of the examination is necessary. Rape can have taken place in the absence of all visible injuries and without a trace of detectable semen. Evidence of ejaculate on clothing, underclothes, furniture, abdomen, thighs, mons or labia majora is not evidence of rape. Semen in the vagina, without other evidence, means an act of sexual intercourse took place, not necessarily rape. It is impossible, with present knowledge, to disprove that coitus or rape has taken place, as is occasionally requested of the physician. During trial the physician-witness' opinion may be asked on possible drainage of semen either into the vagina from the vulva, if she stayed on her back; or by gravity and motion out of the vagina if she was running: both are possibilities, and have been shown to occur, but the likelihood appears minor.

Preventing Infection. (See also p. 252). It is considered sound practice to assume that an unknown assailant was venereally infected. Adequate prevention of the 5 principal venereal diseases (p. 243) is probably offered by tetracycline 0.5, 4 times a day by mouth for 15 (10 to 20) successive days, which is unfortunately too prolonged a schedule for compliance by some women. Adequate antigonorrheal prophylaxis with penicillin—4.8 million units of procaine penicillin G in aqueous suspension intramuscularly as a single dose, one half in each buttock, preceded by oral probenecid 1 Gm. (see p. 250)—will also abort coacquired syphilis during its incubation. This dosage form, however, will worsen the prospects of syphilis treatment if the disease has already reached the primary chancre stage from prior infection.

After the genital examination the woman seen immediately post-rape and not grossly injured needs to thoroughly cleanse her genitalia with soap and water, preferably while squatting. A 2-quart sterile warm water or medicated, antiseptic (e.g., 1:2000 solution of mercuric chloride) douche follows. Some physicians include a thorough swabbing of all accessible parts, partly through a speculum, in the lithotomy position, using a fairly fresh 10 to 20 per cent Argyrol solution, with some of it instilled

---

SIMPLIFIED, RAPID POST-RAPE TREATMENT

An outline for healthy, non-allergic victims of reproductive age who cannot be relied upon to adhere to more complicated instructions.

To soap-wash all parts while squatting.

2-quart cleansing douche (warm water).

Meprobamate 800 mg p.o. stat, repeat 400 mg every 3 to 6 hours for 2 days.

Swab vulva and vagina with freshly made 20 per cent Argyrol solution through speculum; instill some into urethra and hold for a few minutes. Borofax or similar ointment to vulvar abrasions.

Aqueous procaine penicillin G, 4.8 million units intramuscularly, one half into each buttock (U.S.PHS).

Natural conjugated estrogens, 20 mg intravenously; repeated 24 hours later. Or else Depo Provera (medroxyprogesterone acetate) 100 mg intramuscularly if within 24 hours (unapproved).

History and full examination first. Medicolegal procedures next, then treat. Offer return appointment.

---

in the urethra and finger-held in place by the patient for 3 to 5 minutes, for gonorrhea protection. Applications of anesthetic or soothing cream or ointment (e.g., Borofax B-W) or compresses applied locally may be indicated for moderate vulvar swelling and bruises. Mercurial inunctions into the genitalia and surrounding area, although messy, unfashionable and having possible drawbacks, may give some protection against syphilis. Two per cent aqueous Zephyran rubbed in within 3 hours of exposure may help protect against chancroid.

Pregnancy Risk and Prevention. The statistical chances of impregnation from a single random coital insemination have been calculated to lie between 1 in 25 and 1 in 50, thus 2 to 4 per cent (Tietze). The probability is lowest in the second half of the menstrual cycle, beginning approximately 2 days after ovulation; it increases again, beginning gradually with menstruation, until a peak risk is reached near midcycle, very approximately one week after the end of the average menstrual period in a 28-day cycle.

This is made possible because out-of-turn (paracyclic) ovulation can occur on any day of the cycle including days of menstruation; pregnancies have resulted from isolated sex acts, including bona fide rape, which took place during practically every part of the cycle including menses. It is theorized that the emotional stress of the rape experience can induce early ovulation; the possibility of coitus-induced ovulation, as it occurs in some animals, has also been entertained (Clark-Zarrow, Stieve, Weinstock, Wingate-Iffy, others). The administration of large amounts of estrogen over several days appears to be able to prevent pregnancy if given soon after insemination. Changing the hormone balance probably interferes with implantation of the fertilized ovum, which normally occurs about 6 days following conception. Theoretically, only midcycle exposure when an ovum is assumed to be ready and waiting would call for such "morning-after" measures, were it not for the very real possibility of out-of-turn ovulation (see above) and our lack of handy and accurate ovulation tests and predictors. Basal temperatures, pregnanediol determination, etc., are rarely practicable in such cases. Thus it has become the practice to offer estrogen treatment to practically all rape victims of reproductive age. A pre-existing but unsuspected pregnancy, no matter how recent, would not be interfered with by such emergency estrinization.

If unprotected exposure took place not more than 2 (some say 3) days previously, effective doses appear to be ethinyl estradiol (e.g., Estinyl) not less than 2 mg. a day for 5 days; or, perhaps more practicably, diethyl stilbestrol 25 mg. b.i.d. for 5 days. Side effects, in about half the women, are rarely serious: nausea and vomiting, mostly during the first two days, breast discomfort, itching, headache, various nervous symptoms, somnolence and irregular vaginal bleeding are most often reported. A preventive antiemetic is of some help in some patients. For late-reporting rape victims—up to the fourth or fifth day post-rape—natural conjugated estrogens (e.g., Premarin) 20 mg. intravenously on two consecutive days can be used (caution with a history of thrombophlebitis or endocarditis with valve damage!). (See also p. 307).

For those with religious or legal scruples it has been held that post-rape estrinization technically would not constitute abortion, as the results of pregnancy tests taken during the pre-implantation phase would be returned as "not pregnant" by the laboratory (Hellegers). Fairly wide acceptance today of the thesis that human life begins at the end of nidation also tends to remove the abortion label from postcoital anti-nidation measures. For Roman Catholic women it is considered lawful to use any procedure which prevents fertilization from occurring as a result of rape. This includes the use of a cleansing douche immediately after the assault, or as soon thereafter as it is possible to do so (Kelly-Good).

Management. Mild sedation may be required for most women, and exceptionally a minimum of bed rest may be advised. Very young girls may develop a secret fear that they are now unfit to be wives or mothers; or they may harbor superstitions about having "changed into a woman overnight," or that people will see it from (their) face, breasts, "knowing eyes" or "knowing mouth." Girls must be given maximal opportunity to verbalize and ventilate their feelings (e.g., to the mother or, if necessary, the physician). A brief depression is normal; but prolonged brooding or paranoid thoughts must be considered as danger signs. Where nightmares develop following a rape experience, brief psychiatric "abreaction therapy" is usually successful in girls with a fundamentally normal and well-integrated psyche. Even older women who are married and child-blessed may have major anxiety or depressive reactions following rape.

It is not always sound advice, without knowing the personality of the individuals involved, that the raped woman should share her plight with her husband, fiance, or even her parents. The victim's reasoned refusal to do so can often be allowed to prevail without her having to fear that she will lose the moral support of her physician. Increasingly more women today seem to take an unprovoked sexual attack in stride (e.g., "I'm on the pill, I wasn't hurt and my doctor gave me shots for V.D. and said I'm clean. What purpose would it serve to tell my husband? He'd only worry or think maybe I wanted it."). Some victims, often abetted by members of the family, decline to notify the authorities or to permit the physician to do so. Since there is no legal obligation to report such cases, the physician must accede. Such nonreporting lately has tended to be blamed on the unsympathetic or doubting reception all but the youngest and most battered rape victims are alleged to get from male police officers, prosecutor or hospital staffers. However, more victims probably should come forward and make the complaint, mainly in the interest of potential future victims: many rapists are repeaters.

PAINFUL INTERCOURSE (DYSPAREUNIA, ALGOPAREUNIA)

Dyspareunia, by modern custom of usage, refers to genital pain or discomfort during or after intercourse, usually in women. Primary dyspareunia, becoming rarer today, means pain with the first attempts at intercourse; secondary or acquired pain develops after normal intercourse has taken place for a length of time. Vaginismus (vaginospasm) refers to a siege of spasmodic contractions of the muscles about the lower vagina and the perineum (see also p. 271 and p. 420); but other definitions exist.

Vaguely identified psychogenic factors are too often and too indiscriminately named as causes of painful intercourse in females. Unless the pain is near the lower end of the reproductive tract, symmetrical, and not intermittent, to name a few criteria, psychiatric efforts are likely to come up with nothing except perhaps being midwife at any spontaneous cure. However, some women to whom intercourse is chronically unwelcome are distressed more easily, more severely and more persistently by minor degrees of local pathology which would not deter a loving, unruffled or lusty mate; here dyspareunia becomes part of a subconscious avoidance reaction. Women with this type of psychogenically augmented pain are particularly apt to feel sexually incapacitated and to prescribe abstinence from coitus for themselves. This set of circumstances must not be confused with conscious malingering of coital pain which is much rarer.

Pain which is indirectly psychogenic can be experienced by the woman who does not develop genital moisture at the critical time because the proceedings mean little to her; the resulting chafing reinforces her aversion, and vice versa. This is equally true of the woman with spasmodic perivaginal cramping at the intromissory approach; if the lubricated phallus tries to push in, it is painful; this, in turn, makes the fear and aversion worse. On the other hand, a woman who persistently and specifically complains of coital pain, localizing it and ascribing distinct physical characteristics to it is infrequently an "avoider," even if no organic pathology is at first found by the examining physician.

In all cases of dyspareunia it is best to explain the topography and the nature of the lesion in as much detail as is compatible with the patient's ability to understand. Apart from ensuring more intelligent cooperation with treatment, this often seems to shorten the period of recovery as measured by voluntary coital resumption.

Types of Dyspareunia in the Female

Introital Dyspareunia

Pathology, if any, located in the external genitalia or lower vagina. Pain either very well localizable or very vague. Most are younger women, including brides. Includes practically all cases of primary dyspareunia. Causes:

Vulvar Disease. Vulvitis in early diabetes in the elderly, in major anemias, Condyloma acuminatum, Moniliasis. Genital herpes. Bartholinitis or bartholinian occlusion, abscess, neoplasm. Painful midline episiotomy.

Urethral Meatus. Bruising, urethritis, caruncle, eversion, etc.

Insufficient Spontaneous Lubrication. A common cause, but itself secondary to other factors, many of them either deeply psychogenic or overtly attitudinal (e.g., marital disinterest, antipathy, sexual fears, lesbianism, lack of coital foreplay, partner's anticipated impotence). Lack of estrogen in postmaturity, unsuitable contraceptive pill or ovarian malfunction. Heavy over-use of introitus (e.g., prostitute) with tender swollen labia, lower vaginal friction edema, and unrelieved tumescence of plateau structures.

Hymen. Unyielding if intact. Unhealed laceration.

Introital Narrowing (e.g., postmenopausal or post-oophorectomy). Tight episiotomy repair. Following some posterior colpoperineorrhaphies.

Chronic Malimmission. Here phallus has dug a para-introital pouch for itself at either pole of vestibule after years of ignorant practice, thwarted defloration, congenital vaginal bands, or marked hypogenitalism. Infrequent.

Clitoris. Granular Smegma. Adhesions of hood.

Vaginospasm. An indirect cause usually. Spasmodic contraction of perivaginal and perineal muscles can occur reflexly due to anticipated coital pain or overriding sexual fright or aversion, but probably only in the spasm-prone female. Phallic forcing of vaginospasm produces further pain which, in turn, reinforces the next negative anticipation-defensive cramping sequence. See also p. 420.

Vaginal Passage Pain

Somatofunctional as a rule (e.g., hormonal deficit, inflammatory).

Vaginitis. From any cause (e.g., fungal, gonorrheal, chemical). Atrophic vaginitis of elderly.

Lack of Estrogen. Scant lubrication, mucosal changes, metralgia-ex-orgasm.

Stenosis. Rigidity, some shrinking in postmaturity. Post-irradiation. Post-surgical (prolapse repair, etc.). Residual obstetric trauma (scars, etc.).

Various. Vaginal retention cyst following childbirth. Tumors. Cystocele. Sjogren's (sicca) syndrome. Perivaginal implants in endometriosis. Congenital malformations and major hypoplasia (e.g., testicular feminization syndrome) (p. 366). Relative penile oversize only if coinciding with marked vaginal infantilism, defeminizing shrinkage or stenotizing insult. Transient: shrinkage after long continence in the middle years (not universal).

Deep-Thrust Pain

Typical complaint: "penis hitting against something up inside." Average patient somewhat closer to middle age. Acutely painful. Rarely psychogenic, although with missed diagnosis not rarely so labeled. Diagnostic clue: Woman coiting in supine position tends to maneuver self into an extended variant and instinctively approximates legs as much as possible to avoid deep penetration.

Endometriosis. The most frequent cause in this category. Implants in various locations, notably in cul-de-sac and uterosacral ligaments. Tenderness severest at and near menses.

P.I.D. Residual metritis and tubo-ovarian adhesions, etc. due to past gonorrheal infection.

Vaginal Vault (e.g., scarring or tissue rigidity following irradiation of cervix).

Cervix Disease. Chronic cervicitis; changes following conizations; empyema complicating past hysterectomy. Isolated cervical dyspareunia in dispute because of type of nerve receptors.

Uterine Pathology. Some fibroids, other tumors. Rarely moderate retroversion or other malpositions per se.

Broad Ligaments. Tears or scars following traumatic childbirth, abortion, rape. Diagnosis said to be frequently missed; clues: painful hypermobility of cervix, major retroversion, etc.

Tubo-ovarian Disorders. Tumors, adhesions, prolapse of an ovary, most often perhaps the latter. Tubal pregnancy.

SENSITIVITY TO HUSBAND'S SEMEN

A unique, well-studied and much discussed case of spontaneous allergic sensitivity of a young woman to her husband's semen was uncovered in Paris some years ago. A virgin at marriage, patient reacted from the first intercourse, and subsequently, with anaphylactic shock: giant urticaria, edema, asthma, cardiovascular collapse. She is a fraternal twin (Halpern-Ky-Robert). *Immunology 12*:247, 1967

Postcoital Dyspareunia

Here pain either arises or is most noticeable at conclusion of sexual act. Examples:

Chemical or allergic reaction from extraneous substances (e.g., contraceptive chemicals). Pelvic and low back aching discomfort from incomplete detumescence in pseudo-frigidity, coitus interruptus, etc. Painful clitoral spasm following orgasm, of unknown cause; also painful uterine spasm; both in postmature women, both responding to estrogen. Postcoital friction dysuria (p. 242).

Extragenital Pain

Coitus painful, but lesion in vicinity rather than within genital organs. Examples: Adductor tendinitis near the pubic bone (skaters, horseback riders, ballerinas). Vertebral disk disease. Coccygodinia. Caesarean scar, especially with keloid formation. Subacute appendicitis.

One-sided Pain

Most lesions introital. No primary psychogenicity. Here woman characteristically maneuvers body into slightly oblique position and/or pulls up and abducts leg on affected side. Examples: bartholinian abscess, episiotomy repair, anal fissure, preclinical herpes zoster, cyst or cancer of outer vagina.

FOR JOURNAL LITERATURE AND ADDITIONAL READING

Austin, C. R.: Fertilization. Englewood Cliffs, N.J., Prentice Hall, 1968

Barnes, A. C. (ed.): Intra-Uterine Development. Philadelphia, Lea & Febiger, 1968

Benirschke, K. (ed.): Comparative Aspects of Reproductive Failure. New York, Springer Verlag, 1968

Brooks, S. M.: The V. D. Story. Cranbury, N.J., A. S. Barnes, 1971

Comfort, A. (ed.): The Joy of Sex. A Gourmet Guide for Love Making. New York, Crown Publishers, 1972

Diamond, M. (ed.): Perspectives in Reproduction and Sexual Behavior. Bloomington, Indiana Univ. Press, 1968

Gardner, H. L. and Kaufman, R. H.: Benign Diseases of the Vulva and Vagina. St. Louis, Mosby, 1969

Hutton, I. E.: Sex Technique in Marriage. New York, Emerson, 1961

Macdonald, J. M.: Rape: Offenders and their Victims. Springfield, Ill., Thomas, 1970

Moghissi, K. S. and Hafez, E. S. E. (eds.): Reproductive Biology. Biology of Mammalian Fertilization and Implantation. Springfield, Ill., Thomas, 1972

Odell, W. D. and Moyer, D. L.: Physiology of Reproduction. St. Louis, Mosby, 1971

Schofield, C. B. S.: Sexually Transmitted Diseases. London, Churchill Livingstone, 1972

Sherman, A. A. (ed.): Pathways to Conception. Springfield, Ill., Thomas, 1971

Woodruff, J. D. and Pauerstein, C. J.: The Fallopian Tube: Structure, Function, Pathology and Management. Baltimore, Williams & Wilkins, 1969

Zubin, J. and Money, J. (eds.): Contemporary Sexual Behavior: Critical Issues in the 1970's. Baltimore, Johns Hopkins University Press, 1973

CHAPTER 13

Sexual Difficulties in Marriage

Counseling on Sex — Disturbances and Notions — Marital Apathy — Marital Infidelity.

A substantial proportion of both men and women are dissatisfied sexually but have learned not to admit this even to themselves. They resign themselves to endure what they have persuaded themselves is the price they must pay for a reasonably satisfactory domestic existence: an enduring state of sexual semi-satisfaction, and what Greene has called the durable incompatibility of many unions. In a sense, many are afraid to "take the lid off." Although fewer people today are willing to settle for joylessness in marriage, some men prefer a woman with a low level of erotic responsiveness, lest she make too many demands and possibly become a threat to the control and the inegalitarian image of the marriage which the husband is trying to perpetuate (Frank). Or else they have long ago persuaded themselves that this is what they need to conserve their limited libidinal endowment, which in most cases amounts to the rationalization of a misconception. Some women are equally apprehensive of escalating the marital vita sexualis and stimulating an undemanding husband to realization of his full potential, lest their subtle dominance of the resources and affairs of the marriage be endangered either by a newly overbearing phallus pride, or by their own becoming conditioned to greater sexual needfulness and thus, perhaps, dependence.

Much of what is happening to marriage may be the birth pains of a wave of feminism sweeping the Western world; with it seems to go a corresponding surrender of some of the traditional attributes of universal maleness. Sex role versatility, unisex rearing, serial polygamy, multilateral and group marriage and similar manifestations may still be experiments of the few, but reports of their existence are multiplying. Of course, visions are far ahead of what is realistic. "By insisting on the masculinity of men and the femininity of women we have locked individuals in prisons of gender . . ." says Heilbrun; or "the fantasy of one-to-one sufficiency has let us down," declares Comfort. The excesses of egalitarianism have led others to call for partnership-type social contracts to replace marriage, "with separate quarters or separate lovers if desired"; or to assert that ". . . the woman should use the man as a means of obtaining her orgasm, an implement for her to employ if she wishes to do so, her orgasm not being a present she makes him, nor a feather in his cap."

COUNSELING ON SEX

Marriage Counseling Today. The traditional concern of marriage counseling efforts has been to save the marriage. With the ongoing downgrading of the formalized institution of marriage, there is less concern with this today. The focus of what is taught in present-day training centers for professional marriage counselors is on the saving of the spouses, not the marriage. In tattered marriages among the more sophisticated and well-to-do, not too long ago, it was most often the husband who wished to quit and the wife who urged counseling help; today, reportedly, it is more often the wife who threatens to leave or to divorce, and the man who arranges for counseling. Also, there has been little social pressure toward the development of even a minimal frustration tolerance among the very young now entering marriage; as a result, each vexation, each disappointment, each pain cuts deep and can fracture the hull of the marital vessel, unless a basic indifference towards the dyadic commitment itself cushions the impact.

Physician's Role and Nonrole. Where a physician performs his time-honored role as family health advisor he finds himself every so often confronted with disturbances in a marriage situation. Likewise, where he is conscientious in his search for underlying causes of obscure complaints he is bound to encounter significant marital problems from time to time. Remedial efforts directed at these difficulties can be summarized as medical marriage counseling. However, the physician cannot and should not attempt to take upon himself the full weight of a human relationship among any of his patients lest he burden himself excessively or be accused of being meddlesome and thereby impair his own usefulness. It would be equally unwise to let himself be maneuvered into a role where he must continuously intervene and make peace between two quarreling spouses.

One or both members of a severely discordant marriage may offer a physician whom they trust an opportunity to advise them on the desirability of a divorce. Undoubtedly, there are marriages which should not have been contracted in the first place, whose continued existence constitutes a threat to the personal welfare of each member of the family unit. It has been suggested that in such cases it would be a physician's duty to help a couple to face the fact that their marriage is hopeless beyond repair. On the other hand, the concept of what is hopeless beyond repair is subject to variable interpretation. It is believed that an unsolicited suggestion of divorce to a patient should be avoided under practically all circumstances. On the other hand, it would not seem to be proper to voice indiscriminate objections to every couple's divorce plans on the basis of the physician's personal convictions.

Useless Attempts. A conjugal complaint of a sexual nature first of all requires some judgment as to the basic soundness of the marriage. It is rarely possible to graft sexual harmony on an essentially brittle or shallow union, at least not without a concurrent attempt at over-all restoration. This view is widely held. "One may lay it down as a general principle," says Chesser, "that in the absence of love, or of deep respect and good companionship, no attempts at (sexual) adjustment are worth making." Or, "to improve the sexual life of such a (loveless) couple is not usually a worth-while undertaking." (Butterfield). Yet it would be unwise to be dogmatic here. The complexity of marriage relations makes masking of symptoms and complaints frequent. What seems like a basically bad marriage may actually be the result of sexual disarray, or what appears to be a tractable sexual difference may be almost hopelessly entangled with a personality defect. A woman with manipulatory personality traits may use sex in marriage to punish or control, thereby chronically enraging or helplessly humiliating her consort; yet the husband may be consciously aware of—or able to verbalize—no more than a mild complaint, "once in a while, in one of her moods, I get locked out of the bedroom."

Chain Reactions. Sometimes it is impossible to say whether long-standing marital discord has caused chronic sexual maladjustment, or whether sexual difficulties were the primary disrupting factor. Vexatious chain reactions ensue. Two sexually normal spouses may not get along well for some reason, and soon or late this is bound to reflect on their vita sexualis. The wife, resenting the husband, will not welcome his sexual advances; she may evade them or merely suffer them passively. This, in turn, tends to rob the act of much of the pleasurable incentive for the man, and his sexual interest decreases. His approaches become less frequent, or the acts are performed in an increasingly cursory manner. Thus the wife may be left sexually unsatisfied for lengthy periods; as a result, her capacity for tenderness decreases, she may become self-pitying and fault-finding, feel domestically overburdened and generally dissatisfied. The husband, in turn, feels neglected and harassed, and self-pity, resentment and lack of full sexual gratification may combine to lower his resistance to extramarital temptations.

Vagueness and Reluctance. Various obstacles—often mainly communication failure—can interpose themselves between a couple's sexual difficulties and their physician's desire to correct them. Patients may be unsure of how their physician will react to a complaint of a sexual nature. As a result, their approach may be so oversubtle or so overcasual that the physician can easily not understand. He may be presented with a one-word complaint, perhaps followed by a confident "you-know-what-I-mean," and be expected to understand immediately what "not much good," "no feeling," "uncooperative" or "no pep" refers to in the way of sexual deficit; the patient may be greatly disappointed or reluctant at having to go into further details.

Some patients may hush up even the most obvious sexual trouble; their own, for instance, because of a sense of modesty vis-à-vis the physician; or the spouse's because afraid of antagonizing or hurting him (her) by exposing an anxiously guarded private inadequacy to a stranger. The husband is often the more reluctant to discuss marital difficulties with the physician, but he may come to the office or the clinic when told that the purpose is "to improve conditions in the home," or "to talk about the wife's condition." Psychologically, this probably is as it should be. The man is essentially outer—or other—directed, close to being a boy; the woman is essentially inner-directed, always close to being a mother herself; she is thereby more fit for family therapeutic work (Grotjahn). Some patients may allow the physician nothing more than a search for physical abnormalities on which to blame their sexual difficulties, even when the trouble is quite obviously not somatic.

The presenting complaint may be of a sexual nature, such as, "my husband is too direct (not considerate, thoughtless) . . . he cares only about himself (his pleasure)" or else, "he must be becoming impotent," or "I think he is unfaithful." The husband may complain that "she has no interest in sex," "she is cold (frigid)"; or, "we are sexually incompatible." The complaint may also be of a general nature: "she nags constantly," "he does not earn enough . . . does not care how we live," or "she squanders money." The physician in a hurry may give undue weight to the complaint which he happens to elicit first and may miss the point. Actually, the total situation here would require some measure of unraveling before it can be dealt with with any expectation of success.

DISTURBANCES AND NOTIONS

It has been said that a good marriage cannot fail merely because of sexual disarray, and that in the presence of genuine affection any sexual difficulties cannot loom importantly in the spouses' life. This is an unduly romantic view. True, minor sexual difficulties can be bridged; average-affectionate couples usually adjust to each other's differing needs and minor limitations. But where the quality of sexual relations remains a chronic source of vexation or becomes vitiated beyond a certain point for reasons unconnected with love, almost any marriage relationship can become progressively vulnerable to internal and external stresses.

New Baby and Sex. The birth of a child, most often the first, can stress a previously harmonious marriage; the connection between the new baby and the marital difficulties is not always recognized. It begins where a husband feels, or is, neglected in favor of the infant. Men with strong dependent needs may enter into fairly obvious competition with the baby for the wife's interest and affection; symptoms include a succession of minor physical complaints, job neglect, quarrelsomeness, or attention-getting teasing or sulking behavior. The young mother does not always bear these with equanimity. In milder cases the maladjustment is self-limiting, usually within a year.

But at times a usually reserved wife is demonstrative and affectionate toward the new baby to a degree never displayed toward the husband. A major degree of neglect—domestic, emotional and sexual—may result. In these women the experience of motherhood mobilizes latent hostility against the mate and all men. She could have died giving birth, she ruminates, but all he thinks about is his fun; men have all the fun, women the pain, the danger, the chores. Her body has changed, but not his. She suddenly feels angrily unready for the step from girl to mother, forced upon her. Everything now is more for keeps. The fun times on the spur of the moment are gone. He did this. He turns her off. She will just love this baby.

In postpartum depression the young mother is fatigued, listless, apathetic, has lost interest in everything, tends to neglect herself, the house, the child, as well as the husband, is tearful and fearful for no apparent reason, has no appetite, sleeps poorly, feels incapable of warmth and affection for anyone and has no sexual desire. It may be recalled that all psychogenic neglect syndromes of the postpartum period require differentiation from Sheehan's syndrome (p. 357).

Orgasm impairment may follow birth of a child, sometimes the first, but often only after the second baby. See p. 408.

Syndrome of Parental Overdependence. There floats about some younger couples' bedrooms—clearly apparent to one, unbeknownst to the other—the compulsively imaged visage of a binding parent, exhorting, inhibiting, critical or nodding benign approval but, at any rate, intruding and subtly interfering with the spontaneity and mutuality of the spouses' sexual life. It is a major symptom of the syndrome of chronic parental overdependence.

Persistent excessive dependence of one spouse on a parent—most often the mother, occasionally an older sibling—is a serious cause of marital stressing. It seems to occur about equally often in men and women, and must be differentiated from the problem of the merely meddlesome parent-in-law which constitutes a somewhat more tractable situation. The parent in question may or may not be a "domineering" personality; at times he (she) may even impress the physician as a "reasonable" and undemanding person. However, in most cases the parent fosters the dependency situation continuously by subtle scheming, martyr attitudes, psychosomatic invalidism, subtle belittlement of the "intruding" spouse, or even hysterical episodes or veiled self-destructive threats. The most inauspicious type of overdependence occurs in certain mother-daughter symbiotic situations where the mother has devoted herself intensely to the daughter's artistic, public or other success, and feels robbed of her vicarious achievement by the marriage, but clings hostilely to the girl.

Surface symptoms include constant soliciting or accepting of advice from the parent on intimate and domestic matters, regardless of the spouse's known wishes and views; overfrequent visiting, often heedless of ensuing domestic disruption; and frequent, usually unfavorable, voicing of comparisons of the spouse's qualities. It is peculiar of such morbid overdependence that the relationship is not based on any tangible needs for advice or support but is more in the nature of a compulsive-obsessive manifestation.

In all cases where overdependence is pronounced, the outlook for the marriage is practically hopeless, although the causes of the failure may remain unrecognized. Occasionally a very passive and undemanding husband may give the marriage and its vita sexualis the appearance of success. Peculiarly, the death of the parent in question brings no relief; on the contrary, it may mobilize a marked sense of guilt, because hate and death wishes against the deceased had been unconsciously inter-mingled with the clinging dependent ties; thus the death may hasten com-plete disruption of the marriage. However, it is at this point that psychiatric treatment—by dealing with the sense of guilt as if it were a pathologic grief reaction—can accomplish a reasonably complete reversal in a proportion of cases. Forcible countermoves by the perplexed other spouse, such as trying to prohibit contact, moving away, efforts to "buy off" the dominating parent are usually futile or worse.

Quantitative Disturbances. A young wife may present a complaint of overfrequency of relations, either directly ("my husband is oversexed"), or indirectly ("tell him I am too weak and to leave me alone more"), or in some other way. Most such complaints probably mask anhedonia due to fear or aversion (p. 403), or else they are related to pseudofrigidity. A woman who is capable of experiencing orgasm but is frequently de-prived of it (coitus interruptus, early if not premature ejaculation and other lability of potency, her own phobias, etc.—see p. 410) may experi-ence non-satisfaction as an acute distress which it is best to avoid. It would be a disservice to many of the marriages where the wife feels victimized by the frequency of the husband's demands, if the physician merely acted in concert with her and attempted to persuade the husband to desist. Sometimes a naïve or bashful young wife's complaint of "too much" may be meant to indicate local discomfort during the sexual act, perhaps due to a tender urethral meatus or such.

Some wives have entered marriage with a notion that "more than x times a week (or month) is harmful," or that it will impair the quality of the offspring, or simply that it constitutes excess and that all excesses are sinful and must be resisted. Actually, as far as could be ascertained, none of the principal religions and denominations limit the year-round frequency rate of marital cohabitation. Such beliefs sometimes are retained tacitly, persisting throughout married life and constituting the de facto basis for the vita sexualis, the husband accepting the pace set by the wife without question; no problem seems to exist in these cases, and these peculiarly naïve or even irrational adjustments usually come to light only incidentally.

A man may complain that his wife is "oversexed" and, indeed, her sexual drive and appetites may exceed his, although on actually pinpointing coital frequency in such cases more often than not it turns out to be well below the mean for the age group. The couple composed of "a big, lusty, bosomy lass and the hollow wreck of what used to be a man before he was married" most likely belongs to the realm of the fable. The hyperappetitive woman is dealt with elsewhere in this volume (p. 425). Occasionally, a hypochondriacal man may feel himself enfeebled or endangered by his wife's demands, but any postcoital reactions such as palpitations and other autonomic-vasomotor symptoms are as much referable to apprehension as they are to physiologic stress, and, as a rule, respond well to reassurance and precoital sedation. Debility of the husband due to unrecognized chronic disease needs to be ruled out in all cases.

A normal coital frequency rate, by common definition, is any rate which is mutually acceptable to the spouses. An insufficient rate is not acceptable to at least one of the spouses, although no specific complaint may be voiced. In practice the condition amounts to chronic sexual neglect, either mutual or of one spouse by the other; to the physician it is most often of interest where it arises following years of satisfactory adjustment. Individual tolerance for sexual neglect in marriage varies, but, for instance, a healthy couple, 40 years of age, married 15 years, with a history of 2 to 3 cohabitations a week during the first 10 or so years of marriage, but now cohabiting regularly at a rate of only once or twice a month, may be said to have a sexual problem and thus to constitute a medical problem to the extent that the welfare of the family, including preventive watchfulness, has been entrusted to the physician.

Sex Notions. Some couples have no verbal communication on sex matters, and it is also this type of spouse who most often brings a store of uncorrected sex notions into the marriage and innocuously proceeds to act them out, sometimes throughout the married life. Even today's liberated and knowledgeable attitudes from teen age on have had a surprisingly minor effect on some of the old wives' tales which have been the bane of many a marriage among the less sophisticated for untold decades.

The grand-daddy of all sex notions is the engrained belief of many men as well as women that the male "needs" sexual intercourse and the female does not. It implies that perilous social consequences will ensue if a man remains deprived for long. Where two spouses both share such a belief, in any negotiation or disagreement the wife is felt to be dealing from a position of strength. After all, she does not need it; he does (Schimel). In veiled form this notion even seems to have found its way into some of the newer non-dyadic forms of marriage (see p. 274 and 456).

Where a man believes that women are "ready any time," or that they are "cold by nature," habitually cursory intercourse may result. Some naïve wives may share a husband's beliefs of this type. A husband may believe firmly that "nice" girls are less apt to display coital responses than the "passionate type" of girl who is likely to be promiscuous, as adolescent ventures seemingly have conveyed to him. If tacitly forced upon a bride, at times this notion may suffice to inhibit her. She herself may be steeped in the belief—perhaps from fragments of adult talk in past years, perhaps directly through the mother's attitude—that a wife's "passion breeds suspicion (as to her basic virtuousness) in the man." Or restraint may be exercised for such reasons as that it is evidence of having "superior breeding"; or because sexual abandon is the "attitude of a common whore." Her resulting habitually passive attitude (i.e., motionless and generally nonparticipating during intercourse) may, in turn, be a factor in alienating the husband's sexual interest. Equally unfortunate are the notions and excesses which are growing up around the behavioristic approach to sex in marriage which is coming into vogue at present. The climax-counting, good-record-and-attendance, passing-grade numbers games indulged in by some otherwise rational couples can precipitate obsessive suspiciousness, especially in the woman, whenever there is a lessening in one of the parameters of what poses as erotic perfection.

An overly prudish wife may be convinced that it is improper to do anything except to perform intromission in the directest possible way. Faulty indoctrination or misunderstood beliefs may make her feel that it is unchaste even in marriage to view or to be viewed, to touch or be touched, or to be kissed except in the face, thus perhaps disappointing the young husband. Especially frequent is persistent refusal to touch the male organ. The ensuing refusal to guide an inexperienced husband's intromission by hand may result in failure to enter, vulvar traumatization, or loss of erection, especially if combined with reluctance to touch or have the husband touch her vulva. In some of these cases more efficient results seem to be obtained if remedial advice and guidance are directed mainly at the husband to enable him to overcome the young wife's reluctance in a gradual and affectionate manner.

MARITAL APATHY

The presenting complaints are familiar: "my marriage is breaking up because I'm simply too exhausted at night to be bothered" or "he works long (late) hours and is always tired when he comes home" or "sometimes after supper she goes right off to bed" or "he is too bushed for talk or anything else." There is listlessness masquerading as fatigue; disaffection masked by boredom, tiredness, and finally years of marital disaffection become unremitting day's end exhaustion except on special "nights out"—cards, the club, the girls, the boys, bowling. This is a true psychosomatic symptom, barring, with due respect, differences in energy levels, drops in fatigue threshold, anemia, or the hypo set (hypotension, hypoglycemia, hypothyroidism). As the spouses move into middle age, and sometimes long before then, they become lethargic about sex. Interest in late-evening TV or taking a somnifacient, as a custom, spell avoidance of sex, for any of a number of reasons: because it has ceased to be fun, or they don't like the spouse, or they have it with someone else, or because his performance does not permit her to reach climax, or because they'd rather masturbate. It is the opinion of numerous observers that sexual apathy in marriage is increasing as well as supravening at a younger age and that husbands are more lethargic about sex than are their wives.

The syndrome of the chronically tired wife—chronic anhedonic malaise—may be based on many things—dejection, a sense of futility, of nonfulfillment, or domestic overburdening—but in each case the interdependence with the state and conduct of the husband is fairly evident. The man's chronic day's end fatigue is more a thing unto itself. The lazy-husband syndrome, says Norris, is probably the commonest thing of all: after a long 8-hour day he comes home, plops exhausted into chair with a drink and the newspaper or TV set, gets up to eat his dinner an hour later, pecks his wife on the cheek, goes out with the bowling team, has a beer, comes home, watches some more television and plops into bed. There is a widespread tendency to credit men, especially those active in business, the professions or sciences, with a more realistic basis-in-fact for their chronic anhedonia than most of popular opinion is willing to concede to a wife. But it appears dubious that the tensions, the exertions and the worries peculiar to the daily pursuits of men are, by themselves, sexually more incapacitating than the corresponding responsibilities and worries of their wives.

Some Simple Measures. It is not always possible to penetrate to the ultimate motivations underlying psychogenic tiredness or day's end fatigue, but unless conspicuous disaffection exists in a marriage, it appears highly desirable to enlist the couple's cooperation with whatever symptomatic measures seem to be indicated. In some cases it would not be amiss to talk to them in terms of sexual obligation and sexual neglect. Attention may need to be paid to circumstances which make relaxed, unhurried intercourse difficult; to contraceptive practices; and sometimes to a rearrangement of the husband's late-hour activities. Either spouse, if habitually overtired, may be advised to seek a nap before dinner. Some husbands who are frequently overtense from the day's transactions may benefit from 1 or 2 ounces of spir. frumenti or vini gall., in palatable form, around mealtime, on occasions. It has been found helpful in some cases to suggest to such a couple periodic "little honeymoons" or retreats (e.g., an extended week-end together away from home). Even 1 or 3 such excursions a year can spell the difference between continued marital harmony and gradual marital deterioration. However, such trips are probably inadvisable where labile potency of the husband is a contributing factor, especially if they are pointedly planned for purposes of increased sexual activity. Where spouses are already seriously disaffected as well as discordant, and where no spiritual communion remains, remedial efforts rarely are worthwhile.

MARITAL INFIDELITY

(Unfaithfulness. Adultery (legal mostly). Philandering (male, originally). Extramarital relations, episode, transgression, resort, affair, etc. Antiqu. liaison, amour, amorous (illicit, love) affair, cuckolding (by woman).

In prevailing usage infidelity means a sexual relationship of either spouse with a third person, ranging from the most transient and casual (prostitute, party interlude) to the most protracted, emotionally involved affair. Excluded, at least under the law, are platonic relationships, no matter how intimately binding; homosexual acts of married men; and religious polygamy where legal (mostly Mormons and Islamics; custom in both waning rapidly). Technical or unopposed adultery exists by consent, such as the acts of legally or de facto separated but undivorced spouses; participation by both spouses in swinger groups, communal living or multilateral marriages (see p. 456); agreed-upon extramarital resort by the mate of a totally incapacitated or impotent spouse; theologic or legal contentions arising out of the use of donor semen for artificial insemination; in certain nonsexual marriages of convenience; and by extralegal connivance to furnish divorce evidence. Felonious adultery refers to the crime of bigamy. The statutes are not believed to cover transgression in cases of common-law marriage.

Extramarital activity may take place for financial gain, sometimes with the spouse's knowledge or connivance. In other cases a husband may induce or compel his wife to have sexual relations with other men, but with no monetary considerations involved; voyeuristic, sadistic and especially homosexual tendencies have been identified in such husbands. In somewhat similar cases a husband who encourages his wife's infidelity has been held to do so because of his psychic masochism; he uses his wife's infidelity to re-enact his infantile sense of injustice (Bergler). Spurious adultery is encountered in the form of delusional accusations by certain chronic alcoholic, paranoid, impotent, deaf or near-deaf individuals, and in some toxic psychoses (e.g., amphetamines). Spurious self-accusations may occur in severe depressive psychoses.

Incidence. Meaningful statistics regarding extramarital relations are difficult to obtain for obvious reasons. The following seem to be consistent with the consensus of educated guesses and extrapolations of interested observers. By age 40 one half of all married men and 26 per cent of all married women had sexual intercourse with a partner other than the spouse (Kinsey, 1953); a former associate of Kinsey's has said that the female figure probably was low even then and he places the national average of this figure more recently at 30 to 35 per cent (Pomeroy, 1972). Or, by age 40 about one third of all married women and possibly 60 per cent of all married men have had an extramarital sexual experience (Bell, 1971). Or, an interview study of 100 middle-class couples in a conservative Midwestern community found that 28 per cent of the marriages were affected by at least one extramarital relationship (Johnson, 1970).

Acceptance of extramarital resort is increasing, although there is a historians' theory that liberal and puritanical standards in Western morality alternate in a cyclic fashion. Situation ethicism and moral relativism are being increasingly proposed as ideal solutions by theologians and others. A survey of 1272 readers of the Ladies' Home Journal indicated that 74 per cent did not think that a single act of adultery, by either spouse, should necessarily constitute a reason for divorce (Bernard, 1968). In the above-mentioned Midwestern survey 28 per cent of the husbands and 53 per cent of the wives felt that most married persons, even though happily married, would like to experience extramarital intercourse. Others have challenged the proposition that marriage can serve all the needs of a marital couple, and have called it an overloaded social unit. Mutual tolerance pacts, which actually go back to the 19th century, are contained in some model marriage contracts which have been published. Some veteran amoralists are coming into their own (e.g., Ellis, of enhancement-of-life-by-variety repute, maintains that fidelity limits life experience). And, says Francoeur, such terms as adultery, infidelity and fornication are an organic part of a dying pastoral culture which no longer speaks to modern man in any kind of intelligible language.

Couple Exclusivity. In various quarters, notably among the highly educated young, the "you belong to me" approach to married love is being attacked; faithfulness in marriage and coital exclusivity are not considered synonymous; and possessive feelings and jealousy are designated as personal hang-ups. "Enjoy it while it's yours, or the part of me that is yours" is, however, not a feasible attitude for most people, of any age, in our civilization, and there would seem to be little prospect that it will be in the foreseeable future. In fact, it is reported that the greatest wrecker of the new life styles which include group and multilateral marriages is the spontaneous formation of dyadic pairs who sooner or later develop exclusivist tendencies, even though jealous behavior is conscientiously suppressed by those concerned. Swinger groups also have stringent rules of conduct as they try to defend themselves against their single greatest risk: couple cross-infatuation and runaway behavior.

Circumstantial Infidelity. Transgressions of this type remain more frequent in men. The cause lies chiefly in various external or internal (e.g., emotional) circumstances of the moment. These individuals are "seduced by the opportunity." These circumstances usually are unconnected with the marriage itself; in fact, most typically the marriage is good. The personality of the offending spouse is essentially normal, except for the possible presence of minor contributing personality traits, such as a tendency to self-indulgence or self-pity, suggestibility, limited ability to subordinate to higher moral values, or remnants of child-type erotic curiosity. Frequent circumstantial impellents, among men, are a juvenoid desire to be accepted by philandering companions ("regular fellow," "not a sissy,"); a stirring of sexual need combined with provocatively tempting opportunity; a desire for comforting when momentarily despondent or for human communication when momentarily exuberant; or a reassuring intimacy in a frighteningly uninviting, cold distant city. These latter impellents, operative typically when away from the spouse, have also been called the wrong-woman-at-the-right-moment type of infidelity. In the circumstantial infidelity of women this variety of impellent, appropriately reworded, is believed to be the most frequent motive. Circumstantial transgression is facilitated by the temporary weakening—by alcohol, persuasion or example—of those factors which ordinarily tend to inhibit infidelity (e.g., religious, moral or ethical scruples) or fear of complications or of penalities. Where an act of circumstantial infidelity remains undiscovered and penalty-free, it may form the basis of a gradual conditioning process toward promiscuous habits. Each time the individual is confronted again with a similar set of impellent circumstances—nostalgia for human communication, need for comforting, challenge by philandering companions—extramarital resort becomes more nearly reflex. Eventually, the mere presence of abetting factors—alcohol, forcible marital abstinence, remoteness or anonymity of the locale—may act as trigger mechanism. At the same time the inhibiting factors are disposed of with less and less inner conflict. To reverse the process, in emotionally normal men, it may suffice to disrupt any single factor in the conditioning chain.

Infidelity Caused by Marital Factors. Protracted emotional neglect of one spouse by the other is a frequent cause in this category. No actual lessening of affection may exist, but there is excessive taking-for-granted, increasing undemonstrativeness, and gross inattention to the other's emotional needs. In time this may lead to a sense of not being needed, or not being understood, or not being supported morally. With this often comes a sense of inner insecurity, and such characteristic deficit reactions as brooding dissatisfaction, self-pity, resentment, spite fantasies and a vague feeling of boredom. Sexual neglect may play a part, or—in wives approaching middle age—the panic of the closing door. Altogether, thus, a state of negative readiness with respect to infidelity may come into being. If a suitable subject then happens on the scene, an extramarital relationship may ensue. The intensity and the duration of these affairs vary greatly, ranging from a brief, turbulent episode to protracted attachments.

The occurrence, in a previously unremarkable marriage, of a precipitous act of spite or retaliatory (reactive) infidelity, may follow a quarrel, an insult or maltreatment, as well as an episode of infidelity; such insults seem capable of provoking, in either sex, impulsively vindictive thought-imageries of "going to somebody else." But apparently this rarely is, or even can be, carried out, unless there was a candidate accessibly held in reserve.

Affair as Marriage Remedy. There is a body of professional and sophisticated lay opinion which holds that some marriages are best preserved—can be saved, in fact—by extramarital involvement. Says English: "I have seen many people who benefited from, and whose marriage has been helped by, a sexual affair." In an outside affair, according to Clark, one of the spouses may get to know remedies for shortcomings existing in the marital relationship. There has been no dearth of reactions: with great ease, says Salzman, these philanderers convince themselves that an affair is either necessary to maintain their own mental health or a device for allowing them to tolerate a barely compatible husband or wife while still remaining married. On the other hand, it has been said that using affairs to shore up the basic commitment of the marriage is not working any more, mainly because "the commitment is too dry-rotted to support the weight of the bodies bouncing on an afternoon love couch" (Breslin). The fact is that some marriages sooner or later become so dull and unrewarding, even oppressive, as to make openness to a more romantic, meaningful, exciting relationship almost inevitable. Wives especially, with the security of modern contraception and aware of expanded economic opportunities if anything should go badly wrong, have begun to use affairs almost as a health appliance, an antidepressant, an escape hatch, a shaky little secret bridge in and out of the tiresome connubial confines. In fact, in many places, says Schimel, the battle for equality by women has been won and has now entered the stage of overkill.

The offending party is not usually anxious to disturb the domestic equilibrium—there is the house, the children, income and budget, friends, the fear of loneliness—and if there is a choice of affair mates those will serve best who will rock the marriage boat least, meaning someone married or of totally differing background, and with the smallest possible problem in date logistics. On the other hand, some individuals—it is no longer considered certain that these are mostly women—are incapable of tolerating more than one sexual partner at a time, leading usually to neglect of the marital mate or at least to further dilution of the sexual interest in him (her). Some women resort to orgasm-withholding, persuading themselves that thereby they are remaining faithful to one or the other. Others, as they hurry home for same-night marital consumption, have convinced themselves that they are enhancing the marital vita sexualis (vernac. wet deck intercourse). Mutually promised substitution of the lover or beloved in coital imagery enables some spouses to go through the domestic act with seeming animation.

Experimenting. A husband who finds himself constantly unable to arouse sexual interest in his wife or to bring her to climax may develop an urge to prove his masculine capacity elsewhere. This differs from the need for validation in cases of incipient impotence, where early in a progressive organic case a worried man may attempt a sexual act by means of an extramarital, high-arousal experience (pseudorelative impotence; see box, p. 372). A normally sexed wife whose husband performs in a persistently cursory or deficient manner may feel a need for reassurance as to her erotic charms. These needs may develop even where no actual appetite for additional gratification exists. A sexually unresponsive wife may feel impelled to explore the causes and the extent of her own deficiency, by more or less deliberately experimenting with an extramarital partner. She desires, as it were, to find a man who can make her find out what IT is like; if she can do it; and if it is her fault if she cannot. This partly curious, partly chagrined experimentation differs from the compulsive promiscuity of some frigid women (p. 426).

Infidelity in Personality Disorders. Certain individuals, both male and female, act out their infantile and other immaturity traits or their impulse disorders by indulging in acts of extramarital behavior which they appear incapable of checking voluntarily even in the face of marriage-destructive or self-ruinous potential.

In one group infantile-destructive urges which have persisted in the adult personality become mobilized just when (because?) the family and the social situation seem to be most secure and harmonious. A largely joyless, seemingly senseless act of transgression may occur, often so insultingly ostentatious or so clumsily concealed that only unusual for-bearance on the part of the offended spouse can hold the marriage together. However, the act may then be repeated and, unaided, the out-look for the marriage—and usually for all subsequent marriages—is poor.

In impulse-disordered behavior, on the other hand, while the marriage is often smooth and without major sexual dissatisfaction, there prevails in the offending spouse a sense of special privilege vis-à-vis the social norms of behavior. Their egocentricity makes them feel free to suit their whims; they feel no guilt, no sense of disloyalty, as they indulge in a succession of random, usually well-concealed extramarital ventures. The partners tend to be nondescript insofar as they do not seem to possess any assets of charm, culture, appearance or emotional warmth which are not also present in the spouse. Actually, there is nothing compulsive or irresistible about these ventures, and these patients, although not truly curable, often can be controlled successfully by means of long-term management. Characteristically in many the normal sense of ethics is replaced by a tendency to maudlin sentimentalism, especially as regards "sanctity of the family." At intervals some individuals indulge in sense-less, recklessly indiscriminate acts of extramarital bravado; others seem to be impelled periodically to express an underlying sense of rebelliousness through unconventional or independent erotic entanglements. As no un-conscious self-ruinous aim coexists, the marital outlook depends largely on the offended spouse's reaction. In severe impulse disorders with ex-tremely promiscuous tendencies in both sexes no semblance of normal marriage is possible.

Some married men with moderately severe sex-deviate tendencies (e.g., fetishism, masochism) resort to the services of prostitutes if the wife refuses to cooperate with certain variant precoital and coital practices (see p. 212); or where the patient does not wish to degrade her in this fashion; or where she does not constitute a sufficiently provocative partner for the discharge of his deviant needs. The marital outlook is surprisingly good in these cases.

In a number of intercurrent mental disorders, if undiagnosed, seem-ingly inexplicable acts of infidelity may take place. A characteristic ex-ample are subacute, manic episodes in the course of a manic-depressive illness. Sexual transgression may occur in connection with functional (hysterical) amnesia. The amnesia probably most often follows rather than precedes an illicit sexual act (i.e., the act was committed with recognition as yet intact). However, if alcohol was consumed, allowance must be made for a possible prodromal mental clouding effect. One must also allow for sexual victimization as the patient was wandering about helplessly and unattended, while already in an amnestic state.

The Case of Love. It respects nothing—the person's own or the other's married state, age differences, children, habits, infirmities, established social ties—all melt away. Old bonds become like nothing. It comes on suddenly, impetuously ("her first hello gave meaning to my empty life"); or it insinuates itself gradually. It brings tears and romantic hungers and self-accusations, tragic overtones and oceanic feelings, and the terror of illusion betrayed; it preempts all other hungers. It precedes physical sex or follows it, but it can also exist without it. Sex matters little, certainly in the beginning, and it is not true that sexual consummation bursts the balloon of yearning. Such love is an obsession, a force majeur, a disease, perhaps a virus swamping the soul. It makes women give up the good life and men walk away from everything. It can elevate and strengthen just as it can deprive, debase and destroy. Exploitation, dirt, ruin, bondage can follow in its wake, but also felicitous conclusion. It is beyond reason, although reason is not dead, simply overridden. Much learned writing exists on the difference between love and infatuation, but most of it is suspect of being a rationalized apologia pro virtute. At best, the line is difficult to draw. Does the luminous radiance hide the real person of the beloved? Is the longing directed at a living fantasy-object? If the thing crashes, the aftermath is brutal for both members of the married pair-bond involved, regardless of whether the excursionist crawls or struts or sneaks back. Few marriages truly recover.

The Urge to Confess. It has been said, with some justification, that the urge to confess an ongoing or just-ended marital transgression to the innocent spouse, is a greater danger to the average, basically sound marriage than the transgression itself. In theory, confession is a noble and courageous gesture, hopefully evoking powers of forbearance in the other which cannot but strengthen the marriage. In practice, relatively few recipients of such a confession can, unaided, carry the burden of their own aggrieved, resentful or deflated reactions and still remain the same loving spouses. The urge to confide or publish the existence of an erotic relationship, licit or illicit, is peculiarly strong in both sexes. In the presence of romantic love this urge is notorious: from time immemorial both lover and beloved have felt like "shouting the news from the rooftops." But even in lesser involvements there often is a compelling need to confide, to share a feeling of joy, to ventilate doubt or a sense of guilt, to brag or to elicit applause for bravado. Where no confidantes exist, the spouse may be elected for the part. These are often pseudo-confessions, and the results can be truly destructive of the union. However, by relieving his disabling feelings of tension and guilt the errant spouse is also attempting to repair the marriage. Confession to the spouse may also represent a hostile gesture, subconsciously hoping to shock the other into departing. There may be a panicky urge to involve the mate in the affair, perhaps as a rescuer: to chase the tempting devils, to extend forgiveness and to restore the status quo (infantile or panic reaction). Or even an attempt to re-enact a juvenile fantasy, the hope of subtly persuading the marriage partner into accepting a ménage-à-trois, perhaps even a formal triadic marriage, combining the best of two worlds. However, the latter is more often attempted where the straying spouse is a bisexual (p. 501).

Sequels of Infidelity. The effect of exposed infidelity on the average marriage tends to be disrupting. Apart from immediate anxious or chagrined reactions there frequently remains a chronic sense of loss in the offended spouse, which relates to the feeling of exclusive, intimate sharing. Almost equally frequent are lingering feelings of insecurity and a subtle sense of personal inadequacy. Where the adulterous marriage has been merely "patched up" to survive, the offended spouse sooner or later may harass and disquiet the erstwhile offender with accusations and suspicion, often on no other basis than his (her) own sense of insecurity. Among major morbid reactions in the maritally offended one encounters an obsessional preoccupation with having been sexually deprived, even where without substantial foundation, ushering in other obsessional symptoms in the predisposed. Phobic fears of becoming transinfected venereally through coitus may assume a chronic character and can contribute to the fairly frequently observed secondary orgasm failure of wronged wives. A compulsive, usually single, random and pleasureless act of retaliation-in-kind occurs in some basically competitive personalities and may precipitate a chain reaction of its own.

An offended wife who has not genuinely forgiven and forgotten may feel constrained to close her eyes to a past—occasionally even a continuing—adulterous affair of her husband's. What appears then to be philosophic acceptance, especially in the presence of repeated, unasked assertions that the incident is being forgotten "for the marriage's, for the children's sake," may merely mask a protracted state of inner tension or other distress. Some of these distress states are of an insidious and chronic nature, and delayed clinical morbidity is not rare. The nature of this morbidity is protean. The physician, years later, sometimes may not suspect any connection between, say, a woman's chronic anxiety state or colitis or rejection of a child, and a past extramarital venture of the husband's. In wronged men, these chronic reactive syndromes seem to be considerably less frequent; there are indications that they may be most frequent in wronged husbands with strong passive dependent needs.

Abreacting the Shock. The threat of immediate disruption is greater where the husband feels wronged, but chronic repercussions on the marriage are more frequent following exposure of a husband's philandering. In most strata of our society wives lack recourse to certain abreactive devices accessible to men. A symbolic acting-out of "angry departure" from the home, for instance, is a more realistic gesture on the part of the family's breadwinner. In this and in certain other ways he can, in fantasy or symbol, "do something" about being wronged without actually destroying the marriage against his deeper wishes. Such abreactions help to minimize chronic injury to his self-respect; they may also help deenergize and abreact any vindictive impulses that may have arisen. Where the husband has philandered, the average wife's security need for herself and/or the children makes such abreactions usually less feasible or their fantasying less realistic and thus less soothing.

Marriage Disruption. The marriage-disruptive potential of exposed infidelity depends greatly on the reaction of the offended spouse. The general nature of this reaction seems to differ in men and women, although perhaps not for the reasons traditionally advanced. Infidelity by the wife has been assumed to be more serious as she is held to be tampering with her highest biologic value (i.e., the reproductive apparatus). Being supposedly the more suggestible and sexually more dependent party, her affections are held to be more easily and more often seduced away from the spouse than in the case of a philandering man; thus her transgression always would constitute a hazard to the preservation of the family unit and, in the aggregate, endanger the monogamous basis of society. A more acute sense of having been injured usually is expected in an offended husband because remnants of male proprietary attitudes make fear of a "cuckold's repute" a more characteristically masculine emotion. Also, marriages are held to be more likely to survive where the husband was the offender, because of covert retention of a belief in the basically polygamous nature of the male. However, it would seem dubious that among marriages dissolved today because of adultery, unfaithfulness of the wife is more often the cause than masculine philandering. Besides, in either case infidelity is more usually the proverbial straw that breaks the camel's back rather than a prime motive. Observation also makes it appear dubious that unfaithful women are frequently and genuinely the seduced party; or that, excepting the most casual ventures, the extramarital infatuations of men less often break up an existing union than those of wives.

Some spouses react strongly to even casual transgressions early in marriage but tend to be more tolerant in later years; others who may have been philosophic about previous incidents react with anxiety and chagrin to infidelity at a time when they feel their own attractiveness, or their powers, waning. Some spouses will not tolerate incidental affairs, even in the presence of mitigating or pardonable circumstances, but may show little reaction to a protracted involvement, such as a "housefriend-lover" of the wife or an "office-wife" of the husband. Some spouses react only if they believe that the existence of the marriage is threatened by the intruder; others react severely where the marriage has long been of uncertain permanence. Occasionally, even quondam infidelity (i.e., transgression in the distant past but only recently exposed or disclosed) may cause a major reaction.

Reparative Guidance. At times it is feasible to prevent postadulterous disruption of a marriage by means of reparative guidance of the spouses. The physician's assistance in these crises may be sought on the basis of his previous friendly interest in the family's welfare. It is well known that some basically sound marriages can become genuinely and permanently strengthened as an indirect result of an unfaithful episode, especially if reparative guidance has been adroit. Where a couple decide to forget an adulterous incident and to continue the marriage, the situation must be clarified thoroughly. This is perhaps the sine qua non of all genuine marital repair in such cases, although it does not assure by itself a successful marriage. Clarification is accomplished most efficiently when the spouses, each separately, are given an opportunity to ventilate their own thinking and feeling in conversation with a third person who is sympathetic, neutral and preferably experienced in dealing with distressed individuals. It is usually ineffectual, even inadvisable, for two such spouses to attempt sitting down together and to analyze conversationally their own motives and reactions at length, without guidance or restrictions.

A situation may exist where a couple has remained separated following a spouse's angry departure from the home, but where a genuine wish to continue the marriage is suspected to exist. Pride, various anxieties, as well as any number of social or legal pressures may be widening the cleavage involuntarily; they may constitute a compelling drift which neither spouse may know how to reverse. Experienced divorce lawyers, for instance, are said to be able frequently to sense such a drift and may wisely promote reconciliation in these cases. A trusted physician, acting largely as a family friend, may feel justified at times in helping such a couple to make their feelings known to each other.

Legal Position. On the other hand, it is not always appropriate for the physician or other counselor to urge a couple who have already taken some kind of legal steps to "make up and have sex." A single act of sexual intercourse is legally considered as condoning the prior acts which may have formed the legal basis for separation or divorce. Counseling a make-up attempt may create a legal prejudice against one spouse. Copulation while litigating wipes out the (legal) action (Slovenko).

FOR JOURNAL LITERATURE AND ADDITIONAL READING

Abse, D. W., Nash, E. M., and Jessner, L. (eds.): Marriage Counseling in Medical Practice. A Symposium. Chapel Hill, Univ. of N. Carolina Press, 1964

Friedman, L. J.: Virgin Wives, a Study of Unconsummated Marriages. Philadelphia, Lippincott, 1966

Greene, B. L.: A Clinical Approach to Marital Problems: Evaluation and Management. Springfield, Ill., Thomas, 1970

Hastings, D. W.: A Doctor Speaks on Sexual Expression in Marriage. Ed. 2. Boston, Little Brown, 1971

Hunt, M.: The Affair, A Portrait of Extra-marital Love in Contemporary America. New York, World Publishing Co., 1970

Neubeck, G. (ed.): Extra-marital Relations. Englewood Cliffs, N.J., Prentice Hall, 1969

Rosenbaum, A. and Alger, I. (eds.): The Marriage Relationship, Psychoanalytic Perspectives. New York, Basic Books, 1968·

Silverman, H. L. (ed.): Marital Therapy: Moral, Sociological and Psychological Factors. Springfield, Ill., Thomas, 1972

SOME BOOKS FOR THE COUPLE

Birchall, F.: Sex and the Adult Woman. New York, Simon & Schuster, 1967

Butterfield, O. M.: Sexual Harmony in Marriage. New York, Emerson, 1964

Gittelsohn, R. B.: My Beloved is Mine: Judaism and Marriage. New York, Union Amer. Heb. Congreg., 1971

Greenblat, B. R.: A Doctor's Marital Guide for Patients. Chicago, Budlong, 1964

Guttmacher, A. F.: Pregnancy, Birth and Family Planning. New York, Viking Press, 1973

Kelly, G. A.: The Catholic Marriage Manual. New York, Random House, 1964

Landis, T. and M. G.: Building a Successful Marriage, ed. 5. Englewood Cliffs, N.J., Prentice Hall, 1968

Liswood, R.: First Aid for the Happy Marriage. New York, Trident Press, 1965

Naismith, G.: Private and Personal. New York, McKay, 1966

Otto, H. A.: More Joy in your Marriage. New York, Hawthorne, 1969

Rainer, J. and J.: Sexual Adventure in Marriage. New York, Julian Messner, 1965

Saul, L. J. with Powell, K.: Fidelity and Infidelity; and What Makes or Breaks a Marriage. Philadelphia, Lippincott, 1967

CHAPTER 14

Principles of Contraception

Indications — Objections — Prescribing — Abstemious Methods —
Intrauterine Devices — Hormonal Methods — Permanent Methods
— Barrier Methods — Chemical Spermicides — Folk Methods.

Contraception—the inhibition of reproduction—is only one phase of Family Planning (i.e., man's quest to regulate the intervals between births and the number of his offspring). Closely related are the investigation and treatment of infertility and the prevention of fetal wastage and of perinatal hazards.

INDICATIONS

The physician who is giving contraceptive advice is actually doing two things: he is advising a couple, or agreeing with them, that childbearing would be inadvisable at a given time; and he is selecting for them the most appropriate contraceptive method and instructing them in its proper use. The latter function is the concern and the responsibility of the medical professions; the posing of indications is not exclusively in the medical domain. The following contraceptive indications are generally recognized:

Maternal Health Protection.   Here the woman cannot be permitted to conceive because of a health risk, present or projected. Medical progress has reduced these indications, including many of the obstetric, psychiatric, gynecologic and other hazards, but also it has added new ones. At any rate, there exists a number of conditions which require either temporary or permanent contraception to protect the health of the woman because the condition may be aggravated by pregnancy. An example of temporary indication would be incomplete recovery from a physical or mental illness, where the woman is well enough to cohabitate but too debilitated to bear a child. Probably one must include here a history of great, rapid-succession multiparity under circumstances preventing adequate recovery between pregnancies: great multiparity per se does not impair health, but after the sixth or seventh child a steep increase in the maternal invalidism rate seems to occur.

Family Protection.   Anything that protects the health and the vitality of the mother also protects the family unit. Obversely, a risk of maternal invalidism threatens the overall welfare of the family, especially that of existing children. In our time it is desirable that the number and the spacing of children stand in some reasonable relationship to the family's present or potential means of rearing them properly. Proper rearing also demands that there exist in the home at least a modicum of hygiene, cheerfulness and parental harmony; and enough strength, time and animus left over in the parents to follow with affectionate interest the doings of each child, at each stage of its growing up (psychologic birthright). Where a couple is affectionate and devoted, an inability to grant each child its psychologic birthright may cause a type of anguish which often also has a family-decomposing effect. Besides, where each new child constitutes a penalty upon the sexual relationship, cohabitation may become a dreaded, guilty thing, and chronic sexual nonsatisfaction in itself may become an additional source of marital and family tension.

The effect of great multiparity on the future psyche of the children is the subject of controversy; but under ordinary circumstances a large number of children is probably not per se a source of emotional deprivation. This is less true as regards child-crowding. Rapid-succession parity, regardless of family economic status, exposes both infants, the crowded and the crowding one, to a degree of risk as to their psychic as well as physical welfare. With a comfortably situated, vigorous, affectionate mother the risk may be small, but it increases as one moves away from optimal conditions.

Eugenic Indications. The pursuit of eugenics is based on a variable store of knowledge and, occasionally, of fashions; increased knowledge has erased some possible indications and added a few others. A compelling medical eugenic indication exists where a couple cannot foreseeably bring a healthy normal child into the world because of a demonstrable heredopathic risk. In most cases the risk is smaller, as the taint is either recessive or is expected to be no more than mildly disabling or disfiguring. A relative eugenic indication exists during the woman's premenopausal years: unimpeded exposure here leads to the birth of children with a relatively high incidence of anomalies. Where permanent sterilization is employed, some caution is necessary because knowledge of hereditary mechanisms is incomplete, and not all afflictions of limb or mind may be as incurable or as disabling a generation from now as they are now. Temporary eugenic contraception aims at protecting the offspring from exposure, intra-uterine or neonatal, to transmissible diseases such as syphilis while the mother is being cured. The clinical rationale of eugenic contraception is the projected impact of severe morbidity on the afflicted offspring itself, as well as the protection of parents from responsibilities that they are ill-fitted to carry.

Social and Voluntary Indications. Requests for contraceptive advice for self-posited indications are the most common type today. Examples are a newlywed couple's reluctance to interrupt educational or early career plans, a desire to become adjusted to each other, to accumulate some savings, perhaps apprehension of losing personal freedom too soon, or uncertainty, by the couple's own recognition, about the permanence of the relationship. For requests for contraception by unmarried young people including teen-agers, see p. 124.

Demographic Indications. In recent years an ecologic consciousness has arisen; problems of overpopulation and people pollution have become major sources of concern, and the cue-word zero population growth has embedded itself in the life plans and life styles of numerous young people (Lear). Mass contraceptive exploration and prescribing, especially in some of the high-density areas of Asia major, is proceeding with great urgency, as people, ignorant of effective control measures, continue to multiply at a rate which will predictably outstrip the available food resources of the world.

OBJECTIONS

Religious Objections. In the view of the *Roman Catholic* Church any direct intent to prevent conception would be a violation of the natural and the divine positive law as it affects the marital act. The spiritual authority behind this law is not subject to reversal or exception on account of pain or vexation, and to take exception manifests a lack of faith. The Church does not disapprove of married couples making proper decisions about family size and child spacing; but it teaches that such family limitation must be the result of coitus regulation. It forbids all means except complete or periodic continence (rhythm), but also advocates all possible refinements of rhythm technique through biologic research. The encyclical Humanae Vitae (1968) sternly reaffirmed that there must be "openness of the act to the transmission of life."

In continuing to refine its attitude, the Church has long since abandoned the view that sexual intercourse during menstruation and pregnancy is sinful. It also teaches today that conjugal love is a great good and that the procreation of children is not the sole purpose of marriage (Bromley, others). Dissidents within the Church assert the primacy of the individual conscience, and defend the use of any medically sound method of contraception as compatible with Christian morality. An unsolved matter are the progestational oral agents insofar as they are capable of regularizing a woman's monthly flow and thus may be said to correct defects of nature in certain cases.

Jewish legal authorities representing orthodoxy, unlike even Roman

Catholicism, regard the procreation of children as a cardinal duty, a divine commandment given to man; they condemn all limitation on family size but have been known to relax it for important reasons of health, if medically certified. Some Orthodox rabbis believe that once the duty of having children—a son and a daughter—is fulfilled, contraception, including the practice of withdrawal, is permissible. In Reform Judaism no restrictions on the use of contraception exist.

The *Protestant* position in the United States is not unified; however, there is a prevalence of belief among major denominations that in planning parenthood the use of contraceptives, practiced in Christian conscience, fulfills rather than violates the will of God and therefore is moral. It is up to the conscience of the man and the wife to decide the number and the spacing of their children, in a sense of accountability to God and on the basis of competent medical advice; prayer, study and judgment must be used in such planning. Both irresponsible conception of children up to the limit of biologic capacity, and selfish limitation of the number of children are equally detrimental. A few denominations and sects are wholly opposed to artificial contraception; the extreme disapproving views are ascribed to the Hutterite sect.

Psychologic Objections. Freedom of decision as to if, when and how often to have children may place an excessive burden on unstable spouses, resulting in anxiety, inner conflict, or discord. Also, some childless or one-child couples who would be benefited by having a child, procrastinate indefinitely for minor reasons and may miss the most appropriate moment.

Comment: carefully restricted to some vulnerable couples, these arguments are sound. It is probably incumbent upon the physician to discourage contraception where emotional instability of childless spouses appears subject to aggravation because of subsequent guilt feelings over a past wish to control parenthood for reasons which were trivial at the time. In practice this may be difficult to determine except in patients who happen to be in psychotherapy.

The Dysgenic Argument. Contraception, in the long run, may depress the quality of the human race (or nation, or community), as the most desirable portions of the population are more apt to have access to and be more successful in the use of the most efficient contraceptives; while the lowest grades of population, with their relatively larger quota of misfits of every kind, would be unwilling or unable to restrict childbearing to a proportionate extent.

This proposition is arguable in most of its premises. It is not believed to be in accord with the principles of democratic philosophy which assumes that socio-economically depressed status is not a valid indication of potentially increased biologic deficit; that genetic opportunity is equal in all walks of life; and that the existence of an inherently superior minority cannot be assumed a priori.

Moral Objections. The availability of contraceptive advice facilitates, thus encourages, moral laxity—meaning nonmarital cohabitation—by removing the fear of unwanted pregnancy, one of the principal deterrents of promiscuous behavior.

Comment: morality based mainly on deterrents such as fear of pregnancy cannot be considered as being true morality. Humanely, birth of a child out of wedlock is a greater tragedy than a casual sexual relationship is a moral transgression. More strongly put, it is deeply immoral to allow that the birth of a child be made a punishment for sin. Historically, increased promiscuity in the Western world has paralleled increased contraceptive availability for over 100 years.

PRESCRIBING

Contraceptive effectiveness of a method (i.e., a consistently high degree of protection) requires not only that it prevent conception with each sexual act but also that the couple apply this or some equivalent method during all their sexual acts. Intermittent or casual nonuse of a method does not necessarily constitute "patient failure" but also may be classed as method failure or possibly prescription error, because it is evidence of poor acceptability. Casual choice and prescribing of a contraceptive method by the physician tends to encourage casual use (i.e., sporadic nonuse) thereby lowering use-effectiveness. In each case the best possible contraceptive method with the greatest acceptability should be chosen and taught conscientiously. It appears to be dubious philosophy for the physician to adjust the thoughtfulness of contraceptive choice, and the thoroughness of his instructions to the earnestness of the particular indications. If a couple whose ambivalence is encouraged by casual prescribing does not mind playing a game of chance with parenthood, it seems to be preferable that they play it entirely on nature's terms (i.e., without any contraceptive impediment): in the aggregate, a couple's vita sexualis tends to be more successful if coitus is unimpeded.

Contraceptive preference in the past decade has shifted away from barrier and chemical methods; the majority of users today employ oral contraceptives, IUD's or surgery. This has reduced the problem of ill-sustained user motivation: the various indwelling, daily-routinized and permanent methods operate independent of human vagaries leading to use failure, while the prescribing of sex-centered methods—those requiring some action at or near the sex act—must reckon heavily with the psychology and temperament of the user. With the growing shift towards woman-centered contraception in stable unions, the ultimate decision-making role in child-bearing is also shifting subtly, revolutionizing even further the relationships between husband and wife, and accelerating the ongoing alteration of the family system (Liu). There has also been a shift towards woman-centered contraception in the more transitory relationships. College medical advisors have recommended that coeds who do not wish to appear overly available to a date by being on pills or carrying a diaphragm, employ the carry-with-you foam can method (e.g., Emko) for contingency use; unlike the diaphragm it implies no prior fitting. Drug-counter purchase can also be pretended on the heels of an impulse (Revere).

No known method short of panhysterectomy affords 100 per cent protection for any sustained period of time—even simple hysterectomy has not prevented a few tubal pregnancies via a vagino-tubal fistula. To such method failures must be added the human factors: prescribing error which includes failure to adapt the method to the patient's intelligence, habits, facilities or anatomy; inadequate instruction; failure to recheck fitted devices; failure to change prescription under altered conditions (e.g., childbirth, weight gain, divorce), and patient failure: negligence, inconsistent use, inattentiveness in application, or ruinous misuse of a device. Behind such failures one may find ambivalence, even resentment on the user's part, reckless confidence ("won't happen to me" or "just this once"), and especially the phenomenon of WEUP (willful exposure to unwanted pregnancy, Lehfeldt), an inept, unconsciously self-injurious attempt at crisis-solving by emotionally immature or psychoneurotic women and men in reaction to a major stress situation. The method chosen by the physician should be "easy to get, easy to keep, easy to use." For permanent sterilization the best available method is probably vasectomy, although it is not entirely innocuous (Lear). Motivation is usually at its lowest between the first and second baby; both spouses have proven their fertility, and they do not care as much when the next baby comes.

ABSTEMIOUS METHODS

Total Abstinence (Marital Celibacy)

Complete sexual abstinence in marriage, for long periods, is included among contraceptive methods largely as a matter of tradition. Actually, there is little evidence that normally affectionate, healthy couples of early or midreproductive age today are actually resorting to prolonged abstinence solely for contraceptive purposes. However, both retarded and normal but very unsophisticated couples have been known to resort to substitute or to coitus-simulating sex activity exclusively and for many years because of ignorance of contraceptive methods. A full cycle's

EFFECTIVENESS OF CONTRACEPTIVE METHODS

Adapted from 8th Annual Proceedings, Amer. Assoc. Planned Parenthood Physicians, Boston 1970 (Tietze), Nobel Symposium 15 (Diczfalusy-Borell, eds. J. Wiley & Sons), and other sources.

This list is based on theoretical effectiveness which implies usage without error or omission on patient's part. It differs from clinical or use-effectiveness of a method which takes carelessness, ambivalence and other vagaries into account. Methods listed in descending order of estimated usefulness. Failure Rate = Number of pregnancies per 100 women per year of use.

Most Effective Methods.

Failure rate from 0.06; generally less than 1.0

Tubal Ligation (Pomeroy method)
Combined type oral contraceptive (if 1 pill missed: failure rate rises to 1.0)
Vasectomy
Sequential-type oral contraceptive
Temperature rhythm (postovulatory coitus only)
Tubal ligation (Madlener Method)
Oral progestational agents

Highly Effective Methods.

Estimated failure rate from 1.0 to 3.0. IUD failure rate drops to almost 1/3 after 2 years of use

Lippes-Shell loop-IUD
Copper-T IUD
Dalkon I.R. Shield
Large Spiral-IUD
Minipill (type not in use in U.S. at present)
Diaphragm with jelly or cream
Condom
Lippes Loop D-IUD
Double Coil-IUD
Lippes Loop C-IUD

Less Effective Methods.

Failure rate generally above 3.0

Chemical spermicidal agents (foam prob. best)
Temperature rhythm (postmenstrual coitus permitted)
Calendar rhythm
Coitus interruptus

Least Effective Methods.

Failure rate undetermined

Douche
Breast feeding

continence by practicing Catholic couples is no rarity when their rhythm schedule has been thrown off by an irregular ovulation or a faulted indicator.

Rhythm Method

(Periodic continence. Temporary abstinence. Natural child spacing. Vernac. safe period)

This method, the only one countenanced by the Roman Catholic Church, requires that the couple abstain from intercourse on those days on which conception is believed physiologically possible. It halts the input of spermatozoa into the female tract enough days ahead of the estimated ovulation day to be sure that no live sperms are present in the female tract on that day; and postpones the input of new spermatozoa for enough days after ovulation to assure that the ovum is then no longer fertilizable. The interval between the last day from which any sperm might survive to meet the ovum and the first day when fresh sperm will no longer meet a fertilizable ovum constitutes the fertile or "unsafe" period. In the basic 28-day cycle this would, for instance, run from day 10 to day 17, keeping in mind that by general convention day 1 is the first day of menstruation. This must then be extended at both ends to allow for the normal variability of the menstrual pattern. The remainder of time, which includes the menses, constitutes the infertile or "safe" period.

Rhythm is based on the assumption that ovulation in humans usually occurs only once during each cycle, and on the fact that conception can take place only for a short period after the ovum's release from the ovary. The fertilizable span of the human ovum is probably not more than 24 hours following extrusion, after which it begins to degenerate. Human spermatozoa are believed to retain their fertilizing capacity in vivo for no more than 48, exceptionally 72 hours (see also p. 220), although viable spermatozoa have on occasions been found in the female tract up to a few weeks after they had been immitted.

The main problem is menstrual irregularity. The 28 day or "perfectly regular" cycle has turned out to be a myth. In fact, only about 30 per cent of all women have menstrual cycles which are sufficiently regular for calendar rhythm, and most observers now agree that the method is not advisable if the range between the longest and the shortest cycles in a 12-month period exceeds 8 days. Cycles tend to be most regular in women between the ages of 25 and 39; before and after that they become progressively unpatterned. Long-term users of calendar rhythm do better if they re-evaluate their cycle pattern every 5 years. Efforts to control occurrence of ovulation and thus the regularity of the cycle (e.g., the clomiphene method) have not been widely practicable to-date.

However, rhythm counseling has changed somewhat. Temperature rhythm (basal body temperature charting, BBT), although not really precise itself, is supplanting calendar rhythm wherever feasible. With this has come the newer, more rigorous emphasis on the postovulatory (luteal) days as the only absolutely safe phase which, of course, restricts coital opportunities even more. The safe phase begins 72 hours after the temperature rise and generally ends as menstruation ends: the temperature graph cannot predict the next ovulation. In fact, no existing practical method can reliably predict ovulation, although a 72-hour advance warning would be all that is needed. If postmenstrual abstinence is too onerous, the shortest cycle in the preceding 12 months minus 18 days may be used to predict the first unsafe day (Ogino formula), with correspondingly slightly higher risk. In cases where pregnancy must be avoided, abstinence begins when menstruation begins.

Rhythm can offer satisfactory protection to highly motivated couples, carefully selected as regards menstrual pattern and intelligence, and thoroughly instructed in the use of their particular ovulation-indicator technique and its shortcomings (Rock, Poliakoff, others). In well-chosen and well-taught cases couples have done very well on rhythm, without experiencing a diminution of mutual affection, as both spouses sacrifice something to live up to what they expect of each other. Obversely, the method, especially the newer restrictive modality, tends to center sexual attention on the satisfaction of biologic urges and reduces the spontaneity of sexual expression; it calls for marital lovemaking by bookkeeping, by what is due and what is owing; it can make male acceptance grudging and the female stance either defensive or anxiously watchful, aggravating any pre-existing disharmony in the marriage. More recently another worrisome problem has been emerging: a relatively higher incidence of birth defects in accidental rhythm babies. As intercourse takes place further removed from the time of ovulation, and as fertilization occurs at an abnormally late stage of the cycle, either ovum or sperm—depending on whether the faulted act was pre- or postovulatory—may be past their prime and contain a deteriorated chromosome. Conditions such as mongolism (see also p. 198) or anencephaly can result. The strict postovulatory method based on basal body temperature charting would presumably avoid this; unfortunately it is not a suitable indicator-method for every woman relying on rhythm.

INTRAUTERINE DEVICES
(IUD, IUCD)

Modern intrauterine devices are chiefly made of plastic material and shaped as coils, loops, spirals, and shields; closed bows and rings have proven more risky. By and large they are safe and convenient, and have a high rate of effectiveness. The principal side-effects are cramps and bleeding. Using sterile technique the device, which often comes sterilely prepackaged, is placed high in the fundus while stretched or compressed by a special inserter; it then reassumes its original shape. A tail of soft thread emerges into the vagina to help keep track of the device. Spontaneous expulsion, usually early, can occur. Insertion is easiest during menstruation when the cervix is patulous; it is preceded by palpation and sounding. Uterine perforations which can occasionally occur at this time tend to remain asymptomatic unless a bowel loop knuckles through a closed-type IUD and becomes strangulated.

Only fairly recently has it been feasible to fit nulliparous women, including teen-agers, successfully, employing the smaller, lighter, more flexible shield devices (e.g., Dalkon shield), and using a paracervical block for the fitting. Supplementing IUD with foam during midcycle has made security absolute for the nulligravida. Aborting women can be fitted at the time of abortion; postpartum insertion is variably preferred 3 to 8 weeks after childbirth. Large fibroids, unexplained bleeding, recent infection and congenital uterine defects exclude use of the IUD. Complications diminish with growing age (36+), and with parity (3+ children) in younger women. Older women have the highest rate of protection from pregnancy.

The device exerts no significant carcinogenic effect nor causes any tissue damage in humans, from present evidence. If it is well tolerated it need not be removed at all during the reproductive years, although some physicians prefer removal every 5 years or so, and then insert a new one after waiting one cycle. The device does not affect the normal menstrual cycle. Where the device produces a heavy menstrual flow, supplemental iron administration may be desirable. When pregnancy occurs with the IUD in situ, it has not been known to interfere with the fetus and usually is expelled at birth with the placenta. After planned removal pregnancy occurs fairly promptly as a rule: in a cohort of 611 IUD-wearers desirous of pregnancy 1 woman in 3 conceived during the first month; almost 9 out of 10 had conceived within one year after removal. Sexual intercourse is interfered with only occasionally by devices with a long or unwieldy tail protruding from the cervix.

The device acts as a gigantic antigen attracting masses of phagocytes to the endometrial surface within hours of its insertion. The inflammatory response is a sterile one, once the brief initial inserting-bout of bacterial infection is overcome. The actual mode of contraceptive action remains incompletely understood, although there is no dearth of theories. However, it is a true contraceptive response, not a miniature abortion, as it takes place before a fertilized ovum is nidating.

HORMONAL METHODS

Oral Contraceptives
(The pill)

Mode of Action. In this method synthetic female hormones, taken orally, are used to disrupt the ovulation process and otherwise interfere with conception. If taken faithfully, the pills are a highly efficient and practical avenue to the temporary control of fertility. The classical oral contraceptives are basically ovulation suppressants, although they seem to produce so many other antifertility effects that non-ovulation is not always required: they are also capable of rendering the cervical mucus thick and sperm-hostile, they interfere with the capacitation of the spermatozoa, probably disrupt ovum transport before or after fertilization, and the combined type, after lengthy use, may render the endometrium unfit for innidation of any fertilized ovum reaching it. The exact nature of the ovulostatic mechanism is uncertain: suppression of one or both gonadotropic hormones in the anterior pituitary via feedback effect from the high level of circulating exogenous estrogen is a plausible assumption, and/or there may be a direct effect at the ovarian level, and a leveling of the mid-cycle plasma LH surge which normally evokes ovulation.

Composition. More than 20 varieties of the pill, most in calendared or numbered cycle packs, are available in the U.S. Each differs in the dosage and type of the two component hormones, although only 2 types of synthetic estrogen are being used: ethinyl estradiol, and its weaker-by-half precursor, mestranol. Milligram for milligram, the estrogenic potency of ethinyl estradiol is 60 to 75 times as high as that of conjugated equine estrogens (e.g., Premarin), and it differs from them physiologically. However, of the orally active progestational substances a wide variety are in use; they are either derivatives of testosterone or substituted progesterones. Almost all are chemically synthetized from diosgenin which is extracted from the tubers of the tropical yam, mostly in Mexico. Some are more androgenic in effect than others (e.g., while norethindrone and norethindrone acetate may masculinize an accidentally conceived female fetus, norethynodrel, dimethisterone or medroxyprogesterone acetate will not). See also p. 364.

Prescribing. Apart from the new minipill (daily, uninterrupted low-dose oral progestin, without estrogen added) and the long(months)-acting injectable medroxyprogesterone acetate (Depo-Provera), two principal prescription regimens exist: combined pills and sequentials. In the combined method 20 or 21 daily estrogen-progestin pills are taken; 2 to 3 days after the last pill withdrawal bleeding usually begins ("day 1"); on day 5 a new pill cycle is started. The sequentials consist of 15 or 16 high-dose estrogen tablets followed by 5 tablets containing estrogen and progestin. Simplified methods exist such as 21 days on, 7 days off combined pills, regardless of bleeding; or uninterrupted cycles of 28 numbered, look-alike pills, some of them inert. Continuous daily ingestion of a combined-type pill for 2 cycles, to avoid vaginal bleeding during the honeymoon, is believed harmless. Continuous pill-taking for many cycles, imposed on some prostitutes by their procurers to eliminate profitless periods, must be considered gynecologically harmful.

The combined pills are the more widely used. They give better protection against pregnancy and seem to have a lower use-interruption rate. One or 2 forgot-to-take episodes can more often be made up with them. The withdrawal bleedings (pseudomenses) are scantier. Some women on the combined pill are subject to the oversuppression syndrome (i.e., prolonged—more than 6 or 12 months—secondary amenorrhea after discontinuing the hormonal contraception). The sequential tablets are more physiological in use, better tolerated, but less safe in their protection against pregnancy which depends entirely on their relatively high estrogen content. They are less likely to induce such progesterone-excess manifestations as heightened monoamine oxidase activity in the endometrium and other histochemical enzyme system changes, as well as such symptoms as depression (disputed), diminished sexual responsiveness, tiredness, or appetite and weight gains. The progestins have been added to the sequential formulation partly for psychologic reasons—to simulate the monthly bleeding pattern whose absence would vaguely worry most women —and partly to avoid constant unbalanced high-dose estrogen stimulation of the breasts and of the endometrium without a chance to cleanse itself periodically by shedding overgrowth.

Choice. Most pills are either androgenic or estrogenic in effect. This consideration may enter into their selection for a patient. The tall thin girl, or the large-breasted woman with a history of premenstrual breast soreness and bloating, with much nausea throughout her pregnancies who is probably estrogen sensitive, needs a low-estrogen pill with an androgenically more active progestin (e.g., Ortho-Novum 2, Norinyl) (Kistner). The chunky girl, perhaps Mediterranean in appearance, with a tendency to acne and hirsuteness, needs a high-estrogen formulation with the least possible androgenicity (e.g., Oracon, perhaps Provest or Enovid).

Usage. Below age 16 or 17, or until ovulatory cycles are firmly established, the use of contraceptive pills is not indicated. In later adolescence sequentials are preferred, but even more acceptable may turn out to be the minipill which is believed not to affect ovulation. Experienced observers advise to interrupt pill cycles every 6 to 30 months in very young women and allow 1 or 2 spontaneous cycles. The nullipara, her fertility as yet unproven, should also interrupt from time to time. The pill is unsuitable for nursing mothers, but others may be safely started on it at any time postpartum. Couples ready to begin procreation after several years on the pill should change to another contraceptive method several months before that time to reduce the potentially long, vexing post-pill amenorrhea ("University syndrome"). In the premenopausal years with the greater potential need for unopposed estrogen, use of the sequential pills has been advised. The steady use of oral contraceptives will, of course, mask the onset of the climacteric, although there appears to be no harm in this. In all women, on any type of pill, vaginal yeast infections (Candida, p. 255) occur more frequently. The ascendancy of oral contraceptives may have added to the soaring VD rate, as the use of the condom and diaphragm, now declining, provided a certain amount of antivenereal protection (Fiumara). No evidence has been found that use of the pill increases the susceptibility of the vaginal mucosa to gonococcal infection.

Pill and Libido. In most pill users the marital vita sexualis has bene-fited from the obvious gain in erotic spontaneity, and both spouses enjoy sexual relations more. Moderate diminution of sexual interest occurs quite noticeably in some women, most so with a postulated non-androgenic high-progestin, low-estrogen agent—a theoretic combination not on the market—or any agent coming close to this, and more so in women with a labile sex response; libido returns promptly when changing the type of pill or using another contraceptive method. The issue has been obscured by seemingly inexpert question-posing in some patient surveys and by disregarding the underlying mechanism: progestational substances, like the progestational phase of the normal cycle, tend to impede sexual re-sponse progression in women not firmly locked into an affectionately motivated, erotic stimulus-response conditioning system. Such inability to feel pleasure leads, sooner or later, to a degree of sexual anhedonia—apathy, diminished libidinal interest—which in turn translates itself easily into a lessening of the occasions on which sex activity is sought or even granted (see also p. 403). The pills are also reported to alter the quality of the sexual climax in some women. Depression, irritability and lethargy which some progestins seem to induce in a number of women can of their own contribute to sexual disinterest.

Psychology. It has been observed in a number of newly pill-protected marriages that husbands malreacted to their wives' newfound sense of freedom and spontaneity. Some men had never had much sexual interest in their spouses and had played an "avoidance game" largely centered on true or fancied conception problems. Now challenged and faced with clear erotic demands, some men have felt exposed, attacked, defenseless and generally put upon, and reacted with relative sexual impotence. Others, their defenses similarly exposed, have reacted paranoidally, ac-cusing the newly zestful spouse groundlessly of unfaithfulness or even promiscuity. Some husbands of women on pills have felt threatened in their masculine prerogative as control of fertility was taken entirely out of their hands. A deeply felt sense of loss of masculine identity validation—a growing phenomenon in marriages today and not limited to the pill—has led to major marital discord; also to partial withdrawal of masculine affect and its channeling into self-centered orgasmic preoccupation; or even to "servicer's panic."

Postcoital Estrogens

(Interceptive treatment. Vernac. morning-after pill)

This method, which has become fairly well established, is administered to the woman for emergency purposes only (i.e., where pregnancy is distinctly undesirable following inadequately protected sexual exposure, notably in midcycle). Rape, contraceptive method- or use-failure, and single impulsive sex acts are the chief indications. City emergency departments, store-front-type clinics, college health services and private gynecologists and practitioners are the principal providers. See also Forcible Intercourse (Rape), p. 268.

Oral medication must be started not later than 72 (some say 48) hours after intercourse. All estrogens seem to be usable. Often used regimens: Stilbestrol 25 mg (some use 50 mg) b.i.d. for 5 days (some: 8 to 10 days), each dose, if necessary, preceded by 1 to 3 hours by an antinauseant-antiemetic; ethinyl estradiol (e.g., Estinyl) 1 mg b.i.d. (some use up to 5 mg a day) for 5 days; conjugated estrogens (e.g., Premarin) 5 mg t.i.d. for 4 days. For late-reporters (latest: approx. 100 hours post coitum): Premarin 20 mg intravenously, repeated once next day. Clinics may supply a few extra tablets of stilbestrol in case of untimely vomiting, a frequent side-effect (Morris, Kuchera, others).

In theory, only midcycle exposure makes the treatment rational, but practical considerations make it seem wiser to disregard cycle timing and treat all exposed patients of childbearing age, except in case of spontaneously supravening "hallelujah menses." The method seems to work in that the change in hormone balance causes any ovum, fertilized or not, to be flushed prematurely out of its fallopian tube, before the endometrium is ready to receive a zygote, or by interfering with nidation directly (theories). Massive estrinization will not cause a firmly established pregnancy to be aborted, even if only a few days old (i.e., the method is not an abortifacient). Cautions have been posted for women with previous blood clotting difficulties, possibly migraine, and for liver disease (cirrhosis, acute hepatitis) which may interfere with the estrogen-metabolizing function of this organ. It would be safer to have emergency stilbestrol preceded by a rapid pregnancy test, because the daughters of some stilbestrol-treated pregnant women have developed vaginal cancer after adolescence; some authorities doubt if the above dosage would suffice to induce this. Women have been known to ask for, and receive, several applications of the postcoital estrogen method in fairly short order, without ill effects, but the safety of repeated use is not established.

PERMANENT METHODS

Tubal Sterilization
(Tubal ligation)

Surgical sterilization in the woman aims at destroying reproductive function by depriving the ova of access to the uterus, most often by interrupting the continuity of the fallopian tubes. In some states voluntary sterilization is subject to specific laws; in others the procedure is not regulated by name, although such common-law and public policy concepts as mayhem (maim) and battery are ever-present. However, surgical sterilization has been gaining favor rapidly of late, outdistancing the barrier and chemical methods of contraception.

Rules. However, independent medical and administrative staff policies continue in force in the majority of hospitals and clinics where such surgery is to be performed. Clinical individualization is also important. Ideally, the salient aspects of the woman's health, her personality, reproductive history and the couple's marital stability and expectations should be considered preoperatively. Some boards require that the marriage certificate be viewed, and the birth certificates of the children be exhibited. A formerly common formula for approval required that the woman's age multiplied by the number of healthy, living children at the time of surgery must be greater than 100 (others: 120), or else that she have had 2 to 4 caesarean deliveries. Such age-parity formulas denied sterilization to nulliparas, and to most women with only 1 or 2 children. Fixed rules of prior consultative approval often exist, including psychiatric consultation in some of the more enlightened institutions (to briefly probe motives and to rule out mental depression and paranoia). Both spouses must affirm their informed consent in writing, the husband's joinder serving to exclude any future claim that his presumed interest in the fertility of his wife had been disregarded. In cases of divorce or the husband's predecease, potential future husbands have objected to marrying a sterile wife which has caused serious upheavals in some cases.

Technique. All tubal procedures are performed bilaterally, through a single abdominal incision, or transvaginally, within several days of childbirth, following abortion, at caesarean birth, or at other times. The vaginal route is unsuitable if there was previous abdominal surgery. Among the most often used is still the Pomeroy procedure: a loop of tube is tied off with catgut and excised; as the ligature is absorbed, the severed ends retract and separate. It has a high fail rate if done at time of caesarean birth and transvaginally post abortum. In the Madlener technique a loop of tube is crushed and tied off with nonabsorbable suture; there is no excision. The fail rate is fairly high, often due to recanalization via a fistula. In the Irving method the tubes are cut less than 1 inch from the cornual end; the distal portion is buried between layers of the broad ligament, while the proximal cut is sutured deeply into the uterine muscles to forestall formation of a false ostium. The procedure is more difficult and time-consuming than most, but is often preferred with caesarean delivery. Sometimes preferred is the laparoscopic—less often the vaginal culdoscopic—approach ("band-aid surgery"); in laparoscopy electrocauterization and excision are done through the instrument, following inflation of the abdominal cavity with about 2 quarts of carbon dioxide. Recovery is fairly rapid, the scar is small, but the operative risk has been reported as not negligible. Less often used at present are methods such as cornual resection (i.e., excision of the corners of the uterus containing the interstitial portions of the tubes); total salpingectomy; subserosal injections following dissection; or the newer ovariotexy: encasing the ovaries in plastic pouches and burying them in the broad ligaments away from the tubes. Occlusion of the tubes by sclerosing chemicals or by plugs remain experimental methods at present.

Reversal of tubal sterilization cannot be achieved with certainty in spite of the observation that the fallopian tubes appear to have a remarkable capacity to recanalize following physical insult. Although the chances of undoing such surgery by another, reconstructive, operation have improved in recent years—with claims of up to 35 per cent, even 50 per cent, of success—this cannot be promised to a patient and sterilization should probably continue to be held out in each case to the couple as being a definitive procedure. The various types of tuboplastic procedures may succeed in reconstructing tubal patency, but just as in vasectomy of the male this is a far cry from the rate of actual successful pregnancies. In cases of successful reversal a high rate of ectopic pregnancies has been observed.

Libido. The general effects of tubal sterilization do not appear to be remarkable. There are no hormonal alterations or changes in the secondary sex characteristics. Menstruations continue, and in the majority of tuboligated women libido and sexual responsiveness are about the same as preoperatively; in a minority it is heightened, probably due to eradication of apprehensions surrounding conceiving; in another minority group it is lowered, presumably due to anhedonia (see p. 402) in connection with an impairment of the feminine self-image or a sense of guilt or shame.

Simple Hysterectomy

A case for hysterectomy for the purpose of sterilization, in the absence of major pelvic problems, has not been proved, and in women under 30 the procedure is not defensible. The long-term psychologic results of hysterectomy, even without castration, are notoriously bad (see below), but the method continues to be employed and advocated (e.g., "after the last planned pregnancy," says Wright, "the uterus becomes a useless, bleeding, symptom-producing, potentially cancer-bearing organ and should therefore be removed."). Physicians desiring to sterilize a woman for maternal health protection with conventional methods, have had to face existing restrictive rules of hospital governing bodies even where such an indication is permissible by law; often they have found it easier to rationalize a simple hysterectomy on minor pelvic grounds—myoma, moderate cervical dysplasia or such—rather than battle for tubal sterilization. Catholic patients, forbidden tubal ligation, have often pressed for hysterectomy on whatever grounds their physician was able to detect. The classic arguments for elective hysterectomy include the almost absolute contraceptive security; prevention of uterine cancer; and prevention of future pelvic surgery such as is necessary in about 1 tuboligated patient out of 7.

Ill Effects. All women seem to experience hysterectomy as a femininity-threatening event, a profound loss experience, consciously or otherwise (Drellich-Bieber, Hollender, Melody, Wolff, others). This is not related to age, nor to further childbearing which often is not even desired, nor to the number of pregnable years left, although higher parity seems to be a mitigating factor. Psychiatrically hysterectomy is better tolerated when it is a stringent gynecologic necessity than when it is elective-voluntary. The majority of women cope, and within 6 or 12 months are fully re-established. However, a very substantial minority become psychiatrically ill, most often with psychosomatic invalidism and stubborn depressions. Usually not before about 2 years have elapsed does the turmoil become clinically overt, although a skilled observer can often pick it up earlier. Among 45 women with elective hysterectomy 48.8 per cent had psychiatric complications, while in a control group of 41 cholecystectomized women of similar age, parity and ethnic origin only 16.2 per cent did (Steiner-Aleksandrovicz). In a series of 729 hysterectomized and 280 cholecystectomized control patients the rate of psychiatric referral within a 4½-year mean postoperative period was 2½ times higher for the former (Barker). In a series of 190 surgically sterilized women, divided into 3 groups, most of the hysterectomized patients were encountered in the group with the worst psychiatric end results (Barglow). Nor does the physical risk of such surgery appear readily acceptable. In a series of 2,060 sterilizations, operative complications following elective vaginal hysterectomy were 11 times as frequent as after elective abdominal tubal ligation (Hibbard). Caesarean hysterectomy performed only for sterilization is beset by substantial operative morbidity (O'Leary, Pletsch, Pritchard, Ward).

Libido is not significantly affected by simple hysterectomy, and the quality of the postsurgical vita sexualis can often be predicted from the preoperative sexual adjustment, although it takes more than a questionnaire or a few casual queries to obtain a true picture. The mate's emotional support following surgery is important here in most marriages. When enhanced sexual responsiveness is reported, as it occasionally is, this is probably related to the freedom from worry about impregnation, or else due to the coincidental surgical correction of a dyspareunic focus. Diminution of libido, where present, is usually due to sexual anhedonia (p. 402) in the wake of the insidious psychiatric disturbances, notably the depressive syndrome. Generally, the woman with simple hysterectomy seems to retain normal hormonal functioning; unlike in some animals, no alteration of corpus luteum function takes place. But not infrequently the absence of menstruations and consciousness of her diminished gynecic status make at least some of these patients feel vaguely barren, incomplete as women and undesirable, and there may be an earlier-than-usual turning away from an active vita sexualis. Tubal pregnancies have in rare cases occurred following simple hysterectomy due to a vagino-tubal fistula; in other cases innidation of a viable blastocyst, either tubal or in a surgically spared lower uterine segment, had occurred preoperatively (Hanes).

Vasectomy
(Male surgical sterilization)

Bilateral vasectomy as a means of permanent birth control is becoming increasingly accepted; in fact, it is spreading with the speed of a bandwagon phenomenon. Sterilization is effected by interrupting the vas deferens on each side, thus preventing spermatozoa from being present in the ejaculate. This is not a desexing operation. Testicular androgen production is not affected, although this has lately been questioned on the basis of animal experiments. Clinically, secondary sex characteristics—penis, beard, voice, etc.—remain unchanged as do, in the great majority of men, sex drive, erection and ability to ejaculate with orgasm. The ejaculate, except for azoospermia, is probably not changed. A number of minor physiologic and biochemical changes have been noted postoperatively, with unknown significance.

Procedure. Vasectomy most often is an office procedure under local anesthesia. The vasa are ligated and cut in the scrotum through 2 separate or a midline incision, with or without resection, fulgurization of cut ends or interposing of fascia. Special methods, not all successful, include tantalum (Weck's) clips, nonabsorbent intravasal nylon thread or other material for occlusion, or insertion of intravasal turn-on-off microvalves. Minor local complications (e.g., infection or congestive epididymitis) can occur. The operation is more difficult with prior hernia or hydrocele surgery. Postoperative discomfort is minor. Closing sutures are not always used, and a scar is not always detectable on the rugose scrotal skin. The most frequent errors calling for reoperation are sectioning of the same vas twice, and of a spermatic blood vessel.

Effectiveness. The operation is not immediately effective. Spermatozoa remaining in the seminal vesicles and other parts of the excurrent ducts distal to the interruption are eliminated only slowly. This appears to be both a matter of elapsed time and the number of ejaculations; opinions based on observations here remain in flux. Sperm clearance, which is more rapid in younger patients, may be accomplished after as few as 4 or as many as 35 ejaculations, and may take from 4 weeks to 4 months. One, preferably two specimens should be azoospermic before the patient may abandon other contraceptive methods. Search for semen includes 50 consecutive low power microscopic fields of seminal smear followed by centrifuging of specimen at 2000 g for 10 minutes, and fixing and staining a smear from the pellet (Davis-Freund) for further microscopy. In an estimated 2 to 10 per cent of cases motile spermatozoa make a usually transient (for up to 4 months) reappearance, presumably via spontaneous recanalization through local granulomatosis (Bunge); it has led to occasional paternity disputes. Six-monthly reexaminations for 1 or 2 years have been an advisable practice. A late, even years later, complication in 4 per cent of cases (Schmidt) is spermatic granuloma of the epididymis, a tumor-like infiltrate caused by blocked and transmigrated spermatozoa; it comes to notice as a local aching sensation.

Case Selection. The law almost everywhere today interposes no obstacles to vasectomy. Public policy towards male sterilization has shifted radically in the last 10 years. There have been no further judicial determinations calling sterilization an immoral contract or classing it as a form of mayhem. Major insurance carriers and some public welfare programs recognize contraceptive vasectomies as a reimbursable medical health service. However, the physician must take care. Apart from the ever-present breach of contract allegations, some individuals—probably more than had previously been thought—are a poor psychologic risk for this operation and are best excluded by screening, although this, too, appears to be more difficult than had previously been thought. Ideally there should be a stable family unit with children (disputed); both spouses to give informed consent in writing after a personal interview with the operating physician; they accept one or two group counseling sessions and, if indicated, psychiatric consultation; there is a cooling-off or waiting period of 2 (some say 5) weeks, and full acceptance of the no-guarantee, no-reversal reality.

Vasectomy on demand, with no or minimal screening, has been reported by some practitioners and clinics and they were satisfied with their results. However, it does not seem like a good idea. The operation has been equated with abortion, which is unjustified because the latter does not involve permanent destruction of a biologic function. Nor is the physician, as a small radicalized minority will have it, merely a technician serving the unguided will of the people. Today's physician is justified in turning down for vasectomy some of those requesting his services: certainly all teen-agers, single or married; the obviously frivolous; men dragged in by their wives and couples trying to salvage a marriage; men with labile sexual potency; and men who are obviously mentally depressed. On the other hand, being psychotic or an alcoholic or an addict is not by itself a contraindication, as long as competence and ability to make rational decisions can be certified. For the mentally retarded, see p. 199.

Libido. Malreactions. The man with normal libido who is well motivated, who does not fear for his masculinity and who understands the difference between castration and sterilization, retains his libido and his potency; occasionally—unencumbered by devices or precautions, no longer worried about impregnation—he finds it improved. Some go on extramarital sprees ("vasectomy backlash"), perhaps wanting to ward off an uncomfortable feeling that they are no longer real men; perhaps like children trying out a new toy; even rapists have turned up trying to reassure their victims that way. Wives also have gone on promiscuous sprees, or have held sterility over the husband's head as a club ("he has more to lose if we separate"). Worst affected appear to be young married men whose father is a domineering figure opposed to vasectomy, perhaps desirous of grandchildren. Unfortunately, only some of these psychologic malreactions were or would have been predicted on routine screening. By and large, vasectomy is not as entirely free of psychologic and, less often, psychosexual complications for either the patient or his spouse as could be wished, but not as hazardous as some might fear (Ziegler, Lear, others).

Restoration of fertility by surgery is an uncertain undertaking. Possibly, a man asking for reversal surgery should not have been sterilized in the first place. With meticulous vasovasostomy motile sperm reappears in the ejaculate in 60 to 80 per cent of cases, less often with other techniques. However, it is generally agreed that only 20 to 30 per cent of re-operated men can impregnate a woman. The shorter the time elapsed, and the further away from the testes the cuts, the better the chances. One explanation of reversal failure is that reabsorption of obstructed spermatozoa swamps the antibody-forming apparatus and that the body develops significant titers of circulating autoantibodies against its own spermatozoa, disabling them (Henry).

Storing Frozen Semen in one of the commercial cryobanking facilities available today in many large cities may be one way to help alleviate some of the apprehensions of the vasectomy patient, and perhaps of his surgeon.

Long-term observations on stored human semen are as yet sketchy, but there are some unreported cases of human conception after as long as 10 years of freeze preservation; at least 400 children have been born following artificial insemination with stored semen; and the oldest thawed-sperm baby now living and well was born in 1953. However, the viability of thawed spermatozoa appears to depend largely on the quality of the pre-freeze semen, and the genetic adequacy of thawed sperm remains to be established.

BARRIER METHODS

Condom

(Sheath; coitus condomatus, condomistic intercourse (derogat.). Vernac.
rubber, prophylactic or pro, safety or safe, protection, contraceptive,
French letter, etc. Special: skin)

In the U.S., unlike elsewhere, condoms have never been very popular as a customary method of contraception by married couples. Condom manufacture is under Federal Drug Administration supervision. The devices are sold, prerolled and packaged, in drugstores, etc. without prescription. Most are made from latex, a modified rubber compound; some are of nylon; and the most expensive ones ("skins") are made from the peritoneal mucosa covering the cecum of sheep or calves. Better-type latex condoms have an elastic rim to prevent slipping-off during coital thrusting. An increasing number are made with a receptacle for semen at the tip (teat-end, reservoir end, catch pocket). They are sold premoistened or prelubricated. Glans condoms (capot, male diaphragm) are held in the coronary sulcus by an elastic. Saran wrap as an emergency substitute is unsatisfactory and sometimes ends up lying crumpled deep in the vault.

Except in casual encounters or where they serve predominantly for antivenereal protection, condoms are acceptable to male users only if they do not produce major alterations of tactile sensation (i.e., mostly in relation to their thinness); the most expensive condoms have advantages in the more lifelike sensation they permit, but, generally, U.S.-made condoms, by Federal regulation, are exceedingly thick-walled (up to almost 1/10 mm). An adverse effect on female sensation is a frequent complaint; this is probably mostly psychological in that the interposing of foreign material between the genitalia produces the feeling of being deprived of a sense of immediacy and oneness. Objectionable to some is the need to interrupt coital preliminaries, although couples can be instructed to make placing of the device by the wife part of the erotic foreplay; in this way esthetic objections have also been overcome by some couples. However, the condom is not a suitable method for men with labile erective potency. A condom neurosis in worrisome and obsessive-compulsive men has been described (Caprio). Some individuals harbor prejudices such as, "condoms are for prostitutes, not for wives."

An ill-fitting, wrinkled or insufficiently lubricated sheath may irritate the female tract, especially if intercourse is protracted or includes re-insertions which allow moisture to evaporate more quickly. Condoms should be lubricated on the outside with a water-soluble jelly (see p. 207), of contraceptive type if desired, but not on the inside. Petroleum base lubricants (petrolatum, cold cream, mineral oil) attack rubber compounds, sometimes within minutes, and can cause breaks. The female fingernails have been known to cause breaks. If a tear is discovered postcoitally, insertion of contraceptive jelly is called for. Pretesting of condoms by water-ballooning or cigarette smoke for pinhole defects is no longer thought necessary in U.S.-manufactured devices because of good quality control. In placing a condom without a catch pocket, a half-inch should be left detached at the tip to harbor the semen and avoid strip-out during orgasmic thrusts. The sheathed phallus should be withdrawn before the erection is totally lost, and the upper rim should be held by the fingers. In the past condom vaginitis from talcum powder added by the manufacturer or preceding re-use has been observed at times. Powder particles enclosed in granulomatous tissue have been found in the abdominal cavity, carried there through the tubes and causing symptoms sufficiently severe to lead to surgery.

Vaginal Diaphragm
(antiqu. Occlusive, contraceptive pessary)

This was the first reliable method in modern times (Mensinga, 1882) allowing women to take responsibility for their own fecundity. The device, obtainable in drugstores by medical prescription, is a soft, round rubber membrane of cuplike or domed shape with a rim consisting of a compressible elastic wire coil or other spring. It lies diagonally across the vagina, partitioning off a segment which includes the tip of the cervix. It is wedged and held in place under the pubic symphysis at one end and in the posterior fornix at the other. During intercourse the anterior part hugs the anterior vaginal wall. Diaphragm alone is not considered optimal protection, and spermicidal jelly or the less lubricatory cream is now always added to the cervical side of the dome and spread on the rim.

The physician fits the largest size diaphragm which is comfortable for the woman; standard sizes range to 105 mm in diameter (average 70 to 80 mm). Special shapes and sizes are also made (e.g., in cases of mild cystocele or prolapse). The woman is also instructed in how to insert (pass in) the device, lubricated side up, by hand or by a simple mechanical inserter; anatomic models for demonstration are commercially available. Insertion takes an experienced woman only a few seconds. Women with an intractable block against manipulating their own genitalia should not be taught to use an inserter, as the risk of malinsertion is excessive here (Sobrero). The diaphragm can, but need not, be inserted 2 or 3 hours in advance, and must be left in place for at least 5 or 6, perhaps 8 hours (e.g., overnight) after intercourse, but may be left alone for a full day. A rinsing douche on removing may, but need not, be employed. Repeat coitus in the same night must be preceded by a new insertion of contraceptive jelly without removing the diaphragm, and indwelling time is counted from the last exposure. Maximum safe number of ejaculations per application is 3, some say 2; thus the method limits the number of sexual acts per encounter.

The most secure fit of the diaphragm is maintained in the traditional man-above coital position. Apart from the recently described physiologic unwedging of its inner end, under laboratory conditions, at the height of arousal, the risk of displacement is increased most by hasty re-insertion of the phallus during the act, in the woman-above-astride position, and possibly in a very wet or hyperlubricated vagina. A well-fitted diaphragm causes no discomfort to the woman nor, as a rule, to the man during the act. The method has been more acceptable—less readily discarded—to private practice patients than in birth control clinics, even when furnished free. The necessity to guess when and whether to insert, or else to inter-rupt preliminaries for the purpose, has deterred some women; slippery late-insertion through a congested vulva may discourage (Pierson). Others have accustomed themselves to pass in a diaphragm as part of their nightly bedtime routine. The method is considered to be well suited for occasional exposure (e.g., in the "week-end bride"). In the nullipara the device should be refitted every few years, also after each childbirth, after pelvic surgery, and after major weight gain or loss. Not fittable are patients with an intact or a recently deflorated hymen, with major overrelaxation of the vaginal walls, with major uterine prolapse or malpositions, with obstetric lacerations of the pelvic floor, and with chronic constipation.

Cervical Cap
(French pessary. Check pessary or vault cap. Vernacular: cap, cup)

This small device—in three sizes from 24 to 36 mm in diameter—has been popular mostly outside the U.S., although it is available here. It is shaped like a cap and is made of firm plastic (e.g., lucite) or rubber. It covers the cervix and is held in place partly by the narrow rim being wedged in the fornices and partly by suction, although the cervical os does not touch the dome. Hard plastic devices may be left in place from menstruation to menstruation; the rubber model is removed after 24 hours. Spermicidal jelly in the cup gives added protection for about a week; some women add a chlorophyll or other deodorant. The device is sold on prescription following pelvic examination which must rule out major cervical lacerations, cervicitis and pelvic inflammatory disease. Following instruction, self-insertion and self-removal are the rule, although some women prefer to have the physician re-apply the cap. The device is especially suitable with overrelaxed vaginal walls and in nursing mothers.

Various Vaginal Obstruents

Women, in desperation at an imminent and unavoidable exposure, have stuffed handkerchiefs, rags, stockings, panties, several menstrual tampons or whatnot into their vaginal recesses; sometimes so deeply that the cervical os must have remained accessible and pregnancy occurred. More rationally, various types of sponges, tampons or pads of nonabsorbent cotton or cotton wool can be placed in the vagina to act as barriers against insemination. They are usually soaked with greasy or oily substances, or medicated with a simple spermicidal agent. Foam-powder impregnated rubber sponges (foam sponges) have been much recommended: both the sponge and the foam released with each penile thrust in the presence of vaginal moisture act as mechanical barriers. These devices usually have a thread or tape attached for removal, or they may be enclosed in a crochet net for this purpose. Pads are usually recommended to be the size of a palm and the thickness of a thumb. This is considered the simplest, cheapest and most easily taught contraceptive method where large population groups are illiterate, or out of the reach of regular health services. The efficiency of these obstruents may depend on their content in spermicidal substance. Oversized pads may interfere with the sexual act and thus lead to sporadic nonuse; undersized ones may be displaced out of their cervix-blocking position during intercourse.

CHEMICAL SPERMICIDES

Almost all vaginally applied spermicidal (spermatocidal) and sperm-arresting substances now in use also are expected to exercise some mechanical barrier action against the penetration of sperm into the endocervix. This may be accomplished by virtue of their fatty, oily, foamy-viscid or gel base forming a film which covers vaginal walls and structures, including the os, or else because the material—sponge, cotton, etc.—on which some are introduced in the vagina act themselves as barriers. Other chemicals on contact with semen immobilize the sperm and arrest spermigration immediately, rather than rely on mechanical blocking action for part of their effect.

Spermicidal chemicals are introduced into the vagina in various forms: as aerosol-foam cream in special containers; by syringe-type applicator or collapsible nozzle-tipped tube (cream, jelly, gel); by insufflation (foam powder); as soluble, effervescent or foam-producing tablets; in melting suppository form; or as a powder or foaming liquid impregnated into a sponge or pad. Deposit by insertion is made as near as possible to the cervix, although the thrusting male organ is expected to agitate and disperse the substance throughout the posterior vagina. Spermicidal agents usually remain in the vagina in a state of effective precoital readiness anywhere from 30 minutes to 2 hours; introduction must be repeated before each successive sexual act. In the multiparous woman the use of 2 applicatorfuls of cream or foam has been advised, but excessive amounts lead to interference with the sex act.

Some preparations may drain or drip out of the vulvovaginal canal before, during or after intercourse, causing annoyance; others may lather excessively so that foam covers the perineum or even the upper thighs. Some foaming powders or tablets may not produce adequate amounts of foam in the absence of copious vaginal lubrication in the woman; others occasionally can cause itching and irritation. Not infrequently self-injected jellies are believed to end up in the posterior fornix, especially in uterine malpositions and where the woman is not altogether sure of the anatomic relationships inside the vagina; if ejaculation occurs rapidly, the phallus may not have had time to disperse the material sufficiently in the vagina and about the cervix. Not all tablets or suppositories dissolve uniformly. Accidental introduction of spermicidal materials into the uterus by nozzle or applicator is said to have occurred in the presence of extensive cervical tears. The use-effectiveness of the cream-alone or jelly-alone methods continues in dispute; most experienced observers appear to incline toward summative protection (e.g., diaphragm-cum-cream). An exception may be the aerosol foam method which, by wide agreement, is said to have given acceptable protective results by itself, if it is applied within 1 hour before intercourse and the nozzle is inserted deep enough. As a method of opportunity the use of a 10 per cent or stronger salt solution has been recommended; it can be soaked into a cloth or a cotton pad to be inserted vaginally. A homemade jelly can be prepared by heating and stirring together for 30 minutes 1 part of gelatin or flour (of rice, wheat, etc.) and 6 to 8 parts by weight of a 10 per cent or stronger salt water solution and allowing it to cool.

FOLK METHODS

Lactation. Where increased spacing of children is desired, couples in some parts of the world still rely on the supposed functional sterility of the nursing mother. The method which extends the overall duration of postpartum amenorrhea is of unpredictable value and, at any rate, limited: the first 6 weeks postpartum are nonfertile; breast-feeding extends this period to close to 3 months, provided no menstruation occurs. Although first postpartum menses are usually anovulatory, they are ovulatory often enough to let about 1 young mother in 20 start another pregnancy without having even menstruated (Tietze). It is not known if continued breast-feeding after menstruation has returned reduces the likelihood of conception. Lactation is a self-maintaining function via the suckling stimulus which elicits release of various hormones supporting the function, chiefly prolactin and ACTH from the anterior and oxytocin from the posterior pituitary, with participation of all other hormones.

Douche (Vaginal irrigation). Postcoital vaginal douching for contraceptive purposes is of uncertain value, even if a proper douching technic (p. 209) is employed. The principal source of failure is the fact that some semen passes into the endocervix in less than 2 minutes—often probably within seconds—after ejaculation. However, the douche eliminates the bulk of the aftercoming semen without which the front-running sperm's fertilizing capacity apparently is curtailed. Homemade solutions with relatively high antisperm effect include white vinegar, up to 8 tablespoons per quart of water or lemon juice, 2 tablespoons per quart. Not recommended are strong salt solutions; Lysol (½ teaspoon per quart) and bichloride of mercury (1:15,000) because of the danger of overdosing; and ice water, still used occasionally by prostitutes for both contraceptive and antimenstrual effect. Where douching apparatus is unavailable, a slightly acid carbonated beverage may be used from the bottle; or else manual soap-washing of the vaults and the fornices has been suggested as a fairly adequate substitute. The vaults are brought into reach of the fingers when the woman squats (e.g., in a bathtub) and exerts straining pressure downward. Water is an efficient spermicidal agent by itself.

Posterior Urethral Compression (Coitus obstructus or Saxonius). At the onset of the man's orgasm the wife exerts sharp digital pressure on his perineum over the posterior urethra, thus preventing forward ejaculation. Retrograde ejaculation occurs, similar to what is observed sometimes after transurethral resection of the prostate. Later the semen is expelled with voiding. The practice was said to be exceedingly painful for the uninitiated, but some kind of conditioning may take place.

Coitus Reservatus (Coitus Reservans, Male Continence, Karezza, Oneida Method, Zugassant). This consists of a prolonged (2 to 3 hours or longer) sexual act performed in a very gentle, slow, nearly motionless manner; eventually the man's erection is expected to subside without orgasm having taken place. The woman may have an unlimited number of orgasms or may also elect to forego climax. The method, which has to be learned, was first practiced in the United States by a small colony founded by idealistic individuals in the last century. Their experiment was religious, social and eugenic and for a time included a form of obligatory polygamy which aimed at optimal selection of parents of the communal offspring. Intercourse, probably with frequent change of partners, took

place at least twice a week, and the total effect on health, psychic contentment, social functioning and quality of the offspring were at that time
medically certified to have been excellent.

Vaginal Extrusion. The women in some European and other farm
populations reportedly extrude a mucous mass from the vagina after
intercourse if they do not wish to conceive. This mass is presumed to be
an admixture of cervical mucus and ejaculum. Extrusion is effected in the
standing or squatting position by means of down-bearing pressure, coughing, induced sneezing and shaking of the pelvis, while the introitus is held
open by the fingers.

Coitus Interruptus (Withdrawal, Coitus Abruptus. Vernac. to pull out,
to come outside, to take care). The oldest known contraceptive procedure; already mentioned in the Bible (Genesis 38:9). The method consists of the man's withdrawing his organ completely from the vagina
shortly before he feels his climax coming on and ejaculating outside (e.g.,
aside, into a handkerchief, or on the woman's abdomen). Unsafe modalities
include emission on her vulva (ante portas), and semi-withdrawal away
from the os (copula dimidiata). Withdrawn ejaculation can be aided by
a few masturbatory stimuli if necessary. Coitus interruptus rarely is a
medically prescribed method, and its ever-availability, simplicity and
cheapness must be pitted against the dissatisfaction it tends to produce in
its users.

The method has shown up well in several effectiveness surveys—although one may quarrel with their methodology—but it has inherent
weaknesses which limit it to relatively few and selected couples for prolonged usage. The sources of momentary patient failure are ever-present:
the man's timing and control can be impaired by tiredness, reckless moods,
alcohol consumption, being high on marijuana, or simply being "carried
away" by a highly transported female partner. The method is unsuitable
for men who tend to ejaculate rapidly and, of course, in premature ejaculation
(p. 388); in older men whose first ejaculatory jet is devoid of distinct
sensation or whose perception of impending climax has become numbed;
in inexperienced teen-age males who have not yet acquired control; probably in most women with overrelaxed vaginal walls which tend to make
it more difficult for the man to ascertain the approach of his own ejaculation; and in grossly irresponsible, impulse-ridden men as well as those who
are chronically debilitated or feeble.

Although in many sexually vigorous and responsive couples with a
trustworthy husband acceptance by the wife seems to be no problem, for
most women withdrawal probably has little appeal. For them the act is
abbreviated, and phallic thrusts tend to become more hesitant and shallow
rather than impetuous and penetrating as the man feels his climax approaching. A man apprehensive of his control may allow an early orgasm
crescendo to build up to climax, whereas otherwise he may have repressed

it so as to prolong the act. The intense stimulation many women experience from sensing the man's approaching ejaculation is replaced by a vague sense of negative anticipation and futility—the sudden void in the midst of an elan (Flood)—related to foreknowledge of the spouse's withdrawal. If they feel they cannot trust the man's control or his motivation, some women are inhibited in their reactions, as they maintain an anxious, admonitory stance; some admit freely that they pretend early orgasm so as to make the man feel free to withdraw at the earliest possible moment. When a second sex act follows coitus interruptus, a faint possibility of insemination on insertion is to be considered, especially in younger men with copious urethrorrhea libidinosa (p. 173). At least some viable spermatozoa have been found in the anterior male urethra up to 1½ hours after ejaculation, but it is not probable that such a small number of residual sperms can effect fertilization. Urination would presumably eliminate this source of potential method failure.

The possible ill effects of long-practiced coitus interruptus remain a subject in dispute. Occasional practice has no noteworthy effect. Some men with labile potency tend to be sufficiently disquieted by the need for tense watchfulness during the act to experience at least transient loss of erection; but no cases of total absolute or relative impotence are clearly ascribable to the practice of withdrawal. However, there may be accelerated reduction of coital frequency in middle-aged couples relying chiefly on this method. Chronic vesiculoprostatitis occurs in men practicing frequent coitus interruptus, but a cause-effect relationship is difficult to prove. The woman seems often to be deprived by withdrawal, and clear instances of chronic pelvic congestion (p. 412) in those habitually exposed to it seem to be no rarity.

FOR JOURNAL LITERATURE AND ADDITIONAL READING

Bromley, D. D.: Catholics and Birth Control. Contemporary Views on Doctrine. New York, Devin-Adair, 1965

Calderone, M. (ed.): Manual of Family Planning and Contraceptive Practice. Ed. 2. Baltimore, Williams & Wilkins, 1970

Davis, H. J.: Intrauterine Devices for Contraception: The IUD. Baltimore, Williams & Wilkins, 1971

Feldman, D. M.: Birth Control in Jewish Law: Marital Relations, Contraception and Abortion as Set Forth in the Classic Texts of Jewish Law. New York, N.Y. Univ. Press (London, Univ. of London Press), 1968

Goldzieher, J. W. and Rice-Wray, E.: Oral Contraception: Mechanism and Management. Springfield, Ill., Thomas, 1966

Lorraine, J. A. and Bell, E. T.: Fertility and Contraception in the Human Female. Baltimore, Williams & Wilkins, 1968

Peel, J. and Potts, M.: Textbook of Contraceptive Practice. New York and London, Cambridge Univ. Press, 1969

Pincus, G.: The Control of Fertility. New York, Academic Press, 1965

Tunnadine, P.: Contraception and Sexual Life. Philadelphia, Lippincott, 1970

CHAPTER 15

Sexuality past Midlife

The Menopausal Woman — Male Middle Age — Advanced-age
Sexuality.

THE MENOPAUSAL WOMAN

*(Menopause—actually a misnomer as this is only a symptom. Climacteric,
Climacterium. Vernac. change of life, the change)*

Menopause marks the end of the reproductive—but not of the sexual—
life of the human female. Its dominant physiologic characteristic is the
failure and often atrophy of the ovaries, as their sensitivity to pituitary
stimulation fades and the supply of available oocytes nears exhaustion
and deteriorates in quality. The principal sign of menopausal ovarian
failure is the sharp reduction of available estrogen together with a dramatic
increase in the plasma gonadotropin (LH, FSH) levels and a relative
increase in ovarian testosterone. The principal symptom is the cessation
of the menstrual flow.

Age at Onset. The female reproductive system, unlike that of men,
starts its irreversible decline while the other systems are still largely in
their functional prime. Actual onset is difficult to determine. Ovulation,
for instance, normally begins to fail in the mid- to late 30's as more and
more anovulatory cycles are intermingled with regular periods. The
average menopause today occurs at close to 50 years of age and cessation
in the early 50's is no longer unusual. True premature menopause—onset
before age 35—is a fairly rare condition, but in about 4 per cent of women
menopause begins in the mid- or late 30's. By present consensus the functional life span of the ovaries is genetically predetermined, although environmental factors cannot be discounted in individual cases: onset may be
hastened by chronically poor health, chronic stress, poor hygiene, poor
nutrition, urban dwelling and/or strenuous work. The nullipara may
involute relatively earlier, as may the woman with a history of several
abortions. Late-maturers tend to have an early climacteric.

THE OVA

Unlike in the male, the woman's entire stock of oocytes is formed during her fetal life, with a high of about 7 million in existence between the fifteenth and twentieth week of gestation. When she is born she has an estimated 200,000 to 500,000 (other estimates run higher, still others lower) left, of which half are already undergoing atresia. At puberty still fewer remain. The reason for this early, progressive loss is unknown.

Once each month, during the 400 or 450 ovulatory cycles, 10 to 15 (range 2 to 30) follicles begin to enlarge and secrete estrogen; only 1 oocyte matures, becomes an ovum and is extruded, while the others go to waste after secreting estrogen for a couple of days. The theory that prolonged use of ovulation suppressants—the oral progestins—saves ova has not proved valid.

Cessation. Some ovaries cease their function abruptly, others more gradually over a period of years. As the ovarian steroids wane, the adrenal cortex somewhat increases its estrogen production. An estimated 20 to 30 per cent of postmature women produce significant amounts of estrogen even as late as in their 80's; and almost a quarter of all women continue to ovulate after menopause. However, the quantities of cycling steroids they produce are too small to stimulate endometrial changes and break-down bleeding, and what ova are produced probably are no longer fertilizable. The menstrual flow ceases abruptly in some cases, but more usually the pattern is prolonged and irregular. Intervals between menses become longer, and duration as well as amount of flow decrease in an irregular fashion. A very heavy ("flooding") flow at some periods is characteristic of menopause. After 1 year of cessation menses seldom recur; but in some cases pregnancy has recurred unexpectedly after several years of uninterrupted middle-aged amenorrhea. For possible ages at late pregnancy see box on p. 198.

Crisis Time. Not everything that is happening to the woman of 50 or 55 is the result of menopause. The menopause comes at a time of life when many problems arising from the life situation trouble the female. There is lessened attention from the husband who is now in his prime and at his busiest. The empty nest syndrome can become a critical factor; the new, exhilarating sense of freedom may shortly give way to a feeling of letdown, a sometimes irrational sense of being discarded. With her vitality no longer consumed by multiple daily problem-solving, even minor somatic symptoms tend to move into the center of awareness. Sometimes such symptoms persist unduly because they seem the only way to obtain concern from her loved ones. Fear of cancer, of recurrence of a previous emotional illness, perhaps problems of job security, disappointment in a child, or absence of interests or hobbies outside homemaking—all can magnify the burden which the middle-aged woman feels herself carrying.

Where a woman has long been unsure of her husband's faithfulness, diffidence and antagonism on her part seem to grow even without provocation, producing major tensions; this is the point where some such marriages fall apart.

Some single women facing the end of their reproductive potential, experience this with a naggingly regretful awareness almost akin to a sense of grieving, regardless of whether consciously they would have liked to conceive or not. However, of late, more and more nominal spinsters reaching the menopause seem to have discounted and rationalized their status many years in advance, and menopause is no unusual trauma to them. It remains perhaps more traumatic for some childless wives, especially if the husband's attitude in the critical few years can be faulted. Less frequent today seems to be the overburdened multipara who welcomes menopause as a relief from her own fertility, and the woman longing for the change of life to rid her of the monthly inconvenience.

Mortification and Libido. Not all women are equally able to tolerate the awareness that their youth is at an end, nor are they well prepared for the gradual desexualization of their emotional needs (Benedek). Not every woman is able to come to terms with the signs of physical decline—figure, skin, breast contour, features, etc.—without a nagging sense of mortification. The average married woman is bound to have at least some fear about losing her physical attractiveness to her husband. Distress tends to be more pronounced in strongly narcissistic women to whom erotic attractiveness was the main symbol of personal worth. Some women with a history of chronic sexual nonsatisfaction are seized by a sudden, agitating awareness that what they have missed soon they will no longer be able to recoup ("panic of the closing door"), leading some to juvenoid, pseudo-provocative behavior or to age-inappropriate dress and make-up, as the woman frantically overloads her image with cues signaling erotic interest and intent. Prostitution and rape fantasies, not unlike those of pubescence, reappear. Transient hyperlibidinal states, what used to be known as the acute idiopathic nymphomania of the involuting woman, may occasionally be truly appetitive due to the relative preponderance of circulating androgen over estrogen; but more often it is merely a hectic-anxious desire to make up for lost time. A woman feeling freed from worry about impregnation for the first time may relax and respond as never before. If menopause coincides with the children leaving the home, more opportunities for relaxed intercourse may exist.

Sex Life. Menopause exerts no major negative effect on libido directly. However, sexually, any midlife rocking of the boat is most successfully withstood by the woman whose sex life all along was both regular and satisfying. Much depends, of course, on the woman's general state of well-being. If depression impairs her zest for living, if frequent headaches, vasomotor crises, back pains or insomnia undermine her general vigor, less interest in sexual relations can be expected. Much also depends on the mate's interest at this time, on his erective potency, and especially on his willingness to be, now more than ever, affectionately demonstrative. Women who customarily multi-climax coitally, may now attain fewer orgasms, and these more slowly. Dyspareunia—itching, burning, some tenderness, postcoital dysuria—may be an early problem in some women; if it is due to estrogen deficiency—some such symptoms represent trichomoniasis or moniliasis—it responds well to topical and/or systemic estrogen therapy. Vaginal over-relaxation may also become an early problem and require treatment (p. 418). On the other hand, substantial dosing with exogenous estrogen, apart from the sometimes excessive vaginal mucification it produces, can interfere with sexual responsiveness: as it depresses the gonadotropin level by suppressive feedback the failing ovaries, in turn, receive less stimulation and thus produce less of the now prevailing testosterone, which acts as sensitizer of the external female genitalia.

Menopause Questions

When to expect it? Average age now close to 50; early 50s not unusual. Mother-daughter rule not generally applicable.

Lasts how long? Technically, for anywhere from 6 months to 3 years from cessation of flow. Symptoms, if any, may persist less long or longer, or even precede flow cessation.

Positive diagnosis possible? Presumptive diagnosis: 6 to 12 months amenorrhea in middle age; vasomotor crises for first time ever; high urinary gonadotropin level or plasma LH rise plus decline in superficial cells in vaginal maturation index. Vaginal cell index alone considered unreliable. Progesterone withdrawal bleeding test. Endometrial biopsy (D and C).

How to tell menopause if on pills? a) Stop at 48, use local method;

watch for 6 to 12 months' amenorrhea; b) don't stop until after 50, then switch to barrier method for several cycles; c) don't bother to stop and find out; early in the 50s use sequential pills or, after 53, any continuous estrogen with cyclic progestins added every 4 or 6 weeks. Methods such as c) are heavily disputed.

When to omit contraception safely? After 1 year (some say 6 months) of continuous middle-age amenorrhea menopause may be assumed to be fully established. Another rule of thumb: after 12 months of amenorrhea at 48; or 6 months at 50 and beyond. For more positive diagnosis see above.

How late possible to conceive? Pregnancy rare after 49 in U.S. Oldest authenticated present-day mothers of living children were aged 52 and 53. After age 47 80 per cent of pregnant primigravidae are expected to abort. See also p. 198.

What external body changes to expect? Changes usually gradual. Not all changes in every woman. Weight gain (not always preventable). Posture may worsen (e.g., "dowager's hump"), possible osteoporosis. Muscles flabbier. Breasts and nipples lose tonus and substance, may sag (estrogen may arrest but not reverse process). Coarsening of features (irreversible; acromegaloid growth hormone hypersecretion?). Skin dry, inelastic, wrinkled (partly restorable). Hair may gray. Voice timbre more raucous. Hairs under chin and on upper lip, but axillary and pubic hair diminishes and eventually grays (irreversible; adrenopause).

Will symptoms be severe? Best estimate: among involuting women 15 per cent notice nothing, 60 per cent have mild or tolerable symptoms; 13 per cent have major distress from symptoms and changes; 12 per cent are totally disabled unless continuously attended. Most vulnerable and/or least responsive to treatment: those with history of adolescent dysmenorrhea (p. 131) and adult premenstrual tension syndrome. Sequelae of chronic pseudofrigidity (p. 410) often presage major difficulties. Hot flushes worse in asthenic women and with history of autonomic instability.

What symptoms to expect? In practice most symptoms overlap as to etiology and responsiveness to estro-gen or psychiatric medication respectively. Estrogen deficiency: vasomotor crises, dyspareunia, headaches, tiredness, back pain, insomnia. Nervous symptoms: formication, numbness and other paresthesias of extremities; palpitations, irritability, feeling of suffocation (air hunger), forgetfulness and lack of concentration, depression. Caution in underrecognizing beginning involutional psychosis, a serious complication of menopause!

Hot flashes dangerous? Vasomotor crises not dangerous, but severely distressing in 15 per cent of involuting women. A sudden, sometimes stifling paroxysm of heat feeling inundates the patient, rising from trunk to neck and head. "Hot flush," in theory, is heat wave followed by drenching perspiration and chill. Flashes last seconds or minutes, but may be massed, day or night, during emotional crises, following excitement or apprehension, and whenever internal or exogenous heat is increased: after exercise or meals, in hot weather, under warm bedclothes (not proved).

What sex life to expect? Continued good if good till now. Worse if bad till now. Not directly affected by menopause, except possible dyspareunia due to substrinized genitalia. Gradually fewer, slower, shallower coital climaxes attained. Massive estrogen substitution a two-sided sword as regards sexual response (see text). Vaginal overrelaxation may benefit from Kegel exercises (p. 418). If vaginoplasty, middle-aged woman should not request restoration of tight "virginal" introitus as it may deter a middle-aged phallus and cause other discomfort.

Bothersome hypererotism, no partner. If sublimation efforts fail and masturbation is not acceptable: trial with depomedroxyprogesterone acetate 150 mg i.m. 2 or 3 times at 15-day intervals.

V.D.? Quite possible. Rising incidence has not spared the middle-aged.

General hygiene measures? High protein diet. Exercise. Plan meaningful existence to counteract challenge of empty nest. Trust one physician for necessary treatment or referrals. Understand that estrogen probably is not an elixir of youth.

Treatment. The quandary of whether, when, how, what and how long estrogen is to be used in the middle-aged woman remains unresolved, as it has for more than 35 years. The number of contraindications and cautions has shrunk, and the trend is towards more generous and longer administration, certainly in cases of demonstrable perimenopausal deficiency, but proponents of the indefinite-replacement thesis ("menopause is always a preventable deficiency disease," Wilson) do not appear to be prevailing in practice at this time, although they probably do in print. A contrary view holds that the smallest dose of estrogen producing relief of symptoms should be elected, and should be discontinued when the patient is symptom-free. Cyclical adding of a progestin is among the necessary secondary choices facing the attending physician, as is the addition of an androgenic substance in the postmenopause.

Estrogen treatment for menopausal symptoms is effective only to the extent that the symptoms are estrogen-related. However, there are indications that the body's capacity to respond to average estrogen doses is lessened in the presence of emotional maladjustment, and that even temporary stress—emotional and other—make higher doses necessary to achieve the same effect on the same symptom in the same woman. Simultaneous relief of nervous symptoms by nonhormonal means thus can lessen the estrogen requirements. Supportive psychotherapy—encouragement, counseling, an opportunity to ventilate—is the physician's prime remedy here. It is best supplemented by minor psychotropic, notably sedative medication. For reasons unknown the "secret" of therapeutic success here often seems to reside in low dosage (e.g., Bellergal Sandoz 1 or 2 tabs h.s.; or Dexamyl SKF ½ tablet every or every other morning; or phenobarbital 15 or 30 mg q.i.d. every other day).

MALE MIDDLE AGE

Men, as they pass through middle age, do not go through a recognizable phase of physiologic involution. Their gonads remain functional for the most part, although there is a gradual deterioration throughout much of adulthood. Unlike in women, what reproductive decline there is in men parallels or even trails behind the overall aging process.

Male middle age is not synonymous with midlife (35–45) which precedes it. These terms are based on a mixture of social, psychologic and biologic realities, but are not scientific. Much of the 60's today is considered part of middle age, and any survey of senescent behavior and function which includes men below age 65 in its base figures has limited validity. The effect of the recent youth explosion and the developing youth cult cannot yet be assessed, but may be expected to blur the transition from middle to advanced age, and eventually lower the societal onset of middle age again; the societal shift, in turn, would result in appropriate psychologic and biologic downgrading following each other in tandem (theory).

Reproductive System. In the normal male, as he ages, the testicles do not shrink in size; but a very gradual histologic involution occurs affecting the testosterone-producing apparatus earlier than the sperm-producing system. Major individual variations exist in the speed with which the various regressive changes take place. Total testosterone production from all sources declines steadily and very slowly, probably beginning in the early 40's; there may be an acceleration in the 50's, but normally no dramatic drop seems to occur at any time. Testicular estrogen production as a rule remains steady. Measuring the state of the steroid-producing Leydig cells by the ability of the seminal vesicles to excrete seminal fructose, this ability, between 45 and 50, is about half of what it was at 25, and at 65 it has decreased to one third. The cause of the slow fading of the gonadal androgen output is sought in a rising insensitivity of the gonads to pituitary stimulation which, in turn, has been blamed on a gradually diminishing blood flow (arteriosclerosis?) through the structures. Gonadotropin—mostly LH—rises somewhat in men past age 45, but never as steeply as in women. Normal spermatogenesis does not cease abruptly at any time if there has been no trauma, but waning frequency of sex acts is paralleled by deteriorating sperm quality including motility and chromosomal intactness, although the count may actually rise (McLeod).

As regards sexual activity, there are vast individual variations, but as a rule the urgency of relief is lessened now and more readily controlled by mentation. Erections require increased stimuli to be provoked; they occur with less speed and are less easily sustained through an environmental distraction. Precoital mucorrhea diminishes, and may cease altogether in middle age. Longer coitus becomes necessary to elicit ejaculation, the climactic cremasteric contractions weaken, and the vigor and number of ejaculatory jets gradually decreases through the years in normal men. No reliable information is available on changes in the possible ecstatic intensity of the orgasm. Masturbatory changes parallel the coital experience.

Male Menopause. A male climacteric syndrome due to gonad failure seems to occur in not more than 12 to 15 per cent of men passing through middle age. Dominant symptoms are fatigue, irritability, difficulties in mental concentration and recall, listlessness and loss of libido. Less constant are recurrent headaches, insomnia, chest pressure and palpitations without objective findings and sexual impotence. The most characteristic finding, present only in some, is vasomotor crises: hot flashes with or without perspiration and chills, similar to those of involuting women. The male climacteric syndrome is subject to frequent over- as well as under-recognition. Diagnosis by lab test (testosterone, plasma LH) is not always practicable. It has been theorized that some men, for reasons unknown, overreact clinically even to moderate drops in the level of circulating androgen; it is also possible that there is a genetically precoded early exhaustion of the gonads' responsiveness to pituitary stimulation. A diagnostic trial—after precautionary prostate examination—with testosterone propionate 25 to 50 mg intramuscularly every other day for 2 weeks; or 10 to 15 mg sublingually daily, should bring rapid improvement, although the validity of this therapeutic test is subject to a number of exceptions.

Unattended, duration of the symptoms ranges from a few months to several years. Additional psychiatric stress-reactive symptoms tend to set in. Gradual systemic repercussions from the steroid starvation include negative protein balance, demineralization of bone structures (inconstant), redistribution of fat deposits, loss of muscle strength, etc. Treatment preference is given to long-acting testosterone injections, 100 to 250 mg for each of 2 successive months, adjusted individually. Hot flashes respond best to moderate amounts of estrogen, given in short courses. A psychosupportive approach greatly enhances the chances of success of the treatment, but some men require a major course of psychiatric therapy. It seems reasonable to refrain from massive androgenic medication in debilitated men and those with doubtful cardiovascular status, as the effect of the medication may lead to overoptimistic exertion incompatible with their general resistance. The possibility of delayed, transitory depression of the sperm count may be a consideration in an occasional case.

Male Middle Age Crisis. Essentially this is a reaction to the stress or shock of recognition of aging which some men tolerate less well than others. Onset is often remarkably sudden. An incident of coital failure, a chance remark, a rejection may bring sudden realization that age is upon them. In others there may be a gradual, seemingly unmotivated lapsing into restless dissatisfaction, with feelings of inadequacy and insecurity, a downsliding of self-confidence, oppressive awareness that they now face decline. This is a problem in self-acceptance, fed by such widely varying stresses as the loss of fantasy hopes of youth accomplishment, need for reading glasses or discovery of a balding scalp (Marmor). They may become aware of urinary difficulties caused by prostatic hypertrophy and then be unable to divorce their thoughts from sexual worry. Physically they are outworked, outwalked, outplayed by younger men. They feel bewildered, even panicked when more than one task simultaneously confronts them. New instructions, new concepts seem difficult to grasp, new ventures are frightening. Retention and recall show lapses, and they may no longer trust their own mental equipment. Interest in their occupational field, in their own hobbies is waning. There may be awareness that time is being counted as time left now, rather than age achieved. Every rebuff seems catastrophic, every slight reversal the final failure, although others, more likely than not, are unaware of any of these changes.

At home the predominant feeling is of not being important to anyone, of no one truly seeming to care about him. To the children he is, or feels, a mere "wallet that walks like a man." The wife has little interest in him; she has grasped much of the decision-making and the money management; her attitude seems controlling and he feels as if emasculated by it. The marital act seems a routinized chore and the prospect seems to stimulate him less and less, and unless casual extramarital affairs reassure him he is certain that sexually, too, he is over the hill. In some men inner protest and belligerence arise and they begin to rebel; this has been termed the "middle-aged rebellion, the measles of the male's early fifties" (Bergler). They may abscond or pull up stakes; or else the attitude toward the wife becomes disdainful and hostile; she may be treated as a burden, and nothing pertaining to her—her manners, taste, friends, housekeeping, sexual response, bookkeeping, body configuration—meets his approval now. Now she may appear to him as a driving, unsympathetic person without real understanding, incapable of the sort of love—and love-making—which he feels he has always needed and craved secretly.

As an indirect result there may be infatuation with another, usually younger woman who to him seems to possess warmth and responsive qualities undreamed of since his adolescence. Her interest in him is sincere; she may have proven it as a loyal, devoted co-worker or simply by listening fondly to his problems. She admires, thus she obviously understands him. He is needed here: she is patently helpless; a woman alone, exposed to life's adversity; perhaps a small child or two, fatherless. A new set of younger friends, acquaintances anyway, embracing him. He is accepted here, all the way. He rises to new heights of affection, again and again, as not in years. Sometimes all of it is exactly so and deserving, and a new, warmly successful life situation is built from this, and endures.

At other times, perhaps more often, it was all illusory, the let-down shattering: the denial and hiding of the aging process exposed, the idealization of the self, of the body image, and of the new love object lost or never truly attained. There is return to what was, the reality of the years, remorsefully or grimly. But the outlook is bleak.

Other men react with a major sustained promiscuous philandering spree—conquests rather than relationships. It may represent indulgence of the harem fantasies and lusts of mid-adolescence, re-emerging and fulfillable now as means and opportunity have been acquired; staving off perhaps the unconsciously fearsome dominance of the resurrected mean, emasculating mother image; and just possibly an unconscious defense mechanism against the irruption of homosexual impulses. Sometimes the philandering search is part of a hypomanic reaction, imbued with grandiose fantasies, often dangerously uncaring. Promiscuity may result from panic, possibly an unconscious attempt to prove that virility is not really waning, as this would constitute an intolerable threat to the personality. Some men develop subtly paranoid reactions to a growing son and secretly resent his true, fancied or prospective erotic exploits. In others a hypochondriacal syndrome may occur, with multiple somatic obsessions.

Occasionally here one observes the emergence of a previously latent sex-deviate tendency. A latent homosexual component, for instance, may be noted first when the physician's rectal examination causes an acute panic reaction in the patient, quite unrelated to pain or fear of cancer. Other men may feel a sudden and disquieting erotic attraction for a younger male. A latent sadistic component may be evidenced by a husband's sudden and persistent interest in marital relations per rectum. Mobilization of deviate sex interests in middle-aged men probably is never due to surfeit or need for sexual variety or, as an occasional wife may suspect, because another woman has taught him to be a pervert.

The middle-age "crisis" may last several years, and some of its complications, if unattended, may remain indefinitely. Often the outlook for the marriage is not good. In some cases divorce may be sought abruptly by the man, often to the genuine surprise of everyone, even the wife herself. Even where the condition subsides spontaneously without major social or other complications, sometimes the patient is left a noticeably older or beaten man in outlook and attitude, and perhaps also in appearance and sexual behavior. In other cases a distinctly and permanently brittle marital relationship results, the husband remaining devoid of affection, surly or withdrawn. In uncomplicated cases which have been managed carefully, both personal and marital prognoses are fairly good, occasionally excellent.

Management of the phenomenon may tax the physician-counselor's resourcefulness. Often the most immediate need is for explanation and advice to the wife, especially if there are still dependent children in the home. In all but certain severe cases an attitude of toleration and patience on her part may be advised as the most efficient approach. Avoidance of a habitually belittling, overanxious, surly or retaliatory attitude is important. It may be difficult to persuade a wife to "overlook" her husband's interest in another woman, or even to compete with the intruder in catering to him; but if she desires the marriage to survive the crisis, this is sometimes the only way.

Management of the husband varies with the symptomatology. In uncomplicated cases reassurance or ventilation may suffice, but simple explanation is not always well received. Quiet discussion of an "other woman" situation may be very helpful to the patient, and many of these men are quite willing to talk about this with a physician whom they trust. Neither direct suggestion nor moralizing "appeals" to the patient are likely to meet with success in these cases. Nor is it in the ethical physician-counselor's domain to judge and decide if a marriage should be demolished, tempting as it may sometimes seem. Attempts to improve the sexual quality of the marriage are discussed on p. 274. Management of potency failure is discussed on p. 392.

ADVANCED-AGE SEXUALITY

Sexual activity is quite feasible late in life, but the obstacles grow with the years. Many aged persons continue to have, or desire, a sexual life. Where no partner is available, or the environment is not conducive to intercourse, the elderly of both sexes are believed to resort to masturbation with almost the same frequency as the middle-aged. However, those sexually active are a minority, even if a substantial one, and it cannot be concluded that retention of sex activity constitutes the norm to be aimed for in every elderly person. Any professional encouragement in this direction requires common sense and restraint.

A cultural bias against the expression of sexuality in the elderly undoubtedly exists; in fact, the sexlessness of old age is a traditional stereotype: "old age is sexless, and if it isn't it should be." What is considered virile drive in a younger man, becomes lecherous in the older one. Equally suggestible are many of the aged themselves; thus, "it would not be right" is an often heard justification of an asexual existence in the absence of biologic necessity. A person who believes himself too old for sex is not only unlikely to make a sustained attempt but may also shy away from other affectional showings and exchanges. Yet there exists a profound psychobiologic hunger in many elderly persons, often simply for tactile contact; but for many it remains largely ungratified in our culture (J. Weinberg). The need probably is not basically erotic; even the warmth of a child's cuddly hug or handhold sometimes seems to satisfy it. Although the skin's surface touch sensing apparatus has regressed by now, pressure and other depth perception has not, nor has the meaning derived from person-to-person contact. Yet the young and the middle-aged rarely permit themselves more than a perfunctory contact with an aged person, and many are repelled or frightened by it. Such recent suggestions as Foster Grandparents programs or the employment of elderly volunteers to give loving care in institutions for retarded and other hard-to-service youngsters aim, in part, at giving a sublimated sense of intimacy as well as a greater sense of social worth to the elderly.

The Sex Act. In the presenium cohabitation becomes progressively more awkward because of increasing exhaustibility, loss of agility, perhaps obesity, or concern about cardiovascular status. As the husband's potency begins to wane, sexual occasions have to wait more and more on his being ready, which is more apt to be in the morning. Often now intercourse is not so much motivated by sexual desire as by an affectionate wish to comfort the other, to recapture past closeness and express it in physical terms, or possibly as an act of ego-satisfaction, sometimes even bravado.

DUKE LONGITUDINAL STUDY
(Pfeiffer-Verwoerdt-Wang. Palmore, ed.)

The sex activity of 254 elderly volunteers in North Carolina was followed from 1954 to 1969. Two thirds were white, one third black, 131 were women. 101 subjects were single. Average age was 70; ages at onset ranged from 60 to 93. Includes only heterosexual intercourse and libido generally.

The majority showed some progressive decline. A substantial minority maintained stable activity and interest. A rising pattern of sexual interest was encountered in 15 per cent, and of increasingly practiced sexual intercourse in 13 per cent of subjects. The average frequency approached 0 in the late 80's, although exceptions among males had regular intercourse in the 90's, 1 per month or less.

The married are more active (disputed for men); the singles run into too many difficulties, rejections, fears, risks.

Aged men continue to have more sexual interest and activity than aged women. When sex relations cease in marriage, it is generally the husband who is responsible for ending relations.

Among men, about 50 per cent continue to be sexually active between 72 and 77. Among men 78 or older about 25 per cent continue active. Twenty per cent continue active into the 80's and 90's.

The largest age-connected change or transition period concerning sex activity occurs in men in the mid-70's, in women in the early 70's.

Even when men's activity declined, sexual interest showed little age-related decline as long as they were healthy.

As the man passes through the late years, sexual desire, potency and enjoyment become increasingly dependent on his being in good health, rested and having a sense of general well-being, although there are exceptions: men in their 80's and 90's engaging in intercourse out of a driving desire and regardless of minor or even moderately severe ailing. Generally, the old endowed drive survives, but as the man ages his sexual performance becomes more stereotyped. Some men become obsessively protective of their erections, at times almost miserly in employing them even when opportunity is available; old superstitions of the adolescent years are surfacing again and producing anxiety ("don't use it up too fast." "Don't burn yourself out before your time."). In actuality the correlation is essentially positive between early sexual onset, relative frequency in youth and middle age, and vigorous survival of potency.

Erective vigor, and potency generally, diminish gradually. Usually erections occur on fewer and fewer occasions and are progressively less rigid and sustained. One may speak of decline in spurts here, as each intercurrent illness, prolonged emotional upset or major interruption of marital routine seems to leave the aging man a little less potent. However, sudden, total extinction of potency is not a normal manifestation of aging. Some men remain capable of vigorous and sustained erections and performance into the eighth and ninth decades. Also, a proportion of aging men are able to "snap back"; thus, even after lengthy interruptions their capacity can be reconditioned and re-established, although perhaps not quite at the same level as before.

As the man ages his ejaculum gradually becomes scantier, although some emit a more copious but thinner fluid. Ejaculatory vigor diminishes and so does the intensity of sensation of orgasm; in fact, the urge to drive to a climax is lessened, and not every act is carried to ejaculation, apparently without ill effects of any kind. The decline of erection and ejaculation, especially in the presence of arteriosclerosis, is not rarely preceded by a period of irritable disorganization of the reflex mechanism; this may involve such responses as premature ejaculation, ejaculation with incomplete or even with no erection, mild priapism with inability to climax, or occasionally dissociation of orgasm and ejaculation.

The testicles continue their gradual histologic process of involution, notably fibrosis of the seminal tubules, but individual differences are great here: among the testicular preparations of presumably normal men of similar ages extremes ranging from excellent preservation of sperm-producing tissues and interstitial cells to germinal aplasia and absence of interstitial cells might be encountered (Engle). Normal spermatogenesis does not cease abruptly at any time, barring intercurrent pathology, but continues to be active, although the progressive fibrosis of the seminal tubules causes deterioration in the quality of the spermatozoa. Viable spermatozoa can be found even in very elderly men, and very high ages for men effecting paternity have been cited. Frequently the production of viable spermatozoa seems to outlive the ability to have erections.

Female Genitalia. In the woman, progressive atrophy of the genitalia is a major phenomenon of the postmature state, as the estrogen-dependent reproductive apparatus follows the ovaries' lead and regresses. Actual regressed status of the genitalia pertains to the senium, but is well under way in some women by the end of the sixth decade. Untreated with estrogen, the tissues of the vulva become thin and lose their erectility. The labia lose subcutaneous fat; they wrinkle, flatten and regress while the introitus can become increasingly tight and inelastic. Pruritus vulvae and chronic atrophic dermatitis are encountered. The vaginal passage becomes inelastic and shrinks somewhat in all its dimensions. The mucosa loses its rugae and becomes thin, shiny and easily irritated and cracked; intercourse may be followed by staining for a few days and on speculum examination submucosal petecchial hemorrhages are seen postcoitally. In orgasm the uterine contractions may be spastic and uncomfortable. Secretions are now scantier and mucosal transudation is slow to commence. Together with the general pelvic relaxation the thinning perivaginal fibromuscular tunic, especially if stretched and pretraumatized during multiple childbirths, may now be herniated by both bladder and rectum, while the uterus may descend and prolapse. Regularity of genital use seems to prevent much dyspareunia, retards regressed status of the female apparatus, and firms both the potency and the confidence of the aging male partner.

ADDITIONAL READING

Frank, S.: The Sexually Active Man Past Forty. New York, Macmillan, 1968

Gray, M.: The Changing Years. The Menopause without Fear. Garden City, N.Y., Doubleday, 1967

Kaufman, S. A.: The Ageless Woman. Englewood Cliffs, N.J., Prentice Hall, 1968

Palmore, E. (ed.): Normal Aging. Durham, N.C. Duke University Press, 1970

Peterson, J. A.: Married Love in the Middle Years. New York, Association Press, 1968

Rubin, I.: Sexual Life after Sixty. New York, Basic Books, 1965

Saxe, L. P.: Sex and the Mature Man. Gilbert Press, 1965

Wilson, R. A.: Feminine Forever. New York, Evans, 1966

PART 4

Sexual Pathology

CHAPTER 16

Desexing, Cross-Sexing, Intersexing

Syndromes in Men: Deficient Sex Endowment in Men —
Demasculinization and Feminization — Syndromes in Women:
The Sexually Undeveloped Woman — Defeminization and
Virilization — Intersexed States.

Syndromes in Men

DEFICIENT SEX ENDOWMENT IN MEN

In the second decade the boy's testicles, upon evocation by the pituitary
gonadotropic hormones, secrete androgen which, in turn, stimulates the
genital and extragenital characteristics to unfold (p. 89). If no gonadotropin is forthcoming because of pituitary or cerebral defect or damage,
or if no healthy testicles are present, or if they are constitutionally unresponsive, no or little maturation takes place, and an asexual male adult—
sometimes a virtual neuter by phenotype—results. If damage to the endo-
crines occurs only after some development has already taken place, a
partially sexed (hypogonadal) man results.

Eunuch. The prototype of male sex deficiency is the eunuch (agonad;
prepuberal castrate—i.e., an adult male whose testicles had been excised
in childhood). Historically, boys have been emasculated both in the
Eastern and Western worlds for specific purposes; in some of them the
phallus was amputated at the same time.

Eunuchs, some enslaved, provided supposedly innocuous personal
servants and confidants, as well as harem managers and guards, for Eastern and North African potentates. A number of them rose to become
powerful advisors on affairs of state, or high-placed civil servants.

THE UNTREATED EUNUCH

This clinical entity, rare today, is rendered here (as a composite) because the adult characteristics of the untreated prepuberal castrate are
found, in attenuated form, in clinical hypogonads where they give rise to
"eunuchoidal" habitus and traits.

Physique. Very tall with disproportionately long extremities (eunuchal
gigantism); arm span, from fingertip to fingertip, exceeds total height;

soles-to-symphysis measurement exceeds symphysis-to-vortex one; leg length best measured as stature less sitting height (Tanner). Pelvis broad and flaring, circumference exceeds that of inspiratory chest. Shoulders narrow, sloping. Wrists gracile, fingers long. Tendency to connective tissue weakness with loose joints, knock knees, flat feet; weak venous walls (varicose veins, hemorrhoids.) Moderate girdle fat deposit (buttocks, hips, mons pubis); pectoral fat deposit (adipomasty). Development and tonus of muscles poor; easily fatigued. Round-shouldered early. Variants: a tall, lean eunuch: those with a leptosome (asthenic) constitution; obesity in castrates with pyknic constitution.

Appearance. Face: mixture of juvenile and prematurely old; becomes finely wrinkled early. Complexion sallow, no tan is acquired, no acne in teens. Beardless, except some on chin and corners of mouth. Character- istic heavy-liddedness gives sleepy expression. Voice high pitched, or later "breaks," remains cracked. Skin soft and pale; soft down on body, but no hair. Little axillary or pubic hair. Scalp hair abundant, often silky fine; does not recede with age.

Sex Apparatus. Penis size of a child's; appears tinier because of tall- ness. Scrotum small, smooth, unpigmented, wider at its base. Prostate very small or absent. 17-ketosteroids in urine very low, gonadotropin very high. Thyroid function lowered, as a rule. Irreparably sterile. May have erections, but infrequent and weak. May obtain child-type (dry, throbbing) orgasm. Exceptionally ejaculates a little fluid. Easily condi- tioned to passive anal libido.

Personality. Intelligence of average range. Controversy exists as to an "emasculated personality." Frequently found: unassertiveness in manner and bearing, timidity, tendency to social withdrawal. Some are indus- trious, capable of planning and achievement; others are markedly nar- cissistic, moody, excitable, show-offish; or highly irascible; or insidiously or openly cruel. Often lacking sense of higher values and abstract ap- preciation. Some overadapt to social roles in which they were cast. Pam- pered, vain, peevish Mediterranean star singers differed from fellow castrates who failed in singing career. Amiable Skopt taxi drivers in Bukarest presumably had little in common with harem eunuchs living in a confined, intrigue-ridden, erotism-centered society, highly drilled to cruelty-on-demand, erotically overexposed, yet chronically frustrated.

Androgenic Substitution. If replacement treatment with androgen in a castrated boy is delayed past approximately 11 years of age, the syn- drome becomes incompletely reversible. If treatment is delayed past ado- lescence, only a modest improvement is possible; some late effects (e.g., osteoporosis) can be averted or controlled, and some sexual manifesta- tions restored, however.

Religious Castration has been the custom in various parts of the world. In Russia and elsewhere the fundamentalist Christian sect of the Skopts has practiced castration with and without phallic amputation in literal interpretation of certain biblical passages (Revelation 14:3,4; Luke 23:29;

Psalm 51; Matthew 18:8 and 19:10–12). They maintain that Christ, to free the world from original sin, emasculated himself, exhorting his followers to do likewise; that castration is man's only hope to avoid temptation of the flesh; and that future paradisical existence for each faithful, depends on the presence on earth of 144,000 "male virgins," which explains the sect's enormous zeal in proselytizing. Due to outlawing and severe persecution the sect went underground, but their influence is said to be again rising. Skopts permit members to postpone castration until they have fathered one or two sons as a future supply of undefiled males.

Euphonic Castration. In Italy boys were castrated to provide future singers for the choirs of the great churches and private chapels of cardinals and nobles throughout Europe. Although the Church officially disapproved, in the 16th century castrati began to find entree into the papal choir and to displace the Spanish-trained (noncastrate) falsetto singers. Later they spilled over into opera. In the 18th century, the art of belcanto attained high degrees of perfection and purity; operas such as Mozart's *Idomeneo* are partly written for castrati. These highly trained men were able to sing a whole octave above the ordinary woman's voice; they had the clear timbre of boys' voices, free from overtones, but with more power and control due to their adult lungs, and they were able to maintain their voices for decades. The most successful earned large incomes. By the end of the 18th century as many as 2,000 children a year are believed to have been altered in Italy at the request of their parents—mostly the poor of large South Italian cities—and entrusted to managers for voice training on speculation (Hirschfeld).

Variants. Reportedly some eunuchs were capable of virile manifestations. One may conjecture that either a late-emasculated early-maturer was involved, or else that professional emasculators, paid on a piecework-and-survival basis, failed to report an occasional cryptorchid or failed to find a migratory testis; or that an anorchic, preferred because no cutting was needed, may have harbored extratesticular Leydig cells in the scrotum, as many normal men also seem to have. Where the penis had also been removed, castrates had to squat female fashion to urinate, or else used a tube or silver quill they carried with them; some had to wear a removable plug to supplement sphincter function. Removal of one testis in a boy has no notable clinical effects. In animal husbandry castration serves to make animals tamer, fatter and/or tastier.

Life Expectancy. Emasculation (bilateral orchiectomy) prolongs life, at least in institutionalized castrates. In a series of 297 such castrates the prepuberally (age 8 to 14) altered outlived those excised at ages 20 to 40. Estimated aggregate life span of all castrates was 69.3 years as against a matched control group's 55.7 years (Hamilton). Resistance to physical stress is usually above average in early castrates.

Hypogonadism. The male who comes into adolescence—and perhaps adulthood—with testicles which, from childhood, are damaged, atrophic or otherwise subnormal and underfunctioning, is a primary (testicular, hypergonadotropic) hypogonad. If testicular nondevelopment results from failure in the pituitary mechanism, he is a secondary (pituitary, hypogonadotropic) hypogonad.

Primary Hypogonadism. The prototype of testicular hypogonadism is *Klinefelter's syndrome,* discussed among the chromosomal intersexes (p. 367). Rarer is *anorchia;* these boys present as bilateral cryptorchids in childhood, but at 8 or 9 they develop eunuchoidal stature which calls for diagnostic laparotomy without delay to enable the physician to stave off disfiguring eunuchoidal growth and habitus by timely substitution therapy. The anorchid, a genetic male, must have had testicles in utero to be born masculinized, but lost them perhaps due to pre-birth torsion necrosis or disease; at any rate, now his vasa end blindly. *Bilateral cryptorchism* itself exposes the testicles either to pressure in the inguinal canals or to the higher abdominal temperatures, often resulting in impairment or loss of future spermatogenic capacity; but impairment of the interstitial, steroid-producing anlage has not been proved to occur. Nondescent of a single testis interferes with no aspect of male function or fertility; however, watchful school systems exclude such boys preventively from contact sports. Other causes of primary deficits include the *Reifenstein* and the *male Turner's* syndromes, and *necrotic degeneration* and atrophy following double episodes of testicular torsion and unavoidably traumatic orchiopexy, as well as a few other conditions.

In **Secondary Hypogonadism** the anterior pituitary gland fails to secrete gonadotropin or one of its fractions. Many such youngsters have no demonstrable lesion either in the pituitary or in the surrounding brain areas, but the defects in pituitary function are sufficient to prevent sexual maturation. Some of these failures are transient, others permanent. Mild pituitary-hypothalamic failure is represented by partially failed puberty resulting from severe and/or chronic nutritional deficits or systemic disorders of childhood and pubescence. Such disorders can interrupt development, delay it, stretch it out or leave it incomplete; examples are rickets, juvenile hypothyroidism, poorly controlled childhood diabetes or starvation.

Differential Diagnosis. The physique in primary testicular failure invariably is eunuchoidal (i.e., it resembles that of the true eunuch; including gynecoid contour, soft skin, hypogenitalism, scant sex hair, etc.). The appearance of men with sexing deficit secondary to pituitary failure, depends on which tropic pituitary hormones are involved. If gonadotropin failure is the only or principal deficit (selective pituitary hypogonadism) the patient is almost indistinguishable from the testicular eunuchoid, except that tallness may be more marked and sex-linked extragenital

SOME LANDMARKS IN TESTIS CHRONOLOGY

Date		Investigator
300 B.C.	Effects of castration in birds and men compared	Aristotle
1849	Effects of castration on cock's comb; prevented by testis transplant	Berthold
1889	Claim of increased vigor after self-treatment with testicular extracts	Brown-Sequard
1903	Lipid seen in Leydig cells; Lipid nature of testis internal secretion suggested	Loisel
1911	Comb growth in capons by injection of saline extracts of testis	Pezard
1927	Highly potent extracts of bull testis	McGee
1931	25 mg of androsterone isolated from 15,000 liters of human urine	Butenandt
1935	Crystalline testosterone from bull testis	Laqueur
1935	Synthesis of androgens from cholesterol	Butenandt, Ruzicka

From Tepperman, Metabolic and Endocrine Physiology 3rd Ed. 1973 (Year Book Med. Publishers)

characteristics less consistently deficient. Here the testicles, microscopically, closely resemble those of a normal prepuberal boy. Gynecomastia does not occur in these men, except at times following therapy with sex steroids. Associated thyreotropic or somatotropic deficit may influence the appearance of pituitary hypogonads. Differential diagnosis relies—apart from thyroid, adrenal and neurologic work-up, sex chromatin and karyotype determinations, skull x-rays, and testicular biopsy—on hormonal testing, including urinary gonadotropins, plasma LH and plasma testosterone. Biologic stimulation tests with human chorionic gonadotropin (genital growth if under age 30) and clomiphene response (plasma LH increase) are other important efforts.

Treatment of the young adult with deficient sex endowment should not be delayed as results grow less certain with every year that passes. Sexual maturation is sought either by stimulating the gonads by means of gonadotropin, or by androgenic replacement therapy. Unless a diagnosis of primary testicular deficit has been established by test, and especially in younger men, stimulation is the method of first choice. A course lasts 3 to 12 months, with higher dosages being employed in recent years; thereby, approximately 40 months of puberal development are crammed into less than a year of artificial maturation. In some cases such a priming course is sufficient, and both the pituitary and the gonad will remain functional on their own. It has been suggested that these are often cases of extreme puberal retardation who would have pubesced spontaneously eventually, possibly even in their 20's; however, it is today neither feasible nor rational to withhold treatment from a mentally normal, sex-deficient older adolescent or young adult who comes to medical attention. In other cases, following the priming course, development regresses again, although rarely completely.

In primary hypogonads, in whom stimulation therapy would be futile, and in patients not responding to gonadotropin, androgenic substitution is resorted to. Dosage of testosterone is empirical for each individual. Severe hypogonads responding to testosterone medication may prove extremely sensitive to it and react with priapism (q.v.). After fullest possible unfolding of sex characteristics, permanent maintenance of androgenic substitution is necessary. It is believed that the penis will grow as long as the body's bony epiphyses are open, but that when they have closed probably nothing will make the organ grow, no matter how small it is. At times this has added up to a dramatic race between the phallus-enhancing and the epiphysis-closing effects of testosterone. Pubic hair may start growth after 1 or 2 weeks of treatment, and within a month the voice usually breaks. Changes in habitus and muscle strength follow gradually. Beard development (except mustache) lags, and shaving more than twice a week is rarely necessary even in fully successful cases. In pituitary hypogonadism, especially in the presence of suprasellar damage, virilization cannot always be accomplished. Libido may be present, but these men remain impotent.

Substitution therapy does not hold certainty in all cases. The older eunuchoid's genital and extragenital sex characteristics may have lost some of their inherent capacity to develop, even with an adequate androgenic supply. Primary hypogonads on substitution therapy may expect to remain sterile, even if otherwise successfully matured, and the chances of adequate, permanent spermatogenesis seem to be barely better for the patient with selective gonadotropic failure.

Guidance. Therapy should be accompanied, perhaps preceded, by guidance, if severe eunuchoids are to be assisted successfully into normal manhood. Hormone therapy tends to activate psychosexual conflicts and can produce more problems than it solves; the later the treatment is undertaken, the more necessary is attention to the psychologic status. The individual who has been a passive and withdrawn or else an envious or perhaps an enraged cripple for years, developing his own pattern of emotional compensation and peculiarities, is often not capable of coping with a sudden influx of adult-type libidinal strivings. Having built a network of perpetual-childhood fantasies and dependent attitudes around himself, the belated biologic stirrings threaten the nature of all his accustomed relationships. This seems to be as true of those still living in the parental home as of some of those who have contracted an asexual or a feebly sexual marriage.

Nor are all psychosocial abnormalities reversed automatically with induced maturation. As a juvenile, the conspicuously immature or sex-divergent individual may have resorted to stealing or other criminality to show that he is as good as his peers, a real he-man, or for similar reasons of overcompensation. Later, this criminality may have become a fixed, habitual pattern of existence; it may not disappear simply because sexual development is induced. Where timidity, slowness or awkwardness (e.g., in a dystrophic hypogonad) have simulated a feeble intellect, improvement can be expected, especially with appropriate guidance. Certain grossly antisocial, defective, or psychopathic eunuchoids probably should not be treated endocrinally without careful prior psychiatric evaluation and, perhaps, occasionally not at all. The artificially matured hypogonad is not always capable of fully normal and satisfactory sex activity. In the predisposed, libido can channel itself into tendencies of the fetishistic or sadistic type, while normal sex relations continue to hold little attraction, especially where all the attention was paid to the hormone dosing and none to the psychic adjustment. A newly matured eunuchoid probably should not marry precipitously as soon as the sex apparatus seems to be capable of adult performance, unless there is reasonable certainty as to his psychosexual adjustment potential.

DEMASCULINIZATION AND FEMINIZATION

A sexually developed, normal man may lose all or part of his masculinity due to disease or interference: his sexual functions diminish, the secondary sex characteristics regress, and his sexual organs may undergo degrees of atrophy. Psychic changes of rather variable intensity accompany the process. In addition to demasculinization, he may, at times, also undergo feminizing changes, such as true gynecomastia.

Adult (Late, Postpuberal) Castration. The prototype of desexing is the loss of both testicles during manhood. It occurs, today, as a result of gunshot or shrapnel wounds; by surgical extirpation because of mutilating injuries, tumorous growth, bilateral necrosis following adult-type testicular torsion, for treatment of prostatic cancer, in intractable syphilitic gummata or stubborn local tubercular infection; during atrocities by indigenous population; by psychotic self-mutilation; as a bizarre self-help measure by some transsexuals; and, most frequently (not in U.S.), as part of the treatment of aggressive sex offenders, or as a condition of their parole (Sturup).

Clinical Manifestations are not predictable with certainty; they seem to follow patterns which remain incompletely understood. Age at castration is a major factor: young men up to their mid-twenties are affected more seriously; only 1 out of 4 or 5 retain libido and potency in this group, and only men in their sixth decade at the time of excision fare worse, almost all of them seeming to lose every virile manifestation with dispatch. Constitution seems to matter: men with pyknic build tend toward increased fat deposit; while those with leptosome build show more stability in resisting somatic changes. Also, the brain-pituitary mechanism of some men seems to be more sensitive to the sudden shut-down of a major link in the endocrine feedback system. Habitus usually remains recognizably masculine for years, although eventually a pelvic-pectoral fat girdle will form, together with general pudginess, muscular flabbiness and increasing fatigability. The complexion tends to become pale and pasty, the skin does not tan well, and the patient has to shave less often. Body, axillary and pubic hair diminish in time, unless there is substitution therapy, but some men continue to shave after the body hair has fallen out. In time, the voice may become slightly squeaky due to regression of the larynx. A male climacteric, infrequent in eugonadal men, often occurs in these patients when they reach early middle age, including hot flashes, excessive perspiration, lability of mood, inability to concentrate and various other symptoms. In recently castrated older men onset of symptoms of autonomic imbalance may be very rapid.

Sexual Manifestations vary, the only constant features being absence of spermatozoa from the ejaculate, regression of the scrotum if one is present, and most probably shrinking of the prostate. Averaging all ages and types, and without benefit of replacement therapy, about 40 per cent lose potency almost immediately; 30 per cent lose it gradually over a period of years, while it remains intact in another 30 per cent. Among cases of immediate impotence, one half are assumed to be on some psychogenic basis. Libido as a whole depends on psychic state, attitude and nature of previous vita sexualis. Men accustomed to regular relations and devoted to their wives may continue satisfactory and regular relations for years, occasionally for as long as 15 years (in one oft-cited case for 30 years). Even with impotence, libido persists in some men. Where gradual loss of potency occurs, duration of individual erections is imperceptibly but progressively shortened until the act can no longer be completed even under ideal circumstances. Combined with this, one encounters gradual lessening of the amount of ejaculate, but orgasm can remain possible even without ejaculation. The penis may lose some substance. Capacity for masculine affectionate feelings for a woman survive late-castration, although some men must first be helped to overcome the psychology of a beaten man. To be differentiated is sexual anhedonia which may accompany a serious intercurrent mental depression—no rarity during the middle years of these men. Recovery of libido and potency after remission of the depression appears to be slower and less complete than in eugonadal men.

Psychologically, many late-castrates eventually have difficulty with mental concentration, and there may be gradual loss of interest in the broader issues of life. The well adapted seem to become increasingly domestic-minded as they grow into or past middle age. Loss of self-confidence and assertiveness may be marked, perhaps especially if there is much preoccupation with being an inferior or inadequate man. Certain pre-existing personality traits may emerge more clearly (e.g., obsessional manifestations) or a tendency to subtle cruelty. Castrated sex offenders in detention experience euphoria for up to 2 months, due to true or fancied relief from the tyranny of their drives; then a phase—up to 6 to 12 months, sometimes with recurrences—of depression, regressive behavior and cognitive detachment during which they struggle for reintegration, new values, interests and motives and are expected to replan their lives.

Treatment and preventive care of late castration chiefly relies on the timely use of androgenic substitution unless contraindicated (e.g., in prostate cases and, supposedly, in sex offenders). The method does not represent fully satisfactory replacement, possibly because not all endocrine substances produced by the normal testicle are known with certainty. Not all ill effects of castration are reversible nor even preventable. Type of preparation, dosage and dosage distribution vary with individual needs and can be coordinated with psychotherapy which plays a fairly important part in the more difficult cases. Patients who depend on replacement steroids occasionally develop acute capacity to discern, by use effectiveness, what esters, dosage and, in one case, what brand of testosterone they are currently receiving.

Organic Hypopituitarism. A man can be desexed by impaired pituitary-hypothalamic production or release of gonadotropin. The cause is anything that impinges on, interrupts, infarcts, interferes with or destroys the brain-pituitary apparatus in some essential part such as the tuber cinereum, the connecting pathways of the stalk, or 75 per cent or more of the anterior pituitary gland itself. A frequent cause may be head injuries, notably falls and car accidents resulting in some displacement of the brain inside the skull. In a series of 100 pituitary glands from craniocerebral injury cases examined microscopically, 22 had ischemic necrosis of the anterior pituitary (Kornblum). Onset is within a day or two and, similar to Sheehan's syndrome (q.v.), fibrosis follows rapidly. Other causes include pressure from surrounding cysts, primary or neighboring tumors, meningoencephalitis, carotid aneurysm and others. Pituitary insufficiency has complicated massive irradiation, snakebite, influenza and other conditions.

Such impairment most usually presents clinically as a panhypopituitary syndrome (male variant of Simmonds' disease) and may be more frequent than had been believed. It is easily subject to misdiagnosis and underrecognition; also, these patients, with their often characteristic apathy and indifference to their own symptoms, tend to consult the physician late or even not at all. Apart from massive trauma or such, the course of the disease is slow. Symptoms depend on how much of the gland, and what tropins, have been interfered with. Insidious onset of the failure with loss of libido and potency is relatively frequent. In a fully developed, untreated case complete desexing reportedly occurs in half the cases, but numerous signs and symptoms of thyroid, adrenal, metabolic and neurologic deficit may coexist.

Cushing's Syndrome is relatively rare in men. Here intense sexual regression, where present, is characterized by atrophy of the testicles, azoospermia, loss of libido and impotence. Occasionally, a girdle type obesity may emerge with the characteristic obesity of the upper trunk to give an appearance of diffuse obesity, but forearms and wrists remain relatively slender. Enlarged breasts consist of an admixture of pectoral fat deposit and true mammary hyperplasia. Body and sexual hair diminish, but hirsutism may occur in cases of Cushing's disease.

Functional Hypopituitarism. In this somewhat controversial entity pituitary gonadotropin failure produces largely reversible desexing. Its most important cause is protracted malnutrition or starvation. The syndrome has been fairly extensively studied clinically and postmortem in victims of famine (hunger or famine dystrophy, vagotonic hunger syndrome, nutritional desexing), in underfed prisoners of war (castration syndrome in starved P.O.W.'s), and in liberated concentration camp inmates (K-Z syndrome). Related is the refeeding phenomenon (returnees', repatriates', Heimkehrer's dystrophy). It is believed that severe stressing such as starvation causes the hypothalamus to retrench releasors for the principal pituitary tropic functions in the order of their importance for survival ("vital functions are fed first"); suspending activation of the expendable gonads first, then of thyroid function, and only lastly inducing adrenal recession.

Only about 10 per cent of equally starved men are believed to suffer a conspicuous form of hypogenitalism. In the severest ("skin and bones") type of inanition (famine, concentration camps), observers at times could not tell men from women except on close inspection. In severe starvation, the first sign usually is loss of libido, then body hair is lost in patches, the beard thins, and there is diminution of pubic and loss of axillary hair, the latter apparently one of the most consistent signs, in both sexes. The penis loses substance, the prostate regresses, the testes decrease somewhat in size, spermatogenesis is arrested, and there is aplasia of the seminal epithelium and hyalinization of the seminiferous tubules, while interstitial cells are preserved. Eunuchoidal fat deposits may develop. Impotence and infertility have been reported to be reversible after as long as 40 months of starvation; but others have reported continuing sexual disturbances (erective impotence, ejaculatio praecox, inability to achieve orgasm, oligospermia) as long as 4 months after repatriation and after the men had regained their weight ("they looked fitter than they were"). Emotional factors may have played a part: states of prolonged apathy persisting after repatriation of prisoners of war have been described. Where the degree of undernutrition is moderate, there may or may not be testicular atrophy, but probably the penis does not shrink, and hair distribution remains normal in these cases.

In addition to demasculinizing (neuterizing) changes, inanition may produce feminizing stigmata, chiefly gynecomastia. In prison camps with a semi-starvation regimen, a proportion of the men grew breasts, either spontaneously after, say, 18 months and regressing only slowly after liberation; or soon after food packages were received by the protein-starved men; or else a few weeks after repatriation and adequate diet—refeeding phenomenon. The liver normally removes estrogens from the blood and inactivates them by conjugation. In the refeeding syndrome, the gonads may recuperate more quickly than the liver, thus producing a shift in the circulating androgens:estrogen ratio. Simultaneously, damage to the liver's protein-synthetizing function is believed to impair further its estrogen-metabolizing capacity.

Estrogen-induced Feminization. Estrogen, regardless of source, both feminizes and demasculinizes the man. It inhibits gonadotropin production in the pituitary gland which, in turn, leads to testicular atrophy and inactivation. Libido is lost, spermatogenesis is suppressed, and erections and ejaculation are diminished and eventually become extinct when estrogenic input is continued beyond 2 or 3 months. Histologically, the Leydig cells resist degeneration longest, and a few clusters of altered interstitial elements have been seen as long as 2 years after continuous estrinization. As feminization takes hold, the breasts enlarge, areolae and nipples darken, hips and buttocks may become padded; and in some muscle strength becomes weaker; only the voice does not change in the adult, but the scalp hair grows more luxuriant, even filling in some bald spots and corners. Psychic effects of hyperestrinization remain somewhat uncertain. Some estrogen-secreting tumors (see below) have caused major shifts in feeling, yet it is possible that no personality traits develop which had not pre-existed, at least latently. Fears of becoming a woman, of "going to think—feel, act, love—like a woman" may just remain fears or may become obsessive ruminations in predisposed personalities. Mental depression with its attendant apprehension, withdrawal and passivity vis-à-vis people may simulate a feminized personality.

Causes. Such estrogenic flooding of an adult male can occur in the treatment of prostatic carcinoma; when a male transsexual deviate (p. 486) doses himself as a measure of functional self-castration; or when estrogen is prescribed pre- and postoperatively during a sex reassignment procedure for such a transsexual. Much less protracted is administration of estrogen to prevent orchitis in mumps; to prevent postoperative erections in circumcision; in accidental exposure of workers in the cosmetic industry, or in firms that manufacture or repack pharmaceuticals. In cirrhosis and other chronic liver disease one finds testicular atrophy, oligospermia, loss of libido, impotence, loss of axillary hair, female pubic escutcheon and gynecomastia, produced by the alterations in hepatic steroid metabolism. The control of aggressive and deviate manifestations in sex offenders by means of prolonged estrogen administration (see p. 466) while detained or as a condition of their parole is not widely practiced today.

Feminizing Tumors, producing estrogen, mostly occur in the testicles of adult men below age 40. Some interstitial cell tumors cause genital atrophy, gynecomastia, female pubic escutcheon, diminished libido and potency—all reversible after surgery, except possibly the gynecomastia. Among the highly malignant choriocarcinoma-chorionepithelioma group of testicular tumors, some of the most spectacular feminizations, including of the personality ("maternalization"), on record have been described. Rarer still are feminizing tumors (mostly carcinoma) of the adrenal cortex; mostly, they have resulted in atrophy of the testes, gynecomastia and reduced libido; their metastases also secrete estrogen.

Spurious Desexing. A variety of noxious agents can insult the testicles directly; they hurt the seminiferous structures and their fragile, easily disorganized spermatogenic function, while the interstitial (Leydig) cells and their steroid-producing function are much more resistant to direct trauma and stress. Adequate spermatogenesis probably cannot exist in the absence of Leydig cell function, but the Leydig cells are capable of normal activity even though the seminiferous tubules may be afunctional. A portion of steroid-producing cells may survive even diffuse testicular necrosis, or after years of continuous exposure to high abdominal temperatures in cryptorchism. It has been the experience, however, that patients exposed to these insults tend to worry most about their sexual potency which is practically never affected. The following insults may sterilize, but they do not desex.

Elevated Perineal Temperatures interfere rapidly and significantly with sperm output. This hypospermia is reversible unless exposure was unremitting. There is no known effect on sexual function. The spermatogenetic tissue is so thermosensitive that daily wearing of a tight-knit jockstrap, or 15 half-hour exposures to a 150-watt light bulb, or a series of hot sitz baths, sauna baths or such, depress spermatogenesis in a matter of weeks. Even ordinary men's clothing, with its confining-insulating crotch arrangement, is known to cause elevated scrotal temperatures higher by several degrees than those in control groups of nudists, etc. Men with borderline fertility are probably more easily affected. Occupational exposure of the perineal region to heat—professional drivers with under-seat heat flow, forge workers, mill hands etc.—may be at risk. Heat may also be produced endogenously (e.g., by fever).

Varicocele interferes with adequate cooling of the testicles, to the point where sterility is produced in some cases. Surgical correction of varicocele improves some characteristics of semen quality in about half the patients (MacLeod). There is no indication that androgen production and sexual function are involved.

Vasectomy (see also p. 311) is not a desexing procedure. Although the operation interrupts the channel of seminal emission, spermatogenesis continues, but in a reversibly incomplete manner possibly due to some atrophy from back pressure of the unemitted spermatozoa. The ejaculate, azoospermic now, is barely diminished, and there are no alterations in sexual functioning.

Irradiation of the human testicle can destroy the germinal epithelium and spermatogenesis, but it does not harm androgenic function which is histologically insensitive to radiation. This is also true for radiomimetic drugs such as the nitrogen mustards and for the furfurans, as well as for microwave (radar, shortwave cooking ovens, etc.) radiation. However, both local and whole body radiation can affect androgen production in a manner similar to exogenous testosterone administration (McKerns). It triggers off pituitary secretory changes at times. Except in rare cases of panhypopituitarism due to excessive radiation dosage impotence has not been known to occur. Mutagenic effect can occur with fairly low doses; these are most often recessively heritable.

Pressure. Damage to the spermatogenic function may be caused by direct pressure. For example, habitual wearing of tight underclothing may not only heat-insulate but also exert physical pressure on the testes, damaging the spermatogenic function. The androgenic function of the testicles does not appear to be affected.

Syndromes in Women

THE SEXUALLY UNDEVELOPED WOMAN

When a girl emerges from the middle teens without having developed sexually, a female hypogonad results. There is deviance of physique from the norm, nondevelopment of estrogen-dependent sex characteristics and organs, and primary amenorrhea. Almost by definition, hypogonadism and primary amenorrhea are terms not applicable before age 18 (some say 17); before that age absent menarche and puberty are considered delay rather than failure. There are various disorders causing puberal failure, but the immediate cause is always ovarian silence: either there were no ovaries, or they were deficient, or unresponsive to pituitary stimulation, or they atrophied, or have been destroyed, or the pituitary failed to provide stimulation due to damage of its own, or else adrenocortical excess blocked ovarian evolution.

Prepuberal Ovarian Failure. A characteristic though no longer frequent variant is the genetically normal (XX) girl in whom signs of sexual maturation simply fail to appear, either because of a presumed embryonic defect in ovarian anlage or due to unrecognized pre- or postnatal post-infectious (viral) atrophy or other destructive damage of the ovaries. She is a tall, long-legged girl, with characteristic eunuchoidal body proportions—a term borrowed from male pathology. Most typically she has a small, narrow pelvis, no breasts, or some breasts but undeveloped nipples. She either does not menstruate at all, or, in milder cases, the anovulatory menses are persistently scant and irregular. The degree of hypogenitalism varies; the vaginal passage is relatively short and narrow, the labia minora absent, secretions scant or nil. The severe case retains the genitalia of childhood with thin, vulnerable vaginal mucosa, sensitive hymen, shallow fornices, barely palpable anteflexed uterine corpus, and the child-type vaginal pH and cytology.

Vita Sexualis. A mild degree of sexual underdevelopment is compatible with marriage and a regular vita sexualis. In fact, it has been conjectured that minor genital hypoplasia may undergo accelerated maturation in the presence of marital harmony and sexual compatibility (psychogenic self-estrinization?). In the past some vastly unmatured girls were forced or persuaded into marriage, either in the futile hope that this would help mature them, or because the condition went unrecognized or was untreatable, and because certain men especially coveted such childlike or boyish-appearing brides. Genital hypoplasia can lead to severe dyspareunia if intercourse is attempted crudely in the presence of sexual infantilism. One may suspect that the relatively much higher incidence, in the older medical literature, of such mishaps as vaginismus with or without penis captivus, and of introital or vulvar lacerations during the honeymoon, was partly due to a greater number of untreated and reluctant hypogonads assuming bridal status. The majority of greatly underdeveloped girls today come to medical attention before marriage. In mitigation of dyspareunia in as yet insufficiently matured hypogenitalism one may advise a bride to coite by rear entry, female prone or in knee-elbow position, using ample lubrication. However, libido tends to be scant in most hypogonadal females.

Among important causes of primary ovarian failure is **Gonadal Dysgenesis (Turner's Syndrome)** which is discussed among the chromosomal intersexes (p. 368). Having no or rudimentary ovaries, they lack ovarian function, and unless treated their reproductive apparatus remains infantile, no breasts develop and menarche does not occur. Dwarfing and a variety of congenital anomalies are usually associated with this syndrome. However, there are degrees of severity.

Prepuberal Pituitary Failure. Secondary (hypogonadotropic) nonsexing exists when the neuroendocrine control mechanism has been interfered with (tumors, encephalitis, head injuries, congenital lesions), crippling the secretion of pituitary gonadotropin. Lacking stimulation the ovaries secrete no sex hormone, there is no ovulation, and the target organs (genitalia, breasts) do not develop. Extensive pathology in the anterior pituitary may result in deficiency of most anterior pituitary hormones including growth hormone secreting cells, producing the picture of the *pituitary dwarf* with her often total sexual infantilism. In addition to their Lilliputian stature, these young women, if untreated, have the well-known immature, myxedematous midget face, dry, yellowish and early wrinkling skin, childish or shrill voice, absent or scant sex hair and childlike genitalia. Spontaneous development including menarche has been known to occur in some, even as late as the early thirties.

In cases with much hypothalamic pathology, the rare *adiposogenital dystrophy,* similar to that seen in boys, can result. These girls have some degree of stunted growth; there is the characteristic girdle of trochanteric-gluteal-pubic fat, an overhanging abdominal fat apron, pseudobreasts made up mostly of fat. Hands and feet are small and delicate. They have weak muscles and fatigue easily. The skin is pale, delicate, and soft. The genitalia remain undeveloped or develop only in part. Menses are either absent or scanty. This syndrome is not identical with even major degrees of exogenous obesity in young women. In the severest cases, of course, one finds associated disturbances of fluid and temperature regulation, vision, sleep, etc.

The hypothalamic-pituitary complex is also sensitive to many kinds of *functional interference.* Almost any system disorder and deficiency state of the early and middle teen years which is sufficiently severe, protracted or debilitating can at least partially arrest and delay the young girl's innate program of sexual development. Causes include, among others, juvenile hypothyroidism, diabetes of childhood, rickets, and rheumatic fever. The blocking effect of even severe malnutrition on sexual development is in dispute, but the existence of an antipuberty effect due to prolonged psychic stress or emotional disorganization is very strongly suspected. A hostile environment may represent such a stress (war and camp internees, foster home malplacement), or an environment that is merely perceived as hostile (institution, psychotic parents).

DEFEMINIZATION AND VIRILIZATION

A woman who has attained normal sexual development may become desexed again, chiefly as the result of 3 supravening pathologic conditions:

loss of ovarian function, pituitary failure, and hyperfunction of the adrenal cortex. This may or may not be combined with symptoms and signs of virilization. At least partial defeminization usually precedes virilization in the adult woman.

Emotional and personality disorders as well as psychoses, notably depression, often accompany virilizing changes. These are most marked in Cushing's syndrome, less so in polycystic ovarian disease, and least in the adrenogenital syndrome. In a mild case (e.g., temporary pituitary hypofunction associated with long-term ataractic or antidepressant medication in psychiatric patients), apart from minor breast and vaginal regression, one may find a minor change in the quality of the patient's orgasmic response during intercourse. All changes appear to be reversible on discontinuing medication, and reappear on resumption; they seem to be most noticeable in slightly masculinoid women.

In contrast to the self-conscious, defeatist, often strongly depressive personality of the untreated or residual congenital hyperadrenocortical (pseudohermaphroditic, see p. 107 and 363) girl who has grown up with her syndrome, the late-virilizing adolescent or adult patient often has increased self-confidence, at times to the point of pronounced aggressiveness. The endogenously virilized woman here differs from the woman whose virilism is due to exogenous testosterone dosing (see below), in that her psychic reactions tend to be more uniform. The most characteristic psychosexual change associated with defeminization is the triad of loss of libido, dyspareunia and orgasm failure which most often appear in sequence.

The prototype of lost feminine function is bilateral excision of the ovaries in a woman of reproductive age.

Surgical (Artificial, Induced) Menopause. The only constant and immediate sequel of bilateral ovariectomy in the adult female is sterility. As hysterectomy accompanies castration in the vast majority of cases (exception: as therapy in neoplasm of breast), there is also amenorrhea, of course. In time—sometimes rapidly, but most often over several years—there will also be regression of the whole reproductive apparatus in the untreated woman. Vulvovaginal structures (except the clitoris) shrink; the vaginal mucosa atrophies; genital secretions diminish; and the muscles of the pelvic floor become relaxed. The coital passage tends to become uncomfortably stenotic, leading to degrees of dyspareunia in a proportion of these patients. The breasts also regress, but a woman who is nursing at the time may continue to secrete milk.

Abrupt ovarian cessation always precipitates at least temporary disruption of the total endocrine feedback system, although the adrenals soon assume a role in supplying an estrogen-precursor for increased peripheral biosynthesis of estrogen. There may be apathy due to hypothyroidism. There is often much weight gain unless the diet is controlled, and the fat deposit can have a Cushing-type distribution. The voice becomes huskier or harsher, and some body and face hair may appear. Premature graying of the hair is seen at times. Vasomotor and nervous symptoms correspond to those of the involutional syndrome, but their incidence is greater, and they tend to be more severe in surgical menopause, especially in younger women and in those under psychic stress. However, for practical purposes it is difficult to predict which woman will suffer intense autonomic and nervous distress, and which will not. Most observers believe that ovariectomy is followed by a heightened incidence of arteriosclerosis, notably of the coronary and cerebral arteries, at relatively early ages.

Sexual Reactions after adult-castration of a younger woman are not predictable with certainty. Estrogenic cessation per se impairs neither the libido nor sexual responsiveness—these are maintained largely by the adrenal androgens—provided that there had been a satisfactory vita sexualis previously. Yet perhaps as many as one third of these women report that their sex reactions are less complete than they were before surgery. The mechanism of the self-fulfilling prophecy is to blame at times: the woman expects castration to end her sex life and, acting on this assumption, may either not expose herself or inhibit herself. A diminished sense of well-being may make sex activity unattractive, or distressing symptoms, such as nervousness, insomnia, hot flashes or depression, may preempt the mind to the exclusion of everything else. In time, the narrowing of the vagina, the mucosal atrophy, the decrease in genital secretion and the loss of tonus in the levator ani muscles may also make themselves felt and interfere with pleasurable intercourse. Sometimes it is the husband who has negative beliefs about the sex needs of a castrated woman and neglects her sexually. In a few wives the subconscious awareness that coitus no longer has reproductive significance seems to impair both their desire and their reactions. A minority of oophorectomized wives indicate that their sexual desire and responses have increased since the operation. This can occur where previously worry about pregnancy had always been a hindrance to enjoyment; and, occasionally, where the vulva, notably the clitoris, has become more sensitized, thus making pleasure more acutely felt and perhaps desired.

Treatment of the postcastration syndrome begins with preoperative reassurance and forewarning, and a search for unfavorably predisposing states of mind. Postoperatively, the choice and the dosage of estrogenic replacement and sedative therapies is somewhat similar to that in the involuting woman, but the addition of testosterone to estrogenic substitution in these younger women is particularly helpful, partly because it can quickly demonstrate to the patient (e.g., in on-the-table pellet implantation) that their libido is no less than it had been. Small doses of thyroid are helpful. Hypnotics should not be given indiscriminately where an acute, remediable sexual adjustment problem between the spouses exists. Diet regulation, both for weight maintenance and ample protein intake, would be of value. The husband may be advised to resume marital relations as soon as surgically permissible and tolerated by the woman, to help her to overcome possible fears of sexual inadequacy or undesirability.

Premature Ovarian Failure (Precocious Menopause). Complete and permanent failure (diagnosis: consistently high, castrate-type gonadotropin excretion) can occur as early as the late teens. It is probably not rare, and may be familial in some cases. The cause is uncertain; abnormalities of the X-chromosome, including mosaicisms, are sometimes found; the ovaries may be congenitally small with deficient primordial follicles and rapid depletion of available oocytes. The condition produces menopausal symptoms with a high incidence of vasomotor discomfort. Any sexual failure is tied to the rapidity of genital changes to be expected in the younger estrogen-deprived woman. Measures include reassurance, timely estrogenic substitution and, for psychologic reasons, maintenance of cyclic bleeding, (e.g., with courses of sequential progestins).

Irradiation of the ovaries can induce ovarian cessation and menopause, but the effect varies with age or, probably, with the number of viable ova remaining. In a young woman 1400 or 1500 rads, either in single dose or fractionated, may be necessary to produce complete cessation; in middle age as little as 700 rads may be sufficient to destroy all hormonally active ova (Andrews, MacDonald).

Chiari-Frommel Syndrome. Here genital atrophy, especially of the uterus, occurs together with amenorrhea. The cardinal symptom is spontaneous lactation after a puerperium, persisting for years, and low urinary gonadotropin (FSH) excretion. At fault probably is a lesion near or in the hypothalamus which blocks the prolactin-inhibiting center. Evidence of a causative tumor may turn up only years later on skull x-rays. Mental symptoms often coexist.

Pituitary Failure, including **Simmonds' Disease.** Desexing may result from pituitary insufficiency. The cause is any structural disorder which lastingly involves the pituitary-hypothalamic axis and impairs and destroys it: tumors in and around the area, massive infarcts (see Sheehan's syndrome, below), encephalitis, cystic degeneration, abscesses, tuberculosis, sarcoidosis, or following influenza, irradiation, snakebites, prolonged cortisone therapy, trauma producing necrosis, and from causes unknown (Simmonds' disease). Sooner or later all endocrine organs under pituitary control participate in the clinical picture to a variable degree, usually the ovaries first, then the thyroid, last the adrenal cortex. Severity of the picture depends on the rate and the degree of pituitary or pathway destruction.

In severe cases, the untreated woman with Simmonds' disease looks old beyond her years. She is apathetic, and moves and talks slowly; or she may take to her bed. The face has a tired, washed-out appearance. The skin is extremely pale and may be of transparent thinness or else puffy with myxedema. The lateral eyebrows are absent. Nutritional status varies; thinness may exist early in the disease in some patients together with weakness, faintness and low blood pressure. Others remain well nourished; still others are obese. Episodes of voraciousness can occur, during which the patients devour food and even foodlike substances and may "empty the water tap." The ovaries involute, there is oligomenorrhea, then amenorrhea, but without vasomotor symptoms. Internal and external genitalia shrink in substance, the breasts may regress, and axillary and later pubic hair gray prematurely or fall out completely. The libido is diminished or absent, partly as a result of associated hypothyroidism. The patients do not perspire; they are oversensitive to cold temperatures. Mental disturbances are relatively frequent.

Sheehan's Syndrome (postpartum hypopituitarism) is a relatively common variety. The cause is ischemic necrosis of the anterior pituitary following obstetric hemorrhage and vascular shock during childbirth or postpartum. Onset, including somatic and personality changes, may be insidious, over a period of months or years; severe cases have gone unrecognized for up to 15 years. These women do not seek medical attention; if they are taken to a physician, they may fail to follow advice or fail to rouse themselves sufficiently to return.

The young mother does not menstruate again as expected, her shaved pubic hair does not grow back or only thinly so, and her breasts shrink and secrete no milk. She is weak, does not feel well and has no appetite. In a severe untreated case, the genitalia become atrophic, while libido decreases, and sooner or later libido becomes extinct. The labia minora and the areolae lose pigment, the whole body becomes hairless. In the severest untreated cases, fairly rare today, personality changes have been dramatic at times because of the marked contrast with the pre-illness existence. In the earlier stages these women may be so apathetic and dysenergetic that the new baby or other children have to be removed because of neglect. They may lose their entire family, lead a marginal existence until they turn up as unkempt, deteriorated derelicts. Both acute deliroid and chronic schizophrenia-like hallucinatory syndromes have been observed.

Inanition Desexing in women parallels that seen in men. Because the most sensitive function, and the first to suffer, is menstruation, hunger dystrophies are customarily classified among the secondary amenorrheas. Adult ovarian failure due to malnutrition has been repeatedly observed on a mass basis during the past 50 years under such designations as war (postwar, ghetto, refugee, Flucht) amenorrhea and as part of the K-Z (concentration camp) syndrome. In severe cases of starvation under stress, the uterus and the ovaries involute, shrink in size, and at autopsy weigh less, with few follicles detectable on the ovaries. The external genitalia also regress, with spontaneous uterine prolapse not infrequent. In most famines, the breasts disappear, but not invariably ("skin-covered skeleton with breasts"). Prognosis as to restoration of cyclic function is good, even after years of amenorrhea, but only as long as there has not been severe genital atrophy. Gonadal resumption begins about 2 weeks after refeeding. However, minor irreversible residual disturbances and deficits in severely starved women may be somewhat more frequent than has been assumed (e.g., libidinal lability, menstrual irregularities, or vaginal and pelvic tonus changes).

Adrenal Virilism (acquired adrenogenital syndrome) in the adolescent or fully grown female, regardless of age, is produced most often by virilizing adenoma or adenocarcinoma of the adrenals. The degree of virilization corresponds roughly to the production rate of testosterone. The inundation of the female organism with androgen also inhibits ovarian function. The mild case may manifest only non-ovulatory menses, or amenorrhea, and hirsutism. In a pronounced case, pelvic fat recedes, contour becomes more masculine, muscle strength increases, while the breasts may or may not remain feminine. Degrees of hirsutism appear, including masculine pubic hair, and she must shave her beard and mustache frequently. The coarse, dark beard hair, especially on the chin and the upper lip, differs from the finer, longer hair on the sides of the face of the woman with Cushing's syndrome. The skin assumes masculine structure, and acne may appear on the face and the back. The voice becomes first hoarse or husky (one of the earliest signs), then harsh or deep; the Adam's apple (thyroid cartilage) becomes prominent. The hairline recedes at the forehead and the temples, the scalp hair becomes sparse and oily, and at times near-baldness ensues. Thus, the picture of the virago prevails.

Genitality. The labia majora darken and thicken somewhat, the clitoris grows in size and vascularity, and there is gradual hypoplasia of the introital structures, vagina and internal genitals, with menstrual irregularities (nonovulation), or secondary amenorrhea, and sterility. In most patients urinary 17-ketosteroids are elevated. The libido may increase in a proportion of these women, as sexual sensitivity becomes more localized. Vaginal atrophy (stenosis) and shortening—ligamental softening with some uterine prolapse—may cause dyspareunia. In many cases a true increase in libido is not present, but some of these women are more aggressive or outspoken about their desire to experience. Lesbianism in previously normal women does not occur. Withdrawal of erotic interest in men, in reaction to a negative self-image, may occur. A proportion of virilized women manifest no erotic interest of any type.

Prognosis. The longer virilizing-defeminizing changes persist, the less likely is their eventual regression. Surgical removal of an androgen-producing neoplasm will, as a rule, cause ovarian function to return and reduce seborrhea. Some excess hair will remain. Breast atrophy and clitoral hypertrophy are not completely reversible. Laryngeal changes will remain and the voice will not rise appreciably (Segre).

Cushing's Syndrome. Here the chronic production of excessive amounts of glucocorticoids in the adrenal cortex produces the characteristic appearance of this disorder: there is muscle wasting and replacement by fat tissue about the upper trunk, neck and face, leading to the "buffalo hump" and the "moon face." The extremities are spared. The skin of the face is glossy and plethoric-ruddy and bruises easily; there are furrowed purple striae on the body. Patients are weak and tire easily, especially at the end of the day; they do not tolerate stress well. Psychiatric symptoms are frequent. In women there is amenorrhea and defeminizing symptoms in about half the cases, believed to be primary (i.e., by direct effect of the hypercortisonism on the ovaries). Virilization occurs frequently, notably where carcinoma causes the syndrome, and is due to overproduction of 17-ketosteroids in addition to the glucocorticoids. The signs of desexing and virilization usually appear and progress in order. First noted is increasing hair on the face, extremities and lower abdominal mid-line, while the menses become scantier, and periods are skipped. Shortly, the breasts become smaller, and sexual intercourse becomes more uncomfortable because the vaginal mucosa thins and becomes tender, the genital secretions diminish, and the vaginal passage becomes somewhat stenotic. This, together with the increasing feeling of malaise and depression, contributes to a lessening of the libido. In time, if untreated, the ovaries, the uterus, the tubes and the vagina may regress conspicuously, the menses cease, and vaginal smears produce a castrate cell picture.

Polycystic Ovary Syndrome (Stein-Leventhal syndrome). This group of ovarian follicle disorders with gradual anovulation and frequent secondary amenorrhea usually arises in adolescence, but mostly is discovered at a somewhat later age. Degrees of hypogonadism develop together with limited virilization, but the clinical picture is far from uniform. About one half of these women develop hirsutism especially of the face and acquire a male pubic escutcheon, together with acne and obesity; these conditions are slowly progressive, if untreated. A minority develop hypoplasia of vagina and breasts, followed shortly by clitoral enlargement, masculinization of the body contour and a degree of libidinal increase. Subjective psychosexual difficulties are more pronounced in the moderately severe cases; there is the usual anhedonia-dyspareunia-frigidity syndrome encountered in defeminizing syndromes, while the patient's knowledge (or suspicion) of being infertile adds a note of panicky desperateness to her efforts to "prove" feminine competence. However, depressions and personality disorders do not reach the severity of those seen in Cushing's but are more frequent than in the adrenogenital syndrome.

Masculinizing Tumors of the Ovaries are fairly rare. Most androgenic tumors occur during the reproductive period, chiefly arrhenoblastoma; less often the clinically similar hilus cell (Leydig cell) tumors of middle-aged women, diffuse luteoma, and the occasional adrenal-like masculinovoblastoma. They cause progressive defeminization accompanied or followed by deepening of the voice, hirsutism and beard growth, receding hairline, enlargement of the clitoris and, occasionally, acne. Depression of mood frequentiy accompanies the syndrome, apparently even when the patient is unaware of the diagnosis and its possible significance. Libido may be lowered or increased, in an unpredictable pattern; in hilus cell tumors it is lowered. In the same tumors, reversal of sex changes after successful surgery is incomplete (age?).

Exogenous Androgen. Prolonged administration of therapeutic androgens can virilize the adult woman, as well as defeminize her, the latter by suppressing gonadotropin and, in turn, ovarian activity. Hair appears on the legs, then on the face and the remaining body; the skin becomes oily, and the voice deepens; then moderate acne may develop, the hairline recedes, and the clitoris becomes enlarged, more vascular and, usually, eroticaily more sensitive. There may be unusual weight gain, graying of the hair, bald spots, and regressive changes in the vaginal mucosa, with mobilization of trichomonas vaginitis. The effect on the breasts is minor or, at most, uncertain (Hamburger).

Equally uncertain is the amount of testosterone necessary to stop menstruation. In the induced virilization of female transsexuals and in other cases sometimes 100 to 150 mg of long-acting testosterone I.M. a week have stopped the menses, and maintenance doses of 150 to 200 mg a month have kept them suppressed; in others, doses above 500 mg a month of the same hormone were unable to maintain anovulation. Although most virilizing effects disappear on cessation of treatment some changes may be irreversible (voice, baldness, facial hirsutism), and these cannot be predicted. Sensitivity to induced virilization varies individually. Particularly susceptible may be women who have discernible viriloid traits, those with a tendency to facial acne or hirsuteness, and women with a family history of a tendency to baldness among the male members. The effect of androgen administration on the female libido, and on the psyche generally, is not a fixed attribute of the hormone but depends to a major extent on the personality make-up and the total situation of the patient. Although, for example, the clitoris is sensitized, libido is not necessarily increased, or when it is, it does not necessarily furnish heightened pleasure (see also p. 416). A small amount of progesterone added to the testosterone dosage may counteract undesired increase in libido (Benjamin).

INTERSEXED STATES

(Intersexuality, Hermaphroditism, Hermaphrodism.
Vernac. Double-Sexedness)

This is a group of sexual abnormalities acquired in utero or even before, when the male and female gametes first united. Intersexuality is estimated to exist in close to 1 per cent of the population. Here male and female somatic gender characteristics are present in the same person in a variety of combinations, affecting the chromosomal sex, the gonads, the internal genital ducts and organs and/or the external genitalia. Not included among intersexed persons are certain individuals of normal build and genitality who identify themselves counter to their own gender and yearn to be part of "the other half" (transsexuals).

Innumerable degrees of somatic sex divergence exist, ranging from the mildest—first degree hypospadias in a normal male, or an enlarged clitoris in a normal female—to cases of the most complex ambisexuality. Often, genital ambiguity is immediately manifest in the newborn infant; in other cases the discovery is made only later (e.g., accidentally during repair of a child's inguinal hernia, or in an adult being examined for infertility). Sometimes the condition emerges into clinical overtness at puberty. In the newborn infant, any kind of genital anomaly needs to be met with a high index of suspicion. The physician must refrain from haphazardly or summarily assigning the infant to the apparent birth sex, if any type of external genital ambiguity is present, such as what seems to be an empty scrotum, or a degree of hypospadias, especially if the testicles are not in place. Instead, sex diagnosis on a scientific basis should be made as soon after birth as possible. For optimal results gender decisions must be made within hours, at most days from birth. During this period any premature gender statement to the parents must be avoided, as any even faint mention of one gender or the other seems to burn itself indelibly into the consciousness of the parents and nothing will ever completely free them from prejudicial thought processes should the decision go against the original mention (Laybourne-Wurster-Fish, others).

Today the prevailing criterion is empirical (i.e., one of potential future adjustment): whether a serviceable genital organ, most often the phallus, can be obtained and maintained. There is rarely more than clinical-technical regard for the existing genetic or gonadal sex. After all ascertainable data—gonadal sex, genetic sex, external and internal genital structure, estimate of hormone status—have been assembled, the final decision as to sex assignment in intersex cases is still a matter of clinical judgment. Some of these infants are truly "between sexes," but they are entitled to as normal an existence as can be provided, and they must have a sex identity. If a sex error occurs (i.e., a child has been misidentified at birth), there is a margin of 1 to 2 years to reassign with impunity; thereafter the child most likely has developed gender identity largely according to its rearing. A few remain uncomfortable and unhappy and in their teens may spontaneously ask a physician for a revision of gender status. This is a severely taxing decision; alone the surgery involved (e.g., castration, penectomy, mastectomy, panhysterectomy, transplants, etc.) according to the necessities of the case, which may have been easier or even unnecessary in infancy, can make such belated crossing-over a formidable undertaking. The indications for this type of surgery in intersexuality is not to be confused with the sex change surgery of transsexuals practiced in a few medical centers.

True Hermaphrodites are intersexed persons who possess both ovarian and testicular tissue in one of 3 basic combinations: a combined ovary and testis (ovotestis) on each side, a testis on one side and an ovary on the other side, or an ovotestis on one side and a specific gonad on the other. Human intersexes are not able to beget as well as conceive, nor to fertilize themselves; in fact, they are sterile, although in a few cases production of ova and spermatozoa has been demonstrated. Most known cases are genetically female; the most frequent karyotype is 46XX. Although almost all have at least a rudimentary uterus and often ovarian function, the vagina is mostly abnormal (e.g., very small), and the external genitalia often ambiguous. At least one gonad is usually found in the abdomen. Many true hermaphrodites are raised as males; but while puberty brings deepening of the voice, enlargement of the phallus and other masculine puberal traits, the breasts also may develop suddenly together with monthly abdominal cramps accompanied by what may be erroneously diagnosed as recurrent monthly hematuria.

Congenital Adrenal Hyperplasia in the Female, also known as **Female Pseudohermaphroditism.** Intersexing here is the product of an inheritable disease, an inborn metabolic error, in which the genetic female, beginning in utero, is being masculinized by her own excess adrenal androgens. It occurs equally often in boys in whom it produces precocious pseudopuberty (infant Hercules, see p. 20). The masculinization of the female fetus and, later, of the little girl, is progressive, unless treatment is instituted (corticosteroids).

In the newborn female pseudohermaphrodite, the external genitalia may look like those of an overdeveloped male infant. The hypertrophic clitoris (often 2 cm. long) may look like a penis with hypospadias. The labia majora are fused to varying degrees, giving the appearance of an empty scrotum; behind it is located the often deepened sinus into which the vagina and the urethra open. An external opening for urination is most often found at the upper pole of the labial folds. Other abnormalities of the vulva occur; occasionally vulva and anterior vagina are absent. The possibility of a "sex error" leading to faulty gender assignment in this type of case, more than any other intersex condition, has led to making sex chromatin determination an urgent indication in all newborns with what appears to be bilateral cryptorchism. Here, in all cases, the sex chromatic pattern is positive. Some of these infants have an associated disorder of the electrolyte regulating mechanism of the adrenals ("salt losers"), a life-threatening condition.

Untreated Female Pseudohermaphrodites are uncommon today, although late treatment in milder cases and in the delayed (postnatal) variant without genital deformities is inevitable on occasions. Adrenogenital sex errors—girls raised to live, even marry, as males—seem to be exceedingly rare now. The untreated little girl develops sexual pseudoprecocity, but along masculine lines, as adrenal androgen continues to be produced. She has tallness and bone and dental maturation far ahead of her age (p. 19). Pubic hair first grows in the third year of life and has masculine distribution; 3 years later axillary hair appears. After age 6, the skin tends toward seborrhea and acne; a gray-brownish pigmentation is not unusual. In the pre-teens a down develops on the upper lip and the sideburns lengthen. If still untreated, the bony epiphyses fuse at the beginning of the second decade, terminating somatic growth and producing the characteristically short (4 feet 8 inches to 5 feet 2 inches) final adult stature of these patients. Body contour remains completely unfeminine, as in childhood; the pelvis and the hips are narrow, the legs short, shoulders and thorax broad and musculature well developed. The voice now deepens and tends toward harshness. Many of these girls develop scant breasts or none at all, although the areolae darken. There is no menarche at the usual age in the untreated case; it either occurs with much delay, or not at all. Uterus and tubes may be rudimentary or malformed.

In the teens the vagina remains immature and shows no evidence of estrinization. The vaginal opening may be hidden within the urethra, and cyclic "hematuria" may be the only evidence of menstruation. There may be a single perineal opening at the base of the clitoris or on its shaft. The clitoris has kept growing. It may reach a nonerect length of 2 or 3 inches, but usually it is held down in ventral chordee. The organ is very sensitive to somesthetic stimuli, and annoying erections and clitoral masturbation are frequent. The labioscrotal folds are hypertrophic and, if fused from birth, hide the vagina. The adult female pseudohermaphrodite who has never been treated, in addition to her genital abnormalities, tends to be a short-statured brownish-pigmented hirsute individual of android habitus, with small or no breasts. In severe cases reared as boys, there is little or nothing to distinguish her from a man on social occasions, or even on

364 • *Desexing, Cross-Sexing, Intersexing*

cursory medical examination. In the past a number of such girls preferred to live disguised as men. Once they "passed" in that role they suffered less from the depressive moods so characteristic of the maladjusted congenital hyperadrenal female.

Exogenous Masculinization of Female in Utero. This condition, also known as the non-adrenal form of female pseudohermaphroditism, is caused by hormonal excess within the mother: most often when she was medicated or took birth control pills during pregnancy, rarely by maternal testosterone-secreting tumors (e.g., ovarian arrhenoblastoma). Substances known to be capable of masculinizing a female fetus include testosterone, 17-methyl-testosterone, diethyl stilbestrol, progesterone, hydroxyprogesterone, norethindrone, norethandrolone and ethisterone (Schlegel-Gardner). Corticosteroid therapy of the mother has not been implicated. In human fraternal twins, unlike in some mammals (e.g., freemartin of cattle), a male fetus cannot masculinize its female twin. Only one female embryo in 3 is affected by these hormones; a hereditary sensitivity may exist. Exposure during or before the 12th gestational week (from last calculated ovulation) constitutes the sensitive period, except for enlargement of the clitoris which can be induced at any stage; the most critical period lies between the sixtieth and ninetieth days (others: the seventh to sixteenth week of gestation). When a pregnant woman on medication reacts with acne, raucousness of voice, hirsutism or clitoral enlargement the fetus has already been masculinized; obversely this may happen even without maternal changes. Simultaneous administration of estrogenic steroids does not protect the fetus.

Clinically, induced masculinization is more benign than the adrenal type. It is limited to the external genitalia and consists of enlargement of the clitoris, partial or complete fusion of the labia, some pubic hair at birth, and some advancement of osseous maturation. Occasionally the meatus is at the base of the phallus or, rarely, a penile urethra exists. The internal genitalia are not affected; the ovaries are functional. Unlike the adrenal form, this condition is not progressive after birth; in fact, it tends to regress within 6 to 24 months, except for the clitoral enlargement and any actual labial fusion which requires surgical correction later. Precocious pseudopuberty does not occur, and the girl can be expected to have normal menarche (through the urethra) and other feminizing puberal development, including breasts, at the normal time. She will be normally fertile. These infants need to be raised as females, regardless of the appearance of the external genitalia.

Male Intersexed State (male pseudohermaphroditism). In essence these are genetic (XY) males with gonads microscopically identifiable as testicles who have incompletely differentiated genital structure—external or internal or both—because either the fetal testicles were functionally insufficient at the critical differentiating time to organize the wolffian ducts and to promote external male organs, or else these structures and ducts were endowed with some form of unresponsiveness. In accord with the principle that all fetal structures feminize unless a working testicle forces masculine development on them (see p. 4), malformations counter to the gonad arise and can be diagnosed in the baby boy at birth. They range over a broad spectrum, from the simplest—a normal male inside and out except for mild hypospadias—to the moderately severe— internal male sex structures with external genitals simulating the female's: bilateral cryptorchism, bifid scrotum, perineal hypospadias and a very small penis held down in chordee—to the extreme—the testicular feminization syndrome (see below) with internal ducts partly differentiated female, in addition to a completely feminized genital exterior, probably resulting from androgen insensitivity of the end organs.

As the quality of testicle function may still be insufficient in the second decade of life, some male intersexes fail to develop puberally and, untreated, become hypogonadal men. Others masculinize, at least somewhat, at puberty; in cases of sex error (misidentified gender) correction is sometimes not made even then. Once in a while cases of this type will pass fleetingly across a medical horizon. Summarily pronounced female by a delivery room nurse, accepted as such by unsophisticated parents, recipient of only minimal or undiscerning pediatric and school medical attention, shamed or browbeaten into assigned sex-role compliance by bewildered parents following unexpected puberal masculinization, yet never examined medically below the waist, the syndrome, once discovered, may be passed off quickly ("just never developed right, that's all"), and the patient is hurried off by the parents or scurries away, to disappear again from view, perhaps to submerge as the "timid strong girl" in some laundering plant or on the parents' farm.

Management of these patients remains empirical, to be decided from case to case. There is wisdom in assigning the sex of male pseudohermaphroditic infants according to the potential of their reproductive system but failures occur. A disappointed father may reluctantly accept his firstborn son to be a girl, but his rearing attitude may be self-conscious, subconsciously masculinizing and imbued with resentful or wishful fantasies; protective castration is then opposed, even with a tiny penis which cannot be stretched to more than 1 inch or so. When pubescence does bring some isosexing—the voice breaks, acne appears, the penis grows, male sex hair and some facial hair come forth, and masculine contour develops—the psyche may remain female-oriented and in spite of good cosmetic support a psychologically unprepared teen-ager can retreat way back emotionally and socially under these circumstances. On the other hand, some individuals have achieved renown as female athletes.

Androgen Insensitivity Syndrome (Testicular Feminizing or Morris Syndrome). This is an extreme, hereditary form of male pseudohermaphroditism which is no longer considered rare. The cause is believed to be an inherited enzyme defect which renders all cells in the body unresponsive to androgen; the cells respond only to testicular estrogen. It is transmitted through female carriers—patients' mothers—who themselves have scant sex and axillary hair and delayed menarche. These intersexed persons are genetic males—the chromosomal karyotype is 46XY—with undescended but usually normally hormone-secreting testicles. Lacking also the testicular wolffian duct stimulator the genital ductal system fails to differentiate correctly and they do not masculinize in fetal life; nor do they virilize at puberty. The hypothalamus presumably remains female, as the brain cells also are testosterone-insensitive. At birth, and later, the external genitalia in every way are female and the neonate passes as a baby girl, which happens to be as it should be in these cases.

As adults they have been described as hairless women with testicles. They are often attractive, feminine, very tall (eunuchoidal) females with long feet and hands. The voice is essentially feminine, head hair is ample, while beard and body hair are absent; pubic and axillary hair, however, are also absent or scanty. At puberty they develop large breasts, though often with juvenile nipples, which remain firm and pointed upright for a long part of their lives. The testicles are abdominal or in the inguinal canal, and it is there, in the teens during the frequently necessary hernia repair, that the diagnosis is first made by the surgeon. These gonads have a high rate of future neoplasia and are now often removed as soon as the secondary sex characteristics are fully developed; subsequent estrogen dosing serves to control the often severe menopause and to maintain well feminized physical traits including breasts and vaginal mucosa. As a rule, there is no uterus, or at most a uterine rudiment. The vagina ends blind. Its length or shortness is in direct proportion to the degree of testicular insufficiency. Some have a very short vagina, especially the few known cases in whom spermatozoa were found on testicular biopsy. Such cases of partial testicular feminization may be a separate syndrome; here the external genitalia are not clearly feminine but ambiguous, there is a substantial clitoris, and at puberty feminization may not take place. Cases with more pronounced feminine structure have a longer vagina. There is always primary amenorrhea and incurable sterility. The estrogen level in the adult patient is low as compared with a normal woman's. The gonadotropin titer is high.

Interests of these individuals are feminine—dolls, maternalism, libido towards males—and but for the amenorrhea and for the infertility later, some cases might never be, and probably are not diagnosed. They tend to have above-average intelligence; as personalities they have a realistic no-

nonsense outlook. A proportion, during childhood, have tomboyish tendencies and some develop amazon-like traits as adults; these cases pertain to partial testicular feminization, characterized by a large clitoris, mentioned above. Libido of most is typically feminine; they usually get married and have a normal vita sexualis, including orgasm. However, where the vagina is short and this has not been treated, dyspareunia can be marked. These are women for all practical purposes; they should be helped to be better adapted to the feminine role. If the breasts are underdeveloped, long courses of intermittent estrogen administration may be tried, or even plastic surgery. If more sex hair is desired, an androgen-estrogen mixture may be deposited in the tissues. If the vagina is too short for cohabitation, estrogens, plastic surgery and dilating bougies may be of help, although intercourse itself tends to have an enlarging effect on the vagina in these cases. In fact, the presence of a chromatin-negative pattern and of testicles is perhaps best kept from the patient, except that they must know that they will never menstruate nor be fertile.

Genetic (Chromosomal) Intersexes

The most prominent syndrome associated with a sex chromosome aberration in the male is **Klinefelter's Syndrome** (seminiferous tubule dysgenesis), leading to eunuchoidal tallness, atrophic testicles, gynecomastia, some mental retardation and enfeebled sexual manifestations; not every sign exists in every case. Incidence is estimated to be 1 in every 400 to 500 live male births; in mentally retarded groups Klinefelter's is found in 1 out of every 50 to 100 patients.

These are phenotypic males, but most have a female type of nuclear sex chromatin pattern. Their characteristic chromosome pattern is 47, XXY, with many mosaicisms and variants, notably XXY/XY; 48, XXYY; 48, XXXY; 49, XXXXY; even some 50, XXXXXY. The more X chromosomes they have, the more eunuchoidal and hypogonadic they tend to be, as well as increasingly often retarded. An additional Y chromosome tends to add aggressive features to the personality, although these are socially less of a potential menace than some (not all!) of the unrelated XYY males. In the chromatin-positive Klinefelter patient the number of X variants can be assessed by the number of Barr bodies in the body cell nuclei: the latter is one less than the number of X chromosomes; a count of Y chromosomes requires a karyotype.

The most constant sign are small testicles (always descended except in the 49, karyotype), ranging from pea-sized to 2 cm long, rarely more. Size can be conveniently assessed with the Prader orchidometer, a string of graded plastic models of testicle shape, sizes 20 to 25 representing the normal adult range. Testicles are considered hypoplastic if their long axis is shorter than 3.4 cm. Hardness of the organs when present is caused by the patchy sclerosing degeneration of the seminiferous tubules. If patients ejaculate at all, the seminal volume is small, its fructose content low, spermatozoa are absent with only a few reported exceptions, and sterility is the rule.

The penis is usually normal, the prostate small, pubic hair scant or of female type, body hair all but absent, beard late and scanty, the voice is not fully masculine, and habitus either eunuchoidal or gynecoid; most are over 6 feet tall. A few are well virilized and manifest only tallness, small testicles and are libidinally somewhat inert. The frequently present gynecomastia is permanent and bilateral (treatment: mastectomy), but the most sex deficient cases grow the least breasts. Some breasts become as large as those of a young woman. The diagnosis is rarely made before teen age. Plasma testosterone is low, gonadotropin (FSH) production high. Those of the most eunuchoidal build complain of vasomotor crises at an early age. The muscles are weak, posture often is slouchy, and vertebral osteoporosis and its complications set in early. Congenital abnormalities of the skeleton and the central nervous system are not unusual, as are abnormal electroencephalograms.

Most of these men are initially capable of erection, and coitus, and marriage is not rare. However, in untreated patients the libido tends to be feeble and rather infantile, and gradual extinction of potency in the third or the fourth decade is the rule.

Some drift into homosexual associations and may be seduced into a passive type of homosexuality, both in and out of institutions. Their sexual self-image and their gender identity tend to be uncertain. There is an increased frequency of transvestism, pedophilia and exhibitionistic tendencies among them.

The condition is not curable. For androgenic deficits an early, adequate and permanent schedule of substitution therapy is indicated, to improve appearance and muscle status, prevent crippling due to osteoporosis, impart a sense of well-being and, perhaps, restore libido.

Turner's Syndrome (gonadal dysgenesis, Bonnevie-Ullrich syndrome). These are phenotypic female, but most have a negative nuclear sex chromatin pattern; the characteristic chromosome pattern is 45, XO, with numerous variants and mosaicisms. The principal manifestations are sexual infantilism, stunted stature, multiple malformations and fibrotic streak-like ovaries in the broad ligaments.

The majority are borderline dwarfs, averaging 4½ feet or a little more in final height if untreated. Some are merely short-statured, and a few reach normal size spontaneously, but sometimes only in their twenties. Deformities include a webbed neck, elbow deformities (increased carrying angle), large or deformed low-set ears, impaired hearing, and others. Not all patients have all or even most stigmata, and a number have few or none. Often the diagnosis is made only in the teens, although even the newborn has the webbed neck, with a whorled hair pattern growing down the nape, the malplanted ears and the small chin, as well as edema of the hands and the feet. Although dwarfed, the proportions of the skeleton are within normal limits, but many, in addition to being obese, are of stocky build with a boyish, narrow pelvis and a broad, "shield-shaped" thoracic front, and a tendency to marked cubitus valgus. On the brachycephalic skull the face, the shape of the mouth and the receding chin combine to give the patient a doll-like appearance.

Unless the patient has been treated (estrogen mainly), the reproductive apparatus remains infantile. Perineum, vulva and vagina are childlike, the labia minora absent, uterus and cervix immature. Breasts remain undeveloped more often than not, and sex hair is scant. There is primary amenorrhea in the great majority of cases, and these patients are incurably sterile, although a few exceptions have been reported. The gonadotropin (FSH) titer is high. Occasionally there is a degree of masculinization, with hirsuties, an enlarged clitoris, and/or somewhat more animation and spunk or even tomboyishness. While even barely in their twenties, but still untreated, they begin to age externally, looking young-oldish as their facial skin wrinkles and becomes atrophic and thin. Subsequently, hypertension and osteoporosis may appear.

Many are childish far into their teens, generally dull, passive and lacking in drive and originality. A proportion are frankly feeble-minded. Often they mainly desire to please their teachers, parents, doctor, etc., and they depend very much on their mothers. The more they advance, untreated, into the teens, the more they are isolated and excluded, or exposed to rejection, by their peers because of their nonconforming appearance and childlikeness. They develop defensive stances in the midteens, including blocking out. Height and weight worry them more than undeveloped breasts or absent menses, and they may blame all social failures on some particular stigma. A seemingly excessive unconcern ("Mother says it'll come right in the end"; "the lady told me not to worry") is partly due to hysteric-type repression and partly to stolidity. Others become truly apprehensive and depressed, and may have to be removed from school temporarily while being treated. Erotic-romantic interest, if any, is usually years behind the chronologic age; but exceptions, as regards libido, have been seen.

Treatment should not start so late as to find the epiphyses near closure or closed; 12 or 13 years of age is usually suitable. Where the possibility of treatment first comes up in the middle or later teens, apprehension, even resistance or panic about feminization are often present. However, it is probably wasteful to wait for guidance to ready these children for menses and womanly somatic features; results are better when the patient is carefully tranquilized first, then estrinized nolens volens; finally, one makes amends by giving continued attention, as the estrogen enhances her accessibility, her motivation and her ability to respond. Following successful estrinization, which continues lifelong, they mature physically and emotionally, and often manifest substantial maternalism which the most evolved among them channel into adoptive motherhood or child care work.

FOR JOURNAL LITERATURE AND ADDITIONAL READING

Armstrong, C. N. and Marshall, A. J. (eds.): Intersexuality in Vertebrates including Man. New York, Academic Press, 1964

Bremer, J.: Asexualization. A Follow-up Study of 244 Cases. New York, Macmillan, 1959

Dewhurst, C. J. and Gordon: Intersexual Disorders. Baltimore, Williams & Wilkins, 1969

Gold, J. J. (ed.): Gynecologic Endocrinology. New York, Hoeber, 1968

Greenblatt, R. B. (ed.): The Hirsute Female. Springfield, Ill., Thomas, 1963

Joel, K. A. (ed.): Fertility Disturbances in Men and Women. Basel, Karger (White Plains, N.Y., A. J. Phiebig), 1971

Jones, H. W. and Scott, W. W. (eds.): Hermaphroditism, Genital Anomalies and Related Endocrine Disorders, ed. 2. Baltimore, Williams & Wilkins, 1971

Martini, L. and Ganong, W. F. (eds.): Neuroendocrinology (2 vols.) New York, Academic Press, 1967, Espec. vol. 2.

Money, J.: Sex Errors of the Body. Baltimore, Johns Hopkins Press, 1968

Overzier, K. (ed.): Intersexuality. New York, Academic Press, 1963

Segre, E. J.: Androgens, Virilization and the Hirsute Female. Springfield, Ill., Thomas, 1967

CHAPTER 17

Sexual Impotence

Minor Deflections of Potency — Organic Causes of Impotence —
Psychogenic Causes of Impotence — Disorders of Ejaculation —
Treatment of Impotence.

Impotence is the inability to have an adequate sexual erection and to
maintain it to the completion of a satisfactory sexual act. It includes disorders of erection as well as of ejaculation—mainly premature, retarded
and retrograde—but not disorders of fertility.

The Myth of "90 Per Cent." It is no longer possible uncritically to
accept the dictum that most cases of impotence are psychogenic. Diagnosis
by exclusion, even after painstaking organic search, remains an inadequate
rationale for assignment to psychogenicity. In the face of mounting new
insights into sexual functioning—role of limbic system, miniquantification
of hormonal plasma level shifts, techniques of operant conditioning, stress
studies, etc.—such assignment no longer seems an acceptable "out" in
case of apparent zero findings. The oft-cited figure of 90 per cent (psychogenic causes of impotence) which found its way into the medical literature
in the 1950's needs finally to be buried: it simply does not correspond to
what cases are seen in clinics and offices which take a little trouble and
have no axes to grind. The fact is, the cause of impotence remains obscure
in a substantial proportion of cases.

Uncertainties of Classification. The classification of male sexual failure
and nonperformance remains unsettled. For instance, most selective impotence (see box) is psychogenic, but is it always true impotence (i.e.,
wishing to perform, then failing at it)? Often these are primarily cases of
deficient interest—in a certain partner, or kind of partner—leading to nonperformance. The men themselves, especially if unsophisticated, cannot
always indicate if they lack capacity or motivation. The physician cannot
tell either: he must rely on what he is told. The wife may report one thing,
and the patient may tell anything at all so as not to have to admit, for
instance, that his wife disgusts him or that he likes sex with young males

GLOSSARY OF SEXUAL IMPOTENCE

Organic Impotence	Includes structural changes (e.g., paraplegia, Leriche syndrome, status postsigmoidectomy), or disease (e.g., diabetic neuropathy, Cushing's syndrome), or demonstrable function impairment (e.g., Klinefelter's, heroin addiction) anywhere in the sexual apparatus or mechanism.
Psychogenic Impotence	Psychologic factors prevail (e.g., anxious-inhibitory syndrome, aversion to partner, moderate depressive state).
Physiologic Impotence	Interruption or cessation of function in due course (e.g., extinction in old age, sexual satiation).
Non-Performance	Erection normal, but too awkward or painful to intromit (e.g., Peyronie's Disease, painful herpes or other inhibiting dyspareunia).

Borderline cases are difficult to classify (e.g., functional hypopituitarism, injury phobia with phimosis, temporal lobe disease, depressive psychosis—hypothalamic libido suppression).

Total (Complete) Impotence	All sexual functions affected in toto: erection, sensation, forward ejaculation, orgasm, though not necessarily libido (e.g., prolonged estrogen medication, some spinal cord cases).
Partial Impotence	Signifies either dissociation of erection and ejaculation (one without the other), or incompletely rigid, unmaintained, or hard-to-initiate erective capacity.
Absolute Impotence	Involves all sexual modalities: marital and extramarital coitus, masturbation, nocturnal erections. *BY RULE OF THUMB,* most often not psychogenic.
Relative (Selective) Impotence	Examples: paramour yes, wife no; rape yes, lover no; masturbation yes, coitus no; nocturnal erections yes, voluntary erections no. *BY RULE OF THUMB,* almost always psychogenic.
Pseudo-Relative Impotence	Early in progressive somatic impotence of any type (e.g., arteriosclerosis) a worried patient may try to reassure himself by seeking stronger (e.g., extramarital, pornography) stimulation; such high-arousal experience may still carry him through a satisfactory act, while his accustomed situation does not. A cursorily elicited history can mislead the physician. There are other types.
Relative Potency	A normal phenomenon signifying that men can be rendered more or less aroused, thus more or less capacitated, by different situations or partners.

or that he prefers masturbation. Only sometimes do spontaneous remarks tell the story: (e.g., "I just can't make myself do it with her" versus "I want to but it doesn't want to happen"). Besides, if a reminder be needed, a diabetic who cannot erect may still be a bisexual or phobia-ridden; or an impotent man who is emotionally immature, fearful, hostile to his wife and habitually masturbates may still be developing multiple sclerosis.

MINOR DEFLECTIONS OF POTENCY

Transient Impotence. Many normal men experience impotence— usually inability to obtain or maintain erection after a confident approach —from time to time, as a result of fatigue, drinking, anxiety about some happening, or other temporary circumstances; most often it is taken in stride and perturbs neither the man nor his mate. Function is restored spontaneously in a brief period, up to 2 days; persistence beyond that would call for further evaluation.

Sudden Failure. This differs somewhat from transient impotence: it is not explicable by circumstances; either the erotic partner or the situation is new; and there has been much sexual anticipation. These men, often young, manifest no fear of failure, no overanxiety and no history of ejaculatio praecox. Sexual activity in the past has been successful. The failure to erect is complete, although prior petting had produced normal erection. The incident does not seem to repeat itself after proper reassurance, although long-term follow-up observation is rarely available. The cause is obscure. Reassurance, relaxation and a few days' abstinence usually are adequate treatment.

Labile Potency. Potency can be intermittently feeble, or mediocre at all times, without being impaired. Low drive endowment, a subclinical endocrine deficit, or an excessive degree of narcissistic residue in the personality are possible explanations. Some men may have sexual desire, but find it difficult to obtain immediate, spontaneous erections as intromission is at hand although they are capable of satisfactory performance if the wife prestimulates them slightly in a manual fashion and retains a manual hold on the organ during the first half minute or so of the sexual act. For coital positions facilitating the act in the presence of partial erections see page 215. A combination of insufficient motivation and labile potency can produce frequent loss of erection in an overrelaxed or excessively moist vagina, occasionally without being aware of it, as the female tract here does not provide much stimulation. Where coitus is difficult because of an obstructed entry due to vaginismus, a rigid perineum, etc., a husband may be unable to maintain his erection during attempts at entering; the same applies where a wife's markedly unhelpful attitude interposes obstacles to the completion of the act. Some very high-strung men, seemingly forever nervous and tense or on the run to nowhere in particular, have erections sometimes and sometimes not, for reasons no one can easily discern. These occurrences do not constitute true impotence by themselves.

LABILE SEXUALITY IN YOUNG MEN

A borderline syndrome involving traces of hypogonadism and developmental lag, labile potency, emotional immaturity and chronic anxiety

He is free of clinically detectable somatosexual deficits, except that in his late 20's, for instance, he still may not shave but every second day or less, or his voice is "squeaky," or one detects a compensatory vocal straining for depth intended to mask a slightly puerile or a partially cracked voice.

He is much preoccupied with his virility, but usually his potency is labile. Married or not, he tries to avoid sexual relations, and clings stubbornly to the assertion (belief?) that ejaculations weaken the body. Often he is engaged in a strenuous body-building (e.g., weight-lifting) program, and has fully persuaded himself that he must abstain sexually for long periods, so as not to interfere with this.

If he does have sexual relations, the act seems difficult and complicated to him, and he worries about it beforehand. He may suffer from ejaculatio praecox. Nocturnal emissions cause him anxiety; they exhaust him considerably and measurably. After each wet dream he may have an aching feeling in the groin, the lower back or the testicles, or the glans penis may feel numb and aching for 1 or 2 days.

Basically timid and unassertive, he often masks this by being noisily aggressive or, occasionally, haughtily aloof. Hypochondriacal preoccupations and fantasies are common. In confidence he may admit being a coward but his athletic proficiency may allow him to cloak his timidity. Motorcycles may be important to him. A number have not stopped wetting the bed until late in the teens. What laboratory data are available are inconsistent.

ORGANIC CAUSES OF IMPOTENCE

Cerebral and Spinal Causes. Neuropathy

Diabetic Impotence (diabetic neuropathy). Men of all ages with diabetes mellitus become irreversibly impotent with some frequency. Among younger diabetic men, 1 out of 4 are believed to develop impotence and another 10 per cent have some potency impairment; in middle-aged diabetics the incidence is about twice as high. If a diabetic develops impotence, he does so early in the course of the disease; often potency disturbances are its first symptom. In fact, unexplained impotence always calls for thorough testing for latent diabetes. The forerunner of erective impotence in the diabetic most often is retrograde ejaculation; its presence (dry orgasm, milky postcoital urine) probably allows the prediction that potency will be extinguished within a year. Libido is not impaired as a primary damage. The semen tends to be moderately deficient in sperm quality, but early sterility is not the rule. Diabetic men without potency problems nevertheless seem to lose their sexual capacity at a somewhat earlier age than nondiabetics. Impotence coinciding with long diabetic neglect and erratic self-care has a generally poor prognosis, even with subsequent optimal control (disputed). Mild intermittent potency disturbances are believed to parallel periods of unnoticed glycosuric spilling.

The nature of diabetic impotence remains incompletely clarified. There are substantial indications that it is due to peripheral neuropathy affecting the parasympathetic pelvic plexi, nervi erigentes, etc. A few observers implicate changes in the spinal reflex mechanism, microvascular changes, a Leriche-type syndrome (q.v.) due to premature arteriosclerosis, or secondary hypogonadism. Neither insulin nor oral antidiabetic agents nor primary psychogenicity are etiologic factors. Degrees of peripheral neuropathy elsewhere in the body are almost always demonstrable (e.g., position and vibratory sensation in the feet or changes in the Achilles tendon reflex). Neurogenic bladder dysfunction is associated with diabetic impotence with regularity, and neurogenic bladder studies (cystometrogram, hot and cold test, residue and capacity measurements, etc.) have been recommended as a test (Ellenberg). Another possible check, by searching for sympathetic dysfunction due to neuropathy, would show anidrosis with the sweating test (Schellen). Treatment of diabetic impotence is unavailing. Men should be advised of the connection between the two disorders; they may be grateful if either the patient or his wife had previously impugned his masculinity or his love interest or even his faithfulness. If offspring are desired following the appearance of retrograde ejaculation, recovery of live spermatozoa from the bladder for artificial insemination is feasible and must not be delayed. In hereditarily vulnerable men the possibility of future diabetic impotence requires some thought and discussion during premarital examination.

Brain, etc. *Temporal lobe epilepsy*—idiopathic, traumatic or tumorous (glioma), etc.—is associated with weak erection and inability to achieve orgasm, mostly if an anterior lobe is affected. "Global hyposexuality" has also been described in these cases. Surgical excision of the epileptogenic focus frequently produces reversal (see also p. 428). A few observers insist on a primary psychogenic factor in temporal impairment. Neuroendocrine disarray (e.g., in *Pituitary Adenoma*) interferes with sexual function. *Parkinsonism,* especially in the advanced postencephalitic type, can produce impotence. Loss of potency may follow *Head Injury*—with onset sometimes as long as several years later—reportedly most often following blows on the back of the head from behind and above. Gross damage demonstrated postmortem includes post-traumatic cysts, ventricular hemorrhages, scar tissue and sclerotic atrophy (e.g., in the hypothalamic area) or else damage may be disruptive of function without visible anatomic damage. Retired, shuffle-gaited ring-fighters with the syndrome of *Multiple Traumatic Encephalopathy* are frequently impotent. *Arteriosclerosis,* apart from the more obvious aortoiliac occlusion (q.v.), by interfering with the cerebral or spinal blood supply, is believed capable of interfering with the sexual mechanism, for instance by blunting the psychic component and thus disorganizing the act, or by direct disruption —or, possibly, retardation—of the reflex mechanism. Impotence can result when *Myelitis, Syringomyelia, Pernicious Anemia, Spinal Cord Tumors* or *Multiple Sclerosis* (retrograde ejaculation) affect the spinal tract. *Tabes Dorsalis* can produce impotence, now thought to be due to a mechanism of peripheral afferent neuropathy. Irritative priapism in the presence of penile anesthesia was reportedly a not infrequent forerunner of tabetic impotence in the pretherapeutic era of syphilis. *Malnutritional Vitamin Deficiency* (thiamine, niacin, vitamin B12) may involve sexual function via pelvic neuropathy.

Trauma.   *Straddle Injuries* are frequently followed by sexual impotence, including ejaculatory disturbances, when crushing of the pudendal nerve between the pubic arch and the hard object occurs. Whether perineal injury in childhood can cause, or predispose to, subsequent impotence cannot be answered with certainty now, but conceivably a connection may exist. Tear or crush injuries of the bulbocavernous and the ischiocavernous muscles are causes of impotence following shrapnel and antipersonnel mine fragment penetrations. *Pelvic Fracture* (crush), with rupture of the posterior urethra frequently leads to degrees of impotence. *Herniated Intervertebral Disks,* most often at about the levels of T-10 or L-1 but probably also at all other vertebral levels have been known to produce impotence, although some observers believe the disordered sex function here to be a psychogenic addition. At least 1 case of occult discogenic disease at L-4 to 5 with erective impotence as the only symptom has been described, with prompt restoration following excision, although a spina bifida at S-1 remained (Shafer-Rosenblum).

Paraplegia.   Where injury has cut the pathways of the spinal cord so that paraplegia results, there is no motor power from the waist down, all lower body sensation is lost, there is no control over elimination, and sexual function is severely disrupted. Erections in paraplegia are totally abolished only after total local destruction of spinal segments S-2 to S-4 or their roots; and after destruction or even partial transection of the cauda equina, especially its upper 1 inch. In all other cord injuries some degree of reflex erections can occur; the higher the location of the lesion, the better the chances of a good erection. One to 24 months after injury about 60 per cent of paraplegics regain penile erections; more if spinal injury is above T-11, fewer if below. Ejaculation is rare. It is abolished in all lesions which abolish erection in toto, and whenever the lower thoracic and upper lumbar segments (approximately to L-3) of the cord are damaged so extensively that the sympathetic components there are destroyed. Where ejaculation does occur, there is little seminal fluid or else it spills retrograde. Sexual sensation is lost in transection anywhere above the sacral level. A paraplegic who can have reflexogenic erections— via any tactile rubbing stimulus about the penis, perineum, anus and upper inner thighs—must look to ascertain if it has occurred. Coitus is devoid of specific local sensation; in ejaculation he must verify any wetness with his fingers and feel for perineal muscle contractions signifying orgasm.

Fertility is infrequent among paraplegic men even when the ejaculating mechanism is preserved. In most cases rapid spermatogenic arrest ensues, even within days. Disturbance of the circulating androgen:estrogen ratio raises relative estrogen levels and causes gynecomastia in almost one fourth of paraplegic men. For purposes of fatherhood semen has been obtained, after hormonal priming, either by electric stimulation of the accessory glands (active electrode in rectum), or by injecting neostigmine (0.2 mg. or more) intrathecally at the L-4 to L-5 interspace, freeze-partitioning the ejaculate and employing it in artificial insemination. However, the chances of obtaining semen of good quality are not good.

Paraplegics today need not consider themselves out-and-out sex cripples. Modern rehabilitation has prolonged their life expectancy to almost normal; much of living—walking, driving—is within their reach, the major complications of paraplegia—infection, tissue wasting, contractures, mental withdrawal—are being increasingly controlled; and today's style of free ventilation of sexual matters facilitates pooling of experience, more effective counseling and spouse guidance. Predictions as to expectancy of reproductive function have been possible through classification into upper (spastic) and lower (flaccid) motor neuron function, complete and incomplete (Comarr, Wahle-Jochheim). Either reflexogenic or, where possible, psychogenic erections can be used for sexual intercourse in the woman-above or a modified lateral position (p. 215). Some men become self-consciously inhibited (e.g., at the ever-present threat of a bowel accident when straining) or they become bored with the joyless activity and relinquish it or limit themselves to kissing and oral sex; but others, often married, are motivated by imagery, a remembered overall thrill of anticipation, an enhancing ego effect, desire to preserve a sense of closeness in marriage and to permit sexual gratification of the spouse. The more realistic among these men learn to bear the loss of voluptas with equanimity.

Endocrinopathic Impotence

Impaired potency and diminished libido coexist as primary damages in almost all types of endocrine disorders affecting male sexual functions. *Hypogonadism*—chromosomal, pituitary or testicular—includes the non-development or the regression of secondary male sex characteristics together with feeble libido and scant potency. In the *Klinefelter Syndrome* (p. 367) libido is weak and potency becomes enfeebled in adulthood and often extinct at 45, although exceptions occur. Characteristic is regression of erective capacity in tall young men after they have been married one or a few years. On cursory examination little may be found in some except the inevitable small-sized testicles. In the rare *Simmonds' Disease of Men* loss of potency precedes recession of libido with ultimate extinction. In *Hemochromatosis,* a chronic inheritable disease, excessive uncontrollable iron deposits in the pituitary often lead to early diminution or loss of potency and libido, probably through a mechanism of impaired production of pituitary gonadotropin. *Dystrophic Myotonia,* a heredofamilial disorder, in which muscle disease is combined with atrophy of the testicles and related endocrine disturbances, produces impotence and loss of libido in a majority of cases. Pathologic hyperpituitarism, both as *Acromegaly* and as the prepuberal form, *Pituitary Gigantism,* lead to early potency impairment and premature extinction of function, the often large external genitalia (scrotum, penis) notwithstanding; in acromegaly the decline is frequently preceded by a hyperlibidinal period. *Addison's Disease* tends to lead to loss of libido and impotence. *Cushing's Syndrome,* except when due to adrenal carcinoma, impairs libido and potency after an initial period (weeks or months) of marked increase. Untreated *Hypothyroidism* may deprive the man of initiative and libido; in major cases a degree of impotence coexists.

Vascular Causes

Aorto-Iliac Occlusive Disease (Leriche Syndrome). Unexplained, progressive weakening of erection—and a diminished penile plethysmographic curve—can be the first symptom of impaired blood flow due to progressive atheromatous narrowing of the abdominal aorta at or near its bifurcation, or of the iliac arteries just below. Overall, more than 40 per cent of men with stenosis and close to three quarters of occluded cases develop impotence. These relatively young men can initiate an erection, but cannot maintain it. Other early signs and symptoms: leg weariness, diminished pulses, bruits, claudication of thighs and buttocks, changes in retrograde aortogram. The higher in the aorta the obliteration—at the bifurcation or above—the earlier does impotence appear and the more complete and permanent it is, even in otherwise successfully treated cases.

In the most benign form only one of the internal iliac vessels is affected. Progress of the lesion, if any, is not systematic but follows a patchy pattern. Vascular surgery (excision, patching, grafting etc. and sympathectomy), which may be a necessity, unfortunately sometimes produces impotence where none pre-existed and may add a recoverable or permanent ejaculatory disorder. *Abdominal Aortic Aneurysm* produces erective impotence in some patients.

CAUSES OF MALE INFERTILITY
1294 consecutive cases, 1965–1970

39%	Varicocele
14%	Testicular Failure (germinal cell aplasia, bilat. postmumps atrophy, Klinefelter's, tumors and injuries)
11.8%	Semen Volume (mostly too high: over 4.5 cc; 1.8% too little: under 1 cc)
8.6%	Endocrinopathy (mostly pituitary gonadotropin deficiency. Only 0.8% hypothyroid)
7.4%	Duct Obstruction (mostly epididymitis-ex-gc or ex-tbc. Also requests to reverse vasectomies)
5.1%	Sexual Problems (mostly potency disorders)
4.4%	Cryptorchidism
2.3%	Semen and Sperm Anomalies: necrospermia, severe sperm auto-agglutination, excessive seminal viscosity, high sperm density (2 cases: 650 and 720 million/ml)
2%	Ejaculatory Disturbances (mostly retrograde ejaculation. Non-ejaculation in 0.4%)
5.4%	Unknown

L. Dubin and R. D. Amelar,
Fertility and Sterility 22:469, 1971

Genito-Urinary Causes

Compulsive Vesiculoprostatostasis (chronic vesiculoprostatitis; prostato-seminal vesiculitis). A chronic congestive syndrome of gradual onset which often gives the appearance of resulting in progressive weakening of the quality of erection, although complete erective impotence is not a primary part of the syndrome. Ejaculatio praecox and/or pain on ejaculation may supravene. The immediate cause probably is long-continued incomplete or unphysiologic emptying of the accessory glands (i.e., any type of sex practice where the pitch of excitation is not matched by the promptness, the completeness, the spontaneity and/or the intensity of the ejaculatory-orgasmic relief afforded). This occurs in self-inhibiting habitual masturbation of the adult (q.v.), in a vita sexualis long limited to heavy petting, in habitual coitus interruptus with a sexually inert partner, or in habitually hastened or furtive-uncomfortable acts, or those in which the sensory apparatus always strainedly scans for threatening interruptions.

The syndrome is encountered almost exclusively in certain anxious-tense individuals, the same men who tend to compulsive masturbation and neurasthenoid impotence (q.v.). The ongoing debate on which produces what may be reasonably answered by saying that the personality induces poor sex habits, which produce the congestive syndrome, which causes sexual dysfunction, which, in turn, further worries and worsens the psyche and with it the sex habits and so forth in a vicious cycle. All ages are affected, although men in early middle age are seen most often. The primarily consulted specialist tends to be the urologist rather than the psychiatrist who infrequently gets to see such men directly. Since what treatment the urologist has to offer here is, in practice, probably at least as successful as attempted—and often resisted—psychotherapy, there exists scant rationale for referral.

Other symptoms in this psychosomatic syndrome are sacro-iliac ache or a "tired" low back, unpleasant sensations in the glans penis, some urinary urgency and frequency, occasionally minor dribbling weakness of the voiding stream, overflow prostatorrhea mostly after straining at stool, sometimes hemospermia. The prostate may feel boggy or mushy, the seminal vesicles are distended, and the posterior urethral mucosa may be seen to be swollen. Where discomfort is somewhat acute, rapid temporary relief is obtained by rectal digital expression and stripping, especially of the seminal vesicles; such relief is considered pathognomonic. A course of vesiculoprostatic massage and decongestant therapy gives prolonged temporary results, but permanent cures are difficult to obtain. Discussion and explanation of desirable sex habits and related hygiene measures are an essential part of the treatment. The physician who tells this man that "there is nothing greatly wrong" with him withholds from him part of the relief possible in these cases. Inflammatory and pyogenic complications are believed to superimpose themselves frequently on chronic congestion. It has been reported that frequent prolonged riding in bouncing vehicles can produce a somewhat similar prostatic congestion.

Other Prostatic Conditions. Benign prostatic hypertrophy, per se, is not believed to cause sexual impotence. Infection of the prostate may cause painful ejaculation, sometimes ejaculatio praecox, and a sense of postcoital fatigue, but it does not interfere with potency other than discouraging the patient from exposing himself to this dyspareunia. Scar tissue or a small tab or mass in the area of the verumontanum, perhaps following gonorrheal or other urethritis, reportedly causes pain referred to the glans when sexual activity is attempted, or else irritable hyperexcitation and eventual exhaustion of the spinal reflex mechanism—mainly of ejaculation—due to the continuous bombardment with excitatory stimuli. In cancer of the prostate potency disturbances occasionally are the first symptoms bringing the patient to the physician. As the lesion tends to start near the ejaculatory duct, ejaculatory changes (hemospermia?) may be early signs.

Peyronie's Disease (fibrosclerosis of Buck's fascia, plastic induration of the corpora cavernosa). One or more sharply delineated, hard plaques develop on the dorsum, occasionally the sides, of the penile shaft, not affecting the skin. They are painless in the resting stage, but erections become more and more painful, as the plaques cause arching, crooking, or even angular deformity, making intercourse all but impossible. Distally to the plaque the corpora may remain flaccid precluding intromission further. The disease is not rare; mild degrees are fairly common. Occurrence is mostly in middle-aged men, but occasionally as early as the twenties. Onset is gradual. The cause is unknown. Histologically the disorder is related to Dupuytren's contracture of the hand, but without the latter's inheritable pattern; the two disorders occur in the same individual in a proportion of cases. Spontaneous regression occurs in many patients over a period of years (average 4 years), but once deformity has occurred it tends to remain. Treatment has given worthwhile results: high doses of vitamin E (tocopherols, 100 mg TID) potassium para-aminobenzoate (Potaba), forcing steroids into the plaques, small doses of x-irradiation, and some other methods. Secondary psychologic effects, often considerable, require attention.

Malformations and Impediments. Congenital, traumatic or disease-induced penile malformations can produce interference with coital entry, thus nonperformance, rather than sexual impotence: *Amputation* of the membrum, *Cicatricial Contractions* due to burns, *Short Frenulum, Elephantiasis,* etc. Others lead to nonperformance because of discomfort on entering (e.g., *Peyronie's Disease,* q.v., acute *Balanitis,* acute *Gonorrhea,* painful recurrences of *Herpes Genitalis,* or *Phimosis* where the condition may be aggravated by a supravening injury phobia). Pain can be referred from an *Anal Fissure* and block coital intent. In *Hypospadias* of major degree with downward chordee of the organ intercourse is difficult; but as this condition may represent a mild form of intersexing, sexual manifestations may be nonvigorous to begin with. This can be similarly true of the fairly rare *Micropenis.* In *Status Postpriapism* erection may be only partial and insufficient for intromission because of irreversible fibrosing in the corpus cavernosum. External impediments such as a large *Hydrocele* or *Hernia* may interfere with coitus mechanically, but there is no impotence except for secondary psychologic self-inhibition.

Pharmacogenic and Toxic Causes

Side-effects of Medication. Certain drugs tend to interfere with sexual function. The frequency with which this happens is not predictable, nor does it appear to depend altogether on dosage or duration of use. Also, reactions to these drugs vary from patient to patient. The sexual side-effects of drugs appear to be reversible upon discontinuation. Ganglionic blocking agents comprise an important group. As the parasympathetic inhibitors block the vagal outflow from the sacral segments of the spinal cord, they tend to disrupt the sexual mechanism and produce impotence; sympathetic disruption—mainly faulty ejaculation—can be part of the picture. *Antihypertensive,* sympathicolytic blocking agents (guanethidine) may be mentioned here. Many of the modern *Psychotropic* agents—ataractics and antidepressants—produce unpredictable degrees of temporary sexual impairment, notably some monamine-oxidase inhibitors, tricyclics, phenothiazines, and reserpine. Thioridazine hydrochloride is well known for producing retrograde ejaculation, while the antidepressants tend to produce non-erection. On the other hand, it need be nòted that, skilfully employed, antidepressive regimens can be superbly helpful in some types of impotence. *Corticosteroids* in large doses, *Methyldopa* and, possibly, *Epinephrine* preparations are other examples. *Estrogen* (e.g., in cancer treatment) produces impotence as part of its demasculinizing action. *Antabuse,* in the modern smaller dosages, probably no longer interferes with potency. Patients on *Methadone* maintenance often experience impotence for several months. The effect of *Nicotine,* from smoking, on potency remains controversial.

Alcohol progressively ". . . provokes the desire, but it takes away the performance" (Shakespeare, Macbeth). Eventually either the erection fails or, less often, ejaculation is greatly delayed or not achieved, more so apparently with beer. In very large amounts alcohol depresses the sexual reflexes to the point of abolishing them. An occasional anxious-inhibited, or profoundly fearful or depressive individual may use drink as a coping device, to disinhibit himself, to assuage his obsession with fear, or to remove himself from the reality of an unlovely wife or from the awareness of some secret distaste. But sooner or later he may actually need alcohol to make love, and when that happens chances are that he is also well on his way to being an alcoholic.

The chronic alcoholic is often impotent. When he is on a spree he has "no time" for females; if anything, he prefers the company of men to drink, talk and feel good with. When he is on the wagon his marital or love relationship most often turns platonic after a few months and for the next 2 or 3 years he often fares better for a longer period if no great sexual obligations confront him. Both organic and psychologic explanations have been advanced to explain this, but the cause remains largely unknown. The malnourished chronic drinker with peripheral neuropathy is very frequently impotent. This applies also to most alcoholic derelicts; some of them, potent or not, are capable of dangerously aggressive sex offenses. The brain-disordered, alcohol-intolerant pathologic drinker and, perhaps less so, the alcoholized psychopath are either impotent when intoxicated, or else easily and grossly aroused, at which time they are capable of brutal or shameless sexual behavior (e.g., in front of the children at home).

Self-Abuse of Drugs. Men addicted to narcotic, stimulant, psychedelic and certain other drugs are subject to major disturbances of sexual potency, many of them reversible. Sporadic abuse of certain substances also tends to lower sexual efficiency. These syndromes are described on p. 443.

Post-Surgical Impotence

Prostatectomy is followed by irreversible retrograde ejaculation in about 80 per cent of cases regardless of what procedure is used; the causes are anatomic changes produced in the bladder neck. Erective impotence can occur with some frequency following perineal procedures, including open perineal biopsy of the prostate, but not with transrectal or needle biopsy, less often in transurethral and least often in suprapubic prostatectomy, the reasons for this being unknown. However, other observers maintain that erective potency disorder, if it occurs, occurs equally in all types of procedure, and that it is a function mostly of age, prior potency and psychologic expectations. In the perineal approach, care in avoiding trauma to the parasympathetic fibers while dissecting the levatores ani may be a favorable factor, as is the surgeon's hopeful, encouraging attitude (Finkle). Coitus after prostatectomy is usually permitted, even encouraged, about 6 weeks postoperatively.

Bowel Surgery. Extensive lower bowel surgery frequently carries the risk of sexual impotence. Apparently there is no sure way to prevent all manipulatory, resecting or dissecting damage to the pelvic autonomic nerves, notably the nervi erigentes as they course through the perirectal, retroperitoneal tissues. It has been demonstrated here that while nerve damage impairs ejaculatory process, erection is principally damaged by interfering with blood flow through the hypogastric (internal iliac) arterial system. Radical *Resection of the Rectum* or sigmoid for cancer, including pelvic lymph node excision, has a high incidence of complicating impotence—erective, ejaculatory or both. In the less radical surgery for benign lower bowel disease, on the other hand, it is often feasible to preserve sexual function. Surgically induced sexual impairment does not include loss of libido as a primary damage. *Colostomy* and *Ileostomy* have a well-known repute for producing sexual impairment even in young people; however, this is largely, although not exclusively due to the psychic trauma, the ostomate's altered self-image, body and function shame, and phobic concern with acceptability and giving offense. Undoubtedly, the necessary dissecting away of portions of the pelvic neural network contributed to postoperative sexual dysfunction here. *Herniorrhaphy* does not cause true impotence, but some patients, misunderstanding pre- and postoperative cautions, are observed to inhibit themselves sexually, sometimes to a major degree.

Sympathectomy and presacral neurectomy are frequently followed by sexual impairment. Innervation levels vary somewhat from individual to individual, but the principal critical level appears to be at L-1. If lumbar ganglia are ablated on both sides, ejaculatory capacity—but not orgasmic sensation—is lost in more than half the men, although it may return spontaneously after several months. Erective capacity may be lost, and if so does not seem to return. Testicular atrophy results at times due to increased scrotal temperature when vasodilatation prevails unopposed.

Various Procedures. *Castration* of postpuberal men (p. 345) because of tumor, torsion necrosis, gunshot wound, self-mutilation etc., does not necessarily, and certainly not immediately, lead to sexual impotence. However, without replacement therapy, the function remains intact in only one third of these men. *Periaortic Lymphadenectomy* in conjunction with a testicular tumor invariably leads to failure of emission (first stage of ejaculation), less often to erective failure. *Radical Cystectomy* always leads to sexual impairment. *Abdominal Aortic Surgery,* for aneurysm or for aortoiliac (Leriche's, q.v.) occlusive disease, sometimes produces an added complication in the form of erective and/or ejaculatory impotence where none pre-existed.

PSYCHOGENIC CAUSES OF IMPOTENCE

Anxious-inhibitory Impotence. Among the relatively most tractable psychogenic syndromes is the anxious inhibitory impotence of young men. The history shows that they failed to erect or perform on one, perhaps their first, occasion for one reason or another; and that they approached the next occasion with increased apprehension, and failed again. Some kept trying only to fail each time; others stopped trying and may see a physician only years later (e.g., when they find a girl they desire to marry). The patient may be convinced that he is impotent, although most typically he has normal desire as well as erections on noncoital occasions. The syndrome gives the appearance of being chiefly a case of fear of failure, with each attempt resembling a case of pronounced stage fright. However, these men are not always emotionally stable individuals, merely deterred by a chain of unfavorable circumstances. Many are chronically anxious, self-conscious and worrisome young men whose inherent sexual capacity may be adequate but rarely great or of optimal stability. In some the fear of failure syndrome masks more serious psychosexual pathology, especially if the history includes repeated incidents of ejaculatio praecox.

Schizoid Variant. Difficulties are encountered in young men with what may be recognized as the schizoid variant of anxious-inhibitory impotence. These patients often lack unreservedness, perhaps warmth, in their relations to others, including the opposite sex. They tend to be suspicious, demanding and penurious, and some give the impression of being indifferent and affect-cold, perhaps cynical, in spite of their professed anxiety about sexual failure. Actually, many are extremely sensitive, and a particularly gentle and soothing approach must be maintained in the face of their sometimes baffling and provocative indifference and perverseness ("I'll do anything, but truthfully, I don't care about the result,"; "I'm paying you for some manhood, let's see who wins out").

Phobic Impotence. A moderately common cause of male failure is overt but unreasonable fear, which can be from many sources. Additionally, such patients tend to be phobia-prone as well as intrinsically low-endowed with drive, or else possess labile potency. Some men cannot easily shake off a fear that they will hurt or damage themselves through coitus, particularly if they have had a painful or protracted affliction along the genitourinary tract, even though now cured. Following venereal infection others cannot be potent, even in the presence of active desire, with any woman who is even a faintly possible source of infection and, in extreme cases, even with a new bride (veneriphobic impotence). Men working in the exposed trades or handling radioactive material, fear not only sterility but the highly unlikely sexual impotence, and their anxiety may bring on a degree of impotence. Men who suffered acute herniation of an intervertebral disk during intercourse may later be so fearful of a repetition of the mishap that they cannot easily maintain an erection during active thrusting. Some seem to fail because they fear that they will be interrupted, others because of acute apprehension that they will be unable to control the timing of coitus interruptus.

A LIBERATIONIST VIEW

Taught he must be a hero in the world and a superstar in bed, let him fail once and the foundations tremble. Success is so tied to his cock, no show and he's had it. The true measure of a man is neither the number of his war wounds nor the times he's bombed out in bed. The way out is to tear up the sex roles; roles which offer dubious rewards in exchange for heavy responsibilities should be put aside. The solution is political.

S. Julty in Ms. Magazine,
October 1972

Neurasthenoid Impotence. In some men, regardless of age, one observes that both their libido and their potency are easily disorganized under stress; that minor illnesses or disappointments fatigue them regularly to the point of being capable only of partial erection in the presence of desire; and that they are afflicted by unexplained episodes of numbed sensations in the genital area, prostatorrhea, ejaculatio tardata, low backaches or similar symptoms which, in turn, often lead to anxious overreaction and inhibition of all sexual performance. They are essentially in good physical health; endocrine functioning is normal. Many are achievement-conscious personalities but also anxious, hypochondriacal, overconcerned with the day-to-day functioning of their bodies. Most are not genuinely warm individuals capable of sharing love. Frequently they tend to be irritable and find it difficult to concentrate whenever distracted by something affecting their feeling of well-being. This syndrome of irritable weakness, which includes a chronic disposition to labile potency, has long been an arena for indiscriminate claims of cure in the treatment of sexual impotence. However, labile potency is easily improved, no matter what treatment is employed, only to relapse again with the next indisposition or strain.

Deep Psychogenicity. Among the most difficult are cases of psychogenic impotence where the underlying psychic impediment—most often fear, a sense of guilt, hostility, passive-dependent wishes, or aggressive, cruel or destructive impulses—must first be uncovered in systematic psychotherapeutic exploration. In the process there may become exposed such unconscious psychic mechanisms as dread of losing the male organ in "that terrifying cavity," perhaps fantasied as a vagina dentata; residues of sexual overexposure in childhood; or there may be fear of inflicting injury to "this tenderest, most untouchable of places," which actually may mask a patient's fear of his own cruel, destructive impulses. The fantasy that the phallus is so powerful and weaponlike that it could hurt and destroy if used with vigor, or if used at all, may be but the turning-around of a fear of being deprived of the organ by a jealous rival (castration anxiety of the Oedipus situation; p. 14).

Depressive State. Loss of libido, followed shortly by impotence, may be among the earliest symptoms of a major depression. These men, especially at the height of the illness, have no interest in sex, as they have lost interest in virtually everything else. "All is gone, all is empty"; life seems futile, love an effort; there is no warmth for anyone, everything is too much. "Without hope I can't have manliness, it becomes difficult, immensely complicated." All self-confidence is gone; "I couldn't do it, there is nothing left I can do right." Even in milder cases, there is no pleasure in anything; the outlook is bleak ("sex couldn't cheer me up even if it went well"). Erections may be preserved at first, but intromission is not sought. Nocturnal emissions which may occur happen without pleasure or thrill. However, some men, even in a severe state of depression, retain coital potency with their wives, often in conjunction with an anxious clinging need. The patient, or his wife, says that he became depressed because he could not perform intercourse any longer, that he worried himself into wanting to die because he thought he was sexually neglecting and hurting his wife, breaking his marriage vows, going against his religion, breaking the law, driving her into somebody else's arms or similar delusional self-accusations. However, the sequence of events here is thoroughly misrecognized by patient and wife alike. One finds, almost invariably, that onset of the depression preceded the sexual difficulty.

Disabling Women. As women in our society have become more assertive and bold, a proportion of men seem to have become more passive and timid. Women are far more certain of their femininity than men are of their masculinity (Greenson). If there be such a culture-wide trend, it both abets and cloaks deep-seated aberrational qualities in some women which seem to drive them not merely to subjugate their men but to disable them.

Such a woman unwittingly incapacitates her man by, for instance, mobilizing incompletely resolved conflicts in him. Attractive and seductive in her manner, she either competes, or else she derogates and derides, perhaps without realizing it; she demeans his build, his performance, his work, his person, finding fault with many facets of him; but she responds with barely more than indifference to his triumphs, and every expression of approval must be milked from her. She comes to him as an echo of his past, perhaps a fault-finding, erotically loved-feared-hated teacher or mother reincarnate, with whom he is defenseless and feels exposed. This image he cannot get himself to coite with, to possess, to do dirty things to. But impotent nonperformance also becomes his defense ("sex is the club of the henpecked husband"). Seeing a doctor at the wife's urging, he readily agrees that he is impotent and goes along with almost any method of treatment the physician suggests, including psychotherapy. But the curative failure rate is high. He may or may not admit eventually how negatively he feels about his wife's advances, but in the meantime the physician's verdict of treatment-resistant impotence ensures that his wife will leave him alone.

Overdirecting. A source of difficulty for some men is a female personality which in psychoanalytic language has been called the phallic woman. She manipulates and arranges incessantly; if she is sexually experienced— and sometimes if she is not—she may take over the conduct of the sexual act, arranging positions, prescribing his movements and regulating his thrusts like a drill sergeant: she wields his penis, as it were. It derives from what she has read and heard tell the act should be for a happy couple, and she is determined to conduct a happy marriage, to keep his sexual routines from becoming stereotyped and stale, apt to induce surfeit and infidelity, and at the same time to keep herself wholesomely satisfied and thus healthy. When he falters she knowingly diagnoses "you are impotent," an effective way to suggest further failure; or she may issue an ultimatum to produce a regular erection, on pain of her extramarital resort. She may even urge him to try a reputed aphrodisiac. But no matter what she hopes for or professes to want, often she succeeds merely in depriving herself further.

Loss of Enabling Image. Of importance for the sexual capacity of some men is the enabling image of a woman. This is encountered in some sexually labile men. For instance, a woman (wife) may be sexually capacitating as he recalls her previous or present functioning as a maid, an executive, a showgirl, a cook or whatnot, while the same female becomes non-enabling if identified with any other role. The female who wears a uniform (nurse, armed services), or merely has worn one in the past, may enable some men to perform very well sexually, but once the image fades, or the woman is somehow divested of this role, impotence may ensue. The woman who is wealthy enables some men, but once she loses or surrenders her wealth, even if to him, impotence may occur. Changes in the female figure, fatter or thinner, may play a similar part. Conversely, the woman who is poor, "in tatters and starving" as it were, may arouse and enable some men; once she is elevated, perhaps dressed up, she loses the capacity to stimulate them sexually. This can occur with various aspects of the feminine image, ranging to rather extreme forms where these peculiarities merge with sexual deviance.

DISORDERS OF EJACULATION

Premature Ejaculation
(Ejaculatio praecox)

This symptom consists of the man's habitual, seemingly uncontrollable ejaculation during sexual intercourse before the act has started (ante portas), upon insertion, or very shortly thereafter (i.e., it is abortive coitus). Several varieties of compulsory foreshortened sex acts can be recognized.

Habitual Coitus Brevis is a separate manifestation. Here the husband has insufficient coital endurance in relation to the wife's orgasm; it is more a form of sexual neglect than of impotence. These men are either insufficiently motivated to gratify their wives, or they have limited interest in normal intercourse generally (e.g., in habitual masturbation). A proportion are rather passive men whose wives do not display sufficient sexual aggressiveness or do not possess enough sexual interest to gratify their husbands' passive needs. These men seem capable of more sustained performance when a more determined, extramarital partner makes them "take it easy." Coitus brevis is presented infrequently as a complaint by the man himself, unless he does so at the express urging of his wife. However, many such men perform indefinitely in this fashion, and a good many wives believe that all normal intercourse is brevis.

Treatment: this manifestation cannot be treated primarily by chemical or physical means, nor by erotic gymnastics or manipulation, unless the latter serve as a vehicle for psychotherapy which is now often the case. This is a disorder of motivation and compatibility. Although improvement is fairly easy to obtain by a variety of avenues, the long-term outlook in marital pairs is not particularly good: once incompatibility and low-grade performance have become so major as to send the wife to consult a physician, recurrences seem to be the rule as the years go by.

Circumstantial Prematurity. In some cases rapid ejaculation has no clinical significance (e.g., when it occurs sporadically because of extreme anticipation or because of impediments encountered while attempting intromission—vaginismus, etc.); however, where this happens repeatedly, it must be regarded as pathologic. In other cases it is an off-and-on manifestation of labile potency (q.v.). Where erective impotence is less than vigorous, a wife's persistent reluctance to guide penile intromission by hand or other failure to cooperate in overcoming the entrance barrier may be responsible for episodes of prematurity from time to time. Otherwise, a genuine inability to control emission, apart from toxic states and true ejaculatio praecox, may only exist in very inexperienced young husbands.

Treatment: acute situations here do not usually come to medical attention, but those which are seen, respond well to common sense counseling, instruction, reassurance and a period of abstinence. Situations which become chronic are not always easy to distinguish from true compulsive prematurity, and may be treated similarly, although a patient unraveling of the situation would be a more rational approach.

Prematurity in the Elderly. Onset here is gradual, often in the 60's. It is assumed to be part of a stage of irritable disorganization of the ejaculatory reflex mechanism which can precede extinction of potency in diffuse arteriosclerosis. Some observers blame prostatic disorders. The role of psychogenic factors is uncertain, but exogenous disorganization of lifelong sexual habits seems to play a part. Premature ejaculation can be highly annoying to some elderly men; they are insistent about having normal potency restored, but prognosis is poor.

Treatment: supportive—hydrotherapy, diathermy, spa therapy, mudpacks, phosphorus preparations. Small estrogen-progestin doses (e.g., Enovid E ¼ or ½ tab.o.d.) seems to do more here than testosterone. Tofranil (e.g., 10 mg h.s.) may be tried. All this may be combined with guidance toward acceptance. Intercourse, if available, should be spaced judiciously, mostly to reduce the psychologic impact of failure These patients are not to utilize morning erections, if any, for sexual purposes, nor to retain urine to intensify sensation or erection. Prostatic expressive massage has been recommended.

True Prematurity. This is an often stubbornly chronic symptom, present during most or all acts of intercourse but not when masturbating. Onset is frequently in the teens. Its psychogenic nature is widely recognized today, although actually this has remained unproved and the cause of the symptom must at present be considered as being uncertain. These patients tend to be obsessive, often rigid, martinet-like men who seem to live in fear of exposing an underlying passive dependency wish. The symptom has been regarded as part of an interpersonal status and dominance struggle with the person by whom it is primarily evoked. An unconscious sadistic wish—to hurt, to soil or to deprive—has also been postulated. Early malconditioning—via first coitus with a busy prostitute or early lovemaking in uncomfortably cramped vehicles—seems to play no major part in true prematurity. Ejaculatio praecox in some young patients is combined with a history of protracted enuresis, partial erection at the moment of ejaculation, and marked clumsiness and difficulties each time intercourse takes place. It may occur with some frequency in sensory temporal lobe epilepsy (Alvarez). Chronic congestive vesiculoprostatitis (q.v.) can produce a hyperirritable ejaculatory reflex mechanism. Hypersensitivity of the uncircumcised glans is a rare factor. A 2 per cent incidence of abnormal shortness of the preputial frenulum was confirmed by surgical cure (Shapiro).

Treatment of true prematurity: *Psychotherapy* (uncovering type) remains a valid treatment, but results, on the whole, have not usually been better than mediocre in true prematurity.

Semans Method (Southern Med. J. *49*: 353, 1956). Essentially psychologic desensitization. Repeated manual masturbation by the consort, interrupted at patient's direction as ejaculation approaches until sensation ceases, and restarted. Phallus is lubricated. After 10–15 sessions procedure is transferred to acts of coitus.

Masters-Johnson Method. Essentially an expanded Semans method with behavior therapy, built into their Sex Therapy procedure (p. 394). Added has been the squeeze technique: female squeezes the glans, thumb underneath on frenulum, first two fingers straddling coronal ridge from above for 3-4 seconds before ejaculation threatens, then masturbation is resumed. Later vaginal insertion in the woman-above position while motionless, with squeeze maneuver against approaching ejaculation. In next days some thrusting with this technique, then a side-to-side, woman-above position is assumed for continuation. Control technique is expected to be continued for up to a year following Sex Therapy course.

Yoga Treatment. During coitus stomach and bladder to be empty or nearly so. Organ rests against vulva, introduced slowly in 3 to 4 stages; organ rested again inside before thrusting. At each inkling of ejaculation all motion halts and breath is held until sensation passes. During act patient practices "tying the root": pulling all anal and pelvic muscles upward and holding them there; this can be practiced during the day. The mind is to focus on heartbeat or on spot between eyebrows, and is to return to these after each coital stage is accomplished, and whenever ejaculation threatens. Patient to practice very slow urination, up to half hour; but this latter control not considered safe unless learned under Yogi's supervision.

Jacobson Method. Patient to practice muscle contraction as if lifting testicles up in scrotum and into body, in short sharp twitches, several times a day. Muscle can be felt in perineum just behind base of scrotum by finger. Then to try this maneuver during coitus at end of each stroke.

Walker-Strauss Method. Patient to relax perineal muscles, best during urination by deliberately stopping urinary stream, then restarting it, taking notice of ensuing change of sensation.

Medication. Mellaril: either continuously (e.g., 10 mg or more t.i.d.) or precoital dosing (e.g., 25 mg): unreliable; also means correcting a fault with a counterfault. Tofranil: a 2-months course (e.g., 10–25 mg b.i.d.). Sometimes worthwhile; usual side-effects. Tinct. of Stramonium USP (8 to 15 drops o.d. or b.i.d.); little recent experience available. Guanethidine: 1 favorable case mentioned in print. Antiparkinsonians: drug and dose by trial and error; Cogentin may be tried first. Alcohol, especially beer: not recommended. Estrogen: not recommended in true prematurity. Testosterone: not known to be helpful here except in hypogonads.

Caine-type Creams or Ointments (e.g., benzocaine 5 per cent, Nupercainal) by inunction in the glans and shaft, have given unreliable results, and often none. Use of condoms of little help; patient may ejaculate while placing it.

Advice to repeat the act as soon and as frequently as possible, disregarding the incidents of prematurity, is probably more applicable to chronic situational ejaculatio praecox, but worth trying. Frequency of coitus should be stepped up if quality of marriage relationship will support this. Rule of thumb: 2 to 3 times the frequency prevailing 6 months before physician was first consulted. The repeated frustrations this entails for the wife must be considered before advising this.

Retarded Ejaculation
(Ejaculatio tardata or retardata)

These men ejaculate with great delay or not at all, although they have robust erections and wish to achieve climax. Physiologic, transient, intermittent and chronic cases, including young never-emitters, are seen, although the condition is not frequent. Physiologic are dry orgasm in prepuberal boys and the coup sec (Fr.), the last coitus in a close-order series, with accessory glands all but emptied. The pathologic forms have been observed at all ages, beginning in the teens. Most frequently it occurs in patients on various psychotropic medications. Reducing medication brings relief, at most a week later, or remission is spontaneous without change in medication, with occasional recurrences; however, patients have asked that the symptom be left undisturbed pro tem for their wives' sake. In dissolute and other over-exertion the continuous stimulus bombardment of the posterior urethra leads to eventual exhaustion of the sympathetic emissive response. A psychodynamic theory of hostile and phobic withholding, sometimes in association with paranoid tendencies, as a cause of chronic or intermittent retardation has been advanced (Ovesey-Meyers, Friedman).

Retrograde Ejaculation

is discussed on p. 374

TREATMENT OF IMPOTENCE

Whenever a specific systemic or local cause for impotence can be found, treatment is primarily directed at this condition where feasible. In the numerous cases where this is not possible, treatment efforts address the symptom directly. In all cases of impotence in which the cause is uncertain, the physician must—in addition to all other examinations and procedures—spend some time talking to the patient, exploring as relaxedly as circumstances permit what kind of person he is or thinks he is, what is agitating him now as well as 1 year, 5 years, 10 years ago, what faults and virtues he finds in his mate, etc. He may not find anything of massive import, but at least he will be more certain that he has not overlooked a major psychic factor (e.g., overt facultative homosexuality, an agitated depression, syphilophobia or some type of inhibitory situation). If nothing else, the mere airing of the symptoms—at times even the fact that another human being has learned about his "shame" and has not, as these men often fear, laughed derisively or joked offensively—can make a difference.

Beaten-dog Attitude. Many impotent men experience a pervading sense of inadequacy and, if they are married or closely attached to one woman, of guilt. Their distress most often revolves little around their sexual needs, but around the requirements of their ego. Many, desperate and in a frantic search for a remedy, are willing to try anything and easily become victimized by the purveyors of nostrums, gadgets and cures. Some impotent men have almost endless fantasies of propping, reinforcing, or inflating the membrum in one way or another. The beaten-dog psychology may be aggravated by the attitude of the wife who, in spite of initial resolves to be patient and kind, soon cannot hide her impatience, anxiety

COMMUNICATING WITH THE PATIENT
ON MATTERS OF POTENCY

Penis:	organ, private. Vernac. dick, pecker, rod. Vulg. prick, cock
Scrotum:	bag, sack; balls, nuts
Erection:	hard-on, get hard, boner, Vernac. get it up
Ejaculation:	to come, come off, let fly
Ejaculum:	semen fluid, sperm. Vernac. scum, wet stuff
Attempt to direct physician's interest to sexual difficulties:	I must be tired, low blood, nothing going right
Non-erection:	can't get it up, lost my nature, over the hill, nothing happens, it's dead, get no hard-on
Labile potency:	Won't stay up, dies on me, she's not holding my interest, have to imagine things
Retarded ejaculation:	It takes forever, have to force myself
Premature ejaculation:	Can't hold it (back), get overexcited, come right away, too fast
Ambiguous:	No interest, no pleasure, no feeling, no sensation, fun fatigue

and, eventually, scorn and resentment. The anticipation of the wife's expectant attitude and of her subsequent expression of disappointment or scorn, as yet another attempt is made and fails, worsens the impotence even further. Some women who have marked musculine-competitive strivings, experience raging resentment at a husband's failure, because it drives home their dependence on the man for the satisfaction of their needs; this attitude, in turn, only impedes the failing man even further. Some impotent men deprive their wives—and eventually themselves—even further by withholding all demonstrative affection from their spouses; partly fearing that it may be misinterpreted as the start of a love session for which they do not feel ready, partly because they fear they may arouse the woman in this fashion and that she may then make demands, or else because they are overreacting to a fear-fantasy that, out of a sense of guilt, they may allow the wife to dominate them to the point where they may be forced to permit her "everything and anything, maybe even to have another man."

Psychotherapy of impotence ranges from the elementary—a word of reassurance—to the most complex dynamic relationship therapies. As an example of treatment which can be successful without the use of an intensive uncovering approach, one may cite the anxious-inhibitory impotence of young men. In all cases a preliminary general medical examination is necessary even where the history clearly seems to suggest an inhibitory type of failure. The patient is reassured—if at all compatible with the findings—that he is physically normal and that prognosis is reasonably good. He is told to befriend girls actively, or to bed with his wife, as the case may be, but that he must not try to perform a sexual act. It is important to make this prohibition firm, yet without attaching threats of health or prognostic hazard, as a cure may result as the patient acts against the physician's advice; he must be able to act without fear of ill effects at that point. The patient is given ataractic medication (e.g., perphenazine, 2 to 4 mg t.i.d.). He should be seen once a week, ostensibly to oversee the therapeutic regimen, actually to keep him motivated, encouraged and to ventilate anxieties as they emerge.

The prohibition of intercourse is not applicable to all cases of impotence. The rationale includes that the patient is spared additional and disappointing defeats which may reinforce his autosuggested fear of failure; he is made to exchange the yoke of a fixed negative idea—that he cannot perform adequately—for an imposed prohibition: that he must not perform; and at a propitious moment the latter is more easily overcome than the former; also, both the patient and the physician are spared the highly critical and potentially self-defeating "moment of truth" which is inherent in all suggestive psychotherapy, when the patient is told in so many words: you are cured, now act.

The opposite method—encouraging coitus—frequently gives creditable results in the labile and neurasthenoid potency disorders; these men seem to react best if neither pressured nor yet having their surface anxieties and minor somatic symptoms overindulged by the physician. Thus one may resort to a regimen aimed at bringing them back to the most regular possible sexual performance at the earliest time. This approach differs from that advocated by some other observers who favor not exposing these patients to coital attempts as long as they feel listless, fatigued or anxious.

All impotent patients must be cautioned "not to worry the function," meaning to refrain from testing themselves, brooding, anticipating, measuring their function against that of others whom they may subtly question, and from comparing their symptoms and course with what medical case material they may be able to get hold of in libraries or elsewhere.

Dual Team Sex Therapy (Masters-Johnson Method). An intensive 2-week or slightly longer course of treatment of the patient and his wife (or partner) jointly by a male and female co-therapist team. Patients arriving alone have used "surrogate partners" employed for the purpose. Both spouses are treated even if only the husband is believed to be dysfunctional. Emphasis is on frank communication between the spouses, and on no immediate expectation of coital success by any of the 4 individuals in the group, nor must coitus be tried or ejaculation obtained in the early days even if erection occurs.

In a case of erective impotence the couple start out by caressing each other, preferably on the back, extremities and face, then proceed to pleasing each other quietly and undemandingly by alternate genital stroking without performance-mindedness, each focussing attention on the other. Later they progress to manually producing erection by caress, stop until it subsides, then reproduce it again. Finally, as casually as possible, the wife inserts the phallus in the woman-above position with the man remaining passive. She is not permitted to thrust toward a climax at first, but both ease slowly into a coital pleasuring pattern.

Sex therapy, in essence, is a course of programed sex activity employed for men with certain types of erective and ejaculatory potency disorders, and for women with orgasm incapacity, as well as related difficulties. The genito-manipulatory program is structured into a benignly authoritarian pattern of conferences and directives, based on the principles of behavior therapy. Attempts at understanding deeper psychologic factors are purposefully avoided. A medical examination precedes the therapy, although little is known about its thoroughness, especially in those establishments which appear to operate without benefit of adequate medical supervision.

The method, especially the vast publicity surrounding the original venture, helped raise the consciousness of many about seeking help for sexual problems. Sex therapy is a potentially effective treatment, although most of its components have been used previously by others, and to date there has been no way of assessing the sometimes astounding claims of cure, especially regarding durability of results. Sex therapy centers have been proliferating since 1970; the technique is now at risk of deteriorating into indiscriminate commercialization via projected chain clinics, 6- to 10-hour training seminars and diploma mills, lecture circuits, traveling teams of borderline practitioners from many fields, etc. Use of surrogate partners (see above) has led to the influx of part- and full-time "sex therapy aides," "surrogate therapists" or "sex counseling paraprofessionals," most often call girls (and some call boys). A few have degrees (e.g., in psychology), and operate as exclusive intercourse therapists by following the steps in the chapters of the Masters-Johnson book, a procedure these authors did not prescribe. Physicians and allied professionals who either assemble lists of available operators and/or refer dysfunctional individuals to them are coming close to being cast in the role of procurers, as money changes hands at several levels.

Behavior Therapy. This approach constitutes a break with traditional insight-centered psychotherapy. Its focus is on symptom removal, employing a number of conditioning and desensitizing methods. Most recom-

RATING OF PERMANENT SEXUAL IMPAIRMENT

For compensation purposes, permanent impairment exists after maximal medical rehabilitation has been achieved. Values are for men aged 40 to 65. Add 50 per cent below age 40; subtract 50 per cent above age 65. For any urinary function impairment combine with appropriate rating value from special chart.

Impairment of the Whole Man

Class 1: Sexual function possible but varying degrees of difficulty of erection, ejaculation and/or awareness: 5 per cent to 10 per cent .

Class 2: Sexual function possible, with sufficient erection, but without ejaculation or awareness: 10 per cent to 15 per cent

Class 3: No sexual function possible: 20 per cent

> Committee on Rating of Mental and Physical Impairment, American Medical Association. From the Guide to Evaluation of Permanent Impairment, A.M.A. 1971

mended for impotence is active, graded therapy which requires realistic contact with the situation under treatment, rather than picture viewing in the physician's office or such. The cooperation of an understanding wife is required; in essence, she and the patient must lie in bed together nude on several occasions in physical closeness but without any expectation of intercourse on the part of either, and without impatience or criticism. This may be preceded by some alcohol or tranquilizer medication. Anxiety is expected to decrease from session to session.

Nude Encounter Group Therapy. The method, when ethically administered by a professionally trained person and structured with care, is not intrinsically immoral. Participants are not expected to indulge in sexual acting-out. Some are of the marathon type, typically with 15 to 20 members of both sexes—strangers, but including couples—all usually in the nude. Sessions involve orientation, audiovisual contact, mutual skin caressing exploration, then verbal catharsis and review (Apfelbaum, Bindrim, Panzer, Shepard, others). Not to have an erection at a certain point is said to be more embarrassing for a male than to have one. No meaningful results are available as regards cures of sexual impotence. Many other groups, run by unqualified leaders, represent a form of psychologic assault on vulnerable participants.

Testosterone. In theory there is little scope for the use of testosterone therapy in sexual impotence except in the relatively few demonstrable syndromes of androgen deficiency. Especially in psychogenic impotence there was little rationale—except when used for "priming" in conjunction with psychotherapy—for the employment of male sex hormone therapy;

and, indeed, in the past the dosing of certain impotent men with testosterone was no better than whipping a dead horse, or administering a placebo. However, experience with this substance has been undergoing some changes. The use of considerably bolder doses, the unexpected success achieved with them, and a more sober risk appraisal are opening up new therapeutic avenues for a proportion of cases. Although the cause-effect relationship between plasma testosterone ranges and use or use-readiness of the male genital function remains poorly understood, this is no reason to turn our backs on an empirical method if it can alleviate, with relative impunity, a condition which is as serious and about which, in truth, we know as little as sexual impotence.

Examples of bolder dosing would be a course of methyl testosterone 25 mg p.o. daily for 3 months, followed by several weeks of rest, then resumed. Or long-acting testosterone 200 mg i.m. once every 1 or 2 weeks. Or 10 to 16 pellets of testosterone, 75 mg each, implanted subcutaneously every 6 months (Greenblatt). Or testosterone propionate sublingually 15 to 20 mg daily or 25 to 50 mg i.m. 3 times a week (needle: 1¼ or 1½ ins. 21G), preferably the parenteral schedule or a combination of the two. Superior, safe performance has been reported with the newer Mesterolone (not in U.S.), an androsterone derivative which is not bioconverted to estrogen and without inhibitory effect on pituitary gonadotropin production and spermatogenesis.

Existing carcinoma of the prostate may be the only absolute contraindication; testosterone can aggravate it, but there is not even evidence that it can cause it. An enlarged prostate or a family history of prostatic malignancy would impose a cautious attitude. Men with cardiopathy in the recent past or present are not usually good candidates for these treatment courses. Spermatogenesis is reversibly (rebound) suppressed after a time; in long-continued use sterility reportedly can become permanent. Unless fertility is not a relevant problem, this needs to be prediscussed with the patient. Other effects of testosterone are well known (e.g., jaundice—only with methyltestosterone; water retention—give occasional diuretic, reduce salt intake). Polycythemia needs to be watched for. The triglyceride level may rise and need be monitored.

Herbal Aphrodisiacs. Through the ages men, assisted by their women, have sought to obtain or initiate sexual stimulant effect from a multitude of pharmacal substances. Some of them produced priapism-like erections which were too distressing to make coitus possible, or even to make it appear desirable. However, the mere possession of an erection was held to inspire love and respect in a wife. Those substances which endured over hundreds, some even thousands, of years mostly represent herbal products related to spices which contain volatile oils. Excreted through the kidneys, they irritate the genitourinary tract, causing reflex erection by acting on the posterior urethra. By causing mucosal congestion they produce a sense of urethrovesical fullness, urgency, tingling and itching which may resemble sexual arousal. Most exert a deep genital vasodilator effect as well. Some also contain alkaloids which add to the sexual effect. Essential oils, if employed repeatedly or excessively, damage the kidneys, and with pre-existing renal damage they have been fatal to some users. One may mention, as examples, preparations from vanilla planifolia, and rosemary (as oleum rosmarini officinalis). Preparations for inunction into the male organ have been employed for their stimulant effect due to rubefacient-irritant, congestant or vasodilator action. Examples are oil made from the nuts of Pistaccia vera; crushed leeches in oil; salve of cantharides (see below); and black pepper or paprika ointments.

Yohimbin (yohimbine). A preparation deserving further trial, this alkaloid from the bark of the yohimbihi tree (Corynanthe yohimbe) is used chiefly as the hydrochloride or lactate of yohimbimum or as the pure extract. Present indications are that it has some value. Its systemic effects are ergotamin-like and sympatholytic; it acts as a vasodilator and a hypotensive. Its sexual effects, by mouth, occasionally epidurally, include hyperemia and vasodilation in the genitalia, including the testicles; an affinity for sacrolumbar segments of the spinal cord resulting in stimulation of the neural mechanism; and possibly a moderately irritant effect on the genitourinary mucosa. It is usually buffered to counteract its sometimes distressing hypotensive effects. Where effective, yohimbin does not cause true sexual desire, but reflex erection and a vague genital urge.

Damiana. Ginseng. Here alkaloids add aphrodisiac effect to action due to essential oils. Damiana, from the brush Turnera aphrodisiaca, was and is employed as infusion or fluid extract of the leaves and the twigs. Ginseng, an aromatic long and highly regarded in the Orient and elsewhere, comes from the roots of a few selected varieties of the ginseng plant (Panax ginseng or quinque-folium). As the roots tend to suggest the shape of human figures, a symbolic (talisman) value has adhered to it traditionally as a minor part of its effect.

Various. *Levodopa* (L-dihydrophenylalanine), metabolic precursor of the brain neurotransmitter amines (dopamine, norepinephrine). Useful as an antiparkinsonian, it also produces degrees of increased sexual excitability and appetite, and more frequent spontaneous erections in some men, awake or asleep. However, much of the effect is due to hypomanic behavior, the erections are too fugitive and weak to be enabling, and undesirable side-effects occur. It is not a useful aphrodisiac and is not considered a suitable treatment for impotence.

Hydergine, a combination of 3 hydrogenated ergot alkaloids—adrenergic blockers—has been used (not in U.S.) with reported success in the neurasthenoid type of impotence (q.v.) in men below age 40 (hypotensive, easily fatigued, weak erections, scant libido). Recommended dose: 1 ml. i.m. 3 times a week for 4 to 6 weeks, then 2 to 3 sublingual tablets or 10 to 15 drops a day for 3 to 4 months (Joel).

Clomiphene, an ovulatory stimulant, has been used in impotent men; it increases the release of gonadotropin hormones and raises the testosterone level sharply. The dosage used has been 200 mg a day for 7 days. This is not an approved indication for this substance; results have been variable.

Phosphorus, in modern times as lecithin or as glycerophosphates, has been considered as a sexual stimulant by some. It was said to form the erection-producing ingredient of the Oriental birds'-nest soup (nest of the sea swallow, built from edible seaweeds and fish spawn), although this dish was usually heavily spiced also. Phosphorus in ordinary doses is without sexual effect.

Strychnine as its sulfate or nitrate (1/60 to 1/12 gr.) or as tincture (10 to 30 drops) or as extract (¼ gr.) of nux vomica or by epidural spinal injection (e.g., ½ gr. of strychnine nitrate in 5 ml. sterile water) was at one time held in repute as an aphrodisiac. Apart from its generally tonicizing action it was believed to sensitize the spinal centers. Undoubtedly, it can produce substantial sexual stimulation and possibly an ejaculatory reflex following 1 to 3 doses, several hours apart, preceding the act; but this procedure does not lend itself to frequent repetition. The value of strychnine, as regards the actual treatment of impotence, is generally discredited today.

Cantharides (Spanish Fly). An essentially dangerous substance with a long history of repute as an aphrodisiac for cattle and humans which includes hundreds of deaths. Its use for sexual purposes is to be absolutely discouraged. Active ingredient: cantharidin, obtained from pulverized beetles, mainly Lytta vesicatoria (Cantharis vesicatorea) in the Mediterranean, Epicauta vittata, Nemognatha, Mylabris and many other blister beetles in the Western U.S. The powder is recognized by its metallic glitter. Cantharidin acts sexually by producing a joyless reflex erection through irritation of the urethral mucosa. The few observers with cantharidin experience other than treatment of poisoning have said that too much pain and swelling—often blistering—is involved to make these erections useful; priapism, in fact, occurs as a symptom of severe toxicity. The substance has been used as the powder, tincture, ointment or, formerly, as candy (pastilles galantes). Toxicity is unpredictable and not always dose-related. Acute cantharidismus includes severe cystitis, necrotic kidney damage, hemorrhagic enteritis and blistering oropharyngitis. Emergency treatment: gastric lavage, demulcents, apomorphine, analgesics, copious intravenous fluids; no fat, oil or milk by month. Cantharidin, as a collodion, is in recognized topical use in the U.S. for wart treatment. Some experimental uses of the substance exist.

Highs and Ups (see also p. 444). *Marijuana.* A disinhibitant and euphoriant, it also enhances sexual pleasure in some experienced users, but it does not capacitate. *Amyl Nitrite,* a short-acting vasodilator with undesirable side-effects. Increases sexual pleasure perception or prolongs climax when inhaled ("popped") during the sex act. "The mind zooms off for a minute." The jag is most powerful in combination with marijuana. It has not been known to be of help in impotence. *Amphetamine (high dose),* especially i.v. methamphetamine ("speed"). Prolongs erection, produces a more aggressive, even ferocious sex act heedless of own or partner's chafing pain, may induce multiple orgasms in men. It is an enhancer, but probably not a capacitator. Socially and medically undesirable. *Amphetamines (moderate oral doses)* or Ritalin, etc., self-administered, euphoriate and energize temporarily but do little for most impotent men. If carefully dosed, buffered and alternated under supervision they can add occasional impetus in cases under other therapy. Ten per cent to 20 per cent of adults are believed to be perverse reactors (i.e., they are, like children, indirectly sedated by these drugs). *Cocaine,* sniffed or i.v. In high doses induces long erections, sometimes multiple orgasms, but some men obtain no orgasm from their priapism. The come-down is highly unpleasant. The drug is illegal, socially dangerous, but possibly not habit-forming. It has been known to produce an erection in an occasional impotent man, but there is no long-term benefit.

Niehans Cell Therapy. For males and females, and not limited to sexual deficits. For impotence a suspension of Sertoli cells from freshly killed lamb fetus or young bull testicles is administered intramuscularly in series. Hypothalamus and/or placenta cells are sometimes added. The rationale has been called feeble; success claims have been major. In view of the numerous possible causative factors in impotence objective evaluation of results would appear difficult. The product is available fresh, at the Swiss Clinic in Montreux, or as lyophilized cells (brand name Cellorgan).

Mechanotherapy. A variety of sexual devices continue to be available. Relatively most rational are *Supporting Splints,* sleds, perforated covers, stiffener sheaths or artificial hollow phalli into which the flaccid organ is inserted—sometimes by stretching it—or which are held in place by a strap or harness (Wimpus, coital training apparatus, etc.). They are inserted vaginally with manual help after lubricating, although lubrication makes some sheaths slip off. The purpose is to satisfy a sexually deprived wife; also to help overcome the intromission barrier, hopefully leading to a delayed erection so that the device can be discarded. As failure to erect is hidden and no anxious expectations accompany the progress of the act, it is hoped that in time the organ will be conditioned ("trained") to respond with erection to being in vaginam (Dengrove). As conditioners the sleds and sheaths have rarely been known to be effective. Some wives have reported to have been satisfied sexually by the device; others have tolerated it and feigned orgasm so as not to disappoint their husbands and to raise their self-esteem, or because it felt good just to have his laboring nearness and concern. The devices are not illegal if used for medical indications (G.L. Kelly). *Vacuum Pumps,* hand or battery operated, to induce passive inflow of blood followed by application of special clamps or a tight rubber band to prevent premature outflow are potentially dangerous. Besides, the penile drainage system is deep and beyond the reach of rubber bands. Applications of electrified chains, or of belts or whips "to excite the jaded" are old brothel standbys, either useless, or successful through a masked psychosexual sadomasochistic process. Slightly related are the traditional *Aphrodisiac Manipulations* applied to the phallus and scrotal skin; they include gentle scratching, pinching or biting; and a gentle wringing of the erect shaft ("sexual explosion"), obviously of no help to the impotent. *Electrovibratory Devices* for men, most often used by homosexuals, have not been of help in treating impotence.

Surgical Implant. In irreversible complete organic impotence (e.g., following radical surgery, q.v.) a silicone prosthesis—a rod 6–10 cm long, 10–13 mm in diameter, reaching from corona to suspensory ligament, moulded to fit the penile contour, its proximal end unattached—may be implanted in the dorsum penis between Buck's fascia and the tunica albuginea of the corpora cavernosa, to facilitate sexual intercourse, especially intromission. For this purpose the organ is elevated and directed by hand; at other times it rests pendulous against the thigh (Beheri, Lash, Loeffler, Pearman, Tudoriu, others). A reinforcing embedded Teflon rod or a spring can be used. A flexible prosthesis with a hinged joint is considered a practical possibility.

CHAPTER 18

Frigidity

Loss of Libido — Sexual Anesthesia — Orgasm Failure —
Pseudofrigidity — Treatment of Frigidity — Vaginismus.

The term frigidity, as it is used most commonly, is a collective name for
a number of psychosexual deficits in women. One may include lack of
sexual interest, loss of libido and absence of desire for intercourse (sexual
anhedonia; antiqu: anaphrodisia); inability to experience pleasurable feelings during intercourse (sexual anesthesia or, actually, hypesthesia);
inability to reach orgasm during intercourse (orgasm failure, frigidity
sensu stricto); and the related spasm of vaginal muscles when intercourse
is attempted (vaginismus, vaginospasm). These deficits occur in various
combinations. For instance, a woman who for some reason has a marked
aversion to coitus will rarely derive much pleasure from the act and thus
may not reach orgasm. Or a woman who is incapable of experiencing
pleasurable sensations would not be expected to desire coitus greatly.

In normal women libido and the ability to be sexually aroused to the
point of orgasm, once established, are hardy functions. They have survived
vulvectomy, clitoridectomy, ovariectomy and pelvic exenteration (i.e., total
evacuation of all internal and external genitalia, bladder, rectum, and complete autonomic denervation, with no opening remaining on the perineum).
Copulatory satisfaction has been obtained from intercourse into a neo-
vagina made of a length of sigmoid, or from a dimple patiently pressed and
deepened into the perineal skin. Sexual responsiveness frequently survives
bilateral ovariectomy, but it does not survive adrenalectomy or hypophysectomy, which has helped demonstrate that the function in women is
androgen-dependent (see also p. 189).

LOSS OF LIBIDO

(Sexual Anhedonia)

Temporary Inhibition. Lability. Occasional temporary inhibition of
libido, if of well-explained origin—fatigue, illness, worry, a quarrel, dys-

402

pareunia—are a normal part of the vita sexualis. In some highly sexed women nothing much seems capable of suppressing the libido entirely, and after a lapse it returns promptly, while in others, more modestly endowed, the desire is labile and a small hindrance is apt to abolish the sexual appetite, diminish arousability and deflect sexual interest. Here, following protracted interruption, libido seems to reappear only slowly or late. Coitus is not repugnant to these women, and affection for the man may be sincere; the woman appears to be serenely indifferent to the prospect of intercourse, although pleasure sensations, even occasional orgasm, occur. Unless such a woman is motivated strongly by a sense of duty or by affection, she may tend to avoid marital relations and thus impair marital harmony.

Causes of Anhedonia. Between the two extremes of female libidinal anhedonia—temporary interruptions of normal sexual interest, and intractable chronic anhedonia due to aversion (e.g., some married lesbians)—one encounters libidinal disturbances of many degrees, types and origins. Here one finds the woman who is repelled by the act because it causes her pain, as well as the one who uses pain, or some past pain ("I'm still all torn to pieces from the last baby") to mask her noninterest or her revulsion; the woman sufficiently disaffected from her husband so as to resent his advances or at best suffer his exertions while her mind reviews daily odds and ends; the multipara without recourse to reliable contraception who dreads renewed impregnation; the pregnophobic (often actually anesthesiophobic); the tensely anxious female who dreads the act because she is forever worried that a child or co-dweller may overhear or intrude on it; the wife of the alcoholic, resentful of alcoholized sex, submitting passively and with her teeth clenched; wives with total narcissistic unconcern with their own or their mates' sexual pleasure; as well as a variety of non-acceptors of their own femininity and of the feminine role. Undoubtedly, loss of libido can be organically induced—diabetes mellitus and Cushing's syndrome are examples—but psychoreactive deficits are vastly more common. The physician is well advised, as a matter of clinical expediency, to reverse the traditional method of ruling out etiologic factors in an obscure case of loss of libido: he is apt to be more successful more quickly if he excludes major psychologic factors first and proceeds from there.

Depression. In major mental depressions loss of libido is often an early symptom. A severely depressed wife, characteristically anhedonic and sexually unresponsive, may come to feel that she had been depriving her husband sexually, that she was "no good for him" or he too good for her, that he could perhaps find satisfaction with another woman or that she owed it to him to be out of the way forever. In unrecognized cases of major mental depression a single sexual act—a failure to her disordered thinking, proof of her incurable unwomanliness—sometimes pushes the despondent patient, with her irrational feelings of guilt, to self-destructive acting-out. Libido usually returns to normal following recovery, except that in some untreated cases it may not reach its previous level again. In severe, suicidiferous depressions return of libido does not seem to be a reliable sign of full recovery.

Weight. Obesity of long duration, in a minority of cases, is accompanied by seemingly profound disinterest in sexuality; it is uncertain if these girls have learned to inhibit themselves because ashamed of their weight, or if the general passivity and phlegmatism of some such girls is also responsible for their lack of sexual interest. Normal women being forcibly undernourished lose libido quite rapidly (see p. 357). A severe degree of anhedonia occurs in anorexia nervosa of adolescents. In severely obese patients who had been completely inhibited in their sexual awareness, weight loss is often associated with development of sexual feelings (Bruch).

Ataractic Drugs, both of the reserpine and the phenothiazine variety, can cause major degrees of sexual anhedonia, and marked degrees are produced, in some patients, by some antidepressant drugs, even after depression has given way to a more elevated mood.

In Narcotic Addiction, loss of libido is profound. These women seek orgasm centrally, bypassing the genital apparatus and impatiently stimulating the midbrain for their thrill. The confirmed addict has no use—no time, no energy, no feeling—for people or relationships which do not directly aid in the procurement of the drug. The promiscuity of the addicted woman (see also p. 446), is based on expediency (money for drugs), on compulsive self-debasing, and on the severely disorganized state of all inhibitory mechanisms, but hardly ever on an increase in sexual interest.

Endocrine Deficits. Sex-Diminishing Surgery. Many endocrine disorders which affect sexual function also affect sexual response, and all those which impair response also reduce sexual interest. This includes ovarian deficits such as Turner's and the polycystic ovary syndromes; pituitary disorders (e.g., Simmonds' and Sheehan's diseases), adrenal conditions such as Cushing's syndrome and Addison's disease; and major degrees of hypothyroidism. Following bilateral ovariectomy (surgical menopause), unless replacement therapy is feasible, the genital apparatus regresses, the vulvovaginal passage becomes uncomfortably stenotic, and its mucosa atrophies, making coitus painful and eventually no longer sought or desired. Cessation of estrogen output by itself probably does not impair libido or sexual responsiveness, provided that preoperative sexual adjustment had been good. Nevertheless, about one third of castrated women report failing sexual reactions, including loss of interest (see p. 355). In some women surgical sterilization or simple hysterectomy, or an abortion or miscarriage, or even a medical verdict of permanent infertility have been known to lead to progressive loss of sexual interest. The subconscious awareness that intercourse no longer has reproductive significance or that the patient's feminine self-image has been impaired play a part here. At any rate, there is wide agreement today that the cause of anhedonia following sex-diminishing interventions is psychogenic, possibly connected with a re-mobilization of childhood mutilation fears.

SEXUAL ANESTHESIA

Sexual anesthesia—more often hypesthesia—refers to the absence of pleasurable feelings during intercourse. It is never for long, nor significantly, an independent syndrome. Absence of adequate pleasure feelings makes orgasm difficult or impossible to attain; also, where a woman feels nothing during the act, she will frequently prefer not to be bothered, unless a strong wish to gratify or accommodate the man she loves masks her anhedonia.

Endocrine and Psychogenic Anesthesia. Total sexual anesthesia of all genital structures, no matter what the mode of stimulation, does not occur without coexisting loss of libido—in severe hypogonadism (p. 351) or in late defeminization (q.v.) without masculinization. Major degrees of anesthesia occur where extremely one-sided stimulus reliance, usually vulvo-clitoral, is combined with unremitting indifference or revulsion attending vaginal stimulation. This is seen at times in young nulliparas where such repression of vaginal awareness represents the outcome of pronounced tomboyism which failed to reverse completely at menarche, especially if there were sexual experiences in the early teen period producing fear of pregnancy or childbirth (Greenacre). There also exist some emotionally immature, shallow-hysteroid women who desire, and seek, intercourse frequently, although in the severest cases they are totally without feeling during the act. Their motivation is pseudolibidinal (e.g., a compulsive—not loving—wish to please). They profess to be perplexed by this alien, puzzling "thing" which unaccountably blocks normal progression from desire to fulfillment; they insist that a local organic cause must be present, although none is found. In another, conversion-hysteric manifestation the woman has no manifest neurotic symptoms, and there may even be normal, possibly strong, sexual interest and desire. But once intromission is effected the desire ceases, and no pleasure is felt.

Coital enjoyment does not depend on any one structure or surface of the genital tract (see also p. 188). Some women are endowed or conditioned to rely more on the perivaginal submucosal fibres of the levator ani group (the "vaginal" component), others more on vulvoclitoral stimulation. It is possible that the perivaginal sensory structures must attain full physiologic maturation—late in the teens, sometimes later—before they develop optimal capacity for mediating erotic apperception.

Vaginal Overrelaxation. The most important hypesthetic syndrome occurs in connection with vaginal overrelaxation. To the patient herself this may appear occasionally to be a matter of insufficient contact between penis and vaginal walls. However, there is evidence that relaxed walls are also hypesthetic walls, because the submucosal deep-touch nerve endings which are responsible for the greater part of vaginal sensation are minimally represented if their vehicle—chiefly the pubococcygeus—is hypotrophic. Thus probably no degree of bulk immission can completely overcome these women's diminished sensation, although fantasized desire for an elephantine phallus or half-jesting quest for an extender condom with rubber projections (p. 419) is not rare here at a time when urges are intensified.

A proportion of all women have weak and atrophic pubococcygeal muscles, irrespective of age and childbearing. The muscle corresponds to the tail-flexing muscle in simians. It is attached to the pubic bone and the obturator fascia in front, and to the coccyx posteriorly. If it is constitutionally predisposed to weakness, it may not regain normal tonus even following relatively normal childbirth, and especially after several childbirths in quick succession. However, multiple vaginal parity as such does not produce overrelaxation and certainly not loss of sexual sensation and response. With a history of difficult labor the cause of overrelaxation has been found occasionally in visible but unrepaired or in invisible submucosal lacerations. Mediolateral episiotomy—partly because of its use early during the second stage of labor—tends to cause major damage to the pubococcygeal muscle on one side, unless repaired at the time of injury. Such an unrepaired muscle appears to be a major contributor to unsatisfactory sexual function, as vaginal tonus is lost, possibly in a progressive manner.

Frequent pregnancies in the presence of a debilitated state, and heavy lifting or straining following childbirth, also have been found to be responsible for weakness of the pelvic floor. Also, the belief has been expressed that faulty toilet training, both urethral and anal, in childhood may be responsible for spontaneous overrelaxation, but, although anatomically justifiable, this is unsubstantiated; in fact, it is improbable. The same can be said of the theory which would ascribe spontaneous chronic relaxation to atrophy from sexual disuse. Following ovariectomy, in the absence of replacement therapy, relaxation of the pelvic supporting structures is a frequent sequel, together with the gradual regression of the whole reproductive apparatus. For treatment of the sexual deficit due to pubococcygeal weakness see p. 418.

ORGASM FAILURE

(Frigidity Sensu Stricto)

Definition. Flimsy Orgasm. Frigidity, in the strict sense of the term, is the chronic inability to achieve orgasm during sexual intercourse, often in the presence of affection, desire, arousal and coital pleasure feelings. It differs from pseudofrigidity (q.v.) where orgasm capacity exists but the woman is chronically kept from attaining it by adverse circumstances. The presence of a tenuous or flimsy orgasm ("a trace of orgasm") as a regular pattern usually is not considered as being orgasm failure, as degrees of climactic feeling intensity able to fully gratify a woman range through a wide spectrum. Temporarily tenuous orgasm occurs in debilitated women, or probably in healthy women who are tired, tense or distracted during the act by surrounding unrest.

Orgasm Capacity. Controversy persists as to whether orgasm failure is a pathologic condition at all. Some observers feel that orgasm is not an integral part of female sexuality, but a faculty which the individual woman may or may not achieve; and that the doctrine of universal copulatory orgasm tends to stigmatize a proportion of normal women as sexually deficient or disordered. Most, but not all, clinicians today favor the view that orgasm capacity is an integral part of female sexuality, and that its absence constitutes a significant finding, both as a symptom and as a potential pathogen. On the other hand, the recent obsessive concern with quantity in female orgasm attainment seems to have added little to the enhancement of the quality of conscious living. The sum total of benefits to organism and psyche are not known to be greater with multiple orgasms than with one or two. At any rate, says Shainess, no definition of sexual response which uses orgasm as its major criterion can be valid.

The ability to achieve and control orgasm in many human females is believed to improve with experience training (Lloyd). In fact, coital orgasm is not usually achieved by most women when regular coition first begins. This has clinical significance most often in connection with the so-called physiologic frigidity of the bride, a supposed condition of dormant responsiveness in modest, or at least previously continent young women, and lasting weeks, months, occasionally a year or longer. On the other hand a high degree of response readiness and sensuous endowment is encountered in certain other women, often no less modest, although they may need to struggle harder for whatever continence and virtue their life style demands. It would be erroneous, however, to contrast these two women as regards capacity to attain coital climax when establishing the fond, trusting relationship of early marriage. The incidence of chronic primary orgasm failure appears to be about equal in them (i.e., orgasm capacity probably is not chiefly a function of sensuous endowment or temperament). The highly endowed fail more spectacularly, however, and more noticeably, while the erotically unspectacular young female can coast for a long time on the soothing label of benign onset failure.

Secondary Failure. Where orgasm capacity disappears after having been present normally, usually the condition is designated as secondary orgasm failure. Such secondary failure may follow birth of a child, sometimes the first, but often only after the second baby. Labor was often difficult in these cases, but there is no evidence of physical damage. Difficult labor may rekindle a dormant fear of dying in childbirth, with subsequent phobia formation revolving around sexual intercourse: the pleasurable sexual response is feared and rejected, as it were, because it implies another exposure to childbirth and thus to death (parturiphobia). If there had been sexual neglect of the woman, the experience of motherhood tends to mobilize latent hostility against the mate, possibly as a representative of all men.

Relative Failure signifies that a woman is capable of achieving orgasm in one situation or with one man (e.g., premaritally or extramaritally) but fails in the situation at hand. Some women with neurotic sexuality, for instance, seem to enjoy gratification only where they do not love, and love only where the sexual component is minimally present; such women may be impelled to extramarital resort while deluding themselves that love reigns in the home. Another pathologic example is the woman who can get sufficiently aroused to achieve orgasm only by a man who degrades, abuses or even physically mistreats her (see also p. 478); where this is denied her by a kind and puzzled husband, she remains frigid in the marriage.

Psychogenic Inhibition of Orgasm. Probably the most frequent cause of orgasm failure is chronic unconscious self-inhibition of the capacity to love and let go unreservedly during the sex act. The inhibitants are congealed negative emotions such as fear, shame or hostility, residues of a large variety of past traumata, which have become fused with components of the sexual drive. As the component (e.g., coital arousal of major degree) comes up, the inhibitant rises with it. Clinically, the most deep-seated (i.e., most deeply unconscious, or dating from earliest years) are seen in a woman who is physically healthy, endocrinally unremarkable, without traditional psychoneurotic symptomatology, who desires sex, enjoys foreplay and coitus, but as excitement mounts closer to an acme, suddenly and inexplicably, without distress or rancor, all arousal is dissipated, although she may continue the act to please the mate, even pretend orgasm to hasten him to climax. In others coital excitation may be substantial and sustained, but a climax by means of coitus can simply not be reached; it is elusive and at times seems only the thickness of a transparent curtain away, yet nothing overcomes this barrier, including changes in coital tempo or positioning. In some young women—or even middle-aged brides —in addition to orgasm failure intercourse is somewhat unwelcome, perhaps feared from the beginning; here the line of demarcation between orgasm failure and anhedonic libido becomes more difficult to draw.

One encounters, during psychoanalytic uncovering, the residues and late sequels of sexual assault in childhood, poorly handled by the environment; traumatization by enema; crude suppression of erotic interest in childhood; brutality of an alcoholic father toward the mother; menarche-shock in the presence of a hostile mother; incestuous concubinage with the father or father substitute; a mother's habitual depicting married love as a miserable burden—to name some of the most visible factors. In trauma cases it is probably the event less than its subsequent handling which constitute the pathogen. A recent survey finding (Fisher) which seems to indicate that without the father's closeness in childhood there is later no full erotization of female drives, and less orgasm, has been improperly misinterpreted in popular renditions: insignificance of the father image merely tends to be reflected in the sort of relationship possible with the type of man the scantily fathered woman is apt to attract to herself.

Infantile (Hysterical) Personality (psychosexual infantilism, narcissa frigida). Another cause of frigidity is severe emotional immaturity in the form of infantile personality. These patients combine sexual unresponsiveness with a profound incapacity for giving genuine affection or love. Although the extreme form of this syndrome may be rare, milder cases—many of them frigid—are not uncommon. They have an almost obsessional need to be the center in every human relationship and the insatiable recipient of demonstrative appreciation. Although some are markedly promiscuous, others are capable of intense loyalty in marriage. Some develop a set of pseudosexual reactions which satisfies them completely and often deceives the casual observer. What appears like sexual desire may correspond to the emotion of a child desiring and anticipating an exciting present. What may seem like orgasm to the husband is apt to be the sight of the husband's evident pleasure which arouses in them rapturous images of their own desirability, possibly of climactic intensity. Physically, they are, as a rule, fully matured, endocrinely normal and capable of bearing children. Unlike the sexually infantile female, they are totally unresponsive to hormonal therapy. There is no known treatment.

Diabetes. Frigidity as a symptom rather than an independent clinical entity, is encountered in a number of organic conditions such as diabetes mellitus. In a series of 125 diabetic women aged 18 to 40, 35.2 per cent developed complete orgasm failure (against 6 per cent in a similar, non-diabetic control group). All had been normally responsive in the past. Onset was always gradual, over a period of 6 to 12 months, and followed diabetic overtness. Age and severity of diabetes were not factors; increased incidence of depression in diabetics may have been a minor factor (Kolodny).

Local Anatomic Variations. Excessive distance between clitoris and vaginal introitus—more than 1 to 1½ inches between glans and urethral meatus—reportedly tends to reduce coital orgasm capacity, but this has not been substantiated. However, in theory it seems rational to assume that where the coital to-and-fro pull on the labia has a longer distance to travel to exert mechanical clitoral shaft stimulation some of its impetus can become dissipated on the way. Small size of the clitoris is not known to be an etiologic factor in the genetically and endocrinally normal women, although the obverse, clitoral hypertrophy, is a well-known indicator of androgenic flooding and vulvoclitoral sensitivity.

Prognosis.   The cure rate of frigidity, from best data available, hovers between 30 per cent and 60 per cent of treated cases. The best prognosis— in a series of 58 women treated in a psychiatric outpatient department for a presenting complaint of primary orgasm failure by means of short-term, behavior-oriented psychotherapy (52 per cent cured or improved)—obtained in women whose failure began less than 2 years before treatment, after previous normalcy, who had an essentially normal personality, were possessed of strong sex drive with a heterosexual coital aim direction, had a history of premarital intercourse to orgasm with feelings of love and affection for the male partner without negative attitudes towards their own and the male genitalia as well as sexual experimentation, and who sought help by self-referral, motivated specifically by sexual reasons (Cooper).

PSEUDOFRIGIDITY

(Chronically Incomplete Detumescence.
Circumstantial Orgasm Failure)

In some women sexual intercourse can be a highly gratifying experience regardless of orgasm, but the average woman, especially if she is basically capable of experiencing orgasm, has an almost physical feeling of let-down and non-satisfaction when coital arousal is not followed by orgasm and detumescence. Frequently, she feels tense, untender and irritable after the act and cannot relax or find sleep readily. The feeling of frustration tends to be more acute in women who reach a high pitch of excitement during the act. Where such frustration occurs occasionally in the course of married life it has little clinical significance. The resulting tension is either taken in stride or it is relieved by more successful intercourse later.

Frustration Tolerance.   Where a wife is frequently or chronically deprived of coital completion (see causes, below), her reactions consolidate sooner or later into a pattern of chronic tension, and certain other physical and emotional ill effects appear. Deprived women do not become accustomed to the experience of sexual frustration, but there exists a period of grace, a tolerance period, whose length seems to depend both on her constitutional and personality make-up and on the frequency with which she allows herself to be exposed to traumatic deprivation. By educated guess this period in an average-robust, reasonably placid woman engaged in about 2 acts a week would average 1½ to 3 years, perhaps twice this if she practices coital evasion and is comfortable with masturbating from time to time. Thereafter she tends to become progressively morose and irritable or else hypochondriacal and depressive. Over the years she may lose her sense of well-being, become bored, restless, feel overburdened and increasingly lose her capacity for tenderness. She may become tensely irritable with the children, often without herself knowing why. In general, one may say that there is a tendency to mobilize the most unfavorable facets of the underlying personality.

Causes of Orgasm Deprivation. A frequent cause is habitually deficient, perfunctory or overly rapid performance by the husband, especially if coital foreplay is cursory or absent. Another cause is habitually practiced coitus interruptus (p. 320), especially where the wife feels that she cannot rely on her husband's sense of timing, and thus cannot relax. There are noncaring husbands who habitually ask to be brought to ejaculation by hand or mouth and nothing further. A husband with labile potency, including the alcoholic, often cannot make his erection endure through an entire act. Some women remain too shy or inhibited to permit adequate precoital stimulation and caresses.

A slow-to-arouse wife may persist in her naïve belief that women have no orgasm, thus it may not occur to her to encourage the husband to prolong his performance; as the coital experience is pleasurable by her standard, she may assure him that "everything is as it should be." Women have been known to keep their feeling of frustration secret for many years because they felt it to be a sign of abnormal oversexedness. Apprehensive or purposeful self-inhibition of orgasm has been observed in cancerophobia (cervix); guilt over an extramarital venture; as a contraceptive superstition; in young wives severely indoctrinated against orgasm by their mothers ("to hold a man you must not let yourself go"); and in anxious-compulsive personalities exposed to both sexual neglect and an orgasm-conscious world who, throughout the act, remain tensely, futilely, expectant whether "it" will happen this time. No great changes in these patterns have been discerned as yet despite the liberalization of sexual mores.

Sequelae and Complications. Not infrequently resentment is directed also against the "product of joyless conception"; this may lead to arbitrary, unmotivated family limitations, or even to attempts to have pregnancies interrupted for no reason which appears to be rational. The phenomenon of burdensome pregnancy, sometimes accompanied by massive psychosomatic symptoms, also seems to be especially frequent in pseudofrigid women. A previously affectionate marriage relationship may become vulnerable to all manner of petty circumstantial and emotional stresses. Vague feelings of guilt may arise in both spouses leading to increasing brittleness of the marriage. Sexually, such a woman may eventually revolt against the husband's demands, or else evade them, or perhaps remain increasingly passive during the act so as to inhibit her pleasure feelings and minimize the intensity of frustration.

Some women who are left "high and dry" ("up in the air") frequently may resort to sedatives in an effort to calm down or find sleep. This can remain an occasional measure, or else eventually hypnotics are obtained by prescription, upon complaining of insomnia to a physician. In fact, a fair proportion of complaints of insomnia by women of reproductive age, for which no obvious cause can be found, may be related to orgasm deficit. In some cases hypnotics are taken with increasing regularity; at first, only after each unsuccessful intercourse; later, in anticipation of coitus; and eventually, in a way which constitutes barbiturate habituation. In a small number of cases wives have taken a handful of sedative tablets immediately following a perturbing nonorgasmic coitus, as a gesture of distraught overdosing.

Orgasm Deprivation and Money. A wife who has long been left sexually unsatisfied may experience a vague sense of deprivation the source of which is not obvious to her; instead, her sense of deprivation subtly attaches itself to some other incapacity of the husband's (e.g., she may complain of his inability to support her in the manner to which she, often arbitrarily, feels herself entitled). A hostile-vindictive element may insert itself, leading to squandering of "his" money. The resulting financial depletion, in turn, may serve to prove to her that the husband is not adequately taking care of her. Or a sexually long-neglected wife may become so deprived of her sense of personal worth that she is incapable of taking pride in the state of the household and of the marriage as a whole, and practically all budgetary providence and resourcefulness may cease (reactive-depressive improvidence). Some wives to whom sexual intimacy with the husband is grossly repugnant assume an attitude of vindictive exploitation toward him and "his" money, making almost insatiable demands for gifts of money or valuables which they then either secrete or squander (hostile improvidence).

Pelvic Congestion Syndrome. In the pseudofrigida of longer standing one may encounter the pelvic congestion syndrome (pelvic vasocongestion, Taylor's syndrome), a distressing psychosomatic disorder which, in turn, is trailed by chronic malaise and a characteristic dyspareunia (q.v.). The syndrome resembles the formerly recognized but presumably milder "engagement pelvis of young girls" due to frequent petting without release. Not every case of chronic marital orgasm deprivation leads to Taylor's syndrome, nor is every pelvic congestion caused by deprivation, but the connection seems well established.

Gynecologically, there is a characteristic moderate endocervicitis ("weeping cervix") and, mainly in the nullipara, a somewhat enlarged, gaping but rigid external os with a plug of glistening sperm-hostile mucus occupying the canal, a possible cause of lowered fertility. Uterus and ovaries are enlarged and tender, as are the uterosacral ligaments; in late, severe cases the latter may be contracted, perhaps fibrosed. Tender breasts are the rule. During sexual excitement pelvic discomfort increases, the lower abdomen feels heavy and full; the Bartholinian glands secrete profusely. During coitus any contact with the cervix displaces that organ painfully. Postcoitally there may be suprapubic pain hours later, low back pain lasting well into the next day, and even postcoital masturbation is said to detumesce the pelvic organs only slowly and incompletely. The syndrome also has in tow pelvic varicosities, dysmenorrhea, premenstrual tension, excessive vaginal discharge, fatigue, sexual anhedonia and, possibly, a characteristic dream pattern ("just too late . . . just short of").

Spurious Orgasm Deprivation. Some women are unable to, or chronically kept from, attaining a climax, but their feeling of sexual disappointment is quite minimal; nevertheless they are greatly perturbed by the very knowledge or belief that they are frigid. Some are practically sick with chronic resentment and anguished outrage, because they feel deprived of what they believe themselves rightfully entitled to and what the husband, or some other luckier women they know, are able to attain. In a milder variant, orgasm deficit may coincide with a compulsive perfectionistic or a chronically worrisome personality; this woman experiences chronic chagrin at not having a perfect reaction, mainly because she had read or heard that it is abnormal—unhealthy, unfeminine, unliberated—not to have orgasm. This, in turn, differs from the woman who cannot reach orgasm easily because she is too worrisome, or tense or depressive to relax and enjoy.

TREATMENT OF FRIGIDITY

The physician may find the spouses in a state of frazzled feelings and counterfeelings when they are first seen. The wife feels puzzled and inadequate at not being able to respond, and feels she is failing her husband. The husband, too, may feel inadequate at not being able to stimulate her, and feel he is failing her. By that time usually he has tried all manner of maneuvers, positions and technics, varied his approach, prolonged the act, stimulated her manually pre- and postcoitally, all to no avail. Intercourse at this point has become somewhat of a chore which he would, if he could, rather avoid than seek. The woman is not unaware of this, and she may either pretend orgasm at which, being inexperienced perhaps in this sensation, she is not likely to be successful, or else she is becoming increasingly tense and anxious at seeing the marriage become brittle. There are variations of this sequence of events; in any case, frequently the physician is well advised to begin his assistance on a soothing note, including reassurance, explanation and/or encouragement and temporary prohibition of manual stimulation of the wife's genitalia by the husband precoitally.

Selective Treatment. In long-standing primary orgasm failure it is not an absolute necessity to attempt an active correction of the deficit in all cases. An estimate of the patient's frustration proneness and tolerance, based on a period of observation, sometimes may show that reasonable somatopsychic health and marital harmony can be maintained indefinitely. On the other hand, it would seem to be incumbent upon the physician who has a pseudofrigida under his care not to leave her and her family unprotected against the possible ill effects of chronic orgasm deprivation. Where, for instance, early uncorrected pseudofrigidity coincides with a degree of emotional instability in a young wife, practically each month which passes may facilitate development of a secondary anhedonic syndrome which makes the reparative task notoriously more difficult. The frigid or pseudofrigid woman may not come to medical attention before she has developed sequelar symptoms and signs. Where sequelae, emotional or physical, already exist, they demand first attention (e.g., in the pelvic congestion syndrome).

Correction of Coital Technique may require attention in pseudofrigidity, although it is, at best, useless in most cases of psychogenic inhibitory orgasm failure. Advice to the husband, apart from attention to possible ejaculatio praecox, includes prolongation of the act, where it is performed too quickly, through holding back (self-control) by remaining inactive for short periods with the phallus left immitted maximally; attention to adequate precoital as well as intracoital caresses and stimulation; and possible induction of the wife's orgastic release postcoitally through manual stimulation. A husband's self-control usually improves with practice. However, such restraint cannot be expected on every occasion, and in most harmonious marriages such expectations do not exist on the part of the wife. The quality of the penile thrusts may deserve attention. A husband's slow coital rhythm is often more stimulating than a rapid one, even apart from the tendency of the latter to shorten the act. Vigor and full penetration of the individual thrusts are widely reputed to enhance the woman's pleasure. Some husbands, upon being instructed, tend to become overly attentive to their wives' reactions, thereby inhibiting the wife. Advice to the wife regarding improvement of coital participation may be made part of successive visits and conversations, as the physician attempts to gain a picture of all possible factors.

Uncovering Psychotherapy. The task of correcting conscious misapprehensions, fears or other inhibiting emotions—not infrequently accomplished successfully by the alert and patient family physician—must be distinguished from the attempted correction of deep-seated, inhibiting factors. The nature of the latter is chronic and unconscious, they are not subject to spontaneous self-recognition, and almost never corrigible by self-exhortation or simple persuasion. Unfortunately some aspects of this have become distorted in the minds of many, especially as regards the search for the trauma, and what it is supposed to do for the patient. It is fairly easy to cause a frigid woman to recall a childhood seduction, a bloody accident, a brutal father or a nursemaid's horror tales about childbirth; but such memories by themselves have practically no therapeutic value. It is, for instance, incomparably harder to make her re-experience the anxiety, the rage, the despair, the death wishes, or sense of shame, which adhered to the situation; yet only this would constitute a step toward an effective improvement. Thus, in the evidently more deep-seated psychogenic cases, referral for psychiatric evaluation and, if indicated, systematic psychotherapy may be the most valuable service the attending physician can perform for his patient.

Behavior Therapy. Conditioning and desensitization treatment is based on Wolpe's definition of frigidity as a learned habit of anxiety relating to sexual participation. Desensitizing procedures are expected to permit unlearning of the primary neurotic stimulus configuration. Most proficient application may be in conjunction with a modicum of dynamic psychotherapy.

The method elects to disregard the more intricate causative factors in the person and tends to make light of some established differential diagnostic wisdom; it is essentially a simplistic approach, but among its advantages is that it gives results somewhat more often than other methods now in use. There are many modalities which various clinicians have made up as they go along. One combination method with substantial cure claims includes—in less than 20 sessions with a gynecologist—controlled anxiety inhibition by deep muscle relaxation and intravenous barbiturate, used for the presentation of relevant word pictures which progressively agitate the patient in order to strengthen her tolerance for specific negative sex stimuli (desensitization); couple counseling on sex matters (the mate is present throughout the course); and encouragement of emotional expressivity (Jones Jr.-Park).

Dual Team Sex Therapy (Masters-Johnson). An intensive 2-week (longer in most disciple-run branch establishments) course treating the woman together with her husband; the treating team consists of a male and female therapist which facilitates explaining, minimizes a sense of gender bias and during frequent foursome conferences gives each spouse the feeling of having his (her) own spokesperson. Treatment of single women and of lesbians constitutes an ethical dilemma. Results in true frigidity have not been documented. Exercises begin with masturbatory maneuvers, by her own and by the husband's hand guided by the patient, de-emphasizing the clitoris at first. A preferred position is that of the patient leaning her back against the man sitting behind her. Coitus first in woman-above position with slow, exploring thrusts with pauses, wife controlling the pace; later a modified side position and more spontaneous thrusting. Verbal exploration for etiologic factors is purposely kept on a superficial, though diffusely questing level.

Testosterone preparations have been found to be capable of heightening pleasurable coital sensation and response, and in some cases restoring orgasm capacity. The hormone causes an increase in the size, the vascularity and the erotic sensitivity of the clitoris and, to a lesser extent, of the vulva generally. Part of its effect may be due to an increased feeling of well-being and it may exert a beneficial effect in cases of pelvic congestive syndrome. In frigidity no or minimal results may be expected where the woman never had experienced orgasm during intercourse before, although exceptions have been noted. If used successfully without other therapy, discontinuation of the drug is usually followed by relapse, least often perhaps in postpartum frigidity. Beyond vulvoclitoral sensitization, any libidinizing effect of androgen on a woman is not a fixed attribute of the hormone itself (p. 360). Instead, each woman reacts to the experience of a lowered arousal threshold according to her personality, reactions ranging from the stolid woman's "it itches some, I don't mind" to the mobilization of a sense of guilt or to overwhelming urges ("suddenly man-crazy"), and apparently only in a minority to wholesomely joyful utilization of the libidinal enhancement. Some women on the higher dosages of testosterone become irritable and aggressive.

As to dosage requirements there is no close agreement among observers. Taking effectiveness and side-effects into consideration, parenteral preparations seem to work better than oral ones (disputed); high-dose, short, intermittent courses better than prolonged courses or long-acting preparations (disputed); and combination with daily inunction of the vulva, including clitoris and introitus, with an ointment containing, for instance, 2 mg of testosterone propionate in oil per gram of bland ointment base for a period of 2 weeks is of help in some cases without much risk. Testosterone propionate up to 300 mg during a 3-week course (injections twice a week), and resumed after a week's rest, will rarely masculinize or interfere with normal menstruation. Oral methyl testosterone is given in average daily doses of 5–10 mg; or else 10–15 mg b.i.d. for 1 or 1½ weeks, then once daily for the remainder of the month. A high dose course should be followed by maintenance testosterone to ensure adequate exposure to the priming-and-conditioning experience which is the aim of the accompanying psychotherapeutic efforts. Estrogen deficits encountered should be restored before the course is begun and kept restored during the course. Estrogen as such usually has little or no effect on libido and arousability except where psychosexual deficit reflects primary hypogonadism; but very large amounts of stilbestrol—up to 1.0 Gm a day—have strongly libidinizing effect on some women (Kennedy).

Apart from the usual cautions the two most undesirable side-effects are masculinization of the patient, and masculinization of a female fetus during an unnoticed pregnancy. A waiting period in unprotected women before starting treatment, periodic pregnancy tests, or provision for contraception are good practice here. Masculinization—facial hirsutism, loss of scalp hair, acne, deepening of voice, etc.—occur more promptly in certain susceptible women: those with discernible viriloid traits, those with a tendency to facial acne or hirsuteness, and women with a family history of a tendency to baldness among the male members; perhaps these are best not treated at all. Although most masculinizing effects disappear on cessation of treatment, voice changes, partial baldness or mustache and chin hairs can be partly irreversible. Medication should be promptly discontinued as the prodromal signs—oiliness of face, hoarseness or unusual hair loss on combing—are noted. Some women do not tolerate even fairly modest doses. Other side-effects include regressive changes in the vaginal mucosa, diminution of cervical mucus and mobilization of trichomoniasis. Testosterone is not indicated where distinct primary aversion to intercourse exists in the woman; where she is a known homosexual, married or not; in the presence of markedly promiscuous acting-out; and whenever a major mental disorder, including a depressive or a paranoid state, is in evidence.

Various Medications. There is little of value in the general pharmacologic armamentarium, standing alone, for the frigid, pseudofrigid, hypesthetic or chronically turned-off woman. A mild sedative or tranquilizer preceding an anticipated sexual occasion can be mildly helpful in some cases. Modern-type antidepressants should be limited to bona fide depressive states; some of them are unpredictably libido-dousing in effect. Precoital administration of stimulants in clinical doses, by mouth, usually gives disappointing results. Thyroid USP is indicated in hypothyroidism and myxedema; occasional claims for other libido-promoting effect remain unsubstantiated.

Aphrodisiacs. Although mostly used for male impotence in the past (p. 397), a few were held suitable for stimulating the libido and the responsiveness of women. Certain herbals related to spices, with high content in volatile oils, when taken internally and excreted by the kidneys, produced a smarting, itching, hyperemic effect and a sense of urgency; the urge to relieve these sensations may or may not have resembled a sexual urge. Formulae of rubefacient ointments (camphor, glycerine, menthol, ¼ per cent oleoresin of Cayenne pepper, etc.) for prolonged inunction into the vulva were widely available at one time. Preparations containing the spinally acting yohimbin (p. 398) and others continue to be mentioned, but their effect on the female sexual apparatus is highly uncertain.

Drugs. Use of certain "downs" (mostly sedatives), especially when combined with alcohol, after some weeks or months of conditioning and experience, includes lassitude and often enough disinhibition to permit free rein to a voluptuous sense of sexual receptiveness, perhaps urgency, in a proportion of users. These drugs are conducive to passive promiscuity under unfavorable social circumstances. However, essentially they are disinhibitants, and rarely produce coital orgasm where none preexisted. Cocaine, intravenous or sniffed, and high-dose intravenous methamphetamine ("speed") can cause spectacular orgasmic experiences at times, but there are no reliable reports that they can evoke orgasm where none had been achieved previously. Marijuana acts as a mild disinhibitant, as does alcohol in small or moderate amounts; neither lend themselves for routine prescribing preceding intercourse in frigid women (disputed).

Exercises. In sexual hypesthesia due to vaginal relaxation the technique of reeducating the weak pubococcygeal muscle has proved helpful and become accepted (Kegel's tonus restoration). In the flaccid vagina the physician pretests the muscle's body, tone and contractility against his 3 fingers, having patient avoid use of extraneous muscles (instructions: pretend stopping flow of urine or checking a bowel movement; don't press down on abdomen or rectum). The muscle can be palpated against the fingertip along a narrow area of the lower vaginal wall; diastasis of the abdominal recti muscles is often associated with a weak pubococcygeus. The restorative procedure first seeks to establish muscle awareness, by making the patient contract on her own inserted finger. This is followed by regular, frequent exercises of voluntary vaginal contraction, either against resistance furnished by an unbreakable test tube of suitable dimensions, or against the compressible chamber of a perineometer, a form of manometer, which is psychologically helpful. Also recommended have been frequent (20 to 30 times a day) contracting exercises while going about the daily chores. Improvement in strongly motivated younger women can be quite rapid; past age 40 effectiveness seems to diminish with age (Sturgis, others). Faradization of the atonic levator ani muscles is a rational method, but apparently not of any lasting value unless accompanied by systematic muscle re-education; the method has fallen into disuse.

Gadgetry. The battery-operated electric genital vibrator of any shape —penis shaped, facial massage or glove-type—from available experience has caused more mischief than good in the treatment of orgasm failure. It causes enormous orgasms clitorally, in series; but the women who enjoy it most are usually the ones who do not need it and use it as a plaything or a super-pleasurizer. Actual habituation to vibrators can occur (Sherfey). It has been used in conjunction with intercourse for conditioning, but has not been too successful for this. The frigid woman who needs it sometimes develops a panic reaction or becomes obsessed with gadget achievement; the tool intrudes too abruptly and relentlessly into the defensive equilibrium of the patient. Husbands have used it to cut short the manual prestimulation time or to complete orgasm for the woman who lags behind.

It has been attempted to augment the mechanical stimulation of the hypesthetic vagina during intercourse by means of special condom with rubber projections (doigtier, Kitzelfinger). Historically, such devices have included thorn or feather crowns, metallic spines, platelets and balls, affixed to or even surgically inserted into the penis. As the hypesthetic vagina is generally also the overrelaxed vagina, presumably with hypotrophic perivaginal muscles and poorly functioning submucosal proprioceptor terminals, the effect of such objects must be held to be illusory.

Extramarital Resort. Preoccupations with extramarital resort seem to be characteristically present in a substantial proportion of chronically orgasm-impaired wives. It may be no more than an idly curious toying with the possibility of a fling to find out "if orgasm is possible" for them, if they are "really missing something"; but some others are practically obsessed with such a thought. The frigida with relative orgasm incapacity who happens to succeed in finding satisfaction outside the marriage seems to have practically no chance of transferring this accomplishment into the marriage. Some pseudofrigid wives have claimed that, in the same relative situation, they learned to become sexually responsive in this fashion, and that they had transferred such presumed sexual awakening into the marriage by teaching the husband "how to treat me right" (see also Marital Infidelity, p. 283). Even more emphatic claims for an improved conjugal vita sexualis have been made for "release from inhibitions" of frigid women through group sex, either as couple swinging or as organized orgy-type proceedings, with both mates participating (see also p. 458). However, available professional follow-up observations have rarely been favorable for the long term, group sex becoming a source of subsequent conflict and difficulties. Apart from ethical barriers, it would at this time seem inadvisable for the physician to make encouraging recommendations along these lines.

VAGINISMUS

(Vaginospasm)

Vaginismus is an involuntary, often severe and painful spasm of the vaginal muscles upon attempting coitus. The spasms involve the constrictor cunni, the anterior perivaginal muscles and the levators generally. Vaginismus often prevents sexual entry and makes intercourse impossible; the spasm may be fairly prolonged, or it may cease when the sexual attempt ceases. As it represents an involuntary, defensive overreaction, reflex in type, direct acts of will neither bring it about nor can they terminate it. Onset most often is early during the vita sexualis of the woman (e.g., in newly-wed brides in connection with, or shortly after attempted or completed defloration). Such primary vaginismus often persists for an indefinite period and leads to the condition of unconsummated marriage, and, in turn, to months or years of apareunia, or else to malimmission (para-vaginal, nonentrant coitus). Ignorant couples with a reconstructed history of primary vaginismus, and in several cases of thwarted or incomplete defloration of an unusual hymen, have come to medical attention with a complaint of dyspareunia after years of intraurethral coitus, or after the phallus had dug a para-introital pouch for itself at either end of the vestibulum.

Causes. A variety of causes—mostly psychogenic, some due to genital pathology—are encountered in vaginismus. In minor cases the triggering distress is located in the external genitalia—mucosal abrasion, urethral eversion, hymenal hypersensitivity, etc.—and probably occurs chiefly in spasm-prone women; as the trigger is either self-limiting or soon medically attended to, the spasms cease before chronicity occurs. This type of dyspareunic vaginospasm may also occur after the vita sexualis has been well established (secondary vaginismus, a considerably rarer form). Occasionally, spasm reaction to local discomfort persists after removal of the cause, and the symptom then becomes a phobic over-reaction (e.g., due to fear of further pain). Masters-Johnson in their series mention among causes compelled teen-age prostitution, lesbianism, orthodox religious indoctrination (Catholic, Jewish and Protestant), dyspareunia (due to endometriosis, coital resumption in late middle age and a broad-ligament laceration syndrome following childbirth or gang rape), gang rape without dyspareunia and, most importantly, impotence or premature ejaculation of the spouse.

Vaginismus and Impotence. Vaginal spasm which severely and repeatedly thwarts a desirous husband can eventually lead to degrees of sexual impotence or premature ejaculation, just as often as a man with uncertain erective endurance can co-precipitate vaginismus in a high-strung, thwarted woman. Often both spouses contribute to the marital dysfunction in equal measure. Usually, these women cannot relax when intercourse is attempted; after fruitless and uncomfortable attempts the mere approach of the erect phallus (but not necessarily of caressing fingers) may start the spasm. On the examining table, as the physician's finger or instrument approaches, this may cause involuntary tensing and adduction of the thighs, and a minor degree of opisthotonus. The vulva, the introitus, the lower abdomen and the inner surfaces of the thighs may be hypersensitive to touch.

Phobic Vaginismus. Chronic phobic over-reaction can produce vaginismus. The patient may associate sexual intercourse with something forbidden or extremely dirty or dangerous, or there may be unrealistic fantasies about coitus, some of them surviving from mid-childhood. There may be various defloration fears, based on hearsay and misinformation mixed with fantasy. The husband's or first intromissor's initial coital demands may have been excessively awkward or even brutal, or there may have been rape or attempted rape as an initial sexual experience, followed by poor psychologic management of the afterstate. Painful catheterization or traumatic enemas in childhood seem to be important causes of subsequent phobic vaginospasm. There may be severe, chronic pregnaphobia or parturiphobia. At any rate in these women intercourse is unwelcome and feared, although the husband is not necessarily unloved.

Conversion Hysteria. In another, less frequent, type of psychogenic vaginismus, the psychologic factors exist almost entirely below the level of consciousness and cannot be elicited by ordinary means. The everyday personality of these young women seems to reflect no fear or tension. They seem to be calm, pleasant, and genuinely puzzled or normally distraught by their affliction which they may insist must be due to a physical cause ("la belle indifférence," a cardinal sign in some severe hysterics). On questioning it is often impossible to elicit any traumatic incidents. The spasms seem to exist quite independently of the person of the husband: he may be loved devotedly, and it is not unusual that sexual desire is present or even strong in these women. But when the time comes, the normal desire to receive intromission is absent, although in some cases without any distaste or revulsion or fear being felt. The genitalia "simply freeze together." On the examining table there are rarely difficulties. A few seem to be less concerned than one would expect, or even faintly cheerful. Only upon systematic exploration in depth of their psyche does one encounter a florid, often abstruse fantasy life involving the sexual sphere; unconscious hostility to men; sadistic attitudes toward the husband; latent lesbian tendencies; unconscious incestuous fixations; and so forth, with recurrent dreams with symbolic penetration terror (e.g., holding door against a robber or a threatening animal). The nonpsychiatrist is cautioned against haphazard surfacing of such material, and the haphazard use of hypnosis in vaginismus.

Treatment. Although medical orthodoxy would require that gynecologic examination precede all therapeutic attempts, at times it may be necessary to limit the first examination to the external genitalia and a rectal exploration, and not to attempt introduction of a finger or instrument. Allowing the woman to refuse the physician access with full impunity (i.e., without her having to choose between being overwhelmed and being scolded or scowled at) is therapeutically helpful in itself.

First gynecologic examinations in vaginismus should be gentle, using one well-lubed finger, and accompanied by constant reassurance and explanation of what is being done. Others proceed with a general examination from the head downward and after casually positioning the patient insert a pelvic examination in its proper order. Innovations developed in special settings include the husband's presence during the vaginal examination, self-examination with an ungloved finger by the patient, followed by the husband inserting a finger under the physician's direction. Coupled with explanations and reassurance this can help make the patient more comfortable with her own genital structure, give her a feeling of control over her contractions, and may afford an opportunity to help with interpersonal problems of the couple as they emerge (Tunnadine, Stanley). In another method the patient is taught alternatingly to contract and relax the introital muscles against the physician's finger, starting with a request to block the insertion (Kaufman).

If the marriage has remained unconsummated and the hymen unentered, it is of incidental benefit in some cases of vaginismus to attempt initial hymenal dilatation (not hymenotomy; no anesthesia) in the office or clinic in a reassuring manner—running commentary, no hurry or urging, sitting lithotomy position, prewarmed ¾ inch pyrex tube or small Hegar dilator covered with jelly—and to have this continued at home b.i.d. in a warm bath, preferably by finger, while bearing down as if defecating, with rectum and bladder empty. Learning control over her pubococcygeal muscle (p. 418) and discussing progress with the physician is a psychotherapeutic as well as physiologic device.

Marital hygiene measures include that major overt misapprehensions regarding the genitalia, the vita sexualis and childbirth are corrected; the husband is cautioned against undue force or haste in intromitting; and adoption of the supine hyperflexed position by the patient, with a pillow under her hips, with instructions to bear down as if defecating at the time of entry. The rectum and the bladder should be empty. Experimentation with either the lateral or the woman-above positions is often acceptable. There is to be adequate lubrication. Moderate sedation before the act is desirable, but experience has shown that directions such as "take before you expect to have relations" tend to be practically self-defeating. Alcoholic beverages ("to loosen up") before a coital attempt are not a satisfactory method.

FOR JOURNAL LITERATURE AND ADDITIONAL READING

Deutsch, R. M.: The Key to Feminine Response in Marriage. New York, Random House, 1968
Fisher, S.: The Female Orgasm. Psychology, Physiology, Fantasy. New York, Basic Books, 1973
Hastings, D. W.: Impotence and Frigidity. Boston, Little Brown, 1963
Kant, F.: Frigidity. Dynamics and Treatment. Springfield, Ill., Thomas, 1969

CHAPTER 19

Hypersexuality and Pseudo-Hypersexuality

Promiscuity in Men — Promiscuity in Women — Overexcitement States — Habitual Masturbation — Recrudescence in Elderly Men — Sexual Aggression — Pathologic Erections — Sexuality in Drug Users — Prostitution — Group Sex — Various Manifestations — Pornography — Treatment with Sex Depressants.

PROMISCUITY IN MEN

It is normal for many men to have increased erotic awareness whenever their sexual appetites remain ungratified. On the other hand, there are those whose erotic awareness does not abate with satiation: their thoughts begin to concern themselves with a new potential sex mate practically from the moment their present partner is giving indications of yielding sexually. This is the compulsive womanizer.

Observers have long attempted to isolate at least 2 prototypes of compulsive promiscuity; the so-called Don Juan character, after a 17th century fictional personage, and the Casanova type, after an 18th century adventurer and his detailed erotic memoirs.

Don Juan, also called a "skirt chaser," cannot leave women alone but seems unable to relate to any of them as a person. He may keep actual score of his conquests. Sexual possession is his goal, yet for the individual conquest he has no fondness, but mainly disguised contempt. He combines physical intimacy with emotional avoidance, using devices and excuses as his social situation and his acumen permit. He is seen as a man driven to prove or disprove, again and again, some inner doubt or ward off some nagging anxiety. The nature of the drivenness remains incompletely understood, although there is no dearth of theories: a means to dispel unconscious doubts about masculine identification; to reassure him about his masculine adequacy; the equivalent of compulsive adult masturbation in vaginam; a continuing search for the Oedipal mother; an unconscious tech-

423

GLOSSARY OF HYPERSEXUALITY

Promiscuity. Habitual or episodic multipartnerism, in males or females, can be of cultural type (variant life style) or else a compulsive pattern: part of a personality problem or a symptom of a psychic defect or of immaturity. Excessively indiscriminate pairing in females usually is a joyless and compulsive thing; in men, chronic compulsive womanizing more often masquerades as hedonism. In extreme cases females grant sexual liberties to all comers; this excludes prostitutes as they discriminate as to ability to pay.

Overexcitement State (pathologic hypererotism). In males and females. Manifestations range from unremitting sexual appetite to unbridled sex acts, including paroxysms of aggression. Major causes are temporal lobe disease and epilepsy, endocrine alterations, some drug substances, certain psychoses. The syndrome may affect erotic awareness, language, arousal, response, erections in men, impulse control, sex practices and choice of sex object.

Nymphomania. Refers to a female being hyperappetitive, hyperavailable, hyperarousable—either one or in combination. Implies a degree of aggressiveness (e.g., a frenetic urge) but not necessarily high responsiveness. Duration ranges from paroxysmal to chronic. Modalities range from extreme promiscuity to genital insatiability, coital or otherwise. Term held too imprecise for modern clinical use.

Satyriasis. Applies to males. Refers to supposedly insatiable, lustridden, perhaps molestive-minded men, but actually fits no recognizable clinical entity. Owes its name to the Satyrs, goat-legged lechers of mythology, ever-aroused and ever-potent. Term not in clinical use today.

Erotomania. A group of obsessional and paranoid syndromes centered on erotic subjects, more prevalent in females. Often a precursor of a major psychosis. In males, somewhat related, are jealousy syndromes (e.g., as an early symptom of some involutional psychoses).

Sex Mania. Not a scientific term. In the vernacular sex maniacs are deranged males belonging to such diverse groups as sex-graffitomaniacs, coprolaliacs (dirty words), ceaseless smut storytellers, perpetrators of obscene telephone calls, exhibitionists and rapists.

Priapism. In males. A pathologically prolonged erection without sexual desire, often painful. In modern usage term does not refer to a sexual manifestation, but to a disorder of the neural and/or vascular mechanism of erection.

Clitorism (crise clitoridienne). Cramplike clitoral pain, lasting 1–4 hours, with or without tumescence, often following coitus, less often independent of it. Most often in middle age and postmaturity. Probable cause: rapid desexing and virilization in climacteric; often responds to estrogenic Rx. Other causes (e.g., tabetic neuralgia or chronic incomplete sexual detumescence) not definitely established.

nique of denying homosexual impulses; or a coping device for the alienated schizoid in meeting the threat of isolation.

Casanova, by contrast, the "professional heartbreaker," seems to love before he abandons. Each partner is meaningful to him, but not actually in an affectionate way. Although he is less obsessed with sexual intimacy, he is potentially more destructive than Don Juan in his unconscious aim. He seems unendingly compelled to take revenge on each woman to whom he relates. As he seduces and arouses each, perhaps to a high pitch of enamouredness and sensuality, he appears to be recreating, vicariously, the childhood image of a severely frustrating, incestoid mother. As her image recreates itself, the feel of frustration arises with it, producing a feeling of helplessness, panic and anger or rage (theory).

Psychopath. Another type of promiscuous male is encountered among the character disorders (psychopathic personality): endowed with primitive emotionality, surfeit-prone, predatory, with weak capacity to delay impulses, and intolerant of frustration; he tends to look upon his phallus as a power symbol, and uses it as a power tool. It seems to him, as it were, that all whom he does not subjugate mock him. A closely related variant is the sociopathic individual (e.g., the classic predator), either charmingly or brutally acquisitive, disdainful or uncomprehending of the partner's, or anyone's, moral standards, potentially a ruthless exploiter or extorter of the mate of the moment, combining his need to control and possess with a primitive, shallow pleasure aim.

PROMISCUITY IN WOMEN

Related:
Promiscuity in Teen-age Girls p. 154
Prostitution p. 447

Sociocultural Deviance. When it comes to multipartnerism in the female, there is nothing certain as to where sociocultural deviance ends and clinical pathology begins. There are many radically deviant forms of sex freedom (e.g., militant hedonism, adventurism, formalized swinging, group cohabitation). To partake of these may be considered a "now-thing" by a woman regardless of how placid her temperament, how meagerly endowed she is with appetites, or how steeped in romantic-monogamous daydreams she may be. Yet this kind of promiscuity merely represents a trend; label it fringe culture, or social pathology, or sickness of the times; but it is not clinically pathologic promiscuity.

Pathologic Promiscuity differs from its cultural counterpart not so much in the number of sexual entanglements, or whether they tend to be simultaneous or successive, short-lived or protracted, but by its greater indiscrimination, its relative independence from the mores of the immediate environment and its persistence or else relapsing tendency. Such pathologic multipartnerism is maintained in the face of all manner of social and health complications; of the availability of attractive, stable affection (e.g., a loving, vigorously potent husband); of the patient's own apparently sincere resolve to refrain; and of a surprisingly absent, or scant or deviate, libido.

A typology of the adult, promiscuous non-prostituting woman has been attempted repeatedly, but it remains rather fragmentary, and so do the psychodynamics of promiscuity. Among the few fairly well-studied syndromes are the following:

Uncontrolled-dissolute. A group with often major psychopathology when examined closely. In some way the female here gives the impression of riding out of control, or else her attitude is excessively casual and indifferent; a seeming incapacity to care who cohabitates with her and under what circumstances. Clinically one encounters here schizoid psychopaths (Schneider), simple-type schizophrenics, and the genuinely irresponsible, impulse-ridden psychopaths. If promiscuity is episodic, such conditions as temporal lobe disease (p. 427) and manic-depressive illness need to be considered. In these women any tendency to sliding into low-grade prostitution is perhaps largely dependent on what economic resources or individual resourcefulness they happen to possess.

Passive-gullible. Included here are certain mentally retarded and borderline females, others with pathologic degrees of suggestibility and defective judgment. Unlike in other types onset here is often as a continuation of an adolescent behavior pattern. A socially isolated, awkward, mildly retarded girl may crave affection so strongly that a stranger's brief lie of love and flattery suffices; she is primed for acquiescence; "I say yes only to make me warm, to make me feel love." Many of these subnormal females were never drilled and conditioned, at home or in institutions, to espouse the fairly rigid code of moral and social conventions so necessary to the retardate mind. Related are the profound judgment defects of women who acquiesce promiscuously out of a strong need merely to be held, in turn somewhat similar to certain low-libido wives who "trade a cuddle for a coitus" (Hollender).

Compulsive. Several varieties exist. A masculine compulsive acting-out pattern is recognizable when the promiscuous woman acts as if she was repetitiously, tensely, but joylessly using her body to get hurt, disappointed or humiliated in one exact way with the greatest possible frequency. A very resolute, even frantic type of compulsive promiscuity seems to occur among women, mostly married, with latent lesbian tendencies, with their characteristic heterosexual orgasm incapacity. Often misrecognized is the woman who is compulsively yet placidly, almost maternally all-accommodating, almost for the asking. Her habitual complaisance is often over-simplified as "just the result of a generous nature." But her passionate yearning to satisfy all her world's needy male creatures often hides profound self-depreciation and depression. She may be erotically compassionate, a "passive succorer," an "earth mother," but she is also severely compulsive and with what seems to be a high rate of malignant complications (e.g., psychosis, suicide). To be distinguished from compulsive promiscuity is compulsive inciting or coquettishness (see p. 461).

OVEREXCITEMENT STATES

Pathologic states of sexual overexcitement (hypererotism) are not a frequent condition; in clinical practice they are often overshadowed by other manifestations of the disorder which causes them. Conversely, hypersexual behavior sometimes leads to discovery of the underlying disorder.

The symptomatology of these pathologic states is multiform. Men may simply cohabitate and/or masturbate with greater frequency, but true to their usual pattern, or else they may begin to behave out-of-pattern, to masturbate, solicit new or additional partners, perhaps strangers, molest women or attack them sexually, confabulate sexual exploits, or engage in unprecedented oral or anal practices. Children may be molested, peeping resorted to, pornography collected, dirty stories told endlessly, obscene missiles sent, incest committed or sadistic and deviate acts performed. Erections may, in some cases, occur more readily and the refractory period may be shortened. Women may make incessant requests for coital acts to be repeated, or self-stimulation may become frantically over-repetitive. Aggressively crude advances may be made to acquaintances or strangers "by lifting the skirt"; or solicitation may be more subtle but still indiscriminate. Certainly, not all hyperappetitive sensations lead to promiscuous questing, nor does an unremitting state of stimulation always lead to unbridled reactions. The reasons for individual variations in pattern remain incompletely understood; they are part of the ongoing debate as to whether the symptoms of brain, etc. disorders are mainly personality-specific or lesion-specific.

Brain Lesions. Epilepsy. Insults to or disease of the temporal lobes, one or both, recent or past, are increasingly discovered to cause major sexual disturbances, notably hypersexual acting-out. The temporal lobes contain important structures of the easily damaged limbic system, notably the two amygdalas. A blow to the head, residual lesions of encephalitis, tumors, residues of anoxia, hypoglycemia, partial infarction—all may cause limbic disease and interfere with the control of behavior. Diagnosis can be difficult; the standard surface EEG is not always reliable. Right-sided lesions probably prevail in temporal lobe disease manifestations (Geschwind).

Temporal lobe epilepsy, whatever its cause, is most often associated with lessened libido and genital hypofunctioning, but a proportion of patients display hypersexuality. Two forms prevail here: epileptic equivalents and postictal automatism. During prolonged ictal twilight states (i.e., psychomotor equivalent seizures) the patient may commit gross, aggressive sexual acts (furor eroticus epilepticus), or engage in lesser, but for him (her) unprecedented types or degrees of sex activity. It is possible that the patient remains dimly aware of something alien ("not like myself") happening to him, yet there is a sense of relentless organic-type drivenness which can not be resisted. The so-called pathologic alcohol intoxication with its sometimes unbridled, chaotically disinhibited sexual manifestations may actually be such an ictal twilight state precipitated by alcohol (theory).

The postictal type of hypersexual behavior is characterized by amnesia. In its simplest form an occasional epileptic may masturbate repeatedly during the postseizure confusional state; this was also observed following electroconvulsive treatments, before general anesthesia during treatment came into routine use. Occasionally such confusional states are prolonged for hours or possibly longer; then they constitute a postictal twilight state, a state of postictal temporal automatism. One or more atypical sexual acts, including aggressive ones, although perhaps not actual rape, may be committed for which the patient most likely will have amnesia or, when closer to coming-to, only patchy recollection. It remains difficult at present to prove the existence of such a state even while it is in progress. This becomes important after arrest for a sexual offense committed in a twilight state: the offender by then may have recovered normal reality contact and his bewildered inability to explain may be quite genuine.

Following surgical treatment of temporal lobe epilepsy—ablation of part of the epileptogenic lobe—hypersexual behavior, either relative or absolute, and often somewhat paroxysmal, usually seems to replace the previous hyposexuality after several weeks. If the seizures recur postoperatively, hypersexuality ceases (Blumer). Successful suppression of seizures by medication also tends to be followed by episodic hypersexual behavior.

In a number of individuals with extratemporal brain disease or head injury sexual behavior may become altered, although grossly abnormal or paroxysmal antisocial patterns seem to be rare here. These patients become more uninhibited verbally; they may confabulate sexual exploits at length; in the hospital, they may expose themselves and masturbate. This may represent their way of trying to adapt to the stress imposed by their cerebral underfunctioning; these sexual expressions may be the only way in which these premorbidly perhaps rather strongly erotically oriented people can symbolize what seductive or complimentary emotions they feel impelled to express (Weinstein). Some brain-injured individuals may display exaggerated affection (embracing, kisses) on occasions where formerly they would have smiled or uttered a pleasantry. This demonstrativeness is sometimes misinterpreted by the environment; each such manifestation can and probably should be gradually reduced as part of the process of rehabilitation. Hypersexual manifestations have also been observed in the early stages of general paresis and Huntington's disease.

Endocrine Alterations. In the female degrees of hypererotism—but remaining within normal limits—can occur during the middle months of pregnancy, in some pre-involuting and menopausal women and following hysterectomy and/or oophorectomy. These are self-limiting reactions and most have a major psychogenic component which may contribute to the hyperlibidinal response. Androgens introduced into the adult female organism beyond the small amount normally present not only produce degrees of virilization, but may cause an increase in libido which can be substantial in some cases (see also p. 360). The effect of androgen administration on the female libido is probably not a fixed attribute of the hormone as such, but varies with constitutional and personality factors. Although the external genitalia, especially the clitoris, may be sensitized, some women who are stolid or unprepared or do not desire libidinal increases may rather show annoyance at the, to them, vulvar pruritus-like sensations. Others have reacted with apprehension and guilt feelings on perceiving heightened genital stimulation. In some cases androgens can quickly produce libidinization of tormenting acuteness. Ideally, where androgenic increases are unavoidable, any heightened erotism is matter-of-factly or gladly accepted by the woman and worked enhancingly into the fabric of the existing marital sexual relationship. In men, major increases in libido and erective potency, protracted beyond a few weeks or months with signs of Cushing's syndrome, usually point to adrenal carcinoma (Frawley).

Sharp increases in libido can occur in mild cases of thyrotoxicosis, while major degrees of hyperthyroidism appear to have no such effect. Sporadic reports of hypererotic reactions in diabetes mellitus, in both males and females, have been published. Acute hypererotic episodes occur in acromegalic men (e.g., due to pituitary tumors, early in the disorder).

Drug Substances. Levodopa (L-Dopa, L-dihydrophenylalanine), a major anti-Parkinsonian remedy, in large doses has a tendency to produce increased sexual excitement, possibly more so in men. In some, erective potency is temporarily restored or invigorated. L-Dopa is the metabolic precursor of the brain neurotransmitter catecholamines whose brain level rises with the treatment, while serotonin synthesis is inhibited. In some patients all sex manifestations increase, although they are rarely unbridled. Mostly this appears to be part of a general hypomanic reaction, dose-dependent and impermanent; the drug is not considered a true aphrodisiac. With cocaine a sense of grandeur combined with actual hyperexcitation can impel the male user to hypersexual behavior.

Local Hyperstimulation. A variety of minor anatomic conditions of the genitalia have been thought to cause continued sexual hyperstimulation, but few such cases seem to come to medical attention at present. In some women with vaginal hypesthesia, usually due to overrelaxation of the walls, a continued sensation of the vagina being "like a hungry monster" can lead to major hypersexual acting-out, including an obsessive questing for bulk or multiple successive intromissions; the condition tends to be mis-diagnosed as orgasm failure.

Mild pruritus vulvae may be mistaken for a sexual urge by an un-sophisticated woman; itching and appetitive sensations may actually be similar at times. In more discerning patients, and when pruritus is marked, the differentiation presents no difficulty.

Certain irritant-volatile substances (herbs such as ginseng and damiana; spices such as vanilla, rosemary, cloves, etc., see p. 417) taken by mouth and excreted through the kidneys, irritate the genitourinary tract, causing reflex erection and facilitation in men by stimulus bombardment of neuro-receptors in the posterior urethra at the verumontanum. In women local smarting, itching, hyperemic effect, and local mucosal congestion are pro-duced; the urge for relief from these sensations may resemble a prolonged sexual urge. Similarly acting were certain irritant rubefacient ointments of the past applied to the genital organs by prolonged inunction.

Mental Disorders. In schizophrenia sexual excitability and self-generated arousal can be of very major degrees. Mostly this leads to pro-fusely repetitive masturbation but in males it has also led to acts of rape. In schizophrenic women the sharpest increase in libido tends to occur in the early stages of the disease. Because of modern principles of treatment the massive sexual excesses of hospitalized female schizophrenics are no longer seen. In manic psychoses and in major hypomanic states disturbed impulse control and disinhibition can lead to sometimes spectacular sexual hyperexcitability, but the most highly arousable patients are also the ones who are too flighty in their mental processes for sustained attention to any one pursuit and, unlike in the overaroused schizophrenic, their potency tends to be of limited endurance.

HABITUAL MASTURBATION

(for terminology see p. 139)

Sporadic Masturbation in adults, male or female, married or not, is quite common and has no clinical significance. It is most often substitutional when access to the spouse or a sex partner is impeded. In women of reproductive age perimenstrual sexual tension is often relieved in this way. In a proportion of women masturbation can also relieve the uncomfortable pelvic turgidity and some of the accompanying nervous tension which result from coital excitation without orgasm. In men it can serve to supplement a relatively pleasureless ejaculation after the refractory interval. A juvenile masturbation pattern, especially in males, is not rarely protracted into the twenties where circumstances or personality make-up seem to prevent early marriage or other regular connection.

Existential Masturbation. An impression is emerging among some observers that masturbation in men is increasing. Young men, in the most unexpected cases, seem to masturbate almost as much as they have intercourse. Some informal theories heard around staff rooms: Is women's increasing forwardness, their aggressive stance, causing widespread anxiety and diminished function, requiring masturbatory self-comforting? Or do males now of reproductive age belong to transitional generations between patriarchy and matriarchy, no longer sole choosers of their pleasure moments, nor as yet conditioned to perceive a male's noblest function in being called upon to service the female; and is their withholding erections like the fighting of a confused rear-guard battle with a last remaining, alas passive weapon? Or is bisexuality (p. 501) increasing, the homo portion being timidly satisfied with fantasies? Prostitutes and college girls report that more and more men, all ages, involved in casual encounters desire fellatio, which may be considered masturbation per os. Are women liberating themselves out of much genital functioning?

Chronic Self-gratification Habit. This is the most frequently encountered pattern in adult men. In essence it probably represents an acquired coping device of basically frightened, passive, perhaps somewhat affect-blunted individuals with low tolerance for delayed gratification and for discomfort. The average case history shows that these men masturbate more or less continuously since childhood or pubescence with fair, often daily regularity, with occasional interspersed spurts of 2 or 3 acts a day, as they compensate for anxieties, boredom or contretemps by extracting comfort from the body. Occasional masturbation-free days or weeks occur when highly exciting, comforting or novel events, not necessarily of an erotic nature, touch their lives. The pattern persists through marriage, often including the honeymoon. These men tend to have little genuine interest in having the wife or other sex partner sexually satisfied; in fact they seem to prefer masturbation to coitus, or else they tend to convert intercourse into a masturbatory act of sorts, stimulating themselves with various fantasies. Regular masturbation is often carried well into the fifties, even beyond. These men seem incapable of genuinely sharing their pleasure, nor can they bring themselves easily to feel dependent on another person for their satisfaction.

The habit is not truly compelling in these men, and a meaningful incentive can make them refrain easily. However, such incentives are scarce as masturbation here is largely penalty-free: there is little or no sense of guilt, relatively little interference with erective potency, few or no autonomic stress symptoms, nor many prostatic and posterior urethral symptoms of congestion-irritation so frequent in true compulsive masturbation (see below). These men are characteristically surfeit-prone as regards the fantasies which sustain their masturbation; pornography is a major source of replenishment. Deviate sex images are rarely involved.

There is no recommended treatment for this adult habit. These men rarely, if ever, offer masturbation as the presenting complaint, nor do they readily admit it. Where the symptom comes to the surface as part of a wife's marital complaints, any consistent psychotherapeutic effort directed specifically at masturbation would appear excessive in proportion to anything one may hope to achieve. Local or hormonal efforts are pointless here.

Compulsive Masturbation. This type of habitual autosexual practice in men corresponds to what the older French clinicians characterized as "l'onanisme des scrupuleux." These patients masturbate perhaps somewhat less frequently than the preceding group, but they are usually more depressed and exhausted after each act. Listlessness, torpor, fatigue, pressure sensations in the head, dizziness and/or palpitations may last for hours, perhaps a day (Ferenczi's masturbatorische Eintagsneurasthenie; Ger.). They are usually burdened down with much guilt and conflict about their habit; they carry on a continuous inner struggle against it in which they lose out with such regularity that one may speak of the struggle and the act itself as a psychologic unit. Over and over they re-experience the limits of what they consider their will power, each time rekindling anxiety, depression and a measure of self-contempt. They have conspicuous hypochondriacal tendencies which often include the sexual sphere. They have a tendency to disturbances of coital potency, and chronic congestive symptoms of the upper genitourinary tract and accessory glands (p. 385).

Masturbatory fantasies here tend to be stereotyped and not rarely sadistic or bizarre. Socially these men tend to be isolated, and in their younger years they tend to shy away from contacts with the opposite sex; it is also difficult for them to sustain genuinely tender feelings towards women. Many are sensitive to criticism and slight; on the other hand, great occupational ambition and often successfulness are a notable characteristic. Treatment of patients in this group is a delicate undertaking; any remark or procedure which enhances their conflict has a high rate of major psychiatric complications. This is as true for unskilled psychotherapeutic intervention as it is for unwarranted urologic interference. In the absence of opportunities for skilled psychotherapy, simple tranquillizing medication, especially with the benzodiazepine group, can give creditable symptomatic relief.

Habitual Masturbation in the Female. Tension-relieving masturbation is employed by many women throughout a large part of their lives, either sporadically or as a matter of habitual relief. However, most often even frankly habitual female patterns differ psychologically from those of men employing ipsation as a device for coping with life's demands for involvement and feeling. The compulsive type of masturbation in women is relatively infrequent. Indulgence is often daily here, but the pleasure component is rather minimal. An actual struggle against the impulse is unusual, but strong guilt feelings are often present. Even the fantasies have a compulsive quality about them: the same erotic scene may recur indefinitely without a variation. Many are anxious and constricted personalities. It is among the never-marrieds in this group that one finds women who shy away from gynecologic examination even in the presence of medically alarming symptoms because of phobias about recognizability of their "secret." Such detection phobias tend to be projected into the preferred stimulation site, so that clitoral size, color and shape of the labia, or generally the odor and moisture they identify with masturbation becomes the thing to hide.

Resort to dildoes and dildo substitutes is not widespread in the U.S., but battery-operated electrovibratory devices are being used increasingly. As they do not tire the arms they can lead to habitual use for massive sexual self-gratification. They are applied to the clitoris and surroundings and, given the opportunity, a rate of 20 to 50 of such electro-orgasms in a 1 or 2-hour period, 2 or 3 times a week is not unheard of. This habit pattern has been termed "nymphomania without promiscuity" (Sherfey). It may be most pronounced in multiparous women with the "hungry vagina" syndrome (i.e., pubococcygeal overrelaxation with slow postcoital labial detumescence). With prolonged mechanical stimulation a reversible, moderate hypertrophy of the clitoris seems to occur, at least in some cases.

In **Sexual Deviates** masturbation may be the sole or the only gratifying mode of sexual expression throughout their lives; it can thus be called habitual. This is most often the case in fetishists, in primary transvestites, in the homoerotic type of pedophiliac, and in some homosexual and bisexual men and women who shy away from homogendristic sex relationships. In some individuals masturbation is a mechanism of defense against subsurface deviate tendencies; they drain their libido, as it were, to relieve aggressive tension and to prevent escalation into a full-scale, hard-to-control urge which they sense will take them into socially unacceptable territory. Some deviates practice purposeful "prophylactic" masturbation before stepping out or drinking, because they dread what they know from experience their urges will involve them in.

RECRUDESCENCE IN ELDERLY MEN

Some men of advancing age begin to display increased, offensive, molestive or even aggressive sex behavior. Erective potency may be present or absent. Potent or not, a limited number among them are potentially dangerous sex offenders.

Senile. A generally harmless group is found among men with advanced senility who develop a molestive acting-out pattern (paradoxia libidinis senilis); most are close to or past 70 years of age. Advances are made to children in the vicinity, or to children and young women within the household. Such advances tend to be totally indiscriminate, and include daughters, granddaughters, visitors or houseworkers ("grandpa on the prowl"). They are not easily discouraged either by amiable rebuff or by stern rebuke, or they may not even remember the rebuke a short time later, and these situations tend to recur over and over. Serviceable erective potency in this group is most often extinct; on the whole, they are more a nuisance than a menace, although some are quite offensive at times. Indecent behavior in seniles must be distinguished from confusional behavior. Such men may forget to adjust their clothing when getting dressed or after urination; in the latter case the flaccid penis may inadvertently be left grossly exposed. Others may "forgetfully" urinate in an exposed location, and because of prostatic difficulties the act may take so long that it gives the appearance of exhibitionism, especially if children are playing nearby.

Anxious-regressed. In another, larger, socially perhaps more significant group the men are usually nearer 60 or 65 years of age; the offenses here tend to be minor molestation of children, perhaps attempted seduction, rarely attempted rape. This is the anxious-regressed type of elderly sex offender. These are socially and/or emotionally isolated men, not rarely widowers, etc., their appetites persisting, but their virility feared waning and their opportunities narrowing while there is a lessening of the capacity for control. They seek less sexual gratification than reassurance and denial of their regressive reality. A child may be the only subject they dare approach, or perhaps they expect the least rebuff from children. In fact, some seem to be motivated by the desire to give a child pleasure, hoping that the child will be appreciative and accepting toward them. One finds here certain avuncular elderly men who are manifestly fond of children (Kinderonkel: Ger.) but seem to be unable to draw the line between friendliness and molestation.

Cerebral Arteriosclerotic. This is the most pathologic group among elderly men. The degenerative brain changes may be so subtle that neither dementia, nor substantial loss of hemispheric tissue, nor neurologic signs nor major electric dysrhythmias show up as a rule, although the EEG may reflect minuscule, diffuse foci of softening with generalized low voltage slowing. They may appear to be in substantial possession of their intellectual and sensorial faculties, but the cerebral impulse control apparatus is in a state of disarray. There is cortical disinhibition and progressive loss of judgment, moral sense and other higher mental and ethical faculties. However, in principle each patient reacts uniquely to any given cerebral lesion. (Masserman).

The personality change is often surprisingly rapid. The patient may begin to masturbate with increasing frequency, or resort to peeping, sending pornographic missiles, or he may expose himself or otherwise molest children, less often adolescent boys or young women. His own children or grandchildren are not excluded (see also Pedophilia, p. 472). Those who are more disintegrated and regressed may masturbate openly, or indiscriminately proposition strange women. They are sometimes capable of a substantial amount of brutality against a victimized child, quite in contrast to what is known of their previous personality. Their victims tend to be objects of opportunity; occasionally the sclerotic offender kills callously to destroy the evidence. Erective potency here is not always sufficiently sustained to endure through the struggle with a resisting child or woman, but there are periods of potency increase, possibly because the early-stage lesions in the central nervous system act as stimulant-irritants on the neural sex mechanism.

One need mention here the proverbial "dirty old man," the elderly jaded lecher (roué, Fr., Lebegreis, Ger.), largely impotent, in search of ever new females of as young an age as he dare or can afford to dally with, or perhaps desiring merely to look and lick, perhaps to be whipped, and generally in search of high-stimulus perversities and substitute gratification. The condition may be somewhat on the wane; it is also dubious that such behavior constitutes a syndrome sui generis. A fairly large number here are probably the same anxious-regressed or cerebral arteriosclerotic individuals who, economically less favored, resort to various public offenses rather than seek out prostitutes. Others may be surfeit-prone neurotic personalities, or impulse-disordered psychopaths who have reached the stage of waning potency.

Treatment. Control and management of the senile recrudescent man is in large part a matter of individual coping on the part of his family. The nonorganic anxious-regressed patient and the cerebral arteriosclerotic with symptoms of sexual recrudescence, as long as they have not become excessively offensive socially, can be controlled and managed by guidance measures, simple psychotherapy and the use of appropriate medication. Any elderly patient who has manifested major aggression as part of his sexual recrudescence should be considered to be potentially and unpredictably recidivist and thus dangerous for an indefinite period. However, institutionalization is becoming more and more difficult to accomplish for this and any other type of elderly psychiatric patient, and present emphasis is on control by medication, and ambulatory group therapy if feasible.

Medicinally, the true senile recrudescent male requires fairly little; chlorprothixene 25 to 75 mg and imipramine 10 to 30 mg, possibly in single doses at bedtime, may suffice and be acceptable after some initial discomfort. All barbiturates should be avoided. Stilbestrol, 2 to 6 mg daily for a few intermittent 10-day courses has been helpful at times. The anxious-regressed and the cerebral arteriosclerotic patient require more to control major undesirable sexual acting-out. Medroxyprogesterone acetate in fairly long courses suppresses sexual manifestations in these elderly men, although more gradually than the anti-androgens used for men of reproductive age (p. 466). The use of estrogen in this group has not been encouraging. A combination of psychotropic substances (e.g., imipramine and thioridazine), the latter in substantial amounts if necessary, has given fair results. Initial determination of treatment needs is best undertaken in conjunction with a psychiatrist. See also treatment of sex aggressors, p. 439 and p. 464.

SEXUAL AGGRESSION

Related:
The Child as Victim of Sexual Aggression p. 55
Pedophilia p. 472
Teen-age Child Molesting p. 152
Recrudescence in Elderly Men p. 434
Forcible Intercourse (Rape) p. 259
Sexual Sadism p. 478

Sexual aggression is sex activity associated with the infliction of loss, fright, pain or injury. It differs from "sexual offenses" which include all sexual manifestations prohibited by law, even if victimless and between consenting adults. Sex criminals are not a homogeneous group of offenders, and even among aggressive offenders there exist profound differences. Some are ruthlessly asocial psychopaths incapable of feeling concern for others in their impulse pursuits; some are sexual deviates; others are sufficiently emotionally disturbed, mentally ill or brain-disordered so as to be incapable of control; still others are victims of a seductive situation and of their own lechery. Not unlike spectacular suicide or a spectacular burglary publicized in the media, spectacular cases of rape are "infectious"; police departments have spoken of a rash or epidemic of sex assaults in such cases. Alcohol and/or barbituric etc. drugs ("downs") are believed to play a part in about one third of sexual assaults; hard drugs hardly at all.

The Cause of rapist aggression, which may be considered the prototype of all sexual aggression, is not to be sought in overabundant endowment

PRINCIPAL CATEGORIES OF SEX OFFENSES

So-Called Victimless Sex Offenses	Erotic wall writing Incest (adult) Adultery. Fornication (unmarried adults) Adult homosexual relations in private Selling pornography to adults Prostitution (off-street)
Public Nuisance (Molestive Offenses)	Obscene telephoning Zoophilia Exhibitionism (to adults) Homosexual haunting in public Pandering and pimping Frottage Transvestism (disputed) Statutory rape, if ages close Voyeurism (most)
Dangerous Sex Offenses (Non-violent)	Exhibitionism (to child) Child fondling. Fetishism relating to children Voyeurism (some; disputed) Forcible rape by acquaintance Father-daughter incest (disputed) Ephebophilia, active relationship
Violent Sex Offenses	Forcible rape by stranger Pedophilic act with intromission, boy or girl Major sadistic acting-out Any death, major injury or abduction in connection with sexual aggression against stranger

with sexual appetite or potency, nor in prolonged sexual deprivation. At most, these play a minor part at times. One must seek causes at greater depth in the offender: in chronic anger and hostility against women; in defensive acting-out against subconscious passive-feminine wishes; in chronic frustration intolerance with epileptoid rages accompanied by fantasies of punishing; or in intractable sexual anesthesia unless violence and painful struggle capacitate the patient. Clinically, knowledge of predatory rapists' make-up and modus operandi is advancing but not yet substantial; however, the major functional types are becoming somewhat recognizable.

The Irresolute Rapist, also known as compensatory rapist (Cohen-Seghorn) is basically a confused individual. He feels unsure of his sex role, inadequate, and needs to demonstrate his manhood as it were. He feels passive longings, despises them as womanish ("Was I to be a girl? Am I a queer?"). He hates his longing, the confusion, himself, women, manly men; but a basically masculine-dominant orientation is not attainable for him.

Socially a conformist, but not usually an achiever, he is known as quiet or nice to family and neighbors; but he is socially and emotionally isolated. He assaults by threat and frightening but he hopes for acceptance and affection from the victim, perhaps love, a word of praise for his performance, how he has pleased her. They are the talkers, the apologizers, the returners; often they want to make themselves known. They come back hoping for acceptance, but their deeply built-in incapacity to absorb affection from a woman makes it impossible and if allowed close they most likely will rape again. They are by no means harmless; their compulsive self-revelation can produce sudden fright in them, and they may inflict harm in a panic.

The Angry-aggressive Rapist experiences his sexual appetite as an urge which compels him to seek satisfaction by violent means. He seems forever compelled to shape relationships with women by psychologic overpowering or physical assault. He perceives women as angry and rejecting, and fascinatedly hates, perhaps fears them. He must come to their notice if they are strangers, control the situation, degrade them perhaps. He feels excluded and the anger smoulders at all times. On the threshold of a voluntary intimate relationship he may sense—or fantasize—rejection, and his assaultive rage is mobilized. The anger, the emotional warping, may masquerade as many things, even as counter-culture anarchism, "Rape is good . . . to rip off some loving from the bourgeoisie . . . from anyone . . . rape is a statement." Even with a willing female available to him, or the victim compliant, the attacker may compound the rape by brutal assaultiveness (Kozol). Preferably the woman must resist; a regular sex act brings the image of the incestoid-frustrating mother (p. 74) and is repelling.

The Impulsive Psychopathic Rapist is both asocial and potentially antisocial. He has no genuine ties to anyone, he is little concerned with what others think of him, and has no functioning conscience. If he moves on an antisocial track, he may take what pleases him and is within his reach.

THE POTENTIALLY MOST-TO-BE-FEARED SEX OFFENDERS

Pathologic drinkers (pathologic response to relatively small amount of alcohol) especially if epileptoid or socially degraded. Unstoppable, brutal impulsivity during crisis.

Some cerebral arteriosclerotics, in early stage. Potentially very callous and brutal toward victim. Also some other organic brain disorders.

Necrosadists (see p. 480).

Mentally retarded adolescents, if brutalized and goaded.

Fetishistic heterosexual pedophiliacs with compulsive-repetitive pattern. Capable of much brutality. Nigh-intractable recidivism.

Paranoid schizophrenics, with delusions of female mockery, or hearing goading voices.

All predatory rapists, because of notorious recidivism.

In the course of a burglary he may commit rape as just another act of plunder, perhaps as a mere afterthought. He is distinctly stimulus-bound, and his unstable impulse control lets him overreact to both frustration and deprivation. Anger against one woman can be displaced by attacking another woman. His reaction to enforced sexual abstinence quickly generates major tension which at the first occasion he promptly—and ruthlessly if need be—discharges against the environment. He is easily provoked and a surge of unreasoning anger may wash away his meager self-control, but basically he is more cynical than hostile. What makes him dangerous is that he is a punisher; he tends to rationalize his assaultive acts as somehow deserved by the victim. Potentially he is also a callous destroyer of evidence.

The Sadistic Rapist (see also p. 480), in spite of his potential cruelty, feels no anger. He leads a reasonably well-adjusted life, but he suffers from an unrelieved sexual deficit: inability to experience sexual excitement without violence or inflicting pain. Unlike the aggressive rapist he tends to pre-select his victims. He loses interest or is impotent unless she begs him either to spare her, or to punish her for being bad (prostitute), or unless she genuinely resists and must be subdued, choked or threatened at knife-point. His sexual excitement feeds on his own cruelty. The squirming struggle his degrading commands produce delights and pleasures him until, more rarely, the scene escalates to bloody harm.

Treatment by Law.   Most states have enacted Sexual Offender Laws which provide for the detention of sexually dangerous persons (i.e., convicted sex offenders). Sentences frequently are indeterminate (e.g., "from one day to life") and psychiatry is charged with the responsibility for diagnosis, treatment and the all-important risk prognosis which affects release. The laws are a compromise between society's need to protect itself and the recognition that most sex criminals have mental and medical disorders. Some are studied and treated in special sex offender units or sex deviate facilities; examples are the institutions at Bridgewater (Mass.), Atascadero (Calif.), Waupun (Wisc.), Fort Steilacoom (Wash.) and at Philadelphia General Hospital (Penna.).

The singling out of sex criminals is unique in the history of criminology and has not gone unchallenged, even though the trend appears to be towards confining mostly the dangerous and violent offenders, while affording ambulatory psychiatric care to nuisance molesters (Halleck). The psychiatric and legal concept behind the sex offender laws has been called vague (Ploscowe, S. Rubin, Craig, others) and offering insufficient safeguards for personal liberties and due process. It has been charged that the special units of necessity select patients not on the basis of dangerousness but of treatability, so that some of the worst offenders (e.g., the intractable psychopathic personalities) are not included. However, the method has great practical utility, and in a sense constitutes preventive medical treatment

RISK PREDICTION

Psychiatric Prediction of the Future Conduct of Potentially Dangerous Sex Offenders aims at preventing their premature release. It remains more an art than a science; no unequivocal tests or criteria exist. Each offender must be judged from what has become known about him during correctional observation and treatment. It is extremely difficult to assess the risk unless he has already committed an aggressive act. The following findings may, but need not, warrant a heightened degree of pessimism regarding risk prognosis.

Childhood History of triad of bed-wetting, firesetting, cruelty to pet animals (Hellman-Blackman).

Childhood History of alternatingly seductive-frustrating mother and brutalizing—disturbed, sadistic or psychotic—father; possibly either alone.

History of triad of wife and child beating or other unmotivated assaults, pathologic alcohol intolerance, numerous major traffic accidents and violations.

Escalation of sex offenses, notably in voyeurs and pedophiles (disputed). Committing a variety of sex offenses (disputed).

Glueck's Social Prediction Tables, concordance with.

Psychosis. Symptoms of active psychosis: delusions, hallucinations, affect disorder, etc. (disputed).

Fantasies. Presence of massive bizarre, sadistic fantasies.

Guilt. Prolonged, intense protestations of shame, remorse, guilt, self-hatred, yet sustained lack of concern for victim (Kozol, others).

Temporal Lobe Disease, notably episodic dyscontrol syndrome.

EEG. Activation of unstable, nonspecific EEG changes by structured test situation and discussion, read out by automatic frequency analysis (Roubicek; experimental).

Karyotype. An XYY sex chromosome pattern. Relatively large-sized (long) Y chromosome (Nielsen, others).

Abstinence from alcohol, total (disputed). Sex assault in state of sobriety.

I.Q. Very low and very high I.Q. (disputed).

(Sadoff, Kozol). Also, in regular prisons fellow convicts despise and often brutalize sex criminals; as outcasts among outcasts they tend to lapse into deepening self-hatred precluding the possibility of rehabilitation.

The special institutional treatment of convicted sex offenders today is behavior-centered. It chiefly employs group interaction and conditioning technics directed at impulse control. Most serious offenders need external control while undergoing treatment. A preliminary necessity is a thorough examination: a detailed history of the crime, with field investigation if necessary; a thorough health and life history including clues which later may bear on parole eligibility; karyotype, EEG, psychologic tests, blood chemistry and endocrine profile as well as medical, neurologic and psychiatric examination. Such identifiable conditions as frank psychosis, temporal lobe disease or the disputed XYY syndromes require special procedures, of course. The chief criterion of pragmatic cure is successful return to the community without recidivism. There is much forward-looking—and some unpromising—experimenting now in progress with such technics as self-government, aversive technics, hypnotherapy, high-intensity group therapies, counseling of families, carrot-and-stick conditioning, both monasticism and "coed" incarceration (projected), and others more.

Castration of Sex Offenders (e.g., as a condition of their parole) will reduce sexual urges and manifestations in a proportion of cases, but it is a highly uncertain method, somewhat alien to the temper of the times, and it carries the double risk of instilling a false sense of security in the authorities while it renders some offenders even more dangerous. Genuine "taming" of a male adult by excision of his testes cannot, as a rule, be expected (see also p. 345). One major factor is age. The younger the man, the more severely the sex characteristics, libido and potency are affected. Past the mid-twenties there is increasingly less regression and vestiges of function are maintained longer. In the sometimes very dangerous elderly sex offenders there may be little or no change if the psycho-sexual apparatus was functional at the time of surgery. The method probably is totally unsuitable where cruelty or rage played a part in an act of sexual assault, and in the psychopathic character and sociopathic disorders in which even worse antisocial acting-out can be expected to result. The method gives fairly good results in curbing the abnormal sexual manifestations in some postencephalitic syndromes (Jensch). It has been the experience that castration of offenders is followed by a euphoric phase lasting a few weeks to a few months, followed by deterioration and depression lasting 6 to 12 months, occasionally longer, as the man regresses physiologically. This is the period of instability during which psychotherapeutic re-integration has been successfully pursued; it is considered an error to release an offender during either period. A released castrate can obtain fairly adequate hormonal replacement therapy from a physician by misrepresenting his past history. Castration in connection with sex offenses has not been practiced in the U.S. for some time.

Sterilization by vasectomy would not be a rational treatment for a sex crime. Neither the sex drive nor potency are predictably affected by this operation (see p. 311). In a few known cases, it has been imposed by a court to protect future rape victims from insemination where existing laws limited the sentence for the rapist and there was no expectation of rehabilitation.

The Passage of Time is a highly unreliable preventive remedy against the recidivism of certain serious sexual aggressors, if unaccompanied by genuine rehabilitation efforts. Even after many years of state hospital or penitentiary sojourn some such men have committed the same aggressive offense again following their release.

Medicinal Treatment, etc. is discussed on p. 464.

PATHOLOGIC ERECTIONS

Priapism. In modern clinical usage the term refers to a prolonged, pathologic erection not accompanied by sexual desire. It is not a sexual disorder, but a symptom of various disorders involving the mechanism of erection (see p. 174). The name is derived from the ancient deity Priapus whose statues represented him with an erect phallus.

Priapism is a distressing, disabling condition usually requiring hospitalization. It has been observed at all ages, from infancy to senescence, but most patients are adult men before middle age. Onset can be either sudden: one day the membrum does not subside again after a sexual act; or there are preceding transient episodes of unusually prolonged erection. Medically less sophisticated patients may try to cohabitate repeatedly to rid themselves of the erection; but the act gives them little pleasure; at orgasm the semen merely dribbles out; very soon no orgasm can be obtained; soon thereafter even the thought of coitus becomes distasteful; in some cases pain sets in. The membrum remains in a more or less complete erect state day and night, for days, weeks or even many months (reported record: close to 2 years). The erection does not yield to sedatives, somnifacients or even to general anesthesia. Urination remains possible.

A frequent cause is sickle cell disease in black men and, occasionally, boys. Other blood dyscrasias such as tularemia or myelogenous leukemia as well as thrombophlebitic processes can obstruct penile drainage. Neurologic diseases—cord tumors, multiple sclerosis, cerebrospinal lues—may disorganize the erective mechanism. Excessive stimulus bombardment in the posterior urethra due to local pathology can be a cause. In small boys phimosis and rectal oxyuriasis, among others, have produced the syndrome. Hypogonadic adolescents being stimulated with heavy doses of human chorionic gonadotropin may react with a mild form of priapism.

The pathology includes venostasis, gumming and sludging of penile blood, and severe edema of the cavernous septa. Eventually this can result in thrombosis, even irreversible fibrosis and eventual occlusion of the arteriovenous apparatus. Treatment includes a large variety of local and systemic measures, including several surgical approaches, notably saphenous bypass and the cavernosa-spongiosum anastomosing procedures, as the corpus spongiosum is not affected. Local and surgical methods often unavoidably tend to leave the patient with permanent impairment of potency.

Painful Nocturnal Erections. Cyclical nocturnal erections occur normally in most normal men, but rarely awaken the sleeper (see p. 173). Intermittent painful erections during all or most nights are encountered in some middle-aged men. The pain awakens the patient from 1 to 6 times a night. There is no sexual desire. The erection may subside fairly promptly once the patient gets up, walks around, and urinates, if only a few drops; others feel they must resort to cold sponging or a shower to detumesce. The pain is variable in intensity and location from patient to patient. Daytime waking erections are not painful, but they have been so during daytime naps. Coitus during the preceding evening tends to worsen the symptoms. In some men no pain occurs when they sleep away from home, with or without sex activity, only to recur after a few days in the marriage bed. Potency varies, but is most often normal. The condition can last from a few weeks to several years.

No specific cause nor treatment is known. Possible causes include conversion neurosis and anorectal, prostatic or posterior urethral pathology. Most other erection-disrupting pathology does not fit the clinical picture. Psychiatric therapy has helped, but uncertainly so. Symptomatic measures in milder cases may include a cool room, light covers, hard mattress, no double bed, no close-fitting nightwear, sleeping on the side, avoiding intestinal flatulence, bland diet, light evening meal, no alcohol. Neither excess nor restricted fluid intake seem to matter. An occasional somnifacient has been useful, as have been anticholinergic-sedative suppositories. Estrogen or anti-androgen therapy seem remote possibilities.

Various Abnormal Erections. Prolonged, sometimes painful erections can occur following abuse of such stimulating drugs as cocaine, or of amphetamines in large doses. In temporal epilepsy, following surgical ablation of the epileptogenic area, priapism of several hours' duration has been observed in some patients.

SEXUALITY IN DRUG USERS

The drugs in illicit use today still retain a reputation for increasing sexual appetite or capacity or both, in men and in women. With some exceptions this has been shown to be untrue. Also, in all drugs part of the drug reaction results from an elaboration of pre-existing personality traits. Some traits may be intensified, others released or immobilized, while impulse control may become disorganized.

Marijuana (Marihuana; cannabis indica; vernac. pot, grass, etc.). This is not an aphrodisiac, but in about one third of experienced users pleasure appreciation seems to be heightened and erotic objects appear more desirable. Because of distortion of the time sense sexual orgasm, coital or masturbatory, can seem prolonged in both sexes. The euphoria, a sense of gregarious intimacy, heightened suggestibility and the drug mystique itself can help transform a marijuana bash into a "love-in"; but the part cannabis per se plays in this remains vague (Ewing). All effects are dose-related, and probably cumulative. A proportion of heavy users experience progressive loss of sexual interest. Cannabis being a sympathomimetic substance, it has long been suspected of causing one type of effect in sympathotonic individuals, and a different one in the vagotonic constitution. Marijuana is not known to lead to promiscuity or to predatory sexual aggression.

Amyl Nitrite (vernac. snapper, popper). The marijuana effect on the male sex experience can be sharply increased when amyl nitrite is sniffed (inhaled, "popped") just as orgasm is imminent. The interaction results in what has been described as explosive heightening and prolonging of the orgastic experience. By itself the sexual effect is less sharp. Amyl nitrite, a short-acting vasodilator, was formerly used to prevent anginal pain, but has been largely abandoned because of side effects. The drug has its widest use in the homosexual subculture.

Hashish (cannabis sativa; vernac. hash) appears to dampen sexual appetite more often than spur it. This is not in conformity with many reports of hashish orgies in other parts of the world and in days past. Theories advanced to explain the discrepancy remain unconfirmed. Most users in the U.S. co-use other drugs.

LSD (D-lysergic acid diethylamide, "acid"; a hallucinogen). Sexual effects not completely predictable because of frequent adulterant substances; but generally does not arouse or increase libido, although it alters, maybe heightens, sensation and apperception (Isbell). Original claims for its aphrodisiac qualities were withdrawn. In the drug state the familiar seems novel, the banal appears portentous. A non-existing sex act may be hallucinated as an inexpressibly joyous experience. To the chronic LSD user, the "acid head," sexual orgasm no longer appears the acme of sensual experience. Generally, his marked passivity makes him a non-aggressor. However, the response to a hallucinogen can be altered by pre-existing brain damage: unrecognized residues of encephalitis or head trauma affecting the vulnerable limbic nuclei of the temporal lobes can add an element of unpredictability.

Amphetamines (vernac. ups, speed, etc.) euphoriate and energize the moderate or recent user, male and female. The disinhibiting effect may produce more confident sexual performance. Libido may be increased intermittently, especially if combined with barbiturates. An occasional frigida achieves orgasm with her first doses, but after long abuse orgasm is delayed rather than promoted. Long-time heavy male users may have strong erections, but difficulties achieving orgasm, thus prolonging the sex act. A few have multiple orgasms at first. Much later impotence sets in; still later there is loss of interest in sex. All symptoms are reversible following withdrawal, unless the patient enters a prolonged depressive reaction. With very large daily doses bizarrely ferocious sex behavior may be induced, or sex-deviate trends or a promiscuous pattern may emerge ("anything goes"). Aggressive sexual solicitation by males or females can occur. However, in chronic female users libido dwindles to practically nil; their aggressive promiscuity often is accompanied by a paranoid resentment of being used (Greaves, others). In predisposed individuals amphetamines facilitate the emergence of sexual violence. With high-dose intravenous use an orgasm-like rush is felt in the whole body; it differs from the heroin rush in that it precedes a rousing reaction rather than torpor. Amphetamines can produce painful vaginal dryness during the prolonged act, but the hyperstimulated female may disregard it and so may the male.

The amphetamine effect is characterized by sympathetic dominance, but overexposure may reverse-cue the neural mechanisms. As it lessens the perceptive cues concerning the urgency of drives demanding satisfaction, libidinal urges, same as hunger pangs, appear lessened.

Cocaine (coke, snow, jam, C, etc.), sniffed or intravenously. Acute cocaine intoxication causes increased sexual excitability and appetite in most users, especially in females. Intravenously used the "rush" is similar to the amphetamine rush but more quickly dissipated. Cocaine induces a grandiose sense of prowess and ability, and male potency may be temporarily increased at the height of the drug effect. However, flight of ideas and various side reactions interfere with sustained sexual performance; long-time users may develop episodes of painful priapism (Gay). The user, when "high," is a potential sexual predator. Impurities in the powder are believed to be responsible for irritable and paranoid over-reactions in erotic situations.

Barbiturates (vernac. goofballs, downs, etc.; mostly the sodium salts of intermediate-short acting barbituric derivatives). In acute intoxication (e.g., amytal jag), in addition to motor incoordination there can be substantial disinhibition, even to the point of indiscriminate solicitation or exhibitionistic acting-out. However, male potency is not increased. In barbiturate habituation ("barbfreaks") sexuality resembles the regressive pattern of chronic alcoholism (q.v.); men may develop impotence.

Heroin, Morphine, Methadone, Other Opiates. The opiate addiction picture continues to change, and sex activity of drug users changes with it. Users are younger, often in their teens, and the sexual disruption pattern in the teens seems to differ from adults'. There is more group usage, less secrecy; there are more intermittent users as dilution makes the habit less compelling at times. As dilution increases, both side-effects and withdrawal symptoms become milder.

In essence, the opiates desexualize; "horse (heroin) cuts the nature." Addicts, male and female, progressively lose interest in and desire for sex activity. The euphoriant dose probably represents a passive substitute for sex. Intravenous dosing is followed by a "pharmacogenic orgasm," an orgasm-like abdominal thrill or rush. As he impatiently bypasses the genital apparatus the addict achieves orgasm centrally, stimulating the midbrain for his thrill. The resulting sex-inhibiting effect probably is serotonin-mediated.

The male addict on a moderate maintenance regimen, if he is interested at all, has labile potency and ejaculation is often retarded or not achieved. The more severe addict tends to become totally impotent. Users are not sexual aggressors, although their other criminality—to obtain money for drugs—is well known. The severely addicted user, male or female, has no use—no time, no energy, no feeling—for people or relationships which do not directly aid in the procurement of the drugs.

The female addict, if on undiluted heroin, has a high rate of non-ovulation (i.e., secondary amenorrhea and sterility). Libido recedes. She becomes slovenly, often joylessly promiscuous and slides—or is forced—into prostitution intermittently to obtain drug money. However, today among many of the urban teen-age street prostitutes who are users habit and hustling tend to start simultaneously.

Sudden withdrawal of opiates tends to produce sensations of intense genital excitement in both male and female users; this is accompanied, in many, by acute distaste at the very thought of sex activity. Others experience a surge of libidinal feelings (Cushman, Jr.). The male may experience pleasureless erection and ejaculation at the mere touch of the penis. In the post-withdrawal period there may be marked increase in libido; but, in men at least, this is often channeled into autosexual practices or fantasies. Potency returns in most ex-addicts.

On methadone substitution maintenance a proportion of the men appear to have psychosexual disturbances (low libido; no orgasm reached). Intravenously used, methadone produces an orgasmic "rush" reaction said to be almost as intense as the heroin rush.

The opium smoker presents a characteristic picture of euphoric erotic lassitude (i.e., pleasant, mildly exciting erotic fantasies occur which usually do not lead to an urge for sexual action).

Alcohol. All major alcohol consumption progressively ". . . provokes the desire, but it takes away the performance" (Shakespeare, Macbeth). Either the erection fails or, less often, ejaculation is greatly delayed. In very large amounts alcohol depresses the sexual reflexes to the point of abolishing them. It is thus far from being an aphrodisiac, although in moderate, well tolerated amounts it may disinhibit a tense female or a male with an inhibitory potency disorder sufficiently to produce beneficial results. The effectiveness of this "cure" is quickly exhausted, however. Sporadic excessive drinking sometimes serves as a kind of self-administered anesthesia to blot out sexual urges vaguely perceived to be dangerously aggressive or deviant; with this the drinker effectively eliminates all sex expression from his life.

The compulsive chronic alcoholic is frequently impotent. When in remission he seems to fare better for a longer time if no great sexual demands confront him. The deteriorated, socially degraded or derelict male alcoholic rarely seems greatly interested in sex or sufficiently potent as he seesaws between toxic state and withdrawal symptoms. The pathologic drinker (i.e., the epileptoid alcoholic and the alcohol-intolerant borderline patient) at times are excessively aroused when intoxicated and may become either brutally or shamelessly aggressive sexually (e.g., in front of children at home or vis-à-vis a normally unsuitable partner). Women alcoholics, as a group, are not unusually promiscuous, except for female sociopathic problem drinkers in whom the incidence of promiscuity is high.

PROSTITUTION

The phenomenon of prostitution resists comprehensive definition, especially as one approaches upper socio-economic level arrangements. Generally, and perhaps somewhat hypocritically, a female prostitute is a woman who unequivocally earns part or all of her livelihood by making herself available for sexual purposes for immediate cash payment. The term prostitute is inapplicable to a wife or common-law wife with respect to her husband, no matter how exploitatory the relationship. In addition to the usual street, bar, hotel, apartment, house, or wagon hustlers the term covers itinerant (playgirl) operators, professional call and party girls, pseudomasseuses, etc. Probably not includable are a multitude of undefinable venal arrangements such as the kept mistress, exploits of occasional opportunity, last-resort barter by women otherwise employed, nor the rapidly increasing phenomenon of young housewives turning out for occasional daytime assignations for "clothes money," with or without their husbands' knowledge.

Regulation of Prostitution. Two basic social attitudes towards prostitution exist: limited toleration, and repression. Toleration is based on the premise that prostitution is an ineradicable evil, but that it must not flourish unchecked; it has vastly fallen out of favor in the Western world today. Repression (or partial suppression) is the moralistic principle officially adhered to almost everywhere today; it defines an administrative attitude which is inseparable from its underlying philosophy of "abolition with rehabilitation."

Toleration has always been accompanied by one of three classic administrative regulating devices. *Inscription,* no longer in use in the Western World, involved registration of all known prostitutes by the police, compulsory periodic health examinations with issuing of health cards, and quarantining if necessary. The method is degrading and the notoriously

PROSTITUTION: A GLOSSARY

Prostitute: commercial prostitute, pro, prosti, pross (pl. prossies), whore, ho, hooker, hustler, chippie, roundheel. Euphemisms: operator; working, professional, good-time, play, party girl. Harlot; courtesan (returning into use). Tart, scrubber (Br.). Meretrix.

Special Categories: street-walker or hustler, flatbacker (volume, also coitus only), call girl, hotel-pross or -girl, bar hooker, teenie hooker, dumper (has been), knobber (female impersonator), lush worker (drunks), baby pro (midteens, works expensive hotels etc.), bottom woman (best girl in a pimp's stable).

Hustling Life: The game, the life, the business.

Soliciting: whoring, tricking, operating, hustling, turning or servicing tricks.

Customer: trick, date, John.

Procurer: ponce, pimp, mack, player, sweet man, husband or man (euphem.), meat salesman.

House of Prostitution: trick house, cat house, whorehouse, brothel, crib, bordello, call house, creep house (premises for robbing customers).

unreliable V.D. examination gave customers a false sense of security. *Segregation* in a "red light" district or zone has survived only in some seaports, etc. but may be making a comeback. The method allows dubious civic boasts of a "clean town," while certain realty and business interests become de facto partners of the prostitutes; it tends to encourage corruption of law enforcement officers; exposes the girls to crass exploitation; facilitates access to prostitutes for minors; while the district easily becomes a hang-out for criminal elements and various parasitic men. The third method, *licensing,* concentrates the prostitutes in legalized "houses of toleration" (i.e., price-controlled and regularly inspected bordellos). While clandestine brothels and similar premises remain in widespread existence in the U.S., legalized houses are largely alien to the temper of the times. Their principal advantage was that they protected the girls from the crassest forms of exploitation, made access to prostitutes more difficult for minors, and facilitated health examination. However, the method, such as the red light zone, encourages unscrupulous recruitment practices and traffic in young women, gives clients an unjustified sense of security regarding V.D., and stresses the social ostracism of these prostitutes. Where the cost of the license or permit was substantial, and especially if imposed on a sliding scale consonant with fees, the method made the licensing municipality or government a de facto partner of the prostitute or her managers.

Moralistic Repression, the method prevailing today, combines social assistance and rehabilitation efforts with varying degrees of enforcement of anti-prostitution laws. Without its socially conscious, moralistic underpinning, known as abolitionism, the repressive method would in practice merely consist of harrying the girls off the street and generally out of sight while punishing those who are caught. Clearing the streets is not considered to be hypocrisy, however. Suppression of street solicitation is based on the dogma that, as regards prostitution, patronage stands in direct ratio to accessibility and that high visibility stimulates men's desires. Street-walking is also considered offensive to the community; it introduces elements of shabbiness, squalor and violence in the area unfavorable to local business, and as the girls accost strangers they may cause them embarrassment. It creates an atmosphere of general corruption, and continues to be considered a factor in enticing vulnerable teen-age girls into what they perceive as "the easy life," as they see others ply their trade with open toleration. Today's urban street-walking attracts all manner of criminals into a neighborhood; it also entails a spreading risk of assault and robbery by predatory, knife-armed teen-age girls, prostitutes or posing as such, operating singly or in small groups.

Historically, abolitionism is an indirect outgrowth of the Women's Rights Movement. It took its name from their resolve to abolish brothels, red light districts and registration; to abolish the double standard which exonerates the male customers; abolish the causes of prostitution; and eventually prostitution itself. Abolition's ultimate goal, luminous but utopian, was "total prevention": to adjust the attitudes and sex habits of men; to protect vulnerable girls from lapsing into mercenary promiscuity; to punish all persons living off the proceeds of prostitution; and to rehabilitate existing prostitutes.

PROSTITUTION

A Feminist View

"It is foolish to prosecute a woman for a crime in which she is the victim, but it is reprehensible to let a man go free for the criminal act of purchasing another's body."

Susan Brownmiller, 1971

Helping Measures. Almost all states in the U.S. have laws against prostitution and those promoting and abetting it. The preventive-curative efforts of the abolitionist-repressive system have translated themselves for now into such items as rehabilitation centers and clinics, shelters, probation and casework services, crisis intervention teams, group therapy workshops, juvenile police bureaus separate from the vice squads, residential homes and supervised hostels for vulnerable wayward minors, facilities for unwed mothers and a variety of consultation services. Interwoven through these various measures is the ever-present concern of the public health authorities charged with controlling the epidemic spread of venereal disease.

However, it seems safe to predict that the above measures will not give the desired ultimate results (i.e., abolish prostitution). It is quite apparent by now that with few exceptions female prostitution is not truly eradicable, in our civilization and in all modern, Western male-dominated civilizations known to historians, neither in good times nor in bad, in both socialist and capitalist societies, no matter how oppressive the anti-prostitution laws or how libertarian the sexual mores of the culture.

The Milieu. In the lower urban echelons the girls exist in a special circumscribed world, a dirty, tough jungle, a society with its own social structure and snobberies, its own style of talk and dress, its own drinking and drug abuse pattern; a world centered around territorial disputes and arrests ("busts"), and wigs and clothes; around lesbian jealousies and rivalries about the sweet man (pimp) and his other women. Although seemingly the Life is all about money, the value of money is truly comprehended only by those who profit from the proceeds of the prostitutes' toil, and hardly at all by the girls themselves. In the somewhat elevated echelons, the full-time apartment, resort and call girls, existence is less dirty and hectic; but in spite of their superior resourcefulness they share many traits and preoccupations with their nether sisters.

The Prostitute as an Individual has always excited speculation and fantasy on the part of outsiders, male and female. But most of them being notorious, habitual liars, many observations even by respected observers need to be perused with a grain of salt. Some, for instance, change their name so often—even weekly—that they must make an effort to recall their true one. They drift, they live roles, and they tend to resist any effort to render reasoned accounts of anything to themselves or to anyone else. Fantasizing, rationalizing and fabricating are also second nature to the majority of these women. The prostitute has been called lazy, work-shy, shiftless and nomadic, vain, irresponsible, living for the moment and incapable of planning. She has been said to be overly sentimental and endowed with a child's trash-loving mind; suggestible, excitable, unstable and argumentative; greedy and larcenous towards strangers, but loyal and generous to her friends. She has been found prone to alcohol and drug abuse, frigid with all men but one and often lesbian for gratification. But none of these traits are found in all women in the Life, nor does any prostitute have all of them, while many straight women have some of them. Endowed or induced, no generalizing answer is possible and it would be unrealistic to assume that a "timeless prostitute type" even exists.

The most frequent single characteristic which prostitutes have in common, apart from their sexual indifference while practicing their métier, is their deprecation of and hostility to their men customers. Their hostile-predatory contempt is not always subsurface or well disguised. "To love none and despise them all," ascribed to Thaïs, famed hetaera of ancient

Athens, typifies this attitude. The customers are suckers who get nothing for their money ("I got the money, you got nothing"). To most the sexual transaction essentially is not a service performed for a fee but a one-sidedly exploitatory, almost vindictive rip-off on their part, because they really "do nothing" for the money; "I don't really give myself." To do as little as possible for as much money as possible is not a merchandising principle for them but a source of morbid satisfaction. Yet money, apart from some rather primitive barter significance, has mostly symbolic meaning to most of them. As a material thing it tends to be a non-value, something that must be compulsively squandered or given away. Lacking foresight, they cannot foresee the potential future value of money savings to them; or if they see it, they cannot act accordingly. Besides, money is the one thing their pimp loves so dearly to take from them, and it is not unusual for them to feel that they cannot deny him this pleasure.

They feel they give nothing because they feel they have nothing. Much prostituting is built on self-contempt and self-hatred. An often highly unrealistic depreciation of their own bodies, their own sexual attraction, can be found in them, often at the very outset of their careers, coupled with an obsessive sense of worthlessness. Did these pre-exist? Or did they emerge as a result of leading a prostitute's existence? The prevailing belief today is that they preexisted; in fact, that they constitute one of the major unconscious impellents towards mercenary promiscuity. However, little of substance is known about the psychic feedback effect of day-after-day lewd parading and self-debasing on an already disordered psyche.

Entry into Prostitution. What makes a girl first become a prostitute? A well-established part of the answer is that neither money nor libidinal urges are primary impellents in the vast majority of prostitutes. Although some of the early-promiscuous teen-agers drift into the Life, this is, from all the evidence, only another facilitating factor; at any rate, a promiscuous girl who actually likes males and desires or enjoys sex promiscuously, rarely has the psychologic makings of a prostitute. Also, many girls have eyed finery and glittering life styles beyond their reach with envy and convinced themselves that they would "gladly sleep around some" to get them. But between that attitude and the regular practice of prostitution lies a large psychologic gap. In fact, it is conceivable that existentially the two are mutually exclusive. Some girls who have landed early in the superior reaches of the Life may boast, "where else can I have all these advantages, clothes, travel, meet interesting men? I love it, I would not change places with a waitress, a clerk for anything . . ." Except for a few who make a resolute lucky leap to safety and for a few others who basically are more entrepreneuses than whores, the basic drift in prostitution is downwards, and girls such as the above usually stay neither advantaged nor happy for long.

ENTRY INTO PROSTITUTION

Age at Entry: 12–15 no rarity today. 16–18 increasingly customary. Rare after 25.

Psychodynamic Factors: Hostile identification with mother. Contempt for feminine role. Acute disappointment with father (Glover), especially if latter manifestly promiscuous. Severe identity diffusion at puberty (Maerov).

Facilitating Factors: Background (e.g., broken home). Example. Demand and supply (e.g., war, prosperity, nearby camp or resort). Triad of instability, suggestibility, thrill-craving. Exposure to persuasion. Runaway status. Condoning culture. Addiction.

Precipitating Factors: (in teens): Rape. Out-of-wedlock baby. Early marriage and divorce. Prolonged father-daughter incest. Object loss.

Relative Non-factors: Need or desire for money. Libidinal urges.

Critical Age Periods (theory): 3–6 for basic deflection. 12–16 for pathologic "recapitulation" (subconscious re-experiencing of operant factors) and translation into acting-out; latter may precede final drift by years.

The Grossly Disordered. At any point in time a proportion of all commercial prostitutes—at least 20 per cent—are frankly psychotic, pre-psychotic, borderline patients, mentally retarded or frank psychopathic personalities. An unknown number—at least 10 per cent by educated guess—are unredeemable chronic alcoholics and hard-core addicts rapidly approaching derelict or chronic dependent status. By all known clinical standards their ills were present before they found their way into prostitution, unrecognized, unattended or simply intractable. Certain clinical profiles turn up with some regularity: the affect-blunted, unadjustable schizoids; unpredictably suspicious paranoids; the dim-witted, toiling "flat-backs," their semi-alcoholized existence punctured by noisy epileptoid excitement states; erratic, impulsive psychopaths, some vicious, others "chronic victims" unable to learn from experience; manic-depressives, swinging from uncaringly self-destructive depression to manic "give-it-all-away" highs and back again; street junkies who barely allow the customer time to ejaculate before racing off with the money to buy a "fix"; and others.

Fertility. Many of the adolescent females drifting into the Life already have one, sometimes two legitimate or out-of-wedlock children. During subsequent years of prostitution relative infertility seems to be the rule; in one sample of white pros pregnancy as an occupational hazard occurred only in 11 per cent of the females (Gebhard). There are several theories explaining the causes of this one-child sterility: wide use of oral contraceptives (possibly; but non-users are equally infertile; also uneven use-reliability make the pills an uncertain factor here); ubiquitous old P.I.D.

(i.e., postgonorrheal chronic salpingitis and tubal obstruction—not believed a frequent cause in urban prostitutes today); chronic vasocongestive syndrome (a fairly frequent finding today, unproven, but a possible cause); chronic drug and/or alcohol toxicity (a fair possibility in those affected, most so in heroin users); repeated, very early, unnoticed or unreported abortions due to copious seminal prostaglandin input (unproven; known abortion rate in prostitutes is high but mechanism is unknown); and high incidence of sperm-agglutinating and -immobilizing antibodies, both circulating in the blood and fixed in the local tissues, present in promiscuous women due to the plethora of spermatic antigens introduced (considered a strong possibility; each new seminal load would maintain or increase anti-sperm activity in the female secretions; the sterility should, and reportedly does abate several months after such multipartnerism ceases). The validity of the local response theories is being made additionally problematical by the newer patterns of prostitute contact—and, in fact, much other, non-commercial sex contact—consisting increasingly of fellatio only; also by the fact that relatively fewer pros permit coitus without use of condom today. The orosexual pattern may, in turn, be increasing the frequency of cases of chronic sterility-producing pelvic congestion in prostitutes, as the opportunity for even an occasional detumescent orgasm is being further minimized.

Sexual Apparatus.   Attention has been called to the prostitute's early aging skin, her menstrual irregularities, the areolar excitability of her breasts, her large "cockscomb" labia minora, the worn vulva with its smooth, polished look, and the elastic distensibility of her external tract generally leading to nontraumatic labor. These traits have variously been said to "stamp" the prostitute, but no single one of them is present in all of them, and each such trait may be found also in nonprostituting women; besides, most of these traits are becoming infrequent gynecologic findings today. A more frequent and characteristic triad of findings in prostitutes today reportedly consists of an enlarged clitoris, copious noninfectious leukorrhea, and marked tenderness and a bag-of-worms feel on bimanual palpation near the side walls of the bony pelvis produced by chronic venous congestion and accompanied by substantial chronic pelvic discomfort (Melody). See also p. 412.

The protective sexual armamentarium of the more aware prostitute may include gargles, vaginal sprays, disinfectants, surgical cleansing soaps, refusal to kiss and to allow unsheathed coitus, tetracycline self-dosing virtually in perpetuity and/or a weekly medical visit for a penicillin injection. Both I.U.D.s and oral contraceptives are in preferred use, sometimes both. Where a girl's ponce is extra money-hungry, he may have her take a contraceptive pill every day without pause so as to lose no tricking days to undesired bleeding.

PROSTITUTE AND PHYSICIAN

In the U.S. a physician may diagnose, medically advise and treat any woman, including one who holds herself out or is known to be a prostitute. However, as a matter of professional ethics, he may not knowingly examine a prostitute for the purpose of aiding her trade (e.g., by providing her with a certificate of freedom from venereal disease or from communicability of such a disease, which can be used in soliciting).

The Procurer (protector, pimp, ponce, man, etc.) has existed throughout modern times, and possibly before; he can be found wherever prostitutes ply their trade, not excluding urban socialist societies. In the U.S. the typical pimp is a sociopath who lives full-time off the earnings of "his" women; in fact, he takes pride in living well, perhaps elegantly or even flashily on this and in not having any regular occupation. Most prostitutes, in turn, take pride in whatever elegance of life style their man is able to display. Procuring in the U.S. today is prevalently a métier of black men; they control black and white girls alike. Procurers are not identical with organized racketeers who control large groups of prostitutes and their working premises.

A pimp's "family" consists of himself and as many prostitutes ("wives," "wives-in-law") as he is able to manage, often 2 to 5. Each girl may operate under the carefully nurtured illusion that she is the main wife while the others are merely being used, that this is only a temporary arrangement, and that they will wind up as a respectable twosome in a few years, often with the promised recovery of an out-of-wedlock child now in a home playing a large part. In fact, many white newcomers project the black ponce as the future father for a racially mixed illegitimate baby they left behind (Sheehy). The girls turn over all or most of the money they earn while he pays for clothing, health expenses, rent, court fines, etc. He affords them pseudoaffection, sex with orgasmic relief, for each one night in turn, and an illusory sense of belonging (e.g., ". . . a guy I like, maybe my own guy, a guy for myself, a real guy . . ." I. Rubin). It is a compelling, bondage-like attachment experienced by the girl as "love." When he beats them (e.g., for not earning enough or for holding back money) they tend, in time, to accept this as due them. The relationship has also been called a symbiosis of mutual need for contempt, as each despises the other as more degraded than themselves. Not all prostitutes have a procurer at all times. Also, aggressive lesbian hustlers do not tolerate them, but may fill this role, in part, themselves for one or several colleagues.

Pimps recruit new wives in several ways. A wife may be sent back to her old home town or neighborhood to persuade a suitable friend into the Life. Much luring of runaway girls—often rebellious but suggestible teenagers craving excitement—is done on the basis of a personal flashy magnetism, promises of clothes, wigs and jewels, of future riches and glittering adventure, and/or a promise of affectionate caring coupled with reassuring words from one of the other girls in his family. Other prostitutes are inducted by an almost standardized method of rapid (e.g., 4 days) coercion: almost "fresh off the bus" they are taken in, terrorized by being locked up, being subjected to repeated raw, at times rape-like sex by the pimp and 1 or 2 other men, followed immediately by some selected "easy" customers, followed in turn by a gift of stylish clothes, etc. Addicts constitute a source of recruits; other girls are started on addictive drugs by the pimp. Switching of pimps and trading of girls is also quite common.

The Prostitute's Customers.　The lists of names of "regular" customers confiscated from commercial call girls never cease to amaze, especially as to certain men obviously in a position to attract more personalized female companionship at will. In explanation it can be said that among the attractions of prostitution—most of them illusory in the long run—are the expectation of assured discretion; more safety as compared to random pick-ups; relative inexpensiveness if comparing with the courting and dating expenses for nonprofessional companions; and, most of all, the avoidance of "intimacy" which to the mature or successful man with an already complicated life means mostly emotional, social and/or sexual demands and interference with his habits. For some men the resort to prostitution can be called habit-forming; their essential loneliness and sense of isolation is not relieved as they leave the woman who services them but withholds herself as a person. Prostitute sex relieves tension, but does not give positive satisfaction. The men tend to become more lonely; in their acute need they seek out a prostitute again, thus build up no drive, nor an opportunity to meet other female company.

Some of the brighter prostitutes boast that they initiate the young boy properly; teach variety to inexperienced young husbands, thus salvaging or improving marriages; that they provide undreamed-of orgasmic bliss for some; revive the waning powers of the elderly, or the sleeping powers of the timid; and that they comfort the lonely man far from home, protect the sailor from finding attraction in his shipmates, or protect the soldier from the ire of townfolks whose daughters he may otherwise feel compelled to importune. But these boasts are largely in the realm of rationalization. An experienced paramour may be in a position to accomplish one or the other of these deeds, but the social role of the prostitute is basically parasitic, not helping. "They make like they're a social worker, but it's just another hustle." A possible exception is the prostitute's availability— usually for extra money and grudgingly—for the release of sexually deviant needs and urges, notably sadomasochism and fetishism ("freak scenes," "weirdos," "kinky sex"). However, there is no practical way to establish if unavailability of prostitution would expose the community to increased danger from the unsatisfied urges of sexually abnormal men.

GROUP SEX

Commune. Basically a social, not a sexual grouping in search of a satisfying life style, even the "hippie" communes. Sexual styles include the full range from celibacy to free love, but no stable commune has been known to be frankly sex-centered. Both monogamous as well as triadic or other group marriages can be embedded in the communal structure.

Consensual Adultery. Spouses' participation, by mutual consent, in some form of swinging activity. Most usually today both spouses participate, either in the same group, or with the same "co-marital" single mate. There are many motives. A couple may share a venturesome spirit or a willingness to experiment with "just a sex thing"; a desire to act out juvenile hedonistic fantasies; or to keep up with their close friends. Some may want to improve the state of the marital vita sexualis (e.g., by fantasizing recalled swinging images in domestic intercourse, or even by gleaning sexual technics from other swingers—"let's go learn something"). Some seek to repair brittle marriages by shifting to a new extraneous focus of mutual interest; or they expect benefits from seeing the mate become a person visibly desired by others. Some hope for protection against adulterous urges and opportunities in themselves or the spouse. A husband may urge, even force his wife into swinging, because of unfocused prurience, or to avoid family-destructive reprisals for his found-out furtive adultery. Some need reassurance as to their own prowess or desirability. Other individuals, incapable of forming any intimate relationship, use swinging as a safety valve to keep intimacy at a level they can tolerate (Littner).

Daisy Chain. Several persons, often male homosexuals, engaged in simultaneous sexual relations, including genital, oral or anal conjunctions. In a triangle, if 3 participants; in a row or circle if more.

Dyadic Marriage (Dyad, twosome). Usually signifies a conventional married couple.

Free Love. Any open-ended sexual consummating encounter without legal or other commitment (Ramey). At one time applied to young couples living in a sort of trial marriage without legal sanction.

Gang-shack (Gang-bang, line-up). Usually a group of adolescent boys coiting, one after the other, with a girl who volunteered, is paid or was forced (gang rape).

Group Marriage (Multilateral marriage). Fairly rare as an overt formalized relationship, but disguised units are more frequent. A settled conjugal unit of 1 to 3 couples, some with an added single. Most frequent: 2-couple units and M-F-F triads; the latter integrate better than F-M-M triads with their complex male bisexual undercurrents. Partners share not only sex, but residence, economic resources, child rearing and affection. Median age in the Constantines' survey was 31 (range 23 to 59); mostly of college level and above. All try to live up to ideal of equal love, no preferences, but jealousy is said to be a chronic problem. Bedroom set-ups range from 1 bed and 1 room per person to 3 persons permanently in 1 bed; the mode is 2 rooms with 2 people in each. Group sex is not the major mode, and 4-person sex tends to become 2 couples side-by-side, with the men always more uncomfortable: tense, competitive, perhaps temporarily impotent. It may be noted that Masters and Johnson found that women in their laboratory were desensitized to non-privacy during sex much more quickly than men.

Groupies. Girls, usually but not always runaway or delinquent teen-agers, who follow one or more idols—a band, a singer, athletes, etc.—from place to place in their travels, vying for their attention and being available to them. The girls travel and room together amicably. Their sustenance is uncertain.

Mate-swapping. A major aspect of intimate-group swinging. Shifting is strictly temporary, sometimes ritualized and often subject to restrictive rules to protect the basic marriage units; such as partner rotation by lot or schedule, or even no repeats; time limit on intimacies; no outside rendez-vous; no exchange of verbal affection in private. However, extramarital elopements by two newly infatuated swingers are no rarity. See also Swinging, Consensual Adultery.

Orgy (Group sex proper). Composition of carousing groups varies widely. Participants may be communalists, group-spouses (q.v.) or recreational swingers; in semi-public open-end orgies, on the other hand, there is little control over participants and they are a source of various dangers. In theory, "everything goes, anybody with anybody" in an orgy, all together and in one place: hetero- and homosexual activity, exhibiting, viewing, sometimes masochism, while sadistic orgies are specialized, typically ritualized and secretive affairs rarely open to observers. As the men tend to spend themselves fairly quickly, "like kids locked in a candy store," the later main activity is often lesbian. This has also been one of the surprises of the emerging swinger movement: the frequent interest in open female-female sex play even by initially reluctant, prim wives brought into swinging. It has also led to a good many psychiatric difficulties centered around obsessive guilt feelings which emerged later. An instance or two of previously latent male homosexual (actually bisexual) interest, can often be found to emerge in group sex scenes. Private all-homosexual orgies have become commonplace where large but shifting gay populations congregate.

Plural Marriage. Same as polygamy (q.v.). Does not usually include the crime of bigamy.

Polygamy. Formal marriage of a man to several wives. Permitted under Islamic faith, but increasingly restricted by modern Muslim family law. Illegal in U.S., but about 20,000 Mormons practicing polygamy were left in Utah in 1971.

Sex Club. Usually found in high schools. Couples swap dates, pair off and engage in sex activities; occasionally orgy-type activities take place.

Swap Club. A semi-public extension of mate-swapping and intimate-group swinging (Breedlove). Today not usually an actual club but part of a national network, only partly underground, with swinger ad magazines, newcomer introductions and exchanges, regional get-togethers, etc. The purpose is exclusively sexual.

Swinging (The swinging scene). Controlled multipartnerism. Although the term is being over-used to include all manner of promiscuity, open-end group sex and free love with stranger-partners, basically swingers are of 2 types:

Utopian or Ideologic Swingers. This is a minority seeking stable, close relationships, with flexible couple arrangements and often with radical child rearing attitudes (Symonds). It is a total, liberated, experimental life style, part of the sexual freedom movement (Sexual Freedom League). Similar movements have existed in the past.

Recreational Swingers. This involves 2 or more couples who mutually decide to switch sex partners and/or to engage in group sex on scheduled occasions. Many multicouple groups exclude singles; in other cases the smallest unit is a triad of a couple and a single, most often a female. Swingers tend to be conforming, conventional people in everything except sex (Bell). They may overconventionalize the rest of the marriage to compensate (Denfeld-Gordon). Some groups start as close friends, settled couples who sexualize their friendship (Comfort). Other couples join by invitation or, if experienced transfers, by mail (e.g., via wife's photograph). Some intimate-group swingers progress to close social friendship, but the majority of couples are believed to drop out in less than 6 months. The external form of swinger groups varies, but there are almost always rules to protect the basic marriage units (see Mate-swapping). Swinging in a fixed group may be too mechanistic and unmeaningful for sensitive persons (Bartell), thus quickly leading to surfeit and boredom. This, in turn, can lead to escalation into experimenting with drugs, bondage, witchcraft, etc. (Ramey). However, alcohol and pornographic movies are often initially part of the scene. Swinging can become an "addiction," less satisfying as it becomes more compulsive (Grold).

Triad (Trio, 3-way scene, ménage-à-trois; Fr.). Exists both as a settled, fully committed form of group marriage, most often a male and 2 females (O'Neill), and as the smallest unit in recreational swinging. The lesbian component in triads appears to be fairly substantial; swinger ads seeking singles may look for "versatile" female or mention "ac/dc" wife. However, most such wives deny that they are lesbians. Male performance is said to be enhanced in these triads as female-female sex contact is believed to be among the most arousing viewing experiences for males.

Triadic Marriage. A settled conjugal unit of 3 persons, often a couple and a female. The triadic marriage is said to be the relatively most stable (enduring) of the new non-dyadic forms of marriage.

Wife-swapping. Originally signified a stylized social pastime among middle-class couples. Term became unacceptable in 1960s, changed to sexual "mate-swapping" and became part of "swinging." Basic dyadic married-couple structure is preserved.

VARIOUS MANIFESTATIONS

Erotomania (erotic obsessions). This is a group of fairly severe mental disorders, mainly encountered in women. In the relatively most benign form seemingly irrepressible, irrational sex fears are just one item interspersed with other preoccupations. The patients—men or women—fear that they will lose control of themselves and undress in public, shout dirty words in church, grab at people's private parts, or such. They never actually do any of this. In a more serious disorder the patient indicates that she "cannot get sex off my mind," everything seems to remind her of genital or sexual symbols; or she cannot read anything without having to search for, or discovering, hidden erotic or obscene meanings; or she may endlessly doodle or draw sexual symbols. Patients rarely have any marked sexual desire or may even abhor the thought of intercourse; an occasional patient may "try sex to get it out of my mind," but without success. The condition tends to be chronic, not rarely with a drift into schizophrenia. Psychiatric treatment is difficult but relatively successful, except that these patients do not always cooperate well or even agree to therapy.

In the severest (psychotic) form the woman is irrationally convinced that a certain man is in love with her; she may construe elaborate proof of this in her mind, then approach him, pursue him, perhaps accuse him and eventually hallucinate that he visits her (e.g., in her bedroom, at night through a window—Liebeswahn; Ger., syndrome erotomaniaque; Fr.). Related is Kretschmer's Erotischer Beziehungswahn of the aging spinster. In physically handicapped women milder chronic syndromes of erotic reference are not altogether rare. In men, somewhat related are major delusions of conjugal jealousy (e.g., in some involutional psychoses or accompanying a gradual loss of hearing). They seem to be prognostically especially malignant if an incestuous perpetrator is named by the patient (de Busscher). These syndromes are more rarely encountered in women.

Graffitomania (erotic g.). Obscene wall writing and drawing—sexual graffiti, scatology—goes back to ancient times. The scrawled inscriptions, some mildly erotic, others unabashed and explicit, are part of man's urge to leave his mark. Some significant and learned works have been published on the subject in modern times, but clinical information on the habitual perpetrator remains fragmentary. The immature, casual wall artist is of no clinical significance. The true graffitomaniac, for whom any suitable public men's room wall is an irresistible invitation and who may carry a pencil stub for this very purpose, is almost always male, often an anxious-passive personality, and in about half the cases probably has homosexual inclinations. He seeks to shock anonymously, but a number have been known to loiter about inconspicuously to observe the effect on others, but they do not reveal themselves; but other homosexuals have been known to use their own or pre-existing public toilet graffiti as part of their sexual solicitation.

Obscene Telephoning. Published information is scant, but much material is scattered in psychiatric case records. Principal perpetrators, apart from girls of pre-teen and early teen age in giggly groups, are lonely, insecure, and isolated men of various ages. The victim is chosen either by random dialing until an appealing female voice answers, or else from among acquaintances even if known only by remote hearsay. The perpetrator may blurt out an obscene word or question and hang up; in other cases if a hoped-for lengthy exchange develops he may masturbate right then, or the recollected words and voice, with added fantasies, may sustain his solitary acts subsequently. Clinically, the telephonist is close to the exhibitionist (p. 468). Their psychologic make-up is similar, and in some cases offenders have resorted to both modalities. The offender most often resorts to telephoning when the anxiety connected with his ambivalent rage against women has built up to an acute need to be acknowledged and respected by them, even if only for his ability to shock (Nadler). The obscene telephone offender is essentially inoffensive, non-selective and anonymous. However, systematic telephone molesting of a selected victim also occurs; inadvertent encouragement by the victim here has led to subsequent physical accosting in a few known cases.

Scatology (compulsive smut storytelling). A fairly infrequent syndrome seemingly limited to males. Most patients are clinically unremarkable except for a tendency to frequent or incessant telling of erotic stories or off-color jokes. Sometimes the pattern can be so unremitting that patients are handicapped socially and economically, especially where the compulsive need is experienced as beyond voluntary control. Onset is uncertain, but in a few cases could be traced to childhood, beginning as compulsive coprolalia (obscene words), possibly following a bout of encephalitis. It may thus represent an attenuated type of Tourette's Disease (see below). In fact, a possible cause is temporal lobe disease. It is significant that following surgical temporal lobe ablation for epilepsy previously hyposexual men acquired, in some cases, an intense fascination with "talking dirty" and telling obscene stories (Blumer). Similar observations can be made in some cerebral arteriosclerotics. In view of the proximity of the posterior temporal-parietal speech control areas to the temporal limbic structures co-regulating sexual behavior, disarray of the interaction between these areas (e.g., by focal disinhibitory pathology) has gained some attention of late (Money et al.). Treatment cases were largely unresponsive to psychotherapy.

Gilles de la Tourette Disease (Tourette's Syndrome, Foulmouth Disease, Tic Convulsif, Maladie des Tics). In males, less in females. Onset is in childhood with facial and body tics and twitching, later hissing, barking and other vocalizing, and bouts of uncontrollable, senselessly repetitive, loudly obscene language (coprolalia), expletives and cursing. Course is chronic. Intelligence and insight are normal. Believed to be an organic-metabolic brain disorder. Symptomatic and maintenance treatment, best with haloperidol, a potent catecholamine receptor blocker, often in high doses (Shapiro).

Compulsive Inciting. In females. Habitual coquettishness is essentially a non-sexual manifestation. The seemingly indefatigable temptresses of men, the habitual flirts, teasers, proposition collectors—almost predatory in their inciting, almost virginal in their refusing—act compulsively and may, in fact, often be quite unaware of the effect they have on men. Many are so-called infantile personalities. Through the years the woman can again and again act—and feel—surprised, even indignant at being propositioned in return by one or the other of her objects; "why do men always want sex?" she keeps asking. Her sexual responses are discussed on p. 409; for victim-precipitated rape see p. 262. She harbors an obsessional need to be the center of even the most casual male-female relationships. She erotizes the situation by provocative behavior or innuendo, as this seems to be the only way she has of handling her anxiety in regard to men.

Nudism, or social nudism, is a health movement, and has no sexual connotations. It is practiced in outdoor camps by its members, mostly couples with children. Firmly established in the U.S. since ca. 1929. Most camps are governed by strict rules of conduct, and ban the use of alcohol, profanity and physical contact (Casler). Social nudism has been seen as middle-class people's need to transcend the restraints of a culturally imposed value system including detachment and alienation (Holt). Qualified observers find members to be in comparatively sound psychologic health (DeMartino, Weinberg); as a group they are neither undersexed nor oversexed (Serban). In recent years interest reportedly has gravitated from naturalism, sunbathing and physical health to greater concern with interpersonal, companionable relationships. The movement is unrelated to recent experiments with nude psychotherapy and sensitivity training groups.

PORNOGRAPHY

Related:
Exposure to Pornography p. 136

Practically all contemporary commercial pornography is aimed at men. Males are aroused by details of action, while most adult females in our culture respond sexually more to erotic affection and romantic symbols.

To arouse, the material must permit either sex to project themselves into the scene; it must also activate at least some fantasy to be effective. What excites one group generally leaves others cold (e.g., the coyly teasing material which is written to arouse primary transvestites, bores the normal adult beholder—Stoller). That is equally true of material for male homosexuals, sadists, etc. Present-day "normal" hard-core pornography conveys an image of insatiable and forever potent men, of women continuously in heat, and of ever-present opportunities for lustful encounters. After a time

---

OBSCENITY AND PORNOGRAPHY

Glossary

Obscenity: Matter offensive to taste or modesty; expressing or exposing private matters lewdly.

Pornography: Use of obscenity aimed at titillating without true narrative or esthetic justification. Effective only if it has capacity to activate beholder's or reader's fantasy. Tends to escalation into portrayal of the pathologic (e.g., sadism, victimization) and of the unreal.

Hard-Core Pornography: Depicts every manner of sex activity, barring nothing. No pretense of redeeming social value. Pictures, films mostly.

Soft-Core Pornography: Generally excludes details of genital arousal and activity, but designed to arouse.

Erotic Realism (Naturalism): Sex matter incidental to other material (Kronhausen).

Erotica: The treasures of erotic art and literature through the ages, capable of sublimating their creators' own deeper needs while affecting the beholder's emotions. Held above blame by some, by virtue of its superior merit; but also denounced as a system of privileged prurience: "high class erotica is okay, the rest is smut" (Fiedler).

---

all this becomes hopelessly dull and boring for even the most compulsive consumer. He then searches for escalation, and so does the producer who knows his customer material. Almost inevitably, both branch out into the pathologic: sadomasochism, lesbianism, aggression and such; still later they go into the fantastic, just as the Marquis de Sade (p. 478) eventually forced his imagination into a dreary enumeration of improbably ludicrous tortures. At some point the more unstable consumer—perhaps even some of the producers who cater to him—no longer can tell normality and reality from the abnormal; in the least stable latent morbidity may become mobilized, although the habit of instant masturbation probably drains most of the urges before they reach reaction levels (theory; disputed).

U.S. Law. No stable approach to the legal definition of pornography has yet been devised. What is obscene to one judging authority may not be obscene to another. Besides, criteria shift with the shifting mores of the times (e.g., the "visible pubic hair" test faltered vis-à-vis respectable nudist magazines). U.S. Justice Stewart said he could not define obscenity, "but I know it when I see it," which made good sense but not good law. Prevailing legal doctrine, by and large, is based on the prurient appeal standard defining as illegal any materials in which "to the average person, applying contemporary community standards, the dominant theme of the material, taken as a whole, appeals (primarily) to prurient interest" (U.S. Supreme Court, 1957). Prurient interest, in turn, has been defined as "a substantial tendency to incite lascivious thoughts or arouse lustful desire."

The 1957 law has been reinterpreted and amended repeatedly since then. "Community" was re-interpreted to mean society-at-large, to avoid sectional narrowing. In 1966 the Court added an important test: is the material utterly without redeeming social (literary) value, or does it contain ideas worthy of protection? Later it let the states make it a crime to sell "to minors under 17 matter defined to be obscene to them whether or not it would be obscene to adults." Matters perused in the privacy of the home were exempted. "Average person" was re-interpreted to include "pandering to the average member of any recipient group," (e.g., clearly defined deviates such as homosexuals, sadists, transvestites). Finally the court proposed to move the definition of obscenity from content to the manner of advertising and sale and to its intent to arouse prurient interest (i.e., the doctrine of the motive of the sellers, who ". . . make a business of pandering to the widespread weakness for titillation by pornography"). Soft-core pornography usually is exonerated as in the 1963 landmark decision by New York State Justice Shapiro: ". . . there are those who because of lack of education, the meanness of their existence or mental insufficiency cannot cope with anything better (pulp sex novels) to provide them with an escape." In 1973 the U.S. Supreme Court, in essence, abolished redeeming social value as a defense, and left it to state and lesser jurisdictions to determine what is offensive to the average person by local community standards.

Censorship—con: it is wrong to keep pornography from adults who want it; suppression violates the First Amendment to the Constitution; even absolute freedom for adults to read what they wish is not a danger to the state (an Amer. Civ. Lib. Union official). What we regard as lewd merely reflects what is in our minds (Kirkendall). Pornography not being legally definable with precision, there is no practical way of censoring it. "The spectacle of a judge poring over the picture of a nude trying to ascertain the extent to which she arouses prurient interest . . . has elements of low comedy" (Thurman Arnold). Besides, suppression makes pornography even more titillating; it is best to rely on the proven fact that people get surfeited and bored when untrammeled dissemination is permitted. Also pornography is more a release than a stimulus; it helps defuse deviates and maladjusted men, as they act out pathologic drives in fantasy with less need to victimize others. In 1970 a National Commission on Obscenity issued a much-discussed report which widely missed its point; finding no significant correlation between pornographic exposure and antisocial behavior, it advocated repeal of all laws curbing adults' access to sexually explicit materials.

Censorship—pro: no society can be totally indifferent to the ways its citizens publicly entertain themselves (Berns). The First Amendment's guarantees of free speech have never applied to obscene materials (U.S. Supreme Court, 1957). The idea that "everything is permitted" rests on the premise of nihilism. A flow of pornographic material does not necessarily lead to satiety and boredom; its habitual perusal by those who have come to depend on it amounts to a chronic self-reinforcing neurosis (Kristol). Obscenity is a moral issue; political and philosophic assessment is more relevant to establishing a social policy than scientific and utilitarian criteria (J.Q. Wilson). Pornography is steeped in psychosexual immaturity and deficit: it is written by impotent men, distributed by scoptophiliacs, and consumed by prurient boys and men in need of a substitute sex partner or a psychoaphrodisiac (Eliasberg, Karpman, Turkel). As to youth, it has neither been proved nor disproved that their ethical or moral development is impaired by obscene material, but this only applies to "normal" pornography and normal youths. There are indications, however, that continued perusal together with the inevitable escalation of material into the pathologic produces subtle erotic corruptive effects in certain unstable or borderline youngsters (see also p. 137). Although all reasonable observers agree that children should be shielded from access, this is not always practicable where the product is freely offered and accessible to adults.

Pornographomania. Found almost exclusively in males. The true pornographomanic is a compulsive collector, thus he differs substantially from the individual who is interested in such material mainly for the purpose of expedient self-excitation. The pornographomanic's interest can lead to elaborate and sophisticated collection of printed material, pictures, etchings, objets d'art, or curiosa. There exist porno collectors' clubs, and a veritable cult with bartering, hunting for rare acquisitions and busy dealers. Most such true collectors of pornography appear to be sadists, or possibly sadistic fetishists, of an attenuated or sublimated type. In this connection it is interesting that sadists probably are among the most gregarious types of sexual deviates.

TREATMENT WITH SEX DEPRESSANTS

Treatment of hypersexual behavior is directed primarily at the underlying cause. However, a substantial number of cases call for symptomatic control of the social and clinical manifestations, whether episodic or unremitting. Individualization of treatment efforts is obviously of the essence.

Progesterone. Both progesterone and the synthetic gestagens tend to suppress sexual manifestations in men. They reduce both testosterone and LH plasma levels as well as urinary 17-ketosteroid excretion; the testicles become smaller and there is azoospermia after a period. Medroxyprogesterone acetate 20 mg a day has been used or, for prolonged effect, parenteral Depo-Provera or Delalutin. The combination-type birth control pill, ½ tablet 3 times a week has given fair but slow results in a few hyper-libidinized males, without major side effects. In some sexually recrudescent elderly men medroxyprogesterone has given creditable results (see p. 436). In women, progesterone by mouth, i.m. or by implanted pellet, and the combination-type progestins, cyclically but double- or triple-dosed (Greenblatt) have similar clinical effect, but they have not been widely tried and results remain uncertain.

OLDER ANAPHRODISIACS (ANTIAPHRODISIACS)

Saltpeter (niter, potassium nitrate, KNO₃). Used for pickling "corned" meat. Long used in institutions to suppress libido of inmates, but now in disuse in most of the world. Effective only after continued use; single or few doses ineffective. 1 to 2 Gm per dose, diluted; daily maximum 4 to 12 Gm. Possibly effective largely via weakness, lassitude, torpor it produces. Eliminated through kidneys. Poisoning: acute hemorrhagic enteritis with anuria or hematuria, convulsions. Fatality over 50 per cent. Mild toxicity: bradycardia, bloody diarrhea.

Bromides. Not widely used today. Inorganic bromides, notably potassium salt, are fairly effective libido reducers, but disagreeable to use. Organic bromides less toxic, but also less effective. Cumulative effect may induce bromism. Preferred: mixture of several bromides, in intermittent courses, with daily salt intake 2 to 3 times bromide dose. Dosage determined by trial and error; average 2.5 to 3.5 Gm (range 1 to 5 Gm) daily in divided doses by mouth after meals, well

diluted. Unsafe in elderly and in arteriosclerosis.

Carbromal (e.g., Sedamyl, Taborea, Carbrital). Effective in acute hyper-libidinal states, but sedative-hypnotic action and relatively high habituation risk restrict usefulness.

Valerian. For self-dosing in mild cases. Safe, except in urinary tract inflammation. As tincture, fluid-extract, or coated tablets. In U.S. mostly in combination with other sedative substances and herbals.

Camomile Tea. "The anaphrodisiac for frightened little old ladies." Safe for self-dosing.

Lupulin (extract of hops, humulus lupulus). Unpredictably effective. Hops preparations first stimulate, then depress vagal centers. Often combined with bromides, Valerian, etc. (e.g., Neurosine in the U.S.).

Various. Monobromated camphor; Antipyrine; Dicodid: available specific observations are dated. Epsom Salts (magnesium sulfate) 20 to 40 Gm in ½ glass of water, one repeat if desired: a horse cure; gives temporary relief.

Cyproterone Acetate (not approved in U.S.) is the principal remaining substance among the newer anti-androgenics being extensively used outside the U.S. at present, the others having been discontinued because of side-effects. This synthetic inhibitor of testosterone, a progestinic, reduces the sexual drive without inducing feminization. Its use in male sex criminals and adolescent sex delinquents has been successful in Europe, which is apparently not the case with medroxyprogesterone acetate. However, the use of anti-androgenics in convicted sex aggressors while in detention is not wholly rational: the effect is not permanent or even long-lasting, nor does reduced androgenic function ensure control of violent impulses nor of pseudosexual assaults.

Cyproterone acetate acts by competing with and displacing testosterone directly at the receptor sites, or else by inhibiting gonadotropic hormone releasors in the midbrain. It is rapid-acting—onset in less than a week— as it lessens and eventually virtually extinguishes libido, erections and nocturnal emissions. It also reduces spermatogenesis; the testicles become either softer or smaller (Ott). Effects appear to be reversible within 3 months after discontinuation. It is proving medically useful in suppressing inappropriate sex activity in ambulatory patients.

Estrogen in Men. Estrogen is promptly and highly effective in suppressing erections, etc., in normal men, followed by degrees of demasculinization and feminization (gynecomastia, etc.) with continued use (see p. 349). Administration for a period of at least 2 weeks of 5 to 10 mg Stilbestrol a day has inhibited sexual manifestations for a number of months. However, suppression of libido is much more uncertain unless appropriate psychotropic medication (see below) is added; in fact, the combination of abnormally high and insufficiently controlled libido and suppressed erections can produce dangerous aggressive tendencies in some psychopaths. Massive estrogen doses are being used in the palliative pre- and postoperative treatment of some transsexuals (p. 490). Estrogen is not indicated during active development in sexually aggressive teen-agers.

Psychotropic Remedies. Most common sedatives and the minor tranquilizers have no specific value as anaphrodisiacs, short of subduing the total person. However, some of the major psychotropics, both ataractics and antidepressants, tend to produce a sex-depressant effect, although not with reliable predictability. In the general practice of psychiatry this is usually regarded as a side-effect, and for various reasons this approach has only limited usefulness and requires knowledge of complications and their remedies. Thioridazine (Mellaril) has given creditable results in female hyper-excitement states, with dosages varying widely; in men its effect is uncertain or it may be limited to retrograde ejaculation (p. 374). Chlorpromazine (Thorazine) may be tried (e.g., 100 or 200 mg h.s.) or, for prolonged effect, parenteral fluphenazine (Prolixin) enanthate (causes occasional severe depressions). Reserpine can be effective but in the necessary dosage is a high-risk drug (depression). Not formally tested and rather unpredictable are the gradually libido- and male potency-reducing effects of the antidepressants, notably isocarboxacid (Marplan) among the monoamine-oxidase inhibitors and imipramine (Tofranil) among the tricyclics, the latter especially in combination with fairly small amounts of estrogen. However, their use in the absence of the usual psychiatric indications is not recommended. Not rational but at times effective is the use of certain other substances which impair sexual manifestations as a side-effect (e.g., ganglionic blocking agents, high-dose Antabuse, etc.).

Various. Lesioning: bilateral surgical or other lesion setting in the basal nuclei of the amygdalae, part of the limbic system in the brain, is an experimental method of promise but also of potential controversy. Pineal gland extracts have been praised for their anaphrodisiac effect by some investigators; they are not commercially available.

FOR JOURNAL LITERATURE AND ADDITIONAL READING

Bartell, G. D.: Group Sex. New York, P. H. Wyden, 1971

Gerber, A. B.: Sex, Pornography and Justice. New York, Lyle Stuart, 1966

Gilder, G. F.: Sexual Suicide. New York, Quadrangle/The New York Times Book Co., 1973

Gorski, R. A. and Whalen, R. E. (eds.): The Brain and Gonadal Function (vol. 3 of Brain and Behavior). Berkeley, Univ. of California Press, 1966

Heath, R.: The Role of Pleasure in Behavior. New York, Hoeber, 1965

Lieberman, M., Yalon, I., and Miles, M.: Encounter Groups, First Facts. New York, Basic Books, 1973

Monroe, R. R.: Episodic Behavioral Disorders: A Psychodynamic and Neurophysiologic Analysis. Boston, Harvard Univ. Press, 1970

O'Neill, N. and G.: Open Marriage. New York, M. Evans & Co., 1972

Rubin, I.: In the Life. New York, Macmillan, 1961

Sagarin, E.: Anatomy of Dirty Words. New York, Lyle Stuart, 1965

Winick, C. and Kinsie, P. M.: The Lively Commerce. New York, New American Library (Paperback), 1972

CHAPTER 20

Sexual Deviations

(Sexual Deviance, Aberrations, Perversions. Paraphilias.

Deviant Sexual Behavior)

Exhibitionism — Pedophilia — Sexual Masochism and Sadism. Sex Killing. Necrophilia — Fetishism — Transvestism — Transsexualism — Voyeurism — Zoophilia — Various Deviations.

Deviant sex manifestations in this chapter, if habitual or compellingly recurrent, are considered psychosexual aberrations sui generis. The same manifestations may also be the symptom of a more general personality disorder, or a symptom of a brain disease or a psychosis, or due to immaturity of impulse control. None constitutes merely unconventional sex practice, which involves the right of competent consenting adults to engage in private sexual behavior of their choice (see Variant Practices, p. 210). A sexual deviation is said to be compulsory when it constitutes the exclusive or principal sex aim, when satisfying sexual expression is not possible without it, and when its pursuit cannot be restrained by reason, guilt or fear of consequences. While in the majority of patients a single aberrant manifestation prevails, there can be overlapping and coexistence of several manifestations in other individuals.

EXHIBITIONISM

This is a compelling sexual deviation consisting of the display of the (most often erect) penis before one or more strange females, usually in a public locality. The legal term "indecent exposure" is not strictly synonymous with the medical term term exhibitionism; but all exposure constitutes a punishable offense. The term "exhibitionistic," meaning ostentatious or show-offish, is unrelated to the compulsive deviation; in fact, psychologically the two are mutually exclusive. The disorder, which is chronic with usually episodic manifestations, occurs in males about 15 times as often as in females; the latter come only infrequently to medical attention. In the typical case onset is between 14 and 17 years of age. The earlier the onset the poorer the prognosis (Mathis).

The Compulsive Exhibitionist is neither shameless nor even truly aggressive. He is an inhibited, immature personality, inclined to be passive and often beset by feelings of masculine inadequacy. He views women with awe, as a rule. In his daily life he is reticent, frequently overconscientious, diffident rather than outgoing, and sometimes rigidly moralistic. Some are fairly amiable, hard-working men, living unremarkably among their neighbors. Some are men of distinguished accomplishments and repute. Few have antisocial tendencies except for this. A substantial number are married and have children, but their vita sexualis, as a rule, is stereotyped and inadequate, although complete relative impotence is probably infrequent. Many are habitual masturbators.

The Act. The compulsive exhibitionist intends to be seen by and to shock his victims, mostly by the element of surprise. No menace is intended, nor is there a desire to titillate or seduce, and certainly neither wish nor fantasy of the victim responding erotically to the cue; even thinking of the possibility frightens the compulsive exhibitionist. His most frequent objects are girls in late childhood or pubescence ("they seem just old enough to understand and be impressed and frightened but not old enough for me to risk coming closer.") Others expose themselves only to adult women. He rarely desires or finds erotic pleasure from exhibiting himself but acts to relieve a state of inner pressure and tension which has built up during a prodromal period which lasts anywhere from 30 minutes to almost 48 hours and does not vary much in the same individual. The prodrome is a combination of irritability, restlessness, headache and a strange sense of exhilaration, although trance-like or stupefied states have also been described. These traits lend some weight to a newer theory which links compulsive genital display to abnormal discharges in the temporal lobes. However, the patient is conscious and aware although driven, looks for an "opportunity," and plans his line of retreat (although this often goes wrong later).

His performance is stereotyped. Often he returns to the same vicinity, repeats the manner of his approach and seeks out females of similar ages. Some loiter in secluded spots or ride the platforms of public conveyances, but an increasing number today use the automobile; they either approach the victim (or victims) pretending to inquire directions, or they open the car door after maneuvering into the victim's field of view. As they flee the scene they tend to be dangerous drivers. Those operating at night may carry a flashlight to shine on themselves. Others have been known to wear special clothes (e.g., just trouser-legs under an overcoat). After the act relief from the inner tension is almost immediate and does not necessarily depend on an ejaculation. The mere act of exposure, and especially seeing his victim's evident startle, fright or fascination, may suffice, although some masturbate during or after the act, while a few have a spontaneous orgasm while exposed. Relief from tension usually is followed by a feeling of depression and intense remorse. The frequency of the episodes varies. Some will commit the act almost daily for a period of weeks, then become quiescent for months. Others seek to expose themselves with some regularity, the rate ranging from once a week to as little as once or twice a year, or even less.

Upon arrest the compulsive offender will deny stubbornly or explain away the charge of indecent exposure; few other types of deviates are similarly persistent in this regard. As his community life is usually orderly and normal and sometimes exemplary, a great many disbelieving character witnesses are apt to come forward in his behalf, once the nature of the charge has become known; the most determined of these is often his mother. Careless exposure during urgent urination while under the influence of alcohol is the most frequent defense of arrested exhibitionists pleading not guilty at their trials. The compulsive exhibitionist is relatively harmless insofar as he is not likely to become physically aggressive toward his victims, and in that he hardly ever commits other types of aggressive sex offenses. However, the act is potentially more than a nuisance offense. For some of the child victims it can be greatly frightening and disturbing, and for some labilely adjusted girls it is a true sexual trauma.

Symptomatic Exhibitionism occurs in a variety of psychiatric personality disorders. The pathologic drinker; the sadistic type of pedophile (q.v.); certain middle-aged or elderly men with an aggressive pattern resulting from an organic brain syndrome (p. 434); and the multisexual opportunists among the psychopathic personalities—all potentially dangerous sex offenders—may expose themselves at times, yet this is rarely the limit of their antisocial sex repertoire. Here the immediate stimulus to expose usually comes from the environment rather than from endopsychic tension. Their abnormal behavior is essentially opportunity-induced, thus unpredictable, lacks a prodromal phase except for brief titillating anticipation, and if they encounter what seems to them an encouraging response they do not run from it.

Mentally retarded men may expose themselves. The more frequent offender here is the repressed, timid, maladjusted defective who has exhibited his genitalia since childhood days to obtain attention from the environment or to express some crude protest or need (see p. 160). His exhibitionism now, too, is not a matter of expressing sexual need. A much more serious problem is the brutalized defective drifter who displays both cunning and aggressiveness in his approach. Distinct and easily recognizable is the psychotic exhibitionist, male or female. The schizophrenic patient may stand close to an open window and masturbate, apparently without much interest in who is seeing him. The patient in a state of manic excitement may indiscriminately call attention to his (her) exposed parts but be quite aware of who is observing him.

Treatment. One of the practicable approaches is therapeutic management. This is ordinarily a psychiatric responsibility, but some compulsive exhibitionists, with lesser degrees of repressed anxiety, have been managed successfully by their family physicians. Although most of these men are prospective recidivists and seem to know that they are, they rarely seek medical help voluntarily. Sometimes near-discovery may frighten them to see a physician; but as their fright wears off, so does their recognition of being vulnerable and disordered. Under fear of prison sentence or of public exposure, at times they may become anxiously, even tearfully, cooperative; yet if the case is simply dismissed in court, they also discontinue treatment. Unlike many other deviates, the compulsive exhibitionist actually seems to benefit from being sentenced and from remaining in some way under the protective jurisdiction of the court. Punishment itself will rarely prevent his recidivism, but a suspended sentence or lengthy probation, even a limited prison term for a repeated and uncooperative offender, seems to make subsequent treatment efforts distinctly more effective.

The minimal goal of therapeutic management is to enable the patient at first to withstand and eventually to remain unaffected by any welling-up of anxious-aggressive tension. Although exhibitionism is the presenting complaint, it need be discussed only infrequently with the patient. These men are well aware that a social peril is hanging over their heads. Regular recreational and social interests need to be encouraged, especially if he tends to isolate himself from social fellowship. In view of what is at stake the physician need not hesitate to advise major occupational changes where indicated. The patient should not be allowed avoidable opportunities to roam or loiter. It is best to restrict or discourage alcohol consumption. If necessary, use of an automobile, unless accompanied by another person, may be minimized.

The married exhibitionist requires the active and sympathetic moral support of his wife; the outcome of treatment efforts becomes rather dubious where the physician cannot enlist this. The vita sexualis often requires attention, and everything should be done to improve it. On the other hand, the mothers of these men are frequently more hindrance than help. It has even been suggested that, where necessary, the help of the court be invoked to enforce separation of an (unmarried) patient from his mother as a prerequisite for treatment. Sometimes nothing can persuade such a woman to believe that her son is disordered.

Other treatment modalities of compulsive exhibitionism which have proven valuable include group psychotherapy, and acting-out by the psychodrama method if expertly supervised. Claims of cure by hypnosis may need additional follow-up confirmation. This holds equally true for behavior-modifying (e.g., aversion) therapy. Psychoanalytic therapy has accomplished long remissions in some cases. Treatment, largely medicinal, perhaps surgical, directed at a possible underlying temporal lobe disease origin, is being explored.

PEDOPHILIA

Related:
The Child as Victim of Sexual Aggression p. 55
Father-Daughter Incest p. 61
Recrudescence in Elderly Men p. 434
Teen-age Child Molesting p. 152

Pedophilia is a collective term for any type of abnormal erotic interest in a child on the part of an adult, whether in the nature of infatuation, molestation or sexual abuse. The victims, male or female, with a few exceptions (see below) are of prepuberal age. Adolescents are pedophilic perpetrators if the age difference exceeds 10 (some say 5) years. As true compulsive deviance the condition probably occurs only in men. Among women with marked sexual interest in immature boys there is a prevalence of impulse-ridden, somewhat sadistic psychopathic personalities. Incestoid mothers resorting to quasi-seduction of a young son have various psychopathology but are not compulsively pedophilic. Mere non-exclusive erotic dalliance of adult women with young boys is, by tradition, not included. Much overlapping of personality disorders, motives and mental mechanisms is found among the abusers of children; it would be a dangerous oversimplification to regard all of them simply as timid souls whose inadequacy in coping with the complexities of adult relationships has led them to escape into this simpler type of intimacy.

Compulsive Heterosexual Pedophilia (nymphophilia), the prototype in this group of aberrations, is a chronic, seemingly irrepressible disorder of men resulting in undesirable sexual behavior towards little girls, most of them 7 to 10 (range 6 to 12) years of age. Although not as potentially destructive (murderous, etc.) as the brain-arteriosclerotic or the fetishistic child abuser, this is essentially an aggressive pursuer of immature girls who is compellingly driven by an inner tensional urge. As a rule he is body-fixated and untender. His abnormal activities may range from simple fondling or jocular spanking of little girls to periodic rape attempts. He may have a favorite, perhaps a neighbor's child or a relative whom he fondles or otherwise molests, or even seduces, with some regularity; or he may seek out victims in suitable localities. His interest may be centered on the child's buttocks, or on enticing her to expose herself or to view pornographic material, or to manipulate his organ.

GLOSSARY (PEDOPHILIA)

Pedophilia	A collective term for any erotic interest of an adult (or older adolescent) in a child. May be a compulsive aberration with homo- and heteroerotic subvariants, or a symptom of a more general personality disorder. A criminal offense everywhere.
Pederasty	Originally anal coitus of an adult man with a boy, but term has been applied to any adult rectal immission and other sex activities; its use is best avoided by the physician.
Pedicatio	Antiquated medical term for any sexual penetration of a child, but doubtfully also anal connection of any two individuals.
Buggery	Any anal coitus or bestialism (q.v.).
Sodomy (see also p. 211)	Collective non-medical term for every kind of "unnatural" sex activity—oral, anal, animal, children, homosexual, extramarital, adulterous, etc. The term is archaic but still being used in some jurisdictions.
Carnal Abuse (of a female child)	Any "indecent" (erotic) practice or contact with a child's genital organs; some include any erogenous body part.
Additional Information:	Karpman, B.: The Sexual Offender and His Offenses, New York, Julian Press, 1954, pp. 14 ff, 462 Kinsey, A. C. et al.: Sexual Behavior in the Human Female, Philadelphia, Saunders Co., 1953, pp. 370, 508, footnote; p. 262

His general sexual adjustment is rarely good. He has little capacity for fondness for women, is infrequently married, and sexually not very adequate if he is; or he may even be impotent in heterosexual relations. Most have been known to masturbate a great deal, with a prevalence of active or passive girl-fondling, etc., fantasies. Drinking in this group is not usually excessive (disputed; Peters, Swanson, others). Following treatment and/or incarceration the rate of recidivism is high.

Homoerotic Pedophilia. The typical compulsive lover of small boys is not a homosexual; he is probably incapable of being aroused by an adult male. He usually has difficulties in relating to women, yet he may be capable of great fondness for some of them. He may or may not be married and have children of his own. He is rarely impotent in heterosexual relations, although his libido may not be pronounced. These men often appear vastly attached to themselves (narcissism) or rather to their own childhood image of themselves. They may repeatedly shave all their pubic hair, admire or kiss their mirror image, or enjoy masturbating in front of a mirror. Most masturbate a great deal.

The milder case is more comfortable in the company of children, especially boys, than with anyone else. He often has a very winning way with them; some are successful teachers, etc., in institutions or schools for boys. Yet he may be constantly aware of a subdued erotic tension, a readiness to be enamored. In the more severe cases he may be fascinated, almost obsessed, with the sight of little boys, especially if nude; sometimes he can barely tear himself away from looking at their little organs. He may feel overcome or he may feel a strong impulsion "just to touch." The child's penis becomes a fetish and the hunt for it may assume a driven quality. In a few the urge may be directed more crudely at engaging in immediate sex with the child.

Some are veritably in love, now with one boy, now with another, or perhaps with one favorite for years. He behaves as a combination playmate, older brother and a lover with his girl. When aroused he may behave in an uncautious, even reckless manner; when enamored he merely hopes that no one will suspect anything wrong in a young man spending so much time with a young boy, secluding himself with him, perhaps arranging to have him share his room at night. Sex most often consists of mutual masturbation, although not all of them take physical liberties. An occasional one may abuse a male infant as young as 6 months of age, but these are apparently brief and passing episodes.

These patients are aware that their urges are improper and dangerous, and they struggle against them. Unlike compulsive exhibitionists, for instance, frequently they seem willing to accept treatment in private. On the basis of limited data, the condition sometimes seems to abate spontaneously before the patient reaches middle age.

Ephebophilia (Greek, Hellenic, Dorian love). The sex objects here are boys near puberty. The offenders usually are dominant and virile, but often highly sensitive and refined individuals. As a group they appear to be emotionally more mature than the homoerotic child lover. Next to this idiopathic group there is also a symptomatic type of ephebophiliac, mostly multiperverse psychopaths, often markedly depraved and lascivious individuals. Ephebophilia is no longer recognized as a distinct clinical entity, but—quite often probably wrongly so—is grouped as homosexuality by many observers (see also The Teen-Age Male Prostitute, p. 153). In several cultures of antiquity ephebophilia was part of Plato's idealistic concept of kalon k'agathon (the good and the beautiful; a romantic cult of the beautiful young boy); in our society, unless ascetic and sublimely motivated, this is a dangerous and often intractable perverter of vulnerable boys of early adolescent age. In turn, their capacity for exquisitely painful suffering over unrequited love, in a quest with no possible happy ending in our culture, has led more sensitive afflictees among them to suicide or serious suicidal attempts than any other type of sexual deviate, with the probable exception of male transsexuals (q.v.).

Symptomatic Pedophilia. Here one encounters a variety of disordered individuals who at one time or another—a few chronically—resort to the sexual abuse of children. A frequent offender is the labile psychopath with defective impulse control. His overtness may date from adolescence, but others do not seem to become actively offensive until well into adult life. Most characteristically, he is a sexual opportunist. A combination of tempting circumstances can "give him an idea" which he then translates into action with more or less sophistication or aggressiveness. The mere fact that children congregate within his reach can arouse his erotic interest. Some pedophiliacs are mentally ill, such as the unrecognized schizophrenic who is commanded by voices to torment children (Wertham, others), or who impulsively acts out his distorted incest fantasies. The patient, in a state of subacute manic excitement, seemingly jolly, affable, fond of children, may make a child sit on his lap, feel suddenly stimulated and—temporarily incapable of impulse control—may abuse the child. Socially undeveloped retardates loom large in institutional surveys of convicted child abusers (e.g., 25 per cent in one large series—Gebhard-Gagnon) because they are vulnerable to detection. Both chronic alcoholics and pathological drinkers are capable of importuning or assaulting children, possibly because they are latent pedophiliacs. Many types of organic brain disorder—postencephalitic, post-traumatic, arteriosclerotic, Korsakoff's, general paresis—have been known to produce sex-offensive behavior against children; here the disintegration of the moral and social impulse barriers (deteriorated ego control) plays a major part. Epileptic automatism and, possibly, postictal confusion can lead to assault on a child. Hypogonadic men have been known to manifest pedophilic behavior, but neither psychogenic impotence nor adult castration have induced this type of reaction.

SEXUAL MASOCHISM AND SADISM. SEX KILLING. NECROPHILIA

Sexual Masochism

The sexual masochist obtains gratification if he is hurt or humiliated by the partner as part of the ritualized activities. The deviation owes its name to L. von Sacher-Masoch (1836–1895), an Austrian writer who was himself afflicted with this tendency and whose novels (*Venus in Fur,* etc.) deal with the submission of men to cruel and domineering women. The true masochistic deviate is not altogether a passive recipient of pain; he actively schemes, arranges and induces his own humiliation, and he may prescribe the exact degree of physical and psychic suffering he desires. In fact, any painful or humiliating experience imposed on him impersonally, or against his wishes, is unpleasant and mortifying to him: one would not expect the typical masochist to look forward to the dentist's drill unless, if homosexual, he has assigned a sexualized and castigating fantasy role to the doctor, as has happened.

SADOMASOCHISM

The modern contracted usage of the double term has given rise to some confusion. In individuals with attenuated variants of either deviation—the moral masochist and the sadistic character with perversion-tinged sexuality—roles are often interchangeable. Not so in the true deviate. The severe sexual sadist cannot, under any circumstances, tolerate that he himself be used as recipient for pain and humiliation and is plainly revolted at the mere thought; this is inversely true of the sexual masochist. Also, the so-called sadomasochistic pair have rarely, if ever, both been known to be true deviates of opposite type; a true sadist and a true masochist would not fulfill each other's needs.

Criteria for differentiating the full-fledged sadistic deviate: degradation, pain and torture, and the mate's visible reaction to them are the chief sex aims, ends in themselves rather than an enhancing device; sexual gratification is unsought or impossible without such inflicting; and genuine objections or implorations to desist by the mate make the sadist lose interest (disputed); the sadistic psychopath, by contrast, becomes merely more cruel.

Our incomplete understanding of the reciprocal nature of the pain-pleasure mechanism is illustrated by the phenomenon of autosadism, those who turn sadism upon themselves yet are not true masochists; various self-slashers, self-scarifiers, self-flagellators (except cultists) and self-torturers, as far as they are not psychotic or acting in a state of epileptoid automatism.

The Compulsive Masochist is chronically, or recurrently, obsessed with reproducing the one situation that will give him a sense of relief. He seeks not voluptuous genital gratification but relief from a tense urge which impels him to humiliate or debase himself before a sex partner, or to be punished for imaginary misdeeds. The play-acting at most encounters begins with abject begging for kindness, for forgiveness and love. He thereby seems to reenact, in distorted and sexualized form, a complex deprivation trauma of his earliest years. These men are stereotyped and ritualistic about the type of gratification they desire, although they lack the cold and methodical approach to pleasure of sadistic deviates. Some obtain satisfaction from merely exchanging letters with platonic or prospective mistresses or masters in which all manner of humiliating or tantalizing situations are depicted. Or he may return, month after month, to the same prostitute to have himself tied hand and foot, insulted, flagellated, briefly strangulated, or humiliated in some fashion, and then go home relieved and satisfied.

His tense urge may be appeased even when no ejaculation takes place, although he may masturbate or, in some cases, have a spontaneous ejaculation while masochistically enthralled. If he cohabitates with his domineering mistress, it may represent merely another satisfying penalty, a service imposed by her. With all this often he is fairly potent in ordinary sex relations (e.g., with his wife); but intercourse cannot, for long, relieve his underlying craving. In some cases the compulsive masochistic tendency remains latent during the first 4 or 5 decades of life and is mobilized into overtness only by a middle-age crisis (p. 327).

Symptomatic Sexual Masochism differs somewhat from the true compulsive deviation. This type of masochist desires to be hurt or humiliated in order to be aroused sexually. He will not regard his evening of perversities a success unless he has been able to wind up with coitus or similar orgasmic release. His perverse practices, perhaps notably the pain, constitute a sexual enabling device, and he may be impotent without them. A few may yearn to be whipped (flagellated) into a frenzy which will allow them to unloose their sexual impetus, or perhaps their latent cruelty and sadism. These individuals, characteristically, possess both masochistic and sadistic potentialities and occasionally may revert from one to the other (sadomasochism; see also p. 476). Symptomatic masochism is encountered in some impulse-disordered, multiperverse psychopaths, in some cerebral arteriosclerotics and in certain surfeit-prone, basically immature (puerile, arrested) personalities.

Moral Masochism. For the present, sexual is probably best distinguished from psychic or moral masochism and from the masochistic character: individuals who chronically seem to manage to invite maltreatment, defeats, refusals, hardship and martyrdom and who appear to have an exaggerated need to suffer or to be used as the objects of aggression generally. Subconsciously this individual conceives of himself as a despicable failure; he is convinced that he deserves to suffer and he manages much of the time not to get out of harm's way. A sublimated form of sexual masochism in men occurs where a man's love for an unloving, perhaps cruel and exploiting woman becomes more ardently devoted the more she rejects and humiliates him. One needs to be careful to exclude men who are merely passive in their personalities and/or in the conduct of their sexual relations; or couples where an active or generally domineering woman also seems to direct and control the vita sexualis.

Female Sexual Masochism in many ways does not resemble the male's.

Mild, symbolic forms—habitual submissionism, ostensible desire to be hurt during coitus, rape fantasies, pseudocravings for rape—are difficult to separate from hysteroid desires and should not be called masochistic. The female flagellomaniac (i.e., the woman who cannot find sexual gratification without first being beaten or whipped) most often was specifically taught the pleasures of pain by a former lover, perhaps her first. Typically, there was initial reluctance or distaste, then gradual habituation, and eventually sexual dependence on the practice and the pain.

Sexual Sadism

The sexual sadist derives specific erotic pleasure from debasing, tormenting or hurting the partner. The term derives from the Marquis de Sade (1740–1814), a novelist (*Justine; Juliette; Les Crimes de L'Amour; Les 120 Journées de Sodome*), himself afflicted with this anomaly. In its pure form sexual sadism is less often encountered than masochism, but the attenuated variants, including sadomasochism, are fairly frequent.

The true compulsive sadist seems to be impelled, chronically or periodically, to act out his distorted, partially sexualized power strivings; his most satisfying reaction comes from observing his subject's pain, fear or

THE S-M (ALSO S-AND-M, "SLAVE AND MASTER") SCENE

The elaborate torture racks installed in expensive continental brothels mostly belong to another era; today's sadomasochistic equipment is more of a portable nature. In the U.S. until quite recently ordinary beatings, knife cutting, cigarette burns, and most of all, rope-tying constituted the usual resorts; possibly due to the influence of the international cosmopolitanism of certain traveling homosexual sets, refinements in the gadgetry of the perverse are increasingly being introduced.

What the run-of-the-mill hard-core porn magazines and books describe and picture—the boots, spur, spike heel, chain and whip variety of cruelty, or icy women astride motorcycles—is mostly directed at the juvenile mind experimenting autoerotically or otherwise with escalated lechery. It is dangerous to the most labile among them (see p. 137), but it is not genuine B and D (bondage and discipline). Correspondence clubs and privately circulated magazines and news sheets featuring exchange ads cater to the true cognoscenti, the "kinky" or "freaky" crowd which is the dread of inexperienced or non-specializing prostitutes. Enemas, "animal training," handcuffs, paddles, leg irons, rawhide remain the proffered staple activities; all acceptable as long as no marks are left on the body.

Leather is the currently preferred symbol, from motorcyclist get-ups to fantasies of nail-studded leather brassieres. In large cities leather bars and taverns cater to sadomasochists—sadists are among the most gregarious of all deviates—but they are losing their exclusivity to homosexuals who are into leather costuming.

debasement. He often obtains his grim satisfaction even when the whole procedure is only an act—the victim's (usually a prostitute) suffering simulated and paid for. He is methodical and stereotyped rather than impulsive in his abnormal gratifications and his choice of method. De Sade himself meticulously catalogued 600 varieties of inflicting pain, in a tediously pedantic fashion. If he resorts to beating, for instance, the compulsive sadist was—and occasionally still is—the owner of a collection of whips or birch rods of finely graduated sizes, although some of these men may be merely pathologic collectors of torture instruments (i.e., they are primarily fetishists, q.v.). It is fairly certain that the true sadist does not like women and cannot love them in any normal way, although he is capable of adequate heterosexual intercourse. He probably is not capable of true warmth in any human relationship, yet there is no reason to assume that he will be cruel in all of his everyday actions. In the homosexual sadist the morbid traits are more pronounced, and some observers have felt that these patients are often especially difficult and potentially dangerous.

Variants of Sadism. Sexual sadism needs to be distinguished from the more general moral (or psychic) sadism, and from Horney's sadistic character with his intense and unceasing need to discharge aggression against the environment. "Sexual sadism," said Freud, "is present only where sexual satisfaction is completely conditioned on the humiliation and maltreatment of the object." Some moral sadists are also sexual sadists, but the reverse has less often been found to be true. Since aggression normally is associated more closely with male attitudes than sufferance, the physician's diagnostic task is more difficult in sadism than in masochism (i.e., one cannot always recognize with certainty where crude normality ends and aberration begins).

A tendency to degrade, tantalize, humiliate or subdue a spouse as part of day-to-day behavior does not necessarily characterize the sexual sadist, while the same mechanism enacted as part of a sexual scene is highly characteristic. Symptomatic sadism (i.e., sadistic traits) can be associated with such divers conditions as organic brain disease, psychopathic personality, a variety of mental diseases. One may suspect the presence of latent sadism if a man is chiefly, or exclusively, attracted to deformed, disfigured, crippled or otherwise impaired women; is aroused sexually by women who are markedly ungainly, frankly old or dirty, or engaged in menial or dirty work; or if a cultured man becomes greatly interested in a girl who is conspicuously illiterate or dim-witted. It is theorized that these women become attractive because of the relatively debased position in which they are found or fantasied. This is made more plausible by observations that overt sadists derive coital satisfaction either from simulated rape (woman bound hand and foot), or with the woman masquerading as a corpse, this being the summit of debased defenselessness (symbolic necrophilia). The mere reading or picture viewing of beatings, executions, crucifixions, torture scenes, etc., may cause some sadists intense sexual arousal, even to the point of ejaculating.

Necrosadism; Other Sex Killing; Necrophilia

The severest degree of sadism is necrosadism or lust murder. It differs from ordinary sex or rape killing and probably from merely brutal homicide, as well as from the thrill killing of the psychopath diverting himself.

The true sadistic killer acts to satisfy a specific urge which is not chiefly, sometimes even not at all, genital. He is not interested primarily in obtaining coital gratification from his victim, but in inflicting pain, torture or cruel injury on her (him) in connection with an erotic situation. For days, weeks or months preceding the deed he has a mounting sense of internal tension, an anticipatory void, perhaps a feeling of drivenness, which impels him to seek his kind of relief. During this prodromal phase he anticipates, visualizes and often plans for the deed, although he knows right from wrong. As often as not he is married, and usually he is not sex-starved; in fact, he may be very active sexually in various ways, yet such activities only very briefly relieve his tense urge. Nor is he surfeited with other kinds of sex, as may be the case in the totally amoral, multisexual psychopath, the sexual *thrill killer,* who is diversion-bound, or experiments, in a horrible manner.

In his personality the necrosadist is affect-cold and essentially egotistic, which does not exclude that he may be a weepy sentimentalist. Some are surly, secretive or bizarre; others are pleasant-mannered, affable and good talkers (e.g., De River's youthful "sadist raffiné"). As a rule, he is of normal intelligence.

In his deed he seems to act out his obsessional distorted power strivings, perhaps his unconscious rage against women. He is greatly excited as he tortures the victim, as she (he) becomes increasingly defenseless, as he watches her suffer or beg for her life; he may abuse her sexually or merely masturbate at this point. He may become aroused maximally when he sees her, in death, absolutely defenseless and debased. In his fantasy the victim's body can still suffer pain and humiliation, leading him to mutilate and/or sexually abuse the corpse *(necrostuprum).* Most gross mutilations (evisceration, etc.) in these cases are inflicted after the victim's death. Arousal of oral-sadistic impulses may lead to biting or even to devouring a nipple or other part of her *(sexual necrophagia* or *cannibalism, perversio horribilis).* A sexualized obsessional urge to "force something very tight" may have fixated his urge on a child victim because of its immature introitus or small anus. One cannot say with certainty if actual killing is necessarily part of the pathologic urge; from what some lust murderers have indicated, it may not always be. After the deed, relieved of his tension, he usually sleeps and eats well. He may collect newspaper clippings of the occurrence. He has no true remorse, although he may grieve over the victim in a sentimental, sometimes theatrical fashion. If not apprehended he is apt to be a recidivist; his type of victim, approach and mutilations tend to be the same or similar each time.

The *latent necrosadist* starts out committing, for instance, ordinary robbery, or a simple sexual assault. Latent sadistic urges are mobilized as he grapples with the victim, perhaps for her purse, perhaps to overcome her sexual resistance; or as he sees her helpless in his power, perhaps squirming, or begging for her life, or suffering pain. His excitement mounts, he becomes increasingly cruel, draws blood or mutilates. If she has fainted, or if he has killed her accidentally or in a rage, or for purposes of concealment, his excitement becomes maximal, even though he may have ejaculated already. Necrostuprum, evisceration or necrophagia may occur at this point.

Rape killing occurs when the aggressor becomes frightened following rape of a woman, or abuse of a child, and kills in a state of panic. Or a destructive, blindly annihilating rage may set in against the victim who unwittingly aroused his painful doubt of being sexually adequate and masculine. Others—notably the individual with organic brain disease, the amoral psychopath, perhaps the ambulatory schizophrenic—may callously "destroy the evidence" following simple sexual assault. The epileptoid may explode into homicidal rage if he is unable to effect penile immission when attempting rape. Impulsive or affect homicide—some of it extremely gory—may occur in connection with a sex and drinking orgy, notably by homosexuals; a jealous rage is only one of the possible affects which underlie the homicidal furor on these occasions. In brutalized mentally retarded men a homicidal crime may give the appearance of necrosadism. A woman resists or screams; the aggressor in panic or in a rage, or merely by using disproportionate force, may kill her. Finally, in frustration and rage at her staying lifeless he may slash at, tear and generally maim the body. He may run into hiding, but his fear of consequences tends to be dissipated in less than 48 hours.

It is not certain if true compulsive necrosadism occurs in *women*. Certain cases of brutal child murder and infanticide are described sometimes as sadistic because of the brutality and the manner of death inflicted, but most of these would seem to be "affect killings" or the work of feeble-minded, epileptoid or schizophrenic women. Some habitual, apparently motiveless poisoners have been called sadistic killers. Perhaps closest come the brutal injuries sometimes inflicted by a lesbian affect murderess on the body of her erstwhile woman lover.

Necrophilia differs from necrosadism in that abnormal erotic interest is centered on the woman (rarely child or man) already dead. This is the lover of corpses who either disinters them for his purposes, or steals into a funeral parlor, or even finds employment there or in a similar establishment. At one time almost all of these men were thought to be either psychotic, mentally retarded or suffering from epileptic automatism as well as deprived of other sexual resort. More recently an increasing number of cases has been coming to light in which the perpetrators were neither, but seemed to be afflicted with a deviation sui generis. These men may cohabitate with the dead (perhaps least often), or preserve parts of the anatomy (e.g., shrink the head, work skin into parchment or "leather" used in various objects), or "just keep them around to look at," or commit sadistic acts or practice cannibalism on them. Some necrophiliacs have been found to have committed some killings for necrophilic purposes themselves, and the condition is no longer considered as inoffensive as previously thought.

FETISHISM

In this deviation the sexual object is not another person, but a symbol, or fetish.

Compulsive Fetishism, a condition encountered almost exclusively in males, is a fairly rare and malignant perversion in which the libido is fixated on an inanimate object, to the exclusion of other sexual interests. The object, or fetish, is related in some way to the attire or body of women or children. The most frequent objects of the compulsive fetishistic deviate are shoes, stockings, gloves, undergarments, preferably permeated with a specific body odor, and perhaps hair. His need is usually for possession; he is an inexhaustible collector of his kind of fetish; and he may keep books punctiliously about the date and the origin of his acquisitions. Periodically, he looks at, fondles, manipulates, smells or kisses his objects, and these secret "orgies" may suffice to gratify him. Some have spontaneous ejaculation during this activity; others masturbate. Their easy sexual arousability has been noted whenever the fetish object, or merely its image is involved; also observable in a proportion of cases is the promptness with which any sexual arousal leads to climactic ejaculation. Compulsive fetishists seem to harbor a more or less pronounced sadistic component; their masturbation fantasies are frequently of a sadistic nature.

The compulsive fetishist probably goes through paroxysms of prodromal tension during which he feels an irresistible urge to get hold of some specimen of his type. The urge appears to have such compelling qualities that it can resemble the craving of the addict. In fact, cases of coexisting abnormal paroxysmal temporal lobe function have led to newer postulations of a link to an organic brain syndrome. More often, however, the urge is precipitated by the sight of his object which carries the deviate to strong sexual excitement, and he becomes obsessed with the desire to possess it or at least to fondle or smell it.

It is this urge, together with his sadistic component, which makes the compulsive fetishist a relatively antisocial or even dangerous deviate. He seems to get little satisfaction from purchasing store-new objects, although second-hand articles may do, if obtainable. He may pilfer from a clothes-line or burglarize a residence where he suspects or has observed—or may have followed—a woman (child) with the desired object. It is possible that the bodily presence of the fetish may excite him to commit rape, if the situation is opportune. A number of sex killings, perhaps more often of children, have been committed by fetishists; they kill in panic or from fear of discovery.

Symptomatic Fetishism is the presence of—usually more benign—fetishistic symptoms in other types of sex- and personality-disordered individuals. In these men not only inanimate objects but also parts of the human anatomy can assume the role of fetish (*partialism,* from pars pro toto; may include *sexual toucherism,* p. 494). The most frequent objects of the partialist are buttocks. The symptomatic fetishist is abnormal in that he is not attracted to a woman through her parts, but loves the part. However, unlike the compulsive fetishists, they are not irresistibly impelled to possess their object, and some are capable of, and interested in, other modes of sex activity, as long as the fetish is brought into the picture in some way. Here it acts as a stabilizer or reinforcer for genital functioning (Greenacre); in practice they tend to be impotent with the woman (wife) unless, for instance, she cooperates in his ritual and wears the garment fetish, etc., on which the patient then concentrates his imagery.

It is in this group that occasionally one encounters men with incomplete or even eunuchoidal sexual development, which does not appear to be the case in the compulsive fetishist.

At times fetishism merges with cases of primary transvestism, masochism or sadism. It does not constitute fetishism when certain objects produce sexual arousal by thought or sense association (e.g., when a girl's perfumed handkerchief in the possession of a male produces erotic desire in him each time he draws it out). Nor is it fetishism when a man strongly prefers, for instance, women with a certain type of bust, buttocks, hands, feet, hair, nose or, perhaps, odor (Binet's *petit fétichisme*). Many adolescent boys who are infatuated appreciate the girl in a rather partialistic fashion; this is normal.

The Cause or constellation of causes of compulsive fetishism remains unknown, although many theories have sought to explain it. There is fairly wide agreement that the morbid conditioning (misnamed "choice of the fetish") takes place in childhood. It is possible that it goes back to a fixation point during the vulnerable second year of life involving such factors as an inordinately intense parent-child struggle over control of the bowel excrement, intense attachment to a security blanket or stuffed animal, and an erotization of the sense of smell. An unconscious defense against (i.e., an attempt to overcome) mutilation anxiety has been variously suggested as a meaningful factor. In some cases the actions of a seductive, incestoid mother (p. 74) play a part in introducing the fetish into the boy's instinct pattern. The theory of arbitrary coincidence (e.g., a boy first sexually excited in some connection with a leather glove becomes a glove fetishist) has been largely discarded as a cause of compulsive fetishism, although it may play a part in some symptomatic variants. A relationship to the category of the reflex epilepsies has been postulated, especially as regards the fetishist's semi-automatic sexual arousal upon presentation of the fetish object (Epstein).

The Prognosis of the severe compulsive fetishist is not good, especially among those who forego human partners for sexual gratification; a number seem to progress into chronic mental illness. In milder cases symptom remissions may be accomplished by means of psychotherapy including behavior therapy, but true cures have not been claimed. In a number of cases of symptomatic fetishism spontaneous remissions have occurred.

TRANSVESTISM

(Transvestitism, Compulsive [Primary, Fetishistic] Cross-dressing)

Transvestism is the morbid, usually intermittent desire to put on the clothes of the opposite sex. It is a sexual deviation sui generis, with onset most often in the teens, and occurs prevalently (some say, only) in males. It is essentially unrelated to homosexuality, and transvestites tend to resent the inference that they have homosexual tendencies. In some cases symptoms merge with those of transsexualism (q.v.), and the delineation between the two appears to be less clear-cut than some observers will have it. The milder case of transvestism does not come easily to medical or any other professional attention, and it has rarely been included in the reports from clinics now specializing in transgender research. Transvestism is closely related to fetishism (q.v.); in fact, one name recently suggested for the deviation is intermittent cross-gender dress fetishism. A symptomatic type of cross-dressing is encountered in effeminate homosexuals (drag queen) and mannish lesbians (drag dyke). Sporadic cross-dressing occurs in many normal children (see p. 80).

The average compulsive transvestite, to all appearances, is leading a normal life. Often he is married, has children, and is a good family man and provider. He may seem moody, and in some cases he drinks too much. His vita sexualis is adequate, but his libidinal interest is lukewarm.

Occasionally—perhaps once a week, perhaps only a few times a year—his inner tension mounts until it seems to be no longer bearable. If he cannot relieve it by drinking himself into a stupor—milder degrees of intoxication may only increase his urge or make him incautious—he may contrive to send his family away for an evening or a Sunday. He then dresses in his wife's clothes, either a few specific articles—panties, bra, hose or/and shoes—or in one of everything, from underthings and shoes up; or he may bring a complete outfit of his own from hiding, perhaps a gown and wig, or a ballet costume. Often he adds heavy make-up. He may sit quietly enjoying the feeling of exhilaration, or he stands or parades before a mirror, sometimes for hours. His sexual excitement leads him to masturbate, occasionally more than once. Some men afflicted with transvestism have used their offices after hours, dressing up in clothes they kept locked away there. One man kept a rented room for the purpose; two others, both married, visited their aging parents' apartments where they had use of their boyhood rooms.

Some transvestites remain sensitized to a few or one particular article of female attire for many years (no lifelong follow-ups are available); sometimes use of such fetish-like objects is limited to enabling them to have marital intercourse, either by being worn (see also p. 483) or by fantasizing them. The moment when a phallus emerges from under the skirt is a high point—both in marital play-acting and in fantasy. In others the pattern expands progressively until complete feminine cross-dress is achieved and he then may start venturing out of the house. He may go out for a walk, neither seeking nor avoiding the notice of passers-by. Unlike the homosexual transvestite, he neither flounces nor is obvious. He is happiest when he is "just naturally taken for a woman." Some feel equally contented when no one at all sees them (e.g., at night). Some wear cross-dress among good friends, men and women who tolerantly disregard their foible. Some like to visit relatives, stores, perhaps their dentist in cross-dress "as a lark," giving a female name and being delighted at not being recognized immediately, or at the others' astonishment. Some have been known to carry a picture of themselves in female garb and obtain a sense of pleasure from looking at it from time to time. Some find substitute and compromise outlets; they may wear female underwear or masculine underwear made of female-type fabric. Some say they are content because their work permits them to wear a smock or apron over their men's trousers. A few work on the variety stage as female impersonators, although they share this métier with other types of transgender deviates. But at all times the compulsive transvestite remains a male, derives sexual gratification through use of his penis and wishes to remain a male.

The Cause of transvestism remains uncertain. Malconditioning in early childhood undoubtedly plays a major part, making this essentially a derailment on the boy's track to complete, unequivocal masculine identity. In more than half the cases there is a history of having been forced into female dress by the mother or other female as punishment on at least one occasion. However, one must not overestimate the psychologic impact of such one-shot events in childhood, nor underestimate the possibility of the child himself cluing his environment to this particular mode of intrusion. Psychoanalytic formulations, most centering around castration anxiety, have been attempted, but have contributed remarkably little to the management of compulsive transvestism. Some hypogonads (e.g., males with Klinefelter's syndrome, q.v.), manifest transvestic traits. A connection with temporal lobe disease, similarly to fetishism, has been postulated, although relatively few cases with this combination have come to notice.

Treatment. These patients are rarely motivated to undergo treatment; they may give psychotherapy a minimal try in the early years of overtness or when compelled by a court (public cross-dressing by males is an offense in most jurisdictions), but they do not persist. Improvement of the condition has been obtained with various psychiatric techniques, but cures have not been proven. Aversion therapy, the counter-conditioning type of behavior therapy, is probably applicable.

TRANSSEXUALISM

(Transsexuality)

This is a condition of lifelong identification with the opposite sex in biologically normal individuals, with complete mental repudiation of their gender role of birth and rearing, and a consuming urge to cross over and change sex. It is a disorder of men and, occasionally, of women. It is perhaps less of an actual sexual deviation than the other syndromes in this chapter because erotic gratification is not a foreground problem here. Although the condition is fairly rare, it has received a great deal of medical and public attention, partly because its afflictees are the most verbal, not to say vociferous sufferers in the field of sexual pathology, demanding help noisily, persistently and sometimes dramatically; partly because the only known palliative treatment—combined hormonal and surgical sex reassignment—has raised numerous ethical, legal and philosophic questions of general interest; and partly because the etiology of this disorder is of theoretical interest for the study of basic gender biology and psychology, a burning issue in our time.

Clinical Picture. The transsexual is repelled by his own masculinity and may loathe everything that reminds him of it—his genitalia, his voice, his clothes, his work or his name. Most believe that they are women who by some incredible error were given the bodies of men; they are firmly convinced that they are the "victims of a cruel fate," a "joke of nature." Such a patient will resist strenuously any organic or psychiatric attempt to restore his masculine identity, but he will try anything that holds out the faintest hope of producing an appearance in conformity with his "real self." He may canvass physicians, hospitals or clinics about conversion operations; surgeons known to have performed sex-changing surgery have found their mail swelled with requests for help from many parts of the world, some, of course, by cross-dressing effeminate homosexuals, but many by desperately pleading transsexuals who may also employ pseudo-scientific reasoning, or even threats of suicide. These patients have turned to veterinarians and to abortionists with their requests for castration and a few, to force the surgeon's hand, have crudely amputated all or part of their organs.

Genetically, anatomically and physiologically the male transsexual is a man, although dysplastic and immaturity divergences—softness of skin texture, configuration of the features, scantiness of beard, or a slight measure of girdle-type obesity and genu valgum—are no rarity in them. However, if gynecomastia, perhaps darkened nipples, and un-malelike plasma and urinary hormone values are found, one may suspect prior self-administration of estrogen. The ones with the most feminoid habitus pass as females without difficulty; they learn to adjust mannerisms, motor coordination, make-up, etc., a process which is greatly aided by estrogen medication—best balanced by an androgenic supplement (e.g., mesterolone, a newer androsterone derivative—not in U.S.) which also allays much of these patients' tensional symptoms. They shave their body hair and go through long, costly debearding (electrolysis) procedures. However, they appear to have no genuine interest in child rearing and manifest no maternal traits. Surgically altered patients who were married and had fathered children have reportedly sometimes desired to keep these children but in a mother role; it does not work out and marital separation is necessary. Others have adopted children when they married a man postoperatively, but children probably serve them mostly as an additional badge of femininity.

Although in some cases transsexualism is indistinguishable from transvestism, there are some basic general differences in typical cases. The transsexual man, unlike the transvestite, obtains no erotic pleasure from wearing feminine clothing; he has always considered it his natural apparel, even though rarely permitted to wear it. When he cross-dresses it is not a masquerade or a disguise, but he perceives it as an expression of his true self (Walinder). In fact, in at least one transgender center the history of a single episode of cross-dressing in association with sexual arousal is sufficient to exclude the diagnosis of transsexualism (Baker). Unlike the transvestite he obtains no sexual pleasure through the use of his penis. His libido, as a rule, is not very pronounced, but in his masturbation fantasies and in wet dreams, if these patients' usually unreliable reports are to be believed, he senses himself as a female. A proportion marry and have children, but degrees of impotence are not rare. A number abstain because they consider sexual relations with a woman as a lesbian act. They may yearn for a male lover, not as a homosexual would, but as a natural object for their feminine desires. Others have male lovers, but they are often disappointed because often these men are latent or overt homosexuals who sooner or later evince an interest in the patient's penis. Normal men who would desire and love them as they would "any other female" appear to be rare. Other traits differentiating the transsexual from the compulsive trans-vestite are the much earlier (childhood) onset in the former; the ever-present nature of the abnormal urges versus their episodic recurrence in the cross-dresser and, according to a plausible theory, a difference in the history of the nature of the mother-infant relationship (see below). Socially, transvestites most often are well-settled members of society while transsexuals tend to social downdrift, are school drop-outs, have an un-satisfactory work record in about half the cases, and a general social instability directly attributable to their unsettled and unsettling transsexual status. An undetermined number, both pre- and postoperatively, work as female street and bar prostitutes (e.g., they fellate passersby or truckmen, using menstruation as an invented excuse for not coiting).

Causes. According to one plausible theory, from earliest infancy this beauteous, perhaps slightly feminine-responding (p. 80) baby boy stimu-lates the mother to feminize him, by total—symbiotic—intimacy, to an extreme degree. She discourages masculine behavior at every turn. She herself is a basically unfeminine, doleful, disappointed ex-tomboy (q.v.) whose gender-transformation longings were slowly given up in adolescence. The father does not protect the little boy nor introduce masculinity into his life, being the type of man which this type of woman is apt to have attracted to herself; or else, sooner or later, he desists in puzzled disap-pointment and anger at having whatever he has to offer consistently rejected by this contrary-oriented boy. Later, the environment (school, etc.) de-mands a degree of maleness from him. He tends to withdraw and become a loner among his peers, but embedded remnants of a sense of maleness, together with his basic sense of femaleness, create dual-gender awareness and a chronic feeling of unease, dissatisfaction and a sense of unreality which beclouds the judgment in a proportion of cases. He yearns to have the disturbing remembrance of maleness, the feebler of the two identities, excised. But even radical surgery (see below) apparently cannot eradicate it from his subconscious, judging from available dream and fantasy ma-terial in such men.

Another promising and perhaps interlocking postulation, even more difficult to prove in humans, considers transsexualism as an extragenital form of intersexuality (q.v.); derailing of the track to gender identity here would take place just before or after birth, with all body organs but the brain having been fully differentiated. The steroid-sensitive receptor cells in and near the median eminence of the hypothalamus and upper pituitary stalk which govern male-female releasor hormone cycling are bathed in a stress-altered, androgen-poor humoral mixture at the very time a brief critical period occurs during which they are permanently imprinted with their future type of pattern. As the basic brain is the female-patterned brain, masculine psychosexual differentiation cannot be expected to be complete in these cases, but the environment (mother, etc.) must then develop the deficit into a clinically overt gender fault. Another possibility is seen in the mechanism of competitive blocking: a pregnant woman who is given drugs—actinomycin D, pentobarbital, some phenothiazines, weak testosterone precursors—which compete with testosterone for the steroid receptor sites in the brain, would be endangering a male fetus by keeping his brain from being masculinized. The antiandrogens (cyproterone acetate, etc.), in animals, have been shown to cancel the fetal androgens; severe stressing of the mother has also produced steroids in laboratory animals which compete with testosterone for the fetal brain receptor sites.

Transsexualism in Females. These are biologically normal females— educated guesses at their number in the community vary widely—who show a progressive, uninterrupted identification with the activities, interests, mannerisms, dress and behavior of men (Pauly, Hoenig-Kenna, others). It is easier for them than for their male counterparts to live in the role of the opposite sex. Most known chronic female cross-dressers probably are mannish lesbians, but the female transsexual is only technically a homosexual. She does not desire a lesbian mate, but a normal woman she can love as a man would. However, in some cases the distinction appears to be quite tenuous. Female transsexuals request testosterone treatment, especially when they have fallen in love with a woman. They also desire sex surgery, but they are less insistent about it than males. The early intra-family dynamics in these cases are uncertain, although models of characteristic parent-infant triangles have been put forward.

Treatment. The transsexual doggedly wants his genitalia and appearance changed, and he expects his physician, any physician he consults, to aid him in this in the most complete way the state of the art permits. In mid-late childhood these severely feminized boys, if recognized, can perhaps still be treated successfully with psychotherapy as the feminine component of their bisexuality may not be as fixed as it is in the adolescent and adult transsexual (Stoller-Newman). Psychotherapy of the adult transsexual has not proven fruitful; it is also resisted by these patients who have no interest in having their minds masculinized.

Sex reassignment (transformation) surgery is done in a relatively small number of research-oriented hospitals and by a limited number of surgeons here and abroad. In the most careful programs it is preceded by a lengthy period (6 months to 2 years) of observation. The purpose is to eliminate psychotic individuals with delusions of sex change (no rarity), effeminate homosexuals, fetishistic transvestites and other unsuitable applicants; to test the patient's ability to pass and live as a member of the opposite sex (the more unmasculine, hypogonadal the man the better the chances); and to estrinize the organism, including gynecomastia, by prolonged hormone medication. Female patients receive testosterone. Surgery in male patients consists of castration (bilateral orchiectomy), penectomy, construction of a vagina-like perineal funnel lined anteriorly with penis skin treated as a pedicle flap, relocation of urethral meatus and reshaping of scrotal skin to resemble labia. The most sexually sensitive tissue remaining is a short portion of corpus spongiosum in the perineum which may act as an inverted clitoris (Meyer, Jones Jr.). The vaginal pocket must be kept open by daily usage, either coitally or with wooden or plastic forms. In female transsexuals surgery includes panhysterectomy, breast amputation and, if desired, construction of a phallus-like structure with an implanted splint. Functional results with respect to the genitalia have been unpredictable.

Results in operated patients have been reported as largely satisfactory, even good, but there is room for some doubt, including occasional over-optimistic case reporting. Legally and administratively these patients face a host of difficulties, including legalization, civil status, marriage, and concealment efforts involving insurance companies and alteration of documents. By and large, the procedure is very gradually establishing itself as a recognized method of medical palliation in a definable disorder. Homosexual labeling—their homosexuality is only technical, anyway—is inappropriate. Besides, such discriminatory labeling on the basis of deviance of life style alone is counter to the temper of the times. It would also be unfair and irrational not to treat these individuals as members of their newly adopted gender and deprive them of much of the effect of the palliation which they have bought so painfully.

VOYEURISM

(Scopophilia. Peeping or Peeping Tomism.
Mixoscopia when viewing others' coitus)

The term voyeurism, from the French *to see,* was coined by Coffignon who described certain men loitering in a Paris park to view erotically stimulating sights. As an occasional impulse, peeping is almost universal, potentially so probably in both sexes, although it is more manifest in men. In pubescence and adolescence peeping impulses are frequent. If such curiosity massively protracts itself into the late teens and beyond it constitutes an immaturity reaction. It is not voyeurism when an individual (e.g., a new bridegroom or bride) views the sex partner's body in detail as part of coital foreplay; nor when visual stimulation is derived from having intercourse under full illumination or even enhanced by mirror arrangements. Much voyeuristic interest would be expected to have been defused by the growing participation in various types of group sex (p. 456), but except for abreaction of latent homosexual urges this has not been the experience. Perhaps, as the hiding part, the thrill of the forbidden, the secret intrusion into unsuspecting privacy is removed from peeping, it loses much of its libidinal meaning.

Immaturity Reaction. The emotionally immature adult voyeur (voyeurist), the most frequent type, is the typical "opportunity peeper," reluctant to pass up a tempting sight, or looking for opportunities and, if it is fairly safe and convenient, scanning or loitering at length, waiting for "something to happen." Joking to friends he may make sport of his fondness for a certain "window with a view" or other favorite spot, but he anxiously looks forward to an evening, an hour, alone at home to train his binoculars undisturbed on the apartments opposite.

His erotic interest is in women. The more he is able to see or imagine the greater is his sexual excitement. He half imagines the woman might beckon him. If he happens to peep on coitus, his interest is focused on the woman; he identifies with neither of the partners but may fantasy himself making love to her. Many immaturity voyeurs are habitual masturbators. If married, his marital vita sexualis is apt to be as normal as the habitual masturbator's married sex life ever can be (see p. 431). They may come to medical attention when the wife or someone else has caught him peeping a few times and is worried. In the typical patient the symptomatology is rarely severe enough to require elaborate therapeutic management. Although these surfeit-prone men generally desire the women they spot, they do not come forward and contact or accost them because they are afraid, passive and inhibited socially. A voyeur who is sufficiently aggressive to resort additionally to solicitation-type of exhibitionism (q.v.) or possibly to frottage, can no longer be considered to belong to this socially inoffensive group of peeping Toms.

The Compulsive Voyeur is an obsessed or driven individual, a collector of observations who may even keep a record of what he sees, and when and where. He may be a roving deviate, a "maker of opportunities." He has "his" windows, his houses, his spot in the park, or his peepholes which he patrols with some system when the urge is upon him. He hides in bushes, crawls up fire escapes, loiters in certain places or may make his home in a "promising" hotel or rooming house, drilling ingenious holes into walls or knowing where such holes already exist. He may speak of observation posts or neighborhoods which are duds, of probables and of sure things.

He is aroused sexually by what he sees and may masturbate in the process, but there is little fantasy of direct contact with the victim, nor desire to come forward. An important component of the pleasure may result from latent sadism, deriving satisfaction from the fantasy that the victim is nakedly exposed to him, debased, without her armor of costume; that he could humiliate, frighten, terrorize or possibly rape her if he had a mind to. His gratification derives substantially from the fantasy that, unseen, he is inflicting punishment on the woman in undress for being in undress; he can be insatiable at this. He evidences sadistic potential by this attitude, and a few progress to aggressive sex offenses, although as a rule they do not.

Potentially Aggressive Voyeurs. Generally, voyeurism is a nuisance offense, although such patients sometimes expose themselves to social embarrassment, to being arrested as prowlers or loiterers, and to being beaten by irate householders or others. However, certain impulse-ridden psychopathic personalities and some brutalized mental retardates, to name a few, are opportunity exploiters who can translate mounting visual excitement into questing with various degrees of aggressiveness, or become fixated and are impelled to return to the peeping scene as they allow fantasied libidinal tension to build up. Here the voyeur of today can be the rapist of tomorrow. The compulsive peeper who "specializes" most likely is not primarily a voyeur but some other type of deviate pedophilic voyeurs who limit themselves to peeping on children must be judged individually as to their potential aggressiveness (see p. 475 and 440). Those who have interest only in observing women in the process of urination are usually masochists; their pleasurable fantasies revolve around urolagnic practices (p. 495). A number are homosexuals who prefer peepholes in men's lavatories.

ZOOPHILIA

(Zoophily, zoophilia erotica, zoophilic perversion, bestialism, bestiality, bestiosexuality. Animal copulation, zooerasty, zoostuprum—actual intromissive act. Also zoosadism, animal fetishism. Vernac. animal sex play or experimentation. Unsuitable: animal sodomy)

Erotic interest in, or sexual contact with, animals occurs at various ages, in various forms, and in a variety of mental states—from the normal youngster to men with overt schizophrenia; from the feeble-minded rural to the mundanely sophisticated multiperverse woman; from obsessive, perhaps humanizing infatuation to erotic dalliance; from simple copulation to the most cruel, perhaps bloody zoosadism. In many countries outside the Western culture sexual relations with animals are not legally prohibited (Lukianowicz). It is reportedly still a fairly frequent resort of normal but isolated men in mountainous and desert countries. In various cultures and during various eras attitudes toward animal copulation have ranged from toleration to imposition of the death penalty.

The earliest type observed is animal sex play of children and pubescents, the great majority boys. It rarely occurs before 8 years of age and is most frequent in boys who previously had not carried on sex play with other children. The animal most often is a smallish young male dog. The activity may occur only once or twice, a form of sex exploration, or a substitute form of the normal homoerotism of this phase. The act is typically one of masturbation, although it may end short of orgasm; the boy may masturbate the animal and himself, or simply rub his organ against the animal's side; or induce the animal to lambitus phalli; none of these modalities has pathologic significance as such. Boys who are unhappy, chronically tense emotionally, lonely, or bored may be involved more frequently and more protractedly. In essentially normal boys all such activity is outgrown, usually before puberty, although a few very shy and withdrawn boys may cling to it somewhat longer.

In the middle and later teens animal copulation by farm boys constitutes a form of "sex experimentation" and may be on the wane now. The animal here most likely is one of the larger females upon whom intromission may be attempted or performed: calves, ewes, mares. These boys are essentially normal. Where the experimentation is solitary, the activity usually is discontinued after a few attempts.

The majority of men charged (few are convicted) with overt zoophilic acts have been chronic alcoholics, or brain-disordered men under the influence of alcohol, or coarse farm- or stable-bound men of retarded mentality too inept to contact women socially, and some men in acute states of manic or schizophrenic excitement. Cruel or necrosadistic acts on smaller animals, accompanied or followed by masturbation, have been observed; these may not constitute zoophilia sensu stricto. Other cases of sexual abuse of animals by non-retarded, non-psychotic individuals are being reported from time to time (Shenken, Grassberger, Rappaport, others), but substantial other psychopathology was present in those cases, least probably in men who were occupationally involved with animals. Zoophilia as a true compulsive sexual deviation (i.e., a habitual and preferred sex aim) appears to be rare.

Substantial erotic reactions at the sight of racing horses—"sexy, sleek, sensuous, powerful"—or at the stroking of the fur of certain varieties of cats can occur in some women and men. Women have occasionally been known to condition small pet dogs to perform linctus vulvae on them as a form of masturbation. Submission of women other than performing prostitutes and porn artists to animal intromission, usually large dogs, has been reported by a number of observers. Some husbands have compelled their wives to submit to male animals, evidence of homosexual and/or sadistic traits in such men. Impregnation of a human female by an animal, and vice versa, cannot occur because antibodies to species-specific antigenic material (hyaluronidase and other enzyme systems) in the semen prevent it.

VARIOUS DEVIATIONS

Frottage (frotteurism, toucherism, compulsive mashing). The typical frotteur singles out a strange woman in a crowd and appresses his erect membrum, fully clothed, against her posterior, attempting to produce ejaculation in this manner. For him to succeed in this, there must be no contact of words, no silent agreement of the eyes between them. Frottage occurs wherever men and women are closely crowded together (e.g., in buses and subways during the rush hour, at fairs, etc.). Most victims prefer not to make a complaint; they either move away or quietly discourage the offender, which is easily accomplished. Frottage has also been encountered in women, in a small number of cases. Some observers have held frottage to be a variant of exhibitionism and of fetishism (*"partialism"*); however, one may disagree with this view. At least some of these patients distinctly behave like true, compulsive deviates sui generis. Frotteurs who have come to psychiatric attention were emotionally immature, psychosexually puerile young men with labile impulse control and a few are multiperverse psychopaths with a history of other aberrant sex behavior. Most are relatively nonaggressive.

Erotographomania. Obscene and usually anonymous letter writing may occur more frequently than is known to either clinicians or the authorities. Frequent recipient-victims have been teen-age girls, matrons, and female celebrities. Some obscene or highly ambiguous messages are sent on open postcards. The majority of perpetrators probably are males. Among them have been encountered patients with hypomanic and manic excitement states, a few paranoid schizophrenics and, most frequently, men with a disinhibiting type of cerebral arteriosclerosis (see p. 434) in whom latent sadistic tendencies had been mobilized. Homosexual obscene mailing has been described from time to time, but seems to be infrequent.

Vampirism is the act of drawing blood from a living love object by cutting or biting, then sucking or drinking it from the wound and receiving sexual excitement and pleasure from the act, including orgasm (Vanden-Bergh-Kelly, others). It is a fairly rare disorder. Association with schizophrenic symptoms has been described.

Coprophilia is a compelling sexualized interest in the viewing, smelling and eating (*coprophagia,* if direct from the rectum) of the defecation of others. Coprophilia is not rare; coprophagia was not observed or reported in recent decades, but may occur as part of some sadomasochistic transactions.

Urolagnia is sexual excitement associated with the touching, smelling, drinking or other using of another person's urine. It is sometimes part of the aggressive variant of pedophilia, also of masochistic acting-out.

Pygmalionism is sexual interest in statues; a vaguely defined entity.

Ecouteurism (ecoutage) is the seeking of a specific erotic excitatory effect from the hearing of sounds associated with sexual and similar activities (e.g., by eavesdropping, phonographic records or tapes). Toilet sound tapes reportedly are much in demand from specialized porn dealers.

Pyromania (sexualized arson, pathological firesetting, incendiarism, firesetter syndrome). Acute sexual excitement is produced by the setting and the sight of large destructive fires, leading to urination, erection, masturbation and/or spontaneous orgasm at the scene. It is encountered most often in youthful males. Fantasies or viewing of fire are necessary to capacitate some of them sexually. About one half of observed patients are mentally retarded or severely paranoid, a few are frankly schizophrenic. In the others alcohol and sadistic traits play major parts.

FOR JOURNAL LITERATURE AND ADDITIONAL READING

Allen, C.: A Textbook of Psychosexual Disorders, ed. 2. London, Oxford University Press, 1969

Benjamin, H.: The Transsexual Phenomenon. New York, Julian Press, 1966

Gebhard, P. H., Pomeroy, W. B., Gagnon, J. H., and Christiansen, C. V.: Sex Offenders, An Analysis of Types. New York, Harper & Row and Paul Hoeber, 1965

Giese, H. (ed.): Die Sexuelle Perversion. Frankfurt a.M. Akadem. Verlagsgesellschaft, 1967

Green, R. and Money, J. (eds.): Transsexualism and Sex Reassignment. Baltimore, Johns Hopkins Press, 1969

Karpman, B.: The Sexual Offender and his Offenses. New York, Julian Press, 1954

London, L. S.: Sexual Deviations in the Male and Female. 2 vols. New York, Julian Press, 1964

Lorand, S. and Balint, M. (eds.): Perversions: Psychodynamics and Therapy. New York, Random House, 1956

Macdonald, J. M.: Indecent Exposure. Springfield, Ill. Thomas, 1973

Mohr, J. W., Turner, R. E., and Jerry, M. B.: Pedophilia and Exhibitionism, A Handbook. Toronto, Univ. of Toronto Press, 1964

Rosen, I. (ed.): The Pathology and Treatment of Sexual Deviation. A Methodological Approach. London, Oxford University Press, 1964

Stoller, R. J.: Sex and Gender. New York, Science House, 1968

CHAPTER 21

Homosexuality

Homosexuality in the Male: Subgroups and Nongroups —
Characteristics — The Homosexual Scene — Excerpts from the
Homosexual Argot — Causes — Treatment and Management —
Homosexuality in the Female.

HOMOSEXUALITY IN THE MALE

True homosexuality is a compelling, often lifelong psychosexual aberration characterized by affectional as well as erotic attraction toward members of the same sex. Erotic situations involving an attractive woman leave the homosexual indifferent or even fill him with repugnance or vague fear. The overt homosexual is fully aware of his deviant tendencies and usually accepts them, although some remain unreconciled to their differentness throughout life, and a few commit suicide in early adulthood because of it. Nonacceptance of the disorder usually is accompanied by chronic anxiety; it must be distinguished from deliberate dissimulation of the homosexuality to which many resort for social reasons (camouflage). In a number of cases the deviant direction of the sex drive is the principal, perhaps the only manifestation, but frequently it involves various other deflections in the total personality. The meaning of homosexuality for the total life of the individual can be so enormous that secondary existential disturbances or abnormal adjustment reactions are no rarity.

Homosexuality is not the same as homosexual behavior. Not all who frequently intromit into or dally with men are homosexuals (e.g., certain sex-centered youth culture radicals, some aggressive multiperverse psychopaths and borderline sociopaths, certain participants in far-out adult swinger groups and multilateral marriages, or some adolescent male prostitutes). Also, not all who have erotic longing for men are in the gay life, and some—camouflaged or not—remain continent. Only total homosexual behavior—sex with other males, active cruising (p. 512), mannerisms, preference for gay associations and locales, and gay life style generally—is strongly suggestive of true homosexual orientation. In certain types of

496

treatment situations the more euphemistic descriptive term—homosexual behavior—is preferred in order to avoid an antitherapeutic labeling effect and the subtle psychologic snare of the self-fulfilling prophecy which it often carries in tow.

The Physical Appearance of most homosexuals does not differ significantly from what one encounters in any random group of men except for a carefully looked-after and preserved trimness of the figure into middle age or beyond. A minority have pronounced gracile-delicate physiques, and a few are of the broad-hipped gynecoid type, but true eunuchoidal habitus is infrequent. Unusually small hands, a hairless trunk, soft-pale skin, full lips, round eyes or prettiness of the features are either chance findings or part of a gracile-delicate or a mildly neuterized constitution which may have played a psychologic part in the causation. Nor is it unusual that such prettiness on closer inspection turns out to be merely an illusion produced by an artful hair style, posturing of head and neck, habitual lip pursing and similar facial mannerisms.

Their range of intelligence is probably similar to that of heterosexual men, although claims of a predominantly high I.Q. are made for them from time to time. Superior intelligence is sometimes only apparent, especially in the presence of an aptitude for clever small talk. Undoubtedly, the incidence, among homosexuals, of artistic talent and of superior esthetic sensibilities is fairly high, although cases of pretentious dilettantism must be subtracted from this. Historically, there have been among their numbers great political and military figures, as well as great artists.

A LETTER OF SIGMUND FREUD TO THE MOTHER OF A HOMOSEXUAL

April 9, 1935

Dear Mrs. . . .

I gather from your letter that your son is a homosexual . . . Homosexuality is assuredly no advantage but it is nothing to be ashamed of, no vice, no degradation, it cannot be classified as an illness; we consider it to be a variation of the sexual function produced by a certain arrest of sexual development. Many highly respectable individuals of ancient and modern times have been homosexuals, several of the greatest men among them. It is a great injustice to persecute homosexuality as a crime.

By asking me if I can help, you mean, I suppose, if I can abolish homosexuality and make normal heterosexuality take its place. The answer is, in a general way, we cannot promise to achieve it. . . . The result of treatment cannot be predicted. . . .

Sincerely yours with kind wishes.

Freud

Incidence. Reliable figures as to the incidence of homosexuality do not exist. Best available estimates indicate that close to 5 per cent of adult men in the Western world have conspicuous homosexual inclinations of one clinical type or another. Of these one may guess that not less than one fifth are exclusively and intractably homosexual, about equally divided between men with strongly feminine and strongly masculine make-up and identification. The incidence of partial homosexual behavior, but not necessarily of homosexuality, appears to be rising.

Homosexuality is known to exist and has existed in almost every country, culture and race. It is found on every social level, in communities of every size and among members of every vocation, trade and profession. Its prevalence in large cities and certain other localities is due largely to the fact that homosexuals tend to migrate and congregate there.

Subgroups and Nongroups

Compelling (Compulsory, Obligatory, Essential [Br.], True) Homosexuality

If we depict men who are compellingly, predominantly, or exclusively, attracted to other men along an axis of masculine-feminine orientation, the greatest number will be encountered away from the two hard-core extremes, one at each end of the spectrum: at one end the effeminate homosexual, at the other the high-masculinity homosexual; both with fairly fixed patterns of response and behavior, both totally disinterested in women, both with manifestness of some traits in childhood, both resistant to any systematic attempts at changing them, and both probably unmodifiable.

Away from the hard-cores innumerable gradations and nuances exist as regards the relative degrees of masculine and feminine orientation and of phobic aversion to women. Gender orientation determines such items as vocational preference and detectable mannerisms; gynecophobia contributes to the prevailing degree of homosexual exclusivity, ranging from men who never desired to love or make love to a woman to an entrenched pattern of bisexuality (see below). No clear lines of demarcation seem to exist from one end of the scale to the other. What all such males have in common is that their homosexual strivings—not necessarily their behavior —are compelling and predominate, and that self-recognition—but not necessarily "coming out"—occurs in the teens. It should be noted that exclusiveness of homosexual behavior is not evidence of true homosexuality.

Effeminate Exclusive Homosexuality

This is the most patently deviant subgroup. Although relatively few in numbers—an estimated 10 to 15 per cent of obligatory (compulsory, essential [Br.], true) homosexual men—they are the most visible, and those among them who dramatize and flaunt their differentness in the face of public sensibilities and enjoy the outrage they incite, have given homosexuality much of its "bad name." Their largely feminine identification goes hand in hand with a profound alteration of the total personality, including striving, feeling, talents, manner, motility, libidinal patterning, some of the thinking function and, in a proportion of cases, habitus and physical features. They are the model for what used to be known as the "third sex." Homosexual behavior here—no individual in this group practically ever desires or has a meaningful heterosexual experience—is clearly only part of the total deviant pattern; the latter is fixed, compelling and exclusive, and probably untreatable except, possibly some time in the near future, by patchwork rehabilitation—function by function, mannerism by mannerism —of the most obvious behavioral components. Also, practically none of these individuals have a wish to be changed; they have no aptitude for it and have always avoided sustained psychiatric therapy except when impelled briefly by curiosity, compelled by court order or motivated by a caring lover for seemingly unrelated emotional problems. Their differentness becomes obvious at a very early age (see p. 78). These are also the boys who somewhat later (e.g., from age 5) are homosexually seduced and victimized, often repeatedly, as they either seek the proximity of vulnerable pedophilic men (pp. 81 and 473) or else seem somehow more inept than other children in removing themselves from harm's way. It is this frequent tendency which has given rise to the legend that homosexuality can be produced by childhood seduction.

They have little interest in the masculine role, and many like to cross-dress (in "drag"—e.g., for special dances) but unlike the male transsexuals they have no wish to relinquish their biologic and social gender role or their phallus. Their sexual capacity is rarely remarkable, but passive libido, frequently anal, is well developed and responsive in a narcissistic way. The socially most malconditioned among them are irrepressibly larcenous and notoriously mendacious. Many are forever exploited and victimized at every turn. However, unless provoked about something, they can be charmingly animated and witty companions, capable of endless clever small talk. Most of them age badly. The grossly effeminate gay can be dangerously uncaring carriers of VD, often extragenital, and unless motivated by a current lover who cares they tend to neglect VD follow-up procedures.

They do not truly resemble or even understand women, as has been said to explain their predominance in hair styling or fashion design, but it is debatable if out of deeply frustrated spite they uglify women by design. The most effeminate—walking parodies of womanhood—lack creative talent except for a thin veneer; only as one moves toward the center along the masculine-feminine axis does an innate capacity for esthetic appreciation—of surface form and ornaments mainly—arise. Still further away from the extreme, one occasionally encounters truly sensitive as well as creative artistry.

High-masculinity Exclusive Homosexuality

At the other extreme of the obligatory scale one encounters certain well-masculinized, self-assured, sometimes highly aggressive males. They, too, appear to be different throughout much of their childhood, but in the very early years this differentness is almost unrecognizable except by hindsight. However, they have no history of childhood sexual seduction, and during their teen years and sometimes beyond, a proportion cultivate a highly idealistic and ascetic resolve. Others in this group, beginning in their mid-teens, resort to frequent crudely lecherous, even predatory sexual ventures; they manifest much promiscuity and at an early age learn the ways of the questing homosexual male. During adolescence intense infatuations—actually falling in love—with other teen-age boys occur; they can be of disruptive intensity such as is encountered in heterosexual youngsters only 3 or more years later; the constant awareness of a need for secrecy and dissembling, the mental anguish and loneliness which may be involved, probably contribute something to the quality of emotional maturation of such youngsters; others have been seen to lapse into a psychotic break at this time. This type of homosexual has been represented as exaggerating masculine and aggressive traits in order to disprove any feminine component which he despises, but clinically, it cannot be shown to be the prevailing mechanism producing the high-masculinity traits of most of them.

In the ranks of these men one encounters some of the best and some of the worst among homosexual males—men of political, organizational and creative genius, socially responsible professionals and civic leaders, but also criminality-ridden sociopaths; one finds men of action—from gay bar bouncers to Army general officers, also untiring rabble rousers as well as reformers, men of ideas, students of the res politica, teachers at Universities, original researchers. In the college homophile clubs (see below) the high-masculine gay often quickly reach for the helm and then banish all with a trace of effeminacy which they despise. As they are generally quite inconspicuous, the intelligent among them often "wear the mask" in public with great success and for long periods until, for instance, they become homosexually infatuated near their home base and throw caution to the winds. If they live fully "in a closet," they can tolerate only the most platonic of camouflage marriages. The true, far-end obligatory homosexual has few or no mannerisms. In fact sometimes their extreme masculine stance in all matters except erotic interest in women makes them apparent to the experienced observer.

Bisexuality (Nonexclusive Homosexuality. Vernac. ac/dc, Switcher, Bi, etc.)

This is not truly a subgroup but a major variant within the obligatory homosexual spectrum, and usually implies a fairly high degree of masculine identification. Bisexuality differs from facultative switching (see below), which is more a social manifestation, and from the pseudo-married status of certain exclusive homosexuals living in a usually sexless marriage of convenience or camouflage. The heterosexual pursuits of these individuals may range from only one woman in their lifetime (whom they may marry) to moderate promiscuity. Their homosexual component is either uninterruptedly present, or the impulses appear from time to time. According to observations these impulses, at least in some bisexual men, tend to recur periodically. Intelligent individuals can learn to predict these homosexual episodes, even where they do not recur with periodic regularity. For instance, the first sign may be that he seems to notice men more as he passes them in the street or has various dealings with them. Regardless of how satisfying marital life seems to be, gay impulses may come to the fore as "slip-ups" in self-discipline, often with a peculiarly childlike note ("just to see if it still bothers me," or "I had the feeling something interesting was going on [in a homosexual bar, etc.] and I shouldn't miss it"); or they may appear as sudden, unquenchable sex hunger for a male companion, compared with which heterosexual love seems to be a shallow substitute. These episodes may last a few days and then disappear again, although under unfavorable circumstances there always exists the risk that a lingering homoerotic attachment may be formed during this period.

It is disputed whether the intensity of their affectional feelings for women can be quite the same as that of normal men, but for at least some of them this is undoubtedly true. However, the intensity of the sexual gratification with a female rarely, if ever, seems to equal that experienced in homosexual relations. In any marriage or other long-term liaison the bisexual may find himself resorting to homosexual imagery, fantasy, perhaps pornography, or else the use of a fetish (q.v.) device, to maintain interest and potency. In a few men any change in the frequency, the regularity or even the manner of their marital relations seems to be capable of precipitating a critical homoerotic period. A few are inclined mainly toward girls of somewhat boyish appearance, or they may induce such a girl (or wife) to "masculinize" herself in hair-do and get-up, but as a group they are neither markedly passive nor do the women to whom they are attracted seem to belong to any particular group. They are rarely interested in the virago type of girl, and definitely not in homosexual women.

Some true bisexual men manage to stay married long enough to raise children, but the prevailing long-term outcome of these unions is uncertain;

some endure, others do not. In those who are fairly well adapted and camouflaged, homosexual impulses may arise when they are faced with disappointments, tense situations, or emotional upsets in their marital, social or working life. Both success and failure in the economic and occupational struggle can produce recrudescence of homosexual strivings (e.g., a promotion or a demotion, recognition or slighting both have similar effect). Many a bisexual husband who lost an argument with his wife or with a teen-age son, or failed at a meaningful domestic task, has rushed out to cruise for a pick-up or to telephone an old male lover for a date, partly as a vindictive gesture by endangering (in fantasy, at least) the foundations of his marriage, partly in response to a specific and irrational panic process which somehow equates failure, rejection, weakness, not being a man and being a homosexual after all. The supportive long-term management of the married bisexual by a trusted and interested family physician probably is the most accessible tool yet devised in minimizing the destructive effects of this socially high-risk deviance.

Facultative (Late-Induced, Incl. Experimental) Homosexuality

The homosexual mystique can have an unbelievably strong attraction for a fairly vast nongroup of unmatured, impressionable adolescents and post-adolescents who are befriended, subtly at first, by a masculine-oriented homosexual, not very much older than themselves. These homosexuals detest the effeminate gay, but find straight youths exciting because of appearance or some other trait. Given a glimpse and a taste of the gay world, it acts and continues to act as a magnet for these adolescents. What is visible of the gay life seems free and footloose, highly erotized, hedonistic, travel-prone, culture-conscious, dotted with endlessly witty and cynical dialogue, close to the glamorous stage or involved with far-out art; with money which grubbier men must spend in raising children, buying family insurance, or conducting a household being thrillingly available here for conspicuous consumption; a make-believe world peopled by the most handsome, wearing the latest. The ever-present undercurrents of pain and unhappiness pertaining to all homosexuality remain hidden below the glittering surface. The youngster, perhaps as never before, experiences warm attention to what he says, to his troubles—it is really just man to man, all the way, he convinces himself. Random coercion or seduction are not the issue: he is not pushed, or bought, or bribed; the mystique seduces him; he seduces himself. He neutralizes his own feeling of masculine humiliation, beats out his own shame and guilt at being seen in the company of "queers," at making it with them, getting sex that way. But it seems easy to "let go" in this seductive milieu, to want to be part of it. He lets the "silly, smelly-cunted broads" go by the boards, he embraces "all this, for the price of nothing, nothing at all." And suddenly he is into homosexuality.

These are the vulnerable young. Some are smallish and smoothly slim-bodied, in a fairly masculine way; some are muscular and springy; some frail, sensitive and impractical; others more gynecoid in habitus and pouty. It can be argued whether mere unconscious sex appeal brought about their selection or whether some undefinable assemblage of off-norm traits sent them posing in harm's way. Some may eventually have self-emerged spontaneously as gays; but the presumption remains: at a critical moment someone or something tipped the scales the wrong way. Additionally, an unsuccessful date, a girl's rashly thoughtless derision, a couple of passes by obvious gays which revived the old scary saw, "it takes one to know one," may have helped confirm them in a mistaken belief that they were gay anyway. They may be designated as true victims, losers, when their role as protégé or pet lover, often passing through various hands, keeps them from learning a trade or going to school and may spoil them for the role of family man when 10 years or so later they are dropped from all gay favor and may lose much of their homosexual inclination. A few, luckier, had a truly concerned lover who made them go to school or encouraged them not to drop girls completely from their lives. These boys are not true homosexuals nor bisexuals, but individuals with a weakness in the personality which rendered them vulnerable or eager (e.g., for reasons of dependency craving or other nonhomosexual impellent). Many may be designated as pseudohomosexuals, although during the period of their involvement, and some forever, they will identify themselves and be identified as an intimate part of the homosexual world.

In the same general nongroup, acting-out homosexually, one encounters the anti-establishmentarian experimenter, the fringe element in the hippie-type youth culture, still flourishing, although no longer so visibly. Sexual differentness has much attraction for them; as much of their homosexual acting-out is submerged in mixed-orgy behavior, it is satisfyingly far out, yet "not really queer, like loving up by twos" and helping the gays do their thing is almost like having another rebellious-shocking bag of their own. To be hung up on nothing including the gender of the person they make love to, they understand, means to be free; "try a bit of everything, don't be afraid" becomes the enabling parole. Some authority figures encourage them, mistaking increasing tolerance for the gay life style for accreditation as a normal bag. But these youngsters too are probably vulnerable, at least a proportion of them, although it is too soon for long-range assessment.

Situational (Substitute, Faute-de-Mieux [Fr.], Surrogate, Circumstantial) Homosexual Behavior

The traditional observation that normal adult men during prolonged all-male isolation or confinement (prison, work camps, seamen) simply engage in substitute homosexual practices until heterosexual opportunities are restored, appears no longer to be generally valid, except for men who were homosexual to begin with when they took refuge from social pressures by joining; modern communications, mobility and working conditions are said to be the reason for this shift. Of course, in any group of men there will always be those in whom a combination of opportunity—living in unremitting intimacy with younger, obviously sex-famished males—and personal make-up—low arousal threshold and highly relaxed social conditioning—will mobilize impulses of undifferentiated libidinal greed. These multisexual opportunists when operating freely in society are usually included among the psychopaths or borderline sociopaths. When they operate among captive objects—unmatured, often unstable, affection-starved, suggestible, passive, isolated, frightened, flattery-prone or plain mercenary youths, ubiquitous in such aggregations—they become even more predatory.

Conditions in penal institutions differ today. Long-term penitentiaries, usually reasonably well organized and supervised, have only a seemingly irreducible minimum of the traditional homosexual "wolf-and-bitch" coupling and passing around. It is in the shorter-term prisons that new facets of prison sexuality—some reportedly with racial overtones—have come to light. Since the shocking Philadelphia report (Davis, 1968), followed by others, on the prevalence of homosexual rape, debasement and servitude of nonhomosexual youths of slight body build, it is becoming clear that not sexual gratification, but "conquest and degradation of the victim" is the primary goal of the sexual aggressor, often an expression of the same anger which caused the prisoner's original crimes. It is not lustful, expedient choice, but compensatory domination of a weaker male. Perhaps they seek to redeem nagging awareness of their failure as social beings, effective breadwinners, and thus as masculine males, by forcibly having men submit orally or anally to their phallus. They act pseudohomosexually (Ovesey). The victim, to be a satisfying object, must not be gay, although once used and terrorized into masculine degradation the novice "punk" is considered part of the available fag population (up to 10 per cent of prisoners are effeminate homosexuals, reportedly) and like them is passed around and bartered for housekeeping arrangements and as a masturbatory tool.

Cryptic (Masked, Unconscious, Latent) Homosexuality

This is not a subvariety, but the submerged or latent form of true obligatory homosexuality. Use of the term latent does not imply that all men have an underlying proneness for the aberration, except that the environment must bring it out. Emergence into overtness—self-recognition—in most obligatory homosexuals occurs some time before the end of adolescence, but in some such men, for reasons essentially unknown, the condition does not emerge into consciousness, but remains repressed or masked: the patient genuinely thinks of himself as a heterosexual. The latent status may persist throughout life, or homosexuality may emerge as the result of seduction by a man, or similar experience. Sometimes homosexual overtness emerges spontaneously as late as the early 50's; occasionally, such belated self-discovery is accompanied by suicidal or assaultive panic states, or even by frank psychosis. In other cases the newly manifest tendency can be disguised successfully.

Certain behavioral manifestations and some syndromes of psychopathology may in some cases—but by no means in all cases—mask latent homosexuality. These include some patterns of chronic alcoholism; chronic pathologic jealousy; some paranoid personality disorders; some cases of persistent impotence; some cases of marked chronic (heterosexual) promiscuity of the Don Juan type (q.v.); certain instances of the tendency to lead an eccentric hermit's life; and probably many cases of a persistent desire for woman-sharing (e.g., actual or tell-tale peeping on one's own wife's or girl friend's lovemaking to another man, with her infidelity being tolerated or even encouraged). However, in cases of triadic marriage or co-living (p. 458) where the husband arranges for another man to share the sexual activities between himself and his wife, the bisexual condition is usually overt.

Even where a physician is certain, the presence of latent homosexuality should not be suggested to the patient except for definite indications. Although most of these men will resist (i.e., disbelieve) this information, an occasional patient may become unpredictably and seriously disturbed by it.

Characteristics

Onset and Recognition

The most compelling, exclusive types of homosexuality become manifest in childhood, most notably the effeminate type. Most other homosexual variants manifest themselves in the teens, and more or less rapid self-diagnosis is the rule, a sometimes exceedingly painful and uncertain process. At times, initially little more is noted by the boy than "a quickening of the pulses, a lifting of the heart into the throat" at the sight of some particular fellow male. In other cases an intense interest in the male body and genitalia can rapidly change the nature of what had seemingly started out as a typical juvenile homoerotic-phase dalliance (see p. 143). Final self-discovery may occur when the youngster, to prove himself normal in the face of his own nagging doubts, tries to kiss or coite with a female and experiences "nauseating certainty." If he has picked an unsuitable subject (e.g., a prostitute or a "pig"—teen-age girl habitually manifesting all-comers-type promiscuity), his disgust and failure may, sometimes forever, misguide him as to his sexual status, for example if he is a "borderline" case (bisexual potential). Care is required not to equate the mere absence of interest in girls with a budding homosexual inclination.

Later, in adulthood, the important criteria are the nature of the feeling-responses, longings, fantasies, imageries, dreams and certain mental trends. Sexual behavior, even involving frequent homosexual acts, is only one diagnostic criterion, and sometimes a misleading one. Positive evidence would be that the individual is aroused erotically only by members of the same sex. The fact that he is able to carry out coitus with a woman does not exclude homosexuality. In some cases little more is noted than an increased spirit of animation in the company of attractive males, especially after a few alcoholic drinks; while the same number of drinks makes women seem to be even more undesirable.

In masturbation the nature of the accompanying imageries, particularly those occurring just prior to orgasm, are highly revealing. In the true homosexual they seem to remain homoerotic even after he has relinquished homosexual acting-out following aversive therapy. Significant is phobic avoidance of the actual female genitalia or a sense of disgust at any description or even mention of them other than in derogatory terms. Erotic infatuation, or a longing for it, with a member of the same sex does not occur in heterosexual men, although longings close to this—for approval, paternal-type benevolence, and gratitude-for-rescue fantasies—are universal. A seemingly irrepressible obsession with other males' genitalia, and an omnipresent hypererotic awareness—all remarks, encounters, relationships, happenings, etc., are instinctively evaluated, first and last, in sexual terms—are fairly characteristic of obligatory homosexuality. Some of the newer phallometric methods (e.g., by strain gauge) can give valid differential diagnostic results; they are based on continuous measurements of penis volume (or weight) changes as the individual is exposed to erotically suggestive pictures or other stimuli of one kind or another and their local arousal effects, even though minimal, are compared.

Physical Characteristics

Physical findings specific for homosexuality do not exist except for a diminished or absent gag reflex in those who frequently practice fellatio, and anorectal changes in habitual rectal intromissees. In pronounced cases the latter leads to anus infundibuliformis: flattened perianal folds, an anal sphincter patulous and relaxed to the exploring finger but with strong contractility, and enlargement of the rectal ampulla. Masters has added marked hypertrophy of the hemorrhoidal plexi and a flow of lubricating transudate from the congested rectal walls during sexual arousal. The genitalia are in no way characteristic. Clinical hypogonadism among homosexuals probably is found only slightly more often than among a comparable group of heterosexual men. Erective potency seems to be limited in the effeminate, but is pronounced, sometimes wondrously so, in markedly masculine, promiscuous homosexual males. All are subject to disorders of sexual potency, including premature ejaculation similar to what is found in heterosexuals (p. 388).

With the more precise newer hormone assay techniques relatively low plasma concentrations of testosterone and characteristic variants in urinary androgenic breakdown products are fairly consistently being encountered in certain homosexual males, but the significance of these findings is uncertain at present. Reduced sperm counts and, at times, impaired spermatogenesis are also encountered with some regularity. Genetically, except for a small proportion of men with a chromatin-positive Klinefelter syndrome (q.v.), homosexuality in men is associated with a negative (male) sex chromatin pattern.

Mental Traits

Some observers have felt that all homosexuals are endowed with certain characteristic mental traits; others have found them to be "just like other people" except for the aberrant direction of their sex interest. It must be remembered that many homosexuals develop a kind of underground mentality, because in everyday life they must disguise their inclinations habitually and feel continually reminded of being different. Some deem themselves —and act like—a persecuted minority which, indeed, they may be; but there is little evidence for, and much evidence against, the assertion that they would be happy and normal people, if only society's unreasonable and stigmatizing attitude would change. Apart from the aberrant direction of the sex aim, there are certain singular traits which many compulsory homosexuals have in common, whether they are psychiatric patients or not; for these the stigma with which the social structure surrounds the aberration cannot be made the whipping boy. One may mention the tendency to sexualize all relationships; the obsessive fixation on other men's genitalia; a love of artifice and obsession with trivia; their waspishness, petulance and vindictiveness when among themselves, and the compulsive tendency of many to proselytize or "bring out" as well as to overrecognize homosexuality in other males. Some are proud, to the point of superciliousness, to belong to an elite group and tend to glorify their way of life. Those who realize that theirs is a chronic deficit are often thoroughly and chronically unhappy. The fact that they lack the normal man's interest in founding and raising a family helps to make many founder through life without much inner scope, easily unsettled by a shifting mood or a chance experience, even though their lives may be externally productive.

Mannerisms

This is a group of behavioral peculiarities and affectations, involving mostly general bearing, motility, speech and attire, which are found in compulsory homosexuals to varying degrees. A substantial number of homosexual men exhibit no mannerisms of any kind at any time, others lapse into them only when among themselves, when their erotic interest is aroused, or when they feel themselves being scrutinized and admired. Generally, this type of behavior, except among the undauntedly effeminate, has been decreasing, or at least it is more often controlled and concealed when the "mask" is being worn in public; this does not include the small minority of the "flaming" gay who feel compelled to flaunt their differentness in public streets and locales of the more permissive cities.

The Meaning of homosexual mannerisms remains incompletely understood. Many seem to imitate feminine ways, but more likely they are a display of hostility-tinged antifeminine mockery. Even adopting a girl's name or wanting to be addressed as "she" is perhaps more an outgrowth of infantile than of feminine make-up; unlike transsexuals (q.v.) who fervently desire to cross over, what motivates many homosexuals is a dislike for being called by the grown-up "Mister"; if our language had unequivocal children's appellatives many would prefer them to the feminine ones. Certain mannerisms symbolize a self-contemptuous response—submission— to the environment's disdain and hatred. Mention should be made of the sociologists' Labeling Theory: the blatant gay, having just "come out" and being unsure of their role behavior, model themselves according to the way they think gays are supposed to behave (this theory rarely fits clinical observation: e.g., the blatantly effeminate gay almost always are manifest since childhood).

Body Motion. Some affectations have a strongly suggestive biologic basis. For instance, the configuration of the glenoid fossa-humeral head relationship together with the feminine-type suspension at the elbow with resulting "carrying angle" of the arms—quite noticeable in various neuterized males and many effeminate gays—overextends the elbows, rotates the hands outward when the arms are at rest, and facilitates the limpid overextending or extreme bending at the wrist when the forearm is being raised; it also makes such extremities quite unsuitable for ball throwing, catching, straight hammering, rifle shooting, etc., although elaborate patchwork conditioning therapy lately has succeeded in training away some of the crossgender motility, at least temporarily. The effeminate arm movements may have the curve, but practically never the gracefulness, of a true female's motion. Biologic factors may play a part in the shrillness or falsetto in the voice when certain compulsory homosexuals become excited. Whether the tendency to lisp has a biopathologic substratum is undetermined. A tripping, mincing or floating gait with or without swishing of hips may not be biologically based, although a feminine type suspension at the knee joints has been demonstrated (see also p. 105), and hip joint anatomy may also differ. Purely psychologic is the compensatory or defensively postured gait of some when self-conscious in public: walking assumes a peculiarly exaggerated masculine marching quality, the shoulders tensely straight, hands held tightly at the side with absence of associated armswing, the neck fairly rigid and with a resounding step (reinforced by leather heels and/or metal caps before the era of the sneaker), but not quite succeeding in hiding an underlying tripping quality.

Verbal Mannerisms. With the recent influx into the homosexual subculture of essentially psychopathic elements from among the hippie-type youth culture and with the steep rise in international mobility, styles of verbal behavior are now too much in flux to be meaningfully generalized. There often remains a tendency to mannered, overcareful enunciation and/or oversharp articulation which may result in a stilted variety of Eastern Seaboard Cultured, the so-called pseudo-Oxford English pronunciation. In others there is a seemingly difficult-to-control tendency to a rising inflection of sentences; in others again a passion for refinement and purism of language with almost horrified contempt for certain native regional accents. On the other hand, "regional," notably Western, speech is now fashionable in some areas. Substantially unchanged is the tendency among many, when in uninhibited surroundings, to resort to innuendo and indirections, or to be either mordant-ironical, fastidiously prim or gushy-flowery in the "divinely mad—madly divine" manner.

Sexual Pairing and Practices

The love and sex life of many homosexuals is erratic; where opportunities exist a substantial number tend to be promiscuous to an extreme degree. Casual pairing off for sexual purposes is frequent, as is amicable exchange of partners. On the other hand, sharp infatuations and sharply painful jealousies have always been a hallmark of the homosexual condition. Even the jealous killings among them tend to be bloodier, as homicide officers and medical examiners can attest; some are almost stylized in their savagery. Where homosexual men congregate in crowds, between 300 and 1000 sexual encounters per year with a different partner seem to be no rarity. Homosexuals, as a rule, have a distinctly more specific preference for the type (stature, hair color, features, etc.) of sexual partner which appeals to them than does the average heterosexual with respect to women. It may reflect an unconscious search for ego twinship. Although potency disorders of various types occur in homosexual men—but probably not as often as in heterosexuals—there is also a fair proportion of men with great erective potency who, in addition, are kept in a state of arousal by the notoriously ubiquitous erotization of practically all free-time socializing, thinking, conversing, etc. Except for the relatively few who sublimate much of their instinctual drive into other activities of overriding interest, the Number One subject, spoken or unspoken, of most gay men in groups or new pairs is sex. Most homosexuals are obsessively, endlessly fascinated with other men's phallic organs, their size and shape and speculation as to their potency.

V.D. Because of the casual way homosexuals intermingle genitally, they have become major spreaders throughout the Western world of venereal diseases, especially syphilis, in recent years. Gonorrheal proctitis and syphilis in the rectum and anus are not always easily recognized, nor are anal condylomata lata. Some physicians practicing near the gay scene now do serologic and darkfield examinations whenever a male presents himself with a fissure in ano or hemorrhoids which do not look quite typical.

Affairs. The search for a stable life companion, for an enduring and trusted relationship motivates many, but few (some say, none) seem to succeed in our time. The steadier affairs may last a few months, perhaps a year (Saghir). A small number last for several years and even fewer endure for more than a decade. Even romantically based relationships hardly ever involve complete faithfulness of both lovers. These observations apply equally to smaller towns and metropolitan centers. A few small churches specializing in pastoral care of the gay lately have undertaken to solemnize homosexual "marriages" in covenant ceremonies before witnesses; but under the law these are not recognized as marriages. Contrary to widespread belief, these liaisons are infrequently a "husband-wife" combination with an active-masculine breadwinner and a passive-feminine partner who keeps house. A little more frequent are liaisons between an older and a much younger homosexual, but most often both partners meet on middle ground and have similar appearances, inclinations and talents. Many long-term homosexual affairs end amid jealous quarrels; in other cases the two partners will cling together under unpleasant circumstances because of a desperate need for some sort of stable human relationship.

Group Sex. The most recent generations in the gay subculture, in their late teens or barely out of them, seem to be turning to somewhat different nonvalues. They are deriding the bar-and-tearoom bag of "the older guys and aunties" (age 30 and up) and together with a conspicuous interest in drugs, rock and soul, orgy-type sex behavior on private premises has become their in-thing. Under the influence of the more dissolute elements in the youth culture and their "no hang-ups on any style" motto lesbians as well as occasional straight females participate in the group sex, giving it, according to semi-reliable reports, a more facultative, switch-prone character. Underneath, however, the old compulsory entities seem to be emerging unchanged.

Male Prostitutes are available on almost every social level; they range from quasi-streetwalkers to expensively kept youths. Some are homosexuals themselves, but most are sexually normal ex-juvenile delinquents (p. 153) and sociopaths who find it profitable to make themselves available to men.

With the lower grades of these prostitutes the danger of assault, robbery or blackmail, sometimes at the instigation of their procurers, is ever present. Male houses of prostitution (peg houses) are proliferating (Pittman).

Sexual Practices between homosexuals differ, but many maintain a preference for some particular method of gratification. A consistent, well-defined difference between the preferred practices of masculine and passive homosexuals is infrequent: there is almost always some degree of mutuality, and frequently the sex roles are interchanged. The principal exceptions are grossly effeminate males who are in no way capable of even comprehending the masculine spirit and cannot play this role; and highly masculinized homosexuals who are loath to function for long in a feminine role even when play-acting. Preliminary embraces, caresses and kisses differ little from those of heterosexual couples. Methods of gratification include rectal immission usually aided by a lubricant, intrafemoral insertion and scrotal apposition of the phallus. In more casual sexual encounters most often one deviate asks to be fellated while the other is masturbated or masturbates himself, or there is mutual masturbation. Mutual fellatio is not too rare, but successive (alternating) fellatio is more common. The use of phallus-like devices for rectal insertion is not unusual in those strongly conditioned to passive-anal libido; such dildoes are also self-inserted as a form of solitary masturbation. Various electrovibratory devices are reported to be in fairly widespread use by homosexual men.

The Homosexual Scene

The gay subculture in the U.S., and probably in the rest of the Western world, is neither carefree-gay, nor is it quite as grim as it used to be. As subcultures go it is shallow, unstable, and restlessly mobile but has a relatively high rate of social successfulness among its members. It is multifactional and gregarious, but social stratification is remarkably minimal because the unifying deviance cuts through all social strata. Essentially it has a clique structure.

Geographic clustering of homosexuals is increasing (e.g., in large metropolitan and resort centers, in some University towns, in certain blocks in the large cities—"boys' town"—and wherever other gays have nested). In the largest cities they have their own clubs, bars, restaurants, gyms and steambaths, beaches, happenings, newspapers, protective organizations, celebrities, intrigues, gossip and tragedies of which the average citizen knows little or nothing.

The evenings and other free time accentuate the essential emptiness and restlessness in their lives. Unless they have pronounced domestic inclinations (a few), or are totally absorbed in the pursuit of some private project (few), their apartments or rooms seem to offer little to keep them at home including those maintaining fairly stable dyadic affairs. In the bigger cities a substantial proportion of the homosexuals are on the move every evening, roaming, visiting, partying, attending shows, bars or clubs, reaching out for each other's presence, afraid of being left out, and seemingly forever in search of sex.

Isolation vs. Metropolis. Few of those who make every effort to live in continent privacy or fully camouflaged including perhaps sham marriage to a woman can do so for long without at least periods of mingling with fellow deviants; not always so much because of sexual needs, but to feel that their differentness is not as unique and unbearable as it sometimes seems to them. Those living in the isolation of a small community feel particularly oppressed by this aspect of their homosexuality, apart from their fear of being found out. For them it may be dangerous to have even a clandestine lover, although some manage to live in a camouflaged menage (cousins, tenant or roomer, etc.) and may find social acceptance for their occupational or personal worth, unless their manner is too conspicuously different. However, need for perspective on themselves is one of the major reasons why so many deviates migrate to the large cities. There they also feel less conspicuous or may find more constructive employment for any special talents they may possess. Others, of course, move to gay centers and cities for less mature reasons (e.g., hoping to meet "interesting people" there, or because they find "normal people so dull," or because they have a childlike apprehension that they "will miss something that's going on"). A few are city-bound to act out fantasies (e.g., hoping to find a larger audience of admirers or a wealthy lover who will keep them).

Mutual Recognition. The reputed ability of homosexuals to recognize each other at sight when neither wants to risk exposure, is frequently overestimated. Most often, of course, it is simply a matter of being, loitering, in a particular area or place. Or there may be faint mannerisms of pose or attire: unusually shaped beads, a provocative bit of jewelry, a lilting hand motion, or a fluttering of eyelids in startling contrast to otherwise masculine appearance. It may be a lingering, querying or challenging way of scrutinizing other men ("the eyes ask the question"); or an unusually lingering handshake. In conversation with a stranger who has aroused their interest—the intent of such covert contacts usually is sexual—they may resort to insinuations, the veiled use of jargon cues or a seemingly casual touch of the hand to give the other an opportunity to reveal himself. The question, is he or is he not? (i.e., gay, or susceptible to advances, or even merely sympathetic if he knew the truth) is near-automatically, obsessively on their minds with almost any male they deal with. Most are catalogued (e.g., excluded) instantaneously, but when it is impossible for them to decide about a person, he becomes the subject of much speculation and gossip.

Vocational Clustering is pronounced, most visibly in the graphic and the performing arts; interior and other decorating; hairstyling and -dressing, in the fashion industry, and in certain types of retail establishments. Although many homosexuals function well in a variety of occupations, including every profession, and in their camouflaged everyday lives, others are severely maladjusted outside a homosexual setting and homosexual society; the ubiquitous freemasonry of the unconcealed gay offers them social sanctuary in establishments where they will not feel isolated. However, in the gay society which makes a cult of youthfulness, protective benevolence often comes to an end as a protégé ages; he ceases to be a desirable potential lover and in some way must now pay for his sex, and he also must have established himself occupationally on his own by then.

Hardships. Life in the homosexual subculture is harsh in other ways. Easily intimidated and afraid of violence as the less masculinized are to begin with, they are also beset by fears of ever-present real threats on the part of men around them: cruelly marauding teen-age delinquents, pickups who may beat and rob them, organized extortionists, landlords, their own family, employers, co-workers and possible arrest by police. In almost all states the law prohibits homosexual practices between men, by various definitions. However, police departments as a rule do not seek out homosexuals for arrest and prosecution unless their behavior constitutes a public nuisance or offense (loitering, disorderly conduct, or acts involving minors). A debatable police practice is the use of plainclothes officers serving as decoys, waiting to be accosted by a homosexual (e.g., in public washrooms)—entrapment.

The Law. A widespread effort is under way to remove from the penal law sexual behavior between competent and consenting adults of the same sex when privately and discreetly engaged in. A similar resolution was first formulated by the Wolfenden Committee in England in 1957; after much debate, years later, English homosexuals were given this protection which in view of our continuing inability, in the majority of cases, to modify homosexual feelings and impulses seems humane, reasonable and in keeping with the temper of the times. Reason-based objections include the observation that immature, suggestible and perhaps rehabilitable youths-at-the-brink do not suddenly mature as they reach the age of majority; that homosexual behavior can be a manifestation of certain multiperverse psychopathic personalities in whom impunity for one undesirable act may reinforce and facilitate impulses for other, more antisocial acts; and that the law has deterrent value in the case of certain bisexual men and women whom impunity for repeatedly following a homosexual impulse or a beckoning opportunity may condition away from a functioning child-blessed heterosexual marriage, while prohibition can reduce this undesired response.

Armed Forces, Government, Security. As long as our society abides by the inner belief that homosexuality is neither normal nor desirable, its institutions and agencies must reflect this belief and translate it into administrative terms suitable for their appointed function. Humaneness and all feasible degrees of social justice should surround such administrative policies.

In the armed services of the United States homosexual individuals are not wanted, and every official effort is made to exclude them. Officers and men who are found out are separated from the service by various procedures (U.S. Navy Instruction 1900.9; Air Force Regulation 35–66; Army Regulation 635–212 and 635–100 (Officer Personnel)). Participation in a homosexual act is sufficient, but generally 3 classes of type of offense are recognized. Occasionally court-martial upon a formal complaint for actual sex acts performed leads to sentencing.

Gay Liberation protests—that homosexuals be admitted to the services if their sexual inclinations do not interfere with their service activities—notwithstanding, exclusion would appear to be a fair and necessary policy for the armed forces, although there may be less necessity for an associated punitive stance than is thought desirable at present. Many homosexuals have served, and are serving, with honor; but there is no way of screening out, in advance, the highly libidinized and promiscuous, the compulsive proselytizers; there is no way of preventing the arising of a gay clique structure, perhaps of jealous rivalries following infatuation; of a dazzling homosexual mystique attractive to bored, horny, sometimes unstable adolescent and post-adolescent males. Single exposures to this are a fact of life for youngsters in the modern world, and of little consequence; it is the continued, no-escape exposure, day after day, which tends to captivate the most vulnerable.

Nor is it feasible for a military establishment in our time to allow degrees of impunity based on subtle psychologic differences in personal deviance which cannot be specified and administered by the book. For similar reasons the armed services must necessarily ban every kind of homosexual behavior, whether it stems from deviance or from an immaturity reaction: it is impossible for field supervisors to make such diagnostic differentiations on the spot as cases arise. Although in Europe's past active homosexuality was rife in various officer corps, the then existing sharp demarcation between officers and enlisted men did not make for cross-rank spread which remained a grave offense. In today's more egalitarian organizations such spread would perhaps not be rare and if not discouraged must be assumed to be capable of disrupting a military group's morale and discipline severely.

In certain branches of Government homosexuals are frequently not desired, especially if they would have access to security-sensitive data; this is equally true of certain sensitive industries. Most homosexuals living camouflaged must be presumed to be vulnerable to blackmail, and they may be—and have been—compelled to surrender secret information to unauthorized persons under threat of being exposed. Also held undesirable has been the tendency of others who are too conspicuous or unwilling to live camouflaged to surround themselves with "their own kind"; to form tightly knit cliques; or, occasionally, to favor or overpromote protégés who may lack qualifications. It has been held that any time a homosexual engages in sexual expression, this makes him automatically a lawbreaker, thus unsuitable for Government service. The merit of these contentions remains in dispute, but available experience does not seem to confirm that homosexuals, in the majority of cases, constitute a disruptive element in a government—or business, or industrial, or professional—organization.

Homosexual Organizations. A small proportion of homosexuals, led by often vociferous, dominant individuals among their number, have come out of the shadows to plead or try to compel acceptance of themselves as normal persons. In the U.S. the "Homophile Movement" dates back to 1950 and its militantly radical offshoot, Gay Liberation, dates from 1969. Many organizations are part of this movement but there is little agreement between them as to objectives and methods. In principle, there is rejection of the notion that homosexuality is pathological in any sense or is a symptom of pathology of any kind. It must be considered as a preference, fully on a par with heterosexuality. It is not a medical, psychiatric, legal or moral problem, but a sociologic problem involving prejudice, discrimination and bigotry against a minority (Kameny). There is complete rejection of the terms "cause" and "cure," as well as a sometimes vehemently expressed hatred of psychiatry for its influential stance vis-à-vis homosexual preference. Although a few movement leaders are less vehement in their language, the anti-treatment sentiment, except for unrelated or stress-produced ills, is quite general. However, says Hatterer, who has made extensive attempts to change male bisexuals and homosexuals, homosexual radicalism and militant organizations are the best form of psychotherapy available to most committed homosexuals, giving them a greater sense of identity and self-worth. On the other hand, such organizations, especially the ones on campuses, act as a magnet and as reinforcers for immature individuals-at-the-brink, who should not be thus exposed to their propaganda; and as discouragers of attempted change for those clearly unhappy with their leanings, accusing them of disloyalty and desertion from the ranks for seeking help, and taking the wind of hope from their motivational sails.

Examples of moderately conservative organizations active for the homosexual cause are the Mattachine Societies (Washington, New York, San Francisco, Chicago); the Student Homophile Leagues (on numerous campuses); the Councils on Religion and the Homosexual (Washington, Los Angeles, San Francisco, Dallas, etc.); the Society for Individual Rights (SIR) in San Francisco; One (Los Angeles, Chicago, New York); the

Homosexual Law Reform Society (formerly Janus Society) in Philadelphia; the Daughters of Bilitis (San Francisco, Los Angeles, New York, Philadelphia); and others.

Excerpts from the Homosexual Argot

Auntie (old auntie): an aging homosexual male.

Bitch: derogatory jargon for effeminate male homosexual; also used endearingly for same. Also used for feminine partner of a lesbian liaison. Flaming, screaming, mad bitch: extremely, bizarrely obvious effeminate male.

Blowing (going down on, doing someone): fellatio. Also blow job or job. Being blown, taking it: passive fellatio.

Bringing Out: encouraging, helping an undecided, unstable or bisexual youth to recognize ("discover") and/or profess commitment to his own homosexual proclivity. In some cases practically inseparable from proselytizing (i.e., making "converts" by initiating).

Browning (being browned): anal sex. Also corn-holing.

Butch: virile appearing or rough heterosexual male of interest. Also as a descriptive adjective. Also the mannish female in a lesbian couple; the feminine one is femme.

Call Boy: type of male prostitute; also (stud) hustler, street or bar hustler. Customer is trick or score. Turning a trick, scoring.

Camping: exaggerating one's display of hostilely mimicking effeminacy.

Closet, coming out of: for first time professing one's homosexuality, joining the scene or homosexual subculture. Closet queen: a camouflaged homosexual.

Coming Out: initial professing of own homosexuality by associating with a gay crowd; but not necessarily revealing oneself to straight family, employer, co-workers, neighbors, etc. Also not identical with self-recognition as being homosexual (in teens).

Cruising: searching in streets, parks, public lavatories, bus stations, certain bars or other known places of rendezvous ("meat racks") for a casual male sex partner to pick up.

Dirt: pick-up sex partner or male prostitute who cannot be trusted (possible robbery, assault, blackmail).

Drag: feminine attire worn by a man (drag queen); or man's clothing worn by a mannish lesbian (drag dyke); a form of cross-dressing or transvestism, but not identical with primary transvestism (p. 484). Also a cross-dress party or dance. Going on the drag: to cross-dress elaborately.

Dyke: a mannish female homosexual. Bull dyke: aggressive, controlling type of dyke.

Fag (faggot): derogatory term for effeminate male homosexual. Also a male prostitute serving men who is homosexual (most are not). Fairy, fruit, nance, queer, pansy, maricon (Span.), etc., are hostile-derisive vernacular for homosexual men, but not strictly part of the argot; fairy is sometimes, and Mary (addressingly) always, used by homosexuals without derogatory meaning.

Gay: the most widely used vernacular term for homosexual, male and female.

Hair, keeping up or letting down: to deny or conceal—or to reveal and display—one's homosexuality on all or certain occasions. Also, wearing (dropping) the mask.

Homophile: term introduced in last 20 years by major homosexual self-help associations, to replace homosexual in their names (e.g., Student Homophile League of Columbia U., Stanford U., etc.).

Leather (as in leather crowd, leather bar, etc.): pseudosadistic costuming and mannerisms currently fashionable among some homosexuals. A minority's penchant for leather is not costuming, but part of an aggressive motorcycle-related life style. True sexual sadism (q.v.) also occurs among male (and female) homosexuals, sometimes resulting in exceedingly cruel acting-out.

Sister: a platonic male friend, among effeminate homosexuals.

Straight: heterosexual. Also square, less often jam, which are slightly derisive.

Tearoom: public men's toilet or lavatory where homosexuals loiter to be picked up or engage in fellatio on the spot. Not usually frequented by male prostitutes.

Trade: usually an ostensibly heterosexual young male who consents to homosexual practices without desiring reciprocation (e.g., a male prostitute, or sailors on leave earning beer or girl money). See also p. 153. Trade queen: some male homosexuals prefer trade sex to relations with other gays. Piece of trade: derogatory term. Note the highly controversial saying among homosexuals: today's trade, tomorrow's queen.

Causes

The causes of true, obligatory homosexuality remain essentially unknown, although there is no dearth of theories. It can be firmly assumed that no single cause exists; as Adler has said, a single key will not unlock the riddle of homosexuality. In some way it appears to be the result of derailment or dislocation in normal development, perhaps as early as the moment of fertilization, snowballing from stage to stage and eventually involving others (parents) who then in turn subject the infant to cross-reactive behavior of a first, second or even third order. An appealing general formulation suggests that the genotype responsible for homosexuality may operate on the rate of development of the neurophysiologic mechanism underlying the identification processes and other aspects of object relationship in infancy (Hutchinson).

Non-causes. In no case is true homosexuality a matter of "choice," of "preferring," of making a voluntary commitment, or of electing to join a certain life style; all of these have lately been bandied about, often by persons who should know better. The latter explanation would be like describing the cause of a man's deafness as his desire to join the League for the Deaf. Assertions that homosexuality is "a natural thing," "a normal difference like lefthandedness," or an option "against the conventional mode of family life, from bad personal experience or from a rational desire to avoid conformity" contribute little except, as has been pointed out, to make their authors folk heroes of the militant gay activists. Nor is homosexuality, by all reasonable standards, God's way of preventing a population explosion ("More deviation, less population"). A few popular misbeliefs still crop up from time to time: celibacy does not cause true homosexuality, nor does heterosexual or masturbatory surfeit following chronic excess, nor most probably homosexual seduction or assault during the first decade (certain oft-victimized little boys can be shown to be prehomosexual initiators; see pp. 81 and 151). "Frequent jilting by girls," "bad example" or "forced into it" are typical fabrications by gays having to hold still for some reason for somebody's foolish and unanswerable curiosity.

Genetic and Organic Factors. Direct familial occurrence, making homosexuality inheritable, has not been demonstrated in the offspring of obligatory homosexuals who have by now been observed in sufficient numbers. As exclusive obligatory homosexuals do not procreate, they play no part in this. Many homosexuals have a history of late birth order and high maternal age, with a variation in the latter as substantial as that in mongolism (see also p. 198), suggesting qualitative chromosomal changes (Slater); however, the finding also has possible sociopsychologic implications. Genetic relevance is shown by the observation that identical twins are significantly more often alike as regards male homosexuality than are fraternal twins (80 per cent of 66 identical pairs versus 10 per cent of 40 pairs of fraternal twins reported in the literature, C.C. Taylor); however, no twin observations to date have given conclusive results. Promising as to the gender orientation aspects within the homosexual riddle are newer observations on the basic femaleness of the fetus on which any programed future male must force maleness at every relevant junction of development, which obviously makes males more vulnerable to derailment of function; those on the posterior hypothalamus which, some time near birth, passes through a brief critical phase (see p. 4) after which it either continues as a female brain center with rudimentary estrus, or else becomes masculinized, dropping the residual estrus (cycling) behavior; or those on some animal mothers severely stressed during gestation, who then feminize their male offspring (e.g., as regards gender behavior). The importance of findings, with newer assay techniques, of reduced plasma testosterone and sperm production in some homosexuals has not as yet contributed specific understanding to the mechanism of homosexual causation.

Psychogenic Factors. A history of pathology of the parent-infant triangle (e.g., the overwhelming mother, the alienated father; see p. 80) is encountered in a proportion of homosexual men, but also in heterosexuals. It is probable that the male infant carries the cue for this with it and by some inborn gender-alien characteristic perceived by the mother sets in motion the chain of intimate mother appersonation, a mama's boy distaste for father's offerings, father being turned off and ceasing to be available as a masculine model. At any rate, the constellation probably only influences the relative degree of masculine and feminine identification and orientation, not the direction of the sex aim. Another, older formulation, one of Freud's own, perceived some homosexuals as remaining fixated (arrested) between the stages of infantile autoerotism and alloerotism (p. 14); they thus love themselves in fantasy through the person of the lover who must have a phallus similar to their own to make them feel sexually attracted.

The well-known distaste for, actually fear of, the opposite sex—gynecophobia, vaginophobia, *horror feminae*—may be deeply ingrained. It is believed to arise where the scene is dominated by a mother who displays insidiously seductive behavior toward the boy (p. 74); this may be coupled with a tendency to threaten his sex (e.g., by disparaging remarks about the male genitalia, or by threatening to cut them off for masturbation). Especially if there was early accidental observation of parental intercourse, or certain misapprehensions regarding menstruation, the boy may conclude that in the sex act the woman attacks and hurts the man. Fantasies of a *vagina dentata* may arise and remain. By the time he reaches pubescence the boy is fixedly, though probably no longer consciously, steeped in the notion that it is not safe to be a man sexually. Later such a mother may increasingly attach herself to the son and, leechlike, monopolize and drain his remaining masculine strivings.

A similar influence may be exerted on a fatherless boy whose mother is promiscuous but continually disparages her men friends in the boy's hearing; also on boys raised only by females (mother and older sisters, aunts, etc.) who habitually speak of men as worthless creatures merely to be tolerated and only good to be exploited. If there is no significant man figure in the boy's life with whom he can identify as he grows up, sooner or later he may disown his masculine inclinations because of fear, shame or sexual self-disgust.

In another postulated noxious sequence the boy is unduly prettified and girlified from an early age (e.g., by feminine pet names, clothes, hair style or frequent remarks about the pity of not having been born a girl). Feminization by the parents can lead to early confusion about sex identity and make him adopt certain traits and outlooks of the other sex; also, it may be aided by undue maternal emphasis on the need to be pleasing. This sequence comes to morbid fruition before age 7, during a stage when all boys go through a period of fantasizing that the father is a dangerous rival (p. 14); the pre-deviate's impulse is to placate the father by assuming a passive-ingratiating-seductive attitude toward him. At this point the father's reaction can fixate the pattern: if he is a man with much pride in his own athletic-virile physique, prowess and mentality, he may severely reject the boy as a sissy, either by subjecting him to brute masculinizing measures or taunting him or, somewhat later, by disparaging the boy's feeble efforts to feel and act as a boy (e.g., dates). Thus the boy is deprived of an opportunity to identify with a sympathetic male figure when he needs this most. Furthermore, since these are often somewhat delicate and pretty boys to begin with, their seductiveness toward the father can arouse vague erotic impulses in the latter. The effects of this subsurface interplay could be most disturbing as regards the sexual adjustment of the boy.

Treatment and Management

No specific cure for homosexuality exists, but in a proportion of cases various psychiatric treatment methods have shown results of fair to good quality. Many homosexuals are not motivated to seek treatment designed

PROGNOSIS FOR CHANGING OF MALE HOMOSEXUALS WITH PSYCHIATRIC TREATMENT

Factors grouped in estimated order of importance

Bad Prognostic Factors	Favorable Prognostic Factors
Very Bad	*Good*
Onset of self-awareness before puberty.	Late onset.
Feminine identification, effeminacy, much camping, mannerisms of movement and speech.	Not part of gay subculture.
	Masculine identification.
History of several adult homosexual assaults in childhood.	Heterosexual experience prior to coming out.
Poor initial motivation.	Homosexual only under influence of alcohol.
Entrenched in gay subculture and occupation.	No elation after homosexual sex act.
Much sisterly communing with women.	Much anxiety and guilt feeling.
Masturbatory fantasies unremittingly homosexual.	Few or no mannerisms.
Engaged in homosexual prostitution.	*Fairly Good*
	Camouflaged social existence.
	Married or steady girlfriend.
	Heterosexually potent.

Bad	*Fairly Good*
Previous unsuccessful treatment.	Low Kinsey rating.
Age 30 or older (except onset in	Intelligent, well educated.
middle age).	Young age (under 30).
Ongoing homosexual affair or	Good initial motivation.
menage.	
Rare social contact with women,	
phobic avoidance.	

Moderately Bad

Predatory homosexual acting-out, by history.
Revolted by female genitalia.
High Kinsey rating.
Previous psychosis, delinquency.
Poor education, low IQ.
Hostile, rejecting parents or wife.

KINSEY'S RATING SCALE

Based on both psychologic reactions and overt experience

0. Exclusively heterosexual with no homosexual
1. Predominantly heterosexual, only incidentally homosexual
2. Predominantly heterosexual, but more than incidentally homosexual
3. Equally heterosexual and homosexual
4. Predominantly homosexual, but more than incidentally heterosexual
5. Predominantly homosexual, but incidentally heterosexual
6. Exclusively homosexual

From Kinsey, Pomeroy and Martin, Sexual Behavior in the Human Male, Philadelphia, Saunders Co., 1948.

to change them, although they may come for help for unrelated or partly related psychiatric, etc., problems such as depression, impotence or anxiety hysteria. The hard-core exclusive obligatory homosexuals, both the effeminate and the high-masculinity types, must be considered essentially untreatable. But those who are untreatable yet seek help can be counseled and taught to adapt (i.e., to make the best possible adjustment) either wholly within the gay subculture or basically camouflaged within society at large. A physician who is called upon to deal with such an individual will seek to disregard any personal distaste he may have for homosexuals and their mores. If he finds that his animosity persists he should not attempt extensive counseling. A majority of homosexuals, once they have found an understanding physician, remain faithful and excellent patients in every way.

In conversing with a homosexual, it is best to avoid offensive terms such as fag, fairy or queer, even if the patient himself uses them in jest or self-derogation. Some patients may make a single, exploratory "pass" at a friendly doctor (e.g., a seemingly casual touching of his hand or body) not so much because they believe him to be a fellow deviate or actually wish to seduce him, but it is their way of satisfying an obsessive curiosity about some men with whom they have major dealings. If the physician disregards the gesture without flinching or anger and remains friendly, it is almost never repeated.

The most prominent methods at present employed for the changing of homosexuals are intensive (psychoanalytic) psychotherapy, special group psychotherapy, and behavior modification therapy; occasionally a combination of two or more of these. Claims of success which have ranged from 15 per cent to well over 50 per cent are not always reliable, partly because of the inclusion of facultative (including pseudohomosexual, p. 504) individuals in certain cure statistics; these individuals can respond to many nonspecific remedial efforts including acts of will and major religious experiences. Behavior therapy is the most uncritical of the methods as regards cure claims, because, on purpose, no effort is made to explore the type and genesis of a case. However, the figures do convey that a sense of a priori hopelessness is not indicated toward many cases of homosexuality, when first encountered.

Some psychotherapeutic methods have been made more successful by separating the homosexual proclivity into certain major components and attending to these in an order suggested by how importantly each looms in a case, such as phobic reaction to women, obsessive hypersexualized awareness, developmental child-parent relationship disturbances, positive erotic response to males, tendency to self-derogation, homosexual acting-out readiness when discomfited, habitual resort to certain mannerisms, and the sheltering rationalization of happiness in the status quo. In a planned behavior modification program, for instance, the phobia would be treated by desensitization (active graded approach including woman in bed), male-responsiveness by aversion therapy (electropain or apomorphine in conjunction with suggestive homo- and heteroerotic picture slides; female nude pictures sometimes preceded by testosterone injection), habit correction perhaps by posthypnotic suggestion, self-deprecation by assertive training; all combined, possibly, with insight therapy to remove reachable early development factors. The behavioral methods are in line with the turning away from the holistic approach now suffusing all of medicine and the behavioral sciences; they do require a rather high degree of motivation for change on the part of the individual.

Other methods hoping to change the homosexual have included temporal lobectomy (several reports of incidental cures in temporal epilepsy, etc.); hypnosis, standing free (no remarkable results known); and male hormone therapy (no value per se). Sex surgery including castration, such as is performed on male transsexual patients (p. 486) is sometimes requested by severely effeminate homosexual men with transvestic tendencies. They make the rounds of physicians' offices in search for one who will accommodate them. They argue that they are feminine in their affections, attracted to virile-appearing males, and happiest when playing the social or sexual part of a woman; therefore, they should be relieved of the iniquitous burden of physical masculinity. Their insistence is not as extreme as that of transsexuals, however. According to best present knowledge, these arguments are fallacious. Neither castration nor massive estrinization, nor even added amputation of the penis and construction of a pseudovagina will give these patients what they had hoped for. The dubious legality of castration for this indication also should be considered by the physician.

Management of the Homosexual. If changing is not possible or desired, the true homosexual can be helped to accept the permanence of his condition and to make the best of it. If it should still be necessary he probably should be stopped from deceiving himself that he is "not really queer" merely because he feels that his appearance and manner are not effeminate, or because his only homosexual practice has been to have other men perform fellatio on him.

It must be realized that these patients cannot be maneuvered into normal sexual pursuits (e.g., by appealing to their moral sense or good intentions, or by shaming, taunting, frightening or punishing them) except in the context of well-planned, systematic behavior therapy. Equally useless are indiscriminate attempts to stimulate an erotic interest in women (e.g., by encouraging them to attend public dances, watch burlesque shows, look at pornographic material, or visit prostitutes). On the other hand, sometimes it is advisable to encourage them to associate socially with young women with whom they have some interest in common, in order to improve the ability—rather poor in many—to get along with members of the opposite sex.

Adaptation. In the absence of expectations of reversal or substantial remission, adaptive efforts aim at helping the homosexual youth to be and act more mature, to attain optimal self-realization (e.g., in his work or schooling) to avoid untrammeled promiscuity, maintain common standards of public decency, and enable him to enter into more stable relationships. Some homosexuals elect an essentially abstentious way of life based on self-restraint and a concentration of life energies on a humane, social, artistic, academic or professional endeavor, or on religious devotion. On the other hand, frantic and high-strung attempts at complete sexual self-denial, without the necessary emotional maturity, usually end in failure. Solitary masturbation cannot be discouraged in any homosexual patient who feels the need for it.

Family and Church. Alienation from his family and from his church are two major disturbing factors in the lives of some homosexuals. It is probably unwise for the physician to act as go-between for parents and their alienated homosexual son. However, a confirmed homosexual youth who has set out on a seemingly stable affair with another homosexual, including a joint housekeeping ménage can be aided, if necessary, by counseling the families of both friends not to interfere with the relationship. While the ministers of a few churches have accepted pastoral care of the homosexual as their main concern, many others resist the militant demands that they provide separate social activities and services for homosexuals. A number of churches are modifying their attitude toward homosexuality as being contra naturam and thus un-Christian and sinful. "A new morality," said a spokesman for a large Episcopal diocese, "would seem to allow for homosexual relationships in which physical expression between partners determined to do the most loving thing possible under the circumstances could be free of sin; but the new morality has little comfort to offer those involved in loveless sex relationships. . . . They are immoral" (Lassoe, Jr.).

It has been suggested that young homosexuals on the verge of coming out be directed to contact the nearest homophile organization where they could meet other gays, and possibly an older homosexual to identify with and to act as their mentor; in this way they could minimize confusion and anxiety and adapt their behavior away from possible antisocial models. However, a physician should probably not take it upon himself to do this unless a psychiatric consultant has gone on record, possibly after a trial of change therapy, that the youngster is untreatable.

Marriage. The exclusive true homosexual, as a rule, should be strongly advised against marriage, no matter how greatly he seems to long for the comforts of a conventional home or for a child. The belief that marriage can cure true homosexuality is a fallacy. It matters little if the prospective bride is aware of his condition or even expects to pit her feminine charms against his tendencies; such marriages almost always lead to sorry complications for all parties. Exceptions are marriages of camouflage or convenience with a woman who is either totally anhedonic or a lesbian herself, or considerably older than the patient. In these cases he may obtain some of the companionship and ordered existence of marriage without its sexual obligations.

Marriage of Bisexual. Marriage in itself is not to be considered as a remedy for bisexuality; in fact, it should be discouraged unless the patient has a genuine and somewhat time-tested desire to be married to a particular woman. As a rule, there should be a fair amount of sexual attraction toward her, enough to persist through a courtship period of several months. If premarital intercourse has been attempted but the bisexual groom found himself impotent in spite of sexual desire for the girl, this does not automatically contraindicate marriage, but may be treated with or without postponement of the wedding. The bisexual who is not really cured but has been fond•enough of a girl to marry her and is conducting a satisfactory marriage nevertheless should accept the idea that he will have to include certain precautions in the routine of his living lest he imperil his family and social status.

Life should be well ordered and preferably somewhat routinized for the married bisexual. Existing ties with distinctly homosexual circles should be minimized or severed. If need be, certain situations must be avoided (e.g., some patients must not visit public washrooms under any circumstances, or stroll aimlessly about the streets, or drink alcohol except at home or at private mixed gatherings, or spend nights in strange towns away from the family). Some patients cannot tolerate such continued self-discipline as well as others; symptoms of an acute anxiety or panic state, or occasionally a depression can often herald an overstraining of the bisexual's tolerance for the suppression of his homosexual component. It is understood that in all cases where a bisexual marries, but where there is even a moderate possibility of a relapse into a homosexual pattern, the physician will advise the patient to apprise his bride of this; not all bisexuals will agree with their physician on this, but the physician probably should not put himself on record as abetting such concealment.

HOMOSEXUALITY IN THE FEMALE
(Lesbianism. Antiqu. Sapphism)

Homosexuality in females, the same as its counterpart in males, has been a well-known phenomenon since biblical times. The term lesbianism is derived from the Greek poetess Sappho whose morbidly beautiful poems— only fragments have been preserved—represent love plaints and passionate sensuality directed at young girls of the island of Lesbos.

Lesbians have conspicuously less of a social problem than homosexual men. Even normal women commonly engage in demonstrations of tenderness and affection; they share intimacies, walk arm in arm, dance together, or share the same bed. Unlike their male counterparts, homosexual women do not roam about with as much frequency, and the ostentatious minority among them is probably much smaller than the corresponding minority among male deviates. Even the recognizably lesbian couple is apt to arouse much less animosity in the community or among onlookers than is frequently evoked by their male counterpart. In all large cities and scattered in many other populated areas there are bars and taverns where lesbians gather. In the largest cities formal organizations of female homosexuals exist. Female homosexuality and its manifestations are not excluded from the provisions of most law statutes, but it is a rarity that women are arrested and taken to court on homosexual charges.

Newer Developments. It is not known if female homosexuality is increasing, or if more of them are surfacing in today's permissive, liberated atmosphere; at any rate, from all indications homosexual behavior among women seems distinctly on the rise. It received a major impetus with the spread of swinger groups (p. 458) which most wives joined reluctantly at first. The major discovery made at such couple group affairs all over the Western world was the frequency with which the wives entered into lesbian sex activities in the latter part of the evening (see also Group Sex, p. 457). Another newer development is the frequency with which wives and mothers even in their 40's discover themselves to be erotically attracted to another female and either leave home or make some other arrangement with only a haphazard effort at camouflaging their new orientation and venture. More and more often husbands are heard from who are in shock and calling for help because apparently they had not been looking or listening or had tuned out what they did perceive.

Characteristics. Many lesbians will admit that they are different—in fact, some are proud of it—but they will rarely admit that they are disordered. Some lead contented, active lives, but a majority seem to be embroiled interminably in emotional difficulties. Even those who are greatly successful in their employment, in the arts, in business, or have a wide circle of friends still may lead an existence of restless, aimless dissatisfaction. No matter what the more vocal among them elect to proclaim publicly, or what the publicity releases of some homophile organizations wish the people to believe, the personal life of many has been well characterized as a bottomless "Well of Loneliness" (Hall). However, many do not genuinely desire to change from their homosexuality. In character they range along the scale of human differences, from the highest type of civic and personal morality to the most dissolute and socially offensive. Among prostitutes a considerable number have homosexual tendencies, although many are probably not true lesbians. However, a proportion of lesbians do not mind working as prostitutes serving men, either intermittently or as their sole source of livelihood; they have depersonalized their bodies, as it were, while in others a lifelong history of repression of vaginal awareness makes this particular recess of their anatomy, this ". . . good-for-nothing dirty hole," readily surrendered to heterosexual exploitation.

Although some gifted, intellectually superior female homosexuals tend to romanticize lesbianism and to glorify woman-to-woman lovemaking (e.g., as "superior to all other sex, untiring and unlimited, gently moist, tender, slow, inventive, considerate, romantic, thrilling at the heights"— anonym. nurse) there is another side to lesbian relations. Middle-aged women following around a flirtatious, uncaring girl half their age, spending household money on drinks or gifts, being led on by occasionally being allowed to "get down" briefly on the bored girl can be a pathetic sight.

Two grown women reverting to a preteen behavior pattern with hand-holding everywhere, secret messages, dress-alike, engraved presents, and jealous scenes may cause no great social upheaval, but contrast this with the ferocious sexual aggressiveness and dominance of certain bull dykes (e.g., in women's penal institutions). A relationship between two women, Simone de Beauvoir has said, "assumes many different forms; it may be conjugal or romantic; it has room for sadism, masochism, generosity, fidelity, devotion, capriciousness, egotism, betrayal; among lesbians there are prostitutes and also great lovers."

Masculine Traits. Chromosomally, gross-anatomically and physiologically lesbians are women, no matter how mannish the deportment or how masculinized the orientation of some may appear. As a rule, they are neither unusually hirsute or flat-chested, nor are the genitalia undeveloped or the menses absent. Among those who have tried to conceive many have succeeded. In a small proportion of mannish lesbians one observes that gait and motility are of masculine type, the facial planes large, the features coarse, the muscles well developed, and the voice raucous; they also may have an unusually large clitoris with a hooding, caudad-furrowed prepuce. There is little doubt that such features, occurring as a syndrome, represent a form of subclinical virilism (i.e., a constitutional disposition). But, many women with subclinical virilism are sexually normal, and many aggressive-type lesbians have no physical traits that set them apart from the average woman. Much of what makes some mannish lesbians so obviously mannish is the result of ingrained mannerisms. They may wear distinctly masculine costume, use no make-up and few ornaments, try to disguise the bust or develop a taste for cigars. The true virago (i.e., the woman with residual congenital adrenogenitalism) is only infrequently also a lesbian. A virilizing syndrome arising past puberty (e.g., in a young woman manifesting late adrenocortical pathology) has not reliably been known to make a lesbian out of a previously normal woman. Nor can an excessive androgenic level from any other source (e.g., medication) make a normal woman homosexual, even as estrogenic medication cannot make a lesbian attracted to men.

Among the more masculine-oriented lesbians a biologic component among the causes of their homosexuality cannot be excluded. Exposure to sex identity-distorting attitudes throughout childhood, or other psychic factors, determine much of the direction which the libido will take eventually. But there are also indications that little girls with constitutional ungirl-like traits are more predisposed to, perhaps also more provocative of, such undesirable early influences. As to the more passive type of lesbian, a biologic component among the causes never has been claimed by reasonable observers. The typical mannish lesbian is a tomboy (p. 108) from childhood, or else perhaps an earnest, studious or manually gifted girl.

Unlike the majority of idiopathic tomboys, her attitude and feelings do not undergo a change at puberty, but her masculine interests continue, while her somatosexual development proceeds normally. She evades dates with boys but may continue to have intense "crushes" on other adolescent girls. She emerges as an efficient, perhaps aggressive wage earner or business girl, or an authoritative supervisor. Some have great capacity for tenderness toward the girls working with and under them; others are cruel and near-sadistic. When she has creative artistic talent, often she seems to be more capable of translating it into finished and meaningful products than normal women do. She may prefer being called "Smith" or "John" rather than "Miss Smith" or "Jane." In her early adult years, or from time to time thereafter, she may experiment briefly with heterosexual intercourse, but this gives her little gratification. Awareness of her own homosexuality arose within a few years from menarche.

Facultative Homosexuality. Not all homosexually active women are true lesbians; some may be characterized as facultative homosexual women. In certain emotionally immature and arrested personalities a sexual orientation does not become clearly established following the puberal homoerotic phase. Others are psychopathic women, impulse-ridden or multiperverse, who resort to homoerotic gratification as easily as to other types of sex activity, according to the impulses or the opportunities of the moment, including monetary considerations, or merely for kicks or for variety. Others are shallow, hysteroid, basically narcissistic young women to whom involvement with, perhaps the adoration of, an older or more accomplished woman is an intriguing experience and to whom lesbian sex is a fascinating sensual game. The facultative homosexual woman, especially if hypersuggestible, may become so conditioned to homosexual preference that she becomes indistinguishable, for practical purposes, from a true lesbian. This is apt to occur when prolonged and emotionally satisfying erotic rapport with a lesbian coincides with an episode of intense surfeit or distaste for man-woman love relationships.

Lesbian Friendships may occur between two young contemporaries of similar interests and about the same temperament and degree of aggressiveness, but probably more characteristic are affairs where one woman is aggressive and often somewhat older, while her friend is distinctly feminine. The more passive or younger partner may be a facultative lesbian, or simply a pretty, hypersuggestible girl becoming homosexually conditioned and attached. She may be beautiful, occasionally strikingly so. She may have greater talents, greater success, or greater earning capacity than her older friend. But most often she is dependent, has little spiritual depth, and contributes almost nothing material to the menage. Although such role-playing in female homosexual affairs is distinctly lessening today, giving way to an easier camaraderie, it is by no means extinct.

To the outside observer a menage of a butch lesbian and her femme friend seems like the image of a husband-and-wife relationship. The older one has done the pursuing and the wooing, as well as the planning. She appears dominant, protective and solicitous. She arranges and budgets; she may manage her protégé's career, encourage a marriage of convenience, help place her in an easy job, recommend her to a reliable pimp, or place her in a higher grade house of prostitution, as the case may be. Yet, psychologically, they do not represent husband and wife but probably are unconsciously re-enacting a parent-child relationship or rather a caricature thereof.

At all times the femme is the privileged member of the couple. Often she is fickle and capricious where the older one is earnest and devoted. She may display violent jealousy of the parent-lesbian's true or fancied attention to some other girl, while the older one often suffers intense torments of jealousy in silence. The younger one may threaten to abandon the menage and may do so repeatedly for a period, while the parent seems only to be stirred to greater devotion and solicitude, to an almost pleasurable self-humiliation, before the child's accusations, demands, caprices or infidelities. Some such friendships are relatively serene throughout; however, many are only a repetitious sequence of quarrels, accusations and passionate reaffirmations of love. There is hardly anything like it in most heterosexual marriages, and only infrequently anything as lastingly hyperemotional between male homosexuals. Yet these ménages generally seem to last much longer than the corresponding ones between male homosexuals; in fact, there may be only one, or a few, during either woman's lifetime.

Most lesbians seem to turn to an asexual life relatively earlier than normal women, although menages and friendships may persist on a platonic basis. While in the sexually active phase, physical relations between lesbians are carried out in a number of ways. Some couples are, and remain, fully satisfied with mutual embracing, petting and kissing. Mutual genital masturbation, although an occasional resort of many couples, is perhaps the least frequent mode of habitual gratification. On the other hand, oral stimulation plays a major part. A relatively small number resort to some kind of vaginal penetration ("penis games," tribadism, tribadismus internus). Infrequent in the U.S. today is the use of an artificial penis (penis succedaneus, "dummy phallus," dildo—from Italian diletto, godmiche or godemiche—from Latin gaude mihi).

Marriage and Offspring. A fair number, from their early years, are bisexual, or feel impelled to camouflage their orientation by going on dates with males at least occasionally, necking and even having intercourse. Camouflage or social convenience may include a marriage, followed usually quickly by a divorce (this differs from women latently homosexual who "come out" years after marrying). Both camouflaged and latent lesbians, in divorcing, may take their 1 or 2 children along and rear them in a new lesbian ("2-mother") marriage; there exists a Lesbian Mothers' Union, with their own newspaper. The effect on these children, who usually are aware of all the facts, is rarely innocuous, from limited experience. However, some of the younger women declare that they do not mind rearing children who will be homosexual. More often, the true lesbian has no erotic interest in men; she is indifferent to a man's sexual attentions, irritated by them, repulsed, or occasionally even frightened. The more passive homosexual woman who marries a normal man for convenience or social protection, remains sexually frigid and incapable of genuine love for her husband. She does not desire children and, as a rule, does not make a good mother. The mannish lesbian marries infrequently, except perhaps a homosexual, impotent or elderly man. Some of them may greatly desire a child (but without a permanent husband), and may succeed in conceiving or adopting one.

FOR JOURNAL LITERATURE AND ADDITIONAL READING

Bergler, E.: Homosexuality: Disease or Way of Life? New York, Hill and Wang, 1957

Bieber, I. et al. (ed.): Homosexuality. New York, Basic Books, 1962

Caprio, F. S.: Female Homosexuality. New York, Citadel Press, 1954

Cavanagh, J. R.: Counseling the Invert. Milwaukee, Bruce Publishing, 1966

Cory, D. W. (Pseud.) and LeRoy, J. P.: The Homosexual and his Society. New York, Citadel Press, 1964

Cory, D. W. (Pseud.): The Lesbian in America. New York, Citadel Press, 1964

Hoffman, M.: The Gay World: Male Homosexuality and the Social Creation of Evil. New York, Basic Books, 1968

Hooker, E. (ed.): Background Papers and Final Report, U.S. Task Force on Homosexuality. Washington, Govt. Printing Office, 1969

Humphreys, R. A. L.: Tearoom Trade: Impersonal Sex in Public Places. Chicago, Aldine Publ. Co., 1970

Jones, H. K.: Towards a Christian Understanding of the Homosexual. New York, Association Press, 1966

Karlen, A.: Sexuality and Homosexuality. New York, Norton, 1971

Magee, B.: One in Twenty. A Study of Homosexuality in Men and Women. New York, Stein & Day, 1966

Marmor, J. (ed.): Sexual Inversion. The Multiple Roots of Homosexuality. New York, Basic Books, 1965

Ovesey, L.: Homosexuality and Pseudohomosexuality. Springfield, Ill., Thomas, 1969

Parker, W.: Homosexuality. A Selective Bibliography of over 3000 Items. Metuchen, N.J., Scarecrow Press, 1971

Ruitenbeek, H. (ed.): The Problem of Homosexuality in Modern Society. New York, Dutton & Co., 1963

Saghir, M. T. and Robins, E.: Male and Female Homosexuality: A Comprehensive Investigation. Baltimore, Williams & Wilkins, 1973

Socarides, C. W.: The Overt Homosexual. New York, Grune & Stratton, 1968

Teal, D.: The Gay Militants. New York, Stein & Day, 1971

West, D. J.: Homosexuality. ed. 2. Chicago, Aldine Publ. Co., 1968

NAME INDEX

SUBJECT INDEX